SECRET SERVICE

Political Policing in Ca
from the Fenians to Fortress America

Secret Service provides the first comprehensive history of political policing in Canada – from its beginnings in the mid-nineteenth century,
through two world wars and the Cold War, to the more recent 'war on
terror.' This book reveals the extent, focus, and politics of government-
sponsored surveillance and intelligence-gathering operations.

Drawing on previously classified government records, the authors
reveal that for over 150 years, Canada has run spy operations largely
hidden from public or parliamentary scrutiny – complete with all the
usual apparatus of deception and betrayal so familiar to fans of spy
fiction. As they argue, what makes Canada unique among Western
countries is its insistent focus of its surveillance inwards, and usually
against Canadian citizens.

Secret Service highlights the many tensions that arise when undercover police and their covert methods are deployed too freely in a liberal democratic society. It will prove invaluable to readers attuned to
contemporary debates about policing, national security, and civil rights
in a post-9/11 world.

REG WHITAKER is Distinguished Research Professor Emeritus in the Department of Political Science at York University and an adjunct professor of Political Science at the University of Victoria.

GREGORY S. KEALEY is Provost, Vice-President Research, and professor of
History at the University of New Brunswick.

ANDREW PARNABY is an associate professor in the Department of History at Cape Breton University.

Secret Service

*Political Policing in Canada
from the Fenians to Fortress America*

REG WHITAKER, GREGORY S. KEALEY, AND
ANDREW PARNABY

UNIVERSITY OF TORONTO PRESS
Toronto Buffalo London

© University of Toronto Press 2012
Toronto Buffalo London
www.utppublishing.com
Printed in Canada

ISBN 978-0-8020-0752-0 (cloth)
ISBN 978-0-8020-7801-8 (paper)

Printed on acid-free paper

Library and Archives Canada Cataloguing in Publication

Whitaker, Reginald, 1943–
Secret service : political policing in Canada from the Fenians to fortress America /
Reg Whitaker, Gregory S. Kealey, and Andrew Parnaby.

Includes bibliographical references and index.
ISBN 978-0-8020-0752-0 (bound). – ISBN 978-0-8020-7801-8 (pbk.)

1. Secret service – Canada – History. 2. Intelligence service – Canada – History.
I. Kealey, Gregory S., 1948– II. Parnaby, Andrew, 1970– III. Title.

HV8157.W45 2012   363.28'30971   C2012-902319-1

University of Toronto Press acknowledges the financial assistance to its publishing
program of the Canada Council for the Arts and the Ontario Arts Council.

  Canada Council Conseil des Arts   ONTARIO ARTS COUNCIL
for the Arts du Canada   CONSEIL DES ARTS DE L'ONTARIO

University of Toronto Press acknowledges the financial support of the Government of
Canada through the Canada Book Fund for its publishing activities.

This book has been published with the help of a grant from the Canadian Federation for
the Humanities and Social Sciences, through the Aid to Scholarly Publications Program,
using funds provided by the Social Sciences and Humanities Research Council of
Canada.

This book was supported by a subsidy in aid of publication from Cape Breton
University.

This book was supported by a subsidy in aid of publication from the University of
New Brunswick.

Contents

Illustrations follow page 312

Acknowledgments

Over the long period of research that went into the preparation of this book, many people were of assistance, including former practitioners in security intelligence, people targeted by the agencies, politicians, public servants, archivists, fellow academics, university administrators, graduate students, lawyers, and journalists. All assisted in different ways in adding value to this study.

Among these are: Maurice Archdeacon, Jane Arnold, Ron Atkey, Robert Bothwell, Ingrid Botting, Roger Bowen, Jim Bronskill, Mike Butt, Anthony Campbell, Richard Cleroux, Peter Gill, J.L. Granatstein, Lois Harder, John Harker, Bob Hayward, Bob Hong, Ben Isitt, Barbara Jackman, William Kaplan, Zuhair Kashmieri, Gary Kinsman, Amy Knight, Derek Lee, the late Gil Levine, the late Peyton V. Lyon, John Manley, Gary Marcuse, Peter Marwitz, Michelle McBride, the late Mark McClung, David McKnight, Val Meredith, Andrew Mitrovica, Rod Nicholls, Kirk Niergarth, Mark Olyan, Rick Rennie, Graham Reynolds, Kent Roach, Daniel Robinson, Alti Rodal, Philip Rosen, Peter Russell, John Sawatsky, Michelle Shephard, David Stafford, John Starnes, Lorne Waldman, the late Bill Walsh, Fred Winsor, and Glenn Wright.

Special thanks to long-standing colleagues and friends Stuart Farson, Larry Hannant, Steve Hewitt, and Wesley Wark. And a particular note of sadness and regret for Jim Littleton, whose infectious enthusiasm for the project and inexhaustible store of knowledge of the subject were of inestimable assistance and support until cut short by his untimely passing.

Sincere appreciation is also due the University of Toronto Press for its inexhaustible patience for, and support of, this manuscript. Len Husband, our editor at UTP, has been especially helpful; Curtis Fahey carried out a judicious copy editing; and Wayne Herrington watched over the process of turning text into publication. We have also benefited over the years from the institutional support of several Canadian universities – York University and University of Victoria (Whitaker); Memorial University of Newfoundland and University of New Brunswick (Kealey); and Cape Breton University (Parnaby).

This book has been published with the help of a grant from the Canadian Federation for the Humanities and Social Sciences, through the Aid to Scholarly Publications Program provided by the Social Sciences and Humanities Research Council of Canada. Additional support for publication has been provided by the University of New Brunswick, Cape Breton University, and the York University Senior Scholar Research Fund.

SECRET SERVICE

Political Policing in Canada
from the Fenians to Fortress America

Introduction:
Political Policing in Canada

On 26 September 2002 Maher Arar – a Syrian-born Canadian citizen – was detained by U.S. Immigration and Naturalization officials in New York City while en route home to Montreal after a vacation in Tunisia, his wife's birthplace; he was stopped at John F. Kennedy International Airport. Suspected of being a member of Al-Qaeda, the jihadist group that had carried out the attacks on the World Trade Center about a year before, Arar was questioned by the Federal Bureau of Investigation (FBI) and was held in the city for almost two weeks. During this time he did not have access to a lawyer and was visited only once by a Canadian consular official, who, after meeting with Arar, believed that he would be extradited back to Canada, despite the serious allegations put forth by American officials. She was wrong. On 8 October, Arar was taken from his cell at three in the morning and taken aboard a Gulfstream private jet, operated by the Central Intelligence Agency (CIA), and flown to Jordan as part of a U.S. policy known as 'extraordinary rendition'; the next day, by car, Arar arrived in Damascus, the Syrian capital, and was handed over to Syrian military intelligence – which subsequently 'interrogated, tortured, and held [him] in degrading and inhumane conditions' for the next ten months.[1] Word of his disappearance surfaced in the media quickly. 'Amnesty International is concerned by the possible "disappearance" of Canadian citizen Maher Arar,' the international human-rights organization reported on 20 October 2002. 'Although recent reports state that he was deported to Syria, neither the Canadian authorities nor his family have been able to confirm his whereabouts. There are grave fears for his safety.'[2] So grave, in fact, that by the end of October, Canadian consular officials in Damascus began meeting with Arar on a fairly routine basis; accompanied by Syrian authorities at all times, they noted the poor conditions under which he was being held but did not report any instances of torture. Meanwhile, back in Canada, Arar's wife, Monia Mazigh, pressured the federal government to secure her husband's release. On 23 August 2003 Arar – blindfolded – was driven to a new prison, where the treatment was reportedly much better: no torture, no solitary confinement. While at this new facility, Arar met another Canadian and friend, Abdullah Almalki, who told a similar story of detainment, interrogation, and torture. In early October, about a year after his initial detainment, Arar was finally released by Syrian military intelligence, but not before he was forced to sign a written confession that detailed his putative involvement with Al-Qaeda. He was subsequently flown home to Canada.

Almost immediately after Arar's return, public pressure mounted for a full judicial inquiry into this year-long ordeal; especially worrisome was the possible complicity of Canadian security officials in the American policy of 'extraordinary rendition' – which, some critics alleged, effectively 'subcontracted torture.' Prime Minister Paul Martin acquiesced to the public demand for more information in early 2004; a commission of inquiry began its work later that summer and released its final multi-volume report about a year and a half later, in September 2006. Headed by Associate Chief Justice of Ontario Dennis O'Connor, who rose to public prominence after leading an investigation into tainted water in Walkerton, Ontario, the inquiry absolved Arar of any connections to Islamic terrorist organizations. It also exposed the role of Canadian security officials in Arar's nightmare: Not only had the Royal Canadian Mounted Police (RCMP) been monitoring Arar and some of his acquaintances long before that fateful day at JFK airport, but the Mounties had also shared that information with their American counterparts. The information that related to Arar directly ('Islamic Extremist … suspected of being linked to the Al Qaeda terrorist movement') was inaccurate and, in O'Connor's judgment, 'very likely' led to his detention by U.S. authorities.[3] While O'Connor found no evidence that Canadian officials were actively involved in the decision to remove Arar first to Jordon and then to Syria for further interrogation, he did discover that Canada's premier spy agency, the Canadian Security Intelligence Service (CSIS), understood well the fate that awaited the Syrian Canadian once he was placed in U.S. custody – but it did not act to prevent his rendition or act quickly to help bring him home once removed to the Middle East.[4] Withheld by the federal government for reasons of 'national security confidentiality,' that final revelation about CSIS came to light only in August 2007, after O'Connor had successfully convinced a federal court to order the government of Prime Minister Stephen Harper to release it along with some additional documentation.

As the O'Connor probe drew to a close, another controversy involving Canadian spy agencies was unfolding – this time in Afghanistan.[5] As part of the International Security Assistance Force of the North Atlantic Treaty Organization (NATO), which had toppled the Taliban regime shortly after the terrorist attacks of 11 September 2001, Canadian forces were by 2006 situated primarily in Kandahar province, where pro-Taliban insurgents were especially active. From the beginning of the Canadian mission, successive prime ministers, defence ministers, and commanding officers permitted Canadian soldiers to transfer prisoners to the Afghan security service – the National Directorate of Security (NDS) – despite clear and obvious evidence that the NDS routinely tortured those detainees, in flagrant violation of both the Geneva Conventions and an agreement signed with the Canadian government in 2005. Between the spring of 2006 and the fall of 2009, Conservative Prime Minister Harper and his defence ministers, Gordon O'Connor and then Peter MacKay, publicly denied allegations that the Canadian forces knowingly subjected detainees to torture by handing them over to Afghan officials, only to reverse this position as media reports and an investigation mounted by the Military Police Complaints Commission (MPCC) produced mounds of evidence to the contrary. Particularly stunning was the revelation – contained in heavily censored witness transcripts filed with the MPCC – that CSIS, working alongside military intelligence, was deeply involved in all of this: it interrogated prisoners, provided tactical advice, and sometimes recommended which detainees ought to be handed over to the NDS.[6] The release of additional documentation related to the Afghan detainee controversy, and the role of Canadian spy agencies in it, awaits the conclusion of multiparty negotiations that were set in motion by the speaker of the House of Commons, Peter Milliken, who ruled in late April 2010 that Parliament had the right to see all unredacted documents related to the issue.[7]

An earlier version of this Introduction, written before the World Trade Center bombings, began with a joke, the punchline of which was that Canada – peaceful, multicultural, middle-power Canada – actually possessed a secret service. The joke worked (or so we thought) because it contrasted the general perception of Canada as a country with little political intrigue and even less political repression with a historical reality that was more sobering and often truly sensational. Yet, in the aftermath of '9/11' (as the Al-Qaeda attacks of 2001 had quickly been dubbed), the Maher Arar scandal, and the Afghan detainee affair, the joke no longer seems to resonate. Thanks to the O'Connor inquiry and the proceedings of the Military Police Complaints Commission, Canadians now know plenty about their spy agencies and their furtive actions – making a contrast between the milquetoast and the menacing (the crux of our lighthearted earlier draft) awkward, if not impossible, to deliver with a straight face. In contrast, this Introduction strikes a more sombre note, more in tune with the seriousness of the national-security issues currently unfolding in Canada. As the brief sketches of the Maher Arar debacle and Afghan detainee scandal suggest, the 9/11 bombings altered how the Canadian government conceptualized, and acted upon, threats to national security – and did so decisively. Since then, Canadian spy agencies have been drawn into a tighter relationship with their American counterparts and now operate regularly on foreign soil. These twin developments – integration and internationalization of secret service functions – mark a significant departure from the ways in which Ottawa has handled national-security questions for over a century.[8] A new era is just now coming into view, and as the Arar debacle and Afghan detainee controversy suggests, it may prove to be brutal, costly, and even deadly.

The significance of this shift is appreciated best, we think, when it is placed in the broad sweep of Canadian history. Before 2001, Canada did not run spies on foreign soil. Nothing like the U.S. Central Intelligence Agency or Britain's Secret Intelligence Service (SIS) has ever operated under a Canadian flag. Canada has for many decades mounted an electronic eavesdropping operation abroad, under the aegis of the Communications Security Establishment (CSE), but that is part of the new high-tech world of technical intelligence-gathering by sophisticated listening devices, computers, and complex software programs for sorting 'signals' from 'noise,' flagging significant messages, and decrypting coded communications.[9] The Canadian Armed Forces have, like all armed forces everywhere, a military-intelligence arm. In peacetime, Canadian military attachés abroad, like their counterparts the world over, do gather intelligence about other countries' military capabilities. It is not unknown for Canadian diplomats to gather bits and pieces of intelligence about other countries that are not drawn entirely from formal diplomatic channels. But, as for Canadian spies à la James Bond or even George Smiley running agents and operations in exotic climes, there just weren't any to be found before 2001.[10] Canada is not an innocent in this business, however. In fact, for more than a century, Canadian governments have run spy operations, with undercover agents, secret sources, agents provocateurs, coded communications, elaborate files, and all the usual apparatus of deception and betrayal so familiar to aficionados of spy fiction. But instead of conducting such activities abroad, Canadian governments have done so at home, and usually against Canadian citizens. Other countries do this as well – the FBI spies on Americans; MI5 and Special Branch spies on Britons; the French have an alphabet soup of agencies, some not even publicly acknowledged, that spy on French citizens. But Canada is somewhat unusual among major Western nations in so insistently focusing its surveillance activities inwards.

This is, on the face of it, odd. Why have Canadian governments been so fearful of 'enemies within,' when Canada's history suggests strongly that it is one of the most peaceful, well-ordered, uneventful countries in a turbulent world? There have been no revolutions, or even near-revolutions, in this century, and a small handful of local rebellions in the nineteenth century did not require enormous exertions or huge expenditures of resources on the part of the authorities of the day to reassert order. A clandestine separatist movement employing terrorism and assassination had a brief fling in Quebec in the 1960s but was quickly suppressed and disappeared less than a decade from its inception. A peaceful, legitimate sovereignist movement in Quebec may again threaten national *unity*, but it is a bit of a stretch to see it as threatening national *security*. Espionage or conspiracies to influence Canadian events on behalf of the interests of hostile foreign states have from time to time animated Canadian authorities into extreme counter-measures. Foreign threats to Canada have risen and subsequently vanished, from the Kaiser's Germany in the early part of this century until 1918; Hitler's Germany from the late 1930s until 1945; and finally Communist Russia from 1917 until 1989–90. Yet the disappearance of old enemies, or their transformation into friends and allies, seems to have had little effect on the construction of an internal surveillance state. Each successive foreign threat has had the effect of ratcheting up the level of internal vigilance; the relaxation of external tensions has had little effect in relaxing internal controls, but the appearance of a new threat on the horizon has almost invariably brought forth calls for yet more powers and yet more controls. All the while, the attention of the state has usually been directed not so much outwards as inwards – towards potential 'fifth columns' of Canadians who, for reasons of ethnic, cultural, religious, or ideological associations, might be inclined to act on behalf of foreign powers or movements.

This persistent concern for 'subversive' Canadians is tied in part to the country's extremely modest position in international affairs, which has made it easier for successive Canadian governments to leave not only military preparedness but foreign intelligence gathering to other nations – first Britain, then the United States.[11] Moreover, as a land of immigrants and refugees (save, of course, the Native peoples), it is not altogether surprising that persistent anxiety has surrounded the loyalty and trustworthiness of those who have arrived from other shores, carrying their own cultural, religious, and political baggage – and sometimes their own violent quarrels. The great democracy to the south is supposed to be a 'melting pot' where immigrants are transformed into 100 per cent Americans. The dark underside of the melting pot has always been anxiety that Americans could be made over again into enemies within: hence witch-hunts for 'un-American activities.' Canada is not exactly a melting pot, and has often styled itself as a 'mosaic,' retaining the original colours and textures of its peoples in a unique design. Whatever the truth of that metaphor, it has certainly been the case that Canada, with its binational and bilingual character and the relative weakness of any pan-Canadian national identity, has presented a somewhat indistinct face of 'Canadianism' into which immigrants can assimilate. The idea of 'un-Canadian activities' thus seems a little outlandish. This has not, however, led to a state in which, to borrow a phrase, a thousand flowers have been allowed to bloom. On the contrary, the very lack of firm definition of a Canadian creed has, if anything, increased anxiety levels on the part of the political authorities concerning subversives, spies, and saboteurs among the population. After all, if it is unclear what constitutes 100 per cent Canadianism, all the more must *we* worry about ill-defined and possibly subversive 'un-Canadians.'

There is another long-standing difference from our southern neighbours that is related to this lack of clarity. Since Americanism is a democratic, populist creed, so too the struggle against subversion of that creed has most often been a democratic, populist crusade. Hence, nativist movements directed against immigrants, Catholics, Jews, and other 'aliens' sometimes had wide popular resonance in the late nineteenth and early twentieth centuries. In the 1950s, McCarthyism attained the status of a populist assault upon such established American institutions as the presidency and the army. In the mid-1990s, grass-roots 'militias' took up arms and blew up a federal building in Oklahoma City to oppose what they saw as a takeover of America by alien forces – the federal government. American scholars have written books with titles such as *The Paranoid Style in American Politics*,[12] *Red Scare: A Study in National Hysteria*,[13] and *A Conspiracy So Immense*.[14] In Canada, on the other hand, the struggle against subversion has been generally considered a prerogative of the state. Indeed, freelance movements of populist paranoia have never been welcomed in Canada, where crown privilege, executive dominance, and deference to authority have traditionally – though not always – been the rule. This does not mean, as many Canadians have smugly concluded, that Canada is necessarily more liberal and less repressive than the United States. Nor does it mean that strains of a more authoritarian populism have been completely absent from Canadian democracy, as shown by widespread popular support for the RCMP down to the 1960s and 1970s, when the public consensus supporting the Mounties began to weaken in the face of serious revelations of police excesses and wrongdoing. It simply means that political repression in Canada has been largely confined to the 'legitimate' auspices of the state. Hence, our study of the Canadian secret service – which begins in the 1860s, before Canada was actually *Canada* – touches on a good deal of political history, told from both a top-down and a bottom-up perspective.

For most of Canadian history since Confederation, no clear demarcation was made between illegitimate and legitimate targets for investigation: the line between the two was either too blurry to be useful or simply non-existent. Thus, the surveillance arm of the state routinely engaged in amassing secret dossiers on the political activities of Canadians of all sorts. Resources did not always permit these files to be as extensive as the secret police might have liked, but when resources were provided, the police showed quite remarkable energy and zeal in spying on a large number of citizens. A royal commission discovered in 1977 that the RCMP security service maintained a name index with 1,300,000 entries, representing 800,000 files on individuals, including one of the authors of this book.[15] It is now possible through the Access to Information Act to troll through a small part of this vast trove of material which, even in censored form, reveals a mild Canadian version of the same kind of prurient interest in people's private activities, associations, and even thoughts that moved the notorious East German Stasi to pry into every nook and cranny of society for evidence of political deviance. Of course, Canada was never a totalitarian country –

although, during two world wars in this century, efforts were made on the home front to emulate the kind of controls over domestic life exercised by more dictatorial adversaries. Even in peacetime, however, and even without the teeth to inflict the kind of punitive brutality that totalitarian states visit on their own citizens, it is notable that the state in a liberal democracy like Canada has persistently spied on its own people, run undercover agents and maintained secret sources of information within the 'private' associations of civil society, and kept secret files that categorized people in terms of their personal beliefs – with serious consequences, given that people's jobs and careers and their public reputations might be threatened by the information in those files.[16] Nor is it any small matter that generations of Canadians who have exercised their democratic and civic right to express and promote political, social, and economic ideas that might be at some variance with the prevailing orthodox wisdom have had to face the uncomfortable and distasteful possibility that one or more of their colleagues in the common cause might actually be a police spy.

This kind of state activity has been termed *political policing*.[17] Policing politics is inherently anomalous in liberal democracies, but it has been done, and continues to be done, in all of them. What lies behind attempts to police political behaviour is the notion that there are limits to ideas acceptable in the public sphere. Democracies like Canada pride themselves on their openness and on the freedom of their citizens to express themselves; they have even fought world wars to 'make the world safe for democracy' and cold wars against totalitarianism. Yet, from the beginning to the present, certain ideas have been regarded as subversive, beyond the pale: those who espouse such ideas are deemed suspect – security risks – and those who attempt to actually advance or implement these ideas are to be isolated and silenced. Of course, one generation's subversion is another generation's conventional wisdom. Ideas once denounced as heresy, and treated as such, may gradually move into the mainstream. Louis Riel was viewed by the authorities as a traitor, and hung. A century later, Louis Riel Day is a statutory holiday in Manitoba and the idea of the inherent right of Aboriginal and Métis peoples to self-government is widely, although not universally, accepted. Earlier in this century, trade-union organizers fighting for collective-bargaining rights were sometimes treated as Bolshevik agitators; today, collective bargaining is hardly considered subversive but is rather seen as part of the fabric of Canadian society. The reverse process also occurs. In the late nineteenth and early twentieth centuries, racist ideas of white supremacy were standard fare in the most respectable circles of Canadian society; today, political groups espousing such ideas are targets for surveillance by the security service.

There is a common thread that runs down through the years. Just as the regular police are always the front line of defence for the established order, defending power and property, so too the political police are always on the side of the political/economic status quo, suspicious of those who would challenge the powerful and the wealthy. There is nothing here that should surprise us, of course. As the American playwright David Mamet has mused, 'policemen so cherish their status as keepers of the peace and protectors of the public that they have occasionally been known to beat to death those citizens or groups who question that status.'[18] But the story of how the political police have defended the status quo is not well known, deliberately shrouded in secrecy as their activities have been. There is a kind of secret history of conservatism to be deciphered from the records of the security service. What we learn from this secret history is that the established order and the elites that defend it have not contented themselves with arguing their case in Parliament and in the court of public opinion, but have resorted to secret police spies, undercover agents, agents provocateurs, and occasional dirty tricks. We also learn that an interest in legitimately worrisome peoples and organizations often provides the political cover necessary for advancing other objectives, which cannot be attained as quickly, or at all, by democratic means.

If the history of the political police is a secret history of conservatism, the targets of state surveillance form a kind of roster of Canadian radicalism over the decades. From its origins in the late nineteenth century, socialist radicalism, in both the political and industrial spheres, was a long-term target of the secret police. By the time of the Russian Revolution in 1917, 'left-wing' activism had been identified as the grand antagonist of the capitalist order. If Protestant Canada had once identified Rome as the foreign source of papist doctrines propagated to subvert the proper religious order, conservative Canada in the twentieth century identified Moscow as the source of revolutionary Communist doctrine propagated to subvert the proper political and economic order. Any so-called left-wing activity was labelled as being linked to the Soviet Union, and thus fair game for the attentions of the secret police. This focus carried through the interwar years, was perpetuated during the Second World War even when the USSR became an ally in the war against the Axis, and was powerfully reinforced with the onset of the Cold War.

With the end of the Cold War in 1989–90, this decades-long obsession has had to give way to new targets, not without some resulting disorientation. Yet, even before the death throes of Soviet Communism, new threats had begun to intrude on the simplistic 'made-in-Moscow' model of security threats to the Canadian state: Quebec separatism, beginning in the early 1960s, provides perhaps the best example.

A great deal of this book will necessarily focus on the lengthy obsession with the political left. The secret police never developed a very sophisticated grasp of the subtleties of Marxist politics, but they were fairly adept in planting secret agents within the Communist ranks. In fact, they were in on the ground floor near the beginning of the Communist Party and in one form or another they retained a clandestine presence inside the party through depressions, wars, and cold wars. But their proclivity for Red-hunting did not stop there. They were convinced that it was necessary not only to penetrate the Communist Party but also to keep a close eye on every aspect of Canadian life where the Communists might try to spread their influence. This led them to plant or recruit sources of information within myriad private associations, from schools and universities to youth clubs, from ethnic dancing halls to foreign-language study groups, from civil-liberties associations to peace groups. Above all, it led them to honeycomb the labour movement with spies, sources, and agents. The amount of paper produced by Mounties keeping a baleful eye on trade unions in this country is staggering. There was a Department of Labour in Ottawa that kept information on union organization, strike activity, and collective-bargaining agreements, but this was not much more than a small public ornament of the federal government. Beneath the surface was a vast subterranean catacomb of secretly compiled information that far outmatched the scant public databank. If that were all, it would be alarming enough. But there is evidence that from time to time the security service did not rest content with collecting information and filing it away, that on occasion the service – or its friends and sources – may have played more active roles in covertly disrupting, dividing, and defeating unions. This was an activist conservatism on behalf of capital against its perceived enemies; that it was done surreptitiously and unaccountably adds up to a double challenge to the standard rhetoric about the neutrality of the democratic state.

With the growth of the modern state and its large bureaucratic apparatus, the security forces emerged in the 1930s and especially the 1940s with a new role of screening applicants for government jobs as well as screening existing employees seeking promotion to more sensitive posts, with access to confidential and classified government information. Even private firms with government contracts in the defence sector fell under security-screening requirements. To this must be added the requirement to screen the huge post-Second World War inflow of immigrants and refugees and applicants for Canadian citizenship and the anxiety over gays and lesbians in the civil service in the 1960s and 1970s.[19] This not only pumped up the number of files enormously – as well as straining police resources in the process – but also offered the police innumerable opportunities to increase their foothold within the many groups they targeted, to do deals with the objects of their screening to provide information, a typical modus operandi of intelligence services the world over.

Yet the targets of state surveillance did not always take these attentions quietly or without protest. The history of the secret police in Canada is also a history of resistance to being spied upon and interfered with. In some cases, as when Quebec separatism was the target, resistance turned out to be widespread and fierce, and may even have sparked greater support for the cause. And some Canadians, not always themselves the objects of intrusive observation, have undertaken to raise concerns about the violations of civil liberties and the strains on democratic standards occasioned by secret police activities, even in the darkest days of wartime when protest took some real courage. That said, it must also be acknowledged that political policing has not operated in a democratic vacuum. Always there has been considerable public support for secret wars against what many have considered dangerous subversives. Supporters have usually been content with letting the security force do its job silently, behind the scenes, and have asked few questions. If political policing is the secret arm of conservatism, it is a conservatism that has always commanded popular, even populist, support. Taken together with the resistance and protest, this democratic authoritarianism signifies that political policing is an inherently divisive and controversial venture on the part of the state. How could it be otherwise, when the state intervenes in the civil society on behalf of certain interests and against others, and then tries to cover its tracks?

The existence of a secret state within the state has always been a delicate management matter for governments. When things have gone wrong, or embarrassing facts have leaked out into the public realm, governments have often blustered, denied, and tried to cover up. If this fails to calm the waters, carefully controlled public investigations have been launched whose object has generally been symbolic reassurance. Immense legal, bureaucratic, and parliamentary resources have also proven effective to blunt or limit the effectiveness of more independent investigations, as was the case with the Military Police Complaints Commission which opened up the Afghan detainee question to public scrutiny. Periodically – as in the early 1980s and in 2010 – legislated mechanisms for public and parliamentary accountability have had to be enacted. Yet, through all this, the security forces soldier on, doing what they have always done, with more or less circumspection, and with a watchful eye on their would-be overseers.

From the point of view of governments, too much accountability seems threatening, but too little raises its own problems. Sir John A. Macdonald was briefly embarrassed when his handling of secret service funds outside parliamentary channels became public.[20] A century later, Pierre Trudeau's Liberal government of the late 1970s was plagued by recurrent scandals about RCMP wrongdoing.[21] Governments may also fear that their secret police will run out of their control, and even turn, Frankenstein-like, upon their political masters. Precisely this has been alleged to have occurred in Britain in the 1970s when the security service, MI5, was alleged to have plotted to destabilize the Labour government of Harold Wilson.[22] The former director of the FBI, J. Edgar Hoover, is known to have bugged and terrorized not only generations of Americans but successive U.S. presidents as well, not one of whom dared to challenge or rein him in. In this country, it is hard to find credible examples of governments being undermined by their own political police. The latter have generally worked in a fashion complementary to that of their political masters. More to the point, perhaps, are examples of the opposite effect: government misuse of the secret state for its own political purposes. The Trudeau Liberals used the RCMP as 'fall-guys' when their secret war on Quebec separatism went wrong, but, as this book will show, it was a war conceived and directed from the highest levels of the cabinet in Ottawa; the RCMP were only taking orders, even if their own enthusiasm sometimes inspired excessive zeal. The alternatives all boil down to the same point. Whether striking out on their own against their political masters or being misused by the same masters for political ends, secret police with extraordinary powers who act in the shadows are an ongoing problem for a healthy democracy.[23] This is a difficulty that is far from being resolved, but a close look at the history of the Canadian secret service over the past century or more makes two things unassailably clear: the list of those accused of subversion is always miles longer than those actually conducting subversive actions; and without strong, critical, and resolutely independent oversight, spy agencies will do more harm than good. The Arar inquiry made both points painfully clear.

With the terrorist attacks on 9/11 and the subsequent NATO invasion of Afghanistan, the history of political policing in Canada has moved into a new, distinctive era. The Cold War, which for nearly half a century instilled the world of security and intelligence with a pervasive single-mindedness and crusading zeal that to subsequent generations will surely seem as puzzling and incomprehensible as the medieval wars of religion, is now over. Yet, with scarcely a pause for breath, Canadian security and intelligence agencies have been put on the trail of Islamic jihadists both at home and, more important, on foreign soil. 'Events have increasingly required us to operate abroad,' the director of CSIS observed in 2003. 'Extremists respect no barriers either international or moral ... The centre of gravity of threats to the security of Canada has shifted.'[24] From its inception in the 1860s, the Canadian security service has always operated in a transnational context. Not only has it often relied on the British and Americans for institutional support, but it has defined what is, or what is not, a security risk with more than made-in-Canada prejudices and political realities in mind; global as well as local factors have always played a critical role in this respect. However, despite this enduring transnational influence, the Canadian security service has never operated abroad on a consistent basis. And yet now, in the post-9/11 environment, it appears to be doing just that, with serious implications for human lives, human rights, and the operation of Canadian democracy.

What follows is the first attempt at a comprehensive scholarly history of the political police in Canada, from their mid-nineteenth century origins to the present day. Others have examined segments of this history, from particular angles. Journalists John Sawatsky,[25] James Littleton,[26] and Richard Cleroux[27] have all written usefully about the post-war security service; as journalists, they have tended to rely upon interviews as their major source. We draw almost exclusively upon declassified government records and other documentary sources. There is one other major published source on the security service by a Canadian scholar, Larry Hannant's study of the RCMP's role in the origins of security screening, that merits mention; so, too, does the meticulous and groundbreaking scholarship of Steve Hewitt, Gary Kinsman, and Patricia Gentile.[28] There is also an invaluable unpublished source on the history of the RCMP security service from its origins to the late 1960s. This is an official internal history by two RCMP historians, Carl Betke and Stan Horrall, based upon untrammelled access to internal documentation, which has been released in censored form under Access to Information.[29] There are official published sources, including four royal commission reports,[30] a parliamentary review of the CSIS Act,[31] and the invaluable annual reports of the Security Intelligence Review Committee (SIRC), published since 1985–6, along with special reports by that body on specific issues that have arisen with regard to CSIS.[32]

The present-day security service may not appreciate our critical approach, but we think that it is about time that both the hitherto secret and public parts of the record be brought together and assessed within the broad sweep of the 145 years of Canada's experience as a nation.[33]

PART ONE

Origins

1

The Empire Strikes Back

Canada's early experience in the realm of intelligence and security matters, as in other areas of political life, was shaped decisively by its status as an outpost of the British empire.[1] Early experiments in covert policing took place in the aftermath of the Rebellions in Upper and Lower Canada in 1837 and 1838. At that time, the British authorities in Quebec, drawing on the example set by colonial authorities in Ireland and Jamaica, appointed stipendiary magistrates to head up a newly created rural police force with the authority to collect political intelligence and pacify the countryside. Decades later, during the American Civil War, colonial politicians in the Canadas adopted a similar, albeit much smaller, version of this system to prevent American military recruiters from violating Canadian neutrality.[2] Yet it was in the face of other, more threatening political challenges – at once domestic and foreign; nationalist, republican, and anti-imperialist – that the Canadian government undertook a greater, more sustained effort in political policing: by the 1860s, Irish radicals who sought to use North America as a staging ground for an independence struggle growing in Ireland itself were the target of the government's newly created secret police force. Just as imperial ties defined Canada's early political enemies, imperial personnel played a significant role in tracking those enemies down and curbing their influence – a pattern that would persist into the early 1900s (and is the focus of chapter 2). By the turn of the century, as the threat from Irish radicalism waned, the use of spies and spymasters had become a normal part of the federal civil service, tactics that the mother country – imbued with a deep tradition of individual rights and a steely Victorian confidence in the empire's resolve – was more reluctant to employ on its own soil.[3]

The Fenian Threat

The Irish Republican Brotherhood (IRB) was founded in Dublin in 1858. With a political pedigree that stretched back to the United Irish Rebellion in the 1790s, it was an avowedly revolutionary organization that was committed to overthrowing British rule in Ireland and establishing an Irish republic.[4] Yet, as its leader, James Stephens, understood well, success in the struggle at home required the substantial support of Irish immigrants abroad, most notably in the United States where tens of thousands of Irish men and women, many of whom had fled Ireland during the depths of the Famine, swelled the ranks of working-class populations in New York, Boston, Chicago, Detroit, and Cincinnati. Thus, seven months after the IRB's founding, Stephens travelled to New York. With the aid of Irish exiles, he helped to form an American support group, the Fenian Brotherhood, under the leadership of John O'Mahony, himself a seasoned rebel who had participated in the Irish Confederates' revolt of 1848 and 1849. Like its Irish counterpart, the US-wing of the organization – which was named after the *fianna*, mythical warriors in Irish mythology – was overwhelmingly working class; its supporters, some of whom had served in the Union Army during the U.S. Civil War, lived in large northern cities. 'No Irishman could have invented such a scheme. No Yankee would ever have believed in it,' the London *Times* observed sarcastically in October 1865. 'But put American exaggeration and Irish credulity together and you get Fenianism.'[5]

Braced in no small measure by supportive American politicians, who counted heavily on the Irish Catholic vote to win congressional elections, the Fenian organization grew rapidly in the United States in the late 1850s and early 1860s. 'Both Republicans and Democrats will fish for the Irish vote, and therefore wink as much as possible at any action of the Fenian body,' the Canadian prime minister, John A. Macdonald, remarked in 1868.[6] Yet, as Macdonald keenly appreciated, Fenianism found a receptive audience among Canada's urban working classes as well. A year after the organization was founded, Edward Meagher Condon, a representative of its U.S.-wing, contacted Michael Murphy, a cooper and tavern keeper who had established the predominantly working-class Hibernian Benevolent Society in Toronto in 1858. Shortly thereafter, a small clandestine Fenian circle, operating within the context of the association, received formal accreditation from John O'Mahony. By the mid-1860s, the society had extended its reach beyond Canada West's largest city to other locales such as St Catharines, Hamilton,

London, and Kingston – its burgeoning membership drawn to a heady mix of camaraderie, nationalism, and collective action at a time when local and provincial politics often turned on the power, privileges, and prejudices that differentiated the Orange from the Green. 'It is time to cast off the habiliments of wretchedness and come forth clothed in the manly garb of equality,' the *Irish Canadian*, the Hibernian's newspaper, exclaimed. 'We Irish will yet stand erect in Canada.'[7]

For his part, Michael Murphy, who attended the first national Fenian convention in the United States in 1863, walked a fine political line. He spoke publicly of the respectability, dignity, and fealty of the Hibernian Benevolent Society – qualities that justified the organization's existence in the face of 'Orange excesses' and challenges from more moderate Irish Catholic leaders, both lay and religious. At the same time, however, he railed against British imperialism in the 'old country' and publicly sympathized with 'any organization having for its object the freedom and prosperity of the Irish people.'[8] It was a delicate balancing act between loyalty and opposition, one that became increasingly untenable as the U.S.-wing of the organization debated publicly the possibility of invading Canada. With the British government's attention drawn to a battle in North America, so the argument went, Ireland would be vulnerable; perhaps a captive British North America could be bargained for a free Ireland. This strategy, which had circulated among Irish rebels since 1812, was so contentious that at their national convention in October 1865 the American Fenians split into two rival factions: O'Mahony rejected the idea of a Canadian invasion, proclaiming 'war in Ireland and nowhere else,' while his chief rival, William Roberts, endorsed it.[9] A Fenian marching song of 1866 captured the enthusiasm – and naivety – of the latter faction:

> We are the Fenian brotherhood, skilled in the arts of war,
> and we're going to fight for Ireland, the land that we adore.
> Many battles we have won, along with the boys in blue,
> and we'll go and capture Canada, for we've nothing else to do.[10]

Murphy (and other Toronto Hibernians) backed O'Mahony – and as late as March 1866, as rumours swirled in Canada West about an imminent Fenian invasion, he assured marchers in the city's annual St Patrick's Day parade that the Hibernians were loyal to both Canada and Ireland. Unfortunately for Murphy, O'Mahony, who originally opposed the idea of cross-border raids, changed his mind. In an attempt to restore his hold on the Fenian leadership, the American leader launched a feeble attempt to seize Campobello Island, New Brunswick, in April 1866. Significantly, Murphy and other Canadian Fenians were conspicuous by their absence, not because they had lost faith in the cause but because they were arrested in Cornwall, Canada West, en route to Portland, Maine, to join the advancing, if slim and under-armed, Green army. Days later, the Hibernian president and seven others were charged with treason – they were, after all, British subjects assisting in the invasion of a British territory – and put in jail.[11] Little did the prisoners then know, however, that the local police were acting on orders from the Canadian government, which had been watching them for some time.

About a year before the arrest of Murphy and his Fenian comrades, the Canadian government had begun monitoring the threat of Irish radicalism closely. At the government's disposal was a secret police force originally created in 1864 during the final months of the American Civil War to, in the words of one Canadian official, 'find out any attempt to disturb the public peace, the existence of any plot, conspiracy, or organization whereby peace would be endangered, the Queen's Majesty insulted, or her proclamation of neutrality infringed.'[12] At the time of the Civil War, George-Étienne Cartier, attorney general and leader of the Conservative bloc from Canada East, appointed Frederick William Ermatinger, a former lieutenant-colonel in the Royal Montreal Cavalry with extensive experience handling labour unrest and urban crowds, to head up the force east of the Ottawa River. At the same time, John A. Macdonald, Cartier's Conservative counterpart in Canada West, hired Gilbert McMicken, a one-time customs agent, to establish the new Western Frontier Constabulary. From Macdonald's viewpoint, McMicken was a suitable choice for many reasons, not least of which was his extensive first-hand knowledge of life and politics along the U.S. border. After arriving in Canada in 1832 and marrying into a prominent family in 1835, McMicken had built a business career directly connected to cross-border transportation, communication, and trade.[13] Closely tied to prominent merchants on the Niagara peninsula and politically loyal to Macdonald, he became a customs inspector in 1838, an elected member of the Legislative Assembly in 1857, and an excise officer in Windsor in 1864, just two months before assuming his secretive police duties. '[He is] a shrewd, cool, and determined man who won't easily lose his head and who will fearlessly perform his duty,' Macdonald remarked after appointing McMicken to his new post.[14]

As 1864 became 1865, McMicken consulted with customs agents, telegraph operators, saloon keepers, and American officials up and down the border region; under his command were at least fifteen undercover operatives, who filed copious reports from Detroit and Buffalo, London, Brantford, and Sarnia as they, too, watched for illegal cross-border activities of military recruiters, draft resisters, and bounty hunters.[15] When the 'war between the states' finally reached its bloody conclusion in early April 1865, the embryonic secret police did not disappear. Border security remained paramount; only the threat had changed. Raids conducted by British officials against the Fenians' parent organization in the United Kingdom – which closed newspapers, intimidated supporters, and jailed high-profile leaders – piqued the Canadian government's interest in the new question of Irish radicalism; so, too, did the emergence of the 'Canada option' among contenders for the Fenians' American leadership, which prompted worries in the Canadas about the loyalties of Irish Catholics in Canadian border towns. The demobilization of thousands of Irish Catholic soldiers from the Union Army – 'boys in blue' who could make $100 if they signed on with the Fenians – added to the general sense of unease. 'I … now, in consequence of this Fenian business, authorize [sic] you to employ five or six good men more – they should watch the whole frontier, in your beat,' Macdonald wrote to McMicken. 'The Fenian action in Ireland is serious, and the Imperial government seems fully alive to it. We must not be caught napping. Keep me fully advised.'[16]

To keep Macdonald fully briefed, McMicken increased substantially the number of men under his command; by 1870, upward of fifty agents, working both in the United States and in Canada, were attending Fenian meetings, hanging out at Irish saloons, and shadowing suspected 'Irish Rebbles.' Fragmentary evidence suggests that McMicken's recruits were usually men in their late twenties and early thirties who possessed military and/or police backgrounds; of the seventeen agents who can be positively identified, seven were Irish (six Roman Catholics), six were Scottish (one Roman Catholic), and five were English (all Protestants). Paid relatively well, making at least $1.25 per day with all expenses paid, including the purchase of information, some informants nonetheless took up employment in the areas under their supervision in order to allay any suspicions about how they were supporting themselves – and what their real motives were.[17] 'I was impressed with the idea that he was capable and had proven his being a very intelligent Irish Roman Catholic,' McMicken wrote to Macdonald, assessing the credentials of one of his undercover men. 'This, in connection with his integrity and loyalty, led me to engage his services for a time. He was to put himself in communication with the British Consul there [Buffalo] and be instructed by him and through him by me.'[18]

When it came to tracking the machinations of Fenian rebels in the United States, the Canadian government worked cheek by jowl with British consular officials in several large American cities, most notably Buffalo, a key border crossing, and New York, a hive of Green activity and home to O'Mahony's headquarters. Key to this arrangement was Sir Edward Mortimer Archibald, a Nova Scotia-born lawyer who served as clerk to the House of Assembly, attorney general, and Supreme Court justice in Newfoundland from 1833 to 1854 before being appointed British consul at New York in 1857. By 1866, as the Fenians gathered strength in the United States, Archibald had recruited a group of informers – some of whom operated in the upper echelons of the Fenian organization – and tapped his connections with local law-enforcement and customs officials to keep tabs on the revolutionary outfit. Consular officials in other cities, such as H.W. Hemans in Buffalo, made similar arrangements with paid informants and, like their New York counterpart, were often in direct contact with some of McMicken's men. For his part, Archibald forwarded the information he received from this loose collection of sources to various British officials, including the colonial secretary (who, in turn, informed police forces in London and Dublin), the commander of British forces in North America, the lieutenant governor of New Brunswick, and the governor general of Canada, Lord Monck.[19] Combined, the Canadian government and British diplomats marshalled a far-flung and eclectic battery of informants. Drawn from inside and outside the Fenians' ranks and scattered along the Canada-U.S. border, it pumped information through the capillaries of communication that linked governments and law-enforcement agencies on both sides of the Atlantic. Years later, Archibald, a long-time servant of the empire, was knighted for his role in fending off the Fenians – both in North America and in the United Kingdom.[20]

On Canadian soil, responsibility for monitoring the Fenians fell not to imperial civil servants but to McMicken's agents and local police forces. By the end of December 1865, Patrick Nolan, one of McMicken's most reliable informants in Chicago, was recalled to Canada and sent to Toronto, a place where the Hibernian Benevolent Society appeared to be very active. Once in the city, the highly prized secret agent was placed at the disposal of both a local crown attorney and McMicken himself – a development that angered the dutiful and diligent spymaster considerably. 'I feel quite provoked at all this for it is a very difficult thing to find a capable and reliable Irish Roman Catholic who will undertake such service and it is extremely imprudent to say the least to place a detective working in secret in communication with too many,' McMicken informed Macdonald. 'He is apt to become demoralized[,] to think what he has to inform so many is of little consequence and may be got up for the occasion. He loses attachment, as I may say, between himself and the person he deals in secrecy with. He fears for his own exposure and is apt to become careless and indifferent and in some case the result might be a "change of face" to save himself.'[21] How this matter was ultimately resolved is not clear; what is obvious, however, is that Nolan was indeed an adroit and effective undercover agent. Within months of accepting his assignment in Toronto, he had submerged himself in the local Green scene, filing numerous reports between December 1865 and March 1866 that confirmed McMicken's and Macdonald's worse fears: there were approximately seventeen Fenian lodges in Canada West, nine of them in Toronto; the Hibernian Benevolent Society and the Fenians were not the same thing, but there was substantial overlap between the two organizations; and the ubiquitous Michael Murphy was indeed a Fenian supporter and was in touch with like-minded individuals in the United States.[22]

As St Patrick's Day, 1866, approached, Nolan reported that Murphy and a group of supporters were preparing to leave Toronto after the celebration to assist O'Mahony, the American Fenian leader, in a cross-border raid of some kind. Some of the volunteer soldiers, McMicken's highly prized informant added, were currently staying at Murphy's Toronto tavern. Much to the satisfaction of the city's Protestant establishment, the March 17th parade ended without incident; McMicken, too, was pleased for he had met with Murphy shortly before the festivities to ensure that things remained 'unprovocative.'[23] Days later, as Nolan had predicted, Murphy and a small band of allies left Toronto by train for the Maritimes, followed by no fewer than four undercover agents assigned by McMicken. Meanwhile, Edward Archibald, from his consular perch in New York, continued to sound the alarm. Dispatches were sent to John A. Macdonald and Arthur Gordon, the lieutenant governor of New Brunswick, about the possibility of a Fenian incursion across the Maine-New Brunswick border. Gordon also received appraisals from the British colonial secretary, Edward Cardwell, and the commander of British forces in North America, Sir John Michel. 'I know every move of the small Fenian circle in Calais and the names of all the members and have very good information at Eastport and Bangor also,' the lieutenant governor observed.[24] Perhaps not surprisingly, when the raids on Campobello Island finally took place in April 1866, they were easily turned back by British and American authorities. Not only were both governments well advised, as Gordon's observation attests, but the Fenians' much-needed reinforcements from Canada never made it to the battlefield.[25] North of the border, Murphy and the Toronto Hibernians were arrested in Cornwall, Canada West, a move that came at the behest of Attorney General George-Étienne Cartier and Minister of Finance Alexander Galt, who were anxious to contain the Fenian threat before it spread further in their own, largely Roman Catholic, bailiwick of Canada East.

John A. Macdonald was not impressed by his colleagues' decisive actions. Not only did Cartier and Galt not possess the necessary information to convict Murphy of treason, but the ministers' intervention scuttled the ongoing undercover efforts of McMicken and Ermatinger, who had been ordered to pick up Murphy's trail as he made his way east. In government circles, this conflict between open prosecution and longer-range intelligence-gathering objectives later gave way to outright embarrassment as repeated spying efforts, including the use of a jailhouse snitch and the ransacking of Hibernian offices, failed to produce adequate evidence to prosecute the jailed Fenians. Nearly five months after their arrest, Murphy and five of his six supporters escaped from custody by tunnelling out of the Cornwall jail, commandeering a row boat, and crossing the St Lawrence River to Ogdensburg in upper New York State – thereby saving the future prime minister the embarrassment of their going to trial and being acquitted.[26] Still, despite the internal controversy surrounding Murphy's arrest, Macdonald had reason to be satisfied with his handling of the Fenian invasion. Not only had O'Mahony's plan 'to free Ireland on the plains of Canada' been foiled, but the government's tough stand on the issue was playing a role in the ongoing debates over Confederation. Samuel L. Tilley, the former New Brunswick leader and staunch proponent of a federal union, strengthened his successful re-election bid by linking the Fenian invasion attempt to the wider issue of American annexation – a threat that only a strong, national government could turn back. 'You will laugh when you see the Antis are endeavouring to make people believe that you Canadians have sent them [the Fenians] here to aid Confederation,' Tilley wrote to Macdonald in the spring of 1866.[27]

But the Fenians' defeat at Campobello did little to discourage the militant Roberts-wing of the organization, the group which was the first to map out a plan to 'make a strike for Canada,' or scotch rumours in Canada West that an additional raid was imminent. 'Steadfast stand, and sleepless ward / Along the line! Along the line! / Great the treasures that you guard / Along the line! Along the line!' wrote Thomas D'Arcy McGee, the prominent Irish Catholic leader, member of Parliament, and future 'father of Confederation,' after the Campobello raid.[28] As a consequence, the government refocused its attention on the American scene. By mid-May 1866, McMicken had additional men, including stalwart Patrick Nolan, stationed in Fort Erie, Detroit, Chicago, and Cleveland, to name but four locales. For his part, Ermatinger, whose role as a spymaster is little understood, appears to have had informants in Ogdensburg and New York. Many of these agents were in constant contact with British consular officials who, in turn, continued to communicate with Lord Monck; by this time, an inspector from the Royal Irish Constabulary had been assigned to the Fenian file in the United States. With agents active on both sides of the border, Canadian authorities believed that the 'line' was well guarded. 'Three things ... deprive the Fenian threat of their significance,' Monck wrote to John A. Macdonald in the spring of 1866, flushed with confidence. 'They are, First, our power at very short notice to turn out a large body of troops and turn them on any threatened point – Second, the certainty that the Government of the United States will permit no invasion of Canada from their soils nor export munitions – Third, the inability of the Fenian leaders to get together any number of men without our knowledge.'[29]

But the governor general's confidence was misplaced. Canadian authorities were indeed forewarned, but they were not, surprisingly, forearmed. Poor communication between government, secret service, and military officials, coupled with conflicting reports from some secret agents, generated a mix of confusion and complacency in official circles. So too, it appears, did a misplaced belief that U.S. law-enforcement agencies would intervene, as they had at Campobello. As a consequence, the Canadian government, despite its extensive preparations, was unable to prevent additional Fenian attacks in June 1866, one in Canada West (Ridgeway and Fort Erie) and another in Canada East.[30] The Fenians' military manoeuvres in Canada West were devised by Major General Thomas Sweeney, a veteran of both the U.S. Civil War and the Mexican-American conflict. Originally, Sweeney had proposed a more sophisticated invasion strategy which involved multiple raids

in Canada West and a massive deployment of Fenian men into Canada
East; French Canadians, it was surmised, possessed their own complicated history with the British crown and thus would join the armed republican struggle.[31] It did not happen that way. The diversionary attack
on Toronto failed to materialize and its commander was subsequently
dismissed for cowardice. In the southwestern corner of Canada West,
an invasion force of perhaps eight hundred men, about one-sixth the
size that Sweeney had hoped for, crossed the Niagara River on 31 May,
clashed with the Canadian militia on 2 June at Ridgeway, and, significantly, won a modest – yet short-lived – victory; another skirmish later
that afternoon at nearby Fort Erie also went to the Fenians. A day later,
as Canadian reinforcements headed to the area, the Fenians retreated
back across the border where they eventually surrendered to the U.S.
army, which by that time had disrupted their supply lines. By the time
the fighting in the Niagara area was over, twelve Canadian soldiers lay
dead and forty others wounded, while eighteen Fenian fighters were
lost and twenty-four were injured. 'Onward is the order,' read a Fenian
proclamation issued after the battle of Ridgeway, 'and let Ireland and
victory be the watchword.'[32] With Canadian troops fanning out across
the border regions of Canada West, the Fenians shifted their military
focus to Canada East. From Franklin, Vermont, they hoped to assemble
a fighting force of 12,000 men and cross the Canadian border again. Yet
on the day of the attack, 8 June, only 1,000 Fenian soldiers were ready
to go. Undermanned, under-armed, and facing a massive mobilization
of British regulars and Canadian militia sent from Montreal, the seat
of British military power in Canada, the Green army was effectively
pushed back. By early July, eighty-one Fenians sat in Canadian jails.[33]

Against Lawless Aggression

In the aftermath of the cross-border raids, the provincial Parliament
went on the offensive. At its disposal was the Upper Canada Lawless
Aggression Act, which was originally passed after the Rebellions of
1837–8; targeting individuals who attacked the Canadian colony from
a country at peace with Britain, the legislation also reduced dramatically the procedural safeguards ordinarily available to the accused under British treason laws. In early June 1866, the Legislative Assembly
amended the act by extending its reach to Lower Canada and making it
easier for the government to use military, as opposed to civilian, courts
to prosecute alleged aggressors; in August 1866, the earlier amend-

ments were made retroactive, thereby bringing the Fenian actions in Lower Canada, which did not possess equivalent legislation at the time the cross-border offences took place, within the law's coercive ambit.[34] During that earlier, June sitting of the Canadian assembly, lawmakers took other determined steps to deal with the Fenian question. They suspended habeas corpus for a year, and, without the burden of having to establish the lawfulness of an arrest before a judge or court, police in both Upper and Lower Canada arrested about fifty men suspected of Fenian sympathies. What was more, Parliament also passed legislation 'to prevent the unlawful training of persons in Military evolutions, and the use of Fire Arms, and to authorize the seizure of Fire Arms collected for purposes dangerous to the public peace' and made a huge military appropriation – $1,897,085 on a total budget of $7,003,236 – which included $100,000 for 'detective and secret service work'; it added an additional $50,000 and $75,000 in 1867 and 1868 respectively. To the anxious Canadian legislators, all of these measures were both necessary and just; not only had the Fenians undertaken three separate incursions onto British territory, but in the United States the organization's supporters, a coveted cohort for U.S. politicians, still numbered in the tens of thousands.[35] One Fenian picnic in August 1866 in Chicago was attended by 11,000 people, one of whom was the state's governor. 'The Fenians using the politicians and the Politicians using the Fenians,' McMicken wrote at the time. 'It seems disgraceful, however, to see the Governor of the State ... so sunk in demagogueism.'[36]

When it came to prosecuting the jailed Fenians, Macdonald (still the attorney general of Canada West) found himself constrained by a range of legal and political matters. British officials – the secretary of state for the colonies, Edward Cardwell, and his successor, the Earl of Carnarvon – expressed general concerns about strained Anglo-American relations and specific worries about the amended Upper Canada Lawless Aggression Act. The possibility of trials without juries, they both maintained, offended basic principles of British justice and threatened to inflame further Fenian passions, in North America and abroad; Lord Monck, the governor general, agreed on both points. While Macdonald resented this unsolicited pressure from above, he agreed to move cautiously against those 'unlawfully and feloniously in arms'; regular civilian trials, not military courts martial, would be used.[37] Between October 1866 and January 1867, fifty-seven Fenians were brought to trial; twenty-two of them were convicted of lawless aggression and sentenced to hang.[38] Despite the occasional death threat against judges and jurors – 'For every drop of Fenian blood you spill, rivers will flow in revenge' – the trials, from the government's perspective, proceeded smoothly: American authorities paid the legal bills of the accused; overt anti-Catholic sentiment in the courts was kept to a minimum; and unresolved legal questions related to the Lawless Aggression Act were carefully avoided. British justice, it seemed, had triumphed at trial – an impression reinforced later by the attorney general's decision, on the strong advice of his imperial colleagues, to change each of the twenty-two death sentences to twenty years of hard labour in Kingston Penitentiary. 'It will prove to the Roman Catholics of Ontario,' Macdonald observed, 'that I have consulted their feelings in the matter.'[39]

Yet, behind this spectacle of judicial fairness and impartiality, Gilbert McMicken's secret police remained active. With the lion's share of the new secret service budget at his disposal, he maintained at least sixteen secret agents throughout southwestern Canada West in places such as Welland, Thorold, Hamilton, and Windsor, including several informants who routinely intercepted suspected Fenian communications by mail and telegraph. By the end of 1866, however, McMicken's focus appears to have shifted somewhat – from the border zones to key urban centres of Fenian activity in Chicago and New York. The movement of agent Charles Clarke illustrates this change well. As Cornelius O'Sullivan, he infiltrated a Fenian circle in the Ridgeway-Fort Erie area and, along with at least one other agent, provided details of Fenian manoeuvres at the time of the fighting in early June; after stints at several Fenian conventions, he was transferred to Brooklyn where he quickly rose to prominence among local Irish republicans, eventually winning the confidence of Roberts and other influential leaders. His numerous reports chronicled both the political machinations taking place within the Fenian organization after the June invasions and the ebb and flow of the so-called Canadian option. 'You will not see a raid this spring,' he wrote in March 1867. 'I say this from what I heard today from Robberts [sic] himself. I do not care from what source you have your information[,] I know *I am right* and I say it at the risk of your opinion of me.'[40] Other Canadian recruits, such as W.M. McMichael in New York and J.W. McDonald in Buffalo and Philadelphia, developed into extremely successful spies; also useful was Charles Joseph Coursol, a cavalry officer with considerable police and militia experience, who was hired to run special agents on the Quebec-United States border.[41] Much of the intelligence generated by this extensive network ended up with Macdonald, who by the fall of 1867 was prime minister and minister of justice of the new Dominion. And from his vantage point it was clear that the Fenian threat from the American side of the border had not subsided significantly – despite their defeats the previous year – and that there were still many Irish Canadians with access to guns who supported them. As a result, in the first session of the new Dominion Parliament in November, Macdonald introduced a bill to extend the suspension of habeus corpus for yet another year. The legislation passed easily.[42]

A Doomed Man and the Prince of Spies

Other, far-reaching changes were under way too – spurred on by the assassination of Thomas D'Arcy McGee on 7 April 1868. A passionate advocate of Irish republicanism in his youth, McGee immigrated to North America in 1842; after fifteen years working as a journalist and writer in Boston and New York City, he moved in 1857 to Montreal, where he was elected as a member of the Legislative Assembly. By the time McGee started his career in Canadian politics, the radicalism of his youth had vanished completely, replaced by a staunchly conservative viewpoint that drew the ire of many Irish Catholic immigrants, who now saw him as a traitor to the cause of a free Ireland.[43] In the pages of Irish newspapers, in the ranks of Irish societies, and in the streets when he campaigned for office in the mid-1860s, the hatred poured out. Death threats from Fenians were not uncommon; nor was it unusual for McGee to travel with a body guard. For his part, McGee did little to hide his disdain for his erstwhile comrades; he routinely and harshly denounced them in public and called for the execution of the Fenians captured after the 1866 raids, even while Macdonald and Monck pursued a more moderate approach to sentencing in the name of British justice.[44] So perhaps it surprised few people when, in early April 1868, a suspected Fenian sympathizer shot and killed McGee outside his rooming house in Ottawa. 'His only crime was that he steadily and affectionately advised his countrymen in Canada to enjoy all the advantages that our equal laws and institutions gave to Irishmen and to Roman Catholics,' Macdonald told a friend in England. 'He sternly set his face against the introduction of Fenianism into Canada, and he was therefore a doomed man.'[45]

Without the obstacle of habeas corpus, which had been resuspended the year before, the Canadian authorities arrested dozens of individuals. At first, only those directly connected to the accused – Patrick James Whelan, an Irish nationalist and tailor who was then working

in Ottawa – were taken in; within weeks, however, the circles of repression widened further to include men and women who simply
possessed Fenian sympathies, including Patrick Boyle, editor of the
Irish Canadian, and John Nolan, treasurer of Toronto's high-profile Hibernian society (his brother, Patrick, was one of McMicken's spies!).
Anxious to convict Whelan, Macdonald dipped into the secret service
fund, something he would do often during his tenure as prime minister, to help grease the wheels of political advantage: he provided
the prosecuting attorney in the case and at least one putative eyewitness with funds for room, board, and expenses. At trial in September
1868, the crown made much of the gun with burnt powder found in
Whelan's jacket, which suggested the accused had the means to commit murder; copies of the *Irish American* and a badge from the Toronto
Hibernian Society found in his room indicated his likely motive. After
an eight-day hearing, Whelan – who steadfastly maintained his innocence – was convicted of murder; he was hanged in Ottawa the following year, the last public execution in Canada. No public burial was
held for fear of a Fenian demonstration.[46]

In addition to the intimidation of suspected Fenians in Canada, Mc-
Gee's assassination prompted the ruling Conservatives to create the Dominion Police (DP) in May 1868 under the direction of McMicken and
Coursol, the latter replacing Ermatinger who had retired on account
of poor health. Mandated to protect government buildings, investigate
federal crimes such as mail theft, and undertake political policing, the
new force provided a more permanent home for the secret service. It
also provided the institutional context within which McMicken and
Macdonald recruited one of their most impressive undercover operatives: Thomas Beach. Born in England in 1841 to a modest family, Beach
worked in France as a banker in the late 1850s, eventually leaving Europe for North America in 1861 to fight for the Union Army in the Civil
War. Once in the United States, Beach enlisted in 8th Pennsylvania Re-
serve as a private and adopted the name Henri le Caron – a pseudonym that is perhaps the source of David Cornwell's nom de plume Le
Carré. After the war, he settled in Illinois and later took a position as
a medical officer at the Illinois State Penitentiary.[47] On the basis of his
military credentials and knowledge of Fenianism – he had served with
Irish soldiers in the Union Army – le Caron was recruited by British officials in the autumn of 1867 to be a paid informant. He was very good
at his job. Soon after establishing a Fenian circle in Lockport, Illinois,
le Caron was promoted to the rank of 'Major and Military Organizer'

with a mandate to organize throughout the eastern states and a salary of $100 a month.[48]

Early on, le Caron reported to the British Home Office, but as he penetrated the Fenians' inner circles he looked for a closer, more secure contact: the Canadian government. After receiving a letter from le Caron, Macdonald sent McMicken to Detroit in early June 1868 to meet the British spy. 'He will enter the service as an organiser – will accept a position on [Fenian General John] O'Neill's staff – will run the risk consequent upon any actual engagement upon Canadian soil,' the veteran spymaster wrote to Macdonald. 'He is to furnish me from time to time with correct information as they proceed with work and in due season inform me of the actual points of attack with all particulars in order that we may be prepared for them.'[49] Apparently impressed with le Caron's connections, Macdonald authorized McMicken to hire him for $150 a month, but warned: 'A man who will engage to do what he offers to do, that is, betray those with whom he acts, is not to be trusted.'[50] Macdonald's scepticism was misplaced. From the date of his recruitment, le Caron provided the Canadian government with copious and prescient intelligence, often on a daily basis. 'I succeeded in hoodwinking the poor and deluded, together with the unprincipled, blatant, professional Irish patriots,' le Caron recalled in his immensely popular autobiography. '[I was] successful in winning the confidence of almost every Fenian with whom I was brought in contact, and in obtaining the most important information and details.'[51]

By the end of 1868, the Canadian government had, to some extent, carved out a more permanent role for its embryonic secret service: it boasted institutional support in the form of the newly minted Dominion Police, possessed a stable budget with the secret service fund, and depended more and more on the expertise of its own well-paid and highly placed agents than on the observations of well-connected imperial officials. Thus, when rumblings of another Fenian invasion emerged in 1869 and 1870, Canadian government officials enjoyed near complete knowledge of Fenian preparations; some even mused about letting a raid take place, so that the bothersome Irish rebels could be crushed once and for all.[52] The Fenian strategy this time around involved a main invasion at Franklin, Vermont, and Malone, New York, with diversionary raids at Detroit, Buffalo, and Ogdensburg. In the months and days leading up to the actual incursion, which took place in late May 1870, le Caron was in the thick of things: he worked closely with Fenian General John O'Neill, helped to prepare Fenian military strategy, and stashed guns and ammunition at key border points – all the while communicating the Fenians' day-to-day whereabouts to McMicken. (On one occasion, two of Coursol's informants reported on le Caron's activities, unaware that the highly respected Fenian commander was himself an undercover agent.)[53] Not surprisingly, then, when O'Neill and about two hundred Fenian soldiers finally crossed the border from Vermont, they were met by a sizable Canadian force – one that had been called up and prepared well in advance – and were soundly defeated. The presence of U.S. troops in the area, put on alert after President Ulysses S. Grant reviewed extensive intelligence generated by his own sources, sealed the Greens' fate on that day. Months later, McMicken, who was thrilled with le Caron's actions in hindering O'Neill's advance, paid his star informant a bonus of $2,000: 'he was a true hearted Englishman,' he told John A. Macdonald.[54]

Western Opportunities

Down but not out, O'Neill participated in a final campaign against Canada, this time along the Canadian-American border in the west in 1871. Fresh from a two-year stint in jail for his role in the Vermont debacle, the former 'hero of Ridgeway' assembled a raiding party of between forty and eighty men with Fenian connections at Pembina, North Dakota, with the intent of attacking the newly created province of Manitoba. In early October, however, O'Neill's small army was confronted by American authorities shortly after it took a Hudson's Bay Company fort inside the Canadian border; a handful of men, including O'Neill, were arrested and the invasion fizzled.[55] What Gilbert McMicken would later call the 'abortive raid' on Manitoba was not, officially, a Fenian operation. Organized by William Bernard O'Donoghue, who had served as treasurer of Louis Riel's provisional government during the Red River Rebellion of 1869–70, the attack was not sanctioned by the leadership of the Fenian Brotherhood in Canada or the United States, though O'Donoghue was successful in gaining O'Neill's support. O'Donoghue later explained that he viewed the action as an attempt to revive Riel's rebellion. The raiders clearly anticipated that they would gain the support of Manitoba's Métis community, with whom they shared both a religion and an anti-colonial perspective. A Fenian-Métis alliance was precisely what the lieutenant governor of Manitoba, Adams George Archibald, feared, but it failed to materialize. Riel and other Métis leaders, in this instance, remained loyal to the government.

A grateful Archibald became infamous in the eyes of Ontario Orange-men for shaking hands with Riel after inspecting Métis troops who volunteered to help defend the province against O'Donoghue's Fenian-assisted incursion.[56]

In McMicken's own account of this apprehended insurrection, he de-scribes, in a style fit for *Boy's Own Annual*, his surreptitious trip from St Paul, Minnesota, to Fort Garry, Manitoba, during which he slipped by the Fenian raiders; his assistance to Archibald in raising a militia of 'loyal Canadians'; and his unflagging devotion to queen and country.[57] Importantly, the so-called Fenian threat to Manitoba only hastened McMicken on a journey already in progress. Even before the fateful handshake with Riel, Prime Minister Macdonald and other federal politicians were concerned that Lieutenant Governor Archibald was too sympathetic to Métis demands that they be granted the lands guar-anteed them in the Manitoba Act. McMicken was dispatched to, as he put it to Macdonald, ensure that 'actual settlers' received land without enraging 'French half breeds' over violations of their 'fancied rights.'[58] In addition to his duties as Dominion Police commissioner, then, Mc-Micken was appointed to a number of civil-service offices in Manitoba: he was simultaneously an agent of the Dominion Lands Branch, the province's assistant receiver general, secretary of the Intercolonial Rail-way commission, and an immigration officer. While in Manitoba, as Macdonald's intelligence agent, McMicken surreptitiously monitored both Archibald's activities and the security threat posed by the Métis. As lands agent, McMicken proposed a scheme for a random distribu-tion of lands to the Métis that undermined the arrangements already made by Archibald.[59] Deeply loyal to Prime Minister Macdonald, Mc-Micken had with John A's patronage fashioned a long career that (by the late 1860s and early 1870s) effectively combined the public duties of an administrator with the private actions associated with national security – a blending of roles that foreshadowed the tactics deployed by the federal government in the early decades of the next century.

Although the failed Manitoba raid crippled the Fenians as an or-ganization, radical Irish nationalism, in its various guises, persisted in North America. When in the mid- to late 1870s and 1880s the Land Leaguers and the United Brotherhood or Clan-na-Gael emerged in the United States, the Canadian government possessed the experience and institutional means to address the possibility of additional cross-border actions. 'I have some paid agents in the various large cities just now who are employed temporarily, their duty is to report what occurs as

the various secret meetings of these various dynamite conspirators,'
Percy Sherwood, superintendent and later commissioner of the Dominion Police, wrote in 1883. 'I need scarcely tell you that my informants
are of the same stripe and have a finger in the pie. The only way to deal
with this class of crime is to buy up the principals. It goes against the
grain, but has become a necessity.'[60] That the use of undercover agents
had become so routine, so commonplace by that time underscores just
how *un*controversial the formation of the secret service was among
Canada's political leaders. The suspension of habeas corpus, political arrests without charges, mail seizure, secret agents, perhaps even
agents provocateurs – all were present in the formative years of the
new nation-state and all went virtually unopposed, the lone dissenting
voices being those of the victims. The only controversy about the secret
service came in 1877 when Alexander Mackenzie's Liberal government
investigated Macdonald's misuse of the secret service fund. Yet at issue
was not the legitimacy, purpose, or secrecy of the fund, but simply its
misappropriation; even the oversight established by Parliament after
the probe was concluded fell far short of equivalent standards found in
England at the same time.

Drawing on a legacy of centralized authority in Upper Canada – the
'Tory touch' – the prerogative of the federal government to surreptitiously monitor potentially subversive citizens was underwritten by
the 'peace, order and good government' provision of the British North
America Act of 1867, which allowed for a highly centralized state and
made available to the prime minister and his cabinet a wide range of
emergency powers – executive and administrative – to confront threats
to the political and economic status quo. As attorney general in Upper Canada, and later as Dominion leader, Macdonald rarely hesitated
in availing himself of these significant powers: he exerted a firm grip
on his subordinates, personally controlled the secret service fund, and
developed the mechanisms necessary to gather intelligence in recognition of personal, national, and imperial interests. Mindful of these
wider considerations, Macdonald occasionally used the suspension of
habeas corpus with a touch of restraint and moderation; yet the limited
scope of this overt breach of civil liberties was made possible, in large
measure, through extensive covert intelligence by the secret police. The
profound suspicion so prevalent in Victorian England of spies, spying,
and secrecy found few reflections in the Canadian outpost of empire.

By the time of Macdonald's death in 1891, the threat from radical
Irish nationalism in North America had waned, only to be replaced in

the opening years of the next century by another anti-colonial movement that hoped – in a similar fashion – to strike a blow for independence at home by generating support for its cause in North America.
By this time, however, the Canadian government knew how to handle
such political challenges and it was, quite naturally, willing to press
that knowledge into service for both the good of the mother country
and the stability of British rule – the *Raj* – in India. South Asian radicalism, which was based on the Pacific coast yet possessed a global reach,
is the focus of the next chapter.

2

'You Drive Us Hindus out of Canada and We Will Drive Every White Man out of India!'

In India, as in Ireland, opposition to British rule grew steadily over the nineteenth and early twentieth centuries. Active locally and nationally, it came in many forms, adopted a wide range of tactics, and debated myriad issues – notably the possibility of Indian self-determination. 'The methods which the agitators have pursued are singularly like those adopted in Ireland,' Lord Hamilton, the secretary of state for India, wrote to that country's viceroy in 1899 shortly after the assassination of two British officials in the Bombay Presidency, 'an ostensible constitutional party, a virulent and seditious press on the border land of legality, and an inner circle of desperadoes.'[1] Yet those desperadoes, as British officials in London and Calcutta (the seat of imperial rule in India) knew well, were not confined to the subcontinent alone. In England, France, Germany, Switzerland, Japan, and (increasingly) the United States, Indian radicals – typically male, university-educated, and middle-class – mixed with left-wing and liberal intellectuals, socialists and trade unionists, anarchists and civil libertarians, and other immigrants and exiles, many of whom shared their anti-British perspective. 'It is clear that the advantages of America as a training ground for revolutionaries are well recognized by the Indian agitators,' an early report drafted by the Indian government's Criminal Investigation Department (CID) observed. 'In New York especially, a strong colony of discontented Irish … are always ready to take up [with] any movement likely to embarrass the British Government.'[2] Wherever their location, Indian radicals rejected the moderate approach charted by the Indian National Congress, which was founded in 1885, and articulated instead a vision of Indian independence achieved through militant tactics. Canada, too, was home to a vibrant and diverse South Asian community, which included a small group of people deeply involved in the movement for Indian self-rule with political connections that stretched around the world. Like the Fenians before them, they became the focus of intense surveillance by the Canadian government, for its officials feared, as they had in the 1860s, that the politics of immigrants at home might undermine British power abroad.[3]

The 'Hindoo' Crisis

Between 1904 and 1908, about 5,200 South Asians, most of whom were Sikhs from the Punjab, immigrated to British Columbia. Drawn by the promise of work and wages in the industrializing West, they arrived at a time of intense anti-Asian agitation.[4] Spurred on by the inflammatory rhetoric and violent demonstrations of many white British Columbians, which only intensified as the province's economy faltered in 1907, the federal government sought to curtail Asian immigration by raising the head tax on newcomers from China and negotiating a 'gentleman's agreement' with Japanese authorities. For the ruling Liberals in Ottawa, the outright exclusion of South Asian immigrants posed a significant challenge, for, unlike the Chinese and Japanese, they were British subjects and, at least in theory, possessed all the rights and freedoms associated with that status.[5] The wider connection between the condition of South Asians in Canada and the political stability of the Raj was also a key concern. A Canadian ban on Indian immigration would have revealed the hollowness of the rights the crown claimed to safeguard, so the argument went, and likely fanned the flames of anti-imperial sentiment, which burned more intensely inside and outside the subcontinent after Lord Curzon, the viceroy, decided to partition Bengal in 1905.[6] 'Strange as it is,' Prime Minister Wilfrid Laurier observed, 'yet England is now threatened in India … She has endeavoured to lift up and to educate those groping masses, and the consequence is agitators and agitations.'[7]

In March 1908 Laurier dispatched William Lyon Mackenzie King, the young deputy minister of labour, to England to confer with British and Indian authorities about Canada's immigration policy as it applied to the 'Orient.' At meeting after meeting, King laid bare the rationale behind the government's desire to stem the flow of Indian immigrants. In the short term, he told Lord Elgin, the secretary of state for the colonies, there was the immediate fear of additional race riots in British Columbia, which 'might prove most unfortunate both for Canada and the

Empire.' Moreover, he informed John Morley, the secretary of state for India, 'it was in the interests of the Indians themselves that they should be kept out; that they were unsuited to the country because [of] the climatic conditions [in Canada] and their inability to adapt themselves to the new environment.'[8] In the long term, King continued, lurked the real possibility that British Columbia might in time cease to be *British* at all, if immigration from Asia continued. Not only 'was it estimated that of the present male population [in the province], there was one Oriental to every four whites,' but the very presence of 'Chinese, Japanese, or Hindu labour' has dissuaded 'working men and their families' from migrating to the Pacific coast in the first place; thus, the province 'had not been peopled with persons of British extraction to the extent that was desirable.'[9] Finally, King suggested, the use of 'Asiatic labour' was an indirect cause of the growth of 'socialism' in British Columbia, 'the only province in which [it] had made headway,' because it enabled 'rapid' industrialization; the upshot of this phenomenon was a large 'mass of men' who possessed 'no stake in the community' and were thus open to foreign ideologies.[10] Riots, race suicide, and possible revolution: the Hindus were, in King's view, responsible for it all.

After about a month of consultations, King found that imperial officials agreed that it was 'natural' that the Canadian government should wish to restrict Asian immigration: 'That Canada should desire to remain a white man's country is believed to be not only desirable for economic and social reasons,' he reported, 'but highly necessary on political and national grounds.' On the other hand, King reported that all thought it was best to avoid 'enacting legislation in either India or in Canada which might appear to reflect on fellow British subjects in another part of the empire,' since 'nothing could be more unfortunate … than that the impression should go forth that Canada … is not deeply sensible of the obligation which citizenship within the empire entails.'[11] Fortunately, according to King's analysis, the combination of new Canadian immigration restrictions and Indian emigration laws created an 'effective bar' to further South Asian immigration to Canada.[12] Especially effective, King thought, would be a Canadian order-in-council, PC 27, passed on 8 January 1908, which prohibited the entry of immigrants who did not travel by 'continuous journey' from the country of their birth to Canada. Since the only company that had been selling a 'through ticket' from India to Canada was the Canadian Pacific Railway, and since the government had used its influence to convince this company to stop selling such tickets, this measure achieved its purpose: between 1908 and 1915, only about one hundred South Asians were admitted to Canada. [13]

If PC 27 was politically sly, it was legally dubious. The measure was declared invalid by the British Columbia Supreme Court even while King was praising it in England, and the government moved quickly to replace it with a reworded order-in-council, PC 662. The measure was put on firmer legal footing on 27 May 1908, when it was underpinned by an amendment to the Immigration Act passed in the House of Commons.[14] Yet, if the government's extraordinary efforts to maintain the 'continuous journey' stipulations dampened the spirit of anti-Asian agitation in British Columbia – so toxic in the months and years leading up to Ottawa's intervention – on the other side of the racial divide, members of the South Asian community were incensed. Not only did the 'continuous journey' requirements cut them off from family and friends who wished to join them in Canada, but it cast in bold relief the emptiness of the crown's claim – particularly prominent during Lord Curzon's tenure as viceroy – that all British subjects were equal before and under the law. That the Sikhs had remained loyal to the British during the 'Great Mutiny' of 1857, in which Indian soldiers in the Bengal army revolted against their British officers, and had played a key role in the Indian army in subsequent decades only added insult to injury. In this hothouse of intolerance and confrontation, nationalist, anti-British sentiments started to germinate – drawing many in the South Asian community, including a small yet influential group of students and entrepreneurs, into a political debate that was both local and global in its consequences.

Mr Hopkinson

Mindful of the situation in British Columbia and the broader politics of imperial rule in India, especially at a time when unrest was rocking parts of the Punjab and Bengal, the federal government was anxious to keep tabs on this pocket of local agitation, both for its own benefit and the benefit of its counterparts in London and Calcutta. Its principal resource in this regard was William Charles Hopkinson.

The son of a British officer in the Indian army and a Brahmin mother, Hopkinson was born in Delhi in 1880. At the age of sixteen, he joined the Indian police, working first in the Punjab and then later, from 1901 to 1907, in Calcutta, where nearly half of the inspectors – Hopkinson's colleagues – were non-British; it is possible that he worked as a police officer in Lahore, too. Fluent in English, Punjabi, Hindi, and other Indian languages, Hopkinson left the Calcutta police force sometime in 1907 and surfaced in British Columbia later that year (or early in 1908).[15] Shortly after his arrival, the former detective convinced local authorities to shut down a night school for South Asian workers in New Westminster and a newspaper called *Free Hindusthan*, which routinely published anti-British material. Both were run by Taraknath Das, a young university-educated activist who at one time played a role in nationalist protests against the partition of Bengal before turning up in San Francisco in 1906.[16] It is possible that Hopkinson had been on the radical's trail for some time at the behest of India's Department of Criminal Intelligence, which had been created under Lord Curzon. Whatever the impetus for Hopkinson's journey to North America, the Canadian Department of the Interior, which was responsible for immigration, and the federal cabinet understood just how valuable he was in minimizing potential political unrest as an interpreter and spy.[17]

Having all but stemmed the flow of South Asian immigrants to British Columbia by imposing 'continuous journey' requirements, the Canadian government was considering a plan that would relocate those who had already arrived. In the fall of 1908, Ottawa devised a plan to transplant South Asians from British Columbia to British Honduras. The scheme was first formulated by J.B. Harkin, private secretary to the minister of the interior, the summer before. 'It has been pretty well established that physically and mentally the Hindoo is unfitted to compete successfully with whites or with other Orientals in a country like this,' Harkin told W.D. Scott, the superintendent of immigration. '[This proposal] avoids the possibility of a precipitation of trouble in India consequent on the return of Hindoos enraged at their treatment in British territory.'[18] The federal government concurred, and within weeks of receiving the Colonial Office's blessing it permitted Harkin to assemble a delegation to investigate the feasibility of the central American colony. The special group included Hopkinson, who was brought on board as a secretary and interpreter, and two representatives from Vancouver's South Asian community: Sham Singh, a Hindu, and Hagar Singh, a Sikh. It travelled to Belize in late October. From Harkin's and Hopkinson's point of view, the trip, which lasted several weeks, was a great success. The demand for agricultural labour in British Honduras was higher than expected, and by all accounts the South Asian delegates were impressed by the working conditions there and desirous of seeing the scheme through. Or so the trip's organizers thought. Upon returning to Vancouver, Sham Singh and Hagar Singh rejected the re-location plan and went so far as to accuse Hopkinson of trying to bribe them into delivering a more positive assessment. Harkin, who was not in British Columbia at the time the delegates made their views public, was incensed. 'Evidently agitators [are] at work,' he informed W.W. Cory, the deputy minister of the interior, after receiving an assessment of the situation in Vancouver from Hopkinson. 'It is to be regretted that the efforts of the Government to better their condition and ensure their welfare in another part of the British Empire should be thus thwarted by foreign influence, over which we seem to have little control,' Cory replied.[19]

One of the 'agitators' in question was Teja Singh. Married with two children, the articulate, multilingual, and highly educated Sikh (he attended Lahore University and Cambridge) came to Vancouver in October 1908 and quickly emerged as a local leader, helping to create a self-help association for South Asian workers and a trust company to look after community investments.[20] Yet, shortly after Hopkinson's delegation returned from British Honduras, the suspected seditionist made several speeches outlining his opposition to the relocation plan, the existence of corruption in the immigration service, and, more ominously from the government's point of view, 'the present unrest in India.' Teja Singh's remarks, whereabouts, and personal relations were carefully tracked by Hopkinson and forwarded to local officials with the Department of the Interior, who, in turn, kept senior bureaucrats, cabinet members, and the prime minister well informed.[21] Not surprisingly, all of this was of great concern to the governor general, Lord Grey. Like his predecessors at Rideau Hall, he was an aristocrat, a veteran of the civil service, and an official link between Ottawa and London. As such, he handled the voluminous correspondence that flowed back and forth across the Atlantic and advised the Dominion government on issues of national and imperial concern. Indeed, when it came to this particular realm of political affairs, Lord Grey's opinion still carried considerable weight on Parliament Hill, despite the largely ceremonial and administrative character of his position; '[a] vigilant watch must be maintained on all events, statements, and newspaper reports which, if repeated in India, might be likely to inflame the minds of those who are tools and victims of sedition,' he cautioned the prime minister in early December 1908.[22] Sound intelligence was, of course, key to this approach, and the governor general worked hard to ensure that it found its way to the Colonial Office and India Office in London and the CID and viceroy in Calcutta. (The words 'Copy Sent To India' are stamped on many of these documents.)[23]

But Lord Grey was not the only imperial official to play a decisive role in the expansion of political policing in Canada. When Ottawa first proposed the idea of relocating South Asians, Colonel E.J. Swayne, governor of British Honduras and an 'Old Indian officer,' was in London on other business; evidently, he offered up his colony as a possible solution to Canada's 'Hindoo' problem. On his way back to Belize in early December 1908, the governor travelled via Canada and met with the governor general and Prime Minister Laurier, who was particularly enamoured by his guest, a bona fide imperial statesmen: '[he is] the very embodiment of that most valuable class of officers developed by Indian service, trained for war and civil service, honest and true as the sun's light, modest and firm, devoted to the Empire and equally devoted to those over whom they are appointed to rule. Happy the country served by such men, and no country but England ever produced such men.'[24] Political and diplomatic formalities concluded, Swayne undertook his own investigation of 'matters affecting the East Indian Community in British Columbia.' Based in part on discussions with Hopkinson, Harkin, and Mackenzie King, his final report examined the origins of racial strife in the Pacific province, the composition of its South Asian community, and the actions of local agitators, both Indian and white.[25]

Less anxious than Lord Grey about the potential risks posed by the likes of Teja Singh – 'neither his interviews nor his lectures give me the impression of being intended to further the agitation in India' – Swayne nevertheless possessed strong opinions about the future of South Asian immigration to Canada. It should be 'controlled,' he wrote forcefully, because 'the terms of close familiarity which competition with white labour has brought about, do not make for British prestige.' Swayne understood well that, when workers, immigrants, and intellectuals mixed, the result was often an explosive combination of radical ideas, militant tactics, and nationalist aspirations: anarchist bombings in continental Europe and North America in the 1880s and 1890s, not to mention the empire's long-standing troubles in Ireland, were evidence of that fact. 'Socialists of a very undesirable type have made it their business to tamper with the East Indians in Vancouver,' he wrote bluntly, referring to the radical Industrial Workers of the World (IWW) and the Socialist Party of Canada (SPC).

The return of the Sikhs to the Punjab amongst their friends, spreading as they will, new, ill-digested socialistic ideas, and the familiar knowledge of such defects amongst their white fellow labourers, such as labour rivalry would have been only too ready to pick out, cannot but tend to react amongst the military classes of the Punjab, to the detriment of British prestige. As – when all is said and done, looking at our position in India as a whole, it must be recognized that it is by prestige alone that India is held and not by force, the importance of a circulation of labour between Vancouver and India as affecting that prestige is such, I submit, as cannot be wisely overlooked.[26]

In this regard, he concluded, in addition to 'strictly limiting' immigration from India to Canada, it was crucial that the 'doings of the Brahmin section be closely watched' on an ongoing basis. 'I do not think that a better man than Mr. Hopkinson of the Calcutta police could be found for this work,' Swayne stated, recognizing the importance of having another old India hand on the job. 'I suggest Mr. Hopkinson be appointed as Dominion police officer on special duty at Vancouver, for the special purpose of this enquiry, and the Government of India be asked to place him in official communication with the head of the Calcutta police in order to further this work.'[27]

With the support of the Department of Interior, the governor general, and the governor of British Honduras, Ottawa officially hired Hopkinson early in 1909. He was given a permanent position in the immigration department in Vancouver and was assigned to the Dominion Police, although he did not receive a formal commission in the force until 1911. For $100 per month, he was expected to keep tabs on the South Asian community and undertake regular duties as an interpreter. Caught between the rock of local politics and the hard place of imperial concerns, the federal government opted for the same solution it had employed the previous century against the Irish – political policing – to help solve the conundrum. Again immigrant communities were the focus of surveillance and intelligence-gathering operations and again a civil servant combined his legitimate, above-board government duties – in this instance, with the immigration branch of the Department of Interior – with the more surreptitious activities characteristic of secret service work. John A. Macdonald would have recognized this approach instantly and approved of it. Certainly, imperial officials at that time did. Just months before Hopkinson was officially hired, John Morley, the secretary of state for India, had written to Lord Minto (the former governor general of Canada who succeeded Lord Curzon as viceroy of India in 1905) lamenting the absence of knowledgeable undercover agents. 'The whole Indian field is absolutely unfamiliar, in language, habits, and everything else,' he said. 'In short, both you and I can easily understand that the ordinary square-toed English constable, even in the detective branch, would be rather clumsy in tracing your wily Asiatics.'[28]

'High-Handed, Impolite, and Empire-Breaking Actions'

Between 1909 and 1914, Hopkinson was exceptionally busy. His activities, which were initially confined to British Columbia's lower mainland and southern Vancouver Island but later expanded to include Washington State, Oregon, and northern California, were many and varied: he attended suspicious meetings and rallies in order to 'find out their latest move and the methods they are adopting for the bringing out of their countrymen from India'; monitored the movements of community leaders and their supporters within the province and across the Canada-U.S. border; and kept tabs on foreign-language newspapers. Taraknath Das's *Free Hindusthan*, which was then based out of Seattle but printed in Vancouver with the assistance of the Socialist Party of Canada, was of particular interest; so, too, was *Swadesh Sewak* (Servant of the Country), a Gurmukhi-language monthly published by Guran Ditta Kumar, a former college instructor from Calcutta who arrived in British Columbia in 1907.[29] Kumar, a self-described 'Punjabi Buddhist' and 'Worker in the cause of Temperance and Vegetarianism,' first came to Hopkinson's attention as a possible 'agitator' in late 1908.[30] At that time, Kumar was living in Victoria and running a grocery store that had been set up with the assistance of his friend Taraknath Das, whom he had first met in Calcutta. The link between the two men, which was common knowledge within the South Asian community, prompted Hopkinson to pay a visit to Kumar's modest operation in the provincial capital in August 1909. Disguised as a lumberman looking for labourers, the new Dominion Police investigator discovered not only that Kumar sold *Free Hindusthan* and the radical, London-based *Indian Sociologist* but that he was in constant contact with the ubiquitous Teja Singh and Taraknath Das, who was then living in Washington State. The following November, 1909, Kumar surfaced in Vancouver, opened the 'Swadesh Sewak Home,' and started publishing a newspaper by the same name early in 1910.[31] Hopkinson kept tabs on him at all times. 'The tone of this paper gradually became more and more objectionable,' one government official's report concluded, based in part on Hopkinson's numerous assessments. 'It was addressed principally to the Sikhs in the Indian Army in their own language, and was being sent out to India in considerable numbers.'[32]

Hopkinson's modus operandi – the reading of seditious publications, the tracking of suspected agitators – was the stock-in-trade of political policing; it would have been easily recognized by the likes of Patrick Nolan or Henri le Caron. Yet, unlike his nineteenth-century counterparts, Hopkinson actually spent very little time undercover; his public position with the immigration service, not to mention his obvious European appearance, would have made it impossible for him to conceal his identity effectively in any event – his brief appearance as a lumberman in Victoria in 1909 notwithstanding. As a result, Hopkinson relied to a great extent on informants within the South Asian community itself – many of whom were paid – to keep an eye on the movement of prominent people and the tenor of political debates and publications.[33] Occasionally, more aggressive (and overtly criminal) measures were taken to secure better intelligence. On the watch for G.D. Kumar, who later decamped for Seattle, Hopkinson enlisted the assistance of one Umrow Singh who burglarized the newspaper editor's room and pilfered reams of 'seditious papers' – including an address book which had contact numbers of radical newspapers such as the *Irish Independent* and *Bande Mataram* (Hail Motherland), a 'monthly organ of Indian independence.'[34]

But Hopkinson was not simply a spymaster and spy. He was also an immigration inspector, and this dual role was fraught with both tension and danger at a time when Ottawa was making use of its wide-ranging discretionary powers to curtail immigration from Asian countries.[35] Indeed, Hopkinson, like others in his position, possessed the authority to admit, reject, or initiate deportation proceedings against new immigrants – powers that were invaluable for someone concerned both with the administration of immigration policy *and* with limiting the development of seditious behaviour among immigrant communities. In this important respect, not only was Hopkinson deeply lodged in the day-to-day controversies surrounding the enforcement of the landing restrictions for South Asian immigrants, but, ironically, his very actions helped to stoke the unnerving anti-British sentiment that prompted the federal government to hire him in the first place. '[Some of the Hindus will] have nothing to do with me or convey any information of any kind to me,' Hopkinson told his handler, W.W. Cory, in 1912, 'branding me as the man who is responsible for the present state of things and that I am instrumental in keeping their women out of Canada.'[36] For Hopkinson, carrying out this dual role – as secret service officer and immigration inspector – would in the end prove deadly.

From the moment that the federal government imposed the 'continuous journey' restrictions in 1908, the South Asian community mounted a sustained campaign to overturn them, a development that enhanced the profile of committed radicals and brought moderates in touch with more militant ideas and tactics. One of the men who was particularly forceful in his denunciation of federal immigration policy, and Hopkinson's role in implementing it, was Chagan Kairaj Varma, a native of the Porbander district in Gujarat state who came to Canada on a tourist visa in January 1910 after spending several years working in Japan and Hawaii. Known in British Columbia by the Muslim name Hussain Rahim, the middle-aged, Westernized Hindu quickly assumed a leadership role in the South Asian community – an ascent that was driven, in part, by his own ongoing conflict with the immigration service.[37] Shortly after turning up in Vancouver, Rahim established the Canada India Supply and Trust Company and applied for permission to stay in the country. Immigration officials responded to this request by arresting Rahim and initiating deportation proceedings against him. 'You drive us Hindus out of Canada and we will drive every white man out of India,' he said after being apprehended.[38] Hopkinson, for one, took this threat seriously. Later that same day, Vancouver city police located a notebook belonging to Rahim that contained information about explosives and the names of activists from other countries.[39] In the weeks and months that followed this startling revelation, both men found themselves in court as Rahim, like other South Asian immigrants before him, challenged the government's deportation order – successfully arguing that particular elements of the orders-in-council that curbed South Asian immigration exceeded the scope of authority available to the federal government under the Immigration Act.[40] Writing to the prime minister and the secretary of state for India (Lord Crewe), in 1910, the Hindustani Association, a self-help organization that assisted in Rahim's legal defence, laid bare the wider political significance of this narrow technical argument: 'As British subjects, we demand our inalienable rights to reside more freely in the British Empire and request immediate redress against high-handed, impolite, and Empire-breaking actions of local authorities.'[41] As Rahim himself put it, in a letter to the Vancouver *News Advertiser*, 'Hindus share the pains and perils of the Empire and must be allowed to share a few blessings too.'[42]

For Hopkinson, Rahim's legal victory was infuriating for many reasons, not the least of which was that it heightened his prestige in the South Asian community, called into question the legitimacy and effectiveness of the immigration branch, and, by virtue of the issues at stake, provided further grist for the anti-colonial mill. 'The failure ... of the Department to deport Rahim from Canada has so bolstered up his position in the Hindu community here as to make him a leader and a counsellor in respect to all matters concerning their community,' he informed W.W. Cory. 'Canada would be well rid of Rahim and the exposure of his true character would have a very beneficial effect on [the] community.'[43] The 'true character' that Hopkinson had in mind was not simply Rahim's obvious commitment to the 'liberty, equality, and fraternity of the Hindustani Nation' but also his immersion in Vancouver's vibrant left-wing milieu, which was then dominated by the Socialist Party of Canada and the Industrial Workers of the World. Particularly alarming for Hopkinson was the discovery that Rahim had joined the SPC shortly after arriving in the country, helped to form a South Asian SPC local, acted as a scrutineer for the party in a provincial election, and, drawing on the resources of the Canada India Supply and Trust Company, posted bail for several members of the IWW jailed during the free-speech fights in 1912. 'The Hindus have up to the present never identified themselves with any particular Political party and the introduction by Rahim of the socialist propaganda into this community, is, I consider a very serious matter, as the majority of these people are uneducated and ignorant and easily led like sheep by a man like Rahim,' Hopkinson wrote in April 1912. 'The danger to the country is not here but the question is what effect will all these Socialistic and Revolutionary teachings have on the people in India on the return of these men primed with Western methods of agitation and Political and Social equality.'[44]

It was, of course, a rhetorical question for Hopkinson was beginning to see more clearly that Rahim, as important as he was in Vancouver, was but one cog in a much larger political machine. In fact, there were South Asian men 'primed' with both 'Western methods of agitation' and ideas of 'political and social equality' operating up and down the west coast. As a result, Hopkinson eventually expanded the range of his intelligence-gathering activities to include Seattle, Portland, San Francisco, Palo Alto, Oakland, and Berkeley. Early forays south of the border in the summer of 1911 focused on the activities of Taraknath Das, who was based in Seattle yet in constant contact with activists in Vancouver and elsewhere; rumour had it that he was planning a return visit to India with G.D. Kumar – prompting fears that a plan had been hatched to interfere with the royal visit to the subcontinent planned for that December; '[we have] grave suspicions as to his possible complicity in anarchistic or revolutionary movements or conspiracies directed against the government of India,' observed the British ambassador to the United States, James Bryce.[45] Similar suspicions led Hopkinson to spend an additional three weeks outside British Columbia in the fall of 1911, gathering information from U.S. immigration officials and British consular staff in San Francisco and seeking out suspicious individuals whose names first came to light in the notebooks purloined from Hussain Rahim about a year before.[46] Hopkinson wrapped up his lengthy sojourn south of the border in late October, and from his perspective it had been a productive and eye-opening experience. Yet, while he had successfully interfered with Das's plans to travel to India, thereby avoiding a possible incident there, and expanded his intelligence-gathering capabilities considerably, he still worried that the British government did not understand fully the potential threat posed by South Asian immigrants on the Pacific coast. More resources, both financial and human, must be devoted to places such as Washington State and northern California, he told Cory, with a full-time agent – a 'Hindu expert' – stationed at the consular office in San Francisco.[47]

Hopkinson returned to the United States a year and a half later, in 1913, not to investigate Taraknath Das – 'the most active and persistent agitator against the British rule in India that can be found in this country' – but to track Lala Har Dayal, a Delhi-born, Oxford-educated lecturer in Indian philosophy at Stanford University who had been in California for about two years.[48] While Hopkinson perhaps knew of Har Dayal prior to 1913 – he had edited the Paris-based *Bande Mataram* from 1909 to 1911– the decision to place the university instructor under constant surveillance was prompted by the British consul general in San Francisco, who reported that Har Dayal possessed ties to the Industrial Workers of the World and was linked in some way to the assassination attempt on the viceroy, Lord Hardingue, on 23 December 1912; in official circles, Har Dayal's name had become synonymous with anarchism.[49] Once in California, Hopkinson utilized his connections with the U.S. immigration service to monitor Har Dayal's mail, some of which was intercepted en route to India; he also recruited informants at Stanford who kept watch on suspicious political meetings. By the end of January 1913, Hopkinson was convinced that Har Dayal had replaced Taraknath Das as the most dangerous and influential agitator around, an assessment he passed on to his handlers in the immigration branch of the Department of Interior. Less than a month later, at the behest of the Canadian government, Hopkinson found himself in London, where he briefed imperial officials about the current state of anti-colonial agitation on the west coast. Acting largely on the basis of his provocative conclusions, British, Canadian, and Indian authorities agreed that Hopkinson should be more secure, both institutionally and monetarily, and kept better informed.[50]

While the India Office and Colonial Office sought to make intelligence gathered by the Indian government more readily available to Hopkinson in North America, arrangements were also made to have the highly prized informant placed on the India Office's payroll; paid an allowance of £60 per year, he was now expected to report directly to the superintendent of police for Bombay, J.A. Wallinger, who was in London at the time working in the area of intelligence and imperial defence.[51] 'Agitators [have] worked up the Sikh labourers there ... who form such an important section of our Army in India,' Wallinger observed. 'It is the danger of the wholesale contamination of these Sikhs that gives cause for special measures.'[52] Canada's new governor general, the Duke of Connaught – who had been to Canada before as an army officer during the Fenian scares of the 1860s – was not impressed with this revised arrangement. 'The entire system, if system it can be called, is dependent on one man,' he told the Colonial Office. 'If any thing happens to Mr Hopkinson, the work would automatically collapse.' For the governor general, the best way to proceed was to transfer Hopkinson to the Indian government completely; after all, he stated, the uber-agent's work was both costly and increasingly about imperial, not national, concerns. Wallinger disagreed and argued successfully that 'the permanent transfer of Mr Hopkinson to the Indian Government would entirely destroy Mr Hopkinson's usefulness. He is now, by very reason of his multifarious offices ... in a position to do some delicate work for us without having suspicion drawn upon himself. Once he is removed from these offices he would be a marked man.'[53]

Delicate work continued in late 1913, when Hopkinson – now partially compensated by the India Office, but still the responsibility of the Canadian government – returned to San Francisco with the intention of getting Har Dayal deported from the United States. It was a multifaceted affair that involved the high-level intervention of the British ambassador to the United States and the low-level involvement of special agents attached to various U.S. government departments. In this respect, the initiative was emblematic of not only Hopkinson's growing political influence but also the British, Indian, and Canadian governments' heightened anxiety about west coast agitators – anxiety that only deepened the more they watched.[54] Indeed, officials in all three governments knew well that in the months following Hopkinson's first report on Har Dayal, but before his subsequent return to California late in 1913, the committed revolutionary joined the Pacific Coast Hindi Association (which was created by Taraknath Das) and helped to found the Ghadar (Mutiny) movement. The former organization was dedicated to uniting Hindu intellectuals and Sikh farmers, while the latter, as its provocative name implies, called on its supporters to 'return to India and start a Revolution.'[55] The first issue of Ghadar's newspaper, which was read by Indian radicals from Vancouver to Honolulu, San Francisco to Tokyo, Shanghai to Bombay, rolled off the presses in early November 1913.[56] 'Time is gliding on. Oppression and misery have passed all bounds in your country. The whole world is waiting to see when these brave men will rise and destroy the English,' one of the newspaper's editorials read. 'Serve your country with body, mind and wealth. Give this advice to all and follow it yourselves. The time is soon to come when rifle and blood will take the place of pen and ink. Pray for this rising, talk, dream, earn money, eat for it alone.'[57] Yet, despite Har Dayal's connection to this militant publication and the Ghadar movement, he was never successfully deported, Hopkinson's persistent efforts to this end notwithstanding. Instead, after weeks of surveillance and harassment – 'I have been spied upon by British secret operatives, but have gone about my affairs openly' – Har Dayal left the United States on his own volition sometime in January 1914.[58] Arriving first in Lausanne, Switzerland, he later moved to Germany where, in the early years of the Great War, he joined forces with other Berlin-based nationalists – Turks, Egyptians, Algerians, and Indians – to continue the struggle against imperialist rule.[59]

In the wake of Har Dayal's departure, Hopkinson found himself back in British Columbia, absorbed again by the incendiary politics of Canadian immigration restrictions and imperial concerns. In late May 1914, the *Komagata Maru* sailed into the port of Vancouver. Chartered by a Sikh entrepreneur named Gurdit Singh to challenge the federal government's ban on South Asian immigrants, the vessel carried 376 passengers – 340 Sikhs, 24 Muslims, and 12 Hindus. 'We are British citizens and we consider we have a right to visit any part of the Empire. We are determined to make this a test case and if we are refused entrance into your country, the matter will not end here,' Gurdit Singh told the local press, shortly after dropping anchor. 'What is done with this shipload of my people will determine whether we shall have peace in all parts of the British Empire.'[60] Immigration officials 'did' with this batch of immigrants what they had done to scores of others since the federal government first introduced selective landing requirements: they refused to allow them on shore. This action, coupled with Gurdit Singh's resolve to overturn the ban, prompted a long and sometimes violent stand-off which ended on 23 July when the passengers of the *Komagata Maru*, after facing down an attempt by Canadian authorities to seize the ship by force, decided to return to India. Throughout this incident, Hopkinson handled the negotiations between those on ship and those on shore – including senior immigration officials and the immigrants' allies, the so-called shore committee which was led by Hussain Rahim.[61] From the perspective of many in the South Asian community, the entire *Komagata Maru* affair simply reinforced their belief that a toxic combination of fear, loathing, and racial hatred was at the core of both Canadian immigration policy and the broader white society that sanctioned it. What was more, it reaffirmed graphically the hypocrisy of the British empire; Sikhs and Hindus simply did not possess the same rights and freedoms as freeborn Englishmen – in Canada or India for that matter. And Hopkinson, by virtue of his role as an immigration officer and secret agent, was as guilty as anyone in defending this condition of inequality.

In the months that followed the *Komagata Maru*'s departure, several of Hopkinson's informants were murdered. The killings, which were carried out by militants within the South Asian community, provoked violence between Sikhs themselves. On one occasion, one of Hopkinson's supporters, Bela Singh, was attacked while praying at the Sikh temple in Vancouver; in response, he shot and killed two people, including the priest, and wounded seven others before turning himself in. On 21 October 1914 Hopkinson himself was murdered. While waiting outside a Vancouver courtroom to testify in defence of Bela Singh, he was shot and killed by Mewa Singh, one of his local informants and a former soldier in India.[62] '[He] is the last man one would have suspected of committing the deed,' Malcolm Reid, Hopkinson's superior at the immigration branch, wrote to Ottawa. 'No doubt, however, he

was influenced by the local Hindu community. The man is now perfectly cheerful in his cell and to all intents and purposes seems glad
he has murdered Hopkinson.'[63] The courthouse killing received extensive coverage in all of Vancouver's daily papers; outrage filled the front
pages, the editorial columns, and letters-to-the-editor sections. 'This
thing must stop,' the city's mayor told a reporter from the *Province*. 'It
is bad enough having these Hindus kill their fellow countrymen, but
when they shoot our citizens, it has come to the limit of our endur-
ance.'[64] The day after the shooting, city police detained three other suspects, including Hussain Rahim, and charged them with 'conspiracy to
procure persons to kill others.'[65] In the end, however, only Mewa Singh
was convicted. 'I shall gladly have the rope put around my neck,' he
told a priest before his execution in a provincial jail, 'thinking it to be a
rosary of god's name.'[66]

Hopkinson was given a lavish funeral. Approximately 2,000 people –
including delegations of Canadian and American immigration officers,
city and provincial police forces, local fire brigades, and the Orange
Order – joined a funeral procession that wound its way throughout
Vancouver's downtown; a military escort was provided by the Duke
of Connaught's Own Rifles, to which Hopkinson had once belonged.[67]
Through late October and November, government officials in Vancouver, Ottawa, London, and Delhi (the new seat of British government in
India since 1911) discussed the status of Hopkinson's widow and two
children, the circumstances surrounding his death, and the possibility
of drafting a replacement. While they agreed that Hopkinson had died
honourably in the service of the empire and that his family should be
compensated for its loss, they also concluded that his dual role as immigration inspector and secret agent – what Wallinger once called his
'multifarious offices' – contributed directly to his untimely death. Immigration matters and secret service work, it was concluded, should be
separated. 'I am … advising our agent in Vancouver that in the future
we shall confine our energies entirely to the provisions and regulations
of the Immigration Act,' Hopkinson's handler and deputy minister of
the interior, W.W. Cory, reported to the India Office. 'Under no circumstances are our officers to spy or play detective.'[68] Although the Canadian government did not officially replace its star agent on the Pacific
coast, it did permit Hopkinson's former superior at the immigration
branch, Malcolm Reid, to continue monitoring suspected subversives
in an ad hoc way. Sometimes operating out of his own home, he received updates from some of Hopkinson's contacts within the local

South Asian community and officials within the American and British governments. When the Royal North-West Mounted Police (RNWMP) took over political policing from the Dominion Police in 1918, Reid's modest operation was all but closed down.[69]

With the onset of the Great War, imperial officials in London and Delhi were forced to grapple with a new threat to British rule in India. Beginning in the summer of 1914, South Asian radicals in North America and across the Indian disapora, from Yokohama to Panama City, began returning home to mount an armed struggle for Indian independence. 'At the present stage the practical question is not the intelligence abroad,' Sir Charles Cleveland, the director of the Department of Criminal Intelligence in India, observed, 'but how to deal with seditious activities in India.'[70] Urged on by the Ghadar movement, the returnees – about 8,000 in total – were aided in part by the German government, which recognized the obvious benefits of forcing the British to fight in its colonies as well as on the western front in Europe.[71] In Berlin, in fact, the German foreign ministry worked hand-in-glove with resident South Asian radicals to form the Berlin-India Committee in 1914; that group, which was later renamed the Indian Independence Committee, published anti-British propaganda, orchestrated a joint Ghadar-German incursion from Kabul, Afghanistan, into India's northwest frontier to spark a tribal revolt, and sought to procure arms in North America for anti-British fighters returning in India. Ominously, from the British and Indian governments' perspective, the German foreign ministry deployed considerable financial and human resources, through its consular offices in the United States, to strengthen the links between Indian radicals and their Irish sympathizers who belonged to organizations such as the Irish Republican Brotherhood and Sinn Fein, both of which would participate in the Easter Rising of 1916.[72] Two of Hopkinson's most watched subjects, Lala Har Dayal and Taraknath Das, were deeply involved in all of this.

The emergence of this three-way collaboration prompted the British government to expand its intelligence-gathering operations outside the United Kingdom. It created the Security Intelligence Service in 1916.[73] Known colloquially as MI6, the new agency controlled at least two hundred agents in the United States by 1918, many of whom were in San Francisco where the British consular office was poised to confront the Ghadar-German partnership; some MI6 informants occupied leadership positions within the Ghadar movement itself. Headed by Sir Robert Nathan – a former civil servant in India with extensive police experience and one-time private secretary to Lord Curzon – the MI6 mission in the United States worked closely with the Department of Justice, the Department of Labor, and the Home Department, all of which had undertaken their own elaborate investigations of seditious activities on the Pacific coast. Reams of information about 'Indian sedition,' some of it originally produced by Hopkinson, passed between the various government agencies, with Nathan acting as an important conduit. Nathan also received regular communications from Canadian officials in Vancouver and Ottawa. By the spring of 1917, the U.S. government had amassed enough evidence about Indo-Irish-German activities to indict 105 people for violating its neutrality laws, which forbade anyone from launching a military expedition from American soil against an American ally. When the trial finally began the following November, thirty-five individuals – nine Germans, nine Americans, and seventeen Indians – stood accused. In the end, all but three of the defendants were convicted, including Taraknath Das and the German consul general to San Francisco; a smaller trial centred on the same charges also took place in Chicago, ending with similar results.[74] In both proceedings, intelligence first compiled by Hopkinson was introduced as evidence; witnesses arrived from India with the substantial assistance of the Canadian government. With its leaders in jail and membership factionalized, the Ghadar movement would barely survive the war.[75] And by then, its founder – after a year in Germany – had had a profound change of heart. 'The Germans counted upon a revolt in Ireland and South Africa, a general insurrection of all Muslims, and a rebellion in India,' Har Dayal wrote in 1920. 'None of these hopes have been fulfilled. Irish "nationalism," the great Jihad, and Indian and Egyptian "extremism" have been found to be puny forces compared with British imperialism … Co-operation and evolution should [now] be our watchword. The policy of separation and intrigue is futile and fallacious.'[76]

The Burden of Empire

Canada's early experiences in the realm of political policing were shaped decisively by its status as a collection of colonies, then later a self-governing Dominion, within the British empire. Between the 1860s – the focus of chapter 1 – and the Great War, Ottawa was preoccupied with 'subversive' groups and individuals whose real enemy was the mother country itself. While Irish and South Asian radicals possessed different histories under British rule, and drew on different cultural and religious resources to mount their political challenges, their activities abroad were very similar. Routinely crossing the borders between their countries of origin, Canada, and the United States, they dedicated considerable intellectual and financial resources to spreading their ideas, raising people's consciousness, and forging links between those in the disapora and those at home; a seemingly endless supply of clubs and organizations, newspapers and pamphlets, was critical to this process of making political communities across generations and geography. Leavened by the relative freedom available in North America, both groups sought self-determination for their respective homelands: 'Home rule all over the world!'[77] To this end, they rejected constitutional and legal approaches to their particular grievances and cultivated, instead, uncompromising nationalisms grounded in historic injustices, ethnic and cultural pride, and religious ideas – for one, Catholicism, for the other, Hinduism. This political world view was braced in no small measure by an understanding of the ideals deeply set in the British liberal and American republican traditions – liberty and equality for all – and the abject failure of the empire to extend those ideals to all its members. Both Fenians and Ghadarites were familiar with Thomas Paine and John Stuart Mill.

Yet violence was part and parcel of both the radical Irish and Indian movements as well – providing one of the basic frames of reference through which many true believers understood not only their enemy but the correct political way forward. The British empire, they agreed, had been created and sustained by violence – war, conquest, terror, and famine – and thus it must be opposed with violence. In prose and poetry, writers in both movements extolled the need and desire to take direct action, often tying this rhapsodic sentiment to specific moments of collective suffering and struggle, themselves violent in character. For the Fenians, the Great Famine of the 1840s and the failed rebellion of 1848 were important touchstones for political mobilization; so, too, were the nationalist rebellions that swept across Europe in the 1840s and 1850s and the more immediate experiences of the American Civil War, itself an unprecedented North American spectacle of death, grief, and loss. South Asian radicals situated themselves in the tradition of the Great Mutiny of 1857 and frequently invoked the partition of Bengal in 1905 – 'a motherland dismembered … despite the protests of her children' – to bolster their actions.[78] For them, an evolving relationship with the radical labour movement and left-wing political parties was important too, for it brought within their ambit the direct-action tactics of the Industrial Workers of the World, the sophisticated political economy of the Socialist Party of Canada, and the rebel energy of anarchism. All of it, combined, provided much of the grit upon which the struggle for Indian independence in North America would find traction. 'Resistance to tyranny is service to humanity and a necessity of civilization,' observed *Free Hindusthan* in 1910.[79]

Whether Irish or Indian radicals were terrorists or freedom fighters depended entirely on one's angle of vision. From the vantage point of the Canadian government, however, there was no debate worth having: both movements were violent, seditious, and threatened not only the peaceable Dominion but the stability of the empire writ large. Just as Canada's first security threats – Irish and Indian – reflected its status as an outpost of British rule, so, too, did the ways in which the federal government responded to such threats. Indeed, Canada's embryonic secret service, both in the 1860s and early 1900s, relied heavily on Britain's extensive diplomatic presence in the United States to target its foes. By hiring their own undercover agents, and tapping their own connections the American government, British consular officials in cities such as New York and San Francisco monitored potential dissidents and circulated that information widely, first to their home government, then later to Canada and beyond. The role of the British diplomatic corps was supplemented by many imperial civil servants, most notably the various governors general who served as Canada's head of state. Holding a position of little significance today, governors general like Lord Monck and Lord Grey possessed extensive knowledge of imperial politics, served as important conduits for the copious intelligence that flowed between Ottawa, London, and elsewhere, and were strong advocates of political policing as a means to solve both national and imperial problems. Rounding out the imperial contribution to the expansion of the Canadian secret service were a range of other officials drawn from military, police, and civilian backgrounds, from the commander of British forces in North America in the 1860s to the governor of British Honduras in the early 1900s. Only after the First World War, when the nature of Canada's internal security problems changed and its own capacity to monitor dissidents expanded, would the role of this imperial infrastructure diminish.

The ways in which the Canadian government mobilized against Fenians and South Asian radicals were markedly similar – despite the decades that separated the two movements. No vigorous debate among politicians and civil servants accompanied the creation of the secret service in the 1860s; no serious disagreements over its role and function surfaced in the early 1900s either. The occasional arguments that did emerge centred not around the legality of spymasters and spying as political tactics, but on the logistics and particulars of a given undercover operation. Should Patrick Nolan stay in Chicago or return to Toronto? Is William Hopkinson being paid enough? In the absence of any scepticism about the legitimacy of the secret service, Canadian officials were instead enthusiastic about the possibility of defeating an imperial enemy – and the utility of political policing to that end. The Dominion was still a young nation-state, and its ties to the old country remained strong and influential: those at the highest levels of political decision making were convinced that, in pursuing Fenians or South Asian radicals, they were protecting the empire's civilizing mission in the world, its cherished political and legal institutions, its edifying myths and symbols. Believing in and wanting to safeguard this world view was as natural to those in power in Canada as breathing in and breathing out. And, if the attitudes of Canadian political leaders towards political policing were the same in the 1860s as they were in the early 1900s, so too were the strategies adopted by those who handled Canada's undercover operatives. Recourse to secrecy, surveillance, intelligence gathering, and sabotage; suspicion of immigrant groups and their 'foreign' ideologies; and coordination of covert activities with conventional uses of government power had become common practice in Canadian political life as the nineteenth century ended and the twentieth began.

Yet, with the onset of the Great War, the Canadian secret service would undergo a significant transformation: institutionally bigger and financially better supported, it would target an altogether new internal enemy: organized labour and the left. Signs of this shift away from imperial concerns – the Irish and Indians – were evident before the war years, as Hopkinson's increasing preoccupation with 'socialistic ideas' suggests; it was cemented by the immediate post-war era, as the domestic pressures and uncertainties of war, the resurgence of the Canadian labour movement, and the success of the Bolshevik Revolution in Russia in 1917 altered political realities, both locally and globally. In the crucible of the war years and after, Ottawa would suspend civil liberties outright, create a new battery of repressive measures, and, under the pretext of mobilizing the nation for war, move to crush its new and more formidable opponent. Before the Great War was even over, the Cold War had already begun.

3

A War on Two Fronts

R.B. Russell could not believe his eyes. It was bad enough that as a high-profile member of the left-wing Socialist Party of Canada and One Big Union (OBU) he was on trial for his involvement in the Winnipeg General Strike of 1919, a stand-off between the city's working and employing classes that had paralysed the city for six weeks. But now this: one of the crown's star witnesses in this highly publicized show trial, one of eight since the strike's bloody conclusion that June, was Harry Blask, a member of the Socialist Party from Calgary who had been working as an undercover agent for the Royal North-West Mounted Police for over a year. To stalwarts of the struggle like Russell, the presence of paid informants in the ranks of the labour movement, while infuriating, was not a complete surprise – employers had often hired private detectives to keep tabs on union activity. But, as Blask's time underground, important role in securing Russell's conviction, and ties to the Mounted Police made clear, this labour spy was no ordinary, company-hired gumshoe.

Recruited by the force in 1917, Blask was an Italian immigrant whose real name was Franco Zanetti but who renamed himself Frank Zaneth. He was sent underground in the spring of 1918, joining other new recruits whose social class, ethnicity, and language skills, the force thought, made them well suited for work among the country's so-called undesirables: working people who opposed Canada's war effort and, once the armistice was signed, demanded a larger slice of the capitalist pie. Zaneth's first assignment was in Quebec City, where he helped local and federal authorities restore order after violent anti-conscription riots rocked the provincial capital. From there he moved west to Alberta, and after stops in Drumheller and Canmore, Zaneth, now known as Harry Blask, settled in Calgary and submerged himself in the local radical scene. He moved through the ranks of the Socialist Party of Canada and attended the Western Labor Conference, a historic gathering of left-wing unionists that launched the One Big Union. Within a year, Blask was informing his RNWMP handlers of every radical activity taking place in the city, knowledge that proved useful in the wake of the Winnipeg General Strike at Russell's trial. After assisting the crown in convicting the prominent labour activist on charges of 'seditious conspiracy,' and having his cover blown in the process, Harry Blask found that his brief career as a labour spy was, for all intents and purposes, over. But not before he had helped both to undermine domestic resistance to the Great War and to beat back the socialist tide.[1]

Although Blask's stint as an undercover agent was brief, it captures nicely the twin crises that faced the federal government during these tumultuous years – and, importantly, the solutions it employed to help solve them. Of particular concern to Prime Minister Robert Borden's Conservative and later Union governments was the obvious necessity of mobilizing a diverse and politically fractious nation for war. The second, and less appreciated challenge, of these years was the defence of the economic and political status quo against the twin threats of labour militancy and socialism that swept the nation during the Canadian labour revolt of 1917–23. The revolt, which climaxed in 1919 with the confrontation at Winnipeg and a wave of sympathy strikes that followed the arrest of Russell and other strike leaders, was the first significant nationwide challenge to capitalist rule.[2] Taken together, the problems posed by the war – the presence of large immigrant communities from enemy nations resident in Canada, the need for secrecy about the war effort, and resistance to compulsory military service or 'conscription' – coupled with the labour unrest of this period, prompted Ottawa to create the legislative and institutional means necessary to undermine internal dissent. During these years, the federal government was waging a war on two fronts, one in which men like Harry Blask – and the fledgling spy network of which he was a part – played a decisive role. In the crucible of both world war and class war, the Canadian secret service – today associated with the Royal Canadian Mounted Police and the Canadian Security Intelligence Service – was born.

Organizing for War

Among the first actions of the Borden administration after Canada's declaration of war in early August 1914 was to invoke the War Measures Act, a move that assured the prime minister and the cabinet, the 'executive' arm of the federal government, the maximum power possible to pursue the course of war. 'The Governor in Council shall have power to do and authorize such acts and things, and to make from time to time such orders and regulations, as he may by reason of the real or apprehended war, invasion, or insurrection deem necessary for the security, defence, peace, order, and welfare of Canada,' its preamble read, laying out the executive's new authority. Unprecedented in the annals of parliamentary government, the 'orders and regulations' permitted under the act – called 'orders-in-council' or 'Privy Council Orders' (PC) – took aim at a wide range of concerns, including the 'censorship,' 'control,' and 'suppression' of all 'means of communication' and the 'arrest,' 'detention,' and 'deportation' of citizens deemed harmful to the war effort. Significantly, such decrees did not require the approval of Parliament to become law, nor did they – or the War Measures Act itself for that matter – possess either a time limit or independent mechanism for termination.[3] In short, the Borden administration had effectively replaced parliamentary government during the Great War with an 'order-in-council' government.[4]

And it wasted little time in flexing this new all-powerful muscle. Even before the War Measures Act's passage through Parliament, it had issued an order-in-council to regulate the flow of 'enemy aliens' – its phrase for immigrants from enemy nations residing in Canada – out of the country; this decree, coupled with an additional order-in-council passed the next day, simultaneously safeguarded their property and businesses yet also demanded that they turn over all fire arms and explosives. In late October 1914, Ottawa took a far more dramatic step and demanded that all enemy aliens appear for registration and examination before special registrars or local police in major centres. Those men and women deemed non-threatening were either allowed to leave Canada or to remain free under condition they report monthly to the registrar. Enemy aliens considered dangerous or who failed or refused to register were interned as prisoners of war. In an initial wave of enthusiasm, some 6,000 aliens, most of whom were Ukrainians, not Germans, found themselves interned. That most Ukrainian Canadians passionately hated the Austro-Hungarian empire (one of the Triple Entente's enemies in the Great War) made no difference.[5]

All of this took place under the watchful eye of Percy Sherwood, the chief commissioner of the Dominion Police. Born in Ottawa in 1854, Sherwood possessed an extensive background in conventional police work – serving first as deputy sheriff for Carleton County and later as chief of police for the city of Ottawa before being named head of the federal police force in 1885, at the age of thirty-one.[6] Sherwood's ascent to the nation's top police job was matched by an equally impressive ascent within the ranks of the local militia; by 1899, he was lieutenant-colonel of the Ottawa-based Duke of Cornwall's Own Rifles, members of which were involved in the repulsion of the Fenian threat in 1866, suppression of the North-West Rebellion in 1885, and defeat of the 'Boers' in the South African War from 1899 to 1902.[7] A 'patron of manly sport,' 'clever and reliable marksman,' and 'profoundly religious,' Sherwood spent part of his early years with the Dominion Police as an undercover operative on the Pacific coast.[8] Sent west in 1896 to assist the British and Canadian delegations to the Bering Sea Claims Commission, which was sorting out international fishing boundaries, Sherwood skulked around the waterfront districts of Seattle and San Francisco for the better part of a year, looking for any information that might undermine American claims. 'Not a suspicion of my presence here has been manifested by those most concerned,' he told the senior British counsel at the hearings, which were held in Victoria, British Columbia. 'I am enjoying the excitement immensely.' Once the legal hearings ended in 1897, Sherwood shed his disguise, returned to Ottawa, and resumed the familiar duties of Dominion Police commissioner, a position he would hold until after the Great War.[9]

The federal government's decision in the fall of 1914 to monitor, register, and examine enemy aliens was given additional strength the following summer when it created the office of chief press censor to scrutinize and, if need be, shut down publications critical of the war. Under the direction of Major Ernest J. Chambers – a friend of Percy Sherwood's and author of a regimental history of the Duke of Cornwall's Own Rifles – the office took specific aim at the foreign-language press. Initially, it was relatively ineffectual in this pursuit: only the secretary of state, who was responsible for the office of chief press censor, possessed the power to close down a publication and he was, much to Chambers's chagrin, reluctant to exercise this ministerial prerogative. As a consequence, the office was forced to rely on Chambers's own personal contacts to establish both its authority in government and its influence over foreign-language editors. Yet as the war dragged on, and agitation against its escalation grew stronger and stronger, the mandate of the chief press sensor was broadened considerably. Implemented by the Borden administration in 1917, the Consolidated Orders respecting

Censorship enlarged the publication ban to include material hostile to conscription; a year later, the censor's reach was extended further to include anything that might spread discontent or weaken the Canadian people's support for the war. Chambers, who was opposed to any limitations imposed on his office by timid government officials, stepped up the size and scope of his operation accordingly, banning two items in 1914, sixteen in 1915, fifty-two in 1916, fifty-eight in 1917, and fifty-nine in the first eight months of 1918.[10]

In addition to censorship, the government also faced the daunting task of recruiting Canadians for the armed services. At first, finding willing volunteers was not a problem as promises of a quick victory, coupled with a serious economic recession, drew thousands of volunteers – particularly British immigrants – into the army in an initial wave of imperial devotion and war enthusiasm.[11] Nevertheless, as early as the summer of 1915, even before the economy had fully recovered, recruiters began to complain bitterly of difficulties attracting adequate numbers of soldiers, and as the grim realities of trench warfare became more readily apparent on the home front, this task grew only more difficult. Consequently, the Borden government, under heavy pressure from various anglophone patriotic groups, created the National Service Board (NSB) in August 1916 and appointed a director general of national service to undertake a voluntary survey of potential soldiers. In the face of considerable criticism from both organized and unorganized workers, the prime minister assured the country that the voluntary national-service schemes 'were not connected with Conscription. Rather, the idea was to make an appeal for voluntary National Service which would render unnecessary any resort to compulsion.'[12] Conscription, it appeared, was not in the offing. The leaders of the Trades and Labor Congress (TLC), the national umbrella organization of trade unions, accepted Borden's argument and recommended full compliance with the NSB to its affiliated unions, abandoning their original anti-draft mandate, which they had sought and received in August 1916. In the eyes of many trade unionists, especially in Quebec, Ontario, and British Columbia, it was a stunning reversal, one that exacerbated existing tensions within the labour movement and effectively divided it over the progress of the war.

In the aftermath of the TLC leadership's acceptance of national registration, a storm of protest arose from Canadian workers. In meeting after meeting throughout the early months of 1917, the federal government's war plans were denounced and resistance by any means was discussed. Meanwhile, the government went through one final pretense of voluntarism with an attempt to recruit a Canadian Defence Force to provide domestic defence and thus allow the Canadian army to be freed entirely for overseas duty. This force, which aimed to recruit 50,000 men, was allowed to disappear quietly when, after almost six weeks of recruiting, only 200 men had signed up.[13] This final failure, combined with Borden's return from a meeting of the Imperial War Cabinet in England, led to a late May decision by the federal cabinet to proceed with conscription. A Military Service Act (MSA) was introduced into the House of Commons that June and eventually became law in late August 1917. Not surprisingly, the MSA was met with fierce opposition; nationwide demonstrations denounced conscription, and talk of general strikes and even revolution filled the air. 'There were two major views of the War, that of the exploiter and that of the exploited,' roared Alphonse Verville, the sitting Liberal-Labour member of Parliament for Montreal-Hochelaga.[14] The ensuing 1917 federal election turned exclusively on the question of compulsory military service. One of the most divisive, vicious, and passionate campaigns in Canadian politics, it was punctuated by anti-conscription demonstrations but ended in a convincing victory by the pro-war Union government, a victory gained, at least in part, by the enfranchisement of some Canadian women and disenfranchisement of naturalized immigrants from enemy countries.[15]

For the mainstream labour movement, the conscription debate came to a head at the September 1917 TLC convention in Ottawa. The organization's executive took the easy position that, because the MSA was law, labour could not afford to oppose it. Delegates saw things differently; the Resolutions Committee brought to the convention floor a more militant stand: 'This Congress is emphatically opposed to any development in the enforcement of any legislation that will make for industrial conscription, or the interference with the trade union movement in the taking care of the interests of the organized workers of the Dominion.'[16] After a fiery exchange that lasted many hours, general opposition to conscription of manpower prevailed; however, fears of government repression led to the defeat of a more radical motion that labour would back conscription of manpower only if wealth, too, was conscripted.[17] Although the national trade-union leadership bowed out of the struggle against compulsory service, the fight did not end there.

Resistance to the Military Service Act took many forms. The primary and easiest way was simply to apply for an exemption and, of the first approximately 160,000 men called to report, fully 92 per cent did just that. By the end of 1917, some 73 per cent of those seeking exemptions had been successful.[18] Others took more radical action. On the Easter weekend of 1918, Quebec City crowds rescued an arrested defaulter from the hands of Dominion Police officers and proceeded to wreck the offices of the city's two pro-Union government newspapers – the *Chronicle* and *L'Evénement* – and, a day later, the office of the registrar of the MSA. The authorities, who had rushed troops from Toronto to help maintain order, turned them loose on the crowd with fixed bayonets. While the army restored order that evening, the enraged citizenry rioted again the following night and, in the ensuing battle, at least four Quebec City workers were fatally wounded. The riots ended on 4 April when habeas corpus was suspended and all citizens were warned that any arrested demonstrators would be conscripted immediately.[19] Later that summer in Vancouver, thousands participated in Canada's first political general strike, held on 2 August 1918, to protest the killing of labour activist and MSA defaulter Albert 'Ginger' Goodwin. A prominent member of the Western Federation of Miners, Socialist Party of Canada, and British Columbia Federation of Labour, Goodwin had initially been granted a exemption as unfit for military service but while leading a strike in Trail, British Columbia, he was suddenly reclassified and called for active service. He fled to Vancouver Island, took to the hills near Comox, and hooked up with a colony of draft resisters. There, in late July, he was shot, allegedly in self-defence, by Dominion Police special constable Dan Campbell, who was eventually exonerated by a special inquiry. British Columbia workers, however, believed that Goodwin had been murdered and, under the auspices of Vancouver's left-wing labour council, shut the city down in an effective general strike.[20] The Borden government had imposed conscription over the heated objections of Canadian labour, but it had done so at considerable cost: by calling the moderate leadership of the TLC into disrepute, it helped pave the way for the massive labour revolt that peaked in the summer of 1919.

From 1917 to 1923, Canada, like other industrialized countries, was rocked by unprecedented levels of class conflict. The climax of this labour revolt took place in 1919, when about 150,000 workers participated in 428 separate confrontations, including local battles, wider general strikes that shut down entire industries and cities – the largest and most well known taking in place in Winnipeg – and sympathy strikes held in solidarity with the men and women on the picket lines in the Manitoba capital. 'The realization is growing that there is a class war, a war in which there is no discharge,' William Yates, a street railwayman from New Westminster, British Columbia, observed in 1919; 'Let the workingman, the one who produced, have control and we shall see the light of the new dawn,' echoed Resina Asals, a member of the Regina Women's Labor League.[21] From coast to coast, workers in nearly all sectors of the economy, from telephone operators and waitresses to miners and loggers, confronted both employers and the government for higher wages, better working conditions, and union recognition; others called for a 'new democracy' based on production for use, not for profit. Surveying the situation in the 'eye of the storm' in Winnipeg, the commissioner of the Royal North-West Mounted Police, A.B. Perry, remarked: 'The greater number of labour men, and probably the community as a whole[,] are in an uncertain, apprehensive, nervous and irritable temper. Perhaps these agitators are but the foam on the wave.'[22]

The immediate causes of this 'wave' of unrest were legion. While manufacturers continued to make massive profits during the war, wartime inflation pushed the cost of living higher and higher, making it extremely difficult for workers and their families to make ends meet – and priming them for a fight. At the same time, the spread of unionism into previously unorganized areas of the economy gave rise to the notion that collective struggles were not only necessary but indeed just: beginning in 1918, letter carriers in Vancouver, firefighters in Edmonton, civic workers in Winnipeg, and, most alarming of all to the Canadian upper class, police officers in many large cities signed union cards.[23] The sense of possibility generated by these public-sector battles was enhanced further by developments overseas. The Russian Revolution in 1917 and the subsequent tide of revolts across Europe stimulated Canadian socialists who were already battling the government's wartime polices and debating the possibilities of post-war reconstruction. Finally, the working class, which ballooned with new immigrants from eastern and southern Europe in the pre-war years, had by 1919 undergone a notable transformation of its own; it had matured, coalesced, and commenced the process of incorporating these new workers into the movement – Jewish, Ukrainian, and Finnish women and men who often possessed labour and socialist backgrounds. Drawn together in the electrified context of the Great War, these conditions produced an unprecedented level of class conflict. In 1919 alone, the equivalent of almost 3.5 million days of work were lost to industrial strife.[24] The unrest continued in muted form into the early 1920s, as the Canadian economy faltered.

From the anti-conscription agitation to the summer strike wave, the war came home with a vengeance; it certainly did not await the return of the Canadian troops after the November 1918 armistice. Not surprisingly, the unrest of this period aroused the fears of the Canadian government, prompting an intensification of repression and a 'Red Scare' of significant proportions.

From World War to Class War

Internment, which had been used less and less in 1915 and 1916, made an instant recovery. Although authorities had harassed socialist and pacifist opponents of the war in its early years, their efforts grew massively in this period of mounting unrest. Enemy aliens charged with anything related to radical politics – possession of prohibited literature, attendance at illegal meetings, membership in an illegal group – found themselves whisked away to internment camps. Indeed, in February 1919, as heads of state sorted out peace at Versailles and the summer strike wave heated up, the government expanded the camps' potential considerably by allowing any county – or district court judge – on a summary complaint from a municipal authority or any 'reasonable' citizen, to intern on grounds no greater than a 'feeling of public apprehension entertained by the community.' In this context, the suspected alien need not be present at the hearing and was explicitly denied the right to legal counsel. This provision proved quite useful in dealing with radicals. Some thirty-three 'aliens' were interned at Kapuskasing, Ontario, in the aftermath of the Winnipeg General Strike. When the camps were finally closed fully fifteen months after peace in Europe, nearly 9,000 men, women, and children had been interned, of whom only a third, by Ottawa's own admission, could even remotely be considered conventional prisoners of war. Some 80,000 other foreign-born Canadians had passed through the registration and examination procedures without being detained.[25]

As dramatic as internment, however, was the government's suppression of two other democratic freedoms. On 25 September 1918 Ottawa passed PC 2381, an order-in-council that curtailed freedom of the press by making it unlawful to print, publish, deliver, receive, or possess any publication in an 'enemy language'; this blanket restriction was later augmented by a series of amendments that permitted more targeted bans of material not covered by the initial order-in-council. Those who violated the order ran the risk of receiving a $5,000 fine and/or five years in jail.[26] Buoyed by the ever-widening definition of objectionable material, Chambers, the chief press censor, moved against a wide variety of material, most notably that published in Yiddish, Ukrainian, and Finnish; by 1919, the entire foreign-language radical press had been suppressed.[27] Yet more striking than PC 2381 – and its curtailment of freedom of the press – was the simultaneous passage of PC 2384, a decree that drastically circumscribed freedom of association, assembly, and speech for a select group of Canadians, most of whom were foreign immigrants. The government's new list of illegal societies and parties, complete with errors, included the Industrial Workers of the World, the Ukrainian Social Democratic Party (USDP), the Social Democratic Party, and the Socialist Party of North America, among others. Radical organizations that were not explicitly identified in the order were nonetheless covered by a catch-all clause which prohibited 'any association ... one of whose purposes or professed purposes is to bring about any governmental, political, social, industrial, or economic change within Canada by the use of force, violence, or physical injury to person or property, or by threats of such injury or which teaches, advocates, advises, or defends the use of [such tactics].' What was more, this order-in-council made it illegal to 'sell, speak, write, or publish anything,' 'to become or continue to be a member,' 'or wear, carry, or cause to be displayed any badge, insignia, emblem, banner, motto, pennant, card, or any device whatsoever' indicating membership in a prohibited group.[28] With the war against the Kaiser winding down, the war against labour and the left in Canada was ramping up.

Spurred on by the nationwide rise in union militancy, and later energized by the widening array of powers made available by 'wartime' orders-in-council, the Dominion Police participated in a series of arrests, prosecutions, and convictions of alleged 'subversives' between 1916 and 1919. Working to the east of Lake Superior, the force engaged in undercover work in a wide range of locales – from Sault Ste-Marie in northern Ontario to Sydney, Cape Breton, in eastern Nova Scotia – and did so with the assistance of other federal departments, crown agencies such as the post office, and provincial and municipal police forces. Commissioner Sherwood and his assistant, Albert Cawdron, extended the Dominion Police's reach further by making liberal use of private detective agencies that possessed extensive experience in combating unions, including the Pinkerton Detective Agency in New York, the

Thiel Detective Company in Chicago, and the Employers' Detective Agency in Toronto. While the utilization of private help was an expensive way to proceed, Cawdron admitted in a letter to the minister of justice in 1918, the long-term costs associated with the possible triumph of labour radicals – 'a very dangerous, socialistic, and perhaps murderous lot' – were potentially much, much higher.[29]

By the middle of March 1918, Cawdron – who by then had assumed some of Sherwood's responsibilities – had received several briefs from his network of informants. And the news from the field was decidedly mixed. While the Industrial Workers of the World did not appear to be especially active in some locales, the reports suggested, there was a more serious threat emanating from within the ranks of the Ukrainian Social Democratic Party. The extent to which to the Dominion Police understood the true nature of this particular organization – the USDP – is unclear; what is known, however, is that Sherwood's and Cawdron's general concerns about labour and the left were supported by subsequent reports filed by special agents linked to intelligence operations conducted by employers (Hollinger Consolidated Gold Mines in Timmins, Ontario, and the Mountain Lumber Manufacturers' Association in Nelson, British Columbia) and other government institutions (military intelligence, Department of Labour, and Department of Immigration). These briefs suggested increased radical activity among immigrant workers, in both central and western Canada. Although incomplete, and sometimes contradictory, the information turning up in Ottawa made it clear that something terrible, and terribly worrisome, was afoot in the land in late 1918 and early 1919. 'I feel that unless some action is taken to deal with these people, before they get too strong, it may eventually lead to general strikes throughout the country. Further investigation is being made,' Cawdron observed.[30]

The Dominion Police did indeed move ahead with 'further investigations,' and it did so with the assistance of PC 2381 and PC 2384. In early 1919, about five months after the new wartime orders-in-council were enacted, Sherwood met with Joseph Rogers, the superintendent of the Ontario Provincial Police (OPP), and other heads of police to formulate a coordinated plan of attack. According to the head of the OPP, 'at this meeting, it was decided that a systematic raid should be made by the police from the Atlantic to the Pacific' for 'the spirit of Bolshevism is strong among the aliens in this country and the Russians and the Finns are the class that requires the most attention.'[31] And they certainly got it. According to one police report entitled 'Bolshevik Propaganda,' between the fall of 1918 and June 1919, 214 men and women, most of them of Finnish and Slav ancestry, were charged with various offences, including possession of prohibited literature, attending illegal meetings, and being members of banned organizations.[32] As these statistics suggest, Ottawa was – by this time – fighting a war on two fronts: not only had it mobilized to battle the enemy abroad, but, increasingly, the enemy was seen to be at home too. Yet to contain it, the federal government required more resources than the Dominion Police could possibly provide. This stark realization prompted the Borden administration to turn increasingly to the other federally controlled law-enforcement agency, the Royal North-West Mounted Police. Yet prior to the summer strike wave of 1918 and the upheavals of 1919, the future of the Mounted Police was by no means certain.

A Many-Headed Hydra

In the years running up to the Great War, the Mounted Police, which had atrophied significantly with the closing of the frontier and the settlement of the western provinces between the late nineteenth and early twentieth century, were primarily responsible for provincial policing in Saskatchewan and Alberta. In the early years of the war, however, its duties were expanded to include the registration and internment of 'enemy aliens' and securing the integrity of the Canada-U.S. border.[33] At the same time, the Mounted Police were permitted to 'employ men for special service to gather information with reference to the movements, disposition, etc., of foreign settlers' – the funds necessary for this action coming out of war appropriations, not the normal Mounted Police budget. While little is known about the undercover agents hired in these early years, fragmentary evidence suggests that they were keeping tabs on striking coal miners in Crows Nest Pass, Alberta, in 1915 and draft resisters in Quebec a year or two later.[34] While the commissioner of the Mounted Police, A.B. Perry, certainly welcomed the challenge of supporting the war effort, he nevertheless was concerned about the strain that this new, wartime mandate placed on the force's modest resources. 'Owing to the wide distribution and paucity, the Mounted Police cannot be looked upon as defensive; their energies are absorbed in their various civil duties,' he told Prime Minister Borden in the fall of 1916. 'To render it of more service in meeting war conditions its members would have to be largely increased, its ordinary police duties taken over by the different provinces, and its distribution revised.'[35] Borden was sympathetic, and within a year both Saskatchewan and Alberta had created their own provincial police forces; about eighty Mounted Police posts were subsequently closed.[36]

Yet by the time this reorientation was under way, Perry's priorities had started to shift somewhat. No longer completely content with the force's purely domestic role – policing on the Canadian prairies or supervising enemy aliens – he hoped that the Mounties might be deployed overseas to help Ottawa fulfil its obligations on the Western front and elsewhere. Despite the misgivings of Canadian and British military leaders, in the end, the federal government permitted the force to play a modest military role; in May 1918 a cavalry outfit consisting of 12 officers and 726 non-commissioned officers left for Europe. Five officers and 181 other Mounted Police personnel later joined Canadian forces in Siberia as part of the Allies' attempt to bolster counter-revolutionary forces in Russia.[37] By this time, the force's ranks had contracted substantially and many, both inside and outside the service, wondered if it would continue to exist at all. As one member of the force active during these lean years recalled, '[there was a] prevalent rumour throughout the entire Force during my early years of service that the RNWMP would soon be disbanded.'[38] Yet rumours of the Mounted Police's imminent demise proved premature – as renewed working-class militancy across the country, coupled with a realization that the Dominion Police lacked the resources to meet this burgeoning challenge, prompted the Borden administration to explore the feasibility of making the Mounties solely responsible for secret service work.

To this end, the prime minister commissioned Montreal lawyer and long-time Tory C.H. Cahan to draw up a report on left-wing activity in Canada and recommend ways to suppress it. To the country's political and business elite, Cahan's involvement in this process was perhaps not a complete surprise. Born in Nova Scotia in 1861, Cahan attended Dalhousie University, graduating with an BA in 1886 and LLB in 1890. After several years with the influential *Herald and Mail*, he turned his attention to corporate law. 'He was well paid. His legal fees were large – too large for that age,' Max Aitken, the future Lord Beaverbrook, once remarked, commenting on the period in which Cahan handled the affairs of his Royal Securities Corporation. Like his legal fees, Cahan's political ambitions were large too. In 1890 he was elected to the Nova Scotia legislature and served as leader of the Conservative opposition for four years. But his success on the provincial hustings was short-lived; he ran unsuccessfully in two subsequent provincial elections, in 1896 and 1900. Eleven years later, Cahan, who by then was quite wealthy and had moved permanently to Montreal, was working as an organizer for the federal Tories, then under the leadership of Borden, himself an attorney from Nova Scotia. During the First World War, Cahan, who ran unsuccessfully for the federal Tories in 1917, worked his political and business connections to help procure munitions from the United States for the Allied forces – an operation made possible by his presence on the board of Canadian Car and Foundry which was based in Montreal but possessed plants in the United States. Piecemeal evidence suggests that Cahan might have been in touch with British intelligence at the same time – as fears about German saboteurs mounted on both sides of the Atlantic. By 1918, Cahan was looking into questions of subversion at the behest of the Canadian prime minister.[39]

At first, ambiguity, not clarity, characterized the prime minister's sense of what the politically minded and well-heeled lawyer could do for the federal government. Writing to Cahan in May 1918, Borden spoke of 'certain evidence pointing pretty distinctly to ... propaganda in various parts of the country which raises suspicion that it is being carried on by German agents or with German support.' After seeking Cahan's advice on establishing 'some effective organization to investigate the whole subject,' the prime minister hinted that the American example, in which an 'organization of a more or less voluntary character,' operating under the auspices of the Department of Justice, kept watch on enemy aliens, might be the way to go.[40] Although Borden never said so explicitly, it appears that he was thinking about a Canadian equivalent of the American Protective League, an organization that, according to the U.S. attorney general, consisted of 'several hundred thousand private citizens – some as individuals, most of the as members of patriotic bodies, engaged in assisting the heavily overworked Federal authorities in keeping an eye on disloyal individuals and making reports of disloyal utterances.' With the sanction of the American government, members of the American Protective League, sporting badges that read 'APL – Secret Service,' intercepted mail, ransacked offices, acted as agents provocateurs, and threatened, harassed, intimidated, and assaulted those who acted in an un-American way by opposing the war.[41] As a Tory and a Canadian, the prime minister was likely sceptical of the republican and populist character of the league; but, like his American counterparts, he, too, was searching for a way to undertake political policing on a wider and more sustained basis that was affordable, politically viable, and effective. For his part, Cahan rejected the idea of a purely civic organization; he had far more ambitious, state-centred plans in mind.

After about two months of investigation, Cahan filed an interim report with the minister of justice in late July 1918. While he found little to worry about among German or Austrian citizens, he did note that 'there is apparently wide-spread unrest and discontent throughout Canada, which finds expression in labor agitation and strikes, in attempts to avoid the Military Service Act, in mutterings against food prices, in criticism of the treatment of returned soldiers, in the prevalent suspicion that discrimination is shown in the collection of federal taxes, and in general discontent with the administration of the federal departments.' What was more, Cahan continued, bound up in this general unease about the prosecution of the war effort was the specific 'mental unrest' experienced by 'the peoples of Slavic origin in Canada, Russian, Ukrainian, and Austrian' which was, in his opinion, 'directly attributable to the dissemination in Canada of the Socialistic doctrines, espoused by the Russian Revolutionary element, and more recently by the Bolsheveki Party in Russia.' In the plodding prose of a barrister, Cahan pinpointed the origins of the subversive threat in Canada. It was not German, nor was it necessarily linked to the Industrial Workers of the World or the Ukrainian Social Democratic Party – targets identified, or perhaps even confused, by those at the helm of the Dominion Police. Rather, it was Bolshevism, a pernicious political praxis that had origins overseas yet flourished among immigrant communities here at home. The Reds, Cahan was saying, were increasing under the bed, and only by expanding the work carried out by the Dominion Police, and bringing about greater cooperation between it and other agencies, could they be held in check.[42]

The summer strike wave of 1918 no doubt hardened Cahan's suspicions. In the fall, after conducting additional research into 'socialistic propaganda in Canada, its purposes, results, and remedies,' he submitted his final report to the minister of justice, a seventeen-page document which extended and refined his earlier findings. On the whole, he said, the federal government's policy of registering and interning enemy aliens was implemented well, and the commissioner of the Dominion Police deserved mention for his strong leadership in this regard. The problem, however, was that police actions and government policies did not go far enough. 'The Russians, Ukrainians, and Finns, who are employed in the mines, factories, and other industries of Canada, are now being thoroughly saturated with the socialistic doctrines which have been proclaimed by the Bolsheviki faction of Russia,' Cahan observed. 'For several years before the outbreak of the war, the industrial centres of Canada were literally deluged with these publications; and, at present time, I have before me a mass of literature, filled with the most pernicious and seditious teaching, which is even now, in large quantities, being secretly circulated in Canada.' The key, then, was to expand the wartime orders-in-council to cover those ethnic groups most susceptible to this propaganda, apply the 'most stringent measures to curtail the importation, publication, and distribution of such doctrines,' prohibit 'during the same period, the oral advocacy of such doctrines at public and private meetings,' and ban outright 'any society or organization' that advocated objectionable tactics and objectives. To do all of this, and to do it effectively, necessitated not only the expansion of existing enforcement mechanisms – he explained – but the creation of a new, overarching one to better centralize and coordinate the various government departments and agencies currently looking after the War Measures Act. Thus, the hawkish lawyer urged the federal government to create a new Public Safety Branch of the Department of Justice; responsible for the administration of all security provisions, it should be headed by an individual 'in cordial sympathy with the war aims of the government.'[43]

The Borden administration moved quickly to implement many of the recommendations contained in Cahan's final report: in September and October 1918, the orders-in-council came fast and furious. Within a week, the government passed the infamous PC 2381 and 2384 which banned various ethnic, labour, and socialist organizations and their publications; it would not be long before the men and women who were a part of the radical Industrial Workers of the World or who published militant newspapers, like the Finnish organ *Vapaus*, would feel the pressure. The federal government went on to ban strikes for the duration of the war – though public outcry, coupled with a vigorous protest from the labour movement and rank-and-file workers' refusal to cease and desist, led to the decree's withdrawal before its punitive provisions were utilized. In October, the ruling Unionists, fearing the expansion of public-sector unionism into its own ranks, passed PC 2213, which forbade any member of the Dominion or Mounted Police from 'becoming a member of ... or associated with any trade union organization or any society or association connected therewith.'[44] During the same month, the Public Safety Branch, the capstone of Cahan's report, was established for the 'effective administration of the laws, orders, and regulations enacted for the preservation of public order and safety during the continuance of the war, and more particularly to administer and enforce the orders and regulations sanctioned as war measures.' Cahan, who had been angling for a more permanent role for some time, became its first director.[45]

In the weeks and months that followed his appointment, Cahan mapped out a detailed and ambitious blueprint for the new agency which called for a central office staff, a 'Bureau of Investigation' consisting of five secret service agents under the command of the branch director, and the complete reorganization and expansion of the Dominion Police 'sufficient to preserve public order and safety throughout Canada during the period of demobilization, without the necessity of involving the frequent aid of the military forces.'[46] Never a supporter of the American Protective League as a possible solution for the security dilemma in Canada, Cahan nevertheless saw something in the American experience that he liked: the (Federal) Bureau of Investigation which was taking shape within the United States Department of Justice. Both inside and outside government circles, he trumpeted this solution, stressing, as he often did to the deputy minister and minister of justice, the benefits to be derived from a force of secret agents capable of 'prob[ing] very thoroughly the sources of enemy propaganda in this country, the violations of law due to the advocates of social and political revolution, and the general social and industrial unrest throughout Canada.'[47] In a public address before a literary society in Montreal in late 1918, he laid bare what was at stake if a comprehensive plan of attack, one that drew on the resources and vigilance of the state and civil society, was not enacted:

> The revolutionary socialists would burn down the structures that civilization has reared, with all its slowly acquired values, for the purpose of obliterating its obvious defects; but the people of Canada, if they are wise in their day and generation, will devote the energies of Statesmen and of citizens alike to maintain on the old foundations the fabric our fathers have built, with new improvements as the health, the moral welfare, the material prosperity and the political and social advancement of our Nation obviously demand. Radical, revolutionary socialism, which is raising its *hydra-head* and threatening the obliteration of all that civilization has thus far accomplished, can only be stayed by such eternal vigilance as will enable us to discern and to eradicate social evils as they appear, without destroying al that is valuable in the Social System which we have so far developed, amid so much of toil and strike and suffering.[48]

That Cahan employed the metaphor of the many-headed hydra to convey his sense of the Bolshevik menace is particularly striking. A symbol of disorder in ancient mythology, the image of the hydra was invoked often in the seventeenth and eighteenth centuries by the architects of imperial expansion when they spoke of those who opposed the construction of state, empire, and capitalism: the dispossessed and disenfranchised. Perhaps Cahan, like the powerful of earlier historical periods, thought of himself as Hercules, the mythical ancient hero who killed the hydra by cutting off its central head. If this is so, his deft turn-of-phrase captures more than just a personal desire to deliver spit-polished prose in a public lecture; indeed, by invoking the Hercules-hydra myth, Cahan was laying bare his – and the government's – mounting desire to impose a death sentence, to cut down the monster of labour and working-class opposition before it revealed itself in another, perhaps more terrifying and destructive, guise.[49]

But not everyone in the federal cabinet backed Cahan's aggressive agenda. Chief among his opponents was Newton Rowell, one-time leader of the Liberal Party in Ontario, president of the Privy Council, and perhaps the most important Grit in Borden's Union administration. His cabinet portfolio included the Mounted Police. In the fall of 1918, as the federal government passed its repressive orders-in-council and the Public Safety Branch was created, Rowell was actually on a tour of western Canada to, among other things, consult with the commissioner of the Mounted Police about the future of the force.[50] Upon his return to Ottawa he became embroiled in a cabinet struggle over the aggressive steps taken by the government in his absence. While Rowell had no qualms with the general thrust of the administration's repressive measures, he did feel that the legislation had gone too far by including the more moderate Social Democratic Party of Canada on the list of specifically banned organizations. Writing to the minister of justice, he was conciliatory, suggesting that maybe it was just an oversight that this particular outfit was included at all. Cahan, whose Public Safety Branch was located within the Department of Justice, refused to compromise. In several pointed letters to the prime minister, he argued strenuously against lifting the ban on the Social Democratic Party; not only was it a dangerous and seditious organization, Cahan stated, but any repeal would be 'hailed by those followers of the red flag, who are chief exponents of German propaganda throughout Canada, as an indication that they are at liberty in Canada to undermine, without restraint, the very foundation of our social, industrial, and political system.'[51] In the end,

Rowell won the day on this issue, arguing successfully that 'a policy of repression [was] not only contrary to the public interest, but will alienate from government the support of the progressive elements in the community, who, while out of sympathy with the SDP programme, still insist on freedom of thought and freedom of speech on social and economic questions.'[52] As a result, the order-in-council was amended; the ban on other organizations, however, remained.

Cahan's defeat on this issue was tied to many developments, not the least of which was the importance of party politics at the cabinet table. It is not hard to imagine Prime Minister Borden seeking a compromise on this specific issue in order to ensure the stability of the broader war-time coalition of Liberals and Conservatives that had produced the Union government back when the war first started. Cahan's fortunes were likely undermined further by his inability to follow proper ad-ministrative procedures in one area – he often corresponded directly with Borden, instead of the appropriate government minister – and by the staunch opposition of Thomas Crerar, a powerful Liberal from western Canada, spokesperson for farming interests, minister of agri-culture, and future leader of the Progressive Party. '[Cahan's attack] is the very negation of the first principle of democracy,' Crerar stat-ed bluntly.[53] That both Rowell and Crerar had a political stake in the long-term survival of the Mounted Police – the former minister was in charge of the force, the latter politician represented a region with a long association with the 'scarlet and gold' – probably solidified their opposition to Cahan's vision of a new independent federal bureau of investigation. Politics, personalities, and shifting perspectives on the course of state security in wartime and after had thus weakened Ca-han's stature quickly and considerably by late 1918 – to the extent that his additional requests for more agents, more money, and more legal support to fight the 'social revolutionists' were rejected.[54] Frustrated by the government's foot dragging, Cahan resigned in early January 1919. Perhaps if he had some of the political savvy and bureaucratic talents of the young J. Edgar Hoover, the outcome of this debate over political policing in Canada might have been very different.[55]

As the fortunes of the Conservative lawyer waxed then waned, in-terested federal politicians, high-level civil servants, and senior police officials seized the opportunity to reconsider the role of the Mounted Police as the appropriate body to head up Canada's own intelligence agency. Commissioner Perry was especially forceful in this respect. Encouraged by the conversations he had with Newton Rowell during the minister's tour of the west earlier that fall, the commissioner drew up three possible scenarios and presented them to his political boss in late October 1918: 1) shrink the force even further and make it responsible for policing the Yukon and Northwest Territories only; 2) make the Mounted Police a permanent part of the military establishment; or 3) amalgamate the force with all other departmental law-enforcement outfits, including the Dominion Police, to form one federal agency. Of the three options, Perry favoured the last one, and suggested to Rowell that as part of the consolidation process, the Mounted Police would be well suited to enforce all federal laws, look after customs and revenue matters, and, significantly, head up the secret service.[56] Other federal cabinet members, such as the influential conservative Arthur Meighen, liked the idea of a merger too, but he did so for different reasons.[57]

The prime minister was not entirely convinced. He agreed that some reorganization should take place, but not in the way that Perry, Rowell, and Meighen proposed. Somewhat out of touch, Borden doubted that the Dominion Police and RNWMP could be effectively combined – given the Mounties' semi-military heritage and proud traditions. Moreover, he was not convinced that the future of the force depended on whether or not it acquired sole responsibility for intelligence and security matters; perhaps, he opined, its future prospects could be secured in others ways.[58] Thus, the reorganization of the federal police forces, which took place in December 1918 to take effect in the new year, was not as dramatic as it might have been. As a first step, the RNWMP was given jurisdiction for all of western Canada, from the twin cities of Port Arthur and Fort William at the top of Lake Superior west to British Columbia and north to the Yukon; the Dominion Police retained its focus for the provinces east of that imaginary line. Both forces were responsible for the enforcement of federal laws in their respective jurisdictions, upholding all the orders-in-council passed under the War Measures Act and, more ominously, helping civil authorities to maintain law and order. High priority was also given to bringing members of the RNWMP home from Europe, incorporating any Dominion Police officers who were stationed in western Canada into the force, and recruiting new constables in order to expand the Mounties' overall ranks to about 1,200.[59] The Mounted Police, which had dwindled in size and stature in the early years of the war, now had more authority and more reach than at any time in their history. And they would need it, for as the politicians debated the future of the federal police forces, working-class people, who had borne the brunt of the nation's transition to capitalism and mobilization for war, were still on the offensive, marching in the streets, shutting down workplaces, and, by the summer of 1919, paralysing entire cities.

The Creation of the RCMP

In this moment of heightened strike activity and significant internal reorganization, Newton Rowell – the cabinet minister responsible for the Mounted Police – was deeply concerned that neither of the federal police forces, the DP or the RNWMP, was able to provide the government with timely and prescient intelligence. 'It is important that this branch of the Service should receive most careful consideration,' he wrote to his deputy minister, A.A. McLean, 'and that an efficient service should be maintained so that the Government would be thoroughly advised of what is going on in the principal centres where the IWW or other revolutionary agitators might be at work.'[60] The 'principal centres' that Rowell had in mind were located in the west, and, given the Mounted Police's newly acquired responsibility for policing politics in the entire region, he was especially interested in the nature of the Dominion Police's earlier operations west of Lake Superior. That the minister responsible for one federal force was only dimly aware of the surveillance and intelligence operations undertaken by the other federal force underscores the fragmented way that many of these repressive tasks were conducted, both before and after the reorganization. That McLean, upon receiving his minister's inquiry, in turn contacted C.H. Cahan in February 1919 for assistance in the area of counter-subversion underscores this notion further: by that time, Cahan had already resigned his position and his Public Service Branch had been terminated by order-in-council.[61]

For his part, Commissioner Perry possessed a firmer grasp of the obstacles standing in the way of extending the government's access to reliable and timely information about subversives in Canada – and moved to eliminate them. To this end, he helped to end the security and intelligence functions undertaken on an informal basis by other government officials in other government departments, most notably the ubiquitous Malcolm Reid in British Columbia, who had taken over for William Charles Hopkinson after the latter's murder in 1914. At the same time, Perry pared back the role of provincial and municipal forces in this respect and looked ahead to hiring undercover operatives in a serious way.[62] Writing to his 'Officers Commanding' in Manitoba, Saskatchewan, Alberta, and British Columbia in early January 1919, Perry drew their attention to the 'pernicious doctrines of Bolshevism' which were present 'not only across the world, but across Canada' as well. Of particular concern, he continued, were the immigrant communities in Winnipeg, Edmonton, and Vancouver for they were especially 'susceptible to Bolshevik teaching and propaganda.' In this regard, commanding officers were 'to take steps to see that careful and constant supervision is maintained over these foreign settlements with a view to detecting the least indication of Bolshevik tendencies and doctrines.' In this regard, he went on, it was crucial that 'good, trustworthy men' be recruited as secret agents and that they, in a manner 'not to arouse suspicion or cause antagonism,' become 'fully acquainted with all labour and other organizations in their respective districts.' Knowing each organization's tactics and objectives, the 'ways, habits, and antecedents' of its officials, and whether it was open to Bolshevik influence, was at the core of the secret agent's duties.[63]

These external changes to the force were matched by some internal renovations, for the commissioner was well aware that intelligence was valuable to the government only if it was well organized and accessible to authorities in a timely manner. Thus, Perry and his assistant commissioner, W.H. Routledge, attached considerable importance to establishing clear channels of communication, standardizing monthly reports, and creating 'Personal History Files,' a registry of suspected subversives that included 'names and usual descriptive particulars. A photograph if it is at all possible to obtain one without arousing suspicion. Date of arrival in Canada; if naturalized or not; married or single; family; home address; present occupation; particular associations affiliated with and standing in same; present locality of activities; points where he is known to have been in any way active; details of any police records which he may have had; degree of intelligence and education and all other possible information which would assist in compiling a complete record of the man.' At first, Perry and Routledge envisaged a system in which personal-history files would be opened only at the request of the force's national office. But within weeks of introducing the idea, the two senior officers modified their position, and advised local commanding officers to '[start a file on] any prominent agitator coming under your notice.'[64] Between 1919 and 1924, the Mounted Police 'noticed' 2,525 individuals active in 2,287 different locales, an eclectic group of 'agitators' that included men and women, radicals and moderates, clergymen and elected officials, doctors and intellectuals, an Esperanto teacher and a Hindu wrestler.[65]

Out in the field, local commanding officers soon discovered how difficult it was to find the 'good' and 'trustworthy' men that Perry and Routledge desired. 'I have been endeavouring during the month to engage some special agents with a view of getting definite information with regard to alien propaganda and socialistic matters,' the Mounties' commanding officer in Edmonton reported in late January 1919. 'This I have found exceedingly difficult; the right class of man is very hard to get. I have engaged temporarily a returned soldier, W.P. Walker, who has been highly recommended and I think he will make good.'[66] That this local officer found it difficult to find suitable recruits, and thus looked to veterans of the Great War for assistance, is significant for it highlights the hatred of radicals that both the police and many returned men shared. Throughout this rocky post-war period, it was not uncommon for mainstream veterans' organizations, often working hand in glove with local police and politicians, to harass, intimidate, and assault citizens thought to be associated with the 'Bolsheveki menace'; returned men also made good strike-breakers.[67] In short, from the Mounties' perspective, former soldiers – especially officers – were a good bet: not only did they possess military training, but they had served God, King, and Country overseas and were likely to do so again. 'It is a difficult matter ... to ensure efficient work in a new district like this, when one does not know the people on whom it is necessary to rely on for information and investigation,' a report from the Mounties' Vancouver detachment stated, echoing the concerns voiced in the Alberta capital. 'Up to date Messrs. Devitt, Spain, Eccles, Jones, Roth, Hall, Davies, Wilkie, and Lawrence have been engaged, all of whom are either ex-members of the Force or are returned soldiers or both.'[68]

Possessing a military or police background was by no means the sole criterion used by the Mounted Police when assessing potential operatives. Indeed, it was equally important that prospective agents possessed some knowledge of radicalism and the labour movement or, at the very least, were able to insert themselves into 'subversive' circles without raising any suspicion. The short yet intriguing career of Robert Raglan Gosden – who has the unique distinction of being both a secret agent *and* the subject of a personal-history file – illustrates this point well. Born in England in 1882, Gosden came to North America at the age of fourteen. Like many young men of his social class, he worked at a variety of jobs, including miner, logger, seafarer, and labourer – crisscrossing the continent as employment opportunities were available.[69] Given this work history, it is perhaps no surprise that Gosden joined the Industrial Workers of the World, which had grown steadily in the west in the years running up to the Great War. Sometimes dressed in black, the colour of anarchism, Gosden could be found fighting for free speech in San Diego, organizing workers in Prince Rupert and Steveston, British Columbia, and urging coal miners on Vancouver Island to opt for radicalism, not reform, as a way to end their long and bitter strike of 1912–14.[70] The controversy that accompanied this stance had hardly died down when, in 1916, Gosden was embroiled in a political scandal in which he was accused of 'plugging,' or stuffing, ballot boxes for the provincial Liberals. 'I wanted to see the Government in power have some new blood in it,' Gosden told a commission of inquiry. 'I may say there was some satisfaction in seeing the Liberals get in to beat the Conservatives for once. Do you think I don't remember the troubles up on the Island [during the miners' strike]?'[71]

By the early months of 1919, Gosden was a spy for the Mounted Police. His motivations are difficult to assess. On the one hand, it appears that he was attracted by a job that paid reasonably well, required brains and organizational skills, and promised both intrigue and excitement, qualities that were absent from his regular, workaday life. On the other hand, it is possible that Gosden saw political policing as a way to neutralize other radicals tied to the Socialist Party of Canada who had taken control of some important unions and labour councils in the province: they might have been left-wingers, but from his perspective, they were not 'Wobblies,' as IWW members were commonly known. For its part, the Mounties were attracted by Gosden's extensive background in the radical workers' movement; '[this agent has] for many years taken an active part in the IWW and kindred associations, and is therefore peculiarly competent to discuss the leaders in such movements and their aims and objectives,' the commissioner remarked. That Gosden had shown a penchant for secrecy, intrigue, and political double-dealing during the 'plugging' scandal of 1916 probably enhanced his profile as a potential recruit.[72] Identified by his police handler as 'Secret Agent No. 10,' Gosden spent several months travelling through mining communities in British Columbia and Alberta before landing in Calgary in March 1919 as a delegate to the Western Labor Conference.[73]

Gosden's lengthy final report on the conference is significant for a variety of reasons, not the least of which is that it correctly identified leading members of the Socialist Party of Canada as key players in the formation of the One Big Union – an assessment that bore all the marks of his intimate understanding of the left-wing labour movement. In addition to this astute consideration of the Socialist Party's motivations and objectives, Gosden went on to recommend that the state undertake a concerted campaign of repression and destabilization against the newly created OBU. 'After one or two of these leaders had been picked up at various points in a mysterious manner, and disappeared just as mysteriously, the unseen hand would so intimidate the weaker and lesser lights that the agitation would automatically die down,' Secret Agent No. 10 wrote enthusiastically. 'All precedents and policies of the authorities must be swept aside to meet this newer and more subtle form of revolutionary activity.'[74] Easily dismissed as the delusions of a demented ex-radical, Gosden's account laid bare a sentiment that many in government circles understood all too well: a new moment of working-class radicalism was emerging and the state, now capable of wielding the 'unseen hand' of political policing, must act. Perhaps it is for this reason that the report, its bombast and rhetorical excess notwithstanding, was deemed important enough by the Mounted Police to be passed up the chain of command to the Prime Minister's Office (PMO), albeit with a cautionary note affixed.[75]

Gosden was not the only operative at the Western Labor Conference. Franco Zanetti, who also went by the names of Frank Zaneth, Harry Blask, James LaPlante, and 'Secret Agent No. 7,' was present too. Neither a veteran of the Great War nor a seasoned labour radical, Zaneth provided the Mounted Police with other qualities that were critical to the successful penetration of those communities thought to be behind the national labour revolt: his ethnicity and language skills. The son of a cabinetmaker, Zanetti was born in Italy in 1890. At the age of nine, he accompanied his older brother to the United States; the two boys were joined by their family a few years later. They lived in Springfield, Massachusetts. In 1910 Zanetti got married and, with his new wife, moved to Moose Jaw, Saskatchewan, in hopes of acquiring a homestead, which they succeeded in doing in 1912. By 1917, however, Zanetti was back in Springfield: his time on the land was unsuccessful, his marriage had ended, and his future was uncertain. That year he applied to join the Mounted Police under his newly assumed name, Frank Zaneth; he was accepted and in December enlisted at Regina headquarters. Shortly after completing his basic training, Zaneth was sent underground, undertaking his first round of reconnaissance in Quebec City after violent anti-conscription riots had erupted there in the spring of 1918. By the fall and winter of 1918, Zaneth, who now went by the name of Harry Blask, was back out west on the trail of the Industrial Workers of the World. After stops in Drumheller and Canmore, he went on to Calgary where he set about ingratiating himself with George Sangster, a machinist and prominent radical.[76]

As Sangster's friend and comrade, Blask gained access to the Socialist Party of Canada and the wider radical milieu of which it was a part. He turned up at intimate gatherings, participated in union meetings, and, in March 1919, attended the Western Labor Conference. After a brief sojourn in Regina to report directly to the commissioner of the Mounted Police, Blask, who spent a week in jail at the behest of the federal police in order to bolster his credentials as a left-winger, returned to Calgary just as the Winnipeg General Strike was starting to unfold. On 15 May 1919 the Winnipeg Trades and Labour Council called a general strike following the breakdown of negotiations between the city's metal and building trades and its unionized employees. Spurred on by the general climate of unrest following the Great War, and emboldened by a deeper, collective history of class antagonism, 12,000 workers heeded the call to walk off the job; within days they were joined by 30,000 more, the vast majority of whom did not even belong to a union. What began as a conflict over the right to bargain collectively and better wages and working conditions had become something far more explosive: to many workers, this was the opening battle in a longer 'war for freedom'; to their opponents, it was a Bolshevik plot hatched by 'revolutionary unionists,' 'crazy idealists,' and 'ordinary thieves.'[77] Throughout the six-week crisis, Blask reported on what he deemed to be radical goings-on in Calgary, and even discovered the identity of the strikers' own spy in the Citizens' Committee of One Thousand, the employer-state body in the Manitoba capital that opposed the strike.[78]

In the aftermath of the confrontation, as both the state and capital moved to make an example of radicals and quash any remaining public support, a debate raged between the Mounted Police and A.J. Andrews, the chief prosecutor in the cases brought against the Winnipeg strike leaders. Andrews needed Blask as a star witness; the Mounties did not want to disclose the identity of their top labour spy. In the end, Andrews won the argument. On 5 December 1919 Harry Blask testified against R.B. Russell, member of the Socialist Party of Canada and leader of the One Big Union, who was on trial for 'seditious conspiracy.' Broad enough to encompass a wide variety of acts – including organizing a union, writing a pamphlet, and making a speech – seditious conspiracy was, at its core, about silencing those who 'excit[ed] dis-affection against the government, the laws, and the constitution, and generally promot[ed] ill-will and hostility amongst the people and be-tween classes.'[79] After twenty-three days of legal proceedings, which included the presentation of 703 exhibits and the taking of 'voluminous evidence,' the presiding judge left the matter in the jury's hands, but not before making sure that its members understood what was at stake:

> If a man's ideal is Socialism, that is not illegal. But perhaps you may think it not to be nice. It is not illegal, but, gentlemen after hearing the evidence of what Socialism is, may we not remember the words of that illustrious countryman of Mr. Russell, and ask ourselves, 'Breathes there a man with soul so dead, who never to himself has said, this is my own, my native land.' What did our forefathers fight for at Queenstown Heights? For what did they fling back the Americans for the ramparts of the city of Quebec and roll them down the snow clad cliffs? What do you think of patriotism? What do you think of allegiance to your country? What do you think of allegiance to the brotherhood of the world, limiting the brotherhood of the world to the working class as indicated here. Well, I like my country. Do you?[80]

Russell was convicted and sent to prison, and Frank Zaneth, after a brief time undercover in Montreal as James LaPlante, was promoted to the upper ranks of the Mounted Police.[81]

In the wake of the conflagration at Winnipeg, Ottawa broadened the mandate of the Mounted Police, granting it complete jurisdiction in the area of federal law enforcement and national security countrywide. The threat posed by the national labour revolt had clearly trumped any lin-gering doubts about the need for a single agency responsible for politi-cal policing from one coast to the other. Within this wider framework, a new Criminal Investigation Branch (CIB) responsible for the running of detectives and spies across the country was established at Regina head-quarters. A year later, in 1920, the older Dominion Police force was qui-etly merged into the larger North-West Mounted Police to produce the Royal Canadian Mounted Police and the new force's headquarters was moved to Ottawa to emphasize its national role. Once in the nation's capital, the RCMP expanded its security work further both by creat-ing a Central Registry – an extensive archive of the country's so-called undesirables – and, later, by appointing a liaison and intelligence of-ficer (LIO). This position produced weekly summaries of security and intelligence material collected by the force for the perusal of the prime minister and cabinet. Thus, by 1922, with the creation of the Criminal Investigation Branch, the Central Registry, and the office of liaison and intelligence, the security state had arrived in Canada.

From Hot War to Cold War

During the heady days of the Great War and the national labour revolt, the Canadian government deeply feared the Bolshevik external threat and harboured real fears of revolution at home. In response, it created a battery of repressive measures and agencies during the war and in its immediate aftermath. The historical irony of this two-front war is striking: while thousands of working-class men and women were marched off to Europe, ostensibly to defend the rights and freedoms of democracy against tyranny, such highly prized ideals were routinely, and often viciously, violated at home. What began as a war against German aggression ended as a campaign against labour and the left. The Cold War in Canada did not await the revelations of Soviet espionage in the Canadian civil service in the 1940s, but was present from 1918 when C.H. Cahan, at the behest of Prime Minister Borden, created the Public Safety Branch within the Department of Justice. By the end of the Great War, the source of Canada's national-security anxieties had shifted decisively: the enemy was no longer Irish or South Asian anti-imperialism – as it had been in the mid- to late nineteenth and early twentieth centuries – but Communism, and this preoccupation would last for the better part of the new century.

   While the face of Canada's internal enemy shifted decisively with the onset of the Great War and national labour revolt, many of the issues that faced the Canadian state in the realm of national security remained consistent over time. In the early twentieth century, as in the nineteenth, matters of political policing remained lodged in a broader global framework, with Canada serving as both a staging ground for radical movements with transnational connections and an important catchment area for the intelligence necessary to repress those movements, both at home and abroad. Within the Canadian government itself, surveillance and intelligence gathering sat comfortably under the aegis of the crown – operating out of and between several government departments and two federal police forces – and thus was shielded from parliamentary or public scrutiny and effectively depoliticized. Moreover, in the new century as in the old, tensions persisted within each component of the surveillance and intelligence gathering cycle: between political needs and policing resources; between long-term undercover objectives and short-term law-enforcement matters; and between the promise of a star informant and the risks/benefits associated with prolonged and often dangerous undercover operations. Human resources also remained key to political policing in the early years; the association of ethnicity with subversion remained indispensable for spymasters and spies as well. Combined, all of this had by the early 1920s formed a sort of political and bureaucratic pattern or template, which would shape the future practices of the RCMP as it assumed its new role as the sole state agency responsible for political policing.

Outside the ambit of the Canadian state, immigrant radicals were likely aware of some of these continuities, notably the consistent manner in which the Mounties equated ethnicity and radicalism and converted both classifications into something called 'subversion' or 'un-British' behaviour. Thus, with this in mind, they had to live cautiously in the 1920s. Propelled forward by the events at Winnipeg, Ottawa introduced significant amendments to the Immigration Act which allowed for the automatic deportation of 'anarchists' and any other radicals. At the same time, it rewrote the Naturalization Act so that it would be able to revoke the naturalization of anyone, even those of British heritage, who fomented revolution. Changes to the Criminal Code made prosecution possible for anyone who advocated change outside of peaceful, parliamentary channels. Working-class publishers and journalists had to be careful as well. When the office of chief press censor was shut down after the war, its head passed a summary of its activities on to the RCMP with a clear indication of which papers the censor felt should be watched. This list included the *BC Federationist* ('incite[d] the public to violence and revolt against constituted authority'), *Camp Workers* ('extremely revolutionary in tone'), *Ukrainian Labor News* ('objectionable Bolshevist publication ... worth watching closely'), and *Western Labor News* ('created feeling of unrest and discontent'). Needless to say, the RCMP would continue to watch the labour press carefully.[82]

Obviously, the Canadian government cut its repressive teeth during this period and established a clear trajectory in security and intelligence work. But the revolutionary movement learned its political lessons too. For progressive Finns and Ukrainians, the way forward remained quite clear: left-wing political and cultural centres such as the Finnish Organization of Canada and the Ukrainian Labour Farmer Temple Association (ULFTA) moved directly into the fledgling Communist Party of

Canada (CPC) which was founded in 1921. This direction proved most appealing for most left-wing Jews as well, although there was a significant group in that community that remained loyal to more moderate social-democratic traditions. The radical press in these three communities became overwhelmingly Communist in the 1920s. In the aftermath of '1919,' the Social Democratic Party disappeared as its immigrant members joined the Communist Party, while some of its British and native Canadian elements chose to pursue other political agendas. Members of the Industrial Workers of the World and the Socialist Party of Canada, split along ideological lines, became involved with the Communist Party or remained tied to a non-Bolshevik, socialist vision.

Significantly, the state's position on the battlefield of class war, which had remained hidden to large segments of the Canadian workers before 1914, now stood exposed. The economic climate of the 1920s, however, was to prove inhospitable for further labour activism. The state's new repressive apparatus, operating out of the departments of Immigration and Justice and through military intelligence and the Royal Canadian Mounted Police, remained alert. Its practices, initiated in the Great War and the immediate post-war era and continued during the 1920s, would again come to the fore during the Great Depression, the next nationwide period of worker militancy.

PART TWO

Survival and Revival

4

The RCMP, the Communist Party, and the Consolidation of Canada's Cold War

In the aftermath of the Great War and the national labour revolt, what it meant to be Canadian was the subject of intense debate. Throughout the 1920s, politicians sought laws designed to shore up the nuclear family, promote compulsory education, and weed out 'unfit' and 'inferior' immigrants as a bulwark against 'foreign' ideologies. On the job, many employers adopted new, more enlightened approaches to labour relations – company unions, pension plans, reading rooms – in an attempt to stave off further industrial conflict. At the same time, volunteer organizations, charities, and church groups promoted clean living, physical fitness, and Christian values to ensure that the nation's 'human stock' was efficient, modern, and incorruptible. While diverse in origin, and sometimes contradictory in effect, these initiatives shared two common objectives: in the short term, 'normalcy'; in the long term, regeneration.[1] Coercion, the leitmotif of the war years, had given way to consent.

For labour and left-wing activists, the possibility of being harassed or jailed for ideological reasons still existed, but it was by no means as strong as it once was: the war was over, the labour revolt had been crushed, and workers' organizations were, generally, on the defensive. But pockets of radicalism persisted. Down, but not out, a group of radicals established the Communist Party of Canada in June 1921. Inspired by the success of the Bolshevik Revolution, and disillusioned by the divisions that weakened the Canadian left during the war years, the new organization hoped that a disciplined leadership cadre would keep it on the path to revolution. Not long after its inaugural meeting, it affiliated with the Communist International, an umbrella organization of Communist parties that was led by the Communist Party of the Soviet Union. That international body set the framework within which national organizations operated, though rank-and-file activists, many of whom were drawn to the party's spirit of defiance, demonstrated a significant capacity for independent activity. During the 1920s, party members could be found in the mainstream labour movement, in the workplace, and in various organizations, such as the Ukrainian Labour Farmer Temple Association, keeping a culture of opposition alive.[2]

The creation of the Communist Party of Canada did not go unnoticed by the RCMP; in fact, it had an undercover operative at the party's inaugural meeting, held in a barn in Guelph, Ontario.[3] Yet, from the highest levels of the force's command structure in Ottawa to its regional and local offices across the country, the belief that the 'Communist menace' had to be watched, harassed, and intimidated when possible was tempered by a sense that in the relative calm of the 1920s the Mounties had things in hand and thus could focus on developing the administrative and legal framework within which they operated. Courtlandt Starnes, the force's assistant commissioner, certainly saw things this way. Writing to the deputy minister of justice on several occasions in 1922 and 1923, he pointed out that the CPC was a small and politically marginal organization that was now operating in a political environment that – with few exceptions – was uninterested in radicalism, a welcome change from the war years and the era of the national labour revolt. What was more, he added, the very creation of the RCMP, coupled with significant amendments to the Criminal Code, the Immigration Act, and other pieces of federal legislation, meant that powers previously permitted only under the War Measures Act were still available, albeit with greater restrictions.[4]

As Starnes's remarks suggest, the force's evolution in the early to mid-1920s was defined by two important and intimately connected trends: the emergence of the Communist Party of Canada as the sole focus of surveillance and intelligence-gathering operations and the simultaneous creation of the institutional mechanisms to carry out this serious work.

Spymasters

The RCMP was a masculine, military, and, for the most part, white institution – characteristics illustrated well by the personal background of the force's most senior officers. The first commissioner of the RCMP, A.B. Perry, stemmed from United Empire Loyalist stock in Napanee, Ontario, graduated from the Royal Military College, and joined the

Royal North-West Mounted Police in 1883 after a brief career in the Royal Engineers. As a Mountie, he served in the North-West Rebellion, in which a Métis uprising under Louis Riel was defeated, and was commissioner of the old western force from 1900 to 1920 before heading up the RCMP until 1923.[5] Perry's successor, Cortlandt Starnes, was born in Montreal and possessed a Loyalist background too. He also saw action in the North-West Rebellion, not as a Mountie but as a member of the Canadian militia's 65th Regiment. He joined the Royal North-West Mounted Police in 1886 and served as assistant commissioner for a time before holding the top job from 1923 to 1931.[6] The third and final leader of the force during the interwar period was General J.H. MacBrien, who hailed from Myrtle, Ontario. After a brief stint as a Mountie at the turn of the century, he left for South Africa where he fought in the Boer War and later served six years in the South African Constabulary before returning to Canada and the military. During the Great War he rose to the rank of brigadier-general and was appointed chief of the general staff in 1920, a position he held for eight years. After a brief retirement, MacBrien became commissioner of the RCMP in 1931. Known for his role in 'modernizing' the force, he was knighted for his service to the empire in 1935 and died, while in office, three years later.[7]

The RCMP's first intelligence officer, C.F. Hamilton, was cut from the same cloth as Perry, Starnes, and MacBrien. Born in Roslin, Ontario, and a graduate of Queen's University, Hamilton worked first as a journalist, covering the South African War for the *Globe* before joining the Royal North-West Mounted Police in 1913. After taking a leave of absence from the Mounties during the Great War, a period in which he served as deputy chief press censor and director of cable censorship, Hamilton returned to police work just as the federal government was creating the RCMP. He was quickly appointed secretary of the force, a title later changed to intelligence and liaison officer, and served in this capacity until his death in 1933, when he was succeeded by Arthur Patteson, his assistant of several years.[8] An English immigrant, Patteson was educated at Marlborough, a prestigious school, before coming to Canada; like his predecessor, he, too, had served in the Royal North-West Mounted Police before moving to Ottawa to take up his new responsibilities.[9] Patteson died unexpectedly in 1935. His immediate successors were also English immigrants, most notably Charles Rivett-Carnac, who was born in Eastbourne, Sussex, in 1901, served briefly in the Great War, and worked in India before coming to Canada in the 1920s and joining the Mounties. He served in the Yukon for over a decade before being appointed intelligence officer in 1935, a title he held until 1939.[10]

Drawn primarily from the ranks of the anglo, central Canadian, military elite, the RCMP's senior officers flourished at a time when military organizations, and the values they embodied, were held in high esteem. That they incorporated this militarism into the force is significant; not only did this ethos reflect the organization's history as a frontier constabulary, but it imbued the RCMP with certain Victorian sensibilities: its members were supposed to be civilized, chivalrous, self-controlled, virtuous, and manly.[11] With the exception of many undercover agents, the men who enlisted in the RCMP were, like the force's leaders, overwhelmingly anglo: they were either born in the old country or had parents or grandparents who were.[12] 'They are soldiers, for the recruit gets a military training and is taught to ride and shoot and, above all, to obey orders,' Starnes observed in 1923. 'People outside as well as inside of Canada feel that it discharges its duties honestly, fearlessly, impatiently: that its men are courteous as well as inflexible, doing their duty without being rude or overbearing ... There is still romance in the Force.'[13] As the commissioner's remarks suggest, barracks life, with its emphasis on hierarchy, discipline, and punishment, was the lot of the young recruit. Success, therefore, necessitated a near religious devotion, a willingness 'to do disagreeable, or difficult, or dangerous things from which [one] naturally would shrink,' a triumph of the will. Not surprisingly, perhaps, the force accepted only single men into its ranks and required those new bachelor recruits to request permission if they wanted to get married.[14]

While the general public was perhaps not familiar with the biographical details of the force's leaders, it was, no doubt, well acquainted with the Mountie mystique. Indeed, almost from the moment that the old North-West Mounted Police made its historic 'March West' in 1873 to secure federal control over the western prairies, hundreds of books and articles, which extolled the force's achievements, circulated in Canadian popular culture. By the 1920s, the Mounties had been featured in many mass-circulation magazines, which were growing in popularity at the time, not to mention dozens of American-produced feature films (twenty-three in 1922 alone). Whatever the format, the message was invariably the same: in the face of great adversity, these 'splendid specimens of manhood,' as one novelist wrote, built a great nation – the true, north, strong, and free.[15] Bound up in this sentiment of English Canadian nationalism were other characteristics that bolstered its widespread appeal. Promoted as the 'most dapper police organization in the world, the most famous, renowned for their gallantry, their valor, their courage, their traditions, and their esprit de corps,' the Mountie mythology provided a link to a pre-industrial past, a mythical golden age that, by the opening decades of the twentieth century, had been eclipsed by modern society. What was more, with its red serge and British military traditions, it encapsulated English Canada's loyalty to the crown – a sentiment that had surged in importance during and immediately after the Great War when both 'enemy aliens' and the 'Bolsheveki menace' were thought to be at the gates of the peaceable kingdom.[16] 'I'll meet a real, real, man – brave, strong, chivalrous, with great, yes, great ideals – a fairy Prince, a knight of the Round Table,' a Mountie's future bride opined in *Spirit of Iron*, published in 1923. 'They say they don't live now – Oh, but they do! Perhaps the armour's gone but they are knights and Princes just the same.'[17]

Princes in popular culture, but practically paupers in Ottawa. The 1920s were anything but 'roaring' for the Mounties. Although the force played a significant role during the war years, it remained, as its leaders never tired of telling the federal cabinet, underfunded and understaffed. Between 1920 and 1926, the RCMP's *Annual Report* noted, the force's size had been reduced from 1,532 members to only 876.[18] Just two years after it was established, the force was nearly folded into a newly created Department of National Defence – a fate headed off by members of the Progressive Party who believed that the police and military must remain separate lest either organization become too powerful. The force's dicey position is illustrated further by the modest growth of its intelligence and security apparatus, which was constructed with such haste during the Great War. It consisted of three sections: under the auspices of the commissioner there was the Criminal Investigation Branch, the Central Registry, and the Intelligence and Liaison Officer (ILO). At the helm of the Criminal Investigation Branch was the director of criminal investigations, who oversaw the many and varied operations of CIB sections in each of the force's divisions and subdivisions across the country. The Central Registry was, as its names implies, an archive of individuals, organizations, and publications thought to be 'subversive'; registry staff, of which there were only a few, created and updated files, handled routine correspondence and reports, and translated material written in languages other than English. The third and final component of security operations at this time, the position of intelligence and liaison officer, was created in 1922. The only person

in the RCMP whose administrative responsibilities were exclusively in
the area of intelligence and security, the ILO represented the RCMP on
various government committees and produced weekly summaries of
subversive activities. Originally entitled 'Notes on the Work of the CIB
Division' but later renamed 'Weekly Summary: Notes regarding Revolutionary Organizations and Agitators in Canada,' the reports were
intended for the prime minister, cabinet, and senior government officials.[19] This basic framework remained virtually the same for the better
part of the interwar period.

Yet despite its meagre resources, and the absence of any long-term
plan for security from the ruling Liberal government under Prime Minister Mackenzie King, the force sought to shore up its position as the
principal Canadian institution in the realm of intelligence and security
by undertaking a series of external and internal initiatives.[20] In the late
nineteenth and early twentieth century, when the Canadian and British governments exchanged intelligence, that intelligence was about
imperial concerns: Ireland and India. With the Bolshevik Revolution,
however, and subsequent creation of the Communist International, or
'Comintern,' these concerns were displaced gradually by a focus on the
global reach of the 'Red Scare' or 'Red Menace.' As early as 1919, the
British government was interested in the nature and extent of the Canadian labour revolt, as well as the counter-revolutionary potential of
the various citizens' committees which were created to roll back the
left-wing tide. Within a year, regular communication between the two
governments on matters of security and intelligence had been established – the material flowing through both the older, more circuitous
route of the governor general and, as time went on, more direct links
between the RCMP and the appropriate British agency.[21] That the Communist International, and affiliated national Communist parties, dominated these intergovernmental discussions is captured by an extensive
exchange between the commissioner of the RCMP, Courtlandt Starnes,
and the head of Scotland Yard's Special Branch, Sir Wyndham Childs,
in 1922. In the wake of Britain's interception of Moscow-bound materials belonging to the Communist Party of Canada, Childs wanted
more information on the potential threat of Canada's Reds. A similar
dialogue took place a year later, only this time the intelligence loop
included not just the RCMP and Scotland Yard but the secretary of state
for the colonies, the governor general, the prime minister, and the undersecretary of state for external affairs. 'This document is the property
of his Majesty's Government and should be destroyed by burning after

perusal by the individuals to whom it is addressed,' a covering memo stamped 'secret' read, its contents 'dealing with a meeting of the Colonial Commission of the Third International held at Moscow.'[22]

The relationship between Canada and the United States in this regard remains somewhat sketchy. Prior to the war years, and the labour unrest it helped produce, the Canadian government had relied on British consular officials, private detective agencies, and its own secret agents, like William C. Hopkinson, to gather information about subversives who operated on both sides of the border. By the fall of 1919, high-level police officials were drawing the federal cabinet's attention to 'matters upon which consultation with the U.S. Secret Service is advisable'; unfortunately, they asserted, 'the formal channel not only takes time, but presents inconvenience.' Shortly thereafter, C.F. Hamilton went to Washington to forge a 'direct connection' with U.S. officials – in particular, the Federal Bureau of Investigation which had grown in size and scope during the war.[23] While the immediate results of this tête-à-tête are unknown, it is apparent that by the mid-to-late 1920s, Canada and the United states were trading lists of deported radicals, rejected immigrants, and suspected Communists, at least for a time. Inventories of fingerprints and photographs were exchanged as well.[24] A more formal relationship between the RCMP and FBI was finally established in 1937.[25]

In addition to these intergovernmental initiatives, senior RCMP officers sought closer ties with departments and agencies within the Canadian government, in particular, the Armed Forces, which were later combined into a singular Department of National Defence. In the fall of 1920, as the federal government continued to demobilize rapidly both the army and the navy, the chief of the general staff, the director of the naval service, and the inspector general of the air force formed the Defence Committee of Canada 'to co-ordinate efforts in pursuit of a common policy, and, especially, to ensure co-operation ... in the event of war or other emergency.' The 'other emergency' that generals Willoughby Gwatkin, Arthur Currie, and J.H. MacBrien had in mind was, not surprisingly, the question of subversive activity, a worry brought into sharp focus by the confrontation at Winnipeg just the year before. For this reason, they agreed, any post-war planning demanded that a '[high] priority ... went to internal security because of the fear of communism and extended labour unrest.' What was more, it was important that the commissioner of the RCMP, A.B. Perry, join them on the Defence Committee of Canada. He did, and over the next few years the committee undertook two significant initiatives: the creation of local defence committees in each of the country's twelve military districts and of a Subcommittee on Intelligence to coordinate information gathering, pool scarce resources, and set priorities in the area of security.[26]

Modelled after the Defence Committee of Canada, local defence committees consisted of representatives of the army, navy, air force, and federal police. The first local organization was created in British Columbia in 1921 after the RCMP in Vancouver reported that 'disturbances,' even an 'attempted revolt,' involving the unemployed and known agitators were possible.[27] While no uprising actually materialized, Commissioner Perry was convinced that the incident was 'symptomatic of [the] deep unrest and uneasiness' still gripping many parts of the country; by the following year, local defence committees, an idea proposed by Perry and endorsed by his colleagues on the Defence Committee of Canada, had been created in many parts of the country, including Calgary, Winnipeg, Toronto, and Halifax. Expected to fulfil a variety of roles, the local committees were to report on: 'the dangers to be anticipated or apprehended from the several disturbing factors, such as unrest, the activities of extremist agitators, etc.'; 'the force available in the district to deal with any dangerous situation which may develop'; and 'the action to be taken if any emergency arises.' Writing to his commanding officers, Commissioner Perry made it clear that local Mounties should keep the local defence committees informed but must not, in the process, 'disclose the source of your information or the means by which it was obtained.'[28]

The debate around, and subsequent creation of, local defence committees heightened the Defence Committee of Canada's sense that the government needed a more centralized intelligence bureau, one that would help 'avoid duplication of work, and ... ensure that intelligence is communicated, quickly and regularly, to Departments interested.'[29] Indeed, the more committee members talked, the more they understood just how extensive and overlapping each other's own, internal security efforts had become. Within the Department of Militia, Lieutenant-Colonel H.H. Matthews informed the group, a director of military operations and intelligence stood atop a network of district intelligence officers, area intelligence officers, and special agents which reached into many parts of the country.[30] For its part, the RCMP looked after eleven separate districts which, according to a memo prepared by C.F. Hamilton, possessed 'sufficient investigation staff.' 'Decentralized' and 'flexible' in nature, and therefore capable of shuffling secret agents from one locale to another, the Mounties' intelligence apparatus was augmented by a central staff which 'collates, controls, and uses the information obtained.'[31]

With these structures in mind, members of the Defence Committee of Canada established the Subcommittee on Intelligence in early 1922. Staffed by representatives of the Armed Forces and the federal police, the new body 'arrange[d] for complete liaison and interchange of information' and, perhaps most important, 'consider[ed] what details of Intelligence are required ... for ... the security of Canada, both internal and external.'[32] The longevity and effectiveness of the Sub-Committee on Intelligence is difficult to assess. What is significant about its creation, though, is that the subcommittee, like other external initiatives pursued by senior RCMP officers, was part and parcel of an undiminished desire to refine and expand the state's ability to access and assess the acts, attitudes, and behaviour of a certain group of citizens: 'revolutionists,' 'subversives,' and 'Communists.'

This notion is illustrated further by the connections forged between the RCMP and the Department of Immigration and Colonization. As the Great War gave way to the national labour revolt, Ottawa amended the Immigration Act. Under the terms of section 41 of the revised statute, 'any person other than a Canadian citizen [who] advocates ... the overthrow by force ... of constituted law and authority' could be deported; intentionally broad, this provision was given added heft by special powers granted to the governor general, who, under section 38, was permitted to ban 'immigrants ... belonging to any nationality or race deemed unsuitable.' Spurred on by the general anxiety of the war years, the government's amendments laid bare one of the defining features of Canadian immigration policy since Confederation: when it came to immigrant workers, the country had always been a 'reluctant host.'[33] This time around, however, the issue was as much about an immigrant's politics as it was about his or her country of origin. Often justified on enumerated grounds such as 'criminality,' 'public charge,' or 'medical causes,' political deportation required both reliable intelligence and logistical support to be effective, and the Mounties provided both.[34] By the early 1920s, the force was carrying out naturalization investigations on a routine basis and several high-level Mounties, including Commissioner Perry, were appointed as immigration officials.[35] 'We desire to continue the co-operation between your officers and our men,' the deputy minister of immigration told the RCMP's assistant commissioner in 1922, reflecting on the progress made at several recent

meetings dedicated to 'arriv[ing] at a clear understanding regarding assistance ... by members of the Royal Canadian Mounted Police.'[36]

Spies

The force undertook internal renovations, both at headquarters in Ottawa and at the local level, during this time as well. Of particular concern to senior Mounties in the early 1920s was the absorption of the old
Dominion Police into the RCMP. While the process appeared simple
enough on paper, it was far more difficult in practice. A.J. Cawdron certainly thought so. As commissioner of the Dominion Police from 1918
to 1920, he had rejected the idea of amalgamation from the beginning;
yet, once the decision had been made to combine the two forces, he
expected to be appointed the new deputy commissioner. Much to his
dissatisfaction, however, he was installed as director of criminal investigations, a significant position, to be sure, but one that he felt was not
commensurate with his previous status. As a result, Cawdron agitated
among former members of the Dominion Police and lobbied senior bureaucrats to have the amalgamation nullified – actions that were successful only in bringing about his demotion.[37] Louder and potentially
more disruptive complaints came from rank-and-file members of the
defunct federal force. 'On taking command of the Division ... I found it
to be in the most deplorable condition of any organization of its kind
with which I have ever come into touch,' D.M. Ormand, the commanding officer of the RCMP's Ottawa-based 'A' Division, reported in the
summer of 1920. His complaints were aimed at the ex-DP officers who
comprised the vast majority of his staff. 'The men of this division are entirely lacking in esprit-de-corps in its proper sense. At least 90% of them
consider themselves nothing more than watchmen.'[38] Conflict between
commanding officers and recruits was nothing new to the Mounties,
but, as Ormand's report makes clear, this was a clash of occupational
cultures. Over the summer, the men of 'A' Division protested against
low wages, harsh military discipline, and the denial of 'the former
privilege of voicing their grievances as a body' – a pattern of complaint
that climaxed in late August when twenty-eight officers refused to turn
up on Parliament Hill for their morning drill. Angered by this flagrant
show of 'disloyalty,' and sensing that 'some person, either within the
force or outside it, is endeavouring to form a union in this division,'
Ormand fined the dissenters and threatened them with dismissal – a
response that, it appears, stanched the nascent union drive.[39]

While the integration of the Dominion Police into the institutions and culture of the RCMP was problematic, and the calibre of former DP constables thought to be inferior, the merger of the two forces brought with it many benefits, not the least of which was the Dominion Police's expertise in the new science of fingerprinting. Developed in India in the mid- to late nineteenth century, and later adopted by the London Metropolitan Police to track Indian radicals in England, this new method of identification and investigation was introduced to Canada in 1905 by Edward Foster, a Dominion Police constable who learned of the procedure while working for the Canadian government at the World's Fair in St Louis the year before. Less than ten years after Foster first introduced the idea to his superiors, a national police organization dedicated, in part, to promoting the use of fingerprints as a forensic tool was established; so, too, was the Canadian Criminal Identification Bureau, a permanent registry of fingerprints. It was placed under the auspices of the Dominion Police. With the creation of the RCMP, and the dismantling of the old federal force, both Foster, who by then was an inspector, and the fingerprint registry were absorbed into the Mounties' new Criminal Investigation Branch. Over the following decade, the use of fingerprints in routine police work, and in the area of intelligence and security, grew slowly, but steadily, as the police, government, and society grappled with two significant questions: Who should be fingerprinted and why?[40] 'I was glad to be able to accede to the suggestion that Inspector Foster should read a paper here, and commend his proposals to your attention,' Commissioner Starnes told a police conference in 1923. 'In the systematizing, and the universal use of and co-operation with central Finger-Print offices undoubtedly lies one of the roads to progress.'[41]

The other road, of course, originated in the numerous districts, sub-districts, and detachments that the RCMP was busy assembling across the country. In Ontario, for example, 'O' Division was set up in early 1920; with its regional headquarters in Toronto, the division's jurisdiction stretched from Quebec's Eastern Townships in the east to Windsor in the west to Sault Ste-Marie in the north. Farther west, Alberta's 'G' Division was based in Edmonton and covered the northern part of the province. New divisions needed many things, and throughout the 1920s the force set about renting buildings, buying furniture, hiring support staff, and recalling old RNWMP badges.[42] What was more, it established the bureaucratic framework and administrative procedures within which the divisions would operate. Of particular importance were reliable lines of communication between the national headquarters and local operations, especially when it came to intelligence and security. 'The term *SECRET* is to be used for reports of correspondence on such matters as Unrest, etc., and such subjects where secrecy is most essential,' the commissioner informed all his commanding officers in 1922. 'All "secret" communications must be double-enveloped, the inside one and its contents being marked secret, the outside envelope bearing the address only.'[43] This move towards the standardization of communication was as evident inside the (double) envelope as it was outside; as time went on, intelligence reports generated by the districts were typed, properly dated and annotated, and featured a series of stock phrases such as 'I have the honour to report,' all of it, like the 'external' initiatives discussed above, geared towards efficient analysis, indexing, cross-referencing, and storage of incoming intelligence – or, put simply, to improving the production and circulation of knowledge about suspected 'subversives.'[44]

Each division was staffed by a superintendent, who was responsible for administration and communication with headquarters in Ottawa, and a local head of the Criminal Investigation Branch, who looked after, among other things, the division's detectives.[45] In the field, detectives who were attached to the CIB performed a wide range of duties, from trailing prostitutes and smugglers to ferreting out counterfeiters and political radicals.[46] As this brief job description suggests, however, while surveillance and intelligence gathering was important, it was by no means the sole focus of the force's day-to-day operations. Indeed, the majority of new recruits were members of cavalry units, not the Criminal Investigation Branch, and were stationed across the country to 'control such civil disturbances as might occur.' The career of C.W. 'Cliff' Harvison, a Mountie during the early 1920s, illustrates this point well. After completing his basic training, he was stationed in Ottawa, where, in his words, 'the emphasis remained on the handling of riots and unlawful assemblies.' Before leaving the force in 1923, Harvison spent time supervising seasonal workers en route from Atlantic Canada to the west, guarding deportees in Quebec City, and, for a time, working for the Criminal Investigation Branch in Montreal. In that city he was only one of twelve members of the CIB, and he was sent undercover with no prior training in this area of police work.[47] With or without training, the Mounties' 'human sources' were critical to intelligence gathering and thus establishing the force's role as the principal agency responsible for security matters. Some, like Harvison, went underground for a limited time only, before returning to regular police work, while others, few of whom were detectives, spent the better part of their careers submerged among the country's undesirables.

These were the secret agents. John Leopold was one of them. Born in 1890 in Bohemia, Leopold came to Canada in 1912 and worked as a farmer in Alberta until 1918 when he enlisted in the RCMP. He was hired largely on the basis of his ethnicity and language skills; on his application form he professed to be fluent in German and Czech and able to use Polish and Croatian 'imperfectly.' Such abilities, coupled with what RCMP staff doctors judged 'good intelligence' and a 'sanguine temperament,' made him ideal for work among foreign-born agitators.[48] By the early 1920s, after a short period underground, it was clear to his RCMP handler, Gilbert Salt, that the new Bohemian-born spy was very effective. 'He has shown himself capable of neutralizing the efforts of the leaders of the OBU [One Big Union] on many occasions,' Salt wrote to A.B. Allard, the commanding officer in Regina. 'He has discouraged organization work by many tricks.'[49] Allard was certainly impressed with Leopold's record and recommended to Commissioner Perry that he permit Leopold to 'pursue his role to the full extent.' The commissioner agreed. 'The opportunity offered of gaining access to Communist plans must not be allowed to escape us,' he replied. Thus, Leopold 'should throw himself into the movement and his aim should be to obtain an appointment as organizer.'[50] He did, and in doing so, this secret agent and other men like him acted as the force's eyes and ears on the ground, thereby extending the state's gaze into some of the most intimate dimensions of people's lives.[51] The war might have been over, and the labour revolt an ugly memory, but the question of subversion had certainly not gone away.

Corrupting the Working Classes

Throughout the 1920s, hundreds of publications, and thousands of individuals and organizations, were the target of RCMP surveillance, despite the force's slim resources and falling numbers. Between 1919 and 1929, the force opened at least 6,767 subject files on radicalism and 4,806 files on suspected agitators – over 50 per cent of which were created between 1919 and 1924.[52] Consisting of tens of thousands of pages, these registries catalogued potential trouble in nearly every region of the country. 'B.C. Loggers Camp Workers Union (61 Cordova St. Vancouver)' and 'Crows Nest Pass. Suspected Trouble In' read the headings on two files. 'Ft. William General Meeting of Russians and Ukrainians,' 'Jewish Socialist Party, Montreal,' 'Cape Breton, NS, Labour Conditions,' stated the tabs on three others.[53] Conspicuously absent from this database, however, are the activities of far-right organizations such as the Ku Klux Klan (KKK) of Kanada. An offshoot of the violent, secretive society of cross-burning men that was founded in the southern United States after the Civil War, it was particularly active in Ontario, Saskatchewan, and Alberta during the 1920s and possessed a membership much larger than the Communist Party of Canada.[54] In Saskatchewan, for example, where the Klan was strongest, commanding the allegiance of approximately 10,000 to 15,000 people by 1929, the RCMP's coverage was limited. While sporadic references to it appear in the force's register of subject files on radicalism, the information gathered by Mounties in the field was virtually non-existent.[55] Indeed, when the premier of that prairie province sought additional information about 'a Ku Klux Klan' whose 'main object [was] to play upon the prejudices of the people,' he turned to a private detective, not the federal force.[56]

The Mounties' lax approach to the KKK was not the product of sloppy police work; rather, it reflected lessons learned during the war years and after: it was, after all, the political left, not the political right, that toppled the Russian czar and, closer to home, mounted the first nationwide challenge to capitalist rule. Viewed against the backdrop of '1919,' and the general backlash against immigration that followed, it is not hard to understand how the Klan's message of 'higher moral standards,' 'restrictive and selective immigration,' and 'pure patriotism' – in short, 'Canadians for Canada, Canada for Canadians' – would resonate with members of the force, as it did with politicians and the public at large. Communism, not nativism and white supremacy, was the real enemy, and for both the RCMP and the KKK it was the country's British heritage that was at stake. 'The assimilation of our large alien population is of the greatest importance and it demands wise and sympathetic action and constant attention,' the RCMP commissioner stated in 1919. 'We are a great melting pot, but let us see that the slag and scum that refuse to assimilate and become 100 percent Canadian citizens is skimmed off and thrown away,' echoed one of the Klan's most successful Canadian organizers in 1928.[57]

Without the distraction of policing the far right, the RCMP focused its attention on labour and left-wing groups in general, the Communist Party of Canada in particular. Drawn from a variety of labour, left-wing, and ethnic groups, the CPC's membership was small, peaking at about

4,500 to 4,800 members between 1923 and 1925.[58] Of that group, a smaller number of activists could be found, in the words of one party document, carrying out 'mass propaganda, maintaining and broadening the party contact with the masses, preparing and training the reserves of the working class and educating party cadres.'[59] To accomplish these objectives, they joined existing unions and labour councils, created a wide range of affiliated groups such as the Young Communist League, the Canadian Labour Defense League, and the Trade Union Education League, launched newspapers like *The Worker*, and sponsored countless demonstrations, public lectures, study groups, and book sales.[60] Of particular importance to the party's vitality in these early years was the vibrant associational milieu created and sustained by its Jewish, Ukrainian, and Finnish members; the Finnish Organization of Canada, for example, was an important hub for 'Red' Finns in northern Ontario, supporting local co-ops, providing material and emotional support for unionists, and publishing its own newspaper.[61]

Pilloried by their counterparts in the mainstream labour movement as 'clowns,' 'zealots,' and 'sewer-pipe revolutionists,' and largely ignored by unorganized workers who had little interest in radical politics, party activists nevertheless made inroads among garment workers in Quebec, miners in Alberta and Nova Scotia, and loggers in British Columbia. 'I worked in that [logging] camp there and that's where I first came in contact with organization,' a lumber worker who laboured on the Pacific coast in the 1920s recalled. An 'old fellow ... used to talk to me quite a lot, give me stuff to read and all that ... He was a Marxist. He was no anarchist about him. No. And, you see, we organized the boys in the camp.'[62] From the Mounties' perspective, it was precisely this sort of combination – a Marxist, an ordinary worker, and 'stuff to read' – that produced trouble. Not surprisingly, the force added 610 files to its registry of 'Prohibited or Objectionable Literature' between 1919 and 1929. This archive included details of individuals who possessed banned or suspicious publications, including where they obtained their reading material, as well as an examination of individual books, magazines, newspapers, and pamphlets. Just over 30 per cent of the files were started under the auspices of the War Measures Act between 1919 and 1920; from that year onward, the percentage of new files opened each year dwindled before increasing again in 1929 with the onset of the Depression.[63] The publications that filled these dossiers were identified by the combined, though rarely coordinated, efforts of detectives, secret agents, post office and customs officials, and employer and community organizations.[64] 'I have the honour to enclose herewith the following books, taken from a shipment which arrived at the Customs Port of Hamilton, Ontario, consigned to G. Knowles, of Hamilton,' the Mounties' assistant commissioner, Cortlandt Starnes, informed the deputy minister of justice in 1921. 'This party, I may say, is well known to this Department as a radical agitator. I have marked certain of the revolutionary passages which occur in these books and I should appreciate it very much if you would kindly advise me if in your opinion they contravene the Criminal Code in any way.'[65] Laconic in tone and almost pro forma in content, the assistant commissioner's inquiry underscores just how acceptable the repression of 'objectionable' material had become. This was, after all, a routine letter about what, by that time, was considered routine police business; what was once permissible under the War Measures Act was now permitted, with some restrictions, under an amended Criminal Code.

The writers and readers of the left-wing *Ukrainian Voice* understood this reality well. Brought to the attention of the prime minister by the Imperial Order Daughters of the Empire, a conservative women's organization dedicated to 'one flag, one throne, and one empire,' the newspaper was passed on to the RCMP for its 'full and careful consideration' in the spring of 1921.[66] In a short, two-paragraph letter marked 'secret & confidential,' Commissioner Perry reminded the deputy minister of justice of a similar matter that his department and the Mounties' Criminal Investigation Branch had dealt with just months before. In that particular case, a man from Windsor, Ontario, was charged with importing seditious literature 'in the Ukrainian language,' a violation of section 98 of the Criminal Code which banned any material that advocated 'the use of force, violence, terrorism, or physical injury ... as the means of accomplishing any governmental, industrial, or economic change.' Lawyers for the accused were, in their words, 'particularly puzzled': they knew well that the newspapers in question were once banned under wartime orders-in-council, but they were under the impression that, with the end of the war, 'Ottawa no longer ... prohibited publications or [kept] or furnishe[d] a list thereof.' But it did, and newspapers like this one were on it. Thus, Perry concluded, given that *Ukrainian Voice* called for 'the extermination of social classes, the equality of all nations,' it was illegal. What was more, he concluded, the 'Mounted Police should not intervene,' for the enforcement of the Criminal Code, now the sole authority in this instance, was a provincial matter.[67]

Arvo Vaara was familiar with the price left-wing journalists paid for expressing their ideas. A Finnish immigrant who came to Canada in 1909, settled in Sudbury, and joined the Finnish Organization of Canada, Vaara was convicted of seditious libel in 1928 for publishing editorials in *Vapaus*, a left-wing newspaper, that attacked the monarchy.[68] 'Will the King die, [it] is all the same to us,' he wrote. 'The social order will be equally oppressive to the poor, whoever is King. Capital is the one who really rules.'[69] Vaara's opinions were brought to the attention of the local authorities by a prominent missionary, the Reverend Thomas Jones, who believed that this 'Red' Finn and others like him were not just besmirching the crown but, in the process, impeding his godly work among the region's immigrants. The Mounties certainly were not surprised by Vaara's perspective; not only was he the subject of a personal-history file, but *Vapaus* was banned under the War Measures Act, remaining on the force's list of subversive publications into the post-war period.[70] At trial, Vaara was defended by labour lawyer A.W. Roebuck, who later became attorney general and minister of labour in Ontario in 1934 and member of Parliament in 1940. During the trial, Roebuck maintained that the contentious articles might have been 'objectionable, impolite, and inadvisable,' but, given that they did not advocate violence, they were not seditious. The jury, however, believed otherwise, bringing in a guilty verdict after three hours of deliberation. Vaara was fined $1,000 and jailed for six months; his appeal was unsuccessful. 'Avro Vaara is a spokesperson for the down-trodden and the exploited, particularly among the miners of Northern Ontario,' one working-class journalist wrote after the court's decision was handed down. 'When he maintains that the death of King George would not affect the lot of the worker, he is expressing an obvious fact. When he says that Capitalism is the real ruler, he is expressing an opinion which is very commonly held.'[71]

While *Vapaus* and *Ukrainian Voice* were but two of hundreds of publications that came under the state's disciplinary gaze during the 1920s, their predicament illustrates two important trends. The first: when it came to 'prohibited literature,' the RCMP was, for the most part, content to advise and assist other law-enforcement agencies, rather than spearhead its own campaign. This approach reflected many things, including the Mounties' desire not to expose their secret agents, the division of power between federal and provincial governments, and, perhaps most important, Ottawa's post-war policy of leaving 'prosecutions [for subversion] to the local authorities charged with the administration of justice in the Province[s].'[72] For the ruling Liberals, whose hold on power was dependent on the support of the Progressive Party, which championed civil liberties, it was a decision that was as principled as it was political. The second trend: the Mounties' possessed an unwavering interest in the link between ethnicity and left-wing politics. Both *Vapaus* and *Ukrainian Voice* were radical foreign-language publications, and from the RCMP's perspective they were part and parcel of a wider, potentially devastating threat that involved the Communist Party and its affiliated immigrant organizations. Indeed, as the deputy minister of justice, W. Stuart Edwards, remarked in 1922 during an exchange with his minister and the top Mountie, it was one thing for radicals to propagandize, quite another for them to actually organize. 'It seems to me that to allow a lot of irresponsible cranks to make fiery speeches, as is done in the parks of most large cities, is one thing,' he opined, 'but to permit an organized society ... to carry on a private and insidious campaign for the corruption of the working classes of this country with a view to their ultimately bringing about a revolution by the use of force, is quite another.'[73]

From the converted to the merely curious, no Communist, or suspected Communist, was too small, too inconsequential to be left alone by the RCMP. The leadership of the Communist Party of Canada understood this notion well, and thus advised its members and supporters to be careful: 'We all know that thousands of spies are on the job every day in every city bent upon ferreting out our members, our meetings, and work-places. Consequently, beware of being followed when going to an appointment or meeting-place, particularly if you are under suspicion through having been questioned, or arrested.'[74]

During his life on the left, Sam Scarlett was followed, questioned, and arrested – multiple times! Born in Scotland in 1883, Scarlett came to Canada in 1903 and immigrated to the United States a year later. A machinist by trade, he was a member of the International Association of Machinists, an affiliate of the mainstream American Federation of Labor, until 1911; that year, while in California, he joined the militant Industrial Workers of the World and spent the next seven years as an organizer, primarily in the American west. During the Great War, Scarlett, like more than two hundred other prominent Wobblies in the United States, was convicted of various acts of espionage and subversion, and sentenced to twenty-five years' imprisonment at Leavenworth Penitentiary in Kansas.[75] His sentence was commuted in January 1923, and he was sent back to Scotland; eight months later, he returned to

Canada seeking work as a farm hand. By March 1924, Scarlett was active again with the IWW, prompting the Mounties to place him under surveillance, open a personal-history file ('Clean shaven'; 'Long and large nose'; 'Smokes pipe'), and seek the assistance of immigration officials to 'ascertai[n] if he is or is not deportable.'[76]

On 8 September 1924, just moments after completing a speech on 'Industrial Communism,' Scarlett was arrested under provisions of the Immigration Act, which defined who was and who was not a desirable immigrant. From the perspective of the Department of Justice, not only did the accused support the use of violence to affect political change, an offence under sections 40 and 41, but he was 'a person who was found guilty of conspiring during the war against one of His Majesty's allies' and 'who was deported from an allied country on account of conspiring against such country in connection with the war' – which were violations of section 3. On 9 September, a Board of Inquiry in Vancouver found Scarlett guilty as charged and order him deported. The veteran Wobbly was outraged; so, too, was the labour movement, which organized several mass demonstrations to protest the inquiry's use of 'autocratic powers' to trump 'British justice.' Even one mainstream Vancouver daily not known for its sympathy for the labour movement was critical, noting that the trial was held in secret, that Scarlett had no time to prepare a proper defence, and that, most alarmingly, the inquiry's verdict had been typed in advance of the hearing: in short, it argued, even a radical deserved due process! With public interest in the case rising, Ottawa quashed the deportation order and Scarlett was permitted to stay in the country. The RCMP, however, remained vigilant; not only did the force watch this 'cunning agitator,' sometimes on a daily basis, as he criss-crossed the country, but on occasion it passed its intelligence on to employers who were the targets of his considerable organizational skill.[77] Scarlett would later join the Communist Party.

Jeanne Corbin was young activist in Edmonton. A French emigrant who moved to northern Alberta with her family, Corbin joined the Young Communist League, the party's youth organization, at the age of eighteen – shortly after moving to Edmonton from her home community of Lindbrook to continue her education. By 1925, she had piqued the interest of the RCMP's 'G' Division and a personal-history file bearing her name was opened in Ottawa. Corbin was suspected of trying to recruit her high school classmates to join the cause and, in her spare time, teaching radical ideas to children at a local Ukrainian labour hall.

Described by detectives as 'slovenly' and 'forward,' yet highly prized by the Communist Party for her quick mind and facility with language, she spoke at public meetings, sold newspaper subscriptions, and raised funds for the CPC; in 1927 she assisted party stalwart Beckie Buhay in running the organization's Sylvan Lake Camp, a nature retreat and school for children of unionists and party members.[78] A committed radical at a relatively young age, Corbin also wanted to be schoolteacher, a career option that the RCMP, which was concerned with the effect of 'foreign ideologies' on receptive young minds, did its best to close off. 'Has any hint been given to the Educational authorities that she is a dangerous person to be trusted with the teaching of Canadian children?' the commissioner asked his commanding officer in the provincial capital in the fall of 1926, to which the local head responded: '[The province] was very emphatic in assuring me that this person would not be permitted to teach in any school.' After attending normal school – the 1920s equivalent of teachers' college – and working for a short period, she was fired from her position in 1928. Undaunted, Corbin went on to become an influential member of the Communist Party, first in Alberta, then in Ontario and Quebec, in the late 1920s and 1930s.[79] Protecting the young and impressionable minds of students from radical ideas – especially on university campuses – would later emerge as a significant issue for the RCMP in the 1960s.[80]

That the lives of Vaara, Scarlett, and Corbin were temporarily disrupted by the force no doubt delighted the commissioner of the RCMP. But, as he knew well, it was critical that these short-term campaigns against specific individuals or publications be matched by a more patient, furtive, and long-term agenda of infiltration against the Communist Party itself. In Ontario, the superintendent of 'O' Division, Arthur W. Duffus, and the staff sergeant at Toronto's Regional Headquarters, Herbert Darling, had replaced private detective firms with secret agents. By the mid-1920s, there were at least three undercover operatives on staff, though only one 'O' Division agent could be found in the Communist Party and/or its affiliated organizations at a given time, and it was usually for a short period.[81] The information generated by secret agents 9322 (Constable Harry Catt), 9359 (Constable J.T. Goudie), and 643 (unidentified) was consolidated and assessed by Superintendent Duffus. He, in turn, sent a summary of radical activity on to Ottawa.[82] Similar attempts – some successful, many not – to run undercover operatives against the party in the 1920s were undertaken in Quebec, Saskatchewan, Alberta, and British Columbia.[83]

Significantly, the Mounties' undercover operations were complemented by law-enforcement agencies at the local level which, having received the force's intelligence either directly or through an intermediary such as a provincial attorney general, conducted their own anti-Red crusades. Under the direction of Chief Constable Denis Colbarn Draper, an ex-military officer, staunch conservative, and virulent anti-Communist who was named Toronto's 'top cop' in 1928, the police in that city clubbed, beat, and arrested demonstrators, broke into meeting rooms and private homes to confiscate party records, closed down newspapers, and shadowed party leaders. 'If a man persists in wrong doing he must be stopped,' Draper observed after one particularly bloody confrontation. 'We must not allow these foreigners to rule.'[84] The circles of repression in Toronto widened further when both the federal and city police – dubbed the 'Canadian Cossacks' and 'Draper's Dragoons' by some witty radicals – shared intelligence with the Roman Catholic Archdiocese of Toronto, which had, by the early 1930s, established its own, somewhat more subtle, ways of keeping Communism at bay.[85] On the west coast, where the left was particularly vibrant, the anti-Communist activities of the RCMP's 'E' Division were bolstered by the British Columbia Provincial Police and the Vancouver Police Department, which possessed its own specialized Communist Affairs Branch.[86] Operating out of municipal police forces in some of Canada's largest urban centres, anti-Red squads bolstered the RCMP's anti-Communist efforts significantly, and thus deserve additional research.

Of all the operatives working for the RCMP at this time, none was more important than the diminutive secret agent John Leopold, who was based in Saskatchewan and went by the name of Jack Esselwein. In December 1921 he became the district secretary of the Workers Party of Canada, a forerunner to the CPC, and at the same time functioned as an important local figure in the secret underground Communist organization known in Red circles as the 'Z' party. There he gained the confidence of party members and participated in key debates about the establishment of 'open legal parties' and affiliation with the Third International.[87] He became secretary of the Regina local of the International Brotherhood of Painters (and a year later its vice-president), and in 1925 he was elected president of the Regina Trades and Labour Council. The next year, Commissioner Starnes requested that Leopold move to Winnipeg because things in Regina appeared to be quieting down. By 1926, after a mild reprimand from his supervisors for being 'disposed to work alone and without sufficient consultation with his superiors,'

Esselwein was again on the move, this time to Toronto.[88] There he worked closely with the CPC leadership, including Tim Buck, 'Moscow' Jack MacDonald, and Tom Ewen, often taking trips to Montreal, Sudbury, Fort William, and other places for organizational work.[89] He also wrote for *The Worker*, participated in local demonstrations, including one for the release of suspected anarchists Nicola Sacco and Bartolomeo Vanzetti, and worked on a successful Communist aldermanic campaign in Winnipeg.[90]

To many, Esselwein was both a comrade and a friend. Writing in his autobiography, *The Forge Glows Red*, Ewen, who coordinated the party's trade-union work, recalled a time in the 1920s when he travelled from Saskatoon to Regina just to help 'straighten out' Esselwein; according to the local party branch, he had been on 'one long glorious [drinking] binge' and needed help.[91] Party Secretary MacDonald had similar memories of companionship. 'Esselwein lived a simple life. He had his home near the Allan Gardens [in Toronto],' he observed. 'He got around quietly. Occasionally he did a little house painting. In fact, he painted my own kitchen ... [It] was voluntary, a labor of love for a comrade.'[92] Even 'renegade' labour lawyer J.L. Cohen, who thought Esselwein to be 'drab and dull,' was taken in by the undercover agent's act – defending him against a vagrancy charge in 1925.[93] But it was during this period of seemingly effortless movement among the labour movement and the CPC that some party members became suspicious of their comrade for the first time. In November 1927 MacDonald informed Esselwein that the Communist Party had received information from two ex-Mounties that identified him as a government operative. The secret agent vehemently denied the charges, and the controversy passed. Or so Esselwein thought. Within a year, his cover was blown by a mysterious man named 'Otto' and his career as a radical was over.[94]

According to Leopold, Otto was an 'old time resident" and friend from Regina who often worked on his car and did other odd jobs. After selling his property in Regina and moving to Austria (his country of birth) with his family, Otto returned to Canada in 1928 in hopes of securing a patent for a new invention – 'a process for the manufacture of chocolate wafers.' With little money and in need of finding a place to sleep while in Toronto, he looked up Esselwein who gladly agreed to put him up. Not long after, the undercover agent went to Winnipeg on party business, and Otto, having convinced his friend that he could be trusted to stay on in Toronto by himself for an additional two days, 'rifled [his] trunk and betrayed [him] to Jack MacDonald.'[95] The evidence of 'comrade' Esselwein's true identity was turned over to the CPC's Central Executive Committee on, or about, 13 May 1928; he was formally kicked out of the party on 17 May.[96] For his part, Leopold had an inkling that something had happened while he was away. Writing to his commanding officer just days after being expelled, he reported that the 'first intimation ... that there was something unusual in the air' was on 16 May when, at a lecture, Buck and MacDonald 'refused' to speak with him. This, according to Leopold, stood in stark contrast to the treatment he had received just the week before when he spent a relaxing weekend at MacDonald's home with Buck and his wife in a 'very friendly' atmosphere.[97] 'Prior to ... May 16th, there was nothing noticeable as far as the behaviour of the leading members of the party were concerned which would have indicated that all was not well,' he concluded.[98] With his identity revealed – his picture appeared in *The Worker* under the caption 'Stool Exposed!' – and his personal safety at risk if he stayed in Toronto, Leopold was reassigned to the Yukon in June 1928.[99] It was about as far away from his erstwhile comrades as he could possibly get. His exile, though, was short-lived. With the onset of the Great Depression, Leopold was recalled to Ottawa.

The Great Depression

By the early 1930s, Canada had slipped into the economic abyss. For hundreds of thousands of Canadians, the upshot was staggering: between 1928 and 1933, per-capita incomes shrunk considerably – by 36 per cent in Nova Scotia; 72 per cent in Saskatchewan – while the unemployment rate continued to climb, reaching 32 per cent in 1933, the year the Depression bottomed out.[100] For the unemployed, the crisis was compounded further by the rudimentary character of government relief. Bound by a laissez-faire ideology that viewed joblessness as a personal or moral failing, most politicians believed that eligibility requirements for state assistance should be tough, and levels of support painfully small, lest anyone lose their work ethic. The same philosophy underwrote the creation of relief camps. Run by provincial, then federal authorities, the relief camps provided unemployed men with food, shelter, and a meagre stipend; in return, the 'inmates' cut trees, dug ditches, and built roads. 'It was all justified on the grounds that the exercise would be good for us, that working would improve our morale, and that, by providing us with a token opportunity to work for our relief, we would be freed from the stigma of accepting charity,'

James Gray recalled in his poignant memoir, *The Winter Years.* 'None of these dubious propositions had much validity.'[101]

As unemployed rates rose and governments proved unable to cope, the Communist Party emerged as a weighty political actor. The earliest inklings of this phenomenon were evident in Atlantic Canada, where the Great Depression did not await the stock market crash of 1929 but was present much earlier, a brutal denouement to the Great War and the national labour revolt. In industrial Cape Breton, coal miners under the leadership of James Bryson McLachlan, 'an agitator of the worse type,' waged at least fifty-eight individual strikes between 1920 and 1925, turning the county into an armed camp, while in Halifax, Joseph S. Wallace, a journalist closely tied to the left wing of the labour movement, was organizing the Halifax Unemployed Council by 1921; 'work and living wages' – the battle cry of the unemployed in 1930s – was already being sung. Subjected to RCMP surveillance and harassment from the beginning of their political careers, both McLachlan and Wallace eventually joined the Communist Party – and remained under the Mounties' watchful eye.[102] As the economic situation in Canada worsened, working-class agitation, like that in Nova Scotia, spread. And as it did, the question of internal security once again dominated political debate. 'From almost a question mark in 1923 when I first joined ... its stature greatly increased in Canadian affairs,' one high-level Mountie recalled years later.[103] Surveillance, intelligence gathering, and repression, activities that had persisted in muted form into the relative calm of the early to mid-1920s, grew in size, scope, and sophistication as an undertow of anxiety pulled the country under.

5

'Redder Than Ever': Political Policing during the Great Depression

On the evening of 11 August 1931, the RCMP, Ontario Provincial Police (OPP), and Toronto Police Department raided the offices of the Communist Party and the homes of several of its leaders, including Tim Buck, Tom Ewen, and John Boychuk; at the same time, the OPP descended on the home of A.T. Hill, secretary of the Finnish Organization of Canada, in Timmins. In addition to seizing correspondence, publications, and membership lists, the officers arrested Buck and Boychuk on the spot, charging them with being members of an 'unlawful association' under section 98 of the Criminal Code and possessing the intention to carry out an unlawful act – sedition – under section 134. Additional arrests of party members, some in Ontario, others in British Columbia, took place days later, bringing the total number of collars to nine.[1]

At the time of the crackdown, party members were engaged in a 'struggle for the streets' which took aim at miserly relief rates for the unemployed and the politicians who established and enforced them. In Vancouver, the 'Mecca' for the unemployed, the Communist-led National Unemployed Workers' Association orchestrated approximately one hundred demonstrations for 'work and wages' in 1930 alone. 'Arm yourselves with sticks and clubs, give blow for blow. Fight like hell, fight harder than you ever fought in Flanders,' Allan Campbell, a prominent local activist, roared at a street meeting in December 1930. 'We all know that there is plenty of food in Vancouver. If we cannot get it, we will take it.'[2] Similar campaigns among the unemployed were carried out in other cities, including Calgary, Winnipeg, Toronto, Montreal, and Halifax.

Municipal leaders, whose jurisdictions shouldered much of the cost of direct relief, were frantic: when they were not passing by-laws that banned political meetings in languages other than English, they were pressing Ottawa for the legal tools necessary to rid their streets of 'undesirables.'[3] The federal government agreed to help, and section 98, which had been introduced in 1919 but remained dormant during the 1920s, was revived. 'It is a good red-blooded article,' F.R. Scott, a law professor at McGill University, opined, 'with 115 lines of definitions, offences, and penalties, all so obscurely worded that no one can be sure just how much liberty of speech and association survives – except that it is pretty small.'[4] Small was certainly the word in Montreal, where months before the high-profile arrests of party leaders, seven other CPCers, most members of the Young Communist League, were picked up on sedition charges by city police. Some were awaiting trial, others a chance to appeal their guilty verdicts, when the Toronto raids took place.[5] 'The very serious situation which confronts us should be regarded as a challenge to human ingenuity and moral courage – not a reason for counsels of defeatism,' veteran left-wing journalist Colin McKay observed in the *Canadian Railway Employees' Monthly* after surveying the economic and political landscape as whole. 'Progress will be served, but unless men in high places in politics and business show a better quality of leadership than they have in the past three years, the mounting volume of human misery, of thwarted hopes and ambitions, may result in a social explosion.' Indeed it might, as the newfound militancy of the unemployed and the rising popularity of the Canadian left made especially clear.[6]

The social and economic dislocation of the 1930s produced a significant realignment in Canadian politics. Not only did the Conservative Party defeat the ruling Liberals in the 1930 federal election, but entirely new political parties – the Co-operative Commonwealth Federation (CCF), Social Credit, and the Union Nationale – emerged at the provincial level, providing Depression-weary Canadians with alternatives to the political status quo. A more radical challenge came from the Communist Party of Canada. While the party began the 1930s staking out unpopular positions on the extreme left, and finished the decade as champions of social democracy, along the way it spearheaded the struggle among the unemployed for 'work and living wages' – periodically reaching out to more mainstream political allies. Advanced by a variety of Red-led organizations such as the National Unemployed Workers' Association, this activism among the jobless was matched by an equally aggressive campaign for bona fide industrial unions among loggers and longshoremen in British Columbia, coal miners in

Saskatchewan and Nova Scotia, auto workers and furniture makers in Ontario, and garment workers in Quebec. By the mid-1930s, this tactical combination had raised the visibility, stature, and impact of the party enormously: while only a few thousand actually carried a hammer-and-sickle-embossed membership card, hundreds of thousands of others attended CPC-sponsored events and signed the party's petitions calling for radical political reform. Not everyone was thrilled with the CPC's newfound attractiveness. 'What happens to a man's mind in times of depression is just as important as what happens to his body,' the *Montreal Gazette* observed at the time. 'Therefore it is incumbent upon the authorities to safeguard the individual mind from corruption when it is threatened by the spread of the revolutionary doctrine it is known the Communists are preaching.'[7] Authorities in Ottawa agreed.

Beginning in 1929, the Mounties revived their surveillance and intelligence-gathering operations, which had persisted in reduced form into the early to mid-1920s. Other government bodies, like the federal Department of Immigration, became more active too – aiding local, provincial, and federal authorities in 'shovelling out the mutinous'; when employers, citizens' organizations, and mainstream unions joined the anti-Communist fray, the circles of repression widened even further. Fear of the 'Red Menace' breathed new life into old laws, notably section 98 of the Criminal Code and sections 40 and 41 of the Immigration Act, which together defined who was an 'undesirable' Canadian. Initially aimed at those who advocated the use of violence to achieve political ends, the category of 'undesirable' became more elastic as the 1930s progressed – eventually including a person's employment status, country of origin, personal habits, and nearly any form of politics that appeared hostile to the status quo as grounds for expulsion.[8] To Canadians old enough to remember the war years and after, the upheaval associated with the Great Depression perhaps seemed depressingly familiar: economic uncertainty, political turmoil, and widespread unrest among working people. Certainly, the federal government and the RCMP felt this way: from their perspective, 1929 *was* starting to look a lot like 1919. Yet this time around, the Mounties possessed significantly greater resources than their predecessors had a decade or more before: a solid institutional home, substantial bureaucracy, permissive laws, and exclusive control over political policing. Its repressive capabilities were thus formidable – a fact that many Canadians, Communist or not, would come to appreciate as the Great Depression wore on, sometimes with tragic results.

The Communist Eight

Designed to 'strike at the heart of the Communist Party,' the trial of
Tim Buck, Tom Ewen, and the others opened in Toronto on 2 November 1931. The crown's case proceeded on three legal fronts: first, that
the accused were members of the Communist Party; second, that the
Communist Party advocated the use of 'force, violence, or physical injury' and was thus illegal under section 98; and third, that 'two or more
persons' had agreed to carry out the CPC's objectives, making them
parties to a seditious conspiracy. The first issue was solved quickly. All
of the accused, save for Mike Golinsky (Gilmore), who belonged only
to the Young Communist League and was therefore released, admitted to being full-fledged party members. The second and third issues
were dealt with at length. While the crown called twelve witnesses,
its star was Sergeant John Leopold. 'With eyes straight ahead, his red
coat making a splash of colour in the drab surroundings,' the former
undercover agent spoke at length about the formation of the party and
its nefarious objectives. 'The aims ... of the party ... was to organize the
working class of Canada for the overthrow ... of the economic institutions, the state, and the social order in general,' Leopold testified during direct examination, adding later that, for Communists, this change
could take place only with 'the application of force and violence.'[9] This
was the critical element of the offence, and it was driven home further
by Leopold's testimony about the link between the Canadian party and
the Communist International – specifically, that the latter set the CPC's
strategic direction, and the former, by virtue of its membership in the
Third International, was expected to carry it out. A surfeit of documentary evidence, all of which spoke of 'mass-action,' 'armed insurrection,'
and even 'civil war,' was introduced to bolster this point, much of it
scooped up during the police raids in August, much of it written by
Russians, not Canadians.[10]

    For its part, the defence argued three points. First, the Communist
Party was not an illegal organization. Although its early years were
spent underground for fear of state repression, it had operated in the
open since 1924. Over the past seven years, it had, in fact, worked well
within the bounds of the parliamentary system: it ran candidates in municipal, provincial, and federal elections, garnering thousands of votes
and even electing an alderman in Winnipeg in 1926. This argument was
reinforced by the assertion that the party was not at the beck and call
of the Communist International: to be sure, the umbrella organization

set the broad framework within which the Canadian outfit operated, but, like other national Communist parties, the CPC was free to pursue objectives more in line with the Canadian reality.[11] The third and final component of the defence's position was the toughest to establish; not only did it address section 98 directly, but it was the most abstract: What role did violence play in the CPC's agenda? Put simply, the defence argued that party members did not advocate the use of force; rather, they believed that violence was merely a by-product of capitalism's inevitable decline. In this regard, it was the party's objective to prepare the working class for that reality so that the revolutionary moment, when it finally came, would not slip through their fingers. 'We organize the masses so that the masses, while organizing themselves to-day, shall gain every measure that it is possible for the workers to gain under the present system,' party leader Tim Buck explained on the witness stand, 'and, in gaining those measures, will prepare and when Capitalism is in crisis the working class will be able to take advantage of that situation, instead of allowing [the] economy to drop into chaos.'[12]

The judge delivered his charge to the jury on 12 November. 'Something has been said here about this being an unusual law, a harsh law, and that a jury should struggle against convicting a man for violation of an unreasonable law,' he told the courtroom. 'Is it an unreasonable law, a harsh law, to prohibit force and violence; or does the very nature of a free country demand that any changes in its constitution or in its economic systems shall be brought about not by force and violence but by reason, by argument, by legitimate means? Is it a harsh law, or it is but a reasonable law?'[13] According to the jury, it was reasonable: after nearly two hours of deliberation, it found all eight members of the Communist Party guilty as charged. 'The crime of teaching the overthrow of governmental or economic institutions by force is an extremely dangerous crime. It strikes at the very roots and foundations of our organized society in this country,' the judge observed before punishing Buck et al. 'To think that some of you of foreign birth have been here a short time, a few years, and then to agitate to overthrow the constitutional government of this country is something repugnant to one who believes in peace as we have it in this country.'[14] Seven of the accused were sentenced to five years in prison while one other, Tom Cacic, received a sentence of two years; all of them were slated for deportation upon the completion of their prison terms. On appeal, the convictions for 'seditious conspiracy' were overturned; the verdicts under section 98 were upheld.[15]

The conviction of the 'Communist Eight' illustrated the federal government's intent to crush the Communist Party. From its perspective, there was a lot at stake: in the short term, the legitimacy of the government's response to the economic crisis; in the long term, the survival of law, order, and authority, what the attorney general of Ontario once called the 'foundation of Christian civilization.'[16] As moral as it was political, this crusade was facilitated by section 98 of the Criminal Code. A dead letter since 1919, it was comprehensive, shifted the burden of proof to the accused, and criminalized certain beliefs: the accused were on trial not for actually committing acts of violence but for talking about them, even in the most general or abstract way. As one witty radical sang, to the tune of a Great War song:

> The red fire plug. Red underwear.
> Parlez Vous!
> The drunkard's nose and good red hair.
> Parlez Vous!
> Red anything, the Mounties state
> Comes under section ninety-eight
> Hinky. Dinky. Parlez Vous![17]

While the Criminal Code established the legal basis for the arrest of party leaders, the RCMP's intelligence and security apparatus ensured their conviction. Sergeant Leopold was no ordinary witness; what he learned underground was, as the judge made clear in his charge to the jury, critical to establishing the 'principles and aims' of the Communist Party.[18] For this betrayal, party members in Vancouver had fixed a photograph of their former comrade to a bulletin board at CPC headquarters and stuck it full of pins.[19]

Crackdown

By the winter of 1931, it was open season on Communists and suspected Communists; statistics compiled by the Canadian Labour Defense League told the story well. In 1931, 720 people were arrested for political crimes; 155 of them were later convicted. A year later, there were 839 arrests and 200 convictions.[20] Worse, the revival of section 98 brought to life other, equally repressive laws, specifically section 41 of the Immigration Act which allowed for the deportation of recent immigrants who possessed undesirable political beliefs.[21] This was precisely

Ottawa's intention. Between the time the Communist leadership was rounded up (August) and when they went on trial (November), the minister of justice asked senior officials at immigration and the RCMP to help to increase deportations. Drawing on an extensive archive of suspected radical activity, one generated by a network of secret agents, handlers, detectives, and supervisors spread out across the country, the Mounties provided a list of forty foreign-born Communists to the Department of Immigration and Colonization.[22] By early December 1931, after several weeks of investigation and the sharing of intelligence, the department had whittled the Mounties' list down to individuals who, in the words of A.L. Jolliffe, the immigration commissioner, 'have been selected as the most likely ones in which success would be attained.'[23] The men in question lived in Montreal, Oshawa, Toronto, Sudbury, Winnipeg , Edmonton, and Vancouver; it was now up to the RCMP, in a 'clean cut and well defined' manner, to bring them in. 'I think I mentioned to you that the deportation scheme is on foot. I send with this a list of the persons whom it is proposed to lay hands on suddenly,' C.F. Hamilton informed a colleague in Toronto. 'Evidence may be difficult to obtain in some cases, and it would assist greatly if you would scan your mountains of documents for letters by any of them, or other things that could be regarded as evidence. So the Bad Old Force [can] g. t. m. [get their man].'[24]

As in the previous summer, the force planned to 'synchronize raids and arrests so that these may take place in the various centres at one and the same time.'[25] In memo after memo, Commissioner MacBrien briefed his commanding officers on the attitude of the government, the powers available to the force under section 98 and section 41, and the evidence required, including the testimony of secret agents, to prosecute someone under either provision.[26] Out in the divisions, commanding officers scoured their files on radicalism, secured search warrants from local police magistrates, and sent detectives out to locate those slated to be pinched. This final task was by no means easy; not only was the intelligence on file in several divisions incomplete, out of date, or non-existent, but, as one commanding officer reported, the subjects of this dragnet were 'very "jumpy" these days,' making it difficult to conduct further surveillance. Despite these obstacles, the local dimensions of this national crackdown were starting to shape up. In Edmonton, 'E' Division planned an early morning raid, involving 'two search parties of sufficient strength ... to ward off possible interference,' on the Ukrainian Labour Farmer Temple and the Ukrainian Institute; the 'full particulars' of this arrangement, including detailed floor plans of the buildings in question, were sent to national headquarters in late December 1931. Other jurisdictions filed similar updates. In Halifax, where the potential deportees were to appear before a Board of Inquiry, 'H' Division arranged for special escorts and guards to assist immigration officials while headquarters agreed to send Sergeant Leopold to the port city to help. By late February, the Mounties were prepared, in the commissioner's words, 'to have the individuals taken into custody in accordance with the ... Minister's orders.'[27]

At 5:30 a.m. on 26 April 1932, RCMP officers in Vancouver, aided by detectives from the city police, descended on the headquarters of the Communist Party and the eastside rooming houses occupied by some of its members; one local leader was arrested.[28] 'The influence of our raids here on Communist headquarters and a search for certain Communist Leaders had a most beneficial effect,' the RCMP's commanding officer in British Columbia, S.T. Wood, reported. 'The Ukrainians, for instance, held a separate meeting on May the 1st at their own headquarters and the fear of deportation was the most important matter about which they were concerned.'[29] Additional manoeuvres took place farther east as the week progressed. Dan Holmes was picked up in Winnipeg. Polish by birth, and a printer by trade, Holmes, whose real surname was Chomicki, lived in a 'tiny, spotlessly clean' apartment on Selkirk Avenue in Winnipeg, a city he had called home for over twenty years; he was married, had one child, and worked for the *Ukrainian Labor News*, among other publications. According to the RCMP's 'D' Division, he was also a Communist. Between 1923 and 1931, he attended a party convention, hosted a meeting of the Young Communist League, joined the Ukrainian Labour Farmer Temple Association, and communicated with like-minded people, both at home and abroad. In 1926, for example, he wrote to the Communist Party of Great Britain seeking information about reading material – a tidbit of intelligence brought to the Mounties' attention by Scotland Yard, which had discovered Holmes's letter during an anti-Red raid in London. It was a thin file, to be sure, but, from the perspective of the division's commanding officer, it contained enough information to conclude that Holmes was 'an active worker in the interests of Communis[m]' and 'would be a loss to the Party if deported.' Early in the morning on 2 May 1932, he was arrested by four plainclothes RCMP officers, some of whom, it appears, had staked out the apartment the day before while the family was at a May Day picnic. 'All these men were polite and acted in a gentlemanly manner toward myself and [my daughter] Lovey,' Mrs Holmes told the local press days after. 'But they did not show me any warrants either for the arrest of my husband or to search the house. They did not warn Dan that statements he might make would be used against him. They simply came and took him away. They had no right to do such a thing.'[30]

In total, eleven people, including Arvo Vaara, editor of *Vapaus*, were spirited away to Halifax to await deportation hearings.[31] 'Big Round-Up of Communists Is Under Way,' a headline in the *Mail and Empire* read. 'Sudbury Men's Arrest Part of Wide Round-Up Rumored at Ottawa,' echoed the *Toronto Star*.[32] In the House of Commons, J.S. Woodsworth, Labour member of Parliament and one-time subject of RCMP surveillance, called the arrests an 'outrage' and demanded a 'full, fair trial.'[33] A more trenchant critique came from the labour movement; the Vancouver, New Westminster, and District Trades and Labor Council 'emphatically protest[ed] against police lawlessness and extra-legality, as exemplified in the practice of what is commonly known as the third degree, denial of the writ of Habeas Corpus, and all their various practices.'[34] For its part, the federal government – the minister of justice, the minister of immigration and colonization – maintained that it was simply following the letter and intent of the law: these men were foreign-born residents, and it was up to the government to decide whether or not they had a right to stay in the country, especially given their political views.[35] Commissioner MacBrien was far more explicit: 'The best thing to do would be to send them back where they came from, in every possible way. If we were rid of them, there would be no unemployment or unrest in Canada.'[36]

Of the eleven men who appeared before the Board of Inquiry in Halifax, ten were convicted under section 41 and ordered deported; only Orton Wade, who was a Canadian citizen, was discharged. The board's decision turned on one simple, but critical question: Were the accused members of the Communist Party? All of them denied this assertion, and its associated implication that, as party members, they had advocated 'the overthrow by force or violence of the Government of Canada.' Although immigration officials possessed little documentary evidence about individual defendants, they had no trouble proving their case in a more general sense: in Halifax, as in Toronto the year before, the coup de grâce was delivered by the Mounties' key resource on Communism, Sergeant Leopold. The former undercover agent, who, in addition to his exploits in Regina and Toronto, spent time in Winnipeg with Dan Holmes and his wife, provided expert testimony at each and

every hearing, linking the groups that the accused did admit to joining – the Finnish Organization of Canada, for example – to the Communist Party. In the wake of the hearings, all of the deportees appealed
the board's decision to the minister of immigration; an additional legal
challenge, mounted by eight of the ten convicted men, was lodged in
provincial court under Nova Scotia's 'Liberty of the Subject Act,' a statute that dealt with questions of arrest and detention usually handled
at common law. By October 1932, that dispute was before the Supreme
Court of Canada in Ottawa.[37]

With the assistance of the Canadian Labour Defense League, counsel
for the accused made two arguments before the top court. On the one
hand, the Board of Inquiry 'had no jurisdiction in the matter' because
the complaints lodged against the eight men were too vague, covering
a 'multiplicity of offences' without setting out, clearly, the dates, times,
and locations of particular infractions. In short, the charges were too
general to permit a proper defence. On the other hand, the evidence
brought before the board was insufficient to warrant a conviction: Leopold's assessment of the Communist Party and its affiliated organizations notwithstanding, no compelling evidence pertaining to specific
actions committed by individual deportees was ever introduced. The
five judges who heard the appeal were not convinced, ruling that the
appellants were not entitled to the same protections afforded an accused in civil or criminal proceedings. In short, under the Immigration
Act, 'the Board [of Inquiry] has its own procedure.' The court went on
to reject the question of evidence; put simply, it was outside the court's
jurisdiction. What was more, 'their Lordships' continued, had the court
considered that argument, it would not have found in favour of the accused: 'The various organizations, of which the Appellants were shown
to have been members, were, in fact, controlled by the Communist Party, and that, due to such control, their aims and purposes were similar
to the "parent" organization.' With this final decision, and no intervention from the minister of immigration and colonization in the offing,
the ten men were finally deported.[38]

Intelligence Failures

For the newly appointed head of the RCMP, Major-General J.H. Mac-
Brien, the highly publicized trials in 1931 and 1932 were certainly an
auspicious debut. Plucked from retirement in 1931, the former head of
the Canadian military possessed a reputation for being 'honest,' 'frank,'

'sincere,' 'disciplined,' and 'tough.' From Prime Minister Bennett's perspective, these qualities, coupled with his extensive military and political background, made MacBrien an ideal choice for the job, especially given Ottawa's heightened desire to roll back the Red tide.

Yet, while MacBrien was no doubt pleased to see the Communist leadership in Kingston Penitentiary, and rank-and-file members in detention in Halifax, the trials themselves were not, from his perspective, unqualified successes: despite Sergeant Leopold's 'heroic' testimony, there were significant problems within the Mounties' security and intelligence service. In 'O' Division, for example, which was responsible for southern Ontario and thus kept tabs on the national headquarters of the Communist Party, the force no longer possessed undercover agents who had reliable access to, and intimate knowledge of, the party's upper echelons or its affiliated organizations.[39] This problem dated back to 1928 when Leopold's cover was blown; since that time, Ontario's Mounties were forced to rely on plainclothes officers whose surveillance of radical activity, compared to that generated by undercover agents, was rudimentary at best. 'The present situation is not satisfactory,' MacBrien's predecessor observed in early 1931, referring to 'O' Division. 'In one recent instance some of your staff showed what I cannot describe except as negligence.' The RCMP's ability to infiltrate the party was reduced further when CPC members used aliases, photographed meetings, gathered at homes, instead of halls, moved printing presses from place to place, and formed special committees to ferret out police spies ('Every Worker a Defender!'). For the new commissioner, solving the problem meant cleaning house at 'O' Division, a process that included the removal of the commanding officer and director of the Criminal Investigation Branch, and redoubling efforts to recruit secret agents with the skills and stamina to remain underground for extended periods of time, not just in central Canada but elsewhere.[40]

Strengthening the force's intelligence and security role necessitated changes at national headquarters as well. Basic training was overhauled as some of the older, military aspects of the program were replaced with instruction in legal and technical subjects; security screening for civil servants was introduced in 1931; and the first edition of *RCMP Quarterly*, a publication conceived, in part, to counter Communist propaganda, rolled off the presses two years later.[41] Additional staff was added during the early to mid-1930s – a development spurred on, in large measure, by the force's new responsibility for provincial policing in five provinces – and many of those on the payroll were responsible for more specialized tasks. In 1933 MacBrien scrapped the post of intelligence and liaison officer and replaced it with a position entitled simply 'intelligence officer' – a move permitted by the death of long-time ILO C.F. Hamilton. This was more than just a name change; the new job was filled by a member of the force, not a civilian, and was responsible for security matters only; most interdepartmental and intra-governmental responsibilities were stripped away. Three years later, a new Intelligence Section was created within the Criminal Investigation Branch at national headquarters – a move that was mirrored by CIBs in several major cities, including Montreal and Vancouver.[42]

The experiences of the ubiquitous John Leopold, undercover agent turned expert on Communism at national headquarters, captures this transition towards specialization well. So, too, does the career of RCMP Special Constable Mervyn Black. Born in Russia in 1890, Black worked the better part of his life as a mill manager, first in Scotland, where his parents were from, then later in Russia, both before and after the Bolshevik Revolution. After five years in the coffee business in Colombia, Black immigrated to Canada, taking up farming in Saskatchewan from 1925 to 1932. He joined the force in 1933, and, given his fluency in many languages and 'thorough knowledge of the language and psychology of the Russian,' was sent undercover in 'F' Division. Within a year, Black was back above ground, heading up the division's newly created Intelligence Section. 'Practically all my time is engaged in investigating and reporting on radical activities from the reports submitted in my contacts with S.A.'s [Secret Agents], and in keeping the Secret Files, which are in my charge, up to date,' he informed his commanding officer in 1933. Five years later, he was transferred to Toronto – the commissioner asking him to 'take charge of the subversive activities and secret agents in that Division which is the most important from the Communist standpoint.'[43]

As the commissioner's order suggests, the Communist Party remained a potent political force in Canada well into the mid-1930s; indeed, with a membership hovering around the 6,000 mark (and climbing), it was stronger than it had ever been. Ottawa's coercive turn, which was mirrored by equally repressive measures undertaken by provincial and municipal authorities, was – paradoxically – in part responsible for this development. 'I've been in jail before for it [unlawful assembly], but I came out redder than ever,' Pat Lenihan, a prominent Communist in Calgary, remarked in 1931.[44] In a wider sense, the jailing of the Communist leadership, and the campaign against section 98 that began after the trial, invigorated the Canadian Labour Defense League. Under the direction of A.E. Smith, it emerged as a staunch defender of civil liberties and, as such, provided a weigh station for people who were interested in left-wing politics but wary of any association with the Communist Party. Between 1931 and 1933, the league's membership hit the 25,000 mark, up from 10,000 just two years before, and its petitions routinely garnered hundreds of thousands of signatures. This mobilization against section 98, coupled with developments internal to the Communist Party itself, enhanced the profile of party secretary Tim Buck as well. After a riot in Kingston Penitentiary, in which a guard fired five shots into Buck's cell in an apparent assassination attempt, the stature of this 'dauntless leader of the Canadian working class' was bolstered further. Indeed, when 'prisoner 2425' was finally released from prison in November 1934, he was greeted by 4,000 people at Union Station in Toronto; later, 17,000 packed Maple Leaf Gardens to hear him speak.[45]

As significant as state repression was in bringing about the party's reversal of fortunes, its influence paled in comparison to the combined effect of the ongoing economic crisis, the ideological vacuity of the Liberal and Conservative parties, and the initiative of countless rank-and-file activists to organize the unorganized, both on relief and on the job. Their political work took place within a changing tactical context. Starting in the early 1930s, the party, responding to policy changes undertaken by the Communist International, and its own failure to attract a mass following, shelved its revolutionary rhetoric in favour of 'a turn to real, everyday struggles on the basis of the daily needs of the masses.'[46] This was a broadening out process. Among the unemployed, the 'struggle for the streets,' which drew much of its strength from single, unemployed men, gave way to more inclusive block and neighbourhood councils – organizations that campaigned against unfair rent hikes and evictions, high utility costs, and low government relief. Emblematic of the party's turn to 'everyday' issues, a monster petition drive calling on the federal government to establish a comprehensive system of unemployment insurance was launched in 1931; tens of thousands of people signed the list of demands, while thousands of others rallied for their adoption. In the country's hundreds of relief camps, the party's Relief Camp Workers' Union protested against rotten food, overbearing foremen, and demeaning work; strikes were common – low-level conflicts that, on occasion, mushroomed into mass walkouts.[47] 'After five years of unemployment, vast masses of working people are yet forced to live under conditions that could no longer be tolerated in a civilized country,' read a leaflet put out by 'inmates' at Halifax's Citadel Hill relief camp in 1935. 'Hundreds of thousands are condemned to live in a state of semi-starvation, despite the fact there exists the means to more than supply them all.'[48]

Evidence of the party's change in direction, and the tangible results it produced, was evident on the job as well. 'To hold a propaganda meeting on the street corner or in a hall or to stand up in a union local and take a stand is communist work alright, but it is easy,' party stalwart George Drayton observed. 'The hard work consists of building up contacts in the plants, and in the Company Town, etc. This is the true test of a Communist today.'[49] By the mid-1930s, there was plenty of 'hard work' going on. In 1931 total membership in unions affiliated with the Workers' Unity League (WUL), the party's trade-union arm, stood at 12,500 to 15,000; by 1935, it had more than doubled, reaching approximately 30,000 to 40,000. Loggers, miners, garment workers, furniture makers, and labourers, among others, waged hard-fought strikes in many parts of the country, demonstrating a confidence in collective action that the mainstream labour movement, which had *lost* thousands of members during this time, lacked.[50] All of this – the struggle among the unemployed, the push for industrial unions – was fortified by a culture of opposition. Many of the party's new-found members and sympathizers, including a growing number of middle-class folks, attended dances ('Draw for 10 lbs turkey'), study groups (Upton Sinclair's *The Jungle*), and public lectures ('A Proletarian Life') or joined drama groups ('Progressive Arts Club') and party-sponsored organizations ('Working-Class Ex-Servicemen's League'). Entertaining and didactic in equal measure, these activities underscored a simple, and increasingly popular, notion: the working class and employing class had nothing in common – not politics nor poetry – and only through collective action would the masses, in the words of writer and fellow traveller Dorothy Livesay, have the ability 'To crush the boss, the stifler / To rise over his body with a surge of beauty / A wave of us, storming the world.'[51]

While many socialists and liberals found this more moderate, even romantic, vision of left-wing solidarity enticing, especially at a time when Fascism in Europe was on the rise, the Mounties (for obvious reasons) did not. From the force's perspective, the Communist Party's 'Popular Front' strategy was a political charade; its rhetoric of reform hid an unwavering commitment to revolution – as evidenced by recent party activities on some of Canada's most prestigious university campuses. In Montreal, for example, the Mounties had started to scrutinize student organizations at McGill University, joining the city police force whose own 'Red Squad' had been keeping tabs on campus politics as well. While detectives from 'C' Division tended to downplay the significance of groups like the McGill Labour Club, they maintained a small presence on campus throughout the decade. 'I am quite satisfied that you are doing all that is possible at McGill to assist in the control of Communism,' Commissioner MacBrien told the university's principal, General Arthur Currie, in 1933. 'It would be a big help if the University Authorities would control the public actions of some of their professors.'[52] Similar letters were sent to the presidents of Queen's University, the University of Toronto, the University of Manitoba, and the University of British Columbia.[53]

On to Ottawa

Communist-influenced, working-class activism was especially vibrant on the west coast, and so, too, was the response from the RCMP.[54] Prior to the summer of 1931, the common-sense opinion in British Columbia's 'E' Division was that the 'Party machine' in Vancouver was 'a creaky affair and far from smooth working': attendance at meetings was poor, new recruits drifted in and out, and local leaders were, generally, discouraged. What was more, in the opinion of Senior Inspector F.J. Mead, the party's long-term potential among the unemployed was limited: 'The True-Britishers, even though unemployed, will never condescend to the principles and discipline that is adhered to in connection with the Communist Party.' H.M. Newson, the officer in command in British Columbia, agreed, remarking that despite recent clashes between police and protestors in the city, 'we must not lose sight of the fact that there are large numbers of foreigners among the unemployed. They are easily led by agitators.' After the summer of 1931, however, reports emanating from 'E' Division were striking a different note: Vancouver was suddenly volatile. 'I feel that I should place on record my personal opinion, that unless some definite policy is decided upon to alleviate the Unemployment situation in the City of Vancouver by next fall,' Newson told his superiors at national headquarters, 'considerable trouble in the form of the riots may be expected. Communist propaganda is being disseminated and listened to more than ever before, and will bear fruit if not counteracted.' Subsequent reports noted how city and provincial police were handling the situation, where political meetings were taking place, and, perhaps most important, who was in attendance. 'I noticed among the audience that a large number of them appeared to be of the middle class,' Constable J.G. Yendell recounted after attending a 'United Front' rally with 5,000 other people.[55]

It was precisely this kind of mass appeal, coupled with the ongoing potential for violence in the streets, that prompted an intensification of state repression. Commissioner MacBrien boosted the size of the RCMP detachment in Vancouver from fifty to seventy-five men and authorized the division's commanding officer to 'supply information with respect to ... radical activities, when so requested by the Provincial authorities' because 'we do not expect them to keep records of this nature to the same extent and in the same manner as we do.'[56] S.T. Wood, who would later earn a reputation for his aggressiveness in the realm of security and intelligence work, was named British Columbia's new commanding officer in the fall of 1931.[57] Under his leadership, the division's Criminal Investigation Branch was busier than ever. At least nine plainclothes men in Vancouver were routinely attending block and neighbourhood council meetings ('the nucleus has 21 members on the books'), speaking with party members and supporters ('at least six men approached Yendell for signature on the petition'), and contacting informants within the party ('information supplied by Informant Anthony Moximonko'). At the same time, undercover operatives, like Constable Leland Graham, who went by the name of G. Grant, disappeared into local branches of the Canadian Labour Defense League, the Friends of the Soviet Union, and the Single Unemployed Protective Association.[58]

Each informant demonstrated a keen eye for the multiple connections between these organizations and the worsening 'unemployment situation.' Of particular interest was the Workers Ex-Servicemen's League (WESL). Founded in Winnipeg in 1931, the WESL was the Communist Party's answer to conservative veterans' associations such as the Canadian Legion which, in the party's opinion, were 'controlled by commissioned officers and agents of the capitalist class.' In Vancouver, where working-class veterans made up a sizable portion of the unemployed population, the WESL had its own office, lobbied municipal politicians, and supported unemployed organizations and trade unions. And, like the Communist Party as a whole, the WESL's leadership gravitated to a more inclusive political style as the Great Depression wore on; not only did issues such as non-contributory unemployment insurance, free medical care, and better pensions top the local branch's agenda, but its leadership no longer displayed the Red Flag or sang the Internationale – two age-old red rituals – at its regular meetings. As a result, WESL membership in Vancouver increased. By 1935, 2,000 veterans had signed up, and many others were sympathetic.[59] Almost from the day the WESL arrived on the west coast, at least four local Mounties, including, it appears, at least one undercover operative, kept watch, sometimes on a daily basis. With surveillance, of course, came interference. On several occasions in 1932, the force raided the organization's office and seized its records; a year later, when the WESL sponsored a conference on unemployment in Ottawa, Mounties in Cranbrook, Nelson, and Kamloops 'endeavour[ed] to prevent' the delegates' 'journey east.' At the same time, national headquarters shared intelligence with the Canadian Legion – information that its general secretary considered 'illuminating' and 'valuable' for it showed 'the sort of tactics we must guard against.'[60]

Those tactics included reaching out to working-class veterans on Vancouver's waterfront, many of whom had lost their jobs with the onset of the Depression. Between 1931 and 1933, a group of left-wing longshoremen, some of whom had ties to the Communist Party, established a bona fide union on the docks, replacing a company-sponsored association which had been established in 1923. The Workers' Unity League played a key role in this process of radicalization. So, too, did the WESL – its political discourse contrasting workers' proud service in the Great War with their servile position on the job.[61] The Mounties' interest in the waterfront was evident as early as 1931 when twenty-eight RCMP constables, sixteen of whom were on horseback, joined twenty men from the Vancouver Police Department and the British Columbia Provincial Police to ensure that longshoremen did not strike in sympathy with local sawmill workers who were battling their own austerity-minded employer. Intelligence operations on the waterfront, which involved sharing reports with waterfront employers, other police forces, and the municipal and provincial governments, did not begin in earnest until 1933.[62] Within two years, the Mounties possessed a complete list of longshoremen who had ties to the Communist Party, and party members who possessed links to the waterfront. '[Local party leader George] Drayton succeeded in having a new slate of officers, with the exception of one, set up an election held by the Longshoremen's Union,' one plainclothes detective reported. 'This is considered an outstanding achievement for the WUL and was brought about by effective group work.'[63] While this informant was correct to identify the Workers' Unity League as a key player on the docks, he failed to grasp the extent to which rank-and-file longshoremen – most of them 'True Britishers' and veterans of the Great War – supported the opposition movement on their own volition. His report, then, like so many other intelligence briefs produced during this time, not only reduced a complex movement to a single cause – Communism – but, in doing so, fully justified state repression as a means to ending it.[64] The troublemakers were Reds; they would get what they deserved.

Meanwhile, in the province's hundreds of relief camps, sporadic protests were, slowly, giving way to an organized campaign of resistance under the auspices of the Relief Camp Workers' Union and its pugnacious leader, Arthur 'Slim' Evans. When the provincial government first established its relief camps in 1931, 'E' Division's commanding officer believed it was a 'step in the right direction' because the camps would 'relieve to a great extent the embarrassment of having large numbers of men out of work in the larger cities of the provinces.'[65] By 1934, however, it was clear that the relief camps, which by then were run by the Department of National Defence, had failed to solve the 'embarrassment' of political protest; in fact, by bringing thousands of men together and forcing them to work under poor conditions for meagre pay, the relief camps made things worse. Despite early hopes of establishing 'contacts in the labour camps' in order to 'see to what extent the Communist Party of Canada controls the unemployed,' the assistant commanding officer in British Columbia, J.W. Phillips, had to concede in March 1934 that 'E' Division was finding it difficult to secure reliable and comprehensive intelligence: 'The unemployment camps ... are situated where we have no detachments,' he told Commissioner MacBrien, before asserting that 'it is fair to say that most of the strikes and disturbances in these camps were spontaneous, and the result of the natural unrest among unemployed men.' By the spring of 1935, however, as RCMP informants in Vancouver continued to snoop around, the broad outlines of the Communist Party's objectives were clear. According to a confidential report entitled 'Factors in the Relief Camp Situation,' the agenda 'last discussed [by the party] embraced a general strike of (a) mill workers, (b) street railway men, (c) longshoremen, and this was to be staged simultaneously with the concentration of relief camp men in Vancouver.'[66]

On 4 April 1935 it appeared that the general strike was under way. The longshoremen were about to walk off the job, and thousands of unemployed men, heeding the call of the Relief Camp Workers' Union, left the relief camps and descended on Vancouver. At issue were the immediate needs of camp dwellers, such as wages and working conditions, and wider concerns, including the creation of non-contributory unemployment insurance and the abolition of 'Section 98 of the Criminal Code, Sections 41 and 42 of the Immigration Act, vagrancy laws, and all anti-working class laws.'[67] By this time, mainstream church, community, and political organizations – such as the CCF – had added their support to the relief-camp workers' cause and even some editorial writers were starting to sound sympathetic. 'The only wonder is that these poor fellows have not made such demonstrations before,' observed the *Vancouver Sun*.[68] While strikers marched in the streets, and some local politicians pressed Ottawa to reconsider its position on the single unemployed, the Mounties remained watchful. Throughout April and into May, Constable Eric Kusch, a veteran of the force, filed a steady stream of reports – about one every few days. His dispatches were buttressed by information produced by Constable Graham, who was still underground, and other civilian informants; fragmentary, but suggestive, evidence reveals that Kusch and Graham were not alone on this particular beat.[69] After nearly two months in the city – a time punctuated by an occupation of a Hudson's Bay store, a pitched street battle with police, including the RCMP, and a May Day rally at Stanley Park which attracted upwards of 15,000 people – relief-camp strikers decided to leave Vancouver and head to Ottawa to put their demands before the prime minister himself. According to Constable Kusch, this tactical decision was a sign of weakness, not of strength; the strike, he reported, 'would be abandoned immediately [after] the strikers got out of sight.' It is perhaps for this reason that, when the 'On-to-Ottawa Trek' departed in early June, it appears that no undercover RCMP operatives accompanied it.[70]

As the trek moved east, gathering members and momentum along the way, the Mounties scrambled to piece together reliable intelligence. Information on file in local detachments, or produced by their plainclothes detectives, provided some help, but it was, for the most part, of limited value. By the time the travelling protest reached Moose Jaw, Saskatchewan, on 12 June 1935, the force had re-established a covert source, at least for a time. That night, former undercover agent Mervyn Black engaged two men, one of whom was a Mountie from Regina, Constable Henry Cooper, to 'observe the movements of the [trek] leaders, to endeavour to learn the intentions of the Strikers, and to report anything of importance at a pre-arranged point of contact.' Tapping his prior experience as an operative assigned to relief-camp work, Cooper was able to infiltrate the strikers – receiving card number 295 – and filed several reports until his cover was blown about a week later; someone had recognized him from his days on patrol in the Saskatchewan capital. Subsequent attempts to implant another operative, a constable from Winnipeg with no prior underground experience, failed as the trekkers, building on tactics learned after years of state repression, remained vigilant. 'The policy of the leaders is to keep the intentions and plans of the "Strategy" Committee secret from the mass of the rank and file until the very last moment,' Black explained to his superiors. 'Owing to this policy it is practically impossible to obtain advance information of the intentions of the leaders.'[71] It is unclear what happened to the other man Black spoke to that night in Moose Jaw.

Meanwhile, in Ottawa, Prime Minister Bennett and members of his cabinet were in consultation with the RCMP about how to prevent the trek from turning up on Parliament Hill. These high-level discussions began in early June when the trek first left Vancouver and continued throughout the month as the strikers made their way steadily eastward, from Kamloops to Golden, then on to Calgary, Medicine Hat, Swift Current, Moose Jaw, and finally Regina, on 14 June. Three days before the trekkers arrived in the Saskatchewan capital, the RCMP commissioner, J.H. MacBrien, informed local authorities that the federal government wanted the movement stopped in Regina, lest it reach Winnipeg where, as the *Free Press* observed, 'an electric current of anticipation crackled.'[72] The commanding officer in Saskatchewan, the newly transferred S.T. Wood, agreed but warned that a careful approach was needed for there was 'considerable public support for these strikers' in the area.[73] As the force kept a close watch on the strikers in Regina – they were quartered in the city's exhibition grounds and prevented from boarding any eastbound trains – Commissioner MacBrien continued his discussions with the prime minister and some cabinet members. Responding to a direct request from the minister of justice for a comprehensive strategy to deal with the crisis, the commissioner reaffirmed the importance of blocking the strikers' progress eastbound, adding that the RCMP in Winnipeg needed to be ready nonetheless. He also advised that the Mounties in Regina should disperse the trekkers at an appropriate time, while Ottawa ought to discredit its leaders by making the most of their criminal records and connections to the Communist Party. To that end, MacBrien passed along the intelligence the force had gathered about Slim Evans and other trek leaders, who were by then on their way to the nation's capital to meet directly with Prime Minister Bennett on 22 June.[74]

That meeting between the prime minister and the strikers' delegation did not go well, at least from the trekkers' perspective. After listening to lengthy descriptions of life in the relief camps, the failures of government policies, and the demands of the strikers – Evans did most of the talking – the prime minister had had enough. 'So far as work with wages in these camps are concerned the government has made it perfectly clear to you that these [relief] camps were not established for that purpose,' he began. 'I do ask you young men, at your age, whether or not you think you are playing the part of good citizens in a country with the difficulties we have, and with the efforts we are making to try and restore it to normal conditions, and when we are supplying you with the conditions of a home, because you are homeless men … Now you suddenly say: We are going to violate laws and march on Ottawa. March to Ottawa for what purpose? What purpose?'[75] Shortly after posing this pointed question, the prime minister raised the issue of Evans's criminal record, speculated about the hidden hand of the Communist Party in the unemployed movement, and lectured the delegation – 'who have misled and are continuing to mislead their fellow citizens' – about the need to accept the consequences that come with unlawful activities.[76] (Clearly, the RCMP's intelligence was being put to good use.) In the face of the prime minister's forceful presence, Evans, who had called Bennett a 'liar' earlier in the meeting, was equally unequivocal – and unrepentant: 'We realize the responsibility we are confronted with … Our responsibility is we must take this back to the workers and see that the hunger programme of Bennett is stopped.' And with that, the meeting was over. 'I have nothing more to say,' the prime minister stated. 'Good morning gentlemen. We have been glad to listen to you.'[77]

Shortly after the talks broke down, MacBrien advised Wood that 'the Government desired proceedings taken under section 98 of the Criminal Code against the known leaders' and that a 'special agent, Leopold, who had experience in Communist activities' would be in the city soon. While a delegation of strikers met with the provincial government to negotiate a peaceful end to the trek, the Mounties – some on foot, others on horses – descended on Regina's market square on Dominion Day, 1 July, to snatch the trek leaders. A deadly riot, involving hundreds, if not thousands, of people, ensued. Dozens of strikers were injured and one police officer was killed. 'It was a terrible night, downtown Regina a shambles,' one striker recalled. 'Not a store with a window left in, the streets piled up with rocks and broken glass, dozens of cars piled up in the streets with no glass in them, and twisted fenders and bodies.'[78] Just days after the 'Regina Riot,' Wood filed a detailed report with national headquarters which addressed the RCMP's handling of the relief-camp strike. He was particularly concerned with the connection between surveillance, intelligence gathering, and police work, lamenting that the force was 'handicapped in our sources of information in view of the fact that no Secret Agent or informers accompanied the camp strikers into this Province in spite of the fact that they organized in BC and travelled through Alberta.' Wood went on to add that 'it would have been of immense help had informants been placed among these people to begin with and accompanied them on their trek west. This is a point that should be kept in mind for future occasions.' Although Wood never said so specifically, he might have been thinking about the Mounties' incorrect assessment of the strikers' determination when they left British Columbia, or the inability of Mervyn Black, one of the force's more astute spy handlers, to run undercover operatives against the trekkers once they arrived in Saskatchewan. That Wood was forced to rely on the judgment of a private detective hired by the Canadian Pacific Railroad in the days running up to 1 July underscores the extent of the intelligence disaster that unfolded during the summer of 1935.[79] An inquiry into the riot created later by the provincial government fully exonerated the RCMP and local law-enforcement agencies.

The International Brigades

The Regina Riot, and the broader relief-camp debacle of which it was a part, came to symbolize the failure of the Bennett government to solve the decade's single most important issue: unemployment. In the 1935 federal election, the ruling Tories were defeated by the Liberal Party, still under the watch of Mackenzie King. Although the new prime minister ordered the camps closed shortly after taking office, agitation over unemployment persisted.[80] So, too, did the Communist Party's tactical reorientation. In 1935 the Workers' Unity League was disbanded, sending scores of rank-and-file Red unionists back into the mainstream labour movement. Not long after, the RCMP's weekly 'Report on Revolutionary Organizations and Agitation in Canada' was making note of the labour movement's 'swing to the left' and 'profound radicalization.' By 1937, those concerns were heightened by the emergence of the militant Committee for Industrial Organization (CIO) in the United States. A rival of the American Federation of Labor, the CIO's meteoric rise was fuelled, in large measure, by the political shrewdness of Communist trade unionists, and it was coming to Canada.[81] A new section on 'CIO Activities and Industrial Unrest' was added to the RCMP's weekly summaries of suspected subversion, just as militant organizational drives in the auto, steel, and lumber industries were starting up.

Outside the ranks of organized labour, the Communist Party was increasingly focused on the Spanish Civil War, a cause that resonated with liberal Canadians in a way that union politics did not. In 1931 King Alfonso XIII of Spain was replaced by a Republican administration which promised labour and land reform to aid the country's impoverished workers and peasants. Stymied by internal divisions, and a political agenda that alienated both left-wing supporters and right-wing opponents, the government was defeated at the polls by a Popular Front coalition in 1936. By July, the coalition had splintered, and General Francisco Franco, with the blessing of Hitler and Mussolini, had launched a coup d'etat. Popular resistance to the 'Nationalist' onslaught was fierce – aided, within a year, by volunteers from around the world. Under the auspices of the Communist International, the Communist Party of Canada, like national Communist parties elsewhere, raised awareness, funds, and volunteers; so, too, did churches, unions, and organizations such as the Canadian League Against War and Fascism. In early January 1937 the first of the Canadian volunteers arrived in Spain.[82] Organized into the International Brigades, and later the all-Canadian Mackenzie-Papineau Battalion, almost 1,700 recruits – the vast majority of whom were recent immigrants to Canada – heeded the call to 'Defend Democracy in Spain' before the civil war was finally over.[83]

Democratic governments in the West were not so moved. Fearful that any involvement by an outside power might plunge Europe into a wider and bloodier conflict, they opted for a policy on non-intervention; such was the position that Canada, following Britain's lead, took. As a consequence, Ottawa forbade people from participating in the civil war under amendments to the Foreign Enlistment Act of 1870. Ratified in late July 1937, the legal changes broadened the scope of the original act to include Spain and set out penalties for non-compliance: Canadians who joined the International Brigades could be fined $2,000 and imprisoned for two years. A month later, the federal government, acting under the auspices of the amended act, passed an order-in-council banning all travel to Spain. Spurred on by the demands of British foreign policy,

Ottawa's legislative response to the Spanish Civil War was also shaped by domestic political considerations. Not only was the prime minister sensitive to anti-Republican sentiment in Quebec, but, it appears, the minister of justice (Ernest Lapointe) and undersecretary of state for foreign affairs (O.D. Skelton) were listening to the commissioner of the RCMP. Writing in early July, MacBrien explained that 'a feeling prevails among the loyal spirited foreigners ... that recruiting for the Spanish government should be prohibited, it is felt that these youths are being sent to Spain largely for the sake of gaining experience in practical revolutionary work and will return to this country to form the nucleus of a training corps.'[84] The Foreign Enlistment Act, then, would be useful to combat the Communist Party in a more general sense, especially given the King government's recent abolition of section 98.

The RCMP did not wait for Ottawa to criminalize anti-Fascism before it placed both recruiters and volunteers under surveillance. By late December 1936, plainclothes Mounties in Vancouver, Calgary, Winnipeg, Toronto, and Montreal were reporting that volunteers 'for the Madrid Government are being recruited locally by the Communist Party of Canada and that numbers of Finns, Poles, Ukrainians, and Russians, as well as a sprinkling of other nationalities, have applied for passports to their respective consulates.'[85] Early in the new year, months before the passage of the Foreign Enlistment Act, 'passport control' emerged as a low-key yet somewhat effective method of hampering recruitment activities. Passport officers were asked to inform the federal police of any suspicious applicants so that they could determine 'whether or not any of the individuals ... had any connection with the subversive movement in their respective locales.' As a consequence, in some cities, individuals suspected of left leanings were subjected, in the words of one Vancouver lawyer sympathetic to the Spanish Republican cause, to 'lengthy and protracted and trivial correspondence' designed to delay or deny their travels overseas. Similar acts of obstruction were reported in Winnipeg and Toronto.[86]

With the reinvigoration of the Foreign Enlistment Act, the commissioner of the RCMP was hopeful that a wider crackdown on radical activity might be possible – with participation in the civil war providing the trigger; especially worrying, from his perspective, was the possibility of Canadian volunteers returning home after the war with military skills and applying those skills to domestic 'revolutionary work.'[87] Writing to Minister of Justice Lapointe in the fall of 1937, MacBrien sought clarification on this issue of prosecution, arguing that 'through the medium of special informers' it would be possible to secure convictions not only against volunteers, but against 'members of the Communist Party' as well. Lapointe was slow to commit to the commissioner's plan; his caucus, he said, was still examining the question of enforcement. In late December, however, after several men were apprehended in Montreal trying to make their way to Spain, the minister sought legal advice on the powers available to the government under the amended legislation. 'The evidence already compiled by the police as well as other evidence which is not yet in documentary form discloses a vast and cunning conspiracy to violate the laws of Canada,' a legal opinion prepared for the Justice Department stated, before explaining that the Mounties should proceed with charges under the Criminal Code ('conspiracy to commit any indictable offence'), not the Foreign Enlistment Act itself, for that statute contained no useful 'enforcement machinery.' With this memo in hand, Lapointe gave the RCMP permission to conduct a large-scale investigation, which was headed up by Inspector Frank Zaneth, the former undercover agent who helped jail leaders of the Winnipeg General Strike almost twenty years before; he was particularly zealous about the possibility of a decisive move against the Communist Party as a whole, not just a single recruiter or volunteer. The investigation lasted until late March 1938, when it was terminated by the new commissioner, S.T. Wood. Writing to the minister of justice, Wood pointed out that the civil war had shifted decisively in favour of General Franco and the flow of volunteers from Canada had stopped. Thus, any prosecution would 'arous[e] antipathy in the public mind,' he continued, and, in the process 'merely afford the Communist Party an instrument which that organization would put to useful purpose in attacking the government.' In sum, 'under the circumstances no good would result and a great deal of harm might follow.'[88]

With the end of the Spanish Civil War, the Canadian government faced the difficult problem of repatriating the men and women who survived battles at Ebro, Teruel, and Gandesa, to name but three gruesome engagements. Although its position on the conflict had softened somewhat, Ottawa refused to pay the cost of repatriation; it would, instead, permit organizations such as the Friends of the Mackenzie-Papineau Battalion, which were, technically, in violation of the Foreign Enlistment Act, to work on the volunteers' behalf. Not surprisingly, Commissioner MacBrien and his successor, Commissioner Wood, took a hard line on this question: the volunteers should be refused re-entry. Not only had they violated the Foreign Enlistment Act, but, having 'lost their Canadian domicile' while overseas, they should be banned from returning under the Immigration Act. Worse, they were Communists who now possessed military training, making them capable of 'carry[ing] out in Canada what they learned in Spain' – 'guerilla warfare and the building and defence of barricades, etc.' Under O.D. Skelton, the King government's relatively liberal policy prevailed and veterans of the conflict were permitted re-entry into Canada.[89]

The Red Hand and the White Glove

When the RCMP's predecessor – the Dominion Police – confronted Fenians and South Asian radicals in previous decades, it relied on the bureaucratic infrastructure and skill of the imperial civil service. That the enemies in those years were interested in Canada only as a means to further their objectives in Ireland and India made this reliance a necessity; so, too, did the fact that the Canadian government had yet to develop its own, independent expertise in the area of political policing. The Great War and its immediate aftermath changed all of that: by the time the national labour revolt had ended, Communism had replaced anti-imperialism as the source of the nation's security anxieties, and the RCMP had not only been created but given exclusive responsibility for surveillance and intelligence-gathering operations. The onset of the Great Depression, the rise of the Communist Party, and ongoing plight of the jobless presented the force with its first significant, nationwide security challenge since the war years. From one end of the country to the other, in rural and urban areas, in workplaces and other spaces, the Mounties sought to monitor Communists and suspected Communists, gather intelligence on their political activities, and – when circumstances were favourable – remove them from action, either by incarceration, deportation, or both.

At the highest levels of the federal police and Canadian government, there was a clear sense that constituted authority was being seriously challenged by the broad-based working-class activism that rippled through the decade; employers and many Canadians felt this way too. Occasionally, this anxiety over law and order produced more apocalyptic visions, in which local struggles in Montreal or Estevan, Saskatchewan, were transformed into something bigger and more monstrous: a Communist revolution and the end of 'Christian civilization' itself. Hadn't the Communists toppled the Russian czar, defeated counter-revolutionary forces led by Western democracies, and created the infrastructure to export its theories and practices worldwide, through the Communist International and national Communist parties? While some in positions of political authority believed, in their heart of hearts, that the 'Red Menace' in Canada was actually capable of such destruction if left unchecked, others saw in the nightmarish discourse of Communist subversion an opportunity to quash a threat that was comparatively more benign: the drive to expand trade unionism into sectors of the economy where workers' organizations had either collapsed after 1919 or had never existed in the first place. Pitched battles in the streets, agitation in the relief camps, and deadly strikes provided them with the necessary cover to mount a robust defence of the political and economic status quo. Although they understood that few trade unionists were actually dyed-in-the-wool Communists, they also knew that a cultivated fear of the latter could be used to attack the former – and with good results. As one employer warned during a union drive in 1935: 'Beware the red hand under the white glove!'[90]

While the importance of the old country to political policing in Canada had contracted enormously since 1919, it did not disappear entirely. Throughout the Great Depression, politicians, police chiefs, judges, immigration inspectors, and others spoke of the need to defend 'British values' or 'British traditions' against Communist subversion.[91] Code for parliamentary democracy, law and order, and Christian morality, such appeals to Britishness were easily understood by most English-speaking Canadians, for whom the history and emotional appeal of the empire remained meaningful; this was especially true among those at the highest levels of the RCMP. Yet this rhetoric did not belong to the powerful alone; strikers flew the Union Jack, 'vagrants' wore their medals from the Great War, and both argued that union recognition, abolition of the relief camps, and unemployment insurance were precisely the ways to *restore* British values and traditions, which had been undermined by the calamity of the Great Depression, the government's heavy-handed application of the Criminal Code and Immigration Act, and the RCMP's persistent surveillance and harassment of putative subversives. 'We were told that these communists who were arrested some years ago and sent to Kingston penitentiary were dangerous men, that communists were outlaws of society,' CCF MP J.S. Woodsworth told the House of Commons in 1935. 'I am opposed to [section 98], I say it is little less than a disgrace when we find that men who are not proven to have committed an overt act or to have incited violence should be sent to the penitentiary. That is un-British legislation.'[92] The importance of 'British values' as a touchstone for political debate and identity in English Canada would not diminish until well after the Second World War.[93]

With undercover operatives and plainclothes men, the force sought to identify potential subversives, monitor their activities, calculate the likelihood of future actions, and disseminate timely and accurate information to responsible public officials. In two high-profile cases (the arrest of the Communist Eight in 1931 and the deportation proceedings against eleven others in 1932), this 'intelligence cycle' worked. Both operations were planned in advance based on copious amounts of information; communication between national headquarters and the districts was consistent; and coordination with other government agencies – immigration officials, other police forces – was well executed. The result was a significant strike against the leadership of the Communist Party. Yet these high-profile victories against 'undesirables' were matched by several intelligence failures as well. Often the force found itself unable to spy on activists located outside major urban centres, maintain undercover agents in a single organization for any length of time, and assess accurately the strength of a particular organization. All three problems were especially evident in the RCMP's handling of the On-to-Ottawa Trek, which ended with violence in Regina on Dominion Day and a surge in public support for the jobless and their 'Red' leaders. Notably, the actions of activists themselves helped blunt the effectiveness of state surveillance and repression; years in the movement for social justice and union rights had taught them how to guard against infiltration by a secret agent, protect their comrades from harassment and intimidation, deceive curious postmasters and company foremen, and use the law and the courts to defend themselves.

By early 1939, veterans of the Spanish Civil War were returning home. At railway stations and ports across the country, big crowds, some as large as 10,000 people, welcomed them back, for they knew, as the government did not, that their cause was just. Plainclothes Mounties were among the well-wishers, taking down names, assessing the potential for subversion. Although the force was showing some interest in the far right – Adrien Arcand's Parti de l'unité nationale du Canada, for example – it remained preoccupied with the Communist Party, in particular, and the Canadian left, more generally; large numbers of politically active immigrants always made the force curious, if not a bit scared. By that time, another conflagration in Europe was about to begin; the RCMP's surveillance and intelligence-gathering capabilities would be tested once again.

6
Keep the Home Fires Burning,
1939–45

On 23 August 1939 the Nazi-Soviet Pact was signed. Adolf Hitler now had a free hand in the east and conflict seemed grimly inevitable. On 1 September, the Nazi Blitzkrieg was unleashed upon Poland. The days of appeasement and diplomatic dithering had come to an end: on 3 September, ultimatums demanding German withdrawal passed and Britain and France were at war. One week later, following a parliamentary debate, Canada formally declared itself at Britain's side once again.

The coming of war in 1939 marked an important new phase for the security service, as well as for the RCMP in general. Entering a state of war dramatically transformed the role of the secret police. Protecting national security at home suddenly jumped from being one concern among many of a government beset by a multitude of domestic policy challenges to an absolute priority.

Everything was now subordinated to winning the war. This would soon prove to be a modern 'total' war – a war of nation against nation, ideology against ideology, economy against economy, people against people – war without quarter, a war that would only end, after tens of millions of deaths and frenzied destruction on a scale unparalleled in all of human history, with total, unconditional victory enforced by the ultimate weapon of mass civilian annihilation, the atomic bomb. This kind of war imposed enormous, unprecedented burdens upon the belligerent states, few of whom were initially mobilized for such an effort.

Canada certainly was not ready in September 1939 to wage total war, or even, if truth were known, to wage much in the way of limited war. The economy, battered by a decade of depression, was hardly in a promising state for military mobilization. Military preparations were inadequate. Nor did Canada have any external intelligence capacity of its own, apart from scraps gathered by its small number of diplomatic representatives abroad. For foreign intelligence, Canada was dependent upon Britain's Foreign Office and its Secret Intelligence Service, or MI6.

Planning on the Home Front

There was one area alone that had benefited from a fair amount of advance planning: security on the home front. On this matter, the government had prudently set up machinery to go into operation as soon as war was declared. One of the main instruments for implementing this emergency policy was the RCMP and its Intelligence Section. The branch would enjoy the assistance of very extensive emergency powers under the Defence of Canada Regulations (DOCR), cabinet decrees issued under the authority of the War Measures Act – emergency legislation dating from the First War that was more draconian in scope than the wartime emergency powers exercised by the British or American governments. Under the DOCR, large areas of the Canadian economy and society became subject to direct, coercive regulation by the state. Many individual and group rights normally enjoyed in peacetime were suspended for the duration of the conflict. While Canada remained at war, the liberties of individual Canadians and their civil associations were largely at the mercy of Ottawa. For a great many Canadians, committed as they were to the common goal of winning the war, these restrictions were felt only slightly, if at all. But for those whose politics, religion, or ethnicity made them in any way suspect in the eyes of the state, this sudden loss of protection might be experienced as intrusive, disruptive, and humiliating. For the branch of the RCMP charged with responsibility for surveillance of dissenting and radical political thought and behaviour, the DOCR were empowering. Never before – and never again – would the RCMP have at its disposal such extensive, virtually quasi-totalitarian, powers to carry out the political policing of Canadian society.

On 25 August the minister of justice, Ernest Lapointe, received a letter from the commissioner of the RCMP, S.T. Wood, outlining the state-of-war readiness of Canada's national police force and internal security agency. The Mounties reported that they had prepared lists of 'all known potential enemy aliens' and of all espionage suspects: these could be arrested 'at a moment's notice' once the word was given. 'Suspects of lesser importance' were to be kept under surveillance. A registry of enemy aliens would be supplied with information from the RCMP files. Although concerned with Fascists and Nazis (and Ukrainian nationalists sympathetic towards the Hitler regime), the RCMP also anticipated a 'more rigid and extended surveillance of Communist Agitators, particularly those active among industrial workers' and recommended the outlawing of the Communist Party by order-in-council under the War Measures Act. The commissioner also spoke of close coordination between the RCMP, military intelligence, External Affairs, and the departments of transport, justice and immigration, and added that 'liaison is being maintained in all matters of mutual interest with M.I.5, London, England.'[1]

The relative readiness to deal with the home front reflected some considerable pre-war groundwork. Six interdepartmental committees were formed in 1938 to prepare Canada for war: the officer in charge of the Intelligence Section represented the RCMP on four of these committees (defence coordination; aliens and alien property; emergency legislation; and the Official Secrets Act).[2] The Defence of Canada Order 1938 spelled out sixty-nine regulations to ensure national security in war, and a Government War Book was being prepared to provide guidelines for policy. The order did not, however, include any provisions for internment of aliens and arbitrary detention of persons suspected of threatening the war effort. These became a bone of contention over the next year between, on the one hand, senior civil servants with an attachment to civil liberties, and, on the other, the RCMP and the military, which wished to ensure the maximum degree of security to the state in a war contingency.[3] RCMP Commissioner Wood and Deputy Commissioner R.R. Tait were to prove 'particularly adept' at overcoming civilian reluctance. Bureaucratic allies were successfully cultivated, and British intelligence was brought in to enhance the authority of the Mounties' perceptions. Even so, the proposal for arbitrary detention of British subjects thought 'likely' to commit acts hostile to the war effort did not get unanimous committee approval – the only proposal so to fail. Wood wrote to his minister, Lapointe, that in view of the RCMP's experience and expertise in hunting subversives, 'we are in a more favourable position to determine the essentials of the situation ... than certain members of a Committee whose scope of activity is entirely removed from the type of work mentioned and to whom the proposed legislation ... might appear repugnant due to lack of understanding of the subject.'[4] Despite last-minute appeals to Lapointe from 'certain members,' arbitrary detention was restored. The Mounties would go into the war equipped with as full an armoury with which to protect national security as they could reasonably have expected. For this, they had themselves at least partly to credit.

The Intelligence Section: Nobody Home?

Even if the government had made clear its plans and expectations for maintaining security at home, the officers in the small Intelligence Section at RCMP headquarters did not initially register much enthusiasm for the new and expanded role that was being offered. Quite the contrary. The response of three young constables in the section (including a future director of security and intelligence and commissioner, Leonard Higgit) to Canada's declaration of war was to write the officer in charge requesting they be transferred to 'something useful.'[5]

Even more surprisingly, the most famous and dedicated Red-hunter of them all, with twenty years' service both undercover and at headquarters, John Leopold, asked that he be pensioned in order that he might offer his experience to the British. After consultation with the Justice Department, Commissioner Wood refused his request. He was, Wood declared, 'too valuable an asset to the security service to be released.'[6] Since Leopold's 'experience' consisted exclusively in watching the Canadian Communist Party, it is not clear why the British would have been interested. Nor would his background as an immigrant from Eastern Europe have fitted him for the English public-school old-boy social atmosphere then prevalent in British intelligence. Perhaps some lingering sense of being a square peg in a round hole even in the RCMP – less class-ridden than their British equivalents but still led at the top by a senior officer corps of British origin and education – had driven Leopold to seek escape. There would be none. That extraordinary moment in the 1931 *Rex v. Buck* trials when Leopold, in red serge and Mountie hat, strode into the witness box as the Communist 'Jack Esselwein' had sealed his personal fate as the Mounties' career Communist expert. Leopold was their man, whether he liked it or not.

The general lack of enthusiasm evident in the Intelligence Section at the outset of war requires some explanation. The official historians of the security service speculate that internal security was a 'minor although necessary responsibility of the Force.' Most members still regarded intelligence work as 'something of an aberration,' of secondary importance to their regular, police duties. Worse, there was little glamour or glory attached to their job. No one associated their work with international intrigue, fast cars, and fast women. The era of James Bond was still in the future. In truth, the James Bond world would never arrive, except in the fantasy world of Hollywood and spy fiction. If the work of the Intelligence Section was regarded in 1939 as 'dull and boring,'[7] it would remain so, in war or peace. It is curious that the Mounties had at this time so little regard for intelligence as *police* work. In 1939 the force itself was still relatively unsophisticated. Modern police forces have learned to prize the intelligence function as an essential tool of criminal investigation. Lack of sophistication about intelligence would cost the RCMP later in the war, but war also offered a useful learning experience.

'Policemen into Intelligence Officers Overnight'

On the eve of war, the Intelligence Section was not only psychologically ill-prepared but also lacking in basic manpower and resources. In 1939 headquarters consisted of Rivett-Carnac as intelligence officer, Staff Sergeant Leopold, one lance corporal, and two stenographers. There was considerable turnover at the top. Rivett-Carnac was called away to other duties in 1939, leaving the restive Leopold as the only thread of continuity between peacetime and wartime responsibilities. Rivett-Carnac was replaced by Superintendent E.W. Bavin just after the outbreak of war. Bavin, yet another English-born Mountie, served until early 1941 when he retired from the force, his departure hastened by conflicts, apparently over both personality and policy, with Commissioner Wood. Bavin did not depart from the scene, however, but moved to New York to work with Sir William Stephenson's British Security Coordination (BSC). Here, as we shall see later, he provided useful liaison. Bavin was replaced for the duration of the war by Superintendent Alexander Drysdale, a Scottish-born veteran whose service started with the old RNWMP in 1908. Betke and Horrall note that Drysdale, 'like most of the early Intelligence officers,' 'had absolutely no specialized background for the position. Wartime needs turned a lot of policemen into intelligence officers overnight.'[8]

Nor were there trained staff in the regional divisions ready to take on intelligence war work. Young constables and corporals with quick minds but complete novices in the intelligence business were pressed into service. By early 1940, there were three officers, five non-commissioned officers, eight constables, and three special constables assigned to headquarters' Intelligence Section. Intelligence sections in major divisions were also quickly expanded to twenty or so in Montreal and Ottawa, with smaller contingents elsewhere, but in most cases youth, low rank, and relative inexperience prevailed.

The number of agents run by these officers – mainly within Communist and Fascist groups – is still considered classified information, although the RCMP historians note that they were 'operating reasonably evenly throughout Canada.' By early 1941, on the eve of the Nazi invasion of the Soviet Union, the size of the headquarters branch had mushroomed to seventy-nine (although there were still only three officers, including the indefatigable Leopold). There were now no less than twelve functional divisions. Linguistic capabilities had grown to encompass twenty-four languages. By early 1942, with the war now expanded to Asia as well as the USSR, the Intelligence Section at headquarters weighed in at just under 100 (including twenty-nine stenographers and two clerks), double what it had been in early 1940. Thereafter, numbers declined as did the number of specialists – although experts in 'Communism' and 'subversives' remained on the rolls. 'The chief internal organizational effect of the war was thus to increase Intelligence Section staff to the point at which it forced precise definition of Intelligence Section duties and personnel in the Divisions as well as at Headquarters.'[9]

Although nothing was done about it while the war continued, the organizational status of the Intelligence Section within the RCMP was a topic for debate. Bavin had made known his belief that the mushrooming section should be removed from the Criminal Investigation Branch and report directly to the commissioner. Commissioner Wood was opposed to this; the clash of opinions may have had something to do with Bavin's departure. With Bavin in New York, Wood did canvass commanding officers of the divisions in May 1942 for their opinions about divorcing the section from the CIB, but made it clear that he favoured the continued integration of all 'investigative functions.' The emergence of a fully specialized security service within the RCMP was thus delayed until after the war. But the section found itself playing a role within a wider bureaucracy that in effect recognized its specialized status. This had already been evident in the pre-war emergency planning referred to earlier. Then, on 10 November 1942, a Joint Intelligence Committee was formed, comprised of military intelligence representatives from the three services, along with External Affairs (where the Examination Unit, which began Canadian signals-intelligence operations, was housed) and the RCMP. This was the first coordinative body to oversee government intelligence policy; it provided a forum for the

Intelligence Section to work out problems of jurisdiction with other agencies, especially the military. Wartime exigencies also dictated cooperation with government departments over such matters as postal and press censorship.[10] Slowly but surely the security service was becoming an active player on its own in the Ottawa bureaucracy, a development that would become much more pronounced in the post-war years.

The Sabotage Mirage

In the first few months of war, despite the section's limited resources and the apparent lack of enthusiasm on the part of the existing officer staff, the security service faced a number of pressing demands. One of the more mundane functions was to guard strategic locations, such as power installations and key industrial plants. The FBI had warned Canada about extensive potential for sabotage in the event of war, and no doubt there was legitimate concern about such a tactic. In fact, the sabotage scare, often focused on particular groups, whether ethnic or ideological, proved to be virtually non-existent in practice, as the Mounties themselves frequently attested. Nevertheless, prudence dictated intensive preparations to combat any acts to sabotage the war effort. This involved an extensive survey of industrial sites across the country, an elaborate process begun before the war in which the Mounties were pleased to receive assistance from employers, and provision of such elementary precautions as fencing and floodlighting. It also involved the recruitment of special deputies as guards. Necessitated by the Mounties' limited manpower, this was potentially controversial: armed civilian 'specials,' recruited from among the ranks of unemployed veterans of the last war, could set off alarm bells among trade unionists. Inspector Clifford Harvison warned that the often hard-drinking vets would be 'about as hard a gang to handle as imaginable,' but soon Canadians were treated to the unusual sight of rough-looking men with rifles and 'POLICE' arm bands stopping traffic and questioning people near industrial plants. In the end, the practice proved uncontroversial, mainly because the 1,100 specials were screened for criminal records by the Mounties, closely controlled, and kept to mundane duties.[11]

The RCMP did reasonably well at ensuring plant security, well enough to gain the respect of the FBI. Yet, in some other areas, their performance was less satisfactory. Port security was a continuing problem that drew the wrath of visiting British security officials. An MI5 mission to Canada in the summer of 1941 reviewed security controls in effect for the Dominion. The mission was not impressed with what it saw, and it made a number of recommendations to improve standards. Winston Churchill's personal intelligence adviser informed the British prime minister that security in Canada was 'terrible' (Halifax, he was assured, was a 'hotbed of German spies'). At his urging, Churchill sent a special exhortation on the subject to Mackenzie King. Perhaps their experience as an inland police force did not prepare the 'Horsemen' well for the task of securing seaports. Although all of the measures recommended were not put into effect, enough were that the BSC eventually concluded that the Canadian internal security situation had been improved 'beyond measure.'[12]

The Mounties were confident about their ability to pre-empt sabotage, not least because they saw a number of their wartime duties dovetailing together as preventive measures. As will be described shortly, they had prepared extensive lists of potentially troublesome 'enemy aliens' who were quickly swept up and moved to detention camps. Also, with the close cooperation of employers, they began security screening of employees in defence-related industries, with special attention to workers of German or Italian origin with known Nazi or Fascist sympathies. Prevention worked, or so it seemed. Of course, there was little way of knowing whether planned sabotage had in fact been pre-empted by these measures, or if the threat had been exaggerated. So far as the Mounties and the government were concerned, it was a case of better safe than sorry.

Nor did the force shrink from using the sabotage threat as a justification for its extension of security-screening measures, including fingerprinting, especially when a 'fifth-column' panic swept the country after the fall of France in the spring of 1940.[13] There is always an ambiguity in how police use crime statistics: they are happy to show that they have been doing an effective job of containment, but reluctant to show too much effectiveness, lest their political masters decide to reduce the resources allocated to countering the threat. The wartime sabotage threat proved doubly useful to the Mounties: they demonstrated value for money while keeping the threat simmering on the front burner. In one instance, that of the Japanese Canadians, as we shall see, Mountie realism failed to meet the lurid expectations of a sabotage threat entertained by both government and public and they were in effect taken off the case – probably to their quiet relief. Otherwise, counter-sabotage offered the Mounties a good run, unlike counter-espionage and counter-subversion, which were to prove more troublesome.

Covering the Wartime Labour Front

Trade-union activity continued to be a major source of concern for the security service, and, as always, Communists or suspected Communists in unions attracted much of the attention. In wartime, strikes – always a target for close surveillance even in more peaceful times – now became the focus for concern over sabotage of the war effort. So long as the Communists were opposed to the war, the potential for damage to the war effort from agitation among disaffected workers was obvious. After the June 1941 Nazi invasion of the USSR and the overnight conversion of Communists into apostles of national unity in the struggle against Fascism, the automatic identification of Red unionists as saboteurs became more dubious. Nevertheless, the security service was expected to maintain a watching brief on any strike in the country that was of significant size and duration, especially if connected to war production. The *Annual Reports* of the Intelligence Section to the director of the CIB for the war years, for example, devote a considerable amount of space to detailed description and interpretation of events surrounding 'industrial unrest.' Similarly, the *Intelligence Bulletins* circulated within the service were extremely attentive to labour matters, of which they tried to keep divisional officers informed.

It would be wrong to leave the impression that the presence of Communists in unions made the Mounties indiscriminately anti-labour as such. They occasionally bristled when they gained the impression that employers were trying to use them in unfair ways against unions.[14] They were generally careful to distinguish between Reds and more acceptable trade unionists, the latter category including social-democratic supporters of the CCF. After the USSR became an ally, they somewhat grudgingly acknowledged, among themselves at least, that the 'No Strike' and 'Win the War' pledges encouraged by Communist leaders made even Communists good industrial citizens, at least until Hitler was defeated. Specific reports on strikes most often concluded with an indication that the strikers had comported themselves in a peaceful and orderly fashion. Sometimes, the activity of politically dangerous agitators was noted, but, given the rigorous structure of wartime controls, these reports usually concluded with indications of successful criminal action taken against the offending persons by local police or by the RCMP itself. Although labour unions, or at least strikes, were a preoccupation of the Intelligence Section, they were by no means an obsession.

Counter-Espionage: Lost in the Wilderness of Mirrors

The war introduced the Mounties to the shadowy world of espionage and counter-espionage. Alluring but treacherous, the game of spy and counterspy was one for players of experience, patience, and devious intelligence. Canada did not send its own spies abroad – although the Examination Unit of the Department of External Affairs did intercept and decode enemy signals intelligence[15] – but the security service was responsible for countering enemy espionage operations on Canadian soil. This responsibility eventually confronted the very inexperienced Mounties with the intellectually taxing requirements of counter-intelligence, an arcane game where agents become double agents and enemy espionage is turned back upon its perpetrators. The British, with long experience and skilful tradecraft, developed the celebrated 'Double Cross' system whereby Abwehr (German military intelligence) spies were detected and 'turned,' to the extent that British counter-intelligence, in the words of one British participant, 'actively ran and controlled the German espionage system in [Britain].'[16] The idea of the double cross appealed to the Mounties, who had the opportunity in 1942–3 to try their own hand at it – with disappointing results.

In November 1942 an Abwehr agent was landed by U-boat on the Quebec coast. Detected almost immediately and arrested by the RCMP, the agent confessed and ostensibly agreed to become a double agent, codenamed *Watchdog*. The officer in charge was Clifford Harvison (later a commissioner of the force after the war). Harvison in his memoirs[17] bragged about a successful operation, but the truth seems different. Two Canadian historians quote an MI5 Double Cross expert as recalling that *Watchdog* 'made a monkey out of Harvison.'[18] More recently, Canadian journalist Dean Beeby has written an exhaustive and entertaining treatment of the entire affair based on extensive documentation released under the Access to Information Act.[19] Beeby demolishes Harvison's account, painting instead a picture of the Mounties as a police force with limited understanding of the intricacies of the spy world.

Harvison's idea was simple: with *Watchdog* as mouthpiece, the Mounties set themselves up in business with a transmitter beamed to Hamburg. Harvison's main notion was to catch further agents scheduled to land in Canada: a classic police concept of how to use an informant but not one attuned to the Machiavellian intricacies of the counter-intelligence game. While MI5 sent one of their men, Cyril Mills, to direct the operation, he was unable to devote himself full time to supervision, given a number of other duties to perform in Canada and the United States. Through inexperience and inattention, the *Watchdog* operation went sour. Perhaps the German never intended to act as a double agent and was able to warn his Nazi handlers, or perhaps a more powerful transmitter used by the Mounties gave the game away. In any event, *Watchdog* eventually had to be transported to a British prison camp, with Harvison himself as escort. The Mountie was then sent for further training with Special Branch. Beeby concludes with a cutting remark about RCMP rigidity: 'Like the FBI, the Mounties were imbued with the policing ethos that was inappropriate for the gossamer games of espionage. British intelligence had moved beyond mere counter-espionage to the heights of strategic deception, thanks in part to the wartime recruitment of supple minds from law, business, journalism and academia. In contrast, Mountie counter-intelligence continued to be run by cops trained to catch crooks.'[20] This may not be entirely fair: the Mounties were on their own in devising the initial stages of the *Watchdog* operation, and the British had no interest in encouraging their colonial cousins to get on board their highly prized system. However, two other German agents landed in Canada were not converted to Allied use in deception. The 'only successful double-cross operation in Canada' was entirely fictitious – an invention of MI5 (appropriately codenamed *Moonbeam*!) was 'notionally' transferred to Canada to the evident enthusiasm of the gullible Abwehr.[21]

There was another instance of foreign espionage in which Canadians showed greater finesse. A Spanish press officer had been detected in pro-German espionage activity by MI6. The same official later turned up in North America where he attempted to organize another spy network among Spanish journalists and diplomats on behalf of Japan. He was flagged by MI6 for observation, and the RCMP and FBI alerted. This led to an incident in 1943. The Spanish consul general in Vancouver, Fernando de Kobbé Chinchilla, was declared persona non grata for spying on behalf of the Japanese. The RCMP had intercepted cash payments and espionage instructions and paraphernalia for the consul and had acquired evidence that he was using the Spanish diplomatic pouch to send his replies.[22] The consul was quietly returned to Spain. Evidence of the spying was then passed to the British to be used against Spain. As Norman Robertson of External Affairs noted in a memorandum to the prime minister, the information would allow the Allies 'to put the screws' to Franco: 'In the present phase of the European political situation, the threat of exposure of Spanish collusion with the Axis may be a very useful lever in securing further concession from Spain, or if this course seems more desirable, [it] could be used to discredit the present dictatorial regime entirely.'[23] External Affairs officer Tommy Stone (who specialized in intelligence matters) added a note that 'the implied threat of a most disagreeable public scandal might result in a general clean-up of the anti-United Nations activities in the Spanish foreign service.'[24]

In the case of the Spanish consul, it was External Affairs, in consultation with the allies, who guided the RCMP to an appropriate way of handling counter-espionage. With *Watchdog*, the Mounties flunked their own entry test into the spying big leagues. This was hardly surprising. Little in their background as a prairie police force chasing down horse thieves and controlling Saturday night drunks had prepared them for the wilderness of mirrors that is international espionage. They would have to learn, and fast: the Gouzenko spy affair of 1945–6 would soon show that the war was only a prelude to a prolonged era of international competition in which intelligence and counter-intelligence would be leading tools of national policy.

'Lock 'Em up and Throw away the Key': The Mounties and Internments

Nothing in the wartime experience has led to more notoriety for the RCMP security service than the internment of various people under the DOCR. Depriving people of their liberty without the normal safeguards of charges under the Criminal Code, legal counsel, habeas corpus, and a 'day in court' – all possible to some degree under the draconian provisions of the DOCR that put the safety of the state first – was bound to raise resentments on the part of those at the receiving end. Internment of unpopular minorities was widely applauded at the time by the majority. This only deepened the anxieties of affected minorities, especially in retrospect when a new era of post-war multiculturalism spurred feelings of ethnic victimization that could not have been openly articulated during the war itself. The Japanese Canadian community has been offered an official apology by the Canadian government for the forcible relocation and confinement of the entire Japanese population of the Pacific coast and the confiscation of their property. Complaints have been heard about the internment of Canadians of Italian origin,[25] and scholarly arguments have also been made about the efficacy of the internments of German Canadians.[26] In other cases where ethnicity was replaced by ideology or religion as grounds for internment, complaints of serious injustice have also been sounded.[27]

The Mounties were the agents of the state in this matter as in others. The commissioner of the RCMP was appointed registrar general of enemy aliens under the authority of the DOCR. By March 1940, 16,000 'enemy aliens' (Canadian residents of German birth not British subjects by 1922) had been registered through a special branch of the RCMP set up for this purpose.[28] The Mounties were expected to gather intelligence on subversive activities carried out by groups banned under the DOCR by the cabinet, to prepare lists of persons associated with groups designated for internment, and to take such persons into detention when their names were approved by an advisory internment committee of senior government officials. Under an order-in-council of 4 June 1940, RCMP officers were made justices of the peace for the purpose of issuing search warrants regarding illegal organizations. As William Kaplan explains, 'the effect of the new regulation was that any time a RCMP officer wished to search any premises all he had to do was prepare in his own hand an order giving him the authority to enter and search for any reason, or no reason.'[29]

The actual conduct and conditions of internment were not the RCMP's responsibility. The instance of apparent ethnic victimization that has gained most attention – that of the Japanese relocations – was actually outside the internment program as such; ironically, the RCMP were taken off this case precisely because their advice was *not* alarmist about the supposed threat of a Japanese fifth column. Nor were the RCMP particularly hawkish about the threat posed by German and Italian Canadians, despite well-founded concerns about Nazi and Fascist activists among their ranks.[30] However, another group that drew unwelcome attention because of their pacifism and unconventional social customs, the Mennonites (of largely German extraction), were viewed with some sensitivity by the Mounties.[31]

When ethnicity was mixed with left-wing ideology, it was a different story. The Mounties, in keeping with the always dominant anti-Communism of the security service, were implacable in pursuit of pro-Communist Ukrainians, Red Finns, and other ethnic associations of leftist bent. While able to conceive of the notion that most Canadians of German, Italian, and Japanese origins were probably loyal and law-abiding, especially if treated fairly, and firmly distinguished from the potentially disloyal minority of activist troublemakers, the Mounties showed few signs of sympathy for even rank-and-file members of

leftist ethnic associations. One of the groups that did suffer from internments and from property seizures was the Ukrainian Labour Farmer
Temple Association, which had its string of cultural centres across the
country closed and its assets disposed of. The Mounties not only kept
close scrutiny of the ULFTA but invariably interpreted the words and
behaviour of its officers in the worst possible light.[32]

Close to a hundred Communists or those associated with Communism according to the dossiers of the security service were interned in
the Hull Gaol just across the Ottawa River from Parliament Hill. Even
after the USSR entered the war, many of the Communist internees were
kept behind prison bars for close to another year. In this and in the
maintenance of the ban on the Communist Party throughout the war
which will be discussed later, the RCMP were not simply silent agents
but active lobbyists within government against any legitimation of the
Communists. Yet, when it came to drawing up the 'particulars,' as the
official charges against the internees were called, the security service,
which would have contributed the bulk of the evidence, was not always
very precise or even credible. Ludicrous particulars in the case of individual Communists (that X had attended a civil liberties meeting, or
that Y 'associated' with Z, who associated with Y, thus demonstrating
a conspiracy) eventually drew unfavourable press attention. One Communist internee was even charged with contesting the constitutionality
of the notorious Quebec Padlock Law! Despite detailed knowledge of
who was in the party, amassed from undercover sources, evidence of
actual treasonous or even illegal behaviour by individual Communists
seemed hard to come by. Perhaps there was no such evidence, despite
ideological rhetoric that the Mounties no doubt found seditious. Or
perhaps what evidence there was would have pointed to secret sources
the Mounties had no wish to disclose, nor any need, given the expan-
sively draconian scope of the DOCR.

The Mounties did appear to play a hands-on role with regard to surveillance of one group that suffered considerable damage at the hands
of the Canadian state in wartime. The Jehovah's Witnesses were an
unpopular religious sect whose constant proselytizing irritated mainstream religious sentiment, especially in Catholic Quebec, where they
were a perennial target for repressive actions by Maurice Duplessis's
Union Nationale governments. As conscientious objectors, their refusal
to serve in the Armed Forces and to offer symbolic signs of allegiance,
such as singing the national anthem, made them objects of wartime
suspicion. During the height of the 1940 fifth-column scare, the RCMP

advised the government to ban the sect officially, on grounds of subversion, because of what it alleged were its links to Nazism. The advice was acted upon, but Sergeant Leopold – in charge of the dossier – advised against mass internment, in favour of criminal prosecutions. The commissioner of the RCMP publicly castigated sect members as 'active enemies of Christianity and Democracy.' The security service was by 1941 devoting 'endless time to tracking them, second only to the Communist Party of Canada.' Kaplan remarks that the force was 'way out of its depth' and cites its work on the Witnesses as evidence of 'incompetence and stupidity.' By the late fall of 1941, RCMP interest in the sect had begun to wane, and by 1943 they had virtually given up trying to find evidence of disloyal activity among the Witnesses.[33]

This leads to the major criticism made of the RCMP in its relation to minorities: that the force lacked intelligence resources of sufficient quality to properly identify and isolate the small minority of actively disloyal agents of the Axis powers from the wider ethnic communities in which they were hiding. Some critics have gone so far as to deny the very existence of enemy agents. The result is that, in the eyes of these critics, innocent persons were rounded up and interned on the basis of their ethnicity alone: thus, critics argue, the RCMP and the Canadian state in effect abused minorities in the name of WASP hegemony, that internments were a case of 'ethnicity on trial.' The security service was certainly aware of its deficiencies with regard to the Japanese community. In its internal *Annual Report* for 1941–2, the Intelligence Section conceded that surveillance of the community was 'maintained only with difficulty, as due to racial and physical dissimilarities, our sources of contact are limited.'[34] Yet similar arguments regarding the German and Italian communities do not stand up to close scrutiny.

For one thing, the security service did generally possess adequate language facilities to watch political developments in these communities. For another, its surveillance of pro-Nazi and pro-Fascist activities had well predated the war. In fact, it had been acting closely with Norman Robertson and other senior civil servants from the spring of 1938 to monitor such activities. J.L. Granatstein describes this as a 'desultory process of planning' and a 'belated effort' and implies that Robertson had to do some of the Mounties' intelligence work for them. No doubt Robertson, who semi-humorously described his role to his parents as a 'one man *Cheka* or *Gestapo* ... civilian commissar with the RCMP,' did marshal some useful intelligence (including information on Fascists quietly acquired from Communist, and later convicted Soviet spy, Fred

Rose).[35] Yet an RCMP intelligence document on Italian Fascist activities in Canada dated as early as November 1937 offers a fairly impressive overview of how the Mussolini government was organizing pro-Fascist fronts – fifty-eight pages replete with names and details, with special attention to the methods whereby the Italian regime exercised control over Italians living abroad.[36]

By the time Italy and Canada went to war, the Mounties were well prepared. According to an internal RCMP memorandum, 95 per cent of the Italian Fascists were 'known to us': 'We have complete files and enough evidence to warrant their immediate arrest.'[37] As Michelle Mc-Bride, author of a well-documented thesis on the internment process, puts it: 'Essentially, in the Italian communities, the Canadian government interned those who[m] the Italian community told them to arrest.'[38] A crucial point was to draw the line between leaders and the rank-and-file followers. The Registration of Enemy Aliens was a key surveillance tool. Fingerprinted, the dangerous could be detained while the 'sheep,' in the words of a Justice Department official, could be 'kept track of.'[39] Once Canada was at war with Italy, the DOCR permitted the seizure of documents that pointed police towards further arrests.

It is hard to square this account with the image of a force too ill-informed to finger those likely to cause trouble or potentially vulnerable to Mussolini's agents. Indeed, despite retroactive protestations of innocence, it does seem that most of those rounded up in 1940 were indeed linked to prior pro-Fascist activities, and did thus constitute prima facie threats to national security in a war in which Italy was an enemy state.[40]

Similar points could be made with regard to pro-Nazi activity among Canadians of German background, although the latter community was less concentrated and more dispersed than the Italians. Robert H. Keyserlingk indicts the RCMP for interning farmers and workers, whom he assumes were unlikely to be effective agents of Nazi sabotage or subversion. Yet he admits that almost all of those who were swept up in lightning police raids before dawn on 4 September 1939 (prior to Canada's official entry into the war) were in fact members of pro-Nazi organizations. Further, while Keyserlingk derides the arguments of the RCMP that such action broke the back of potential Nazi subversion of the war effort,[41] he assumes, along with other critics, that because little or no such activity was ever uncovered, no threat existed in the first place. It is surely equally reasonable to conclude that prompt action had pre-empted such activity by removing those whose previous links with pro-Nazi or pro-Fascist organizations would make them the nucleus of any enemy-directed plots. After all, Nazism and Fascism were racial ideologies that claimed the loyalties of 'blood brothers' across the seas.

Although the numbers interned swelled as a result of the fifth-column scare in 1940, releases speeded up in subsequent years. The internments were more remarkable for their relative selectivity than for putting 'ethnicity on trial,' striking not at the ethnic communities in general but at the ideologically suspect minority – in stark contrast to the events of 1914–18.[42] The Japanese experience is, of course, a notorious exception, since this community was indeed severely penalized on the basis of their ethnicity, but, again, the RCMP played no active role in that sorry tale. Where they were directly involved, the RCMP might actually be given some credit for the relative selectivity the state did demonstrate.

Gearing up the Panopticon:
Security Screening of Civil Servants

The war provided a major push towards another role for the security service that would prove of lasting importance, both for the service itself and for Canadian society: security screening of public employees. The notion that the state should have some means of testing the reliability – or somewhat more controversially, the loyalty – of its employees was, especially in the emergency conditions of wartime, unexceptionable. The growth of a modern state bureaucracy presented challenges never faced by the relatively small, patronage-dominated civil service of the nineteenth century. Pressures generated by the First World War had sparked the introduction of the merit system of selection and advancement to the Canadian public service. The Second World War force-fed the growth of an unprecedentedly large, increasingly specialized bureaucratic apparatus, with many bureaucrats necessarily privy to 'secrets of state' (an expansive enough concept even in peacetime Canada but even more comprehensive in wartime). Unlike the patronage appointments of the past, politicians could no longer vouch for the loyalty and reliability of individual applicants. Some more generalized and institutionalized system was required to screen applicants and eliminate, or at least reduce, the numbers of those who presented potential risks to the security of the state. Hence, the rudiments of a screening system that began to appear in the 1930s took on greater scope and more definite shape during the war, and finally culminated in the late 1940s in a formalized system deeply embedded in the practices of government, where it remains in modified form today.

From the start, it was the security service that operated the system, devised and applied the basic criteria, and kept the ever more voluminous files that accumulated as a result. Indeed, security screening became one of the central bureaucratic raisons d'être of the security service. More than that, it was also a crucial information link to any number of other functions, with data matched with that in the espionage, terrorism, and subversion dossiers.

That the history of the security screening system should be inextricable from the history of the security service is no accident. Simplemindedly, a screening system might be taken to be politically neutral in the same way that, say, screening for infectious diseases is neutral. The analogy, however, is entirely misleading. Criteria for reliability of civil servants are, and always have been, political – not in the older patronage sense of partisanship, but in the ideological sense. Bureaucrats might, in the privacy of their own homes and their own thoughts, be Liberal or Tory or CCF or Social Credit, or apolitical. They could not, even in private, uphold 'alien' ideologies, like Fascism, Nazism, anarchism, and, especially, Communism, for these were associations that were *risky*. The people associated with such ideas were dangerous to the state, because they were deemed to hold a higher loyalty to the regimes that embodied these ideologies: Hitler's Germany, Mussolini's Italy, or Stalin's USSR. They might be spies; they might seek to overthrow or undermine their own state in the interests of these powers.

Such suspicions might, of course, be well founded. In assessing such risks, was it not prudent, as governments have always insisted, that doubts about reliability be resolved in favour of the state? In wartime conditions, such arguments were forceful indeed. But an important point should be kept in mind. The criterion for assessing risk being entirely political/ideological, significant power was being granted to the state to define arbitrarily the limits of legitimate political expression in the society. The assignment of the security service to the task of screening, even in a context of general direction by an elected government, meant that considerable discretion in defining legitimacy and illegitimacy was being vested in what were, after all, secret police. Screening necessarily involved the most intrusive penetration of the private lives of its subjects: information was gathered and filed concerning their beliefs and those of their families, their books, newspapers, and magazines, their friends, their clubs and associations, the conduct of their civic obligations, their behaviour as citizens. Thus, if the *text* of the screening system was the legitimate protection of the state, the *subtext* was the political policing of Canadian society.

Given the deeply ingrained anti-Communism of the Mountie mind, it comes as no surprise that the security service put more of its energies into detecting 'Communists' than the apparently more immediate threat of those whose ideological allegiances were to Berlin and Rome rather than Moscow. Nor is it surprising that the commissioner of the RCMP should make a highly publicized public statement warning that Reds posed a greater threat to national security than pro-Nazis, even in a war against Fascism.[43] Privately, Mountie intelligence estimated the numbers of Canadians open to Communist influence in the mid-six-figure range.[44] Meanwhile, the security service was quietly applying these political criteria through the screening system.

This double identity of text and subtext, with its attendant ambiguities, surrounded the introduction of security screening with a furtive air of things done in the shadows. Larry Hannant has brought this deliberately obscured process into the light of historical analysis.[45] One of the most significant facts unearthed by Hannant is that the screening process, begun in the 1930s, was undertaken by the RCMP without a specific cabinet directive. This did not mean that the Mounties were acting on their own, but it did mean that no cabinet guidelines or directions existed as to criteria and procedures. Nor was there any mechanism for ongoing cabinet supervision. The police were in effect the last word on the loyalty of public employees. During the war this authority was extended to the Armed Forces, to plants engaged in war work (where company security officers, many ex-Mounties, expanded the RCMP intelligence network into the private sector), and even to Great Lakes shipping, spurred by the presence of the Communist-led Canadian Seamen's Union (CSU). Its reach within the civil service proper was extended to cover virtually all departments and agencies, with the significant exceptions of External Affairs and the Prime Minister's Office, where the mandarins' old-boy snobbery threw up defences not available to less exalted mortals. Tens of thousands of Canadians were now routinely subject to the vetting of the political police. In the late stages of the war, the arrival in Canada of refugees, mainly Jewish, from liberated Europe led to new security concerns: the RCMP were called in to screen the newcomers (mainly for Communist links), thus prefiguring what was to be a huge post-war growth industry in security screening of immigration and citizenship applications.[46]

There is no question that the Mounties were eager to expand this role. As Hannant points out, they were opportunistic in gaining approval for extensions of the system. Singularly unimpressed with the fifth-column panic in the spring of 1940, they were nevertheless prepared to seize on public hysteria to justify widening the scope of security screening. Moreover, they readily capitalized on new technologies of surveillance to 'sell' their services as screeners. Most controversially, this involved mass fingerprinting of applicants and employees, along with an auto-mated system for fingerprint identification – a practice they success-fully introduced even though, as they were uneasily aware, they had no specific authority to do so. Although there was resistance to what many considered an unacceptable intrusion into personal privacy (fin-gerprinting carried with it a distinct aura of implied criminality), the RCMP grasped the opportunity to initiate an invaluable mechanism of surveillance that might eventually be extended to the society as a whole. Curiously, there was no credible case for the use of fingerprint records to identify *political* security risks, even if it did address a lesser concern for screening out persons with criminal records. Yet it seems the Mounties were able to use their security role to advance techno-logical innovation in police surveillance and vice versa: a happy coinci-dence for a force that, like its American counterpart, the FBI, combined policing and security functions within the same organization.

Hannant's exhaustive account of the wartime security-screening ex-perience demonstrates convincingly that the Mounties developed pro-fessional expertise in the area. The image often advanced by critics of incompetence does not stand up to closer scrutiny: 'While the RCMP was certainly inexperienced and probably incompetent in some aspects of the security intelligence field – especially counter-espionage – quite the opposite verdict must be rendered in the area of security screen-ing.'[47] Evidence of their professionalism can be glimpsed in their ef-ficient management of information about the system. Assisted by the secrecy in which screening was shrouded, the Mounties strove, with great success, to seal the process hermetically from publicity, whether from Parliament, press, or public. The reach of their surveillance was being extended into private-sector workplaces, as well as into sections of the public sector never previously scrutinized so closely. Yet this reach was largely one-way: the Mounties brought more institutions and persons into greater transparency before their inquisitive gaze, while maintaining the opaqueness of their own operations to the eyes of out-siders – including their fellow public servants.

This was precisely the nineteenth-century dream of Jeremy Bentham in his celebrated Panopticon – the concept of a prison in which each prisoner is subject, or believes himself to be subject, at all times to the intrusive one-way gaze of the warders.[48] The fact that it was responsibility not of the RCMP but of the employer, whether government department or private company, to actually remove a security risk from employment, that is, to exercise direct coercion, is precisely in line with the panoptic logic. The RCMP merely watched, gathered information, and provided advice, silently and in the shadows. The effect was to induce political discipline through pervasive, diffuse fear of the consequences of risky ideas, friends, or associations. Totalitarian states enforced political discipline through the cruder forms of police state coercion. In fighting the Nazi state, Canada was also groping towards a more effective, non-coercive, form of discipline. The RCMP proved to be able students of the new science of political surveillance.

The Doorway to a Wider World

One of the biggest changes war brought to the Mounties was the door that opened on a wider world. That door had been partially open before the war, with linkages established with MI5 in Britain and the FBI south of the border. But global war brought a far more intense level of international liaison, with formal lines of cooperation and more face-to-face working relationships with colleagues from abroad. In retrospect it is now clear that 1939–45 represented some early steps in the long-term process of the globalization of policing and security.

The *Watchdog* fiasco did have one important implication for the RCMP's role in the world of intelligence. The arrival of Cyril Mills from MI5 proved to be a significant step in the tightening linkage of the RCMP to the British and American counter-intelligence network. Mills stayed on in Ottawa for the duration of the war and was employed as MI5's point man in liaison with Washington, to which he made frequent trips.

There is a rather complicated background to the growing continental connection in wartime security and intelligence, involving two competing players in Washington (J. Edgar Hoover of the FBI and 'Wild' Bill Donovan, who fashioned the Office of Strategic Services [OSS], the first U.S. civilian intelligence agency to operate abroad), as well as William Stephenson, the Canadian whose British Security Coordination was the initial point of contact between the British government and the Americans on North American intelligence matters. Stephenson, whose role was much later magnified out of all proportion by his journalist/biographer William Stevenson and by his own retroactive efforts at self-promotion, was in fact an important figure, especially during the period prior to America's entry into the war, when his BSC worked at identifying and counteracting pro-Nazi activities in the Western hemisphere as well as fostering pro-British attitudes in American opinion.[49] In the spring of 1940, Hoover told an Interdepartmental Intelligence Conference (combining representatives of the U.S. civilian and military security and intelligence units then operating) that 'the British and Canadian intelligence services in the United States appear to be particularly well organized and that these services have been furnishing considerable information to the FBI.'[50] It is not clear just what Hoover had in mind with his reference to 'Canadian intelligence services,' although he may have elided Canadian and British in his mind, given Stephenson's Canadian nationality and the latter's propensity to recruit Canadians for the BSC staff in the no doubt well-founded belief that they could operate in the United States less obtrusively than Englishmen. He may also have been referring to the RCMP. As Thomas Troy points out, Canada was strategically 'vital': 'Halifax was a major starting point of convoys across the Atlantic. Canadian intelligence on the identification and movement of known and suspected spies, saboteurs and couriers, and disaffected workers, sailors, cargo handlers, and others was essential to the establishment of a pool of intelligence without which the security job could not be done.'[51]

With American entry into the war, the United States was less disposed to tolerate the operations of even friendly foreign intelligence on its shores, and moved to take full charge of its own security and intelligence affairs. The question was: Who would control domestic security operations? Donovan wanted to become coordinator of information in the Western hemisphere, working with the State Department, the BSC, and the Canadians. Agreement in principle was reached on stationing Donovan's representatives at 'certain key points' in Canada so as to facilitate access to vital information. Hoover was brought in to talk about liaison with RCMP. Donovan recommended a joint intelligence committee of representatives from the departments of State, War, Navy, and Justice; his own Office for Coordination of Information; and Canada's Department of External Affairs. To be located in Washington, its 'primary concern' would be the defence of the United States. Hoover was outraged and was able to obtain a presidential directive on 29 December 1941 that reaffirmed the responsibility of the FBI to operate its Special Intelligence Service in Canada, Mexico, and Latin America and that also directed all other intelligence agencies to clear 'any intelligence work' in these areas with the Bureau. He was authorized and instructed to convene meetings of the various hemispheric intelligence agencies to coordinate intelligence activity.

Hoover could no longer tolerate Stephenson; with his bureaucratic triumph over Donovan on jurisdiction in the Western hemisphere, the BSC's days were numbered.[52] The BSC continued to carry out certain duties, especially vetting of personnel, on behalf of MI5 in the United States, but Mills was the major official contact with Hoover of the FBI on counter-espionage matters.[53] This international dimension was to become highly important in the handling of the Gouzenko affair in 1945–6. Although Mills had by this time returned to London, his place in liaison was taken by Peter Dwyer, an MI6 officer stationed in Washington who later came to Ottawa as the leading civilian official coordinating Canadian security intelligence and counter-espionage operations in the 1950s.

Before his organization was marginalized at Hoover's insistence, Stephenson drew upon RCMP assistance, particularly the temporary loan of personnel, including the head of the Records Branch seconded as a 'filing expert.' Another expert who left the RCMP to take up a permanent post with the BSC in the spring of 1941 was Superintendent Ernest W. Bavin, not, as we have pointed out, on the best of terms with Commissioner Wood. Nonetheless, in his new position, Bavin was still of use to the Mounties, since he 'discovered and communicated to the Force material of interest in BSC files.'[54] Bavin also accompanied an MI5 mission to Canada in the summer of 1941 that reviewed security controls in effect for the Dominion, as indicated earlier.[55]

On the matter of internal security, as opposed to counter-espionage, where they were more inexperienced, the RCMP did bring some expertise of their own to international liaison. This was particularly true in their relations with their counterparts to the south. Since Canada was already at war for more than two years before Pearl Harbor rudely forced American participation, the RCMP had some backlog of experience in running the domestic side of a military conflict that was of interest to the FBI. Direct if intermittent liaison between the two forces had begun in the late 1930s. Hoover visited Ottawa in late 1940, more than a year before the United States was drawn into the war, and conferred with the RCMP director of criminal intelligence. The agenda was 'almost entirely devoted to security tasks' – including espionage, Nazi fifth columnists operating out of the United States with designs on Canada, the reliability of Japanese residents, subversive American organizations, and 'what to do about hundreds of Canadian and thousands of American passports known to be in the hands of Moscow.'[56]

Following Pearl Harbor, liaison became formalized and permanent. In April 1942 Assistant Commissioner W.V.M.B. Bruce was posted to Washington as the first regular liaison officer; a U.S. counterpart was established in Ottawa. That August, the Mounties sent representation to a Western Hemisphere Intelligence Conference, where guidelines for liaison were agreed upon. The officers were to interpret the policies of the two forces to each other, and advise on the usefulness of particular investigations. To facilitate this, full mutual access to security files and to senior personnel was granted. A cipher machine handled encrypted communication between the two offices. The need for further hemispheric security conferences was obviated by this immediate, direct, and secure link.

It is apparent that throughout the rest of the war a great deal of information and advice passed back and forth between the FBI and the RCMP and an unprecedentedly high degree of policy coordination was achieved. There were specific matters that demanded a close working arrangement, such as the Alaska Highway and Canol pipeline megaprojects, which passed through Canadian territory, and required closely coordinated security arrangements in wartime conditions. There was also considerable exchange of technical expertise and technology with regard to security screening and fingerprinting. Despite the disparity in the size of the two countries, and in the resources of the two police forces, these exchanges were by no means one-way. The Americans understood that in some areas they had things to learn from the Mounties, such as in matters of maintaining security around important public facilities and industrial plants. Nor did American advice and influence sweep across the border unchecked or unmodified. Differences in the political institutions and the political culture of the two countries were reflected in the thinking and practices of their respective security agencies. The Mounties took some things from the FBI but not others, and some things they did take were modified for the Canadian environment. For instance, the FBI diffused information from its files widely to local police forces and even to private industries involved in war work. Despite some pressures from Canadian companies to do likewise, the RCMP preferred to keep much closer control over its security files. Similarly, the RCMP resisted the FBI practice of planting undercover agents directly in war factories, preferring informal watch-dog units set up by internal factory security teams.[57] It was a different style of operation, and the Mounties generally maintained their own approach.

Hannant correctly identifies what he calls a 'myth of RCMP incompetence in security intelligence matters.'[58] As he makes quite clear, the details of FBI-RCMP wartime liaison demonstrate the flimsiness of the charge of incompetence. The FBI certainly did not appear to share in such a notion. The source of this myth seems to lie largely in the department of External Affairs and in particular in Norman Robertson, from where it has spread into academic interpretation, as in J.L. Granat-stein's biography of Robertson.[59] To be sure, External had some reason to doubt the Mounties' competence in counter-intelligence, but security intelligence was another matter.

There is a different interpretation possible of External's attitude, which rests more on inter-bureaucratic rivalry than on administrative competence. External plainly resented any establishment of direct liaison between the Mounties and the FBI unmediated by its own offices. The first hemispheric security conference had been coordinated through External, as protocol required. Shortly, however, External learned to its irritation and dismay that its offices were being bypassed. External asked the RCMP in October 1942 for copies of the minutes of the two conferences that had been held. Deputy Commissioner R.L. Cadiz indicated that the request would be referred to the FBI for consent to release. Robertson was livid, and fired back a blistering letter to Commissioner Wood. 'I cannot agree,' Robertson bluntly asserted, 'that the views of [Hoover and the FBI] should be solicited in this matter.' He added a short constitutional primer: 'The Secretary of State for External Affairs is responsible for the conduct of the international affairs of this country.' If the offending letter had already been sent, it should be promptly withdrawn. A chastened Cadiz recalled his communications with Washington, sent External copies of the minutes in question, and added that 'the error made in this connection is regretted.'[60] The issue resolved itself, although not to External's satisfaction, when formal international conferences were superseded by the direct liaison described earlier. In effect, External was cut out of the loop by this day-to-day institutionalization of international police cooperation.

Not surprisingly, External did not appreciate this development. Mandarins like Robertson tended to express their displeasure by looking down their noses at the Mounties and questioning their competence. Intuitively, the diplomats seemed to have understood that one aspect of their traditional prerogatives was slipping from their grasp. The kind of liaison established by the RCMP with the FBI in wartime (and, to an extent, the kind of relationship they had already established earlier with MI5 in Britain) presaged the international cooperation in security, intelligence, and policing that would occur in the post-war world. Supranational coordination in these fields has largely developed on a substate level, that is, directly between the relevant agencies in the cooperating countries, often with little notice or attention at the formal government-to-government level, and with little concern for diplomatic formalities. In forging its links with the FBI, the Mounties were in tune with the times, while External, for all its snobbish disdain for the 'Horsemen,' was fighting a rearguard action.

The Mounties Play Bureaucratic Politics

As the international-liaison story indicates, the Mounties were no slouches in getting their way in Ottawa's bureaucratic politics. Indeed, their international linkages were themselves ultimately to prove a very useful card in the Ottawa game, as we shall see in subsequent chapters. The war also gave them some training in how to form political alliances and to act as an effective lobby-from-within regarding policy decisions they saw as important. They did have some influential adversaries, not only in External Affairs but also in the Prime Minister's Office. Officials in the PMO, notably W.T. Turnbull and Jack Pickersgill, were scornful of John Leopold and the security service, sneering at their 'Reds-under-the-bed' mentality and questioning their competence. In 1942 Turnbull suggested to Prime Minister King that the RCMP harboured too many 'men like the notorious Sergeant Leopold, whose jobs would seem to depend on continuing to uncover Bolshevik plots.'[61]

There was no doubt that the Mounties remained deeply concerned about 'Bolshevik plots,' even during a war against Fascism, and this obsessive anti-Communism fostered a somewhat chilly attitude towards them in certain government circles at a time when Stalin was an ally against Hitler. For instance, the Intelligence Section's periodic *Security* or *Intelligence Bulletins* had been regularly distributed to senior government officials. Not everyone in the select circle of official Ottawa which received the *Bulletins* was impressed by their contents, or by the

RCMP's concept of intelligence. Henry Ferns was serving as a young official in Mackenzie King's office in the spring of 1940 when he came up against the face of Canadian intelligence. As Ferns later recollected:

> Political intelligence in the Canadian government was characterized by boneheaded stupidity. I was not alone in this opinion. A few weeks after I entered the Prime Minister's Office, an RCMP constable came to my room bearing a large brown envelope marked SECRET. He saluted and asked me to sign a receipt. This I did. With some awe I carried the envelope to Pickersgill and asked him what to do with this. Jack gave one of his loud guffaws, waved his hand with a flourish and said, 'That's the *Perils of Pauline*. Throw it in the file, but read it if you want a laugh.'
>
> I went back to my room and opened the envelope. Inside was another envelope together with a receipt returnable to the RCMP attesting to the fact that I was about to open the second envelope. Inside this envelope I found a mimeographed pamphlet bound in a green cover bearing the arms of the RCMP. About 80 per cent of the items were extracts from Canadian newspapers concerning the movements and utterances of Communists, supposed Communists, and various trade union officials. Some of the items I had already seen among the daily circulation of the Prime Minister's clipping service. There were a few items on various priests and pacifists, and nothing at all about various splinter groups in Quebec opposed to Canada's entry into the war. It was something of a mystery to me how the RCMP ever found the home-grown Fuhrer, Adrien Arcand, let alone arrested him. After reading this intelligence bulletin a few times I began to follow Pickersgill's advice. I simply 'threw it in the file.'[62]

Ferns went on to note that the discovery of Soviet espionage in wartime Ottawa came not through the counter-espionage activities of the RCMP but through the defection of the Soviet cypher clerk Igor Gouzenko in 1945. The RCMP, he suggests, were instead 'taught to see Communists at work wherever men and women assembled to talk about civil rights, trade union problems, poverty and peace.' Ferns was not an entirely neutral observer. He had himself become a Communist while studying at Cambridge in the 1930s amidst that famous generation of Cambridge Communists. He maintains that his party ties had dropped away before he took up his duties in the PMO, but he retained a certain distance from some of the conservative shibboleths of official Ottawa. Indeed, he was later driven out of the civil service and later yet out of Canada for his alleged left-wing sympathies.[63] But his doubts about RCMP 'intelligence' were shared by others in the PMO.

Jack Pickersgill had prepared an analysis of the *Intelligence Bulletin* for the prime minister in late November 1939. This was passed on to King a year later by James A. Gibson, another PMO official, with approval.[64] Pickersgill noted that in wartime 'the detection of espionage, of plans for sabotage, and of subversive activities is the most important aspect of intelligence work in connection with the maintenance of internal security.' Such work was 'presumably divided' between the RCMP and military intelligence. The latter reported no information to the prime minister. The RCMP, on the other hand, reported regularly through the *Intelligence Bulletin*. Pickersgill's analysis of a single issue of the *Bulletin*[65] revealed a number of serious deficiencies:

(1) an inability to distinguish between 'facts' and 'hearsay';
(2) an 'anti-Red complex' which has a striking resemblance to that of the notorious Dies Committee[66] in the United States, with the same tendency to label labour organizers, mild radicals, etc., as Communists. It may be noted, for example, that French Canadian Liberal candidate in a recent provincial by-election was described in one of the Bulletins (not the one analysed) as a member of a Communist-controlled organization;
(3) no discrimination between legitimate social and political criticism and subversive doctrine;
(4) an almost exclusive pre-occupation with so-called subversive organizations, and, even in this field, very little information about Nazis or Fascists;
(5) no evidence of any suspected sabotage or espionage;
(6) no suggestion that there is any co-ordination with the Military Intelligence, or with the Immigration authorities, or with the Department of External Affairs, or even with the Censorship.

It is evident that the police are attending and reporting on often completely harmless meetings, and spying on the daily activities of peaceful and law-abiding citizens. In itself this may not be very serious, although it would seem to be undesirable in a free country. It is, however, somewhat disturbing to discover that the police are setting themselves up as self-appointed censors of political opinion in the Community, especially when they regard the mildest expressions of liberal views as evidence of Communism.

What is more disturbing is the evidence of a total lack of capacity, education and training required for real intelligence work, and a failure to appreciate the direction from which serious danger may threaten us.

It may well be that there are Communists in Canada who are engaged in espionage or in planning sabotage, but they will presumably be working secretly and will obviously not be among the so-called 'agitators' who are sufficiently well-known. It is more likely that there are secret German agents in the country … From a casual reading of these 'Intelligence Bulletins' one would scarcely realize that Canada was at war with Germany; there is not the slightest hint that anything is being done in the way of intelligent and well-directed 'anti-espionage' work.

Pickersgill suggested the need for greater coordination and liaison between various government agencies with an interest in aspects of intelligence and security under the overall direction of an intelligence branch located in the Department of Justice, to which the RCMP would report. The civilian director of intelligence, 'with an adequate conception of the real function of intelligence work in war-time, could probably direct the energies of the police into channels which would enable them to contribute effectively to our internal security without creating public uneasiness about the development of a police-state.'[67]

It may have been the attitudes of prime ministerial advisers like Turnbull and Pickersgill, given a strong boost by the international situation, that led to a sudden change of policy with regard to the circulation of the *Intelligence Bulletins*. At the end of 1941 (a few months after the Nazi invasion of the USSR), all distribution beyond the RCMP security service itself came to a halt. Moreover, Mounties came around to offices where the *Bulletin* had previously been transmitted and removed all earlier editions dating back to the beginning of the war. Since documentary evidence is lacking on this decision, it remains unclear just what was behind it. Probably the government no longer found the regular anti-Communist litany of much interest. The Mounties went back to talking to themselves – if indeed, given the earlier testimony of Henry Ferns, the *Bulletin* had ever actually had much of an external readership. Intelligence is a product to be consumed, normally by the governments that employ intelligence agencies. The RCMP *Intelligence Bulletin* was a product consumed in-house.[68]

Yet one should not mistake the forces at play in the pressure cooker of wartime Ottawa. While the Mounties had their detractors, they also had natural, instinctive allies who shared their anxieties and readily consented to their definition of the real enemy. Britain was often cited by liberal Canadian officials as an example of relative tolerance of dissent, despite the close proximity of Britain to the Nazi threat.[69] Canada, far from the direct threat of invasion, was more jittery. During the 1940 fifth-column scare, many Canadians in influential positions seemed to panic and calls for repression of dissent were rampant. Nor did they die down entirely with the waning of the scare. Although some might sneer at the 'Perils of Pauline,' there was no gainsaying the fact that the RCMP expressed a mood which had far wider roots than in the police alone. Indeed, despite the existence of some critics with liberal reservations within the government, and despite Mackenzie King's private expressions of a liberal conscience in his diary, the King government in general and the Justice Department in particular strongly supported the Mounties.[70]

The best example of the political leverage that the Mounties could exercise involves the issue of the legalization of the Communist Party following the alliance with the USSR. A legal party at the war's outset, the party had been declared an unlawful association under the Defence of Canada Regulations. The Nazi invasion of the USSR created a new political situation of which some people within the government, including Lester Pearson, believed Ottawa should take advantage. If the Communists had been suddenly converted from opponents into advocates of the war, Pearson suggested, Ottawa should not allow its natural contempt for such hypocrisy to cloud its judgment. Why not use the Communists as allies of convenience, especially where they could be of particular use – as in trade unions where they had begun demanding no-strike pledges under a win-the-war-first philosophy?[71] Although certain observers claimed to have detected a strain of fellow-travelling naivety – or worse – in the officials who argued in this manner,[72] the Ottawa mandarins were under no illusions regarding the nature of the Stalinist state but were pragmatic realists who wished to take advantage of whatever opportunities presented themselves to push the war effort through to a successful conclusion.

The RCMP, however, had quite a different perspective on the question. The change in status of the Soviet Union did not convince the RCMP that any change was indicated in their long-standing attitude towards the Communists.[73] By December 1942, the *Intelligence Bulletin* was editorializing about the lies and hypocrisy of the Communists and justifying the continuing ban on the party.[74] In August 1944 the *Bulletin* greeted the news of the dissolution of the Comintern with the assertion (no doubt quite correct, it should be pointed out) that this meant absolutely nothing for the international reach of the Soviet Union through the agency of local Communist parties.[75]

Given these strongly held views, it is hardly surprising that the force opposed the public campaign to legalize the Communist Party as a friendly gesture towards Canada's Soviet ally, a campaign that led to a parliamentary committee recommendation to lift the ban. The ban was never lifted by cabinet. An examination of the pressures swirling around the government on this issue indicates that the RCMP found very crucial political allies in the form of King's Quebec ministers and his Quebec caucus, backed by the passionately anti-Communist Catholic Church, and the pro-business right-wing of the cabinet led by C.D. Howe.[76] The Mounties thus showed that they could successfully play bureaucratic politics on an issue that really mattered to them.

The fact that the Communists continued to operate under the guise of the Labour Progressive Party – and indeed under that name elected their first (and last) MP in the person of Fred Rose (later convicted of Soviet espionage) – might seem to indicate that the anti-Communist victory was a hollow one. But to the RCMP it was important that no overt legitimacy be granted the Communists, and the official ban on the party did give the Mounties a useful lever with which to control their public, if not their clandestine, activities. Moreover, the issue of the legalization of the party was above all one of symbolic politics. The Mounties, like their allies inside and outside government, took the symbolism of legitimacy seriously. And they won.

The Mounties' Good War

By and large, the security service had a good war. The Intelligence Section, which had started the war so hesitantly and reluctantly, strengthened its place and expanded its role. The Mounties may not have been very successful at counter-intelligence, but on internal security they showed considerable aptitude. They forged links with a powerful international ally in J. Edgar Hoover and his FBI, and they fought off the unwanted attentions of jealous bureaucratic rivals in Ottawa. They showed on an issue that mattered that they could win bureaucratic infights and could effectively line up external allies in the cause. With their role in security screening, they were establishing themselves in a strategic position in the development of a national security state that would emerge as a permanent feature of post-war Canada. They were able to take advantage of draconian wartime powers to greatly extend their surveillance of Canadian society; yet the undiminished lustre of the image of the Redcoats – and the popularity of the war against Hitler – left the Mounties largely untouched by any resentment of their more intrusive role in the political policing of Canadian society.

PART THREE

Cold War Canada

7

The Ice Age: Mounties on the Cold War Front Line, 1945–69

The Mounties' experience of war had been one of greatly increased responsibilities and powers. With the return of peace, the emergency wartime powers would disappear – although not immediately, as we shall see. But the responsibility for protecting national security against the threat of a hostile totalitarian power was recreated in peacetime. Only the name and ideology of the threatening power was different. The long-term challenge to the security service in the post-war era was to discharge its responsibilities effectively without the aid of emergency wartime powers. In fact, the RCMP was to be a central element in the construction of something never seen before in Canada: a peacetime national security state (or 'national *insecurity* state,' as it has been perhaps more accurately dubbed).[1]

The Great Ice Age

For Canada and the RCMP, the Cold War began behind the scenes with the defection of Igor Gouzenko from the Soviet Embassy in Ottawa in September 1945, and publicly with the revelation of the round-up of a number of suspected Soviet spies in February 1946. Of course, for the Mounties, there had always been a state of 'cold war' with Soviet Communism since the Russian Revolution of 1917, a war that had spread into Canada with the founding of the Canadian Communist Party in 1921. As this book has made clear, Communism had always been identified as the primary enemy of Canadian national security by the RCMP, even when Soviet Russia was a military ally from 1941 to 1945. The public mythology of the Cold War – the great bipolar contest for the soul of humanity, the life-and-death struggle for supremacy between irreconcilable ideologies and ways of life – did not teach the RCMP anything they did not already know. The official, historical Cold War (1946–7 to 1990) did, however, provide a national and global mirror for the Mounties that seemed to reflect back a faithful reproduction of their own instinctive anti-Communism. These years of Cold War, especially the first two decades, offered a kind of apotheosis of the essential RCMP philosophy. Chateaubriand once remarked of Lafayette that he had only one idea: 'Luckily for him, it was the century's idea too.'[2] Luckily for the Mounties, their one big idea was the idea, if not of the century, then at least of the half-century.

Sometime in the 1960s this sharp picture began to go out of focus, the world began sending back confusing signals, certitudes faltered. The following two decades were less reassuring, reflecting back an increasingly fragmented portrait of reality. Finally, at the close of the 1980s, the truly unthinkable happened: Communism and the Soviet Union collapsed and disappeared ignominiously from the stage of history. This left the security service with an embarrassment: What does one do when the darkness that defined one's own light is gone? Is this really the end of history? Or, more mundanely, was it the end of security intelligence and the need for political policing? To a security agency, outright victory over the forces of subversion and disorder they are sworn to combat might seem at first glance a pleasing reward for years of dedicated struggle. Yet, in another sense, nothing could be more alarming, since it could call into question the agency's own raison d'être.

We now know that bureaucratic survival instinct and an unexpected degree of intellectual flexibility would rescue the service from the downside of too complete a victory. New threats to security have replaced the old Red Menace. These developments will be the subject of later chapters. For now, we can examine the era of the Cold War in its purest form (1945 through the 1960s) in order to glimpse the security service's historical self-image in stark relief.

Igor Ex Machina: The Gouzenko Spy Affair

The Gouzenko affair of 1945–6[3] put Canada on a domestic Cold War footing even earlier than the United States or Britain. For the RCMP, which had always conceptualized the Communist threat primarily in terms of subversion and revolution, the revelation that the USSR had been carrying out extensive espionage in Canada during the very period of the Grand Alliance against the Axis came as both a minor embarrassment and an unexpected windfall. The damning documents that Gouzenko had stuffed inside his clothes before departing the Soviet Embassy building for the last time clearly demonstrated Soviet duplicity, as well as disloyalty and betrayal by Canadian agents and sources. They were also mildly embarrassing to the Mounties, who had not been able to detect Soviet spying at work in the nation's capital. The Mounties had already flunked their initial test in the world of counter-intelligence, the *Watchdog* fiasco (even if that failure had been largely covered up). And now it seemed that the very enemy they had always warned about, Soviet Russia, had been stealing Canadian secrets right under Mountie noses. Security screening had apparently not worked to detect and eliminate pro-Soviet civil servants and military personnel ready to betray the trust the country had placed in them.[4] Judgment should not be too harsh, however. Counter-espionage was a fairly new game for the Mounties. Moreover, even for experienced services with considerable resources and expertise, it is not at all uncommon to find that the greatest coups come not as a result of the counterspies' patient and painstaking efforts but as unanticipated 'walk-ins,' defectors who simply show up at the front door, as it were.

Any slight embarrassment was more than compensated for by the opportunities presented by Gouzenko's fortuitous arrival on the door-step. Above all, the picture Gouzenko and his documents painted of how Soviet espionage operated provided the crucial, persuasive link between the Mounties' ideological anti-Communism and the interests of the state. The military intelligence (GRU) network in which Gouzenko had been a modest cog targeted as potential sources and agents Canadians ideologically sympathetic to Moscow. The precise mechanism for recruitment was identified by the Kellock-Taschereau Royal Commission, both in its secret hearings and in its public report (much of the text written with skill and deliberate design by the leading anti-Communist Cold Warrior in External Affairs, Arnold Smith),[5] as Communist 'fronts' and Communist-led 'study groups.' There Canadians of leftist views in potentially useful government or military jobs were carefully recruited and gradually drawn by Communist talent spotters into passing on classified information to the Soviets. The commission focused relentlessly on one alleged 'front' organization, the Canadian Association of Scientific Workers (CAScW), which the security service had already penetrated and reported on well before Gouzenko's revelations.[6] The CAScW was quickly destroyed by this harsh public spotlight.

The close linkage between the Communist Party and Soviet espionage was dramatically highlighted by the trial and conviction for espionage of the only Communist elected under the party banner to the House of Commons, Fred Rose, and by the subsequent conviction of the party's national organizer, Sam Carr, on espionage-related charges. In brief, not only was Communism a *subversive* movement, as the Mounties had always strenuously maintained, but it led directly to *treason* against the state on behalf of what was now revealed to be not an ally but a hostile power, the USSR. The Gouzenko affair was the first to point to treason for ideological reasons, a notion that would become paradigmatic of the early Cold War, especially after the revelations of the Burgess-Maclean Cambridge spy ring in Britain. It thus made the case with utmost clarity that the struggle against Communism was the highest priority of the national interest – just as the Mounties had always maintained.

The timing and circumstances of the Gouzenko affair could not have been more propitious. Gouzenko's defection came just after the end of the war but before the formidable panoply of wartime emergency powers had been dismantled. Secret orders-in-council under the authority of the War Measures Act laid the groundwork for the extraordinary exercise of arbitrary state power and disregard for normal liberal-democratic safeguards of due process and individual rights that was to characterize the handling of the affair. After a lengthy period of debriefing in secret, during which time the RCMP had the chance to pursue Gouzenko's leads and watch the suspects, as well as consult with their British and American counterparts, they were given the go-ahead for a round-up on 16 February 1946, after a mysterious leak to the American media precipitated the need for action. Black-jacketed members of the anti-narcotics squad struck before dawn and swept up thirteen persons, along with their personal papers and effects. They were taken away to the Mountie barracks in suburban Ottawa, where they were held incommunicado, without legal counsel, without habeas corpus, and interrogated repeatedly under electric bulbs that blazed night and day. One of the detainees was greeted by Inspector Clifford Harvison, who exulted: 'We've tangled with you Reds before, and you have always screamed if we laid our hands on you, but this time, by God, we've got you!'[7] Indeed they had.

After exhaustive, and no doubt exhausting, interrogation by inspectors Harvison and M.E. Anthony, the thoroughly frightened and bewildered detainees were dragged before the Kafkaesque secret hearings of a royal commission, initially again without legal counsel and advice on their rights, to face aggressive questioning concerning their past behaviour, their friends and associates, and their motives. A weighty report was then published publicly naming over twenty Canadians as having acted as spies for Soviet Russia. Next, a series of criminal trials began (the most sensational being that of Communist MP Fred Rose) that kept the affair before the public for a number of years. As it turned out, only half of those charged were ever convicted of any of the variety of charges brought against them. As a rule, those who had cooperated with the RCMP and the commission were convicted on the strength of their own words; uncooperative witnesses went free. Some, including the RCMP, have drawn from this the inference that the restrictive rules of evidence in court had allowed manifestly guilty parties to escape. A more nuanced judgment is that the royal commission had exceeded the bounds of propriety in publicly naming persons as traitors concerning whom there was only circumstantial and insubstantial evidence, despite the extraordinary methods of investigation. Moreover, despite the lurid atmosphere whipped up by the media at the time, alleging the theft of 'atomic secrets,' the actual substance in terms of what the Soviets attained seems relatively minor league. This in fact is pretty much what Soviet government officials said at the time, when, obviously taken by surprise, they admitted the passage of some information but downplayed its significance.

The relative insignificance of the espionage, however, was not the point. Under the Official Secrets Act, it was the unauthorized transmittal of information to a foreign power that was at issue, not its substance. A number of Canadian public servants had clearly broken their oath of secrecy and had cooperated with a foreign state against the rules of their own country. Nor could there be much doubt that, for those who had acted in this way, some measure of political or ideological motivation was at the bottom of their behaviour. From the security service's point of view, the salient points of the affair were that the Communist Party of Canada had been publicly excoriated and discredited as an instrument of foreign espionage against Canada, and that a stern and menacing warning had been issued by the highest authorities in the land that Canadians should be very careful indeed about any left-wing ideas or associations. In helping bring about this salutary result, the Mounties had been able to take full advantage of the draconian wartime emergency powers at their disposal. They could also draw comfort from the apparent willingness of the Canadian state to employ the firm smack of Prussian-like authority in dealing with a peacetime threat to national security.

If the willingness to use Star Chamber methods represented an official affirmation of the seriousness with which the Mounties viewed the Red Menace, the Gouzenko affair also provided the RCMP with another, unusual, benefit of a different kind. In the United States, J. Edgar Hoover assiduously worked at constructing a public image of himself and his FBI as the public protector against the twin threats of crime and subversion. Hoover crusaded against Communism, both directly and by indirect inspiration, in print, on the airwaves, and on the Hollywood screen. He also surreptitiously fed witch-hunting congressmen, like those on the House Committee on Un-American Activities, active both before and after the war, with material from the FBI's voluminous files. In the late 1940s and early 1950s, Hoover treated the likes of Senator Joseph McCarthy as snarling pit bulls to be kept on a steady diet of raw meat. All this served to reinforce and intensify the anti-Communism that was already a staple element of American culture.

The RCMP envied neither Hoover's self-promotion nor his cultivation of freelance anti-Communist demagoguery. In fact, as good Canadian public servants in the British tradition, the Mounties disliked vulgar populism and mistrusted even ideologically correct agitation exercised outside their direct control. For them, anti-Communism was, when all was said and done, best left as a crown prerogative. Nevertheless, Hoover-style media crusading did have the undoubted advantage of impressing appropriate values on the public mind, something the RCMP was generally constrained from doing, both by the parliamentary system of government and by its own reticence. The Gouzenko affair offered, momentarily but at a crucial moment of transition from war to peace, the best of both worlds. Action was taken with maximum secrecy, with near-absolute priority given to efficiency in serving the interests of state, and with minimal concessions to individual rights. And then an official government report was issued that spelled out all the anti-Communist lessons the RCMP could ever wish to impart to a naive public, including the dangers of 'leftist' thinking and of innocuous-looking 'progressive' groups that were in reality subversive fronts for Communism. The report, moreover, was a media sensation of its time, not only in Canada but around the world. Others would draw from its pages material for more journalistic exposés of the Red Menace (even a Hollywood movie starring Dana Andrews as an improbably dapper Igor Gouzenko), but for the Mounties the report's value lay in the official, respectable imprimatur that it gave to the public diffusion of the anti-Communist moral.

The anti-Communist mission of the security service might also be said to have benefited from another, unanticipated, spinoff of the Gouzenko affair. Gouzenko himself demonstrated a grasp of public relations and the potential use of a media image that was somewhat surprising for a young cipher clerk from a country where there was no free press. He actually advised government officials about how the odyssey of his defection could be exploited for best effect.[8] With the assistance of a ghost writer, he produced a best-selling autobiography.[9] Ostensibly fearing retribution from KGB assassins, he hit upon a veritable media coup by donning a bag over his head for public appearances. With this, Gouzenko became a cultural icon, he and his story an indelible and vivid part of Canadian popular mythology, a living legend that embodied the moral fable of Communism versus freedom. Needless to say, this provided a most useful marketing image for the RCMP's anti-Communist campaign.

It is ironic that the usefulness of the RCMP's public identification with the Gouzenko myth hid an altogether different reality in the actual relationship between the famous defector and the police. Responsible for guarding Gouzenko and his growing family, the Mounties found the defector to be pushy, self-important, and endlessly demanding. The force insisted finally that a man whom it had come to view as a tiresome ingrate be taken off its hands. For his part, Gouzenko, who with Russian suspicion had always distrusted any police, countered with accusations that Commissioner Wood (an indefatigable anti-Communist of the purest stripe) was actually a double agent in charge of the Soviet espionage operation in Canada! The Mounties were discharged from their thankless responsibility as the Gouzenko family keepers. Of course, this reality was never made known to the public, until years later when journalist John Sawatsky's oral history of Gouzenko gave an opportunity for some of the Mounties, since retired, to blow off their accumulated resentments about the man behind the myth.[10]

Operating the Security-Screening Panopticon

The Kellock-Taschereau Royal Commission did not make a large number of recommendations, but the few it did make were closely followed by the government. Among these was an admonition to develop a proper security-screening system to prevent the very kind of thing that had been revealed by Gouzenko. As pointed out in the previous chapter, the Mounties had already been doing security screening of much of the civil service, the Armed Forces, and sections of the private sector to boot. Yet this had obviously not been good enough. Moreover, clearances had been done in something of a policy and administrative vacuum. With the example of the spy scandal before their eyes, and with the emergent Cold War imposing stricter security standards on all countries, the government of Canada sought to establish screening on a more normal and established footing, with clear guidelines from cabinet and a senior coordinative body to supervise the process.

An advisory Security Panel was established in 1946 that included representatives of the three military services as well as the RCMP, with a small permanent secretariat and chaired by the cabinet secretary (the clerk of the Privy Council). This was the peacetime successor to the Joint Intelligence Committee on which the RCMP had sat during the war, although the Security Panel was directed solely towards domestic security issues and not to foreign-intelligence gathering. The panel was to prove an important point for ongoing policy coordination between the security service and senior bureaucrats, as well as with military intelligence people (with whom they sometimes had a prickly relationship). The first major task of the panel was to advise the cabinet on the outlines of a screening system. After lengthy deliberation, a cabinet directive was approved in March 1948, although it was to be kept strictly secret.[11]

The RCMP security service was to be at the heart of the process: it would continue to do the investigations and identify potential security risks. It had the experience, and the files, and, to top it off, the government was keen to associate the high prestige the Mountie image still carried in Canadian public opinion with a program that might potentially attract public criticism for snooping into people's private lives. As it turned out, security-clearance investigations were to take two forms: for less important clearances, a simple file check against security-service records on subversive organizations and activities; for more sensitive requests, the file check would be supplemented by a field investigation, usually involving direct interviews with neighbours, co-workers, acquaintances, and so on. It was the latter kind of investigation, impossible to keep from public notice[12] and with unfortunate connotations of gathering up potentially malicious gossip,[13] that particularly concerned the government. The authority and prestige of the Mounties could be counted upon to counteract these adverse consequences.

Although Commissioner Wood had been quoted in the press as looking forward to a civil service 'purge' parallel to that being initiated in the United States, and had even exhorted civil servants to carry out 'constant vigilance of their office associates,'[14] the government had no intention of following the American example. The Truman administration launched the Loyalty-Security program in 1947, under which federal employees were expected to demonstrate not only a negative absence of risk but positive loyalty to the United States. The Canadian government did not want to impose loyalty tests on its employees, nor did it wish to see scores of employees at all levels of government fired as disloyal, as was to happen in the United States over the next few years. It wanted an altogether quieter screening process, under which those identified as security risks were never hired in the first instance, or if already inside, would be shuffled into areas where they would have no access to classified information, or be allowed to quietly 'retire' to the private sector. Above all, the government did not wish to see a politicized screening process that would offer material for demagogues to attack the government for being 'soft on Communism.'

By and large, the Mounties were content with this approach. They, too, feared anti-Communism running out of the control of the state. And they were satisfied with the establishment of firm guidelines for screening that gave cabinet authority to anti-Communist criteria. One publicly announced aspect of the policy was that 'persons who were members of or associated with the Communist party should not be employed by the government in positions of trust or upon work of a confidential character.'[15] A modified cabinet directive of 1952, which remained in force until 1963, specified the exclusion or marginalization of any applicant or employee 'who by his words or actions shows himself to believe in marxism-leninism.'[16]

Although the Mounties lost responsibility for screening Armed Forces personnel, which the military themselves would henceforth undertake, they gained the right to screen External Affairs and the Prime Minister's Office, which had previously been off-limits – indeed both External and the PMO were on a list of 'vulnerable' departments where all employees would have to be screened irrespective of their specific job. To be sure, department and agency heads retained the right to make final decisions about the disposition of security cases, but this had always been the practice. Occasionally, the RCMP and a department might differ over a case, the most notorious being the tragic story of Herbert Norman, the diplomat who leaped to his death in Cairo in 1957

(discussed later in this chapter), but generally the Mounties respected
the formal limits of their role as advisers. The more serious issue was
that in most cases – External Affairs perhaps being the exception – it
was unlikely that Mountie advice would be rejected by departments,
few of which were in a position to question the marshalling of evidence
prepared by the men with the files and the expertise on Communism.
The principle of civilians exercising the final decision-making authority
was probably honoured more in theory than in practice.

There is other evidence that there was more than met the eye in the
Mounties' formally subordinate role in screening. The civilians on the
Security Panel were always careful to insist, even among themselves,
that adverse security reports on a civil servant ought never to go beyond the secret counsels of government. If, for instance, an employee
with an adverse report could not be given a lateral transfer into a position without access to classified material (which would be the case for
any employee of the so-called vulnerable agencies), it was deemed preferable that he or she be persuaded to resign rather than be fired. The
employee would be given a good technical reference and would find
little difficulty in securing a position in the private sector. So the theory went. In practice, the Mounties pursued 'security risks' wherever
they went, routinely informing employers of the suspect status of their
new employees. Many former civil servants, their footsteps dogged by
zealous Mounties, found considerable difficulty in securing steady employment.[17] It is not clear what motivated this apparently vindictive
behaviour, apart from misplaced moralism on the part of the police.[18]
But the high principles enunciated by the civilians looked less liberal in
the actual experience of those on the receiving end.

The Security Panel justified another dubious aspect of Canadian
screening practice by professions of liberalism. Unlike the American
and British practices, Canada for many years did not allow for appeals
to any neutral, outside body. Appeals could be made to the department
heads, or the minister, that is, the same officials who made the final
decision in security cases. One cabinet minister in the early Cold War
years later smugly declared that he had 'never heard of an unjust result.'[19] This practice was contrary to principles of natural justice, but
it was justified on the grounds that any appeal procedure would open
the system up to outside scrutiny and thus prejudice the reputations of
public employees with adverse security reports. It was true that American appeal boards sometimes turned into fishing expeditions in which
appellants were offered the chance of saving themselves by turning in

others, although this did not happen in the United Kingdom. In any event, a close reading of the declassified documentation reveals that liberalism was not the leading reason for the no-appeal policy. More to the point was the anxious concern of the RCMP that they never be put in the position where their confidential sources of information would be revealed – as they might in the context of cross-examination in an appeal situation. Like all security intelligence agencies everywhere, the RCMP viewed their sources as sacrosanct, their identity to be protected at all costs. The government agreed, and would not even try to fashion an appeals procedure that might balance the rights of individuals to natural justice with protection of police sources. Not until 1984 and the CSIS Act civilianizing the security service would any independent appeal process be allowed.

The 'Fruit Machine'

Despite the decisively anti-Communist rationale for screening, it soon became apparent that there was a kind of developmental logic in the system that tended to expand the categories of risk. When the Mounties sent in their first set of reports to the Security Panel under the new system in 1948, it turned out that the largest number of positive results were not for political cases at all but for what the Mounties termed 'moral' lapses or 'character' defects. Civilian officials were annoyed at this and complained about moralizing on the part of the police. The panel was of the opinion that the screening process had been set up in order to catch Communist spies, not typists who had given birth to children out of wedlock, or clerks with a gambling habit. The Mounties had an answer to this: any employee who had something in their past or in their private life they wished to conceal was a potential target for blackmail by unscrupulous Communist spymasters. This was, at a certain level, an unanswerable argument, once the higher logic of the system had been assimilated: the revised 1952 directive included 'character defects' as a formal risk category. The civilians acquiesced to a screening system that would regularly turn up two categories of 'positive' results: yellow forms for moral problems and pink ones for the 'politicals.' Indeed, the RCMP representative on the Security Panel once admitted that at most 1 per cent of the total public-service workforce might be in any way infected with Communist associations;[20] there were always more who were subject to character defects and moral lapses.

The argument about vulnerability to blackmail was an element of the formal or official text. It barely concealed another, unofficial subtext. Surveillance of the workforce has always been for purposes of 'discipline,' and this usually includes a form of *moral regulation*. The Cold War offered an ideological umbrella for the moral regulation of society, and security screening a mechanism for the specific moral regulation of public employees. Nowhere was this more apparent than in the nexus that was constructed between political and sexual 'deviancy,' the latter category almost entirely coincident with homosexuality. Officially, homosexuality was a vulnerability that invited exploitation by forces hostile to the state. Coming right behind this bland technical argument and quickly crowding it out was the voice of moral outrage: homosexuality was an abominable perversion, the sexual counterpart to the political deviancy of Communism – and inexorably connected to it, at a level that did not require rational explanation but could be 'felt' by all right-thinking persons. That this is no extravagant theorization is apparent from the active and relatively autonomous role the Mounties took in expanding the screening system in the late 1950s and early 1960s to purge the public service of 'sexual deviants.' This discreditable affair, aptly described by a later prime minister as 'odious,'[21] offers the spectacle of a real-life parody of screening as a social and political phenomenon. It might even be funny, were it not for the very real victims, many more in number than ever suffered from straightforward political screening.[22]

In the initial stages of screening there had been no explicit mention of homosexuality as a risk factor. Civilian officials appeared uninterested in pursuing this matter. It was the RCMP itself, prodded by the FBI, which pushed strongly for making sexuality a leading criterion. Moreover, they turned to 'science,' or what passed for science in the field of psychology, to prepare studies on 'deviancy.' In what must rank as the single looniest venture of their entire history, the security service even devised, with appropriate 'scientific' advice, an infamous 'fruit machine' to detect deviant tendencies in persons tested.[23] In this grotesque farce we can glimpse the inner logic of the screening phenomenon. The power of the Panoptic eye that was to survey all and sort the docile from the risky, the normal from the deviant, was grounded in the prestige of rationality and science. Screening was to detect, with regularity and predictability, the signs of risk. The fruit machine was the ultimate embodiment of this Benthamite dream: just plug in the subject and the machine will look into the soul and register its reading. The machine, of course, was utterly useless for its stated purpose. Behind the trappings of scientism was nothing more than the politics of prejudice. But prejudice was here legitimated by the state, with the power to exercise severe sanctions against the unfortunate individuals who fell under the disapproving gaze of the screeners.

Technological failure did nothing to dampen the frenzy of the hunt, which mounted in the 1960s. A special squad and a separate filing system were set up in 1960 to carry out the gay hunt in Ottawa. By the beginning of that decade, 113 civil servants had already been dismissed or forced into resignation. In the *Annual Report* of the security service for 1959–60, it was laconically noted that some resignations had occurred at 'high levels in the public service.' Yet the same report (carrying a 'Top Secret' classification and destined only for the eyes of senior RCMP brass) also indicated that there was only a single case on file in which 'an *attempt* was made' by a hostile intelligence agency to 'compromise a Canadian government employee' through homosexual blackmail or entrapment![24] Obviously, the security rationale was no more than pretext. By 1967, the RCMP had amassed over 8,000 files on known 'or suspected' homosexuals, of which less than 3,000 were actually employed in the public service. In other words, the ostensible government security rationale did not prevent the zealous Mounties from attempting surveillance of homosexuality in Canadian society as a whole.

As for the government sector itself, by the late 1960s, an average of about a hundred adverse reports were being turned in per year. The main method to ferret out suspected homosexuals was, *pace* the preposterous 'fruit machine,' the tried and tested non-technological one of fear and intimidation to extract 'confessions' and browbeat the 'self-admitted' to pass on more names. The Mounties seemed somewhat amazed at how successful these crude methods were: 'one extremely interesting aspect of this inquiry,' according to the 1959–60 *Annual Report*, 'is the reliability of homosexuals as sources of information ... It has been the Force's experience that their naming of an individual as a homosexual, whether their information was obtained by personal contact, hearsay, or the "homing instinct"[!], is substantially correct.' The total number of civil servants dismissed or forced out of the government on these grounds cannot be reconstructed from the files, but it certainly numbered in the hundreds.[25]

The Department of External Affairs – long a suspect area for the Mounties – seems to have been a particular target for this purge. One leading diplomat, John Watkins, who while ambassador to the USSR in the mid-1950s had been the object of an attempted KGB homosexual

entrapment, later died while undergoing interrogation in 1964 by the
security service as a suspected spy. Watkins, one of the more intelligent and perceptive diplomats, had admitted his homosexuality to the
RCMP but insistently denied that he had ever betrayed his country.
Indeed, no evidence of any betrayal has ever been produced, and one
of his interrogators, Leslie James Bennett (later himself to be dismissed
from the service after wrongfully being identified as a Soviet mole),
indicates his own conviction that Watkins had in fact held fast against
the Soviet blackmail attempt.[26] Other figures in the diplomatic service
were forced into early retirement when confronted.[27] The Mounties,
who tried at one point to get a cabinet directive requiring the dismissal
of all homosexuals from the public service, could not line up the Security Panel behind their 'rigorous' line, and the then prime minister,
John Diefenbaker, wondered if matters of character could not be treated
differently from security risks. The latter suggestion was 'rejected.' One
deputy minister queried the idea of depriving the public service of 'brilliant individuals whose homosexuality would be more than adequately
neutralized by proven discretion in behaviour.' In the end, the RCMP
had to pursue its vendetta against gays and lesbians without clear directions from the civilians. As the security service historians note with
apparent irritation, 'character weaknesses, and homosexuality in particular, remained obvious matters of security risk which however evidently suggested enough uncomfortable questions about civil liberties
to impede the imposition of the full extent of procedures necessary to
maximize security.'[28]

The rationale for the 'vulnerability' of homosexuals rested, of course,
on the existence of societal prejudice. In relentlessly pursuing gays
and lesbians, the Mounties were acting as the cutting edge of that very
prejudice. By the 1980s and 1990s, a more rights-conscious society and
a more open and aggressive gay and lesbian community created a climate in which blacklisting on grounds of sexual preference was no longer sustainable; non-discrimination is now official policy.[29] The era of
the fruit machine in the late 1950s and early 1960s can now be recognized as a dark age, both for the RCMP and for a society that the RCMP
faithfully, if over-zealously, reflected.

The Witch Hunters Go to the Movies

The mixture of disgust and anxiety with which the Mounties viewed
sexual 'deviates,' especially gay men, might perhaps be expected from

a virtually all-male paramilitary police force with a relentless emphasis on toughness and other macho values. But gays were not the only category to fall victim to police attitudes of suspicion towards those whose lifestyles set them apart from the mainstream of society. Artists and intellectuals ('long-hairs' or 'high brows' in the mixed metaphors of populist discourse of the era) were similarly suspect. Where artists and intellectuals were employed by the state, this friction could become inflammatory. Such was the case with the National Film Board of Canada (NFB), the site of a major anti-Communist purge in the late 1940s and early 1950s.

The purge at the NFB is a story with two quite contradictory versions. First is the official line put out by the government at the time, and retailed by official apologists since. In essence, this story goes that there was a security problem in the NFB in the late 1940s, which was cleaned up by prompt and humane intervention. Three security risks were terminated, and then the organization was quickly and painlessly rebuilt as a vital element in Canadian culture. The official version was always contested by another which instead saw a McCarthyite witch hunt at work in which many creative filmmakers were driven out and effectively blacklisted. With the accumulated oral evidence of the victims of the purge and the release in recent years of a large number of documents relating to the NFB 'security' crisis, it can now be stated quite confidently that the official version amounts to no better than a cynical cover-up. The unofficial version has been fully verified.[30] Security screening was pretence for an ideological purge. The specific role played by the RCMP security service in this purge says a great deal about the political policing of Canadian society in the deepest ice age of the Cold War.

The RCMP did not initiate the purge, which seems to have had multiple roots. Some went back to John Grierson, the charismatic Scottish documentary filmmaker who was the founding father of the NFB. Grierson had made too many powerful enemies in wartime Ottawa, and when he was caught, in a most circumstantial fashion, in the fallout of the Gouzenko affair, he was thrown to the wolves: the security issue, however, stuck to the NFB after his departure. External Affairs bore a grudge against the agency for intruding on its turf;[31] the departments of trade and commerce and national defence had their own reasons for wishing to squeeze the NFB out. Behind these Ottawa actors stood two sets of private interests, the powerful Hollywood lobby and the less imposing but locally influential private film companies in Canada. The security issue was the pretext for a savaging of the agency by its many enemies. The purge became public knowledge late in 1949. Grierson's successor as NFB commissioner, Ross McLean, who had shown some courage in resisting the onslaught of the witch hunters, was forced to step down; Arthur Irwin, editor of *Maclean's Magazine*, was brought in with explicit instructions to clean out the 'Reds.'

Well before the purge had officially begun at the top, the RCMP had been readied to investigate subversive activities among the filmmakers. As the formal screening regime was initiated in 1948, the Mounties were already going beyond the requirements of specific screening requests on NFB employees to do a wider profile of possible Communists throughout the organization: in effect, following up leads according to police procedures. Detailed organizational charts, with names of incumbents, were obtained; from these, pictures of Communist networks were drawn up. It is not clear from the documents if this wider investigation was authorized from above, or was attributable to the Mounties' own zealousness. Certainly, no one in authority seems to have placed any dampers on this initiative. What is remarkable is the scope of the surveillance. Not content to simply check names against their files, or even to carry out specific field checks on individuals, the security service mounted an intensive spying operation, maintaining close to non-stop surveillance of individual employees after work, reporting on their movements, contacts, and activities. The indefatigable John Leopold directed operations as if this were a major counter-espionage campaign against Moscow Centre, a secret war of spy and counterspy through the streets of Ottawa.

Bulky dossiers were compiled, with information on employees' political activities and opinions, information rife with highly judgmental commentary by the Mounties (including such unanalytical categories such as 'Parlour Pink') which did not hesitate to draw frequently invidious interpretations of motives and which tended to show a strong, if not prurient, interest in matters having to do with employees' alleged sexual behaviour and marital difficulties. Lengthy, highly tendentious psychological profiles were drawn up of the agency's top brass: Commissioner McLean was portrayed as a weak personality type with an inferiority complex, who was being deftly manipulated by a 'Big Four' of behind-the-scenes Communists. The investigators obviously had very little sympathy for, or understanding of, artists with left-wing ideas and were quite prepared to translate their disdain into accusations of Communism and disloyalty.

In the summer of 1949, the Security Panel rather bizarrely declared the NFB to be a 'vulnerable' agency on a par with External Affairs, National Defence, the PMO, the Privy Council Office (PCO), and the RCMP itself: every single employee, no matter how insignificant, would henceforth require security clearance. When the new management settled in place in early 1950, the Mounties were ready with extensive reports on all the security risks. The commissioner was presented with a list of thirty-nine employees identified as Communists or Communist sympathizers. After consultation with Norman Robertson, Irwin agreed to the dismissal of only three. Reportedly, the RCMP was miffed by this apparent rebuff to their professional judgment. The number of dismissals, although not the names, was disclosed in Parliament and has been subsequently used as evidence of liberalism tempering the zealousness of the RCMP.[32] In fact, any evidence of liberalism in this affair is scant. It has always been obvious that the numbers purged went well beyond the three cited. Most NFB employees were on short-term contracts; non-renewals of contracts were not registered as 'dismissals.' Many chose prudently to resign so as to avoid the stigma of dismissal as security risks. There was, by all accounts, an atmosphere of intimidation throughout the NFB that silenced political dissent (this was duly reported in the Mounties' files) but also discouraged dissidents from continuing in the agency. Today, through access to the RCMP files on the NFB, we can now assign a firm number to those purged. In 1959 an internal security service report looked back at the history of the 1948–50 investigation and concluded that it resulted in a 'so-called clean out and resignations of some 40 employees.'[33] This number, be it noted, is rather close to the number presented to the commissioner in 1950, and, in tracing the paper trail through the declassified files, it seems quite likely that the two lists were almost entirely identical. In other words, the Mounties did get their men, and their women too. There is serious doubt about any alleged rift with the civil servants on the grounds of liberal criticism of Mountie methods. It seems that, in zealously hunting down the 'Reds' in the Film Board, the Mounties were doing the job assigned them.

The force did add its own imprint on the affair. Interviews with some of those purged indicate that the Mounties vindictively followed them into the private sector, encouraging a kind of employment blacklist. This had no known approval from the Security Panel but can be put down to an excess of self-righteousness on the part of the police to punish political deviancy without end.

The Globalized Panopticon

The Cold War offered the security service a number of windows on the wider world, but none institutionalized ongoing linkages with other security and intelligence agencies more effectively or brought more international perspective to the inner confines of the security service than the security screening of prospective immigrants to Canada and applications for citizenship. Immigration screening presented the dream of a kind of globalized Panopticon; it has remained a crucial function of the security service to this day.

Screening immigrants and applicants for citizenship by political criteria was not a new activity for the RCMP – in some forms it had gone back to well before the war – but what was new was the sheer scale and volume, as well as the requirements for systematization and for permanent international liaison. The volume was a result of the huge inflow of immigration to Canada in the post-war era: over five and a half million immigrants arrived on Canadian shores from the end of the war through 1987. The 1950s was the decade with the second-highest ratio of net migration to total population growth in the twentieth century, exceeded only by the first decade of the century when the intense program to populate Canada's prairies was at its peak. There was something else that distinguished the Cold War era: there were unprecedented numbers of refugees among this flow, starting with some 100,000 'displaced persons' from the refugee camps of Europe in the late 1940s and early 1950s. Refugees had *political* reasons for fleeing or refusing to return to their homelands. The acceptance or rejection of refugees rested squarely in the context of the emergent Cold War in the late 1940s.

The main thrust of immigration screening was decisively anti-Communist at its post-war inception and was to remain so for some four decades. The concern was simply to screen out from the immigration and refugee inflow any Communist Party members, anyone professing views seen to be pro-Communist, anyone related to Communists, anyone who associated with Communists, and certainly anyone who had ever belonged to any organization that was Communist-inspired or Communist-led. Secondary targets for a few years after the war were Nazis, Fascists, criminal collaborators, and war criminals, although, as we shall see, this concern diminished rather quickly. The formal public text justifying this kind of screening stressed the dangers of trained Communist espionage and sabotage agents infiltrating the immigration inflow, establishing themselves in the host country from whence they could eventually wreak great mischief. The subtextual agenda was ideological: Communist *ideas* must be kept out. In the United States, the McCarran-Walter Immigration and Nationality Act of 1952 formally ensconced anti-Communist ideological criteria at the centre of American immigration policy. In the words of its Senate sponsor, the witch-hunting Pat McCarran, if the immigration 'stream is polluted, our institutions and our way of life become infected.'[34] Canadian officials were just as alarmed about infection by Communist germs, but, characteristically, they chose to screen out the pollution in a less public, more secretive, manner. This is where the Mounties came in.

Canada did not *legislate* immigration security. Rather, it was done entirely under the cloak of administrative arrangements, arrangements that were themselves kept secret. Nor were those ruled inadmissible or ineligible for citizenship on security grounds ever to be told the real reason. RCMP security service officers were posted abroad to Canadian visa offices to interview and investigate applicants for immigration, but these officers were to be under cover as 'immigration' officials – under cover, that is, to applicants but not to the police and security officials of the local country with whom they were in liaison. Applicants would be checked against local police and security files and/or with American and British intelligence. Elaborate but secret rules governed entry. And, once in Canada, immigrants then faced a second screening when they applied for citizenship. Again, it was the security service, with its vast files and its inquisitive interest in the politics of ethnic and immigrant groups, that carried out the security investigations, raised objections where appropriate, and prepared the security cases for deportation – all of these functions being discharged with the maximum possible degree of secrecy.[35]

Fears of the Communist infection of Canadian society did not stop there. Even temporary visitors to Canada were seen as potential threats to national security; elaborate 'look-out' lists of politically undesirable foreigners, including many internationally known scientists, artists, and writers, were prepared and unobtrusively placed at the disposal of immigration officials at ports of entry. Certain union organizers from U.S. international headquarters were effectively banned from Canada by administrative fiat. In the 1960s and 1970s a number of foreign academics were hindered or in some cases prevented from taking up positions at Canadian universities on the murky basis of never-admitted security criteria.

It comes as no surprise that activity shrouded in an impenetrable fog of secrecy and official obfuscation should turn out on closer inspection to conceal things that are cause, or should be cause, for embarrassment. The workings of the system were as arbitrary as would be expected given the insulation from publicity, criticism, and even judicial review. This arbitrariness manifested itself in many injustices against individuals, deprived of natural justice, denied knowledge of the case against them, turned away from the gates with the homily that 'immigration to Canada is a privilege, not a right.' It was also manifest in the unequal incidence of security screening of immigrants from certain countries, such as Italy, France, and Greece, where strong indigenous Communist movements existed, or in the cloak 'security' offered for the exercise of ancient prejudices, such as anti-Semitism. The security service operated in this process with what amounted to impunity: its judgments were rarely challenged by civilian officials, and when they were, the Mounties invoked the sanctity of their foreign sources of information as unanswerable grounds for insisting that the civilians mind their own business.

One result was that the security operation was a kind of secret state within the more open immigration bureaucracy, one that sometimes worked at cross-purposes with the stated policies of the department. The officer in charge of the security service in the early 1950s, George McClelland, put the problem succinctly: 'Mass immigration and good security cannot go side by side. You can have mass immigration with mediocre security, or good security and trickle of immigration.'[36] By and large, mass immigration prevailed, but persistent efforts to enforce 'good security' forced delays and backlogs and added a good deal of frustration to the process – for both immigration officials and their clients. The rejection rate on security grounds was not huge: under 40,000 out of some two million immigrants who entered Canada in the first two post-war decades. The fallback, citizenship screening in Canada, ran into considerable political flack and a certain amount of bureaucratic resistance. Of 700,000 applications from 1951 through 1963, 1,391 were rejected for security reasons.[37]

In the hands of the RCMP, anti-Communism was fairly single-mindedly applied as the main criterion for exclusion and deportation. Between 1946 and 1958, just under 30,000 applicants for immigration were turned down on security grounds, a number that the RCMP were careful to point out exceeded the highest estimates of membership ever attained by the Communist Party of Canada; the juxtaposition was deliberate. To be sure, the anti-Communist priority was approved by the cabinet and overseen by the civilians working with the RCMP on the Security Panel. Still, the Mounties had what amounted to a blank cheque in carrying out the policy in specific cases. They certainly had a freer hand in applying the anti-Communist gospel to screening on a global scale than they had in domestic, civil-service screening. Given the importance of immigration to the face of post-war Canada, it could be said that the security service played a certain modest but not insignificant role in helping mould the ideological cast of the country by screening out left-wing immigrants and encouraging anti-Communist newcomers. Its influence could also be felt in discouraging left-wing political activity among immigrant groups in Canada, as the impact of security screening of citizenship applications spread a chill over certain kinds of ethnic political action. These latter effects are impossible to measure, but the RCMP were quite clear that they anticipated such positive influences from its screening. Of course, anti-Communism did not have to be artificially cultivated among many of the post-war new Canadians, especially those from Eastern Europe whose anti-Communism was visceral and drawn from bitter personal experience. But it is the relative absence of political progressivism in the post-war wave that suggests a distinct silencing effect of immigration and citizenship screening.

Any questions about the inherent ideological biases of the screening system can be settled by examining the sharp contrast between the extraordinary welcome and assistance accorded the displaced persons fleeing the Red Army in the late 1940s, and the refugees from Hungary in 1956 and Czechoslovakia in 1968, on the one hand, and, on the other, the ill-tempered delays and prevarications surrounding the acceptance of refugees from the murderous Pinochet coup against a democratically elected leftist government in Chile in 1973. Right-wing refugees from Communist oppression were exemplary; left-wing refugees from right-wing oppression were suspects. That was the moral that underlay immigration screening, the lesson that was being imparted through the operations of the global screening Panopticon, and so far as the historical record would indicate, there is no reason to believe that the Mounties ever felt any qualms about teaching that lesson.

One other element of immigration screening demands some attention. Communists were not the only prohibited class under the secret regulations governing immigration clearances. Nazis and war criminals were supposed to be barred as well. Yet decades later a royal commission of inquiry found that a goodly number of persons about

whom there were strong enough cases to warrant criminal prosecution for crimes against humanity had somehow slipped through the
net in the early post-war years to find undeserved refuge in Canada.[38]
If this was another example of anti-left bias, it was not in any obvious
or straightforward way. The anti-Communism of the security service
did not automatically lead to a pro-Nazi bias, or even a blind eye to
possible war criminals. In fact, it was successive decisions by Canadian
governments that relaxed restrictions against various categories of Nazis in the early 1950s, decisions that seem mainly motivated by foreign-
policy considerations given that by then West Germany was a rearmed
NATO partner. These decisions were usually opposed by the RCMP
when their views were consulted. Some idea of what the rank-and-file
officers thought about this may be gleaned from the language of an
internal report in 1948: 'The scheduled deportation of obnoxious Nazis
did not take place. The Department of External Affairs has apparently
had a change of heart and decided to let the Nazis remain in Canada as
an antidote to Communism.'[39] The Mounties tended not to see Nazis as
security risks as such (which was not unreasonable in the absence of any
Nazi regimes), but they did tend to view them as highly undesirable as
potential citizens. They were also deeply sceptical of collaborators from
the former Nazi-occupied states, on the assumption that someone who
had once betrayed their country of origin might well be a risk to do so
to their adopted country as well.

It is now well known that some former Nazis were assisted to find
new domiciles by American and British intelligence in exchange for anti-Communist intelligence; the same was done for Nazi scientists who
were considered valuable assets in the emergent Cold War.[40] It is also
known that some of this activity did take place in Canada, although
the dimensions and the details remain cloudy. There was a small, super-secret, high-level group sometimes known as the Defectors Committee (composed of Peter Dwyer, senior security official in the Privy
Council Office, a Security Panel staff functionary, and a senior RCMP
security service official, according to the best information available).
This committee shepherded certain individuals (number unknown)
past Canadian immigration controls at the behest of the American and
British 'cousins' who had incurred some obligation to these persons.
There is shadowy evidence that this operation was actually unknown
to the RCMP officials in the field: inadmissible persons were run past
them with false documentation presumably provided by higher-ups in
the know.[41] Although it seems very probable that the complicity of the

security service was secured at the top, it is likely that most of the working security service were deliberately kept in the dark. In short, this appears to be one instance when the security-screening machine was intentionally short-circuited, in the interests of a higher logic of anti-Communism. If persons guilty of odious crimes against humanity were smuggled into Canada as a result of this 'higher logic,' there is good reason why the operation was so secret: public opinion would never have accepted it. Nor, perhaps, would the ordinary security service officer have been comfortable with such knowledge.

The Sorcerer's Apprentice

One of the most striking characteristics of the screening system was that virtually from day one it ran out of control. The rapid extension of criteria from political to moral was one spectacular example of the system's expansionist proclivities. The application of screening to immigration and citizenship widened the panoptic gaze to the whole globe and enormously increased the screeners' workload. Even within Canada, the system's scope went beyond the confines of the government sector alone. Two areas outside the state were immediately brought into the screening ambit: defence industries and Great Lakes shipping. Both sectors had been subjected to screening during the war, but war powers offered a cover for a great deal of state intervention that required renewed justification in peacetime, especially under the more formal screening regime set up in the late 1940s.

Screening employees in the private sector working on defence contracts was an obvious necessity once the Cold War was under way. Canadian defence spending and defence procurement, after an immediate post-war downturn, shot up to unprecedentedly high levels during the period of Canada's limited commitment to the Korean War (1950–3). In the latter half of the 1950s, it went into relative decline. Even after this point, however, defence-related industrial work was always an important enough component to bring a substantial portion of the industrial workforce under security screening at one time or another. After the Canada-U.S. Defence Sharing Agreement of 1959, most Canadian defence work was in the form of subcontracts for Pentagon programs: screening had to adhere not only to Canadian standards but to American ones as well.

Industrial screening thus continued into peacetime the extension of RCMP surveillance into the private sector begun in the war. Not surprisingly, many security service officers over the years found their way into early-retirement positions as industrial security officials, thus forging closer links between the private and public sectors. This linkage bore potential dangers for a publicity-shy government, however. Private-sector industries were often unionized and subject to collective-bargaining agreements. Screeners would not have the same relatively free hand they had with public-sector employees who did not attain collective-bargaining rights until the late 1960s. For one thing, some form of appeal process was inescapable, despite the rejection of such procedures in the government sector, since dismissal of workers could be subject to union grievances. For another, there were certain trade unions certified on various shop floors as bargaining agents that were labelled as 'Communist-led' by the security service. If membership in such unions were made the official basis for dismissal, the unions might have a legitimate case for anti-union prejudice. The worst possibility from the security service's point of view was that, in the course of appeals, it might be forced either to divulge its sources or to abandon its action. These issues came to a head in an embarrassing incident in the early 1950s: an employee of A.V. Roe Aircraft was fired as a security risk, and his case was taken up in Parliament. Thereafter an unwritten stipulation was enforced on all defence contractors that workers identified as security risks not be dismissed but simply removed to non-defence work. At the same time, a collective-bargaining clause was negotiated with the Communist-led United Electrical Workers Union in which the union accepted transfers out of defence-related work on security grounds. This was a precedent followed elsewhere, and with it defence-industry screening settled into the quiet, non-controversial mode that both government and its security service wanted.

Settling into a routine did not mean that the system was inconsequential: from 1948 to 1960, 750 workers were denied employment on security grounds in defence industries, and a 'further group of files' indicated over a thousand workers identified as security risks who had been transferred to non-classified areas of production.[42] But this was a typically quiet Canadian purge. Rather than use security as an excuse for a public, state-led assault on Communist unions or Communist union activists, as was the case in the United States with its Taft-Hartley law, the Canadian government chose to come quietly to a modus vivendi with Communist trade unionists within the context of the strict application of security criteria. Despite their anti-Communism, there is no evidence of RCMP discomfiture with this arrangement. As always, they, too, preferred a made-in-Canada solution that avoided publicity, while keeping the Communists under their watchful eyes.

The screening of seamen on the Great Lakes was an altogether more bizarre story of how public policy could be made hostage to Cold War fantasies. During the war, screening in this sector had a clear rationale: the then dominant Canadian Seamen's Union was Communist-led and thus held by the Mounties to represent a potential national security risk. After the war, the Seafarers International Union (SIU), led by the notorious labour thug Hal Banks, was imported into Canada from the United States for the express purpose of running the CSU off the waterfront. Although high-level government complicity is evident in such matters as Banks's criminal record being ignored by Canadian immigration, and although the Mounties maintained voluminous files on the CSU as a subversive Communist union, there is no evidence in the files of active RCMP support for the SIU against the CSU in any of the sometimes violent clashes that marked the SIU's strong-arm drive for dominance. In any event, with a doomed strike in 1949 that took on international dimensions, and with the Trades and Labor Congress pulling the rug out from under the CSU, the Communist-led union suffered an irreversible defeat and soon vanished altogether from the waterfront.

Strangely enough, it was in this context of Communist debacle that the government in 1950 began a renewal of security screening on the Great Lakes. Most peculiarly of all, screening was rendered utterly superfluous by Hal Banks's notorious Do Not Ship List, a kind of pre-screening blacklist employed in SIU hiring halls – which after the CSU's rout in 1949 controlled all hiring on the Great Lakes. The requirement to screen thousands of seamen, almost none of whom were ever found to have Communist associations, imposed a heavy additional workload on the RCMP security service, and also forced the government to set up an appeal process to which it was opposed on principle in the public sector.

Why such an empty but costly charade? The answer is simple: pressure from the Americans. The whole senseless exercise was simply an extension into Canada of the U.S. Magnussen Act, which the SIU had earlier relied upon to help crush Communist rivals on American docks. Canadian security officials glumly acquiesced with American insistence, and the Mounties dutifully set about a pointless exercise. Nor could they easily get out of it: screening ground on through the 1950s. Later in the 1960s, Hal Banks became an object of the state's attention for corruption and racketeering and the SIU was eventually put under trusteeship.

The screening system thus grew inexorably outward, into the private sector and onto the international plane, at the same time as the criteria expanded to encompass moral as well as political risk categories. From the very beginning, it was also apparent that the system was out of control even within the government sector. Departments and agencies interpreted screening as a mechanism for satisfying that most characteristic of bureaucratic desires, finding safety in the face of risk (in popular usage, 'cover your ass'). The bureaucratic rule of thumb quickly became: 'when in doubt, classify.' As more information was placed under secrecy restrictions, more civil-service positions required security clearances, and more civil servants, and applicants for the civil service, fell under screening requirements. There was an internal dynamic that drove departments and agencies towards upgrading security classifications to require a greater number of field investigations, as opposed to simple file checks. This was obviously much more labour intensive for the security service (and much more likely to bring it into sometimes invidious contact with the general public over screening matters).

The inevitable result: the entire post-war history of security screening has been one marked by chronic backlogs, frustrating delays, sporadic efforts to cut back on the volume (that never succeed in the long run), and insistent complaints from the security service about case overload and insufficient resources to do the job effectively. For an eleven-year period between 1951 and 1961, the security service was called upon to carry out 2,627,114 security clearances (28.3 per cent in the public service; 46.8 per cent in immigration; 14.6 per cent in citizenship; 9.2 per cent in defence and related industries).[43] With this kind of volume, it is fair to say that security screening has never ceased to be an administrative problem for the federal government. For their part, the Mounties constantly grumbled that their own high ideal of security protection was not being met. As the RCMP historians put it: the security service 'was in the anomalous situation by 1966 of having regularly increased its efforts and manpower over two decades in the fields of government, visa and citizenship security screening without ever being permitted to do the extent of work necessary appreciably to diminish the security risk.'[44] Sometimes it was tough to reconcile one's ideals with the imperfections of the real world.

Yet security service complaints about overwork should be taken with a grain of salt. For one thing, the clearance backlog was a gold-plat-

ed all-weather argument for more money and more personnel for the
service. After all, the Mounties had been asked to do this job: surely
the government should provide them with the tools? For another, the
Mounties never seriously argued within the councils of government for
reducing the number of clearances required. Indeed, as in the case of
the gay purges and in that of immigration screening, they were actually
advocates of expanding the scope of the system. They may never have
been quite as hawkish as their screening counterparts in the Armed
Forces, but there is no question that the Mounties viewed screening as
an important part of their raison d'être. To understand why this should
be so, it is necessary to examine the deliberately concealed subtext of
the system.

In the world of counter-espionage, it is a commonplace that the greatest successes never become public. When a spy is detected, his or her
best possible utilization is to be 'turned' or 'doubled,' that is, ostensibly
to continue in place but now under the control of the counter-espionage
agency. What is less well understood is that the same modus operandi
was also attached firmly to the screening system. Although denied by
the service, there is abundant evidence that screening has not been just
an end in itself (that is, the public justification) but an invaluable means
to the security service's own ends of extending its surveillance of 'subversive' activities, a tool of political policing.

It works like this: a positive report comes in on the subject of a screening request. At this point, everything could go by the book, and the
report would be passed on to the department for a decision. Alternately
– and this course of action would be based on a careful judgment call –
the security service could speak to the individual in question, indicate
that they are in difficulty, that their career or their citizenship hangs in
the balance. Then, sometimes subtly, sometimes crudely, a carrot is dan-
gled. Perhaps the subject could be cooperative, helpful to the service.
Perhaps, in that event, the difficulty might be put on hold. Cooperation
means that the subject continues, say, to belong to the very association
that brought the positive risk report in the first place, but now passes
on information to the service. In short, the subject becomes a source: in
effect, a double agent.

This modus operandi has been utilized extensively over the years
with citizenship applications to provide penetration of immigrant organizations about which the security service is suspicious or merely
curious; it has also been used in civil-service cases as a means of opening windows on various, mainly left-wing, political groups and asso-

ciations in civil society. From the point of view of the service, screening is strictly complementary to its task of political surveillance in the broader sense, offering a mechanism for penetration; on the other side, the deeper and wider the political surveillance, the better the job of screening that can be provided the government. From the point of view of the subjects of this kind of pressure, the picture is less comforting. Cooperation may mean disloyalty to and betrayal of their friends and associates; in some cases it may even mean personal danger. In either event, it means living a lie. Non-cooperation means risking loss of career and, in citizenship cases, deportation. Refusal to cooperate may also trigger vindictiveness from the secret police. To people fleeing to Canada from totalitarian or authoritarian states, this can pose an ugly Hobson's choice.

Security screening is, on closer examination, like those Russian dolls that nest one inside the other. Open one explanation and there is always another hidden inside. But the one certainty is that the security service is always there, always has been there, at every level, watching.

Mounties Go Shopping in the Global Intelligence Bazaar

The Cold War had a nationalizing impact on Canada from which the RCMP security service benefited institutionally in relation to the provincial and municipal 'Red squads' that had flourished in the interwar years. With the exception of Quebec – always in practice, if not in name, a distinct society – provincial and municipal anti-Communist activity waned in the post-war era in deference to the security service with its burgeoning dossiers and its superior technology of surveillance. Quebec City and Montreal Red squads continued to operate, sometimes in cooperation, but sometimes on their own agendas, through the 1950s, armed with the special power of Premier Maurice Duplessis's notorious Padlock Law, until that statute was ruled ultra vires by the Supreme Court of Canada in 1957. By the 1960s, attention to subversive activities in Quebec had turned to Quebec separatism; RCMP involvement in that matter is the subject of a later chapter. Until then, Quebec was the sole provincial exception to the nationalizing impact of the Cold War on Canadian political policing. In tracing this nationalization, one contributing cause stands out above all others: it was precisely the international nature of the Cold War and the international nature of the efforts of the Western allies to counter the Soviet Communist threat that centralized security intelligence in Ottawa. If Communism posed a global threat, it could only be those elements of the new Canadian national security state in closest touch with the international Western defence and intelligence networks that could muster the expertise and information to fight the Communist threat within Canada. Enter the RCMP security service, displacing the more localized and ad hoc anti-Communist policing of an earlier, more provincial era.

The RCMP found the greatly expanded networks of liaison with foreign security intelligence and police forces highly advantageous. No doubt they thereby gained access to a fund of intelligence to which they would never otherwise have been privy. This was especially helpful given the absence of any Canadian equivalent of the CIA or the SIS, that is, a central agency devoted to gathering and interpreting external intelligence.[45] Simply put, Canada did not have a great deal of intelligence on many parts of the world available from its own sources and was consequently reliant upon exchanges of information from friendly foreign agencies. Fighting the Cold War on a global front, as in immigration screening, did provide the Mounties and the Canadian government with reasonable access to what others had gathered, on the basis of common membership in the Western anti-Soviet 'club.'

There were two downsides to this situation, however. First, Canada was somewhat vulnerable to manipulation and disinformation, given its relative inability independently to cross-check intelligence that had to be largely taken on trust. This was a shortcoming pointed out by the McDonald Commission on the RCMP in 1981.[46] Second, Canada did not get foreign intelligence for 'free'; it had generally to provide something in exchange. In immigration matters, the RCMP had good-quality information available on Canadians (that, after all, was the security service's mandate). The transfer of such information to the U.S. authorities was, from the security service's point of view, value for money, given the relative wealth of intelligence it received in return. On the other hand, the barring of Canadians (usually, but not in all cases, of left-wing persuasion) at the U.S. border under the notorious McCarran-Walter restrictions (later repealed) was a constant irritant for Canadian governments, one made even more invidious by the certainty that in many instances decisions were based on RCMP information. The Mounties were unhappy about the lengths to which the Americans were sometimes prone to go in using their files, and the unseemly provocations to Canadian public sensibilities. By the late years of the Cold War, the prominence of Canadians barred at one time or another from entering the United States became a highly visible public scandal: those so treated included Pierre Elliott Trudeau (on whom the FBI maintained a file, even while he served as prime minister) and the popular writer Farley Mowat, who characteristically parlayed his experience into an entertaining book, *My Discovery of America*.[47] A much darker scandal surrounded the Herbert Norman affair, discussed in detail later.

Despite occasional embarrassing side effects, the security service was in no doubt of the value of its international connections. Becoming members of the Western intelligence club conferred numerous advantages. It enhanced the prestige and position of the security service within the RCMP. Although in recent decades, concerns over international organized crime in the form of money laundering, narcotics, the illegal arms trade, and so on have greatly widened the international exposure of the RCMP's criminal investigation division, in the 1940s and 1950s the security intelligence dimension of international liaison was stronger, and this enhanced the position of the security service, especially after it became a separate division in 1956. The international connection also enhanced the service's profile within the wider councils of government. In policy debates around such issues as immigration, for instance, RCMP advice, weighted with the real or conjured prestige of American and British opinion, was not always followed, by any means, but it was followed more than it might otherwise have been without its influential foreign backing. Since the RCMP could legitimately cite the privileged nature of their sources abroad, their arguments were often difficult for less privileged bureaucrats to confront.[48]

One of the characteristics of the international cooperation in intelligence that came with the Cold War was the growth of direct and close relationships among the various agencies in the different Western countries, short-circuiting the official state-to-state channels of formal communication through foreign ministries and heads of state. A thick web of these substate relationships eventually warranted the description of an international intelligence 'community.'[49] To the Mounties, this 'community' was real, warm, and supportive, cemented through regular liaison, international meetings and conferences, training sessions outside Canada, exchange visits with much wining and dining and socializing, and above all the confidence that came with having powerful friends abroad who were engaged with them in a common enterprise.[50] This was an international policy community of like-minded bureaucrats who sometimes had more in common with one another than with the sometimes unsympathetic public servants and politicians they had to deal with at home.

For the RCMP security service, the relationship with their foreign 'cousins' had grown particularly important by the late 1950s, when the Cold War became institutionalized and the Canadian government showed less and less day-to-day interest in how they did their job. After the initial flurry of cabinet and inter-departmental innovation in the late 1940s when the machinery was being set up, detailed interest at the top waned and the service was increasingly frustrated by lack of action on its recommendations for tightening security standards or intensifying general vigilance. There was some resentment that its officers were being treated like tradesmen expected to provide their services but not bother their employers with details. To shift metaphors, like jaded marriage partners complaining that their spouses fail to understand them, they might find comfort elsewhere.

The Hoover Connection

There was an international Western alliance, but one nation loomed over all others in power and prestige. Canada had long-standing ties with Britain, and the RCMP had close and enduring links with its British counterparts. Yet, living as Canada did in the direct shadow of the United States, the hegemonic leader of the 'free world,' there was no question that the Cold War would lead inexorably to enhanced American influence over Canadian policies and institutions.

The direct relationship of the RCMP security service with the FBI was a kind of condensation of the overall Canadian-American relation in the era of Cold War. The two forces had a great deal in common. They were both criminal-investigation and law-enforcement bodies. Each had moved into security intelligence as a sideline that became an increasingly important aspect of policing. The two agencies had a history of liaison, going back to the 1930s, that had been solidified and formalized in the war. They shared a common conviction that Communism was a mortal enemy that demanded extraordinary counter-measures to defeat. There were differences as well. The two forces came out of very different political cultures: the British-Canadian tradition of deference to the authority of the crown did not leave much room for the kind of free-wheeling entrepreneurial empire building that FBI Director J. Edgar Hoover pursued so successfully. Nor did it allow for tolerance of the rabble-rousing populist public-relations image building that Hoover zealously worked at. Hoover became a law unto himself, a rogue bureaucrat who bugged and blackmailed presidents and other politicians and manipulated the federal government with reckless impunity. In short, Hoover was a monster and under his direction the FBI was a force that intimidated and terrorized American democracy. These things are now known and acknowledged in the United States.[51] In the 1950s and 1960s they were not generally known. The RCMP did recognize and dislike certain vulgar and abrasive aspects of Hoover's behaviour, and they certainly did not wish to emulate in Canada the uncontrolled spasms of McCarthyism that wracked the United States in the early 1950s under Hoover's orchestration. But Hoover was, when all was said and done, a very powerful friend, one they did not wish to lose or alienate. The uses of the Hoover connection were never more startlingly demonstrated than at the very outset of the Cold War, before the Gouzenko affair became public. American and British intelligence had been directly involved in the debriefing of Gouzenko, and a secret agreement had been struck between Mackenzie King, President Harry Truman, and Prime Minister Clement Attlee on how the affair should be handled. Then, at the beginning of December 1945, Mackenzie King made an unusual decision to strike out on his own. Instead of employing the War Measures Act and creating a royal commission of inquiry, King decided to speak to the departing Soviet ambassador: Stalin should be told that Soviet espionage would not be tolerated. The Soviet military attaché and some of his assistants would be expelled, but the Canadians implicated would be investigated in departmental inquiries with RCMP assistance.[52]

RCMP Commissioner Stuart Wood was appalled at this initiative. He fired off a four-page letter to his minister, Louis St Laurent. He had numerous objections to the proposed course of action, but the two most powerful were that, without the use of the War Measures Act, it might be impossible to gather sufficient evidence to produce convictions and, as a result, the Communist Party would get off the hook: internal departmental inquiries would not serve to discredit Communism publicly. 'If by reason of high political and diplomatic considerations,' Wood wrote, 'it is thought that [the original plans] are not in the best interests, or possible, it is strongly emphasized that for the time being, at all events, no action should be taken and the subject be treated as an intelligence matter for present purposes pending further developments.' These arguments made no apparent impression on the prime minister, but just hours before King was scheduled to meet with the Soviet ambassador, Wood came up with the argument that could not be turned down. At a meeting with King, St Laurent, and two senior civil servants, Wood dramatically announced that Hoover had just called from Washington. Leads from the Gouzenko affair had suddenly, it seemed, pointed to Soviet penetration at high levels of the Treasury, the White House, and the intelligence services. This information was 'so grave' that Hoover had concentrated 'all FBI activities on this case.' The FBI director 'would prefer postponement,' Wood asserted. Faced with this second-hand suggestion of Hoover's will, the resolution of the prime minister of Canada to follow his own course wilted immediately. King meekly backed down, no questions asked.

If King had pressed Wood with further questions about the relationship between the Gouzenko affair and the alleged high-level moles in Washington, he would have found little other than vague generalities.[53] Nothing seems to have come of this 'grave' information, nor is there any evidence of the FBI committing 'all' its resources to this hot lead. Indeed, it is not even clear from the documentary record if Hoover had imparted any specifics to Wood, or indeed if the latter had even talked to Hoover. No matter, for the RCMP it was a case of 'mission accomplished.' The mission, however, might have failed without the invocation of Hoover's heavyweight reputation. King, for his part, was entirely ignorant of the world of spies and counterspies, and clearly felt out of his depth in cross-examining his commissioner. Even if we grant that King's unexpected initiative was quixotic and ill-advised, it was a made-in-Canada solution undertaken by the prime minister. The RCMP commissioner had headed off this initiative by invoking the word of his counterpart in Washington, clearly in the service of a policy perspective shared with the FBI. All in all, it was an extraordinary sign of the power of a new *Internationale*: that of the security and intelligence confraternity.

A Witch for the Burning: E. Herbert Norman

The case of Herbert Norman sums up, tragically, the vicious undercurrents that played around the Cold War conflict, especially the dilemmas of security screening and the loyalty scare and the dangerous ramifications of the RCMP's close linkage with J. Edgar Hoover's FBI. The known facts are simple, the interpretation of the facts complex and tricky. The facts: E. Herbert Norman was a distinguished scholar of Japanese history, a diplomat in Canada's foreign service, with a record of work in intelligence for Canada during the war and as an adviser to General Douglas MacArthur during his pro-consulship of Japan in the late 1940s. In 1950–1 a U.S. Senate committee publicly aired charges that Norman was a security risk with a Communist past. Norman was subjected to intensive probes of his loyalty by the RCMP and External Affairs in 1951–2, and pronounced safe. In 1957, while he was serving as Canada's ambassador to Egypt, the Senate Committee once again revived the old charges. Norman committed suicide in Cairo on 4 April 1957. Despite an initial revulsion that swept Canadian opinion, both official and public, directed at the United States and its witch-hunting congressional investigators, the question of Norman's loyalties did not end there. In the 1980s two scholarly books on Norman took radically opposed perspectives, one vindicating and one challenging his loyalty.[54] Finally, in 1990, a retired diplomat and academic was given full access to secret documentation and commissioned by the Department of External Affairs to report on the issue of Norman's loyalty: he concluded unequivocally that Norman had always been a loyal servant of his country.[55]

The intersection of the Norman affair with the security service was around the issues of security screening and foreign liaison. Norman entered External Affairs at a time when Mountie security clearances were not required by the department. Following the war, Norman was posted to the American occupation force in Japan. Here he fell afoul, not of General MacArthur, but of MacArthur's intelligence officer, Charles Willoughby, who began an investigation of Norman which, given Willoughby's ultra-suspicious mind and extreme right-wing outlook, was certain to conclude, as it did, that Norman was likely to be a Soviet agent. This investigation coincided with a renewal of activity on an FBI file on Norman that dated back to the war. It was 'information' – or perhaps 'disinformation' might be a more appropriate term – from these files that began leaking to the Senate committee in 1950–1.

When the charges were first aired, Norman was recalled from Japan to answer questions and face an extended series of intensive probes into his past and his security status. These investigations were under the joint supervision of the RCMP and of External Affairs. The two agencies, with a certain backlog of tension and unease in their relations with one another, had rather differing perspectives on the need for a Canadian security probe on Norman. For senior civil servants in External, the investigation was an unhappy necessity, forced upon them by the Americans. They had little or no doubt that Norman was innocent of the charges, but they had the dread feeling that they would never convince J. Edgar Hoover.

The Mounties, on the other hand, were embarrassed, not only by the fact that a potential high-level Canadian security problem had to be pointed out to them by the FBI, but even more so because the FBI had uncovered a couple of alleged links to Norman in the Gouzenko evidence – evidence that the Mounties themselves had passed on to their U.S. counterparts years earlier. These links were slender, to put it charitably,[56] but they were, in the ethos of the age, enough to create 'doubt' about Norman. It was their failure to detect these warnings themselves that was at the root of the Mounties' embarrassment.[57] But, given American expectations that Norman's head would be served up on a platter, there was further embarrassment awaiting. The Mounties had no authority to declare Norman a security risk, even were they to arrive at such a conclusion. They could only advise External, and the latter were not likely to cut one of their own loose when the evidence was so circumstantial and tendentious.

Terry Guernsey, considered one of the security service's ace anti-Communist investigators, was given the Norman dossier. He was not, however, allowed to interrogate Norman without an External official with intelligence responsibilities, George Glazebrook, present as a babysitter. Guernsey, judging from the record of one interview that survives, probed Norman's past without much subtlety or sense of historical context or nuance. Norman had been at Cambridge in the 1930s and had been a Marxist. He was frank about his sympathies at that time, but he flatly denied ever having been a Communist Party member. This denial later served as a focal point for the insistence of Norman's detractors that he had lied, and that his supporters in External, especially the minister, Lester Pearson, compounded the lie by reiterating it publicly. In fact, not even MI5 in Britain could come up with any party card. Norman's denial of membership seems *literally* true. Still, there is no doubt that he had been a practising Communist at Cambridge. The problem was that, under the cabinet guidelines regarding security screening, any confirmation of past Communist Party *membership* ('card-carrying Communist' in contemporary discourse) would automatically disqualify a civil servant from clearance. That would have effectively ended Norman's career in External Affairs. If Norman's conscience was clear that he had never betrayed his trust while in government employment, and if the senior officials in External had full confidence in him, there were powerful reasons for somewhat narrow literalism regarding party membership. Norman had not lied, although he might, to use a latter-day bureaucratic phrase, have been economical with the truth. This satisfied External but was unlikely to have satisfied the Mounties. To the latter, all the circumstantial evidence of Communist ideas and associations in the 1930s were sufficient to create powerful doubts about Norman that they probably felt should be resolved in favour of the state. To make matters worse, there was the FBI reaction to be considered if Norman were left in place.

Norman was left in place in 1952. He had his 'Top Secret' clearance restored and was even given a higher, 'SA' clearance. It is true that his career went into brief hiatus with a posting to New Zealand, but by 1956 he was back in the centre of things as ambassador to the hotspot of Egypt during the Suez crisis, where he helped broker relations between Egyptian president, Gamal Abdul Nasser, and the Western powers. The FBI was incensed. The Canadian government had made it quite clear that any further official American muckraking about a Canadian who had passed Canadian security standards would be unacceptable. However, as Canadian officials feared, Hoover could not be trusted to abide by diplomatic niceties. Information about Norman in FBI files predictably found its way into the hands of the congressional witch hunters. The Senate Internal Security Subcommittee twice raised Norman's name, in 1951 and then again in 1957, this time fatally. This would have been cause enough for Canadian fury, but what was worse was that the FBI information included an RCMP report on the Norman case passed to Hoover on 17 October 1950. This transmission of security intelligence on a Canadian was, in one sense, merely the business as usual of intelligence exchange between the RCMP and the FBI in their close and by now highly institutionalized international liaison: as was well known and well understood, Canada had little to bring to this exchange other than information on Canadians. In this specific case, Norman was a Canadian in whom the FBI had expressed strong interest. Indeed, the FBI had goaded the Canadians to investigate Norman in the first place. Unfortunately, this initial report was inaccurate in numerous instances, and indeed was later disavowed by the RCMP after further and closer investigation. But it was this report that, in Roger Bowen's words, 'followed Norman to his grave.'[58] In fact, Lester Pearson, then in New York at the United Nations, had desperately cabled Norman Robertson in External to prevent the transmission of the report to Hoover, but it had already been sent, replete with unsubstantiated allegations and factual errors. The evil genii were out of the bottle.

With Norman's shocking suicide, the Mounties were doubly embarrassed: first in the eyes of the FBI, then in the eyes of the Canadian government. To make matters worse, Pearson had blood in his eye and retaliation in mind. Pearson, it should be understood, was not only genuinely saddened and appalled by the tragic death of a friend and colleague, but was also aware of a very ugly undertone in the affair that was at best only dimly appreciated at the time by anyone outside the small circle of players. Pearson knew that it was he himself who was the real and ultimate target of the Washington witch hunters, with Norman more an unfortunate stalking horse. William Rusher, counsel to the Senate subcommittee and later the publisher of the American conservative magazine *National Review*, made clear in his memoirs that Pearson had been the big game he and the senators had been after.[59] We also know now that the FBI had been accumulating a file on Pearson marked '*Espionage, R*[ussian]' that in its declassified form is about two inches thick.[60]

Cognizant of the fact that it was RCMP evidence that had passed through Hoover's hands and into those of the Senate inquisitors, Pearson wanted to put an immediate stop to the bleeding. He signalled his firm, if not bitter, intention to send a sharp note to the U.S. government threatening to deny U.S. access to any security information on Canadians unless the Americans could guarantee no passage of such information beyond executive control. This presented a serious threat to the RCMP, which would thereby face a breakdown in the intelligence exchange that had been built up so carefully over the years. The commissioner, L.H. Nicholson, scrambled to enlist Justice and External officials in an effort to dissuade Pearson. Pointedly, Nicholson noted that the Senate subcommittee already held 'access to security information derived from RCMP files about other extremely recognizable high Canadian government officials which could be most damaging if the Subcommittee decided to retaliate with further disclosures.' This thinly veiled reference to Pearson (and to senior civil servant Robert Bryce, also a Washington target) might have been calculated to make the government think twice about the costs of precipitous action, but it may also have raised a question in the minds of the officials to which it was addressed about just what the RCMP were doing passing 'damaging' intelligence on Canadian public servants to the FBI in the first instance.

In the event, having brandished this challenge, Nicholson was taken aback to hear from External officials that Canada might, in further retaliation, 'publicize damaging evidence against well-known Americans' passed in confidence to the RCMP from the FBI. Pearson's note was sent to Washington. Matters were rapidly getting out of hand,

and Nicholson hastened to assure Hoover of his 'continued complete confidence in FBI integrity [!] and a hope for continued cooperation to mutual benefit.' The storm eventually died down with somewhat lame assurances from the Eisenhower administration that they would do their best to forestall any further breaches of confidence by the legislative branch, despite the constitutional separation of powers. As usual, Hoover emerged unscathed, and the RCMP-FBI relationship continued in the spirit sought by Commissioner Nicholson. Herbert Norman's death did not shake this relationship, although it did little to enhance relations between the RCMP and External Affairs.

Norman's death should have been on someone's conscience. Hoover and the senators accepted no blame, viewing the suicide as proof of Norman's guilt. What of the Mounties? John Sawatsky's informants reported that, when news of Norman's suicide reached Mountie headquarters in Ottawa, there was 'open and unapologetic rejoicing' in the corridors. When a civilian rebuked the celebrants, 'a Mountie shot back: "Whose side are you on?"'[61] Sawatsky also claims that Norman's name was the first to be entered into the service's mysterious FEATHER BED file (see chapter 8) on alleged pro-Communists in the government.[62] In his official report on the affair in 1990, Peyton Lyon (who had apparently unrestricted access to relevant documents) writes instead that the RCMP was satisfied with External's resolution of the security question in Norman's favour. 'The RCMP did nothing to resist External's decision, and the files suggest a high degree of mutual respect, at least at that time and at the top level.'[63] These two versions, obviously incommensurate, may both be overstated to a degree. Terry Guernsey, the Mountie who intensively interviewed Norman in 1950–2, did not retroactively challenge the appropriateness of the External decision.[64] On the other hand, the 'top level' correspondence Lyon examined was no doubt marked, on the Mountie side, by a deliberate coating of bureaucratic and diplomatic decorum, as befitted a highly sensitive and delicate negotiation with serious ramifications for both parties.

There may well have been some deliberate masking of real feelings. Perhaps the truth is that, while the Mounties may never have been of one mind on Norman's guilt, they would inevitably have been more suspicious than External: suspicion is, after all, second nature to security officers. Perhaps the most striking observation about the Mounties and the Norman affair is that, at the end of the day, it was the link to Hoover's FBI that the Mounties valued most. Herbert Norman the man was the forgotten party. But, in any event, Norman had long since ceased being a human being and had become a 'case,' a security file, a construct of bureaucratic forces. While the man took his own life, the case went on. For the Mounties, the bureaucratic imperative in the Norman case was above all to preserve their international links, as well as to shore up their relations with their Ottawa masters.

8

The Coyote, the Roadrunner, and the Reds under the Bed: Communist Espionage and Subversion

In the only book-length account of the counter-espionage campaigns of the security service against Soviet intelligence, John Sawatsky speaks of the service's 'seeming impotence against the KGB': 'Like the coyote flubbing his attacks on the defiant roadrunner, whatever the Security Service did failed to defeat, much less faze, the Soviets.'[1] Is this judgment fair and accurate? It *may* be, but then again it may *not*. In no area of security service activity is there less hard information available upon which to base judgments. Records relating to counter-espionage are particularly vulnerable to the censors under the Access to Information Act; little, if anything, of any substance survives the scissors-and-black-ink brigade. Sawatsky's book was based entirely on unattributed personal interviews with security service operatives, either retired or still active. He appears, by all accounts, to have done a good job of accurately reconstructing *some* of the counter-espionage cases, but veterans of the service will cryptically state that there were other cases of which he was unaware.

Apart from the severe limitations of documentation, there are other difficulties that stand in the way of confident observations on the effectiveness of espionage and counter-espionage operations. One of the great frustrations of professionals in the trade is that successes tend to remain secret while failures quickly become public. The celebrated 'Cambridge ring' of high-level Soviet moles in Britain – Kim Philby, Guy Burgess, Donald Maclean et al. – represented a spectacular malfunctioning of British counter-espionage. This story has been front-page news time and again and has spawned its own steady publishing industry for decades. Yet real successes – for instance, double agents who stay in place, feeding disinformation to the opposition, subtly fostering disruption and misdirection in the rival agency, feeding back invaluable parts of the picture of what the hostile agency is interested in – necessarily remain, and must remain, jealously guarded secrets of state.

The Canadian security service's role in the great game of Cold War espionage was somewhat circumscribed both by territorial and bureaucratic jurisdiction and by its rather modest role in the wider network of Western security and intelligence. Although the RCMP security service's mandate was always rather hazy, the force was never intended by its political masters to engage in external intelligence gathering as such; nor was it equipped to do so. This, for a long time, did make its focus parochial. In the globalization of international conflict opened up by the Second World War and the ensuing Cold War, however, the service's focus could no longer be narrowly on Canada alone. If threats to Canadian security were global in origin, then neutralizing those threats, or even gathering information on them, could not be confined to Canada. To a limited extent, the service could draw upon intelligence collected by the Communications Branch of the National Research Council, later the Communications Security Establishment. But the CSE was itself closely tied into the Western intelligence network, its targets often allocated by agreements with its senior partners, rather than by the Canadian government. By and large, pertinent external intelligence would be drawn from friendly foreign agencies through exchanges of information. Within this framework, the task of the RCMP security service was to cover Canadian territory against penetration by hostile intelligence. In the context of the Cold War, that, of course, meant near-exclusive concentration on the activities of the Soviet and Soviet Bloc agencies.

Protecting Canada against Soviet Bloc espionage did double duty: Canada shouldered its new post-war responsibilities to the Western alliance, and the Mounties were given additional punch in pursuing what they had traditionally pursued: Communist subversion. The security-screening system was legitimated and reinforced by Canada's international obligations. Memberships in NATO and the North American Air Defence Command (NORAD), for instance, brought with them security specifications and standards to be applied to Canadian participation. NATO had a particularly comprehensive set of standards (codenamed COSMIC in the 1950s), and security service personnel not only were expected to apply these standards but were from time to time posted to European NATO headquarters for closer liaison. U.S. standards, of-

ten stiffer than Canada might have preferred, were imported directly
into this country sometimes via the Armed Forces acting as conduits for
American demands, and sometimes via the RCMP reflecting the FBI's
concerns. Failure to comply fully with security requirements would expose Canada to the censure and, possibly in serious cases, sanctions of
its allies: this was an argument that was of powerful assistance to the
Mounties in intra-bureaucratic conflicts.

The Pontecorvo Effect

Yet security screening was at best a flimsy and inadequate barrier
against the penetration of hostile intelligence activity. The civilian fram-
ers of the screening system knew this, said so, and expected further
problems even with screening.[2] The Mounties also understood the limitations of trying to screen out dedicated spies sent by sophisticated and
resourceful agencies which would design the profiles of their agents
precisely to slip through the screen. As early as 1950 they had a lesson
in hand. Bruno Pontecorvo, an atomic scientist who had worked at the
Chalk River nuclear plant before moving on to nuclear research in the
United Kingdom, suddenly vanished and turned up as a defector in the
USSR. While no one was ever able to prove that Pontecorvo had passed
information while at Chalk River, the suspicion had to be that a scientist with a sufficiently strong ideological affinity for the Soviet system
to eventually defect would certainly have been under pressure to have
done what Klaus Fuchs and other secretly pro-Communist nuclear scientists had done to assist Stalin to acquire the Bomb. So what had gone
wrong with screening?

It seemed there had been an 'after you, Alphonse' comedy of errors
between the RCMP and British security, each deferring to the other
but neither actually undertaking a real screening. Part of this stemmed
from a failure of Sir William Stephenson's wartime British Security
Coordination to do an effective vetting of Pontecorvo as a participant
in the nuclear research in Canada that fed into the Manhattan Project.
Pontecorvo passed Stephenson's screeners. In fact, the British director
of the 'Tube Alloys' (that is, atomic research) project reported to his
assistant that the BSC had provided an 'unusually enthusiastic report'
on Pontecorvo. This proved unfortunate for both the RCMP and MI5,
which took BSC clearance as adequate.[3] After his disappearance, the
FBI said that it had passed information to the BSC in 1943 indicating
that Communist literature had been found in Pontecorvo's house in

the United States; it was impossible to check this because the BSC had been disbanded.[4] On the other hand, the highly security-conscious Leslie Groves (the U.S. general in charge of the Manhattan Project) complained in 1945 about 'foreigners' working on the Canadian project and insisted that they either take on citizenship or leave. Pontecorvo assumed citizenship and stayed; Groves pronounced himself 'pleased.' In any event, Pontecorvo did have Communist relatives and associations in his native Italy, a point that could have been readily verified had anyone bothered to follow up.[5]

Moles, Marxism, and Money

The Pontecorvo affair offered an embarrassing commentary on the shortcomings of vetting. In a deeper sense, however, it was also a misleading guide to the emerging real world of Cold War espionage.

Pontecorvo, if he had been a spy, was ideologically motivated. If he had been identified as a security risk, it would presumably have been on the basis of his Communist relatives and associations. Klaus Fuchs was unearthed as perhaps the most serious atomic spy of all in early 1950 (this may in fact have precipitated Pontecorvo's flight later that same year): Fuchs was a dedicated Communist who was initially fingered as a security risk when his father accepted a teaching post in East Germany. The Rosenbergs in the United States were similarly motivated by ideology. In 1951 Guy Burgess and Donald Maclean skipped Whitehall to turn up in the Soviet Union, initiating the lengthy unveiling of the 'Cambridge Five,' each of whom (first Kim Philby, then Anthony Blunt and John Cairncross filling out the full roster) had been sent on a lifelong mission of Soviet espionage in the higher levels of the British civil service by deep ideological commitment to a Communist ideal. Given all of this, it did seem reasonable enough in the 1950s to see Communist ideology at the root of why people would betray their country – just as the Gouzenko royal commission had warned. Certainly, the RCMP rested comfortably with this view since it so vividly confirmed their commitment to combat Communist subversion as the real, long-term threat to internal security in Canada.

We now know that the ideological traitor was largely a product of time and place, a very special set of circumstances never replicated again.[6] The 1930s, the era of worldwide capitalist crisis, the rise of Fascism, and the drift to war, had generated a small but historically significant number of people who dedicated their lives to assist a dream of a socialist world, who identified their dream with the Soviet Union, and who were willing to give long, clandestine service to Moscow and to betray their own countries as their contribution to that dream. By the 1950s and 1960s, however, the ideological allure of the USSR to Western intellectuals had all but vanished. Latter-day moles and spies for Moscow tended to act out of mercenary greed (like the Walker family and Aldrich Ames in the United States) or because they had been cynically manoeuvred into cooperation by blackmail or entrapment and so on by KGB spymasters. Soviet Bloc intelligence services adjusted their modus operandi to suit the new rules, carefully grooming those they wished to plant with impeccably non-Communist credentials.

The Mounties, along with their colleagues in allied nations, were chasing false hares if they seriously considered security screening to be proof against penetration. In fact, they did not think it to be anything of the kind. As W.L. 'Len' Higgitt, officer in charge of the Counter-Espionage Section, explained to his superiors in 1952, 'we feel a person who has been sent to Canada as a Soviet agent, or with a view to eventually becoming a Soviet agent, is not likely to be one whose background, upon enquiry, will show any unusual or suspicious circumstances, but will undoubtedly be a person whose background has been well prepared so that nothing abnormal will become visible from even the closest scrutiny.'[7] The Mounties also understood very well the key role screening played in the political policing of Canadian society, and were pleased enough to use the Cold War espionage scare as a legitimating cover. Yet Western security and intelligence agencies were also victims of their own deceptive rhetoric as well. The image of the ideological traitor was burned so deeply into the U.S., British, and Canadian services (most powerfully reinforced in 1963 when the prince of spies, Kim Philby, a man who had been a key figure in Atlantic triangle intelligence operations in the late 1940s, was revealed to be a Communist agent) that mole hunts patterned on the old ideological model wracked and poisoned the services of all three countries through the 1970s, led by such near-pathological figures as James Jesus Angleton at the CIA and Peter Wright at MI5.[8] Victims who fitted the abstract picture of 'spies who might have been' were sent for sacrifice: in Canada, diplomat Herbert Norman was driven to suicide, and Leslie James Bennett of the security service was driven out of the service and out of the country – only to be issued with an official apology and financial compensation years later (these cases are discussed later in this chapter). Some of these problems may be glimpsed in the strange story of the notorious FEATHER BED file.

As You Make Your FEATHER BED …

According to Sawatsky, FEATHER BED began as a gleam in the eye of Terry Guernsey in 'B' Branch (Counter-Espionage) in the early 1950s. Guernsey noted that Gouzenko's revelations had related only to GRU, or military intelligence, operations. Gouzenko himself had indicated his general knowledge of a parallel network run by the KGB's predecessor civilian spy agency but had no specific information given the rigorous separation of the two networks. Guernsey's idea was to detect KGB moles in senior government positions by developing profiles of youthful Communist links in the 1930s and 1940s and then working forward. Allegedly the RCMP hierarchy turned down his proposal, fearing that 'such a search would embarrass the Force in the eyes of the government.' Guernsey apparently kept the idea alive by maintaining a file in his own possession, but it was slender, with few entries. The first was Herbert Norman, whom Guernsey had interviewed in 1951; the second was the late undersecretary of state for external affairs, O.D. Skelton, the man who had built the Department of External Affairs almost singlehanded. One or two other senior civil servants also made Guernsey's list. The potential for FBI-style McCarthyism was obvious in such a project, and it is not surprising that the RCMP hierarchy was cool to institutionalizing it.[9]

Such reluctance gave way, however, with Norman's suicide in 1957. FEATHER BED was formally initiated on 3 March 1958 as a file housing a list of 'suspect or known communist sympathizers employed by the Federal Government' drawn from the service's punch-card index. The Research Section was assigned the task of determining if anything parallel to the Alger Hiss/Harry Dexter-White pattern in the United States, or the Guy Burgess/Donald Maclean pattern in Britain, had occurred in Canada. Common factors appeared to be that Soviet moles were 'practically all college graduates of the 1930s and at one time or other had some association with the Communist Party' followed by a general pattern of employment in government departments targeted by Soviet espionage: wartime agencies and foreign affairs in the postwar period.[10] This, of course, described the career of Herbert Norman. FEATHER BED seems to have initially been a project to point to other potential Normans.

The Research Section was too busy to pay much attention, and a year later FEATHER BED was transferred back to 'B' Branch and put under an analyst who took charge of looking seriously for suspects fitting the profile. By June 1960, forty files had been completed: 'five persons who were prominent civil servants deserved special attention.' The material had at first been kept in the officer's own safe, but by 25 April 1962 a general file under the name FEATHER BED was opened. Within a few months, approximately one thousand individual files revealed sixteen 'senior' public servants in 'positions of trust and influence who had in varying degrees communist affiliations or backgrounds of activity.' By 1968, FEATHER BED had grown to become a separate section, with particular attention directed at following up the Gouzenko leads from 1945–6 and at identifying Soviet 'penetration and disinformation.' Some of the best and brightest minds in the service were drawn into this mushrooming project, which drew in the Counter-Subversion as well as Counter-Espionage sections. Ironically, one of its directors was Jim Bennett, later to be wrongly fingered himself as a Soviet mole. FEATHER BED carried its momentum into the 1970s: by 1972, '74 investigative leads were being processed on individuals or organizational files.'

This peak of activity coincided, not accidently, with the Angleton witch hunt in the CIA and Peter Wright's rampage through MI6 and MI5 in Britain: tracking alleged deep-penetration agents motivated by pro-Communist ideology was definitely the thing to do in the Western counter-espionage trade in those days. But it was a self-destructive drive that finally consumed itself in an excess of paranoia and suspicion. Angleton was forced out of the CIA at the end of 1974, and Wright's career in MI5 came to a close shortly after. FEATHER BED's momentum could not be maintained. By 1975, the project had either exhausted itself or enough material had been returned to other sections that FEATHER BED, as such, became dormant. Ironically, it was only with its demise as an active program that FEATHER BED, by the late 1970s, became a subject of some notoriety in the media, with questions being asked in the House of Commons. Rumours abounded that cabinet ministers and Prime Minister Pierre Trudeau were in the FEATHER BED file. The solicitor general was assured by the RCMP that these rumours were 'not correct.'[11] Whatever the truth of the rumours, FEATHER BED added to the impression of a J. Edgar Hoover-style operation spying upon the government itself. It could do the RCMP no good in the eyes of the public, and certainly not with their political masters. Since there is no evidence that FEATHER BED ever turned up a single case of espionage that could be acted upon, the whole project appears in retrospect as a fiasco.

Prisoners of Their Own Rhetoric?

Were the Mounties as counter-spies prisoners of their own rhetoric? The Cold War did that to people. But then again the Great Game was also one that called for realism, professionalism, and a fair appreciation of the tactics of the adversary. On the strategic plane, the Mounties may have harboured dubious assumptions about unlimited Soviet plans for world domination and enslavement of free people everywhere. Certainly, the Soviets believed, or professed to believe, equally lurid interpretations of Western motives. On the tactical plane, on the other hand, only concrete results mattered. Here the Mounties had to play catch-up in the late 1940s and early 1950s. They had to show the Canadian government that they could prevent repeats of the Gouzenko affair and they had to show the Allies that they could be trusted to defend their patch of turf on the wider playing field.

In the early days, prospects for the Coyote facing the elusive Roadrunner were not bright. There was a huge imbalance of resources available to the two adversaries. Soviet espionage operations were global in scope and pampered by the Kremlin in comparison to other elements of the Soviet bureaucracy. Ottawa was slow to respond in concrete terms to its own strictures about the menace of Communist espionage revealed in the Gouzenko revelations. While internal security procedures and anti-Communist purges were in place by the late 1940s, the necessities of carrying on counter-espionage did not immediately open up the purse strings either of the RCMP hierarchy or of their political masters. Indeed, there were continued questions about the suitability of a paramilitary police force carrying out counter-intelligence operations, as the *Watchdog* fiasco during the war demonstrated. The tendency to see matters primarily in law-enforcement terms – especially when the security service was still housed within the Criminal Investigation Branch – was not a good start. Nor did the human resources initially allocated by the RCMP to the task seem encouraging. In the early 1950s the Counter-Espionage Section numbered a mere four officers at headquarters under the direction of Terry Guernsey, who was acutely aware of the shortcomings of his small, untrained staff. With the death of one veteran officer in 1951, there were only three men left in the service whose experience went back continuously to the early war years. In 1952–3 the Counter-Espionage Section, in its contribution to the preparation of the *Annual Report* of the service, openly lamented its situation: 'One serious lack in the operation of an efficient Counter-

Espionage system is very apparent. *We do not have properly trained inves-tigative personnel* ... A proper appreciation of the basic requirements of intelligence investigations, the most efficient methods of obtaining and assessing intelligence information and an appreciation of the methods of operation of enemy and allied intelligence organizations, is lacking.' A 'few' members, 'through years of painful trial-and-error methods, reached an approximation of the full requirements.' But these were so few and overburdened that they could not pass on their experience to the junior members, who were left on their own 'to chart their own course through the difficulties of an investigation, almost entirely unin-formed and ill-equipped for the task.'[12]

Gradually, however, the tools and resources were grudgingly ad-vanced and the Coyote learned through 'painful trial-and-error' to cope with the machinations of the Roadrunner. Part of the answer was better training and the introduction of civilian analysts into the section, a point that will be explored later in this chapter. Part was simply gath-ering experience and a depth of institutional memory, along with the confidence gained from the realization that the adversary was not su-perhuman and made mistakes that could be capitalized upon by care-ful, solid work. As we shall see, there were problems caused by Soviet penetration of the security service, but this happened to the 'cousins' in London and Washington as well. In the end, the Coyote gained a fair amount of professional expertise. By the 1960s, the RCMP security service had won itself a modest but respected place on the Western se-curity and intelligence team. When the security service was detached from the RCMP in 1984, there were discreet expressions of dismay from old allies in Western capitals.

Canada was probably not a very important Cold War target in and of itself. The country was not the site for scientific developments of stra-tegic East-West significance. The nuclear connection was peripheral, despite some of the sensational publicity around the Gouzenko affair. Later, secret developments in defence technologies of intense interest to Soviet espionage involved Canadian firms at best only in small sub-contracting roles for specific aspects of projects. To be sure, in later Cold War years there was some Canadian-developed commercial technol-ogy that was of interest to the Soviets. And, of course, the KGB was a huge bureaucratic empire that would spy on Canada simply because it was there. But, most of all, Canada would be a terrain for espionage and counter-espionage because it was a link in the Western alliance: Canada may not have had a lot of secrets of its own worth stealing, but it did share in the secrets of its Allies and could therefore be one particular pressure point for Soviet inquisitiveness.

Illegals, Legends, and Sell-Outs

Canadian passports were a favourite Cold War currency for Soviet spy operations. Efforts at passport control proved difficult, especially when legitimate documents were being released to persons with carefully faked identities as Canadian citizens. Canada was a major staging ground for 'illegals': trained Soviet operatives who entered the country illegally and then spent years carefully building up 'legends,' false identities as Canadians, before being activated for service as spies now unlikely to attract notice. Such agents might not even be intended for service in Canada, but as 'Canadians' they might easily enter the United States or European countries. As late as 1996, after the collapse of the USSR and Soviet Communism, two such Russian illegals were discovered building their legends in Toronto, and were deported; in 2010 a large number of illegals were nabbed in the United States: the bureaucratic mills grind on. For the decades of the Cold War, these kinds of operations were a major preoccupation of the Counter-Espionage Section of the security service. Canada was a country of mass post-war immigration, which lacked any national, centralized record-keeping system identifying individuals. This made it a particularly attractive target for such operations. For instance, there was no central matching of birth and death certificates, making it very easy for illegals to assume the identities of deceased Canadians, acquire social insurance and Medicare numbers, establish work records, pay taxes, draw on social benefits, and so on, thus gradually filling out a profile that would be very hard to detect as false. And, of course, 'Canadians' could freely enter and leave the United States undetected, which was very useful.

One such illegal landed in Canada in the early 1950s and was established with the identity of a young Russian immigrant who had returned to the USSR in the 1930s. 'David Soboloff' (codenamed *Gideon* by the RCMP) proved less trustworthy than his Soviet handlers expected. He began an affair with the wife of a Canadian soldier, and refused to move to the United States, as per his orders. Finally, *Gideon* simply phoned the RCMP and revealed his status. At the security service, Terry Guernsey decided to initiate a classic counter-intelligence response by running *Gideon* as a double agent. It might have worked, except for a shocking development in 1955: a member of the security service, James

Morrison, who was heavily in debt from extravagant spending and racetrack gambling and already in trouble for misappropriating secret RCMP payments, sold *Gideon*'s name to the Soviets for $3,500 (about a year's salary for a Mountie officer at the time). *Gideon* was recalled to Moscow for a 'temporary' visit; his Ottawa handlers, unaware of the danger he was in, gave him a choice: quit now and get a new Canadian identity or go back and continue to play the double agent role on behalf of the service. Unwisely, *Gideon* chose to play a little longer. When he failed to return, it was assumed that he had been imprisoned, interrogated, and executed.

When the Mounties learned of Morrison's apparently lethal treachery, they were understandably furious, but they were also concerned not to air their dirty laundry in public. Morrison was dismissed from the force but not charged with any offence. In 1982 journalist John Sawatsky made the story public for the first time, although Morrison's identity was hidden under the codename *Long Knife*.[13] Under pressure of negative publicity, the government eventually prosecuted Morrison decades after his transgression, and secured a conviction. Morrison is the only security service officer ever put away for selling out the service to the KGB, even if it took the RCMP more than thirty years to act against him. His motive had nothing to do with ideology but everything to do with money.

Neither Morrison nor *Gideon*'s Mountie handlers had any reason to doubt that he had perished. Then, decades later, a ghost from the past returned. In the late 1980s, the RCMP security service's successor agency, CSIS, was startled to receive word via British intelligence officers that *Gideon* had contacted them using a password long ago entrusted to the double agent if he had to escape the USSR. As CBC television news revealed in 1997,[14] '*Gideon* had survived. He spent 25 years in Soviet Gulags and emerged as a non-person doing whatever menial work he could find to keep himself alive ... In the late 1980s, as Communism was crumbling and the Soviet Union was in a state of confusion, *Gideon* acted. He made his way from his home near Kiev to the city of Riga in Latvia. And from there he contacted British Intelligence asking to be brought out ... A short time later, using false papers, *Gideon* was smuggled out to the west.' Prime Minister Brian Mulroney arranged for *Gideon*'s return to Canada. The government decided that it owed *Gideon* a pension payable from the time he had first returned to Moscow, with interest accumulated for all the years he had been unable to collect it. The man who had originally entered Canada illegally as a Soviet spy is now a bona fide Canadian, honoured by his adopted country, living in comfortable retirement in Ottawa.[15] By the time *Gideon* returned, Morrison, too, was released from prison. He was never told that the man he betrayed had survived.

The Morrison case serves to highlight a problem of which the Mounties were uneasily aware. The counter-espionage war was a shadow war involving tactics that might be questionable from a legal standpoint. Even when the field officers were doing their duty and following their orders, unlike Morrison, they might well find themselves brushing against ethical and legal questions. In 1950 Sergeant Len Higgitt, then the officer in charge of the Counter-Espionage Section and later a commissioner of the force, wrote to his superiors about what it meant to 'fight fire with fire':

> To be successful in Counter-Espionage work it is often necessary to adopt very unorthodox methods which do not fit in with our regular mode of operations. In this regard it is a matter of real and constant concern to the members of the Counter-Espionage Section of Headquarters Special Branch, that they often have to request, or at least feel they should request, rather unusual courses of action by our field personnel well knowing that by complying with the request the investigator may be seriously jeopardizing their own futures in the Force if through bad luck or human error their operations are discovered by those persons against whom they are directing the investigation. Such discovery could lead to most embarrassing incidents and possibly legal action against the members concerned. It is to be hoped that some official notice can be taken of this situation and some overall directive laid down for guidance. Again it is to be stressed that extraordinary measures and methods must be used if we are to effectively cope with extraordinary situations. To some extent the axiom of the 'end justifies the means' is very true in Counter-Espionage operations but the personal risks to the operating members must be recognized before they can be expected to extend themselves in connection with these matters.[16]

Higgitt was alluding to an endemic problem in the security service in general that would eventually become the subject of the McDonald Commission on RCMP 'wrongdoing' in the late 1970s. His plea for a clear directive from above was never heeded, at least until the new civilian service was created as the RCMP's successor in 1984.

Working at the shadowy margins of legality without clear authorization was enough to cause endemic anxiety among the officers in the field. But associated with this was another disturbing aspect of security intelligence work, especially counter-espionage: the work could literally lie at the margins of life and death – as the *Long Knife* episode so grimly illustrates. Running secret sources and double agents was a very risky business, especially for the sources and agents, but that anxiety could extend to their handlers as well, who had to contend with troubling responsibilities, not to speak of moral dilemmas. According to an internal report on morale problems in the security service in 1963, while the lower ranks were sometimes subject to 'severe emotional disturbances' caused by a combination of boredom and obstacles to career promotion, the responsibilities of their commanding officers led to problems of a longer-term variety 'likely to have detrimental consequences for their health at more advanced ages.' According to the RCMP historians of the security service, among the relatively small number of commissioned officers engaged in the security work of the force to 1966, 'several cases can be documented to testify to the significance of health erosion.' The man in charge of the service in the late 1940s and early 1950s, George McClelland, later wrote to an officer retiring on health grounds: 'Only those of us who went through some of those experiences together will really understand how much of each of us was consumed in some of those difficult operations which we had to carry out.'[17]

Questions of propriety and moral responsibility aside, were there other illegals identified and successfully 'turned' by the service? If there were, there has never been any public notice made of the fact. But, then again, such public notice would be highly unlikely under the circumstances. When the two Russian illegals were identified in 1996, they were returned in the full glare of publicity. The service seems to have been signalling to their old adversaries that they preferred to call off the game, once and for all. In earlier decades, while the Cold War continued, such a course of action would have seemed unprofessional. Turning the agents would have been far more enticing, if feasible. Whether this has actually occurred, and how often, must remain a matter of conjecture, at least until a decision is made to be more forthcoming on the secret Canadian history of the Cold War.

Chasing the Roadrunner 'Diplomats'

Soviet Bloc espionage concentrated a great deal of effort on enlisting locals as sources, agents, or, best of all, moles in influential positions.

From the counter-espionage perspective, the weak spot to strike at in such operations was the communications link between such locals and their handlers. It was notorious that Soviet Bloc embassies were well stocked with phantom 'diplomats' who were in practice intelligence operatives. In the case of the Soviets themselves, this picture was further complicated by the presence of two parallel networks, the KGB and the GRU, which tended to keep their operations watertight from each other as well as from the regular diplomatic staff. Igor Gouzenko had worked for the GRU section, but he told the Mounties that there were separate networks of which he knew very little. Just as the Soviet spymasters had relied on operatives with diplomatic cover to control their wartime networks, so too they continued to rely upon their diplomatic staff throughout the Cold War to recruit and run Canadian sources and agents. These 'legals' posed an obvious espionage threat, but they also presented the RCMP counter-espionage team with an opportunity for surveillance of spy operations.

The first hurdle was to limit the numbers of Embassy personnel and to contain their movements within manageable areas. In conditions of the Cold War it was not difficult to get Canadian government agreement to restrict establishments and to put strict limits on the movements of diplomats. Permission had to be sought for trips outside their area, and itineraries were to be strictly followed. A decades-long cat-and-mouse game was played in the streets of Ottawa and its environs, in which the Mounties followed, filmed, bugged, recorded, and analysed the movements and contacts of Soviet Bloc 'diplomats.' A key feature of this surveillance was the development in the 1950s of the civilian Watcher Service that replaced an earlier Mountie Surveillance Unit. The Watchers developed a good deal of expertise at carrying out surveillance without detection, enough indeed to gain the professional respect of security services in other countries.[18] Of course, Soviet intelligence agents were well schooled in counter-surveillance tactics: a silent war was going on of which virtually no one but the direct participants was aware.

One of the aspects of fighting this secret war that caused a great deal of anxiety in the security service was the blurred line between legality and illegality in the methodology of counter-espionage. An example of this is mail interception, something viewed as an important tool. Until 1954 this presented no problem: under the Defence of Canada Regulations enacted during the war, postal interception was acceptable as an emergency measure. The relevant regulations actually remained in force for almost a decade after the war, but expired in 1954. After this point, the Mounties were, in effect, on their own. Their mail-opening operation, codenamed CATHEDRAL, was particularly useful to the Counter-Espionage Section, and the men in the field had no intention of suddenly dropping such a tool just because of a dubious legal context. The RCMP did, however, seek repeatedly through the late 1950s and into the 1960s for some directive or guideline that would give official sanction to actions that they realized had the potential to get individual Mounties, or their cooperating sources within the Post Office, into legal trouble if ever discovered and made public. They never received any such sanction and complained that mail opening was 'the one major resource that is denied us.'[19] This did not in fact mean a resource whose *use* was denied: CATHEDRAL did operate from 1954 onward, and indeed into the 1970s, sometimes even against the express orders of the RCMP hierarchy[20] (see chapter 10). What the RCMP wanted, but did not receive, was official *legitimation* of the use of mail opening. This sort of problem would eventually come home to roost in the scandals of the 1970s and the official inquiry that recommended the 'civilianization' of the security service under a specific legal mandate. But for the Cold War years in which the Coyote and the Roadrunner battled secretly through Canadian streets and back alleys, the imperative for the Coyote was clear: do what was needed to do and don't worry about the niceties.

The Counter-Espionage Section was particularly interested in the specific communication points between the Soviets and their local contacts, because it was there that they could catch them red-handed. The tradecraft of spying – dead-letter boxes, laundered trails, encrypted communications, and so on – offered vulnerable points for counter-espionage breakthroughs. These sometimes did happen. For instance, by means of a surveillance trap set near an Ottawa shopping centre in the 1960s, Bower Featherstone, a civil servant with a gambling problem, was detected selling classified maps to the Soviets, tried, and convicted. More generally, when the Soviets were caught in flagrante, there might be a round of diplomatic expulsions. Expulsions, especially on a large scale, had the advantage of at least temporarily disrupting the spying networks. External Affairs might not always be happy with the practice of declaring Soviet diplomats persona non grata, because the Soviets would invariably retaliate against Canadian diplomats in Moscow. 'PNG wars' were ultimately pointless in any event, since the KGB and GRU would simply resume the same old game with a new set of players.

Another surveillance trap in the 1960s alerted the Mounties to the Soviets' use of a Vancouver postal clerk, Victor Spencer. Spencer, a somewhat confused left-winger with intertwined personal and social grievances, was an exception to the rule about ideology being replaced by money as the motivation for cooperation with Soviet espionage. His lowly position in the bureaucracy did not allow him access to any secrets, however, and his open espousal of pro-Communist ideas had attracted the attention of the RCMP as long ago as 1950 when the security screeners had turned in a 'pink sheet' on him as a risk.[21] Not holding a sensitive post, he was left in place and not, of course, informed of his security problem; his career in the Post Office was from that time on, in his eyes, unfairly impeded. His problems may well have stemmed from his security status; ironically, his resultant embitterment contributed to his willingness to betray his country. The Soviets showed poor judgment in trying to employ such an unimportant person with such obvious political liabilities. Both Spencer and his Soviet handlers fell into the Mountie surveillance trap in May 1960. The Counter-Espionage Section concluded that the 'KGB are preparing to establish an illegal resident in the Vancouver area, with [Spencer] destined to function as an illegal support agent to the illegal resident.'[22] The Mounties set up shop carefully awaiting future developments.

This particular operation turned bad when the Criminal Investigation Branch, looking for a criminal conviction, took the case away from the security service. Since the information he had provided the Soviets was little more than public knowledge acquired from libraries and other open sources (which the Soviets themselves could have consulted directly!), his grilling only showed the CIB that a conviction under the Official Secrets Act would be doubtful. Besides, by this time Spencer was dying of cancer, and the publicity that would be generated by the spectacle of the Mounties beating up on a dying and rather pathetic old man would hardly constitute a public education in the Soviet espionage threat to Canada. He was, however, quietly fired from his job and lost his pension, since he had not acquired sufficient time. Meanwhile, two Soviet diplomats were expelled (one of whom was in fact connected to the Spencer case) and a reference made to an unnamed civil servant.

Eventually an investigative reporter tracked Spencer down in a cancer ward in a Vancouver hospital, and the whole shabby story became a media event across the country, with emphasis on the government and the RCMP as ogres threatening a dying old man. For a time the security service actually hid Spencer from the media, earning his gratitude for protecting him. Publicity, however, mounted to the point where the prime minister, Lester Pearson, telephoned Spencer and asked him if he wanted a public inquiry into his grievances. Spencer died before the Wells Commission report appeared; as it turned out, the commission pointed out Spencer's espionage and argued that the government had treated him fairly under the circumstances.[23]

The Great Mole Hunt (Canada) Ltd

The Spencer affair had been a public-relations disaster, one that contributed, along with some other scandals, to the creation of the Mackenzie Royal Commission on Security in late 1966. But what troubled the security service most was something not publicly known: the Soviets had cut Spencer off before he had been picked up for questioning. It seemed that they had been tipped off that they were under surveillance. This mystery simply added to a number of other problems associated with too many of the counter-espionage cases. Could it be that the Soviets had penetrated the RCMP security service itself, and were confounding their best counter-espionage efforts? The spectre of Kim Philby, head of the Russian desk at MI6, was too graphic a lesson to pass up. When the Angleton mole hunt accelerated in Washington, the pressure became irresistible: the traitor within *must* exist and *must* be uncovered. James *Long Knife* Morrison was long gone. And surely some greedy overspender looking to cover rubber checks was not the material from which a wily, devilishly clever mole who could worm his way into the very heart of the anti-KGB force was likely to come? This might-have-been mole must be a secret Communist traitor, a Philby clone. This was the conclusion of the inner logic of the Cold War to the last generation of true believers. If a Philby did not exist, it would be necessary to invent him. All that remained was to apply the tradecraft of counter-intelligence to the specific task, and identify the Canadian Philby. Operation GRIDIRON was launched.

Leslie James Bennett was born to a working-class family in the coal-mining district of South Wales in 1920. Growing up in a world of poverty and class conflict, Bennett was naturally enough a Labour Party supporter. When the war came in 1939, young Bennett, with some engineering training, was conscripted into signals intelligence, where he served in Malta, Egypt, and Italy. After the war, he was offered a job in the new Government Communications Headquarters (GCHQ), the heart of British post-war signals intelligence. In 1947 he was posted briefly to Istanbul as the ranking GCHQ man in the British mission. His equivalent in MI6 was the new station chief, Kim Philby. The two met from time to time, not surprisingly, but they seem never to have discussed business. Philby, well-bred Oxbridge high-flyer, was apparently indifferent to a junior person of working-class origin from an intelligence branch in which he held little interest. After additional postings in Asia, and after picking up an Australian wife, Bennett returned to GCHQ in Britain in 1952 as section head responsible for the Middle East.

Seeking a change of scenery, Bennett and his wife immigrated to Canada in 1954, expecting a position in the Canadian equivalent of the GCHQ, the Communications Branch National Research Council (CBNRC). That did not come, but an introduction to the two leading civilians in the security service, Mark McClung and Don Wall, led to a position in that organization instead. Bennett went to work for Terry Guernsey in 'B' Branch (Counter-Espionage) as a research analyst. For the next eighteen years, Jim Bennett was involved at the heart of the war against Soviet espionage in Canada, from 1958 on as head of the Russian desk. When evidence of Soviet penetration led to a mole hunt, suspicion inevitably settled on Bennett.

Of course, Jim Bennett best fitted the profile of a Kim Philby. He was British, he admitted having once had Labour Party sympathies, and, worst of all, he had actually met Philby himself! Although he had long since shed the socialist ideas of his Welsh childhood, Bennett was not a right-winger like so many others in the intelligence profession. Once in the 1960s at a party in Washington, D.C., hosted by the MI6 station chief, Maurice Oldfield, Bennett had fallen into heated debate with Jim Angleton and Angleton's aide Ray Rocca on the subject of the late Senator Joe McCarthy, whose reckless witch-hunting activities Bennett detested. Angleton and Rocca defended McCarthy and eventually an incensed Rocca took a swing at Bennett. Angleton restrained his aide, but the CIA's manic mole hunter had put Bennett down as a 'pinko' suspect. Ever since Angleton had been humiliated by his own close association with Philby (from 1949 to 1951, when Philby was posted to Washington, the two had dozens of bibulous working lunches at fashionable Harvey's Restaurant), he had become obsessed with British traitors. The Americans swung into action to reinforce GRIDIRON, with Bennett as prime suspect.[24] Through CAZAB, a closely linked, super-secret group of counter-intelligence officials from Canada, Australia, New Zealand, Britain, and the United States who met together every year and a half and were in regular secure communication with one another on matters of mutual interest, Bennett became widely known within the Western intelligence network as a possible Soviet mole.[25]

There was, to be sure, considerable circumstantial evidence suggesting that Bennett was the mole who had alerted the Soviets to various operations that had gone mysteriously wrong: as head of the Russian desk since 1958, he would necessarily have been in on all the counter-espionage operations. Some of the evidence pointed the other way, but this was ignored. Finally, in 1972, Bennett had his security clearance lifted. He was taken to a safe house where he underwent five days of interrogation. There was no proof of betrayal, certainly nothing that could remotely be used in court. So the interrogators focused on his past, trying to establish a profile of a Philby-like long-term mole, recruited during the war or even before. Intimate details of his marriage (simultaneously breaking up) revealed to Bennett that they had been bugging his bedroom. Bennett, in the memory of the then director of the security service, John Starnes, who was in overall charge of the inquiry, 'conducted himself with great dignity and strength of character.'[26] Yet, at the end, Bennett was asked to leave the service.

In his 1998 memoirs, Starnes is adamant: 'Exhaustive investigation led to the conclusion that there existed not a shred of evidence that Bennett had ever been a KGB agent.' There were, however, as Starnes ruefully recalls, rumours originating within the service, and deliberately leaked to the media, which made Bennett's retention virtually impossible. That these 'doubts' had spread to allies, especially the Americans, made Bennett a liability, whether or not there was any truth at all to the suspicions. Thus, in the classic logic of the national insecurity state, Starnes regretfully concludes that 'the matter was a personal tragedy which, in the final analysis, it seemed to me had to be resolved in the interest of the state.'[27]

Bennett was offered a 'medical' discharge. Desultory efforts were made to find him another, non-secret job in the civil service, but Bennett, his world collapsing around him, fled Canada, and finally ended up in Perth, Australia, living on a medical pension and what work he could pick up. Everything had been hushed up, but eventually rumours started circulating about a Soviet mole. A novel appeared fictionalizing the story; Bennett sued and won.[28] Then, in 1982, John Sawatsky's work of investigative journalism, *For Services Rendered*, laid out the story to wide public scrutiny. Sawatsky did not draw conclusions but left little doubt in the reader's mind that the Mounties had got the wrong man.

Gilles Brunet was the apparent antithesis of everything Bennett represented. He was not British but a native-born Canadian. Far from having a suspicious past with left-wing traces and a close encounter with the devil Philby, Brunet was the son of a Mountie, J.J. Brunet, who had been the first head of the Security and Intelligence Directorate when it was established as a separate division in 1956 and who had finished his career as deputy commissioner. 'One of us,' Brunet was marked for a brilliant trajectory in the force. He joined the security service in the early 1960s. At the Russian desk, he won promotion in 1966 for investigative work that led to the conviction of Bower Featherstone. The following year, Brunet was enrolled by the service in a Russian-language course and scored top marks. In 1972 an internal assessment report was glowing: 'Sgt. Brunet is well above average and clearly shows that he is capable of assuming heavier responsibilities. He is a very aggressive and resourceful investigator and has developed to a remarkable degree the ability to recognize the significant[,] thereby getting to the crux of a problem and permitting him to cope easily with unexpected developments. In addition to being fully bilingual, he is fluent in Russian, which is a valuable asset in his current position. This is a solid member who is making a most valuable contribution.'[29]

But something funny happened to Gilles Brunet's irresistible rise in the force. A year after the above report, Brunet was thrown out of the RCMP. This had nothing to do with Soviet espionage. Along with his old security service sidekick, Donald McCleery – a tough guy from the wrong side of the tracks in Montreal, a cowboy operator never properly socialized into the hierarchical ethic of the Mounted Police – Brunet was believed to have been too close to shady Montreal underworld connections. Refusing to back off, McCleery and Brunet were cashiered in December 1973. Later, the pair, now running a private security firm, made an abortive attempt to blow the whistle on RCMP dirty tricks in Quebec (see chapter 9). Brunet's promising career with the Mounties had ended very badly. But just how badly was not known until Jim Bennett was publicly exonerated in 1993.

It might have turned out very differently, and Jim Bennett might never have been put through his private hell of wrongful accusations of treason. Gilles Brunet could have been snared as the real traitor as early as 1968, just months after he volunteered cooperation with the KGB as a mercenary in January of that year. According to retired security service officer Peter Marwitz,[30] Brunet had already managed to do serious damage to Canadian interests, including betraying listening devices planted in the Soviet Embassy in Ottawa, disrupting RCMP surveillance of Soviet activities, and fingering a Canadian military attaché in Moscow for expulsion for spying. Then in May he was almost exposed by his own wife, with whom he was on shaky grounds because of his drunkenness and philandering. After he returned drunk late one night, his suspicious wife, seeking evidence of an affair, searched his vehicle and found over $2,000 in twenty-dollar bills neatly folded into an envelope – an amount equivalent at that time to about one-third of Brunet's annual net salary as a Mountie corporal. Unconvinced by Brunet's prevarications about the origins of this extraordinary sum, she contacted the security service and was interviewed about her husband's highly suspicious behaviour. It appears, however, that Brunet had already preemptively warned the service that his jealous and vindictive spouse might try to discredit him. An internal security report was opened on Brunet, but it was kept under the control of only three persons. Whether through his personal influence or, as Marwitz speculates, because Brunet managed to burglarize the office and safe in which the report rested, by September the report was 'lost.' Brunet's charmed double life as an untouchable traitor continued unimpeded for another five years while suspicions aroused by the effects of his activities settled instead on the innocent Jim Bennett.

Brunet was finally unmasked, as is so often the case in the shadow world of spies, by another spy. In 1985 veteran KGB officer Vitaliy Yurchenko defected at the Americans' Rome embassy. Although he later re-defected, Yurchenko was extensively debriefed by the CIA. Since he had been deputy chief supervising all North American KGB residencies, Yurchenko knew KGB operations in Canada inside out. He was very frank during his debriefing, and among the other gold nuggets he offered was the fact that there had been a KGB mole operating within the RCMP security service during the Bennett years. Yurchenko revealed his name. It was not Jim Bennett. It was Gilles Brunet. Proof was offered the RCMP when Yurchenko revealed the name of Brunet's KGB case officer. After Brunet's dismissal in 1973, the Mounties, who had maintained surveillance on him, observed him meeting with a Soviet official. This was the very man named by Yurchenko.[31] In 1993 the Canadian government sent a representative to Perth, Australia, to offer Jim Bennett an unconditional apology and a lump sum of financial compensation. Confirmation was eventually forthcoming that Gilles Brunet had been the real mole.

There are a number of lessons in this sordid tale. Suspicions passed Brunet by time and again because he was 'one of us.' Moreover, there was a deeply held but false sense of confidence within the RCMP that the paramilitary force with its special mystique was somehow bullet-proof against treason. Civilian employees of the security service who had never undertaken the rigorous Mountie training and lacked the Redcoat esprit de corps were in this view vulnerable to KGB manipulation or subversion, but members of the force were not. It was partially on these grounds that the RCMP brass successfully fought off the civilianization proposal of the Mackenzie Commission in 1969–70 (see below), even as Brunet continued to leak RCMP secrets to his KGB handlers. There was another dimension as well that deflected attention from Brunet and focused it on Bennett: the traumatic impact of the Philby/Burgess/Maclean defections on the time-honoured British connections of the RCMP. The security service had grown up closely entwined with its British counterparts, with some equivalent coolness in relation to the Americans. The exposure of the Philby ring, with its implications of treason among well-born Brits, shook that connection and drove the security service into a closer embrace of more sceptical American attitudes about the unreliability of the British. Bennett was British, while Brunet was a Canadian uncontaminated by known links to the likes of Philby.

Yet another dimension, highly significant at the time, was the widespread belief in Western counter-espionage – a belief powerfully reinforced by the Cambridge ring – that spying for the Soviets was most likely motivated by ideology. Brunet was innocent of ideological motives. According to the former head of foreign counter-intelligence for the KGB, General Oleg Kalugin, the Soviets had paid 'hundreds of thousands of dollars' to their RCMP mole (Marwitz calculates Brunet's earnings from the KGB as more than $2 million in 1997 dollars). Brunet, it turns out, lived well beyond his means, with a particular fondness for expensive holiday jaunts to Mexico. His tombstone (he died young in 1984 of a heart attack) is adorned with a drawing of Acapulco and a martini glass.[32] While the Mounties, like their American and British counterparts, were chasing alluring spectres of ideological traitors from the long dead past, the real treason under their very noses wore the very contemporary, but disappointingly sleazy face of commonplace greed and self-indulgence. The real mole was just another *Long Knife*, but far better situated to cover his tracks and to inflict real damage.

Jim Bennett's shadow profile in the counter-intelligence files was no more than an ideological construction, a melodramatic Cold War plot device, a mole that might have been, but never was. Jim Bennett the man was destroyed, two decades of loyal service to Canada thrown into the trash bin, his marriage wrecked, driven into lonely and penurious exile and old age far away on the other side of the world. Gilles Brunet's shadow profile did not match the script, and so he escaped suspicion, although more mundane associations with questionable underworld elements did trip him up (and thereby ended his usefulness to the KGB). Why a man like Brunet should have thrown away so many advantages and such a promising career for the rewards of martini glasses at Acapulco poolsides must remain a puzzle for psychologists. Canada's real Kim Philby is an enigma untranslatable into Cold War discourse.[33]

Last of the Old-Time Spies? The Professor with a Double Life

There was still one last spy from the old Philby mould lurking under cover in Canada, in, of all places, the Economics Department at Laval University in Quebec City. Although his work for the KGB began in the 1950s, his secret double life would not be uncovered until 1979 by the RCMP Counter-Espionage Section, which then strangely left him alone. His public comeuppance did not take place until 1982, and it was not in Canada, but in the United Kingdom, where Professor Hugh Hambleton was charged with passing NATO secrets to the KGB from 1956 to 1961 and with continuing espionage activities until 1979.[34]

When he stood up in the dock at the famous Old Bailey courthouse in London, Hambleton hardly looked like a James Bond, or even a Kim Philby. A bland sixty-year-old bespectacled professor with a research interest in the economic decline of Spain in the seventeenth century, he had attracted little attention over a career of teaching with occasional stints in government. Apart from having served with the French Resistance behind enemy lines in the Second World War, he seemed to all appearances to have lived a quiet life. Perhaps the excitement of his wartime activities had left a taste for the clandestine world, perhaps a left-wing family environment in Ottawa where Soviet diplomats were frequent visitors had inclined him to radical sympathies. Studying in Paris in the 1950s, he was contacted by one of those visitors, now working as a recruiter for Soviet intelligence, who persuaded Hambleton to apply for a job with NATO, where for five years he copied and deposited thousands of secret documents in dead drops all over Paris. Tiring of the constant danger to which he was exposed, Hambleton cut off his Soviet handlers in 1961, telling them he was returning to his academic studies.

Soon he was back in Canada, teaching at Laval. In 1967 a reluctant Hambleton was drawn back into the KGB fold by an engaging, gregarious 'illegal' going by the name of Rudi Herrmann. For the next decade, Hambleton undertook a series of global consultancies from the Middle East to Latin America, all the while collecting open-source intelligence for the KGB. In 1975 he was whisked away for a training session in Moscow. Hambleton claimed to the American writer John Barron that he had even been taken to a private dinner with the head of the KGB, Yuri Andropov (later president) – although whether this is fact or merely Hambleton's fantasizing is unknown. But Hambleton's globetrotting spy career came to an abrupt halt at the end of the 1970s. Rudi Herrmann had been unmasked by the FBI in the United States, and turned. Leads were opened onto the trail of the agents he had been handling. Frank Pratt, a respected spy catcher in the Security Service, led Operation RED PEPPER to uncover Canadian links. In November 1979 RCMP officers landed on Hambleton's apartment in Quebec City with a search warrant, after months of surveillance.

Although expectations were roused that Hambleton would be put on trial, the Trudeau government, recently returned to power in the 1980 winter election, announced that no charges would be brought. Hambleton remained a free man and was able to continue his teaching. The Conservatives were enraged and charged that the Liberals were coddling Communist spies, as did some of the right-wing media. But then the story faded. Behind the scenes, a more complex story of counterintelligence was being played out. Hambleton had readily confessed to his Canadian KGB activities, which were not of a nature that could bring prosecution under the Official Secrets Act. He had cagily refused to divulge anything concerning his NATO days, which involved passing secret documents. Hambleton was offered a deal, or what was designed to look like a deal, that he would not be prosecuted and in exchange would agree to talk about his NATO days, under the guise of immunity. This was, however, immunity only in Canada. NATO allies were brought into the game, as Hambleton chatted away about what he had done from 1956 to 1961. In 1982 he unwisely travelled to Britain where he was met at the port of entry by a Special Branch officer (alerted by the RCMP) who warned him that he might face prosecution if he entered the United Kingdom. He ignored the warning, and was later arrested and put on trial under the British Official Secrets Act, convicted, and sentenced to ten years. Eventually freed on compassionate grounds, he returned to Canada.

Publicly, the Hambleton case appeared to be yet another embarrassment for Canada's record in catching Communist spies. The Canadian version of the Official Secrets Act had been failing in court for a number of years, and the Liberal government wisely decided that it did not need the aggravation of yet another failed prosecution. The more devious game being played behind the scenes eventually resulted in Hambleton's conviction, even if it left the unfortunate impression of Canadian softness on Soviet espionage. The security service seems to have played this case with reasonable skill, given the legal constraints.

So Many Reds, So Many Beds ...: Counter-Subversion

If any image has survived the end of the Cold War ice age, it is that of the zealous Mountie checking under every bed for lurking Reds. The Mounties had always had 'subversives' in their sights, and they were always pretty sure about their colour – flaming Red. With a Cold War on, they had every form of official sanction and legitimation for pursuing their obsession. And pursue it they did, with a passion and a scope that is remarkable to behold. Never before, and probably never again, would they have the opportunity and the capacity to penetrate so far into Canadian society, to extend their surveillance into the nooks and crannies of Canadian life, and to do so, for the most part, sheathed in public invisibility and legal impunity.

In 1977 a royal commission discovered that the security service maintained a subversive name index with 1,300,000 entries, representing 800,000 files on individuals.[35] In 1986 the government ordered the Counter-Subversion Section of the newly civilianized security service to be closed, its voluminous records destroyed, passed to the National Archives, or dispersed to other sections. But just what were they doing in those years when they could accumulate secret files on perhaps 7 to 8 per cent of the adult population of Canada? Were there really that many Reds under that many beds?

Historians can now troll through the files transferred from the Counter-Subversion Section to the National Archives. These files, which represent only a fraction of the material stored in that branch at the time of its dissolution, are nonetheless so voluminous that following all of the files through the cumbersome and time-consuming process of Access to Information requests would be a lifetime's scholarly work. For this book, we have chosen to pursue samples, small cross-sections, of the material potentially available. We have also benefited from the response to requests made by other researchers pursuing interests of their own. Censorship of declassified documents seriously erodes their usefulness, especially in the case of more contemporary, politically sensitive files, but a picture still emerges of a surveillance regime that was at the same time both expansive in scope and minute in its focus.

Take one example: the Ladies Auxiliary, Sudbury Local, International Union of Mine, Mill and Smelter Workers. For years, conscientious Mounties in the Sudbury detachment of the security service earnestly and meticulously compiled files on every meeting and every development in the Ladies Auxiliary. If $50 or $100 were donated to charities, the Mounties recorded the exact allocation of every dollar (and ominously noted from time to time that $10 or so were 'unaccounted'). If the ladies held a bake sale, there was an entry into the RCMP file recording how many cookies were sold, and the net profit. If a resolution passed regarding some matter of public interest (say, smokestack emissions), Mountie watchers duly entered into the files a summary of discussion and a breakdown of the vote. All of this would then be transmitted to headquarters in Ottawa.

The trigger for all this attention was simple: the Mine-Mill union had long been targeted as Communist-led. Indeed, in the late 1950s Mine, Mill was the object of a vicious decertification struggle, with the more conservative Steelworkers union, the CCF, the Catholic Church, and the RCMP all ranged against it. To the Mounties, there was no question that any organization associated with Mine-Mill was, ipso facto, a Communist front. Ergo: intensive surveillance of the Ladies Auxiliary. That was the *text*; the *subtext* is much more ambiguous. There *appears* to be nothing whatsoever in these tedious files to justify the slightest suspicion about the union women. Perhaps they occasionally showed somewhat more leftist attitudes than would be expected from, say, an Anglican Ladies Auxiliary. On occasion they arranged to have politically suspect entertainment for public events, such as foreign-language folksingers. To which they might have replied, had they known about these astonishing dossiers, 'It's a free country, isn't it?' Of course, it is possible that in the censored sections of these declassified files, there might lurk seriously incriminating evidence of subversive or revolutionary activity. It is possible, but it is not, in all honesty, very likely. In any event, nobody in the Ladies Auxiliary was ever charged with offences such as espionage, sabotage, or sedition, or anything else to the best of our knowledge. Were the Mounties simply behaving stupidly, senselessly carrying on like automata constantly bouncing off the same wall? That, too, is possible, but even if the activity seems objectively foolish in retrospect, let us at least grant them that they must have had their reasons at the time for behaving like this. Clearly, something else must be going on, something other than what appears on the surface.

Today a Sewing Circle, Tomorrow the World

First, there are the imperatives of the Cold War to consider. Communism was the mortal enemy and it was both external and internal. Communists in Canada were the fifth column of the USSR. Communists might be spies or saboteurs, but it was most likely they were *subversives*. It is true that this term is nowhere defined under law, and that many have questioned its coherence as a concept.[36] In watching subversives, the Mounties were not concerned with law enforcement, nor were they concerned with philosophical issues. To the political police, subversion was the process whereby the moral fibre of the state and society was undermined by the covert activities of those forces seeking to overthrow the liberal capitalist system. They might not be able to define subversion to the satisfaction of political philosophers and legal scholars, but they knew a subversive when they saw one. In a Cold War, all subversives were directed by Moscow. It is no surprise that, in the late 1940s and throughout the 1950s, the Counter-Subversion Section of the service was also known straightforwardly as the Anti-Communist Section.

Armed with these marching orders, the Mounties would inevitably want to keep a close eye on the Ladies Auxiliary of the Mine-Mill union local. They would not presume that any woman who belonged to this organization was a Communist; it might even be that very few if any belonged to the party. The point was that the organization, affiliated to a Red-led union, was by definition a front for the Communists, who would use it to subvert Canadian society. In an internally circulated admonition, Mounties were warned about the Communist tactics of infiltration and subversion: 'Whether it is an international movement or a small town women's sewing circle, the reds try to get in and if they are successful, they exert every effort to get to the top. And their tactics are extraordinarily successful.' Suppose, the writer ruminated, some people want to set up an association but lack the skills to carry this out. 'Usually there is a Communist handy who does know about these things and he or she is welcomed into the group.' Presto! Another organization 'with a completely innocuous political purpose ... can be used to whatever ends the Party desires.'[37] There are a number of problematic assessments contained in this line of reasoning, of course – that ordinary people are no more than putty in the hands of skilled Communist operatives; that one rotten apple can turn an entire barrel bad; that Communists possessed super-human talents at manipulating and controlling large numbers of people. None of these propositions were ever tested empirically, but the security service apparently saw no need to test them. They were true, by definition.

Equally problematic, and no more tested, was any linkage between the presence of Communists in an organization and the achievement of Communist goals in the society. Just what were the Communists going to *do* with the Ladies Auxiliary, Sudbury local, presuming that highly proficient Communist operatives were actually pulling the strings? When the members voted to donate money to the Canadian National Institute of the Blind, was this laundered Moscow gold that would taint the recipient? Again, the answer to this puzzle is tautological: the extension of Communist influence was to the Communists an end in itself; since Communism was subversive, any such extension of influence must be subversive. The leading civilian analyst in the security service in the 1950s, Mark McClung, once proposed a study of the aims of Communist penetration of the labour movement. His Mountie superiors found this pointless: Why waste time and resources on something that was obvious?[38] Communist union activist Bill Walsh once proposed a similar study to the Communist hierarchy: What were their aims in seeking to extend their influence within the union movement? Ironically, Walsh met the same indifference as McClung.[39] And so the two little armies battled on: one infiltrating, the other watching. The generals on both sides may have had a hazy idea of the point of the conflict, but they did have a firm conviction that the troops must continue to be sent over the top.

The Mounties in a PROFUNC

There was another, more concrete, reason for assiduously gathering information on the likes of the Ladies Auxiliary. Building up the dossiers on Communist, Communist-front, and Communist-infiltrated organizations had specific utility for the important task of security screening. It was precisely through surveillance of a multitude of organizations that, for instance, citizenship-application screeners could come up with positive results: that, for instance, X had attended meetings of the Ukrainian Canadian anti-Fascist war veterans, or some such, and that Y and Z, known Communists, were on the executive of said organization; that therefore X constituted a risk to national security.

Another concrete reason for systematic surveillance of Communist targets was that the RCMP were charged with the responsibility for compiling lists of subversives to be rounded up in the event of a war emergency. Government emergency plans, enumerated in its War Book, drew on the wartime experience. Machinery was created for overseeing rosters of persons earmarked for internment and organizations marked for banning. By 1954, 2,700 people were on the internment list, with 2,200 on a top-priority list and the remaining 500 on a lower-risk second rung. These had been approved by an inter-departmental internment committee, but the Anti-Communist Section had produced 6,500 names, almost 4,000 of which were awaiting approval. These thousands of names made up what the section referred to as its PROFUNC ('Prominent Communist functionaries') files. Plans were formulated for internment camps to be ready to receive and hold these potential fifth columnists. The lists were also intended for censorship purposes. As time went by, the number of candidates nominated by the RCMP for internment continued to number in the thousands (over 5,000 in the early 1960s), but the numbers approved by the committee continued to remain a small proportion of the total (some of those names persistently rejected by the civilians on the committee for lack of 'firm evidence' were placed on a 'special cases' list by the Mounties to be searched for evidence if an emergency broke out). In 1963, by mutual agreement, the overall approved list was pared down to about 1,000; the number awaiting review and assessment was reduced to 500. A special 'crash plan' list of 160 targeted for immediate round-up in the event of a surprise emergency was also pared down. Photo-ID information was provided for the main hit list so that Mounties in the field could recognize their targets. RCMP headquarters produced a *PROFUNC Manual* instructing divisions in their responsibilities. 'A complete set of PROFUNC cards, photo-ident cards, the original blanket and individual orders, and copy of Censorship Watch List and Special Advisory Committee on Internment file' were, after 1958, stored (and regularly updated) in a secret emergency government headquarters (the 'Diefenbunker')[40] near Pembroke in the Ottawa valley.[41]

Like old soldiers, old bureaucratic programs never die, they just fade away. PROFUNC lingered on for decades to the point where most members of the service had long since lost sight of its very existence. Finally, in the early 1980s, as the service was in the process of being transferred to the new civilian agency, the forgotten program was administered the last rites and put to final rest. In its prime, PROFUNC was a voracious consumer of personal information on Canadians. All this data did not come out of thin air. It came as a result of the extensive surveillance of every corner of Canadian society where Communists might be operating. It came through the careful gathering and compilation of every small piece of information that might prove significant when put together with other pieces of information that by themselves might also appear unimportant or innocuous. It came from identifying 'secret' members of the Communist Party who did not appear anywhere on party literature or on membership lists. It came from watching and noting meetings of, among a myriad other groups, the Ladies Auxiliary, Mine, Mill and Smelter Workers, Sudbury Local.

I Was a Communist for the RCMP

This was the strategy of the anti-Communist war. But what of the tactics, the specific weapons used? Technical surveillance (wiretaps, planted listening devices, and the like) were part of the armoury; there were few, if any, legal constraints, given the lack of a specific mandate for the security service. But this kind of surveillance had limits: in the 1950s and 1960s the technology of listening devices had not evolved to their current level of sophistication; installation often involved risky break-and-enter ('black bag') jobs, and targets could take their own counter-surveillance measures. Human sources, especially those highly placed, offered the highest returns. Although names are buried deep in the classified files, it is evident that John Leopold was not the only deep penetration the Mounties ever made of the Communist Party of Canada. In the early 1950s the minister of justice made a thinly veiled reference to his cabinet colleagues about a source or sources of information within the Communist Party that the Mounties were anxious to protect.[42] Pat ('I was a Commie for the RCMP') Walsh went public with lurid stories of his alleged undercover operations. The force, as per standard policy, would neither deny nor affirm Walsh's role, but there is reason to think that he did indeed act as a source while ostensibly playing a role as a Communist organizer.[43] There is also an indication that the service had an intelligence asset near the top of the Canadian Trotskyist movement.[44]

It may be unlikely, although possible, that an undercover Mountie, as such, was a long-term mole in the party. It is rather more likely that highly placed Communists were enlisted (by what means remains unknown) to act as sources. Such a mole or moles would, of course, be invaluable sources of information. There is always the possibility that such a source or sources might also have acted as agents of influence, Mountie tools to disorganize or neutralize the party. This is pure speculation. But there is convincing evidence that such sources did exist. Just as it has plausibly been argued in the case of the U.S. Communist Party that FBI penetration had rendered it virtually paralytic,[45] one must assume that all the resources and all the bureaucratic zeal in the security service dedicated to battling the Communists did indeed pay off in terms of human sources. Ironically, the Communists probably did more to destroy themselves by using their only elected MP, Fred Rose, as a courier in a Soviet espionage operation; by their slavish devotion to Moscow; and by expelling dissidents instead of allowing internal democracy, as during the fatal crisis of the Hungarian revolt and the de-Stalinization revelations in 1956. Yet, however devastated they might be from within and without, the Communists always had one audience who took them utterly seriously and gave them credit for an influence in Canadian society that the Communists themselves would have sold their souls to possess: the RCMP security service.

The question of highly placed moles aside, what is quite extraordinary about the vast collection of dossiers on Canadians and Canadian organizations amassed in the Counter-Subversion Section is the amount of complicity shown by large numbers of people in police surveillance of their own associations and activities. It is simply inconceivable that the volume and detail of information gathered in these files could have been gathered without the active assistance of thousands of ordinary people, rank-and-file supporters, officeholders, organizers, envelope lickers, fundraisers. To return to the Ladies Auxiliary, it beggars belief to imagine that the intimate details of decisions taken in tiny meetings held in a variety of locales, including school basements, kitchens, and living rooms, could possibly have been derived from bugs and wiretaps – or that the security service could afford the vast expenditure of resources, human and monetary, that would be involved in such a immense operation, multiplying the Ladies Auxiliary by all the thousands of other targets across the land. On this basis, Canada would indeed have been the first fully 'wired' nation in the world. The explanation for the intimate detail in the dossiers is less dramatic – but, in a different sense, astonishing enough. It is perfectly clear that, for all of these reported meetings, *there was someone there*, someone who to all outward appearances was a member of the association, a friend and colleague of the others, who was going home at night and reporting to her RCMP contact everything that had transpired. Multiply this by thousands for organizations across the land, and we have a picture of a country honeycombed with secret informers. That is surely the most remarkable, if not chilling, aspect of the surveillance encapsulated in the 800,000 files discovered by the McDonald Commission. The RCMP darkly warned of the numbers of dupes, sympathizers, and fellow travellers who could allegedly be manipulated by the hard core of Communist Party activists. The security service, too, constituted a hard core of activist investigators, but beyond them spread out an army of secret informers and collaborators.

To be sure, the service did not succeed in gaining inside human sources in every organization it was interested in. The quality of information varies a great deal from dossier to dossier. In some cases, what appears is little more than public information, as interpreted by service analysts. But for targets that the service was particularly interested in – and here labour unions seem to have taken pride of place, with ethnic organizations following somewhere well behind – it was often quite successful in tapping informative sources. This directs us to the question of the motivation for people to lead what were in effect double lives: as members of organizations and as after-hours informants to the police. Some guesses can be hazarded. Mercenary motives may well have been at play in some cases. The service would pay for good information; indeed, there was even reason to push for payment, since the exchange of money was also a mechanism of control over informants. There is no doubt (security service denials aside) that security screening was sometimes a useful mechanism for developing sources. In other cases, there may have been idealistic or ideological motives at work – people genuinely concerned about Communist influence, real or imagined, in their unions or associations, or people whose idea of public spiritedness extended to secretly informing on their fellows. The Mounties, be it remembered, were an organization with very high prestige in the eyes of the Canadian public (which is one good reason why the government in this era retained their services as an internal security force). Surely, many must have reasoned, it could only be high-minded and patriotic to assist the Redcoats in protecting Canada against subversion.

To the extent that ideological motivations were in play, the whole picture of political policing in the Cold War era takes on a different colouration than the somewhat simple-minded 'RCMP v. the People' images that appeared in the 1970s. Focusing on the labour movement, it is evident from the almost staggering scope and detail of the files on labour unions (the finding aids alone for the declassified files transferred from the Counter-Subversion Section to the National Archives are hundreds of pages long) that the security service had extensive help from within the unions. One can only assume that many conservative and social-democratic unionists did cooperate voluntarily, presumably out of anti-Communist convictions, not to speak of internal union rivalries. Moreover, conservative and social-democratic unionists did openly and enthusiastically carry out their own public anti-Communist purges – a process avidly observed (at the least) with deep approval by the RCMP.[46] Secret cooperation with the RCMP was just another method of fighting the Communists. The implication is that political policing was not simply something brought down from above or from the outside, but a process deeply implanted in Canadian civil society. The state could not politically police the society without enlisting popular cooperation. The RCMP security service was intervening in alliance with some elements of the society against others.

'Who Killed Cock Robin?': The Surveillance Chill

This intervention had very concrete results. For one thing, despite credible security service protestations that it was not interested in spying on 'legitimate' (that is, non-Communist) groups, the effects necessarily spread farther than the ranks of the 'Reds.' Even in their internal *Intelligence Bulletin*, security service officers were occasionally reminded that trade unions were perfectly legitimate organizations, and that the service had no interest in tracking collective bargaining, or even strikes, as such.[47] Despite rare mistakes, and despite invidious criticism directed at them from time to time, they were by no means witless anti-Communists who could not distinguish between social democrats of the CCF-NDP variety and the bona fide Leninist article. On the contrary, they recognized the CCF-NDP precisely as a useful bulwark against Communist influence. The one intrusive investigation of the NDP focused on the Waffle, a left-wing dissident movement within the party in the early 1970s: the Waffle was in fact expelled by the party leadership, thus confirming a certain shared world view between establishment social democrats and the security service.

Yet there is a major objection to the notion that counter-subversion activities were precision strikes against specific targets. Tracking Communist influence in the labour movement, for instance, inevitably resulted in a surveillance profile that differed very little from tracking labour in general. Certain 'Communist-dominated' unions came in for special attention, but other unions, even some fairly conservative ones, were watched in case the Communists, ever-resourceful, tried to spread their influence. The security service had to 'stand on guard,' and given the expansive notion of the capabilities of the enemy, there could be few areas of Canadian life where vigilance was not required. The files on trade unions held in the RCMP vaults may have outmatched in volume and detail the files held in the Department of Labour. Certainly, no library or archive could match the Mounties' holdings of left-wing literature in the form of books, newspapers, magazines, pamphlets, broadsheets, posters, and notices. Perhaps it might even be some comfort to old veteran leftists to know that they always held at least one deeply attentive and respectful audience.

If the search for subversion took the service so far and so wide, it was inevitable that a great deal of information (and misinformation, given the certainty that mistakes and errors of fact would accumulate) was being gathered and held on people and organizations who were not in and of themselves targeted as subversives. One example that became a public issue in the late 1950s and early 1960s was RCMP surveillance on university campuses.[48] This will be discussed in greater detail later (see chapter 10). At this point, suffice to note that concern about police spying on faculty and students was widespread enough to call forth policy responses from both the Diefenbaker and Pearson governments. Behind closed doors in 1961, Conservative Justice Minister E. Davie Fulton ordered a halt to campus investigations while permitting the service's continued use of existing sources. After the change in government in 1963, Prime Minister Lester Pearson arranged a meeting between the Canadian Association of University Teachers (CAUT), the national student union, and the RCMP, and arrived at an informal agreement that became known as the 'Pearson-Laskin Accord,' supposedly limiting the Mountie presence on campuses. The accord failed to achieve its stated objective, but the very fact that both Conservative and Liberal governments had been moved to intervene demonstrated the sensitivity of taking the hunt for subversion into universities.

The Counter-Subversion Section did not rest content with watching the institutions of civil society alone. It also watched other government agencies closely for signs of subversion. Throughout the 1950s, CBC programming was an object of almost prurient interest. The International Service was, like the National Film Board, purged of 'pro-Communist' elements. The domestic service was threatened from time to time, and the careers of particular people suffered, although never on the scale of the NFB.[49] But looking into the declassified files of the security service, it becomes apparent that the Mounties were not just after individual security risks, as they understood that term; they also fancied themselves cultural critics who reviewed the offerings of the CBC for hidden subversive messages. For instance, in the *1952/53 Annual Report* of the security service, two pages are devoted to an ideological deconstruction of various CBC broadcasts. A play called 'Who Killed Cock Robin?' was 'quite consistent with Communist propaganda' because it suggested, among other sins, 'opposition to war and support of peace.' Another script 'represented various Canadian Government Departments as being incompetent.' A television play by Ted Allan (who was indeed a Communist) was 'reviewed by members of our Toronto Office' and judged by these critics to be 'Communist propaganda.'

To be sure, the RCMP critics did not possess the kind of baleful influence exercised by the U.S. free-enterprise witch hunters like the authors of the notorious *Red Channels* who could destroy an artist or entertainer's career with a single public listing. And yet in the same internal report there is an indication that the CBC had cancelled a scheduled production of an opera to be conducted by Ivan Romanoff when the president of the CBC, Davidson Dunton, 'received a complaint' that this production was produced by 'subversive elements.' Apparently, the opera was based on the work of the Russian writer Gogol, the anniversary of whose death was being celebrated, you see, by the Communists! Dunton bowed to the pressure. The implication, even if not spelled out, is that the 'complaint' came from the Mounties, who were patting themselves on the back for preventing a Red opera from infecting Canadian ears.[50] In short, the Mounties were not merely cultural critics but cultural critics with clout. If this was censorship, it was a typically Canadian variant: unlike the Americans who did these things noisily and in public, the RCMP-inspired censorship was silent, behind the scenes, discreet.

There were many CBC personalities with RCMP dossiers whose names might surprise later generations. A future senator (Philip Deane) and a future governor general (Adrienne Clarkson) were the objects of suspicious interest, as was popular author Farley Mowat.[51] Yet RCMP intelligence had its limits. One of the most prominent personalities in

CBC television's first decades was the 'Weatherman,' Percy Saltzman (indeed his was the first face seen on screen in the inaugural broadcast of the network). Saltzman appears to have passed under the RCMP radar because, apparently unbeknownst to the Mounties, he was a lifelong sympathizer with Marxism and Communism.[52]

There is an argument that all the record keeping of the service was really quite innocuous since it hardly ever *acted* on the material collected.[53] This completely misunderstands the workings of surveillance as a control mechanism. The knowledge that one might be watched and *could* be disciplined for political misbehaviour (screening alone was a powerful system of sanctions) instils inner controls and self-censorship. Intensive surveillance is a *chilling, pre-emptive* device. When one adds secret cooperation with the police, the chilling and debilitating impact on political activity can become quite pronounced. Paranoia and destructive mistrust can take over movements and organizations when the possibility arises that fellow activists may be secret police spies. Whether such effects were justified by the threat to national security is one question; the impact of the silent surveillance is another. The Mounties were not wasting their time, and taxpayers' dollars, in operating their anti-Communist Panopticon. Anti-Communism was official public policy, pronounced and implemented by the government of Canada. The officers of the RCMP security service were tools for that policy: willing, enthusiastic, and, on the whole, reasonably effective.

It is easy enough, looking back in post-Cold War retrospect at Mounties solemnly compiling information on a ladies auxiliary or student club, to ridicule their efforts. It is certainly fair to question the value, and even the ethics, of such activity. Eventually the government of Canada itself came to the conclusion that this kind of state surveillance of civil society in a liberal democracy was unworthy and unwise. But in carrying out their counter-subversive duties in the Cold War, the Mounties were by no means Keystone Cops. They were policing Canadian politics, just as they had been asked to do.

The Organizational Question

The Cold War represented a gold-plated organizational opportunity for the security service and the RCMP that housed it. The officer-in-charge of the service, Charles Rivett-Carnac, explained to his Mountie superiors in 1947: 'The safeguarding of the internal security of the Dominion, bearing in mind the promise of events in the international field and the situation regarding subversive activity as a national and international problem, appears to assume a position of predominance over all other subjects, not only now but more especially in the future. With regard to this point there seems little room for discussion, and it is as well, perhaps, to bear this carefully in mind from the standpoint of our own very definite responsibilities in the matter.'[54] The language might be a bit stiff but the lesson was obvious. With the Cold War, the RCMP had a tiger to ride. But how would they manage it?

The Mounties were, of course, a highly visible part of Canadian mythology. In the post-Gouzenko era, the popular image of the Mounties changed. 'Getting their man' had most often meant getting the criminal. Now it also meant getting the subversive, the spy, or the traitor.[55] The RCMP traded on their image, but the government profited as well: the Mounties were eminently marketable packaging for a set of internal security policies that might not always be palatable to a society used to being relatively free of government snooping. It might seem to be a good deal all around. But there were problems with the marriage of Redcoats and Red hunters. Were the police, especially a paramilitary force like the RCMP, equipped to mount an effective security intelligence service? Was the 'police mentality' appropriate for this kind of work? The idea that the service would be better off 'civilianized' was a criticism with a certain lineage, beginning with critics of the RCMP during the war and slowly gathering speed during the 1960s until a royal commission recommended that major step in 1969. Another fifteen years, and another royal commission, were to pass before civilianization became a fact. But even in the first two Cold War decades, when critics of the RCMP were relatively quiescent, civilianization was a kind of underground theme played out within the confines of the force. The security service was a bureaucratic agency seeking an appropriate organizational form; the tension between policing and security concerns was there inside the RCMP as well as outside.

The security service became Special Branch in late 1946, a change in more than name in that it could now create its own sections within. The first officer-in-charge of the new branch was that indestructible thread of continuity, John Leopold. Leopold was, however, only an interim choice until a more senior and respected officer could be assigned. Leopold's limitations were apparent when he submitted a report proposing changes 'which failed, however, to transcend the framework with which he was familiar, merely advocating the addition of a number of personnel here and there at Headquarters.' Leopold's thinking reflected years of 'retrenchment in RCMP establishment' but was hardly forward looking.[56] Superintendent Rivett-Carnac, who had headed the section in the late 1930s, was soon brought back in, and, after touring the divisions, he reported on reorganization in January 1947. Rivett-Carnac was critical of a degree of disorganization that had set in with war's end. He criticized a failure to attract the 'best analytical minds' and pointed to the lack of professional training, with only 'crude' apprenticeship on the job and constant transfers discouraging the development of experience and expertise. Rivett-Carnac also expressed concern about better public relations for security work; interestingly, he specifically cited educating the rest of the force about the role of the Special Branch. It seems that 'regular' Mounties had a tendency to sneer at the 'spooks,' a situation obviously not conducive to good morale in the branch. A crucial recommendation was that Special Branch units be separated from the CIB. 'Success,' Rivett-Carnac asserted, 'will never be met with until the Special Branch work in the field is divorced as far as possible from criminal investigation matters.'[57] The latter point was an oft-echoed theme of reorganization, but one long resisted by the RCMP hierarchy, for reasons that remain unclear. Approval in principle was given to the report but there was no urgency regarding implementation.

By late 1947, the Special Branch, which had rebounded considerably from its immediate post-war contraction in manpower,[58] was given a new officer-in-charge, George McClellan, later a commissioner. McClellan had a mandate for gearing the branch up, and the dynamism to do the job. McClellan did the obligatory tour of the divisions and provided a series of reports to the commissioner. He echoed a number of his predecessor's concerns about training and career development, and he, too, pointed to the 'ridicule' to which Special Branch officers were subjected by other force members. McClellan recommended, once again, that the branch be separated from the CIB and be given increased personnel to handle its accelerating workload. Although manpower was made available only grudgingly, the main recommendation on separation was effected on 10 July 1950. McClelland was henceforth to report directly to the commissioner, except on financial matters where the DCI would continue to supervise.[59]

New sections were created. 'B' dealt with Counter-Espionage and 'A,' with responsibilities for screening, took most of the additional manpower. In addition, there was 'D' (the Counter-Subversion or Anti-Communist) Section and 'C,' a catch-all that accounted for everything else. An important step was approval by Treasury Board to hire civilian analysts. Civilians might offer some intellectual leaven to the much-maligned police mentality, but the force was not very good at utilizing them. In 1951 a Research Section was created under Leopold as director. Mark McClung and Don Wall were hired to prepare 'briefs, histories, digests and appreciations' for internal use and for the Joint Intelligence Branch, the Joint Intelligence Committee, and military intelligence. After an initial burst of activity, 'the Section settled down to a rather pedestrian routine of updating briefs, and noting and circulating periodical articles of interest as well as documents received form external agencies.' The Research Section declined while civilians were seconded to work in the 'A', 'B,' and 'D' branches. It petered down to a single person by the end of the 1950s and then vanished.

Civilians found their opportunities limited within the force, and advancement difficult outside in the civil service, given the isolation of the RCMP from the rest of the bureaucracy. 'Resignations were common after very few years of service: continuity was lost, collective experience never gained,' write the RCMP historians.[60] By the 1960s, management attention turned towards upgrading the educational qualifications of regular members of the force and a definite policy of phasing out civilians took hold. Part of the problem may have stemmed from a crisis forced in 1955 by the leading civilian in the branch. Mark McClung, son of the redoubtable pioneer feminist Nellie McClung, was not one to take a back seat easily. Asked to prepare a report on how civilian analysts could be more effectively utilized, McClung instead launched a 108-page opus that catalogued the inadequacies of the police mind for intelligence work and the stultifying hold of the police hierarchy. This lesson was unlikely to be appreciated by its immediate audience, but McClung went further yet and proposed an elaborate, even grandiose, blueprint for a new Internal Security Service staffed by civilian professionals, with a corresponding police wing, rather like Britain's MI5 and the Special Branch of Scotland Yard. Although he tried to appease the sensibilities of his superiors by allowing that the new Internal Security Service ought formally to answer to the RCMP commissioner, it was obvious that, as a relative newcomer and civilian with no operational experience, he had overstepped his bounds and committed what the rank-conscious hierarchy considered impertinence.[61] The head of the Special Branch, Clifford Harvison, and the commissioner, L.H. Nicholson, 'emphatically' rejected McClung's main recommendations.[62] McClung believed that this marked the end of his effective role within the branch, although he hung around for a few years more.[63]

There is a view that McClung had developed a progressive vision ahead of its time that had been rejected by a less than perspicacious RCMP hierarchy.[64] This view seems to be based mainly on the testimony of the loquacious McClung himself, who gave numerous interviews over the years presenting his side of the story. Unfortunately, this sheen does not survive a close look at the McClung memorandum itself, which was not as well-thought-out as its author seemed to believe. Indeed, Harvison had little difficulty pointing out gaps and inadequacies in the plan. When the McDonald Commission examined the memorandum years later, it backed Harvison's criticisms.[65]

Still, McClung had identified a real problem, even as his own alternative misfired. The force could not effectively engage the talents of civilians, nor had it always been able to transform policemen into efficient security and intelligence professionals. This structural problem would continue to fester for many years more. In the immediate aftermath of the McClung report, however, there was some internal response. Harvison was asked to prepare his own report covering the questions McClung had been supposed to answer. Harvison's solution lay in expanding and upgrading manpower from the force itself. Organizationally, Harvison recommended that Special Branch be elevated to directorate level, so that divisional officers would report to the security and intelligence director at headquarters on operational matters, not to divisional commanding officers. Moreover, in the absence of the commissioner, the director could take authoritative decisions on his own. On 1 November 1956 Special Branch officially became the Security and Intelligence Directorate and the four sections became branches, permitting further differentiation and specialization of functions.[66] The security service had freed itself of the last vestiges of the criminal-investigation shell that had once housed it, although it would take almost thirty years more before it broke free of the RCMP itself.

Training Better Spies

If the force was going to hold on to the security service and concentrate on making Mounties better intelligence operatives and analysts rather than bringing in and holding any more than a minimum of civilians, then it was obvious that *training* would be crucial. This was especially the case in counter-espionage, which required very special skills (as Terry Guernsey had argued forcefully), but it was also true for the directorate's other security intelligence functions as well. As Mounties, all members would, of course, undergo the force's basic training, supplemented by at least three years in regular duties. They would probably not learn very much there of specific use in the shadow world of intelligence. Indeed, critics (some within the force) over the years argued that what new recruits brought with them from their basic training might actually be in some cases counter-productive for security and intelligence work. The orientation towards the detection and apprehension of criminal activity might be a hindrance when it came to the more analytical and imaginative skills required for counter-espionage. Similarly, the orientation towards immediate results instilled in young Mounties could work against the patience required for surveillance. The work of the security service bore little relationship to the glamorous Hollywood dream world of James Bond; 'boredom' was a common complaint in the lower ranks – not surprising in light of their training and expectations of life in the Mounted Police. What was needed was on-the-job training not only to impart the necessary skills but to help the younger members learn about the larger picture and how their specific tradecraft fitted into it. As numerous complaints from the Counter-Espionage Section made clear, apprenticeship in action was not good enough.

Continuous training dates from 1953. What began as summer classes at headquarters were extended on an annual rotational basis. Divisions were encouraged to give refresher courses with headquarters' help. By the end of 1961, a series of specialized courses in specific security and intelligence techniques were under way. In the early 1960s, a new program was launched whereby selected officers began to attend university full time to obtain degrees, mainly in political science. At the same time, civilian positions were reclassified to be filled with regulars from the force. The thrust of these reforms was clear: the specialized skills for security work were to be developed as far as possible within the force. The vanished Research Section was revived again in 1964, but this time to be staffed with the most 'carefully selected and trained regular members,' chosen for appropriate university education and aptitude for research work.[67]

This internal skills upgrading had certain limitations. For one thing, the officers sent for university degrees did not always fit easily back into Mounties' routine. A good number of the 1960s graduates later left the service, apparently finding the work and the working conditions unsatisfying after their personal vistas had been widened by university experience.[68] Nor did the new emphasis on internal training necessarily expand the somewhat circumscribed intellectual horizons of the force. For instance, in 1960–1 a compulsory reading program was instituted for 'all members employed on security and intelligence duties' designed to make security and intelligence personnel 'more politically conscious and to give them a much deeper insight into the reasons why they are performing the work they are now engaged in' and to improve 'efficiency' by arming them with a 'much better idea what to look for when they go about their day-to-day work.' There was even an intention to institute some form of testing of what they had learned. While this sounded impressive, the actual list contained six books. Apart from Canadian and Australian royal commission reports on Soviet espionage, the list included a standard but limited 1950s textbook on Communism, a book by the abrasively anti-Marxist American writer Sidney Hook, and a two-volume propaganda work produced by the U.S. government entitled *The Communist Conspiracy: Strategy and Tactics of World Communism*.[69] Nothing there would challenge the already well-entrenched *idées fixes* of the security service.

The Sorcerer's Apprentice: Information Management

One of the major ongoing problems faced by the security service through its various organizational manifestations was information management. The very lifeblood of surveillance as a state activity is information processing. Gathering information, from both overt and covert sources, is only the start of the process. Data must then be sorted, stored under appropriate categories in a form readily retrievable for the crucial next step of analysis and interpretation. Next, intelligence must be refined into a finished product for its ultimate consumer, the government that pays the bills. Gathering information was, in a sense, never a real problem: the tools were available and were used. But, for the first fifteen years of so after the war, the second stage of the process, storage and retrieval, was a major problem, attributable largely to technological limitations. Until the era of electronic data processing, or the computer age, had fully arrived, storage and retrieval were problems of paperwork, or more precisely, of a paper blizzard. Surveillance was like the sorcerer's apprentice: once set in motion it generated unceasing flows of data, but without the means of controlling or regulating the flow. The 1960s were a transition era in data processing until by the 1970s technology itself finally took the sorcerer's apprentice off the hook and a major bottleneck in the intelligence cycle was finally resolved.

As early as 1953 the problem had become glaringly apparent: the 'simple expansion of information on Communist subversion was recognized to have reached optimum value,' according to the internal history of the service. 'Processing the sheer quantity involved was proving impossible, negating the point of collecting it in the first place. Quality of intelligence was perceived to be suffering for the sake of quantity.'[70] By this point, the Counter-Subversion Section had amassed 21,000 active files on individuals and 2,300 on organizations. Weight reduction was called for: in 1954, 17,000 'less active' individual files were 'deactivated temporarily.' By 1958, a review was initiated to identify files on hundreds of organizations and thousands of individuals to be 'deadsheeted' and destroyed. New technologies in this era helped to control the flow, but 'never sufficiently.' A punch-card system was instituted in 1955 to 'supplement' the paper case-history files and was soon extended to all files.[71] Punch-carding was not enough. In 1961 the Counter-Subversion Section contained 26,000 case-history files, and 6,700 'simpler' files on individuals with 6 or more 'subversive' references, but 13,000 more had graduated to the second category 'without the manpower available to effect the transfers.' Another information-management problem was that all files had to be housed in the Central Registry. This was a cause of persistent frustration on the part of the Security and Intelligence Directorate, particularly since by the 1960s only a small part of Central Registry work was *not* security-related. Registry staff doubled from 1953 to 1963, and most of the additional personnel had to be dedicated to filing security and intelligence information. In 1964 an entirely separate section was established within the registry to house security and intelligence files, mainly for security reasons. But it was obviously unsatisfactory for security and intelligence information storage and retrieval to be under a separate section of the force, which had other concerns to respond to than those of security and intelligence alone.

The answer to these administrative dilemmas lay in technology. In 1963 consideration was first given to electronic replacement of the punch-card system. By the 1970s, data was being systematically keyed into computer files. Paper did not disappear immediately (only in the 1990s did completely paperless files appear), but electronic data processing solved the flow-management problem. Freed by the computer, the surveillance machinery could finally kick into high gear. Thus it was that the McDonald Commission was shocked to discover the subversion databank in the late 1970s that contained information on 800,000 individuals. Technology enabled the fulfilment of an Orwellian dream of surveillance that had eluded an earlier generation of watchers.

All of these administrative developments point to the accelerating growth and influence of the security service from the 1950s through the 1960s. Although CSIS chooses sometimes to interpret the Access to Information Act as allowing the exclusion of information on numbers of officers and employees over the years in the different divisions of the security service (and the information commissioner has not challenged this practice when it has been questioned), the McDonald Commission in 1981 produced a graphic depiction of the historical development of overall manpower: 'The number of persons involved in the RCMP's security intelligence work increased rapidly in the years following World War II. From the small group at headquarters, which constituted the Intelligence Section at the end of World War II, Special Branch had grown considerably by 1951. By 1960, [the Security and Intelligence] Directorate's membership had tripled and doubled again by [1970]. In a little over 20 years, the RCMP's manpower specializing in security intelligence activities had increased more than fifty-fold.'[72] Security intelligence was a growth industry in the Cold War era.

The Watchers Watched?

The period from 1962 to 1968 was a somewhat chaotic era in Canadian politics, with the Tory government defeated over the issue of nuclear weapons and a series of minority governments marked by scandals and a high degree of partisan rancour. Somewhat unexpectedly, national-security issues were drawn into the partisan battles, and with them the RCMP. Near the end of the decade, the force found itself for the first time in the uncomfortable position of being a subject of a royal commission investigation. Watchers do not like to be watched. It would get much worse in the 1970s and 1980s, but the Mounties did not much care for the first experience.

Part of the problem was the changing ethos of Canadian society. There was less unthinking conformity with Cold War values, more questioning of authority. There were 'New Left' movements appearing that did not owe Cold War allegiance to Moscow or Peking. In Quebec a sometimes violent separatist movement had burst on the scene that did not fit readily into any Cold War mould. Intrusive federal surveillance of Quebec politics was a prescription for trouble unforeseen in Cold War days. There was also growing popular concern about civil liberties and individual rights that would eventually result in the Charter of Rights and Freedoms. These developments subtly changed the context within which the security service operated, but the service did not change its mentality and practices anywhere as quickly as the society was changing. This was not, however, the immediate cause of the calling of a royal commission. Rather, it was the manner in which the security service had been drawn willy-nilly into the partisan arena. When the political police become a partisan issue, matters can quickly spin out of control. 'Non-partisan' commissions of inquiry are a tried-and-true Ottawa method of trying to deflect partisan attack when the heat gets uncomfortable. The RCMP security service was a reluctant hostage to this familiar process.

Sex and Espionage: The Gerda Munsinger Imbroglio

The sad affair of George Victor Spencer has already been described. Embarrassing as the sordid story was in itself to the RCMP and to the Liberal government of Lester Pearson, it had landed in the middle of a series of scandals and embarrassments that beset the Pearson cabinet and was pounced upon by opposition and media in a charged partisan context. The impression was widespread that Spencer was a 'little guy' victim of arbitrary and unfair action by a ruthless Big Brother state. Spencer, the popular view went, had never been charged, never had a day in court, yet had been in effect tried and convicted in secret and had his pension taken away; in any event, the poor man was dying: was there no compassion? In this drama, both government and RCMP were scripted as the heartless heavies, Spencer the hapless victim.

The prime minister was not entirely deaf to this narrative. Pearson had been on the receiving end of 'security' concerns over the Norman affair and, as we have earlier noted, was the subject of a witch-hunting FBI file, of which he was well aware. His ambivalence was apparent in Liberal caucus discussions. And, for mysterious reasons, the microphones in the Liberal caucus room somehow were wired to be heard in the Conservative caucus room! That the Conservative house leader was Erik Nielsen, a former RCMP officer, has led to some speculation, but however this bizarre situation had occurred, Nielsen made good political use of the knowledge of Pearson's ambivalence to force the calling of an inquiry.[73] Pearson, as we earlier indicated, finally telephoned Spencer and asked him if wanted an inquiry.

Even before the specific Spencer inquiry was actually called in March

1966, the RCMP had learned that as early as December 1965 the government had been contemplating the possibility of going further and calling an inquiry into the entire security field. Commissioner McClelland was appalled at such a prospect and peppered the minister of justice and the solicitor general with his objections. In a four-hour meeting on 30 December with the two ministers and their senior officials, McClelland, flanked by his deputy commissioners and Assistant Commissioner William Kelly (in charge of the security service), made the case for keeping political hands, and eyes, off his boys. The prestige of the Mounties would be dragged through the mud, morale in the force would suffer, and the service would be impeded in fulfilling its responsibilities to protect national security. And all this damage only to appease parliamentary and press criticism of the Mounties for handling the Spencer case as all espionage cases had been handled since the war, in conformity with government policy. McClelland told the Liberal ministers that ministerial direction of security matters since the Liberals had come to office had been 'negligible'; he implied that, if they wanted to look for blame, they should begin with themselves. But McClelland was defensive as well as aggressive. In a revealing moment, he expressed anxiety that a public inquiry might reveal such potentially embarrassing matters as RCMP treatment of homosexuals as security risks.[74] The Mounties had every intention of keeping such skeletons firmly in the closet, as it were.

As the commissioner was well aware, the RCMP had already been drawn into the partisan fray, although not yet publicly. In November 1964, harassed by Opposition scandal mongering, Pearson had accepted Transport Minister J.W. Pickersgill's advice and instructed the RCMP to provide him with 'details of any investigations made by them during the last 10 years in which a [government] member was involved.' McClelland delivered the requested report to Pearson on 2 December 1964. From it, Pearson learned of an affair between the former Conservative associate minister of defence, Pierre Sévigny, and a German-born prostitute in Montreal, Gerda Munsinger. This 'sordid' matter, in Pearson's phrase, became a concern because of a 'security' connection: Ms. Munsinger had allegedly acted as a low-level Soviet agent in Germany. Yet Diefenbaker had merely scolded Sévigny when he had been apprised of the affair, and left him in his 'most sensitive' cabinet position, even though he was now a 'vulnerable person from a security point of view.' Believing that he now held something over Diefenbaker's head, the prime minister called in the Opposition leader

on 10 December 1964 and used the Sévigny matter as a threat to warn
Diefenbaker off more scandal accusations against the Liberal government. For his part, Diefenbaker countered with what Pearson himself referred to in his diary as Diefenbaker's 'own form of blackmail':
Diefenbaker had long since come into possession of 'a very important
security file – from Washington' on Pearson (presumably Pearson's
FBI file). Just how the former prime minister had obtained this file is
unclear. He may have received it via the RCMP, since he told Pearson
that it coincided with his coming to office in 1957; he may just as easily
have received it directly from Washington sources such as Hoover who
may have been trying to spread some American-style witch hunting
to Canada. Pearson, unfazed, in effect dared Diefenbaker to use it. As
historian J.L. Granatstein comments: 'This interview between the Prime
Minister and the Leader of the Opposition had surely been extraordinary. Each man tried to blackmail the other with secrets from security
files, and neither emerged with any credit whatsoever.'[75]

This meeting was, of course, secret. Through 1965 and into early
1966, the pursuit of scandals continued, as did the festering knowledge
in the Tory Opposition that the Liberals knew about the Sévigny matter. Then on 4 March 1966, when Pearson finally gave in to demands
for an inquiry into the Spencer affair, his justice minister, Lucien Car-
din, who had publicly opposed any such inquiry, blurted out under
duress in the Commons that the Tories had their own problems, referring to the 'Monseigneur' case. At a press conference, he named
Munsinger and Sévigny and pronounced the matter 'worse' than the
sex-and-security Profumo scandal in the United Kingdom that had
dominated headlines for months in 1964. Munsinger herself was found
alive and well in Germany by an enterprising reporter and added the
information that she had also slept with another Tory minister, George
Hees. The cat was truly out of the bag, and the press went on a binge.
Mr Justice Wishart Spence was appointed to inquire into the affair.
The Spence commission quickly developed the reputation of being a
partisan instrument to discredit the former Tory government, and the
Conservatives withdrew from participation. When Spence reported in
September 1966, he declared that Sévigny had been a security risk, although not disloyal. It was revealed in the report that the RCMP had
advised the then Conservative justice minister, E. Davie Fulton, that
the affair did not constitute a security breach. Surprisingly, Fulton was
chastised by Spence for taking the RCMP's advice, and not investigating further.[76]

Forever Amber: The Mackenzie Royal Commission

Both the Spencer and Munsinger affairs had been formally about 'security' but steeped in partisan considerations. Something more was needed to lift the fog of partisan politics and free the Liberals from further 'security' scandals. Despite Commissioner McClelland's active opposition, on 16 November 1966 a Royal Commission on Security was appointed to 'inquire into and report upon the operation of Canadian security methods and procedures.' The commission was headed by Maxwell Mackenzie along with two other commissioners, Yves Pratte (later head of Air Canada and later yet a Supreme Court justice) and M.J. Coldwell, the former leader of the CCF, the predecessor of the NDP. The Coldwell appointment, according to Sawatsky, 'sent shock waves through the RCMP.' It need not have. Coldwell was the quintessential Cold War social democrat who had always loathed Communists;[77] he became, Sawatsky concludes, 'the conservative anchor on the commission and often argued against some of the more liberal proposals of his two fellow commissioners.'[78]

The Mackenzie Commission uncritically reflected a thoroughly Cold War view of the world. It held no public hearings but relied almost entirely upon the RCMP for its information and its interpretation of security issues. It reported in 1968 to the new Liberal Prime Minister, Pierre Trudeau, and some, although not all, of its findings and recommendations were made public in a slim 116-page volume in June 1969. The published report,[79] coming as it did at the close of the 1960s, reads like the pure Cold War mentality caught forever in amber. The commissioners began by declaring that, 'although it is true that we face a more complicated and fragmented communist world than we did at the time of Gouzenko's defection nearly twenty-five years ago, none of the evidence we have heard suggests to us that recent developments have led to any significant changes in the adversary relationship that continues to exist between the communist powers and the west in terms of intelligence and subversive operations and security defences. Canada remains the target of subversive or potentially subversive activities.' Although they recognized that the Communist world was itself split between the USSR and China, they insisted on the appropriateness of using the 'admittedly simplistic terms "communism" and "communist."' They went on to paint a picture of 'Communist subversion' insidiously spreading out through Canadian society through the infiltration of such institutions as trade unions and universities as well as peace groups. 'Detente' was a ruse by the Communists to intensify their penetration.[80] No one who had immersed themselves in security service files and reports since the 1940s could possibly mistake where this world view came from.

The specific recommendations were generally hard line, in some cases opting for policies that went well beyond existing practices – for instance, requiring fingerprinting of all subjects for security clearances, including private-sector workers. Although the Mounties' fruit-machine campaign had begun to wane, and despite McClelland's earlier concerns about 'embarrassment,' the Mackenzie Commission went out of its way to point to homosexuals as security risks and insisted they be barred from all 'higher levels of classification' and from 'posting to sensitive positions overseas.' The commission further suggested a series of changes to stiffen and toughen security clearance criteria regarding immigrants, public servants, and industrial workers in the defence sector.

If all this seemed to confirm and legitimate what the RCMP had been saying and doing for years, there was one recommendation that blinded the RCMP brass to any other virtues of the report. Indeed, given that Mackenzie reflected RCMP thinking so faithfully on most matters, it was all the more embarrassing to the force when the commissioners recommended that the security service function should be detached altogether from the RCMP and be, in effect, 'civilianized.' In making this case, Mackenzie's argument was of a nature that could not but infuriate the Mounties. Accepting the Mounties' basic Cold War world view and their definition of the nature of the threats to security, the commissioners then argued that the Mounties were the wrong people to do the job. At one point Mackenzie went so far as to suggest that the RCMP had been too diffident and timid in making the case to government about the true magnitude of the Communist threat and of the 'dangers of inaction.'[81] This was odd, to say the least, but Mackenzie did have more substantive points. The main problems – of which the force itself was well aware – were the limitations of the training and specialized expertise available to police trying to be security intelligence officers. Mackenzie made much, no doubt quite rightly, of the huge difference between police and security intelligence work, and of the inflexible police structure which rendered the RCMP ill-suited to the special requirements of intelligence. With some prescience, given the RCMP scandals that were to unfold in the succeeding decade, Mackenzie noted that the blurred line of legality inevitably surrounding security intelligence work was hardly ideal for a law-enforcement agency. What was needed, Mackenzie concluded, was a new agency staffed increasingly by university graduates without law-enforcement powers and answering directly to government without mediation through the RCMP.[82] Mackenzie wanted a more effective instrument than the RCMP to implement the logic of the national security state.

The case for civilianization that was to be elaborated a decade later with much greater amplitude by the McDonald Commission and enacted in 1984 was thus first laid out with precision and brevity in Mackenzie in 1968–9. This was a bitter pill for the Mounties to swallow, but in the context of 1968–9 it was a much easier one to contend with, and reject, than was the case later. The security scandals of the 1960s had not besmirched the RCMP in any visible public manner; rather, it was the politicians who had caught most of the mud. The Mounties still had a large fund of credit in Canadian society on which to draw and powerful friends and allies within the state. The top brass made the decision to fight the civilianization recommendation tooth and nail, and they wheeled out all their top guns, including the articulate Bill Kelly, then head of the security service, to do battle.[83] Some of the arguments marshalled to buttress their case do not read well in retrospect. Most embarrassing was the claim that a civilian service would inevitably be penetrated by Soviet espionage. The smug assumption that the paramilitary structure of the Mounties somehow made them proof against penetration showed a hubris that would eventually be rudely deflated with the bitter knowledge that one of their rising stars, born to the force and the security service, Gilles Brunet, had been in reality a duplicitous tool of the KGB – and this at the very moment when they were boasting about their impenetrability. The Mountie brass also, of course, passed over the lamentable instance of *Long Knife*, who had shopped the star double agent *Gideon* to Moscow, but the civilians knew nothing about this act of betrayal and would certainly not be told.

The Mounties proved effective lobbyists in their own case and soon lined up their supporters within the councils of government. Recognizing that discretion was the better part of valour, the government decided to leave the Mounties in charge after all. Having won the fundamental victory, the force then dug in for a second fight, this time to prevent even the publication of the civilianization recommendations in the public version of the report. The fight was fierce, but this time the Mounties lost.[84] They would have to bear the blow to their self-esteem inflicted in the public airing of Mackenzie's arguments against their jurisdiction over security intelligence. And, after the indignity of a public debate, they had one final blow to contend with: in 1970, as a compromise between Mackenzie and the Mounties, the government appointed the first civilian director of the security service. John Starnes was carefully selected to appease RCMP feelings. He was a relative of a former RCMP commissioner in the 1920s, Cortlandt Starnes, and he had spent his career associated with intelligence, first in military intelligence during the war and then in External Affairs. In practice, Starnes would prove to be very supportive of the security service, but the very appointment of an outsider sent a clear and unwelcome message to the Mounties: the RCMP security service was being put on probation.[85]

Go Together Like a Horse and Carriage

Why did the RCMP fight so tenaciously against civilianization and to maintain their responsibility for security intelligence? Why, for that matter, had they pushed so hard to maintain the dominance of regular force members over civilians within the service? Later, in the early 1980s, key figures in the RCMP hierarchy would come to the conclusion that the security service was a liability that they were best rid of, to limit further damage to the public prestige of the force. But, at the end of the 1960s, they clearly regarded the service not as a liability but as a distinct asset. It is not hard to see why. So long as the Cold War held its grip over the nation, security intelligence and political policing added to the prestige and lustre of the force's public image. The service situated the RCMP closer to the centres of executive decision making on national-security questions in Ottawa than if they had been a mere police force. And, above all, it intimately connected the RCMP to a wider Western intelligence network. It is surely no accident that no less than four directors of the security service during the 1950s and 1960s later became commissioners. The security service was not the only jewel in the RCMP crown, but it certainly was an asset worth fighting to keep.

PART FOUR

Separatists, Scandals, and Reform

9

National Unity, National Security:
The Quebec Conundrum, 1960–84

When the Mackenzie Commission reported publicly in 1969, the commissioners devoted a mere three paragraphs (out of 306) to 'Quebec, separatism, and security.' They noted that, to the extent that a separate Quebec state was sought by legal and democratic means, 'it must be dealt with in a political rather than a security context.' However, if any evidence existed of 'subversive or seditious' intentions, or if there were any indication of foreign influence, then the federal government had a 'clear duty' to gather intelligence on such threats and take appropriate security measures to protect the integrity of the federation. They did find seditious tendencies in 'certain quarters.' These they quickly identified as emanating from Communist and Trotskyite infiltrators who were seeking to 'exploit separatist sentiment.' Foreign influence on secession was also identified as coming from 'certain communist countries.'[1]

Trapped in the mental ice age of the Cold War, the Mackenzie commissioners missed a very real domestic threat to order and security that had been growing throughout the 1960s: a violent urban guerrilla wing of a Quebec secessionist movement that was born and nurtured not by any external Communist bogey but by the long and tortured history of Quebec's relationship to Canada. The same fevered atmosphere of political ferment that had brought Quebec in short years from the 'Quiet Revolution' under the Jean Lesage Liberals (1960–6) to the birth of a sovereignist political party in 1968 also bred revolutionary movements impatient with party politics and constitutional processes, ready to use bombs, kidnapping, and political assassination to spark radical change. Just over a year after the Mackenzie Report's publication, the 1970 October Crisis plunged Canada into the most serious security emergency in its history, but one that bore not even the most distant marks of the Cold War. The Mackenzie Commission, with little or no inkling of a post-Igor Gouzenko world, had been peering into the future through the rear-view mirror.

If they had been paying attention, the commissioners might have noticed that the new Liberal prime minister, Pierre Elliott Trudeau, was a deeply committed partisan in a kind of Quebec civil war that pitted federalists against nationalists who had raised autonomist demands into calls for outright independence. In this contest, the Trudeau Liberals would shift security priorities away from the old Cold War obsessions and direct them much closer to home. Moreover, in this bitter contest, hard-and-fast distinctions would not always be drawn between threats to national *unity*, which emanated from the emergent Parti Québécois (PQ), a lawful and democratic political party, and threats to national *security* that emanated from the more extreme and violent forces at the fringe of the independence movement.

The Not So Quiet Revolution

In June 1960 the Quebec Liberal Party, led by a former federal cabinet minister, Jean Lesage, ended sixteen years of rule by the Union Nationale of Maurice Duplessis, an era later characterized as the *grand noirceur*, or Quebec's dark ages, in which conservative Catholicism and quasi-authoritarian nationalism dominated the province. The Liberals ushered in a new era of *épanouissement*, an opening up of Quebec society to rapid modernization that quickly became known as *la révolution tranquille*, or the Quiet Revolution. As the Quebec government brought in such innovations as the secularization of education and the nationalization of hydroelectricity, there were other, less controlled, forces unleashed by the winds of change. The Rassemblement pour l'indépendance nationale (RIN), founded in 1960, brought the demand for the outright independence of Quebec from Canada into the streets. More revolutionary left-wing tendencies began to coalesce in the fall of 1962, culminating in the foundation of the Front de libération du Québec (FLQ) in early 1963. Soon bombs began exploding in a violent campaign to force independence.[2] In April the violence claimed its first victim, a sixty-five-year-old night watchman and war veteran at a Canadian Army recruiting centre in Montreal. The FLQ issued a communiqué: 'Unfortunately, a revolution cannot be carried out without bloodshed. A man is dead, but the revolution will go forward.'[3] Joint operations by the Quebec and Montreal police and the RCMP security service netted the arrests of twenty-three of the top leaders of the FLQ in June 1963. Despite this setback, the FLQ gathered strength throughout the 1960s and peaked in the October Crisis of 1970 with the kidnapping of British trade commissioner James Cross and the kidnapping and subsequent murder of a Quebec cabinet minister, Pierre Laporte. The federal government invoked the War Measures Act, citing an alleged apprehended insurrection. Following the release of Cross and the apprehension and conviction of the FLQ cell responsible for Laporte's murder, there was a marked diminution of terrorist activity and its complete disappearance by the mid-1970s. By this time, however, a clandestine 'countering' campaign against the FLQ and other radical groups, led by the RCMP under federal government direction, was expanding into illegal acts and 'dirty tricks' by the agents of the state.

In parallel with the growth of a violent revolutionary wing of the secessionist movement, there was another development in the 1960s, ultimately far more significant for Quebec and Canada – the emergence of a sovereignist movement that strictly followed a legal path and respected democratic norms and practices. In 1967–8 René Lévesque, who had been the leader of the left-nationalist wing of the Lesage Liberals in the early 1960s, helped form the Parti Québécois; he subsequently led the PQ in the Quebec election of 1970, just months before the October Crisis was unleashed. Within six years, the PQ gathered wide enough public support to come to office as the government of Quebec and to hold the first referendum on 'sovereignty-association' in 1980, with a second, close-run referendum held by a second PQ government in 1995. In retrospect, it is clear that the October 1970 Crisis signalled a historic turning point for the sovereignty movement. The violent path to separation was abandoned, a casualty both of decisive action by the Canadian (and Quebec) states and of the would-be revolutionaries' own reckless excess in murdering Pierre Laporte in cold blood. While it lasted, however, the FLQ represented a threat to national security as well as to public safety, thus demanding policing in the traditional sense as well as security intelligence assessments. The RCMP, in their guise as both the national police force and the security intelligence service, were the federal government's appropriate tool for responding to this threat. But the parallel growth of the legitimate sovereignist movement complicated matters a great deal, and not just at the perceptual level. The federal nature of the Canadian state, and the identification of the national government with the anglophone majority, makes the matter of federal surveillance of Quebec political activity particularly controversial. In the 1960s and 1970s, federal officials did not always make clear and appropriate distinctions between the two tendencies; intrusive surveillance was directed against both, although with varying degrees of intensity.

In the late 1960s, the RCMP's political masters began nudging the force towards a new, and very dangerous, kind of political policing: one that would result in covert federal interventions in the political life of Quebec. The question of federal interference in Quebec affairs had always been a very sensitive matter, but in the highly volatile atmosphere of Quebec in the 1960s and 1970s, it was the match in a powder keg. By the mid-1980s, the volatility had finally died down, but a succession of explosions had resulted in the end of the RCMP security service and the birth of new civilian agency with a strict legislative mandate and extensive forms of accountability and external review over its activities. The Mounties had stood guard over Canadian society for over half a century of depression, World War, and Cold War without attracting any politically significant degree of criticism. What finally tripped them up were not the foreign or foreign-influenced enemies they had traditionally targeted, but their new intervention in the political affairs of the eternally uneasy partner in Confederation, Quebec. Policing exotic subversives was one thing; intervening in the domestic politics of a Canadian province would prove far more troublesome for the RCMP's image as an impartial, apolitical police force.

There was another dimension to the political policing of Quebec that would further bedevil the RCMP. When Ottawa's political masters directed the surreptitious undermining of the Quebec sovereignty movements, their bureaucratic servants learned that they could be left holding the bag when things went awry and public embarrassment resulted. The familiar intelligence principles of the 'need to know' and 'plausible deniability' would prove valuable devices for shielding the politicians from the political consequences of their own policy directives. This would be uncomfortable, if not sometimes exasperating, for the Mounties. A police force expected to operate at arm's length from political direction under the often cited, but perhaps not always observed, principle of police independence, the RCMP were expected to take responsibility for their actions in initiating investigations and laying criminal charges. As a security intelligence agency, on the other hand, they took direction, albeit secret, from the government of the day. Police independence was a double-edged sword, freeing the force from politicization in criminal law enforcement but offering a cover in security intelligence operations for the political masters to deflect criticism onto their administrative servants. The fit was awkward enough that the RCMP brass would eventually welcome a structural reorganization that hived off the security service entirely from the force, despite the cost in the tarnished image of the Mounties.

Federal surveillance of Quebec became controversial in another way: in the aftermath of the October Crisis, federal ministers from Quebec, including the prime minister, let it be known that they considered the intelligence on Quebec separatism gathered by the RCMP security service to have been inadequate, if not worse.[4] In effect, blame for the crisis was directed at an intelligence failure. What followed in the 1970s was a much more aggressive and intrusive pattern of intelligence targeting of Quebec separatism by the security service. This blew up in the face of the government with a series of public scandals of RCMP 'wrongdoing' – actions that went beyond lawful limits or were seriously questionable from the standpoint of liberal-democratic ethics. A federal commission of inquiry[5] recommended the civilianization of the security service, that is, its detachment from the RCMP and its establishment as a civilian agency with a legislative mandate. This was done in the Canadian Security Intelligence Service Act of 1984. In short, the RCMP security service took two 'hits,' from opposite angles – first, for allegedly inadequate intelligence on Quebec prior to October 1970; second, for overzealous and overly intrusive actions following 1970. Given the seriousness of the Quebec situation, the cumulative effect of these two perceived intelligence failures was fatal to the RCMP security service as an organization.

In this chapter, we will focus initially on the period up to and including the October Crisis. Blaming the RCMP for the intelligence failure has not been unanimous – a minority view has considered that the government should have accepted greater responsibility and pointed fewer fingers at officials.[6] But accounts critical of the RCMP constitute the received wisdom on the subject.[7] To be sure, the RCMP had built-in limitations in their understanding of Quebec and of threats not related to the Cold War. Yet this is not the whole story. Today, through the use of the Access to Information Act, it is possible to examine material from the security service files and thereby gain greater insight into the quality of the intelligence that the service had gathered.[8] As is often the case when original documents are declassified, the received wisdom turns out to require revision.

Identifying the Home-Grown Threat

Given the revolutionary nature of the FLQ goals, the federal government, in the form of its security intelligence service, would obviously be called upon for threat assessments. The security service was an
integral part of the RCMP, which, as a federal police force, were also
concerned with questions of public order and criminal acts, such as terrorism. Thus, the RCMP's investigative interest was from the start related to both its security-intelligence and its law-enforcement functions.
Constitutionally, the Mounties could play only a secondary role to the
Quebec provincial police, le Sûreté du Québec (SQ), and the Montreal
Police in the latter field, while in the former they had primary responsibility. There were serious barriers facing the RCMP security service as it
turned its attention to the emergent terrorist problem. There was a pronounced ideological predisposition of the security service to see security threats primarily, if not exclusively, in Cold War terms: espionage,
terrorism, sabotage, and subversion were all instinctively linked with
Communism, and foreign interference almost always meant Soviet
Bloc machinations. It was initially hard for these veteran Cold Warriors
to grasp the significance of an entirely domestic revolutionary movement. Other barriers were cultural and linguistic. The RCMP were very
much an 'anglo' force with few francophone officers, especially in the
security service, and not especially at home in the Quebec milieu: to the
Mounties, Quebec was simply not *chez nous*.[9]

At some point during the mid-1960s, Sergeant R.A. Vaughan of the
Research Section of the security service summed up some of the initial
problems faced by the force in Quebec.[10] The separatist movement, he
wrote, 'has created a situation ... that is unique, complex, and extremely
sensitive for the police forces ... This is particularly true for the RCMP
which is looked upon by separatists as the agent of a "foreign" power,
i.e., the federal government.' During its early stages of development,
the separatist movement was 'not a target for penetration by this Force.'
Thus, despite early indications of violent potential, the development
of the FLQ was 'not anticipated.' The FLQ bombings were viewed as
criminal offences, and thus prime responsibility fell to the SQ and the
Montreal Police: 'The RCMP was relegated to a role of assistance when
it was requested by the other police forces.' Vaughan added that if, immediately after being arrested, FLQers had been interviewed by the
security service, 'much useful information concerning the FLQ as a
subversive organization might have been uncovered.' To facilitate coor-

dination of criminal and intelligence information, the Inter-Directorate Liaison Section (IDLS) was set up in early 1964. At this point it became apparent that the separatist movement as a whole had to be assessed, 'including the seemingly more moderate sections.' Vaughan spoke of 'considerable effort on the part of the IDLS to locate suitably motivated potential sources for further development,' and added that coverage (a year or two later) 'has improved and should continue to do so.'

The first RCMP threat assessment of the FLQ and other terrorist groups was filed on 22 July 1963.[11] A covering letter to the solicitor general indicated the highly tentative nature of the analysis, which in typical Cold War terms heavily stressed possible Communist linkages with the FLQ. Yet the various police forces were beginning to makes inroads into the FLQ. On 12 April 1963 the RCMP had cooperated with the Montreal Police in the so-called 'Good Friday' raids that netted twenty arrests. Then, on 1 June, a highly placed paid informant for the Montreal Police paved the way for the arrest of twenty-three other militants. In 1964 the RCMP cooperated with the SQ and the Montreal Police in the formation of the Combined Anti-Terrorist Squad (CATS), which soon netted further arrests that broke up a nascent Armée de libération du Québec and another fledgling group, the Front républicaine pour l'indépendance, and dealt a heavy blow against the FLQ. By this stage, the federal police were clearly on the ground and running.

In September 1964 a security brief on 'Separatism and subversion in Quebec'[12] was prepared by the security service that showed a more sophisticated grasp of the various currents and factions swirling around the separatist movement. It was an 'extremely complex' situation involving a complex of clandestine and legal organizations, and a proliferation of groups splitting and reforming, sometimes genuinely but sometimes to confuse the police. Another brief in the same month analysed, in some depth, seven open and five covert organizations.[13] Names of individuals in these briefs are censored under the Access to Information Act, so it is difficult to gain an appreciation of the scope of the security service's knowledge, although Montreal Police penetration operations[14] must have already yielded considerable intelligence that would presumably have been shared. 'The underground movement has three levels of operation – those who actually participate in the terrorist activity, plus a "planner" group, and a group of "theorists" who promote and direct this activity. Arrests to date bear this out, for, as one group of terrorists has been eliminated, the survivors have been quickly reorganized into a successor group, and as long as the upper echelon, the "planners" and the "theorists" who are operating under the cover of the seemingly legitimate separatist organizations, remain free the terrorist activity will continue.' At this stage, the 'seemingly legitimate separatist' movement was dominated by the Rassemblement pour l'indépendance nationale. The radical RIN's mantle later passed to the relatively more moderate and respectable PQ, and the RCMP's difficulty in distinguishing between the terrorist and legitimate wings of the movement was to prove much more troublesome.

At this time the security service remained preoccupied with left-wing socialist tendencies of the RIN and the possible connections this might mean with the Communists. Every use of the term 'national liberation struggle' seemed to set off the force's Cold War alarm bells, since this was a phrase widely used by Communist or pro-Communist Third World revolutionary movements. Yet the Mounties admitted that there was 'not much evidence that separatist leaders have "openly" co-operated with the Communist party.' Separatists, they granted, had no intention of relinquishing control of their organizations to Communists, and for their part, the Communists did not want to risk the adverse publicity that would come from association with terrorism. Yet the Security service could not give up the idea that Communist influence might be felt in 'more subtle ways' that might not even be understood by a substantial segment of the movement. In this report there are even nine heavily censored pages on Trotskyist involvement. An updated version of an earlier brief was subjected to a lengthy critique by Donald Cobb of the Montreal division of the security service who insisted that it had failed to appreciate fully the dangers of Communist influence over the movement. The paper was expanded and rewritten to reflect Cobb's concerns.[15]

The 1964 briefs had an important policy result. The final version was presented to the Security Panel – the coordinating body that administered government security and made recommendations to cabinet on policy – on 23 September 1964.[16] The RCMP were concerned about a security clearance for a civil servant posted abroad who was an open member of the RIN. The problem was that the government had given no directives to the RCMP indicating that membership in a group like the RIN could constitute a security risk. Yet the RCMP suspected that there were links between the RIN, as an open, apparently democratic, separatist movement, and the terrorist groups like the FLQ. The panel concluded that, when conducting security clearances, the RCMP should include in their reports the fact of membership in organizations like the

RIN 'together with such detailed information concerning length of attendance, degrees of involvement, and other pertinent information as
was available in order that Departments, on whom final decision for
the clearance rested, could consider the necessity of further investigation as they would do in cases of information concerning membership
in the Communist Party, Front Organizations or character weaknesses.'

Although it was not formalized in a cabinet directive,[17] this decision
was crucial for RCMP surveillance of Quebec political life. The Security Panel had given the green light to the security service to compile
dossiers on separatists, and it had explicitly agreed that these could
include those belonging to open and legal groups such as the RIN, as
well as to clandestine terrorist organizations, at least so long as the
former were suspected of clandestine ties. A subtext was that this also
provided opportunities for the security service to recruit sources from
within separatist groups: the threat of losing a security clearance and
thus a livelihood could be a powerful inducement to cooperation.[18] Indeed, there is reason to believe that in the mid-1960s the security service became much more active in infiltration of the FLQ. Under the
Access to Information Act any reference to the identity or indeed even
the existence of human sources of intelligence is rigorously excluded.
However, the quality of intelligence seems to pick up quite distinctly
around this time, as does the level of political analysis.[19] Lists of sources
of information, although heavily blacked out in the declassified versions, seem to indicate that while many open sources were consulted,
at least as many or more may have been secret.

Louis Fournier, the best published source on the FLQ and very well
informed on police infiltration, mentions a successful RCMP penetration that may have begun as early as 1966.[20] Fournier speaks of 'one of
the most productive "human sources"' recruited by Donald Cobb in
1968, whom he dubs the 'Taxi Driver.' This source enabled the Mounties to draw up organization charts of separatist networks, and to give
detailed information on personalities (psychological profiles, meeting
places, favourite haunts, and so on). Later, Fournier claims, the 'Taxi
Driver' was of considerable assistance during the October Crisis.[21] Other RCMP sources were alleged but not confirmed. One limitation under
the Access to Information Act is that personal files are exempted until
twenty years following an individual's death. For events in the 1960s
and 1970s mainly involving activists in their twenties and thirties, this
is a serious barrier. However, one leading FLQ militant, François Mario
Bachand, who was among the first waves of arrests in the early 1960s

and continued as an activist until he fled Canada in 1969, was subsequently assassinated in Paris in 1971, an event to which we will return later. Bachand's security service file is now available and has been declassified.[22] Through it one can gain some appreciation of the quantity and quality of intelligence on separatists available to the RCMP. The paper file comprises 10 volumes and is about 2,400 pages in length. A printout of the computer file on Bachand itself runs to about 90 pages of information coded into such categories as name; street name; description; property and residences; itineraries of movements; purpose of movements; outcome of events he had been associated with; correspondence received; employers; Unemployment Insurance records; groups involved with; his role in them; demonstrations attended; and so on. 'Miscellaneous' includes such personal matters as 'frequently uses propanity [sic], talks about sex in a smutty manner, not mature and discreet,' 'has complexes of insecurity and non confidence in himself,' 'habitual liar,' 'only hobby is reading.' Such information could only come from well-placed human sources familiar with the subject – indeed one of these may have been an alleged RCMP source who had a major dispute with Bachand.[23]

The quality of the intelligence is perhaps most apparent in the parts of the Bachand file relating to his leading role in the McGill Française movement in 1969. This movement was directed to the goal of making the venerable anglophone institution of McGill University into a French-language institution. Dossiers were sent by the security service to the solicitor general, the Security Panel, and other senior government officials indicating that a mass demonstration at the gates of McGill was to be the cover for a commando raid on the computer centre (this raid was prevented). The security service was acting on information gathered on the leadership cadre, among whom Bachand was prominent. This information included highly detailed plans (which rooms to move through to reach the target, how the operation was to be financed – ironically through federal government funds via the Company of Young Canadians). At one large meeting, one RCMP and four Montreal Police officers secretly filming the proceedings were detected and forced to leave. But the Bachand file indicates that they had excellent information concerning even small, secret strategy meetings; these could only come from a human source.

A threat assessment on Quebec separatism at the end of 1969[24] examined twenty-two organizations from the traditional and very conservative Société Saint-Jean Baptiste to the radical proletarian Taxi

Liberation Movement. By this stage, the security service had dismissed the Communist bogey as irrelevant, indicating definitively that it had 'no evidence' of any Communist role. The RIN was now defunct, but there was a much more formidable legitimate arm of the independence movement in the newly formed Parti Québécois. The Mounties were less than alarmed about this development, at least from the standpoint of revolutionary threats: the PQ, the report indicated, 'has scrupulously adhered to an ethically and constitutionally correct approach to the Quebec question'; despite the presence of certain individuals of 'dubious political background,' there was no evidence of 'hostile intelligence activity.' The Mounties were interested only in the terrorist and subversive elements: even though the PQ 'poses a distinct threat to the integrity of the Federation, it will not be dealt with in any detail.'

The 1969 assessment is also notable for a tone of relative liberality in its interpretation of the wider 'movement.' For instance, with regard to the McGill Française and Bill 63 (language law) demonstrations, the report concedes that such protests 'may have merit from a participatory democracy point of view.' However, they also 'serve to envenom the atmosphere, increasing both the scope of radicalism and the cost to the taxpayer of containing it.' McGill Française was known to have violent ulterior purposes, but the worst was averted by police action. In light of the impending crisis of the following year that was to call forth the War Measures Act to counter an 'apprehended insurrection,' the security service was coolly realistic about the scope of the terrorist wing, which illustrated, in its words, 'dramatically how a handful of determined youths could wreck destruction and instil fear in the populace *to a degree highly disproportionate to their numbers*' (emphasis added). What it did *not* detect was any indication of a mass revolutionary base.

Another interesting aspect of the 1969 assessment relates to the question of foreign involvement in the separatist movement. Under the Access to Information Act, information about foreign governments is often exempted. One brief on 'Foreign involvement in the Quebec separatist movement' that is undated but appears to be from the mid-1960s[25] contained at least sixty-five pages in the original but has only about seven left after the liberal application of black ink by the censors. It does seem that initially the security service was particularly attentive to evidence of Communist Bloc involvement. Cuba was cited as having links to terrorist activity, as was Algeria, then the Mecca for national liberation movements everywhere. But Communist and other leftist states apparently showed little substantive interest in the Quebec situation. By the end of the 1960s, foreign interest was seen as stemming mainly from France, 'which has been interfering in Canadian affairs since 1963' (and had done so quite publicly with de Gaulle's infamous *Vive le Québec libre* speech in 1967).[26] The federal government had already expelled the French national Phillippe Rossillon, virtually dubbing him an agent of the French secret service.[27] It never could find the smoking gun of French involvement in the separatist movement. One problem was Canada's lack of a foreign intelligence service that might have gathered information on French intentions. The security service did try to enlist the help of American and British intelligence, but it was politely rebuffed.[28] The search for French interference did, however, offer other grounds for maintaining surveillance, not only of the terrorist organizations but of more legitimate groups like the PQ. The PQ might be a legal party, but if the French were seeking to use it for hostile purposes, a watching brief would have to be maintained by the RCMP.

The RCMP and the October Crisis

The charge that the RCMP had failed to provide the government adequate intelligence is especially focused on the events of October 1970. The validity of this depends on how one interprets the nature of the crisis set off by the kidnapping of Cross and Laporte. If it is assumed that Quebec in 1970 was in a 'pre-revolutionary' phase in which one or two sparks could ignite a conflagration (that is, if there was indeed an apprehended insurrection), then it may well be that the police failed to warn the civilian authorities. On the other hand, if October is viewed essentially as a case of a 'handful of determined youths' wielding a political impact 'to a degree highly disproportionate to their numbers' (in words of the 1969 assessment), and the invocation of the War Measures Act an overreaction (either panicked or deliberate), then the case against the RCMP is very considerably weakened.

If we consider the October Crisis simply at face value as a political hostage crisis, the question of whether the RCMP provided the government adequate advance warning based on security service intelligence, can be answered – in the affirmative. It is true that they were not able to prevent the kidnapping of Cross and Laporte, nor the latter's murder. To suggest that the RCMP had failed if they could not prevent the two hostage takings, however, is to set impossible standards for any security intelligence service in similar circumstances (similar reasoning would, for instance, label the British security forces in Northern Ireland during the 'Troubles' as abject failures). A more appropriate question would be: Did the security service provide adequate advance intelligence *warning* that kidnappings were planned by the FLQ and that people like Cross and Laporte were potential targets? Here the answer is an unequivocal yes.

A few months after the conclusion of the crisis, the director general of the security service, John Starnes, was in the process of reading Gérard Pelletier's *La crise d'octobre* and 'came upon a remark by Pelletier in the book that the police were totally unprepared for the kidnappings which took place in October 1970.' Starnes was incensed at this implication of incompetence and asked his staff for documentation on this question.[29] The result was a dossier of evidence to the contrary and a letter from Starnes to Solicitor General Jean-Pierre Goyer early in 1972 that attempted to set the record straight.[30] This dossier makes very interesting reading.

In the first part of 1970 the police foiled two kidnapping attempts, first against an Israeli consul and then against the U.S. consul in Montreal. One of these plots was uncovered by accident in the course of an unrelated investigation, the other by good police work. The security service went to some lengths to be sure that senior government officials were aware of the implications of these failed plots. In April 1970 Assistant Commissioner J.E.M. Barrette made the point very clearly.[31] The combined police forces (RCMP, Montreal Police, SQ) were preparing a contingency plan to cope with any potential kidnappings. Citing the current fashion for political kidnappings among urban guerrillas in Latin America, as well as the evidence from Quebec, the security service extrapolated basic victim groups. Most likely were foreign diplomats and Quebec political and governmental leaders. Ten days later, the director passed on this information to the solicitor general, George McIlraith. This was six months before the FLQ kidnapped a British diplomat and a Quebec cabinet minister.[32]

Did the RCMP know who was likely to undertake kidnappings? A document dated 21 May is heavily censored but *may* be a list of individuals, including photographs, suspected of being possible kidnappers. We know that in October the RCMP had the names of most, if not all, of the actual kidnappers, based on cumulative police evidence and their human sources (the 'Taxi Driver' and possibly others), but lacked the knowledge of the exact location of the hostages. Paul Rose, of the Chenier cell holding Laporte, had been under police surveillance which unfortunately was broken by Rose's evasive actions. The Mounties, employing good police work, were eventually able to track down and free Cross, and the kidnappers and killers of Laporte were subsequently apprehended and convicted. The capacity of clandestine terrorist cells to hide hostages in a large metropolitan area, it should be noted, has been demonstrated time and again in various parts of the world, from Beirut to Rome.

The contingency plan set in motion in the spring of 1970 involved a twenty-four-hour hot line to the Department of External Affairs and FBI liaison and control of movement across borders. It should be pointed out in light of the advance warnings, and especially the two foiled plots, that no watch was placed on the homes of foreign diplomats in Montreal, with the result that the kidnappers of Cross met no resistance when they knocked on his front door. If this constituted negligence, it was the fault not of the RCMP but of the government of Canada for failing to take its security service's warnings seriously and offer appropriate protection to its threatened foreign diplomats. The kidnapping of Laporte presented an even more egregious spectacle of negligence. With the FLQ already holding Cross, another group of terrorists, who had heard about the kidnapping on their car radio while holidaying in Texas, rushed back to Montreal, drove to the home address of the minister of labour, found him tossing a football on his front lawn with a nephew, and hauled him into their car. It turned out to be a tragic turn of events, but it was not the responsibility of the RCMP to guard Quebec officials.

When the crisis was over, the Strategic Operations Centre (SOC), set up to coordinate Ottawa's response, took a considered look back.[33] On police and Armed Forces operations, it concluded that although 'certain deficiencies and possibilities for improvement' had been pointed out by agencies themselves, 'in general *this was the side of government operations which was best prepared and acquitted itself with great credit'* (emphasis added). Listing the various warnings provided by the RCMP, the SOC stated that 'sufficient (although not complete) information was *available* to forewarn the government of the possibility/probability of an "October Crisis"' and to 'warrant some preventive – or at least preparatory – steps being taken prior to such a crisis breaking out.' Why this did not happen was a complex question to which a number of answers could be given. Among these: the 'lack of any mechanism for proper *political evaluation* of information put forward by the RCMP, and of any political input to this information,' and the lack of political mechanisms to *react* to this information. This suggests the classic problem of the lack of effective coordination between intelligence agencies and the consumers of the intelligence product, governments.[34] Add to this the 'instinctive belief it can't happen here,' and we have a recipe for governmental inaction in the face of warnings.

After the PQ came to office in 1976, a special investigation was launched into the events of October 1970 under the direction of Jean-François Duchaîne, who reported in 1980. Despite the refusal of the federal government and the RCMP to cooperate with the inquiry, Duchaîne was clear that, of the three police forces involved, the RCMP were the most knowledgeable and the most professional. It began with numbers: the security service had some 300 officers from the Montreal detachment alone, while the combined anti-terrorist forces of the SQ and the Montreal Police amounted to no more than 45 (this latter number was later augmented). Moreover, the Quebec forces conceded that RCMP security service was 'le mieux équipé pour faire face à la situation' (the best equipped to deal with the situation), while the SQ and Montreal Police found themselves in a panic as they faced a crisis for which they were largely unprepared. Of the three police forces, the RCMP were 'le seul qui possédait un service de sécurité d'une certaine ampleur' (the only one to possess a security service with some scope).[35]

The superiority of the RCMP was nowhere more apparent than in the preparation of the list of detainees to be picked up under the War Measures Act. This assertion, admittedly, flies in the face of the recollections of the major political players in the process, but it can be substantiated by the documentary record. As to the denials of the RCMP's role, we may start with the recollections of former Prime Minister Trudeau in his 1993 *Memoirs*. There he insisted that the role played by the RCMP in the preparation of the list was a 'very minor one': 'I know that because I obtained, a short time before the arrests, a list of the people the RCMP wanted to keep under surveillance. I wanted to see the list not so that I could substitute my own judgment for that of the police, which was not my role, but simply to inform myself about the kind of information the RCMP was gathering. Now, this list consisted almost entirely of the names of members of Maoist and Trotskyite groups, none of which appeared later on lists of prisoners arrested under the War Measures Act, from which I conclude that those on the RCMP list were never bothered.' Trudeau then went on to conclude, incorrectly, that it was the SQ and the Montreal Police who made up the list, which was 'too long and badly verified,' while at the same time identifying the latter forces, correctly, as responsible for the arrests of activists and protestors who 'not guilty – or even capable – of criminal activity.'[36]

The problem with this is that we have no idea exactly when or under what circumstances Trudeau obtained this RCMP list. He says that it was a list of people the RCMP wanted to keep under surveillance, but we do not know for what specific purpose. That this list was almost entirely made up of Maoists and Trotskyists fits Trudeau's general indictment of the Mounties being allegedly stuck in a Cold War time warp, but it does not fit with what the records indicate about the level of RCMP intelligence on the separatists. Nor does it make much sense if we are to interpret Trudeau's list as that of the preliminary list of detainees to be picked up immediately under the War Measures Act, given the chronology of facts as are now known.

An initial list was drawn up by Michel Côté, legal counsel to the city of Montreal, in consultation with the Montreal Police, and used as the basis of the formal request by Mayor Jean Drapeau for the invocation of the War Measures Act, but there were not enough names to justify the emergency powers. More names were subsequently added in consultation with the RCMP. The SQ was also expected to contribute to the list, but it did not have extensive enough dossiers to do the job; the RCMP security service was called in to help. There followed a somewhat bizarre scene: SQ-RCMP 'collaboration' was illusory; the SQ officers were ushered into a room where they were presented with names drawn from files held in another room by the security service to which direct access was denied the SQ. According to Duchaîne, the SQ never had any direct access to the intelligence used in drawing up the lists.[37]

Duchaîne did sharply criticize a certain destructive competition that developed between the RCMP and the two Quebec police forces in the course of the investigations, citing the 'strange' attitude of the RCMP towards sharing information with the SQ.[38] Some of this may be attributed to the inevitable, if deplorable, turf wars that always crop up between different police organizations working on the same terrain. There was, however, another dimension to the RCMP's reluctance to share information with the SQ: the Mounties had evidence that the SQ had been infiltrated by one or more FLQ sympathizers.[39]

Another intriguing aspect of the list of detainees is the question of political input. The RCMP arranged a consultation on their list of 158 detainees with two of Trudeau's closest Quebec lieutenants, Jean Marchand and Gérard Pelletier. This was a 'gesture of courtesy,' but the Mounties were also ready to take advantage of these men's intimate knowledge of Quebec politics and personalities. Both Pelletier and Marchand later leaked to selected journalists an account of this meeting that suggests they were shocked by many of the names and insisted on reducing the list. One account has Marchand crossing out a 'ridiculous' name and Pelletier a 'few.'[40] A more expansive version has an 'incredulous' and 'horrified' Pelletier crossing off 'name after name.'[41] Yet another, a very sympathetic biographer of Trudeau, suggests that the list was sharply reduced down to about two dozen, but that the police then went out and arrested hundreds regardless.[42] It is true that the Quebec police, especially outside Montreal, were excessive in round-ups under the special powers and that the number of arrests did go far beyond the numbers specified in the lists prepared by the RCMP and the Montreal Police. But the retroactive accounts of Marchand and Pelletier are flatly denied by the sworn testimony of senior RCMP officials before the McDonald Commission. Commissioner Higgitt recalled that there was 'no change.' Inspector Joseph Ferraris was explicit: Pelletier had questioned two names but withdrew his objections when they were explained.[43] These two accounts are mutually exclusive, although sworn testimony before a royal commission does seem more credible than non-attributed leaks to journalists. At stake is the credibility of security service intelligence. But, as we shall see in a moment, it was not the RCMP that wanted a dragnet under emergency powers but the government. The list of detainees was as much, or more, to legitimate the decision to invoke the War Measures Act as it was to assist in the police work of tracking down the kidnappers.

Apprehended Insurrection? Invoking the War Measures Act

Two particular versions of October 1970 cast the security service in an unflattering light. One, stressing alleged incompetence, suggests that the War Measures Act provided the police with special powers because they could not do the job under normal rules.[44] The other, stressing a more conspiratorial view of the secret police, suggests that they seized the opportunity offered by the crisis and the emergency powers to strike a blow against the entire independence movement, especially the PQ.[45] Neither version has any basis in fact. The reality is that the RCMP never advised the invocation of the War Measures Act, were not consulted as to its usefulness, and would have opposed it – if they had been asked.

In-camera testimony before the McDonald Commission by senior security service officials makes clear that the force was out of the loop in the decision to invoke the emergency powers. Joseph Ferraris, a veteran of the security service (mostly in Quebec) and a member of 'G' Ops – the special operations unit – had a key role to play at the time of the crisis. Ferraris later told the McDonald commissioners that the RCMP and the security service in particular thought that the War Measures Act was dangerous in the sense that it 'donnait trop de pouvoir' (gave too much power). This power was especially misused by local police in Quebec, over whom the RCMP could exercise no control. Worse, he maintained, it probably 'delayed our finding Mr Cross by about two or three weeks, or maybe a month' because it diverted trained manpower from police work to administering the War Measures Act and picking up and questioning people not directly connected to the kidnappings. Ferraris sardonically summed up his scepticism about the use of the act: 'Pas besoin d'une bombe atomique s'il y a une ... une émeute sur la rue Sainte-Catherine (you don't need an atomic bomb if there's a riot on St Catherine Street).'[46]

Commissioner William Higgitt was, if anything, even blunter. He made it clear that he had never been asked for his opinion on the efficacy of invoking the War Measures Act; the only point on which he offered advice was the mechanics of implementing it. While he granted that it conferred certain advantages on the police, he added that there were many disadvantages, not least of which was the excessive powers granted the Quebec police and the misuse of these powers that could go on unchecked (many more people were arrested than the RCMP thought reasonable). The commission pressed for documentation of the 'apprehended insurrection'; Higgitt said there was none. Indeed, he went further to insist that he would 'have stopped somewhat short of using the word "rebellion" or an "open rebellion"' – 'I had, I guess, greater faith in the people concerned than that.' The commission was puzzled: 'It does strike one as passing strange that in what was one of the great crises in this country's history, there was no apparent file opened concerning the apprehension of insurrection.' Higgitt was unfazed: 'apprehended insurrection' were 'words foreign, quite foreign to us as [far as] I'm concerned.'[47]

Here we come to the crux of the issue that lay between the government and its security service. In invoking the powers of the War Measures Act, the cabinet was answering formal requests from Quebec and Montreal, but these requests were really prompted by Ottawa. If they did not stem from the requirements of the federal police, whence did they come? Even today it is not possible precisely to locate the rationale, but we can say with confidence that the decision came from the prime minister and his inner circle of Quebec ministers and advisers. Some light has been cast on the government's motives by the publication of the late Don Jamieson's memoirs. As a member of the Trudeau cabinet in 1970, Jamieson was near the centre of decision making, and he recalls a sense of unease over the War Measures Act. He remembers Trudeau as being particularly scornful of the alleged weakness and vacillation of Quebec premier Robert Bourassa and the softness of Quebec nationalist intellectuals like Claude Ryan of *Le Devoir* who was arguing for concessions to the FLQ and drawing in trade unions and the PQ into some kind of projected 'provisional government.' Trudeau's Quebec colleague Jean Marchand was in a state of agitation about a violent revolution about to break out. Trudeau no doubt never believed *that* (even Marchand was soon admitting to his colleagues that he had momentarily gone off the deep end), but he did worry about an erosion of the federalist position in Quebec. Jamieson believed that, from the moment Cross had been abducted, Trudeau 'saw the incident as an issue on which he could stand or fall, and through which he might be able to assert the federal position in a dramatic manner.' Laporte's kidnapping 'crystallized' Trudeau's position. 'The PM saw that if he did not move decisively and immediately, his whole posture regarding Quebec and federalism would lose credibility.' Ministers who took him at his word about an apprehended insurrection wanted documentation and support to justify their government's action. Trudeau was, in Jamieson's words, 'surprisingly unresponsive.' No specific rationale was ever developed. 'Subsequent events made his reason ... very plain. *It was his growing awareness, and perhaps concern, that very little in the way of concrete evidence was going to turn up*. No evidence could be publicly documented that would assert without question the existence of an organized plot.' Police sweeps failed to turn up 'the kind of evidence that would justify the action we had taken ... This was the main reason for Trudeau's reluctance to initiate any kind of preparatory work on a general defence of our motives.'[48]

If Trudeau and his close Quebec colleagues had decided on the War Measures Act as a kind of *coup de théâtre* to intimidate the separatists of all stripes and stiffen the backbone of the federalists, this may help to explain their dismissive if not hostile attitude towards the RCMP. This can be glimpsed in Jamieson's account of the infamous RCMP cabinet briefing that various ministers later described as a fiasco. Jamieson joins the pack: 'From a police standpoint, it can only be described as a disaster.' Ministers were dissatisfied with the quality of the intelligence, and got only 'disquieting' answers to questions on police operations. There were, it should be noted, some mitigating circumstances. The director of the security service, John Starnes, was unavailable at this time because of serious illness, and the Mounties had been given almost no notice of the briefing. In the midst of a crisis requiring their full attention, they did not have time to work up a brief appropriate to the audience and the circumstances. But were the politicians' judgments justifiable?

There appears to be no surviving record of this meeting as such. There is a copy of a written brief, dated a few days later, that is likely a polished version of what was delivered verbally to cabinet.[49] It gives a not unreasonable summary of the situation, including an up-to-date list of names of suspects arising out of the earlier foiled kidnap plots (which turned out to be accurate). It also includes an interesting section on foreign influences, pointing out that, in cases like the FLQ, foreign influences were 'more insidious and less apparent than the traditional outside interference of one nation in the affairs of another.' 'The rigid control of international communism ... is not apparent'; instead, the brief speaks of terrorist groups around the world with a 'common bond of belief in guerrilla tactics' gaining strength and encouragement from each other 'often through nothing more tangible than the news accounts of their exploits and the revolutionary writings and statements of their leaders.' The cumulative effect of these influences on Quebec revolutionaries has no doubt 'given them the impetus to emulate their international heroes and "prove" themselves within this milieu by engaging in ever escalating acts of terror.' The RCMP did *not* detect a pre-revolutionary climate or a situation teetering on the brink of anarchy.

Given that the leads the police were working on turned out to be successful, the disdainful characterizations of the briefing by ministers seem unfair. But perhaps the problem was that the police and the politicians were talking past one another. To return to Jamieson, the key point in the breakdown in communication seemed to be when ministers pressed the commissioner on what his force had been able to uncover that would justify the invocation of the War Measures Act. 'We were all shaken very badly by his reply: "he had no such evidence."' Perhaps sensing he was on delicate political ground, the commissioner went on to speculate that 'the total pattern' of the climate of unrest in Quebec justified the government's action. Jamieson now realized that the prime minister – who had absented himself from this meeting – had already known that 'in concrete terms, we did not have a compelling case to put forward.' Another Quebec minister, Jean-Luc Pépin, then advanced a scholarly account of how revolutions are fostered by unrest and disorder undermining confidence in governments, that protesters who would have otherwise taken to the streets and deepened the disorder had been deterred by the War Measures Act. This 'lucid and orderly presentation,' Jamieson recalled, 'gave us a good deal of comfort.' The ministers left the meeting 'very disturbed' by the RCMP presentation. They had placed so much trust in them, and then found that 'they did not have the type of straightforward, unqualified answers one would expect from people *who had exerted so much influence on the government when crucial decisions were made.*'[50]

If the ministers expected a justification of the emergency powers from the RCMP, they were bound to be disappointed. If they were under the misapprehension that the Mounties had exerted 'so much influence' on the government, they would be resentful as well. Perhaps their mistrust and resentment would better have been directed elsewhere. In retrospect, from the vantage point of four decades later, the outlines of a different interpretation of the events of October can be discerned. An alternative explanation might go like this: Two terrorist cells initiated a political hostage crisis. The RCMP saw the crisis as requiring good, patient, careful police work to solve. The Quebec ministers in Ottawa chose deliberately to escalate the political magnitude of the crisis to justify emergency powers as a means of intimidating the nationalists and separatists, with whom the federalist Quebecers were locked in a bitter conflict for the allegiance of Quebec.[51] The October Crisis was in this sense an episode in a kind of Quebec civil war in which non-Quebecers were mainly spectators. The RCMP security service was a somewhat reluctant participant and then a scapegoat when the government later found itself in difficulties justifying its actions.

There is little evidence to be found in declassified files to justify the charge that the security service had failed to warn the government of the possibility of such a crisis, or had provided inadequate intelligence on the terrorist groups that mounted the October actions. Once the crisis was in motion, the government then demanded an alarmist intelligence product to justify the extreme countermeasures it had resolved to take. This was not the first, nor would it be the last time that a government, in Canada or elsewhere, had insisted on intelligence to fit its political agenda, even as that agenda shifted. The October Crisis may have represented a major intelligence failure, but that failure, if such it was, cannot be laid at the door of the lead intelligence agency, the RCMP security service. Intelligence failures must be assessed in the context of the entire intelligence cycle, which crucially includes the government as both the employer and director of its intelligence agencies and the consumer of the threat assessments prepared for it alone. To take one of the most spectacular historical examples of intelligence failures, the failure to anticipate the Nazi invasion of the Soviet Union on 22 June 1941: it was the refusal of Soviet dictator Josef Stalin to credit the numerous warnings of impending German invasion provided by Soviet intelligence that lay at the heart of the overall intelligence failure. If accurate intelligence is not acted upon, failure results.[52] Government only compounds the failure if it then demands intelligence skewed to justify its later overreaction to its initial failure.

The picture that comes to light from declassified RCMP files ironically reinforces one of the conclusions of the Duchaîne inquiry. Appointed by a PQ government, and annoyed at the refusal of the RCMP, through the federal government, to open its files, Duchaîne nevertheless reflected that 'cette obsession du secret, qui est caractéristique de la GRC, est, à notre avis, plus nocive à cette institution que la lumière qui pourrait être faite sur la nature réelle de ses activités.' (This obsession with secrecy, characteristic of the RCMP, is, in our opinion, more harmful to the institution than the light that could be shed on the real nature of its activities.)[53]

From an October Crisis to a Quebec Crisis: 'Countering' the Separatists

In the wake of the October Crisis, the federal Liberal government directed a major offensive against Quebec 'separatists.' This offensive had both a public and a secret face. The public face was led by the prime minister, Pierre Elliott Trudeau, once considered a Quebec radical (and the subject of security files held both by the FBI in the United States and by the RCMP in their notorious FEATHER BED dossier) but now a crusader for the integrity of Canadian federalism, along with his leading Quebec ministers, Jean Marchand and Gérard Pelletier among others. The public face rose in visibility after the formation in 1968 of the Parti Québécois led by René Lévesque, incorporating members from the now dissolved RIN that had long been the subject of security service scrutiny. As a legitimate, legal political party that sought the goal of Quebec independence through lawful means, the PQ soon emerged as a powerful antagonist of the Quebec federalists in a great debate over Quebec's future. In the Quebec elections in 1970, just prior to the October Crisis, *Péquistes* won seats in the National Assembly for the first time. Only six years later, the party swept to office on a rising tide of francophone support. In 1980 a referendum was called asking for a mandate to negotiate sovereignty-association with the rest of Canada. Trudeau, briefly deposed by a minority Tory government in 1979 but now returned to office with a renewed majority mandate, campaigned successfully against the sovereignty option, which garnered only 40 per cent support.

The public face of the national-unity campaign against sovereignty was largely waged in terms of ideas and principles, a campaign for which Trudeau, the so-called philosopher king, writer and polemicist as well as politician, was pre-eminently well suited. But there was another, secret, face that was directed against separatism as an illegitimate, violent challenge to the integrity of the nation. This was the challenge that had been raised by the FLQ in the 1960s, reaching its apogee in the October Crisis. It was a challenge not only to national unity but to national security. Clandestinely organized terrorist groups capable of bombing, kidnapping, assassination, and intimidation of the state, perhaps drawing on covert foreign support and threatening the delicate fabric of social order, called for extraordinary measures in response, measures that should best be shrouded in secrecy, carried out in the shadows, denied officially. This was a job description for the operatives of the RCMP security service, but the Mounties' marching orders were not merely secret, they were deeply *ambiguous*. Were their targets strictly limited to the obviously lawless and violent extremists among the separatists, or did they include the apparently legal *Péquistes* who *might* have connections with those threatening national security, or who *might* have links with foreign operatives attempting to influence Canadian events clandestinely? What were the limits of the secret powers to be exercised by the Mounties against those who sought to undermine democracy and the rule of law? What would happen if the secret methods of the defenders of national security strayed over the line into illegality and impropriety, challenging the very values of democracy and the rule of law? What would happen if such actions became public knowledge? What if it became known that the federal state had been waging a secret war employing methods of dubious legality against not only the violent separatists but also the law-abiding, legitimate ones as well? And finally, would a government, armed in advance with plausible deniability, assume responsibility if the nasty stuff hit the fan, or would its clandestine foot soldiers be left to take the fall?

All these eventualities came to pass, and all these questions came to be asked. Scandals and official investigations ensued, with the ultimate result that the RCMP were forced to abandon their security service; a new civilian security intelligence agency was born; and new accountability rules and mechanisms were put in place over the way in which the federal government protects national security. Canadian federalism, still including Quebec, survived reasonably intact, but the same could not be said for the security intelligence system. The question of ministerial knowledge of and responsibility for what was done in the secret campaign against separatism is more obscure. We will try to draw some of these threads together in the account that follows of RCMP security service activities in Quebec in the 1970s.

The Federal Government Gropes towards a Policy on Separatism

Federal government consideration of how precisely to view the different forms of Quebec separatism went back to the government of Lester Pearson. On 23 September 1964 the Security Panel deliberated at length over the problem of government employees who belonged to open, legal separatist groups. Some participants argued that screening reports should be confined to those who were associated with violent, illegal groups. But the majority held that the RCMP should include in screening reports information on membership in open separatist groups, along with details of that membership. Although this recommendation does not appear at this time to have reached cabinet level for decision, the McDonald Commission pointed out that the Security Panel failed to specify how detailed information on membership in legal separatist associations was to be collected: Was the security service to rely solely on open sources, or was it to investigate in a more intrusive manner? The security service took the Security Panel's use of the highly ambiguous phrase 'separatist/terrorist activities or movement' to begin reporting on both legal and illegal separatist associations of government employees in April 1965, but this was without any official sanction by cabinet directive.[54]

On 24 July 1967 French President Charles de Gaulle made his infamous *Vive le Québec libre* speech during an official visit to Canada, and was told in no uncertain terms by the federal government that he was no longer welcome. On 14 August, Prime Minister Pearson called a meeting of the Security Panel to consider ways and means of improving the intelligence on separatism available to the government. Separatism was identified at the meeting as a threat to Canada greater than that posed by Communism. Three overlapping dimensions of the threat were identified: terrorists; constitutional separatists; and foreign interference. Deputy RCMP Commissioner William Kelly, according to his record of the meeting, took away with him the impression that the RCMP would be expected to provide more and better intelligence on Quebec than they had so far produced. The security service concluded that it had a broad mandate to investigate all forms of separatism, and set about to do so. However, there was unease at the highest levels of the force at the absence of any clear and specific mandate from the government. Senior RCMP officers believed that they were being pushed into moving from being a defensive to an 'offensive' service. The new intelligence requirements would force it to expand its intrusive domestic surveillance as well as to gather intelligence outside Canada, the latter being something the Mounties had little experience in. They 'were very worried about the political consequences if surveillance of this kind were publicly exposed and considered that the Force should not enter into this new area without new terms of reference.'[55]

Despite qualms, the RCMP had little choice but to fulfil the new requirements, as ambiguously formulated as they were. In 1968 the security service was instructing its officers in Quebec to gather detailed intelligence on the new Parti Québécois that was in the initial stages of formation. This intelligence was to be on all aspects of the party and its membership, and not confined to links with terrorists or foreign governments. As political intelligence, it was distinguished from a continuing 'police interest' in 'subversive' individuals associated with the party.[56] Such an expansion of the boundaries of political policing still lacked official sanction, but the new prime minister, Pierre Elliott Trudeau, veteran of federalist-separatist battles, was about to take a more hands-on approach.

The Philosopher King's Symposium on Separatism

A meeting of the cabinet's Committee on Security and Intelligence on 19 December 1969 laid some of the crucial groundwork. Don Wall, the assistant secretary for security and intelligence in the Privy Council Office, first ran a draft 'Top Secret' memorandum on 'Current Threats to National Order and Unity – Quebec Separatism' past the prime minister, which was then circulated to ministers on the committee. The purpose of the memorandum was to set out the problem in general and identify areas where 'corrective action' could be taken. Wall thought it important to establish at the outset that the problems discussed in the paper 'must be dealt with in the larger context of the priority problem of National Unity … and its subsidiary problem of Law and Order.'[57] The PCO thought it appropriate that the issue should be under the 'control and direction of the Prime Minister,' with support personnel housed either in the PMO or in the PCO.

The stated purpose of the paper circulated to the ministers[58] was 'to consider such further action as might reasonably be taken by the federal government to understand and deal effectively with the disruptive forces at play in Canada, and particularly in Quebec, which threaten the order and integrity of Canada.' The late 1960s was a period in which new and unfamiliar forms of protest and social unrest were on the rise. So-called New Left movements in English Canada were challenging a security service fixated on the Old Left of the Communist Party (itself increasingly irrelevant). We will look more closely at how the forces of law and order attempted to cope with the English Canadian New Left in the next chapter. But for the Canadian government, the most threatening form of social and political unrest was clearly emerging from Quebec. In Europe some radical groups were turning to more violent forms of protest that were morphing into urban guerrilla movements like the Baader-Meinhof/Red Army Faction in West Germany and the Red Brigades in Italy. In the United States, the black ghettoes were aflame. In Canada, violent political action had already appeared with the FLQ and other Quebec 'revolutionary' groups earlier in the 1960s, and fears of serious escalation would be fulfilled in October 1970.

Clearly, attention would be focused on Quebec as the fulcrum of potential political violence. But as the memorandum to the ministers was uneasily aware, this potential could not be isolated from the wider context of political unrest in Quebec that affected all levels and all classes of Quebec society. The memorandum enumerated some of the economic and social strains strongly affecting Quebec, and then noted the 'political difficulties' faced by a beleaguered Union Nationale provincial government on all fronts, including 'more "open" conversions to the Parti Québécois on the part of "respectable" middle class people.' 'In light of these factors,' the memorandum stated, 'it is clear that the problem cannot be dealt with entirely within the "security" context as it is usually understood. It is therefore my [the Prime Minister's] intention to have the whole matter brought before the Cabinet Committee on Priorities and Planning in the near future, in order to determine how the various aspects of the problem can be dealt with in an integrated and coordinated manner.' The immediate priority was to gather more and better information about the problem, analyse it, and put it to effective use. To this end, the memorandum set out two general principles for policy direction: any action must be 'such as to command a widespread consensus in all parts of the country and must be in full accord with our legacy of freedom and responsibility within a Parliamentary democracy'; and there must be 'full agreement at all levels among the governments concerned as to the basic objectives and complete understanding that they can only be fulfilled in a spirit of cooperation, not competition.'

The paper then immediately moved to a contentious matter: the employment of 'separatists' by the federal government. It quoted the Mackenzie Commission recommendation that the federal government 'should take (and be seen to take) steps to prevent its infiltration by persons who are clearly committed to the dissolution of Canada, or who are involved with elements of the separatist movement in which seditious activity or foreign involvement are factors.' Separatism should be understood as equivalent to subversion, and appropriate actions taken to bar separatists from employment in sensitive positions. The 1969 memorandum interestingly raises the question of determining the 'public *and private* position which the government should adopt in relation to separatism.' A section of the memorandum that follows is redacted, citing section 14 of the Access to Information Act on privileged information on federal-provincial relations,[59] so we do not know which sensitive inter-governmental issues were being brought to the attention of the ministers. But the reference to a private, as well as public, position of the federal government is intriguing.

On the question of intelligence gathering, after pointing out the importance of open sources and analysis of social trends, the document skates around the issue of the RCMP's role in Quebec. Dependency on Quebec police sources was seen as a limitation, but when it came to 'other actions that the Force could take to obtain more intelligence, particularly [redacted],' it was noted that this would require 'specific governmental instructions,' not to speak of operating in a milieu in which 'political loyalties are often uncertain and divided.' 'It is probably beyond the capacity or functions of any security service,' the paper lamented, 'to provide all of the information necessary for federal planning and action … in the larger context of National Unity and Order.'

A section on 'needs for particular kinds of information' is blacked out in its entirety.

Armed with this paper, the meeting of the cabinet's Committee on Security and Intelligence convened on the afternoon of 19 December 1969, attended by the prime minister as chair, the ministers of External Affairs, National Defence, Justice, and Treasury Board, the solicitor general, and the secretary of state. Accompanying them were a range of deputy ministers and other senior officials, including the commissioner of the RCMP and the current head, as well as two future heads, of the security service.[60] Trudeau opened by pointing out that national unity had been set as a cabinet priority, and that it had to be considered together with the related problem of law and order. This was a grave and urgent matter, the prime minister cautioned, 'bearing in mind that no modern state would allow a threat of this magnitude to its unity and integrity without mounting a consistent and coordinated defence against it.' At the same time, the 'danger of backlash inherent in all these policies and the procedures flowing from them would need to be carefully assessed.' On intelligence, 'sources of information other than the RCMP would have to be developed.' Trudeau recommended an overall planning and coordination unit to oversee federal responses.

Justice Minister John Turner stepped in with useful advice concerning the differences between the two priorities. Law and order referred to activity by terrorists, but the 'problem posed by the Parti Québécois was not necessarily related to the problem of law and order but rather to the problem of national unity.' It was necessary to deal with these problems in different ways 'in order to avoid conflicts and the danger of being accused of using law and order as an anti-Separatist tool.' Gérard Pelletier, secretary of state, suggested that 'where police action was clearly required it would be welcomed by the mass of the population of Quebec, including the Parti Québécois, who were playing a respectable role and attempting to eliminate violent persons from that Party.' But Pelletier, always sceptical of the RCMP, wondered what resources the Mounties actually had in a Quebec milieu with which they were not closely identified. He added that, if their contribution could not be greatly improved, it would be preferable to leave matters in the hands of the local authorities.

The RCMP's minister, Solicitor General George McIlraith, bristled at this, saying that Pelletier's comments were 'disturbing' and pointing out that the RCMP provided a good deal more intelligence on the problem than did 'all the other Police Forces concerned' (which was probably true). More pointedly yet, McIlraith insisted that the problem was not lack of intelligence; he noted that 'there was already *far more available than was being put to effective use*,' citing intelligence provided to the PCO 'on a regular basis concerning the activities of certain members of [redacted].' McIlraith also entered into a dispute with the minister of defence, Léo Cadieux, over the potential use of military intelligence against separatism in Quebec. The solicitor general considered using the Armed Forces to spy on the civilian population of Quebec a very bad idea. For his part, Cadieux wanted to see the military role in Quebec expanded, and cited the use that could be made by the federal government of 'aid to the civil power.'

At this point Trudeau intervened with a more nuanced argument: it was necessary to distinguish between the law-and-order problem, which included aid to the civil power, and the general problem of national unity and the question of separatism in particular. We needed, he suggested, a great deal more information on the first problem in order to deal effectively with the second. He then went to make a crucial argument, one that linked the separatist problem with a more familiar one from the Cold War past: 'In the past, Communism had been considered such a menace to democratic structures that the police had been empowered to gather information on Communist activities in Canada. This being the case, and the Federal Government being dedicated to the maintenance of Canada as a nation … [redacted].' We do not know exactly how Trudeau concluded, but it would seem that the symmetry of his sentence would lead logically to the conclusion that he was recommending intrusive surveillance of the Parti Québécois by analogy to the Cold War surveillance of the Communist Party, which, like the PQ, was an ostensibly legitimate and legal party. This seems to have been reflected in the concerns of ministers Pelletier and Turner, who both quickly inserted caveats regarding the dangers of treating legitimate separatists as if they were terrorists. 'There was nothing in the criminal law,' Turner reminded his listeners, 'to prevent "peaceful subversion."' Perhaps slightly chastened, Trudeau replied that it would be necessary to fight separatists, 'but perhaps not in the same way as revolutionaries would have to be fought.'

It was time for an impartial mandarin to bridge the gap between ministers. Cabinet Secretary Gordon Robertson observed that the Communists had been seen as a legal party that was also a 'potentially subversive force,' and that 'protective government action' had been taken 'as distinguished from protection against criminal acts.' Robertson indicated an analogy between the Communists' allegiance to a foreign power hostile to Canadian national interests and the separatist adherence to a future independent state that would emerge from the break-up of Canada. RCMP Commissioner William Higgitt, of a more practical mind, said that he would require 'clear direction from the government before embarking on the same investigative activities against Separatists as he now conducted against Communists, because of the extreme sensitivity of the problem.' Despite the lack of such direction in the past, the RCMP could provide documentation on separatist organizations, but 'the problem was not so much that of obtaining more information but of putting to use information already available.' As to taking further action to 'gather information by clandestine means, this was of course possible, but he would feel obliged to point out the risks involved.'

The committee did not come down firmly on one side or the other, noting that the tools for dealing with peaceful and violent separatists 'may have to be different' and that 'the risks involved in new federal initiatives [should] be carefully balanced against the probable positive effects.' The ministers settled instead for a bureaucratic solution in considering how to set up the coordinating centre that the prime minister had recommended, while punting downfield to the Priorities and Planning Committee (effectively the inner cabinet in the Trudeau years) the important question of defining precisely what the federal attitude towards the various forms of separatism was, and 'whether that attitude should be publicly expressed in terms of a policy statement.' The RCMP were directed to beef up their recent report on the state of separatism in Quebec by providing a 'basis on which positive counteraction might be taken.'

Years later in his *Memoirs*, Trudeau reflected on the meaning of his 1969 memorandum. In retrospect it seemed to him 'quite clear' that, when he directed the RCMP to gather information on the separatist movement in Quebec, and on separatist influence within Quebec society and government, he was thinking primarily about the violent separatists. But the RCMP had to 'understand that violent separatists could come from and find support in good, middle-class Quebec, and that they must not hesitate to pursue their inquiries within that milieu.' The prime minister was admonishing the 'higher levels of the RCMP [to] become better educated about the very nature of separatism.' This almost sounds as if Trudeau was inviting the police into an academic seminar, an impression that is strengthened when he adds: 'Of course, there was *no question of encouraging them to make inquiries into legitimate democratic opposition parties as such, and even less of encouraging them to resort to illegal methods.*' Yet, on the very next page, he notes that the FLQ were attempting to infiltrate the PQ and other peaceful organizations and the public service; this infiltration had to be checked 'using every means the law put at our disposal': 'It was in such a climate that I made my pronouncement. When certain police officers concluded from my words that they had to spy on every activity of the Parti Québécois, they were mistaken. The Mounties had the right, and even the duty, to keep track of anyone they suspected of treason, even if such suspects were members of a democratic party. But they ought not to have targeted the party as a whole. As soon as I learned of any case of abusive surveillance, I demanded that it be stopped.'[61] While there is no reason to question Trudeau's sincerity, it is not unreasonable to question the clarity of the instructions given the police in applying subtle distinctions between varieties of separatism when they were explicitly directed to look for the bad guys in every organization and every milieu in Quebec society.

Coming virtually on the eve of the October Crisis, the December 1969 memorandum and meeting take on considerable significance in retrospect. Debate between ministers over separatism may have had some of the aura of an academic seminar, but the outcome would have concrete consequences in the real world. After the imposition of the War Measures Act with its accompanying state of emergency and suspension of civil liberties, and the introduction of armed soldiers to patrol the streets of Montreal, instructions would emerge from Ottawa to give more precise form and substance to the secret war against separatism that the cabinet had begun to plan at the end of 1969. Taking the December meeting as a base point for the Trudeau government's position, we can find much that later emerged about this secret war encoded in a discussion which had yet to take on the note of extreme urgency it would later assume. Consider: the uneasy linkage of the national-unity and national-security questions; the blurring of the lines between the legal Parti Québécois and the terrorist wing of the separatist movement; the somewhat sinister analogy between the Communists in the Cold War and the PQ in the war against separatism; the studied ambiguity about RCMP methods and authorization for actions that might bear unspecified risks; and, finally, the opacity of the proposed mechanisms and lines of authority and responsibility. All these were themes that would resurface again and again over the next few years, and would become highly contentious matters of dispute before commissions of inquiry and in political debate.

The Institutional Response: Government

The Trudeau cabinets were preoccupied by the process of government, so it is no surprise that one of the ways they chose to proceed with the separatism problem was to create a new structure for policy coordination, as the Security and Intelligence Committee had recommended in December 1969. Already in 1966 the Department of the Solicitor General (SOLGEN) had been set up as an umbrella ministry for law enforcement, partially as a result of the spate of security scandals that had beset the Pearson government at the time. This reorganization was supposed to enhance ministerial responsibility in security matters, and in 1971 the government went a step further by creating the Security Planning and Research Group (SPARG) in SOLGEN under the direction of Robin Bourne, assistant deputy solicitor general, ostensibly to assist the minister in assessing the security intelligence reports provided by the RCMP. Speculation in the media and in Parliament that SPARG was a parallel civilian security service, indicating a lack of confidence in the RCMP, was in fact groundless. SPARG was never an intelligence-collection agency and never played any operational role. Nor could it fulfil its role as analyst of RCMP reports because the RCMP never fully cooperated with SPARG. The RCMP had no intention of allowing anything that smacked of interference by outsiders in their ongoing operations.[62]

In 1972 the overall direction of security policy was reorganized. The Security Panel and the Intelligence Policy Committee, mainly focused on external intelligence, were combined to form the Interdepartmental Committee on Security and Intelligence (ICSI). The ICSI was designed with a much closer relationship between domestic and foreign security in mind than had been the case in the past. International terrorism and the activities of foreign intelligence agencies in Canada pointed in this direction. The ICSI's membership was at the deputy ministerial level, including the RCMP commissioner, and was chaired by the cabinet secretary. A new Security Advisory Committee (SAC) was formed under the ICSI umbrella, with close links to the RCMP. According to McDonald, SAC 'became in effect a principal bridge between the Security Service and government.' It was chaired by Robin Bourne, and the vice-chairmanship was assumed by the director general of the security service. SAC was responsible for producing security intelligence assessments almost exclusively based on information collected by the security service, on a quarterly basis prior to 1976 and on a weekly basis after that. These reports gave ministers in the Security and Intelligence Committee the opportunity to view regularly the RCMP security intelligence product. This committee was also supposed to receive annual reports from the RCMP detailing the work of the security service, although this obligation was not always fulfilled.[63]

The Institutional Response: RCMP

In March 1975 a growing sense of unease on both the civilian and the RCMP side concerning the lack of a clear mandate for the security service, especially in regard to the activities of RCMP officers in the grey area of legality/illegality, led to cabinet approval for a new mandate for the service, not in statute but in the form of ministerial guidelines. These guidelines indicated that the security service was authorized to 'maintain internal security by discerning, monitoring, investigating, deterring, preventing and countering individuals and groups in Canada where there are reasonable and probable grounds to believe that they may be engaged in or may be planning to engage' in: espionage/sabotage; foreign intelligence activities or foreign-influenced activities in Canada; violent governmental change; terrorism; or 'the use or the encouragement of the use of force, violence, or any criminal means, or the creation or exploitation of civil disorder' to accomplish any of the above.[64]

As a cabinet directive, the mandate did not bear the authority of law. In particular, it provided no authority to act contrary to law. Thus, when the service was directed to 'monitor, investigate, *deter, prevent, and counter*' individuals and groups, it was being provided with apparent official approval for a very wide range of methods and actions that lay potentially outside the law, even for law-enforcement officers – without arming these officers with legal immunity. The director of the security service, in a letter sent to all senior officers in the service on 22 May 1975 explaining his understanding of the new mandate, indicated that 'members of the Security service must act within the limits of the guidelines and within the limits of the law.'[65] In practice, 'deterring, preventing and countering' could not be contained within the 'limits of the law.' If the security service was to be effective in fulfilling the tasks set it under its ministerial guidelines, it would have to place concerns about the limits of the law on the backburner.

The most important institutional change within the security service to accommodate the new focus on Quebec separatism was the creation in September 1970 of 'G' Branch within the 'C' (Quebec) Division. The director general of the service, John Starnes, set out the terms of reference for the new branch: 'To be as fully informed as possible on:

All Separatist/Terrorist activities in the province of Quebec
All activities of foreign powers which may affect the position of Quebec in Confederation
All activities by subversive organizations which touch on the Quebec problem
Developments of a subversive nature among the French speaking population of other provinces

Starnes did not stop there. 'G' Branch would be tasked to obtain 'adequate information' and 'develop sources in all organizations and among all persons supporting the separation of Quebec.' 'Clearly,' he insisted, the PQ – precisely because of its success in gaining support – 'must be regarded as a *prime target*.' Focus should be on those activities within the party 'which clearly are subversive' and 'have as their aim the break-up of confederation,' leaving ambiguous the question of whether the goal of separatism was itself subversive, or just the pursuit of separatism by illegal means. This is not an unimportant distinction.

The ambiguity was only deepened when Starnes went on to specify that the new branch 'should build up an intimate knowledge of the party, its structure, its finances, its aims and those responsible for its direction.' This kind of information on a legal political party was necessary because, 'among other things,' it could 'identify those elements in the party who may attempt to subvert it to the achievement of a separate Quebec by any means, including the use of force and terroristic acts.' Thus, another layer of ambiguity was added: Was the role of 'G' Branch to prevent the subversion of the PQ by violent separatists or to prevent the subversion of Canada by the PQ? Nor did Starnes stop with the PQ. The branch was also tasked to investigate other political parties to identify members 'who seek a separate Quebec *by any means*' (again, did 'any means' include peaceful means, or only violent means?). Finally, Starnes, in a covering letter transmitting the terms of reference, stated that 'the resources available to us in "C" Division will have to be utilized to the full if the government's priority of maintaining *national unity* is to be aggressively pursued.'[66]

Starnes later testified at the McDonald Commission that 'we were not targeting the Parti Québécois as such, and we were very careful not to.' The commission found it hard to reconcile this later statement with the 'broad references to political concerns about the future of Confederation' found in his instructions to 'G' Branch, especially when the commission learned that the security service routinely collected intelligence on the PQ as well as on the Quebec Liberal Party throughout the 1970s, even extending to breaking into PQ headquarters and stealing and copying party membership lists (see below).[67] It is hard indeed. It is even harder when, as we will see, 'G Ops,' that is, operations by Section 'G4' (known even within as the Dirty Tricks Division or DTD) against separatists both legal and illegal, often straying outside the law, became notorious enough to help bring about two commissions of inquiry, one in Quebec and the other the McDonald Commission we have just quoted. Finally, with the coming of the PQ to office at the end of 1976, 'G' Branch was shut down. But 'G' Branch was not the only section of the security service deployed in the secret war against separatists. 'D' Division, the Counter-Subversion Branch, was also operating on the ground in Quebec in the 1970s, sometimes on the same turf as 'G Ops,' sometimes under the umbrella of what was called the 'Special Operations Group.'

The Quebec experience helped raise serious doubts about the whole concept of targeting 'subversion,' a term never properly defined in law and open to such potential misuse that critics have questioned its fundamental validity.[68] Events unleashed in Quebec in the 1970s under the name of combating separatist subversion greatly heightened these concerns.

The 'Dirty Tricks' Era: Barn Burnings, Break-Ins, Burglaries

At first the 'G Ops' and 'D Ops' war against the separatists remained in the shadows, as intended. But in the summer of 1974, a single thread was pulled that began to unravel the tight veil of secrecy. An RCMP constable by the name of Robert Samson was injured when a bomb he had been attempting to plant at the Montreal home of an executive of a supermarket chain had exploded prematurely. This was not an RCMP operation: Samson had been moonlighting as a freelancer for a Montreal *mafioso*. Discharged from the force, and hauled before a court to face charges in 1976, Samson on the witness stand hinted darkly that

he 'had done worse things for the RCMP than plant bombs.' Pressed
for details, he referred to an earlier unsolved break-in at the offices of
the Agence de Presse Libre du Québec (APLQ) which he said was a
joint operation of the RCMP and the SQ, the purpose of which was
to steal documents and files on Quebec left-wingers: the APLQ, Samson explained, 'always had a fairly big list of Quebec leftists.'[69] This
piqued the interest of journalists, who began digging around Samson's
allegations. The federal solicitor general, Warren Allmand, and Prime
Minister Trudeau expressed concern but were quickly reassured by the
RCMP commissioner, Maurice Nadon, and the director general of the
security service, Michael Dare, that the APLQ matter was an isolated
incident. It was not the first time that such reassurance was given the
politicians, and it would not be the last time that it would prove highly
misleading. The APLQ was far from an isolated incident; rather, it was
typical of a pattern of lawbreaking in the name of fighting separatism.

After Samson's testimony, the Quebec Justice Department started an
investigation of the APLQ affair and eventually laid charges against
three police officers, one from the RCMP, one from the SQ, and the third
from the Montreal Police (they were all given absolute discharges). In
the Quebec election on 15 November 1976, the PQ was elected to office.
The new sovereignist government began to show a more active interest
in questionable activities of the federal police in Quebec, and in 1977 it
appointed Jacques Keable to head a judicial inquiry into the APLQ and
related matters. Keable's investigation caused consternation in Ottawa,
both in the RCMP and in the cabinet.

As troubling as all this was for the peace of mind of senior RCMP
officials, potential defections from within the ranks added to the growing anxiety. In 1977 two former security service officers from Montreal
arrived in Ottawa with dangerous stories they were threatening to tell.
One was Donald McCleery and the other Gilles Brunet, many years
later unmasked as the Soviet mole in the security service (see chapter
8). McCleery and Brunet had been discharged from the force in 1973 for
too-close connections with certain Montreal underworld figures and
had been fighting their dismissals in the courts and seeking to appeal
against their discharges to the solicitor general. When they were granted a meeting with the deputy solicitor general, they let it be known
that they had information on criminal offences committed by RCMP officers. McCleery spoke about a secret 'Dirty Tricks Department (DTD)'
or G4 in Montreal, naming the officers involved, that had carried out
a kidnapping, burned an FLQ hideout, and stolen and hidden dyna-

mite – all acts that could have sent the officers to jail if they had been known. Illegal mail openings were also mentioned, and Brunet added further allegations. The solicitor general, Francis Fox, was brought into the picture, since there was some concern that the two former officers were threatening the government with blackmail. Instead, it appears that they were merely trying to convince the minister, who had recently made public statements about the APLQ break-in being an isolated incident, that the RCMP had lied to him on that issue, and consequently might have been lying to him about their individual cases. However, in the course of pursuing this matter, Fox specifically interrogated the RCMP brass about the validity of the dirty-tricks allegations, and was assured once again that there was nothing in it, that the allegations did 'not ring a bell' with them, but they promised to investigate.[70] Based on their assurances, Fox again made a statement in the House of Commons following the discharge of the three police officers charged in the APLQ affair that this was an isolated and exceptional incident and that the 'directives of the RCMP to its members clearly require that all their actions take place within the law.' He went on to say that 'in a democratic society, Mr Speaker, it is essential that those on whom, like the RCMP and the Security Service, falls the task of enforcing the law and protecting our basic liberties, can count upon the complete support of the people. This support, in return, must be based on the faith that those protecting these rights do themselves feel bound and indeed are bound by our laws in fulfilling their duties.'[71]

Behind the liberal public face of the solicitor general, there was growing disquiet among the senior bureaucrats and the senior officials of the RCMP. The McCleery-Brunet allegations were not being cleared up by investigation. Justice and SOLGEN officials acknowledged that criminal offences may have been committed. The danger was, as Superintendent Archie Barr of the RCMP recognized, that 'if the process was allowed to unfold on a piecemeal basis,' a distorted picture could emerge that would do the RCMP considerable harm. Unfolding on a 'piecemeal basis,' was, however, just what was being threatened by media leaks and, above all, by the Keable Inquiry appointed by the PQ government in Quebec. Barr and other senior RCMP officials penned a memorandum suggesting the desirability of having an 'impartial tribunal that would see the Security Service in a more favourable light than would the general public if cases arose, one by one, sometimes in criminal proceedings.' They were also anxious to make clear that the 'inadequate working mandate' provided the security service may have forced 'many totally loyal and dedicated members to resort to methods which were at least unorthodox and often bordering on illegality to carry out the duties required of them by the Canadian people.'[72]

It was now clear to the government that, as in the words of the White House press secretary in the Watergate scandal, 'previous statements on this subject are now inoperative.' Francis Fox was compelled to rise in the House on 6 July 1977 and admit that his previous assurances that the APLQ affair was an isolated incident were unfounded. He now reported that, according to the RCMP commissioner, 'it would appear that some members of the RCMP in the discharge of their duties to protect national security could well have used methods or could have been involved in actions which were neither authorized nor provided for by law.' Consequently, and on the specific recommendation of the commissioner, the solicitor general announced the creation of a 'commission of inquiry into the operations and policies of the RCMP security service, on a national basis,'[73] which soon became known as the McDonald Commission, after its chair, David McDonald, an Alberta judge. With Keable in Quebec, and McDonald in Ottawa, the floodgates were now opened on revelations of unlawful security service methods, most of them, although by no means all, having taken place in Quebec.

We offer the following synoptic summary of operations in Quebec that slipped over the line of legality. This is not necessarily a definitive or exhaustive list, since some operations remain shrouded in secrecy even to today. The ones enumerated here are those that reached public notice, through Quebec or federal inquiries; legal actions taken by the Quebec government after 1976; investigative reporting; or memoirs and recollections of participants.[74]

- Operation BRICOLE: The 1972 break-in and theft of over 200 files at the APLQ.
- Operation HAM: The 1975 break-in at the Montreal office of the PQ; the party's computerized membership lists were stolen and copied.
- Operation CHECKMATE (previously called TENT PEG and ODD-BALL): Fake communiqués purporting to issue from the FLQ were fabricated and distributed by the RCMP. One in particular, fabricated by the chief superintendent in charge of 'G' Branch, Donald Cobb, urged violent action and denounced former FLQ leader Pierre Vallières for joining the PQ and turning away from violence, yet this was not identified as a police fabrication when reported to Ottawa.

- Informers were recruited from within the FLQ by coercive, gangster-like tactics in 1971, including kidnapping and physical intimidation.
- A privately owned barn had been burned in 1972 to prevent a meeting between the FLQ and the U.S. Black Panthers.
- Dynamite had been stolen in 1972 and stored on RCMP's member's property in an attempt to discredit a political group.
- Operation PAUPETTE: The security service was aware that thirteen communiqués from one FLQ cell had been issued by an undercover operative (Carole de Vault) run by the Montreal Police, but failed to inform federal officials of this fact when reporting threat assessments.
- Operation CATHEDRAL: Postal workers were enlisted in unauthorized mail openings.
- Illegal access was gained to government files on citizens, such as tax records, and the information used against them.

Some of these operations were Canada-wide, and will be discussed further in the next chapter. But it was Quebec that appeared to be the target for the main thrust of a wave of political policing outside the law. And it was Quebec, the province in which the sovereignists (or separatists as the federalists preferred to call them) enjoyed widespread popular support and were in provincial office after 1976, where this kind of federal intrusion was most sensitive, if not volatile. In particular, it was operations like HAM, specifically targeting the PQ, which roused the greatest concern. Rough tactics against FLQers and other potential terrorists might have been forgiven – after all, people had died as a result of the actions of the self-proclaimed 'national liberation' guerrillas; few Quebecers of whatever political persuasion wished to see Quebec descend to the kind of bloody sectarian anarchy that afflicted Ulster or other zones of communal conflict. But the idea of the federal secret police targeting a lawful political party that had gained the support of the majority of francophone Quebecers was an entirely different, and more troubling, matter – not to speak of constituting a very major political embarrassment for the Trudeau Liberal government in Ottawa in its crusade to combat the sovereignist challenge to federalism.

A crucial question with regard to targeting the PQ was authorization: Was this targeting the result of political instructions from government, or was it a decision made by the RCMP without political authorization? Earlier we addressed the ambiguity around this issue going back to cabinet committee discussions in 1967 and the analogy drawn between the PQ and the Communist Party, the latter legal but subversive. When

'G' Branch was set up in 1970, its guidelines were extremely ambiguous, perhaps deliberately so, concerning any operational distinction between the legal party and the 'subversive' elements that might be associated with the legal party or might be using the legal party as cover. A key tripwire for the security service was the security screening of public servants. Although the Mounties had been reporting information relating to separatism in security clearance files since the mid-1960s, apparently in response to informal instructions from above, there had never been any formal authorization. Neither Cabinet Directive 35 (the then secret guidelines governing appropriate criteria for establishing security risks) nor any policy statements made by the prime minister or any other minister provided authority for examining separatism when conducting security clearing of civil servants, as the Security Advisory Committee noted at a meeting on 14 November 1972. No final decisions, however, would be based on separatist information without the advice of the PCO, indicating the high degree of sensitivity associated with this matter. In December 1972 SAC further specified the scope of information on separatist links as: 'Separatist sympathies, associations and activities on the part of the subject will be reported as will significant separatist information on relatives and associates.' Although this was circulated to deputy ministers, it never reached cabinet level, and it failed to provide a formal mandate to the security service to collect separatist information, or provide any guidelines on how such information should be collected.[75]

By 1974, the PQ had emerged as a formidable political force, poised as the alternative in waiting to the Quebec Liberal government. The security service recognized that the political implications of targeting a party like this were contentious, and clarified its policy on 3 June 1974. 'The forces actively working at destroying the unity of the country' had to be analysed, so that the security service could become a 'meaningful depository of this data which the Government could rely upon before taking decisions affecting national unity.' Operational guidelines flowing from this objective included restrictions: no coverage of electoral activity; no collecting of membership lists;[76] 'selective' clippings; 'minimal' investigation of financial resources; 'analytical' review of PQ/labour union relationships and PQ activity within pressure groups. At the same time, the service should: investigate leads suggesting foreign interference; 'isolate radical elements operating under PQ cover'; investigate federal government leaks; and, significantly, tighten 'security concerning the reporting of investigations of PQ activities.' There should be 'no discussion of our policy on PQ' with the SQ or the Montreal Police.

Although the new guidelines were initially intended to be discussed with the solicitor general, Director General Michael Dare decided that this was unnecessary. His reasoning on this point seems somewhat opaque: the information gathered would be reported to the minister 'as required from time to time,' he argued, and besides, the prime minister 'has expressed to me his concern regarding separatism … We must all realize that the unity of our country is vital to the federal government.' Thus, a new policy was enacted within the security service on a highly sensitive political matter without consultation with the minister and any discussion or approval at cabinet level. The expression of 'concern' by the prime minister was deemed sufficient to authorize a domestic spying operation on a legal political party that was soon to assume provincial office. Moreover, as the McDonald Commission noted, this policy failed to distinguish between the 'political and security implications of Quebec separatism.'[77]

By 1975, the federal cabinet began to formulate a policy with regard to security service surveillance of the PQ. Unfortunately, as McDonald commented, this initiative resulted in 'great confusion' for the security service and for the public, and 'perhaps even for the policy-makers themselves.' The problem was that the general direction to investigate separatism and the specific mandate to do security clearances were somewhat contradictory. A year after the internal guidelines on separatism were brought in, on 9 June 1975, Director General Dare reported on a conversation he had had with Prime Minister Trudeau, in which the latter had insisted that the security service did not have a mandate to investigate the PQ as such, unless the party was pursuing objectives other than separation by legal means. Dare then sent instructions that 'all enquiries being conducted on the Parti Québécois and its members cease' unless they fell under other parts of the mandate. However, a few days later, Dare questioned whether this new instruction conflicted with the 1972 Security Panel requirement to report on separatist information for screening purposes. The question never seems to been resolved higher up.

By 1976, Dare considered that the information in security service files on the PQ was so out of date that accurate information on separatism could no longer be provided in security screening cases. A letter from Dare to SAC to that effect somehow was leaked to the media, with a reference to Trudeau's advice to Dare the previous year. The result was a

6 May 1976 headline 'Trudeau Halts Screening of Civil Service Separatists.' This led critics in Parliament to question the propriety of the prime minister giving personal instructions to the security service. Trudeau insisted, rightly, that it was a cabinet directive not his personal instructions. He did go on to say he did participate in the cabinet discussion and 'I do not mind admitting that I was one of those who would argue that a democratic political party should not be under systematic surveillance by the RCMP.' This was the view of the government, as established by the Cabinet Committee on Security and Intelligence in a meeting chaired by the prime minister on 20 March 1975, which concluded that, in the case of a legal party that advocated the dissolution of the federation by peaceful democratic means, security service surveillance should occur only when it seemed justified 'in the light of the approved categories [for targeting].'[78]

In March 1976 the Cabinet Committee on Security and Intelligence discussed the security-screening implications of the 1975 decision on PQ surveillance. In a decision that was later ratified by the full cabinet, membership in or support for the PQ was ruled relevant to screening. McDonald comments: 'The Cabinet Committee did not explain how information about a person's separatist leanings or associations was to be available if the Security Service could not systematically collect such information.'[79] Nor did it indicate how surveillance of legitimate targets within the PQ, such as terrorists or foreign agents, could be carried on without conducting surveillance of the party itself, now apparently prohibited.

Once the PQ was in power, the security service had to adopt a 'low profile in discharging our mandate within Quebec,' in Director General Dare's words to the Interdepartmental Committee on Security and Intelligence. Dare did promise to *enhance* intelligence collection in respect to foreign interference, minority tensions, 'terrorist and revolutionary power bases in Quebec,' and penetration of the federal government by separatists who might be trying to undermine federalist responses to the PQ. The security service would continue to monitor closely 'subversives' who might lurk within legitimate parties. At the same time, Dare promised to maintain dialogue and liaison with Quebec authorities 'with the aim of preventing misunderstanding regarding the role of the Security Service,' as well as to maintain and promote 'our long standing working relationship' with provincial and municipal law-enforcement agencies (despite the earlier 1974 directive *not* to discuss the security service policy on the PQ with these same police forces).

1. Wood engraving depicting the funeral procession for Thomas D'Arcy Mc-
Gee – member of Parliament and 'Father of Confederation' – held in Montreal
in 1868. A strident critic of Irish republicanism, McGee was assassinated in Ottawa in April of the same year, more than likely by a Fenian. His death prompted significant reforms to the Canadian secret service, then under the auspices
of the Dominion Police.

2. Under the pseudonym Henri le Caron, Thomas Miller Beach infiltrated the Fenian Brotherhood in the United States in the 1860s and 1870s, at the behest of British and Canadian authorities. Le Caron's long career as a spy ended in 1888 when he was subpoenaed to appear before the Parnell Commission, which was then investigating Irish radicalism in the United Kingdom. This sketch, which depicts Beach giving testimony before the commission, appeared in *The Graphic*, a weekly illustrated newspaper in London.

COLONEL SIR PERCY SHERWOOD, K.C.M.G., M.V.O., A.D.C.

3. Following Gilbert McMicken, Percy Sherwood served as commissioner of the Dominion Police from 1885 to 1919. During the Great War, Sherwood over-saw the Canadian government's monitoring and internment of 'enemy aliens' – Canadians who, on account of birth, ethnicity, language, and/or political affiliation, were seen as threats to the war effort. This image was drawn in 1922 by Arthur George Racey, long-time cartoonist at the *Montreal Star*, as part of a series depicting eminent Canadians.

4. Dressed in his Canadian Immigration uniform, William C. Hopkinson (far right) looks on as H.H. Stevens, the member of Parliament for Vancouver (centre), speaks to reporters during the *Komagata Maru* crisis in 1914. Beginning in 1909, Hopkinson was also a highly prized undercover operative along the Pacific coast; Canadian officials routinely sent his reports about South Asian radicals to their British and Indian counterparts. In October 1914 Hopkinson was killed by one of his own (formerly) loyal undercover contacts.

To Mr. C.H. Coleman
with sincere regards
C.H. Cahan

5. Appointed by Prime Minister Robert Borden as 'Director of Public Safety' in 1918, C.H. Cahan was deeply involved in post-war debates about the future of the Canadian secret service. A prominent corporate lawyer and stalwart of Conservative Party politics, Cahan favoured the creation of a stand-alone undercover police service, much like the United States' Federal Bureau of Investigation. Cahan resigned from his position in 1919, after the prime minister granted the RCMP sole responsibility for national security.

6. An Italian immigrant, Frank Zaneth joined the Royal North-West Mounted Police in 1917 and began work as an undercover operative among labour organizations shortly thereafter. His testimony played a critical role in the conviction of leaders of the Winnipeg General Strike of 1919. While the focus of Zaneth's undercover work shifted in the 1920s and 1930s, he remained a virulent anti-Communist, playing an important role in the surveillance of Canadians who volunteered to join the Spanish Civil War.

Rules for Underground Party Work

1) Don't betray Party Work or Party Workers under any circumstance.

2) Don't carry or keep about you, names and addresses, except they be in good code.

3) Don't keep any incriminating documents or literature in your rooms openly.

4) Don't take unnecessary risks in Party Work.

5) Don't shirk party-work because of the risks connected with it.

6) Don't boast of what you have to do or have done for the Party.

7) Don't divulge your membership in the Party unnecessarily.

8) Don't let spies follow you to appointments or meetings.

9) Don't loose your nerve when in danger.

10) Don't answer questions if arrested, whether at preliminary hearings or in court.

1) The unpardonable crime in underground party work is the betrayal of it or of its workers. For a comrade to give information to the government is outright treason, regardless of the influences means and tortures used to extract it. Make up your mind **not to be a traitor.** No condemnation, no punishment is strong enough for a traitor.

2) (a) To be caught with plainly written names and addresses of comrades, party workers or places is very nearly the same and at least in effect quite the same as betraying them to the government. Such names and addresses should never be written out plainly. Carry in your memory as much as you can. Make your notes merely "memory-aids". And whatever you must write down, do it in good code for numbers is very useful at all times. Make up a word of ten letters or two words of five each (but none that make sense) such as "verga Dsihw" (no letters to be used twice) and then use "v" for 1, "e" for 2, "r" for 3, "w" for 0 and so forth.

(b) Be sure in all cases to have and to know the correct addresses. It is absolutely dangerous to have to ask the way to a party-address from passers-by, or from the janitor and occupants of the very building of your address. It is also dangerous to make mistakes in party-shipment or mail addresses; important shipments and mail are not only lost, but are delivered into the hands of the government; party shipping methods are disclosed; the correct addresses are spoiled; and consequently to cap it all the real addressee may be arrested. Always when giving, taking or using party addresses, look twice to make sure that there are no

7) Party work, agitation and propaganda, even the collection of Party-funds from outsiders and the getting new members for the party, should be carried on without divulging ones membership in the party. It is sufficient to say in some cases that you endorse and support the party, in others that you have connections with party-members. Only when you bring a new member to the probationary group, do you have to reveal your own membership.

It is all right for you to be known as a "red" in you own shop or union—that is too general to be made the basis of prosecution; but you should not be known as a member of the Communist Party.

8) We all know that thousands of spies are on the job every day in every city bent upon ferreting out our members, our meetings and work-places. Consequently, beware of being followed when going to an appointment or meeting-place—particularly if you are under suspicion through having been questioned, or arrested.

Do you know that comrades who are indicted are sometimes purposely released to act as unconscious bait for spies to follow them and discover our meeting-places, workers, etc. This does not mean that they should keep away from all Party-Work, but that they should be especially careful and circumspect. Do you know that in order to track our work, the police authorities will open our letters, photograph or copy them, and then send them through to us nicely closed again. They do not hold them up altogether because that would put the comrades on their guard.

Do not beget a false sense of security because for some length of time, no raids or arrests are made—it may be the calm before the storm. They may be gathering information, and collecting the threads of our organization in order to swoop down upon us suddenly.

9) Presence of mind, self-control and preparedness for emergencies count for much in underground party-work. Prepare in advance for any incriminating situation you are likely to be in. Always prepare a good answer for a sudden—"what are you doing or looking for here?"—"where are you going"—"From Where?". Destroy, as far as possible any material evidence if it seems that you will be caught. But be sure the occasion is not a false alarm.

10) Avoid arrest by all possible means but if you are arrested and if they have sufficient evidence that you are a Communist and therefore as a deadly enemy of the present order, subject to supression and imprisonment, but first to be put through the Third Degree to be grilled for information regarding the organization—then refuse absolutely to answer any questions. (Ask for a lawyer. You have the legal right. And you have the legal right to refuse to answer questions).

This course of action has been proved best by the experiences of

---

7. Issued by leaders of the Communist Party of Canada in the 1920s, this pamphlet warned rank-and-file supporters of the dangers associated with being a party member, especially the likelihood of arrest, police brutality, and infiltration by government spies. 'We all know that thousands of spies are on the job every day in every city,' section 8 (above) reads.

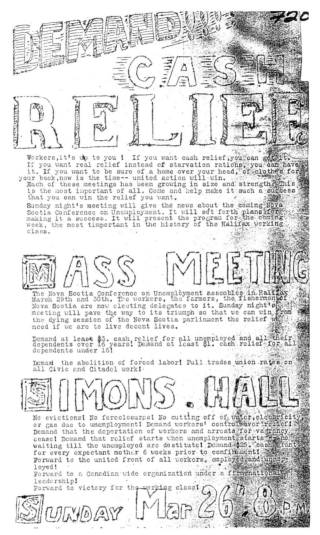

DEMAND CASH RELIEF

Workers, it's up to you ! If you want cash relief, you can get it.
If you want real relief instead of starvation rations, you can have
it. If you want to be sure of a home over your head, of clothes for
your back, now is the time-- united action will win.
Each of these meetings has been growing in size and strength. This
is the most important of all. Come and help make it such a success
that you can win the relief you want.

Sunday night's meeting will give the news about the coming Nova
Scotia Conference on Unemployment. It will set forth plans for
making it a success. It will present the program for the coming
week, the most timportant in the history of the Halifax working
class.

MASS MEETING

The Nova Scotia Conference on Unemployment assembles in Halifax
March 29th and 30th. The workers, the farmers, the fishermen of
Nova Scotia are now electing delegates to it. Sunday night's
meeting will pave the way to its triumph so that we can win from
the dying session of the Nova Scotia parliament the relief we
need if we are to live decent lives.

Demand at least $3. cash relief for all unemployed and all their
dependents over 16 years! Demand at least $1. cash relief for all
dependents under 16!

Demand the abolition of forced labor! Full trades union rates on
all Civic and Citadel work!

SIMONS HALL

No evictions! No foreclosures! No cutting off of water, electricity,
or gas due to unemployment! Demand workers' control over relief!
Demand that the deportation of workers and arrests for vagrancy
cease! Demand that relief starts when unemployment starts -- no
waiting till the unemployed are destitute! Demand $25. cash grant
for every expectant mother 6 weeks prior to confinement!
Forward to the united front of all workers, employed and unemployed!
Forward to a Canadian wide organization under a firm national
leadership!
Forward to victory for the working class!

SUNDAY Mar 26 8 P.M

8. The focus of government-sponsored surveillance and intelligence-gathering
operations since the Canadian labour revolt of 1917–23, the Canadian left was
especially targeted during the Great Depression, as political action among the
unemployed, influenced largely by the Communist Party, spread across the
country. This leaflet was produced by the Halifax Unemployed Council and
distributed among unemployed men living in the Citadel Hill relief camp; the
HUC was infiltrated by RCMP operatives from 1922 until at least 1937.

9. In British Columbia, agitation among the unemployed was particularly vibrant. A massive strike involving roughly 1,500 of the province's federal relief-camp inmates was organized by the CPC-affiliated Workers Unity League in April 1935. That strike later led to the On-to-Ottawa Trek, which departed Vancouver in early June of the same year. No doubt an undercover RCMP officer was among the demonstrators pictured above at this May Day parade in the 1930s.

10. By the time Arthur H. 'Slim' Evans (above) helped to organize and lead the On-to-Ottawa Trek in the spring and summer of 1935, he was widely recognized by workers as a stalwart of the union struggle and by the Canadian and American governments as a dangerous radical. A former member of the Industrial Workers of the World and One Big Union in the 1910s and early 1920s, Evans was a prominent member of the Communist Party during the Great Depression; he led the trekkers' unsuccessful delegation to meet Prime Minister R.B. Bennett in late June 1935. Under constant surveillance by the RCMP throughout the 1930s, Evans went on to raise funds for the International Brigades fighting in the Spanish Civil War and organize smelter workers in Trail, British Columbia.

11. Employing draconian emergency powers under the Defence of Canada Regulations, the RCMP's Intelligence Section during the Second World War incarcerated Canadians of German and Italian descent suspected of Fascist sympathies and undermining the Allied war effort. The five Italian-born men pictured above, all of whom lived and worked in industrial Cape Breton, were interned in Camp Petawawa in Ontario, alongside hundreds of other suspected 'fifth columnists.'

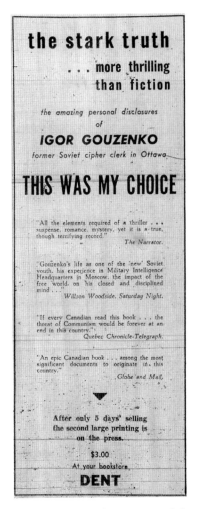

12. Igor Gouzenko was the man whose defection started the Cold War – in Ottawa. Gouzenko quickly became a poster boy for the new anti-Communism, as this ad for his 1948 autobiography shows. His story was featured in a Hollywood movie, *The Iron Curtain*, improbably casting the glamorous Dana Andrews and Gene Tierney as Gouzenko and his wife, Svetlana. Later, Gouzenko cemented his iconic image by appearing in public with a bag over his head, ostensibly to foil KGB assassins. Despite his symbolic status, Gouzenko and the RCMP did not get along. The Mounties were finally able to wash their hands of his protection – to their relief, since they found him an overly demanding charge.

13. External Affairs Minister Lester B. Pearson, future winner of the Nobel Peace Prize and prime minister of Canada, greets Canadian diplomat and leading Japanologist E. Herbert Norman in Tokyo. Norman was hounded to his death in 1957 by American anti-Communist witch hunters, leading to outrage in Canada and questions about the role played by the RCMP in his persecution. Less well known publicly was that Pearson himself was the real target of J. Edgar Hoover's FBI.

14. Until 1984 the security service was part of the RCMP, which held an iconic place in Canadian mythology, a romantic role echoed in Hollywood films like *Rose Marie* (1936) starring Nelson Eddy and Jeanette MacDonald. The Mounties worked hard at maintaining their positive image with its famed Musical Ride and in events like this one featuring the Mountie float in the Santa Claus parade, Toronto, 1960.

15. Scene from the 1985 National Film Board docudrama directed by Donald Brittain, *Canada's Sweetheart: The Saga of Hal C. Banks*. The film exposed the Cold War scandal of official complicity in importing Banks, a notorious American labour racketeer, to crush the Communist Canadian Seamen's Union. The NFB was itself the target of a largely secret anti-Communist purge in the late 1940s carried out by the RCMP.

16. Anti-Vietnam War poster: in the 1960s, RCMP political policing faced an altogether new challenge in the form of 'New Left' activism among students and young people unaffiliated with 'Old Left' Cold War subversion. Heavy-handed Mountie surveillance on university campuses stirred hostile reactions to a force once considered symbolic of Canada.

17. Leading theorists of the FLQ, Pierre Vallières and Charles Gagnon were imprisoned first in the United States and later in Canada under the War Measures Act in the aftermath of the October Crisis of 1970. Vallières later renounced the use of violence to achieve Quebec independence, but the federal government and its security service experienced difficulty in distinguishing clearly between threats to national security and threats to national unity.

18. The murder of Quebec labour minister Pierre Laporte following the imposition of the War Measures Act underlined the grave challenge to national security posed by the FLQ in the October Crisis of 1970. Here Prime Minister Pierre Trudeau is seen at the funeral of Laporte in Montreal. Quebec premier Robert Bourassa, who had asked Trudeau to invoke emergency measures, is just to Trudeau's right.

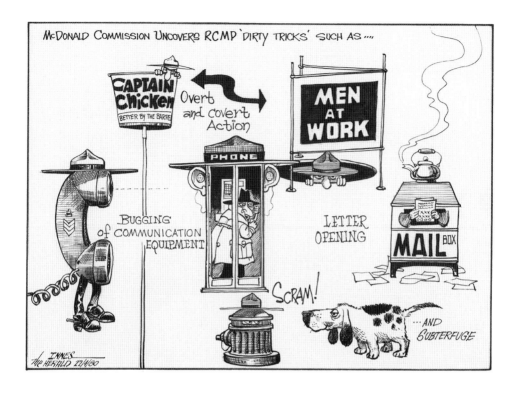

19. The RCMP image began to suffer public embarrassment when the security service came under the harsh spotlight of the McDonald Commission into RCMP wrongdoing. Media coverage was often unflattering, as seen in this 1980 cartoon in the *Calgary Herald*. The McDonald Report recommended the 'civilianization' of the security service, which was implemented in 1984 with the creation of CSIS. Senior Mountie brass had already decided that getting out of political policing would be good for the force, although the RCMP still retain responsibility for enforcement of laws against terrorism and espionage.

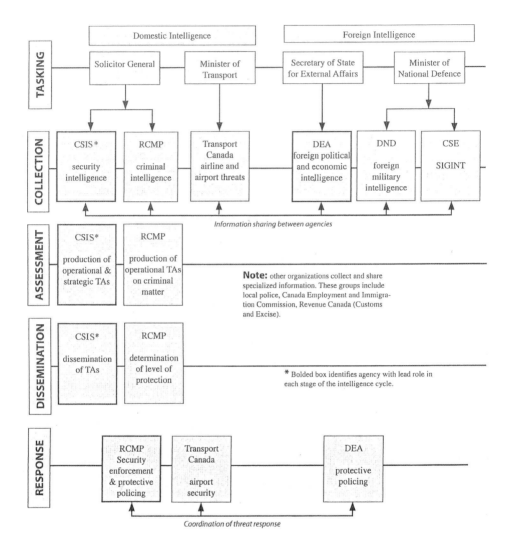

20. In the mid-1980s, the delineation of responsibilities for the detection of terrorist threats and for security measures to prevent terrorist acts was overly complicated, with confused lines of jurisdiction and communication, as indicated in this organizational chart prepared for the Air India inquiry. Counterterrorist organization proved ultimately ineffective, as tragically shown in the Air India bombings.

21. A piece of the fuselage of Air India Flight 182 that was blown out of the sky off the coast of Ireland in June 1985, killing all 329 persons aboard. Air India represents Canada's worst intelligence failure. A quarter-century of investigations, trials, and a commission of inquiry have failed to convict anyone of direct responsibility for the bloodiest terrorist attack in Canadian history.

22. A New York City firefighter looks up at what was left of the World Trade Center following the 11 September 2001 attack by Al-Qaeda terrorists which took close to 3,000 lives. The events of 9/11 brought on a declaration of a global 'War on Terror' by the United States that replaced the Cold War as the focus of Western security and signalled dramatic changes in the structure and functioning of Canadian security intelligence and political policing.

23. Maher Arar reveals the story of his kidnapping and extraordinary rendition by the United States and a nightmarish year of torture in a Syrian prison at a news conference in Ottawa in November 2003. He is watched by his wife, Monia Mazigh, who fought courageously for his release. Arar's case shocked the country and prompted a commission of inquiry and an official apology and compensation from the government of Canada for the complicity of Canadian officials in the abuse of his human rights.

24. Through his Afghan interpreter, a Canadian soldier questions a village elder during a sweep for Taliban west of Kandahar, Afghanistan, in 2006. Canada's combat mission in Afghanistan, which cost the largest number of casualties since the Korean War, was wound down by the summer of 2011. The mission also called for an unprecedented number of (armed) CSIS agents collecting intelligence and assisting the mission, greatly expanding the service's operational role abroad.

An attempt by the RCMP to reinterpret the 1975 guidelines in light of the changed political situation in Quebec failed to achieve ministerial approval, perhaps in part because of loose language about targeting 'subversive, or *other activities aimed at effecting secession.*' The deputy solicitor general raised some uncomfortable but prescient questions: 'Is it in fact a proper function of one element of a national police force to collect information about a provincial government? ... For how long would it be possible to keep this activity from public knowledge? In other words, is the value of the information collected going to be worth the political damage done to the Federal Government and the long-term damage which will probably be done to the RCMP by public disclosure of this activity? The RCMP cannot afford to become suspected of "political spying."'[80] When these words were written, the barn door had long since been opened. Operation HAM had been carried out in early 1973, a direct assault on the PQ. The Keable Inquiry was extremely interested in federal involvement in that break-in, and when the former director general of the security service, John Starnes, was called to testify, the truth finally emerged. It was a security service operation, approved by Starnes, without the knowledge or approval of the RCMP commissioner, the solicitor general, or the prime minister. Starnes's rationale for keeping the lid on this operation was that 'involving ministers might have given the operation an apparent political flavour it never was intended to have.'[81] Eventually, eleven members of the security service were charged with various criminal offences, but in the end most charges were dismissed on the basis of unreasonable delay in bringing them forward, with others disposed of on other technical grounds. But the political damage had been done. The image of the federal secret police breaking into the offices of a legitimate sovereignist political party to access and copy membership lists, with or without sanction from the highest federal authorities, was one that did lasting harm to the cause of federalism in Quebec. The security service may have thought that it was defending federalism, but it had shot itself, and federalism, in the foot.[82]

French Minuet: The Strange Case of Claude Morin, Informer 'Q-1'

The prescient admonitions of the deputy solicitor general in 1975 concerning the risks that would be incurred by the practice of federal 'political spying' in Quebec aside, political spying – worse, sometimes unlawful political spying – was exactly what the security service had been doing and was continuing to do in Quebec, regardless of occasional scruples on the part of the politicians and senior bureaucrats, and shifting rationales by the security service bosses. Nowhere is this more apparent than in the strange case of Claude Morin, RCMP informant extraordinaire, codenamed first *Q-1*, indicating his prized importance to the security service in Quebec, and after 1976, with intended or unintended irony, *French Minuet*.[83]

In early May 1992, sensational revelations emerged that the RCMP security service had had a paid source at the highest level of the PQ cabinet, indeed by many accounts the second most important minister after Premier René Lévesque, and the architect of the PQ's constitutional strategy that culminated in the 1980 referendum on sovereignty-association. Claude Morin had a varied career, as an academic beginning in the 1950s; an influential adviser to the Lesage Liberal government in the early 1960s when he helped shape the policies of the Quiet Revolution; and the deputy minister of federal-provincial and intergovernmental affairs from 1963 to 1971, playing a key role in the constitutional negotiations of the era. In 1972 he joined the new Parti Québécois; in 1976 he was elected to the National Assembly and named minister of intergovernmental affairs, a post he held until 1982 when he returned to his academic career.

When Morin admitted in a Radio Canada interview with Normand Lester in 1992 that he had indeed spent years talking secretly to the RCMP before and after he had taken up duties as a PQ minister, the revelation was profoundly shocking. Worse was the admission that he was a *paid* source, receiving in all perhaps $10,000 to $12,000, a source with assigned codenames, which put the relationship past any suggestion of merely casual encounters. (It even emerged later that the RCMP had filmed Morin taking payment.) It is still unclear just when this relationship began, or on what basis. When Morin first began meeting with the RCMP, while he was deputy minister, he may well have been doing so in a fully official basis with the full authorization of his government. But after Morin had left government service and had joined the PQ as its leading constitutional thinker in the early 1970s, meetings with security service officers from 'D' Division (Counter-Subversion) and 'G' Branch took on a different, more clandestine, tone. After assuming ministerial office in the PQ government in 1976, the meetings continued, with Morin assigned the new codename of *French Minuet*, finally being terminated in 1977.[84]

The PQ leadership, including René Lévesque, had known about this relationship at least since 1981 and PQ Justice Minister Marc-André Bédard apparently even earlier.[85] But the public revelation quickly cast Morin as an arch-traitor in the eyes of many sovereignists. Morin is seen as having been 'the eye of Ottawa' within the PQ government, a mole (*taupe*) planted by Trudeau's spymasters. This is certainly the view of Norman Lester, who broke the story.[86] Morin attempted damage control by releasing to the press in 1992 a notarized statement about his role he had had prepared in 1975.[87] There followed in 2006 a book, *L'affaire Morin*, in which he attacks his critics and tries to explain, or rationalize, his behaviour.[88] Instead of being Ottawa's eye on the PQ, Morin claims that he was acting as the eye of the PQ on the federal intruders. The Mounties may have been trying to gather intelligence on Quebec, but he, Morin, was actually a double agent, playing a clever counter-intelligence game with the cops. They would try to pry out of him information on his PQ colleagues and their plans, but he would instead winkle out from them what Ottawa's intentions were and what the RCMP were planning for Quebec in the way of political espionage and countering and disruption of sovereignist activities. In his apologia, Morin boasts about how, when the Mounties asked him questions, he responded with questions of his own, implying that he, rather than his interviewers, was setting the agenda.

According to Richard Cleroux, who interviewed Morin's RCMP handlers, Morin was held by them in high respect, and his political and diplomatic intelligence was valued for its own sake. He was never treated as if he were some low-grade informant brought onside by coercion, blackmail, bribery, or any of the other devices used in the spy trade – although they were careful to establish a cash nexus in the relationship. Certainly, the RCMP were concerned, especially in the early period of the relationship, to focus their questions to Morin not on the PQ or individual *Pequistes* but on foreign connections, especially those that might involve foreign interference or espionage. There was interest on the part of the Counter-Espionage Branch in the 1970s in the possibility that French intelligence had been penetrated by the KGB, but whether questions to Morin from the security service's 'D' (Counter-Subversion) Branch on French activity were actually about the KGB, or were merely a hook to get him to talk about French interference in Quebec – a subject in which 'D' Branch had an intense interest – is unclear. What is clear is that a focus on French interference, while appropriate, would lead ineluctably to a focus on the PQ targets of French interference,

and hence a focus on at least some *Péquistes*. This was indeed the case
with regard to minister Morin's chief of staff, a PQ activist and cabinet
minister in a later PQ government, Louise Beaudoin, whose apartment
was bugged by the RCMP in the 1970s, allegedly to watch her husband,
François Dorlot, who was suspected – on what appears to be rather thin
evidence – of being a French agent.[89] It does seem that, as time went
on, Morin may have spoken more to his Mountie contacts about his PQ
colleagues, perhaps in part because Morin thought he could thereby
pre-empt other, less trustworthy, sources being utilized. Was this a result of Morin's effective control over the process, or a clever strategy by
his handlers to draw him into talking about matters that he had never
intended to talk about? The Morin affair is also the Morin enigma.

Trying to crack the enigma, at this distance, may be mission impossible. There are, however, a few points that can be made with some
degree of confidence. There is no evidence to suggest that Morin was
acting as a traitor to Quebec and to the PQ, no smoking gun of any
federal government action that could be traced to the betrayal of privileged information by Claude Morin. The lurid accusations of Normand
Lester against Morin are unsupported by the facts or even sometimes
by logic: Morin has no difficulty in dismissing these as 'légendes, sottises et calomnies' (myths, stupidities and slanders). It is fair to assume
that Morin was and is sincere in his interpretation of his own motives.
But can we accept at face value his evaluation of the success of his self-
described 'counter-intelligence' operation?

More persuasively than Lester, Cleroux suggests that Morin gravely
underestimated the intelligence of his RCMP interviewers, described
by Cleroux as among the best minds in the security service. Despite
his intentions, Cleroux asserts, Morin was used by the Mounties more
effectively than he was able to use them.[90] Which raises a further, delicate, question: How could so accomplished, educated, intelligent, and
able an individual as Claude Morin be so foolish as to place himself in
a position that at the very least almost cried out for misinterpretation,
and at worst left him vulnerable to manipulation by forces antithetical
to his own principles? How could a man of these qualities show such a
lack of judgment as to accept cash payments, and leave himself open to
being filmed taking the money?

We are forced to delve into matters of individual psychology, dangerous ground for outsiders. Morin has sometimes been described as
vain and arrogant. Vanity certainly shows in his self-justifying writing, and a certain amount of arrogance may very well have character-

ized his attitude to the *flics* (cops) he was dealing with. Morin seems to have suffered from a syndrome not unfamiliar to successful people, the 'smartest guy in the room' fallacy. The Mounties he sat down with were hardly his broad equal in terms of culture, education, and academic, administrative, and political accomplishments. But what they did know, very well, was *their own agenda*, what they wanted to get from Morin, and how best to get it. Their world may have been narrower, less glittering than his, but in their world they were in charge. Morin is reputedly an aficionado of spy novels, and it does seem that he liked to play spy games. A book he published about the lessons of his years as constitutional negotiator for Quebec with Ottawa[91] titles successive chapters with terms drawn from the world of espionage (double agents, deception, and so on). Perhaps a certain vanity persuaded him that he could play these Mountie spies to his and his party's benefit. But they were the professionals, he the amateur, however gifted. In the end, *l'affaire Morin* may be less about treason and betrayal than about how very smart people can sometimes do very foolish things.

From the RCMP point of view, there is one other lesson to be drawn from this strange and sometimes inexplicable affair. We have already suggested that the RCMP had better intelligence on the FLQ prior to the October Crisis than they have been given credit for. Often derided, even from within the federal cabinet, for being out of touch with the Quebec milieu, they had been given what amounted to a virtual blank cheque to aggressively counter and disrupt precisely because it was believed they were lacking in good intelligence sources. The Morin affair suggests that the image of clueless anglo cops was off the mark. They had successfully cultivated, and to some degree manipulated, the second most important figure in the PQ in the 1970s. The only higher prize could have been René Lévesque himself. Whether it was appropriate for a federal police force to behave in this manner is a separate question. That they were good at the job they undertook at the federal cabinet's behest is incontrovertible.

End Game in Paris: Was Political Murder on the Security Service Duty Roster?

In 1998 a book was published by Michael McLoughlin that made the most sensational charges yet about security service actions against violent separatists.[92] One of the FLQ terrorists who had gone into exile to avoid arrest was Mario Bachand, whose RCMP intelligence dossier was discussed earlier in this chapter. On 29 March 1971 Bachand was murdered in his Paris apartment, a crime that remains unsolved. McLoughlin argues that this was a political assassination ordered by the RCMP security service and carried out by its undercover agents posing as FLQers. The book made a brief splash in the media and then disappeared from sight. But this is a serious charge, indeed a charge of a more serious crime than any of the other transgressions investigated by McDonald and Keable. Is there a plausible case that the security service actually carried out political murders in the name of national security? Could the RCMP security service be described as a Latin American-style death squad?

The first thing to say is that McLoughlin is an excellent researcher with a solid documentary basis for much of a well-written book. Much, but not all: when it comes to the actual murder of Bachand, the documentary trail grows faint and is replaced by circumstantial evidence and speculative explanations. McLoughlin rationalizes the lack of a smoking gun in the manner of conspiracy theorists: the absence of evidence must indicate that it has been suppressed – they would, wouldn't they?

The assassination thesis is implausible, for a number of reasons. It is difficult to discern why such an extreme measure could have been justified against a figure in futile exile and a movement in disarray. In 1971 Bachand represented no real threat to anyone other than other divisive factions in a group in rapid decline and dissolution. McLoughlin adduces an alleged threat of assassination against Robert Bourassa on a planned visit to Paris, but this seems far-fetched in light of Bachand's visibility and the heavy security accorded any foreign dignitary. Another striking implausibility is that the RCMP, which had been engaged in a bitter shadow war with French intelligence since at least 1967 over French mischief in Canada on behalf of Quebec *indépendentistes*, would dare to mount an assassination on French soil. McLoughlin argues, with equal implausibility, that French police and French intelligence were actually colluding with the RCMP. What would lie behind such a remarkable reversal is unexplained. Finally, there is the sheer implausibility of the security service planning and carrying out a politically motivated murder. Whatever else one may say about the security service over the decades, cold-blooded assassination has never been on the charge list. We see no reason to believe that Bachand represents the sole exception, or why this fringe figure should justify such anomalous behaviour.

Radio Canada in 1997 presented a documentary that concluded that Bachand had been murdered by another FLQ faction, that the RCMP had nothing to do with it. McLoughlin is dismissive of this investigation, citing evidence that some FLQers were cooperating with the RCMP. Even if they were, and even if those who carried out the murder had shadowy ties from time to time with the RCMP, the application of Occam's Razor would still eliminate police-directed murder as the less likely explanation than the simpler and familiar tale of factional strife among despairing political exiles. The verdict on McLoughlin: not proven.

Plausible and Implausible Deniability:
What Did the Politicians Know?

In light of the political consequences of security service activity in countering separatism and 'subversion' in Quebec, and in light of the illegality of some of the methods employed, crucial questions must be asked: Were the security service's Quebec follies the result of an RCMP running out of political control; or were they the result of a force directed by its political masters to overstep the lines of legality in order to defeat separatism, and to blur the lines between the objectives of protecting national security and national unity, in order to fulfil the political agenda of the party in power? There has been no shortage of pro-sovereignist commentary in Quebec ready to endorse the latter proposition. The Liberal governments of Pierre Trudeau are seen by these commentators as having engaged in a war without quarter against the national aspirations of Quebec, a war that had a secret, dark underside in which the Mounties acted as subordinate tools in a ruthless federalist campaign.[93] On the other side, accounts of the federalist-sovereignist struggle by English Canadian commentators tend to gloss over the secret war in favour of the open conflict of ideas and policies, which leaves less room for embarrassing questions about Liberal national-security practices. As for the Liberals, once the scandals had become public, they were happy to leave the RCMP as the lightning rod to draw most of the criticism – a position that the McDonald inquiry seemed prepared to go along with.

It is possible to dismiss the hard-line sovereignist picture fairly readily, especially when it is argued, as it has been in Quebec from time to time, that the War Measures Act in 1970 was intended as a warning that any peaceful, constitutional move to independence would be met by military intervention. In fact, Trudeau was quite clear during the 1980 referendum campaign that a democratic expression of the will of the Quebec majority to separate would have to be accepted, in sharp contrast to his handling of the terrorist challenge posed by the FLQ. It is also clear that even the most intrusive interventions of the 1970s against the PQ, Operation HAM and Claude Morin's role as *French Minuet*, were motivated primarily by a desire to collect intelligence on foreign interference and the presence in the party of people otherwise targeted (as terrorists, subversives, and so on). Moreover, it would be contrary to rules of prudent statecraft, not to speak of long-standing Canadian practice, for political leaders to give direct, explicit orders to the police to intervene clandestinely against a legitimate democratic political party.

At this point, however, we can draw an equivalent line against Liberal apologetics. There is an old principle in the intelligence world that has repeatedly offered governments and politicians a handy way to evade blame when operations go awry: *plausible deniability*. In a command hierarchy, those at or near the top may be able to avoid responsibility for instructions carried out below when the instructions are of a general nature, without specifics. Since intelligence operations are carried out in secret, attempts to reconstruct authorization post facto may be difficult. In criminal law, plausible deniability refers to lack of proof *beyond a reasonable doubt*. This does not imply innocence, and the Liberals' plausible deniability for RCMP activities in Quebec does not necessarily imply innocence on their part.

We know that the raid on the APLQ (BRICOLE) was carried out without cabinet approval. Indeed, it was carried out without the prior knowledge and approval of the director general of the security service, John Starnes – a fact that 'irritated' Starnes. We know that the raid on the PQ offices (HAM) was carried out with Starnes's approval, but without the knowledge of the RCMP commissioner, the solicitor general, and the prime minister. We know that, even within 'G' Branch, the officer in charge was not always kept informed of specific operations on the ground. We know that individual RCMP security service officers had relatively wide latitude for front-line decision making. Operating under the cloak of extreme secrecy could lead to an attitude of near-impunity for conduct.

We also know that operations of dubious legality and propriety were carried out within the context of ambiguous instructions from above, from ministers and cabinet committees. There were instructions not just to assess and analyse but to 'counter' the separatists; there were ambiguous analogies drawn between the Communist Party in the Cold War and the PQ in the present era; there were conflicting instructions to collect intelligence on separatists but not to collect intelligence on the chief separatist party; and there were conflicting instructions about looking for subversives, terrorists, foreign agents, and so on operating within legitimate parties, along with constraints on looking at these parties as such. After October 1970, when Liberal politicians blamed the RCMP security service for allegedly failing to provide actionable advance intelligence on the FLQ, and when the federal cabinet decided that the protection of national unity was to be a high priority, the marching orders to the security service in Quebec were reasonably clear: go out and counter and render ineffective the separatists. Ministers did not want to know details of how this was to be done, but they did want results. There is no reason to believe on the basis of the available record that the Liberal ministers ever deliberated over the implications for liberal democracy in authorizing a secret war against separatism. But plausible deniability did prove convenient when operations went sideways.

The McDonald Commission examined a somewhat lower-threshold question of the role of the politicians in relation to the security service: apart from lack of evidence of active direction of wrongdoing, did ministers 'have knowledge of illegal activity combined with a failure to stop it or deal with it in some way,' or were they 'willfully blind' to wrongdoing? Unfortunately, the *Third Report* of the commission, on '*the Question of Governmental Knowledge*,' is unusually opaque and diffuse, not to speak of fragmented and disjointed thanks to extensive redactions which subsequent Access to Information requests have largely failed to redress. It is difficult to escape the conclusion that the opacity is deliberate, that the commissioners had little inclination to shine a potentially unflattering light on the Liberal ministers but preferred to focus critical attention on the security service. Why this might be so is a matter of some dispute. Critics have pointed to the known Liberal ties of the commissioners. Others have suggested that their primary focus was on gaining acceptance from the Liberal government for the sweeping reform agenda they were proposing (see chapter 10); finger-pointing at Liberal ministers might have queered that pitch.[94]

The Paper That Never Was

Any doubt that the commissioners wished to divert attention away from ministerial knowledge is dispelled by the curious case of the commission paper that never was. In the archives of the commission rests a paper, numbered '11,' entitled 'Submission of Commission Counsel: Government Knowledge of RCMP Activities Not Authorized or Provided for by Law,' and dated 12 February 1981. Affixed to the front is a cover page with an advisory that, 'although this document is identified as Paper No. 11 and was prepared by Commission counsel, it did not become an official exhibit of the Commission. Notwithstanding the way it is worded, it does not represent the views or findings of the Commission.' Even more curious is a reference to this paper that came up in the closed commission hearings. At the mention of a Paper No. 11 that 'did not see the light of day,' Commission Chairman McDonald intervened to say: 'I should rephrase that: it not only did not see the light of day: it never came into existence.' The witness then responded: 'Yes, of course, I accept that: that Paper No. 11 did not come into existence because it was never conceived.'[95]

Years later, John Starnes, former security service director general, came across a puzzling reference to the paper that was never conceived and requested it under Access to Information.[96] With some redactions, mainly for solicitor-client privilege, it was released, and for a paper that never existed, it makes interesting reading. The question commission counsel considered was whether ministers and senior public servants 'were made aware in a general way (without being provided with or requesting specifics)' that the security service 'had or was engaged in activities that were not authorized or provided for by law.' To answer this question, the paper addressed a wide variety of testimony it had heard as well as key documents from the cabinet committees on priorities and planning and security and intelligence in late 1970. In these documents, seen by ministers and senior officials, there is reference to the possibility of illegal activities by the security service, particularly break-ins for surveillance purposes and the likelihood that undercover human sources in terrorist groups might be required to commit criminal acts to maintain their cover. In particular, there is evidence provided that Solicitor General George McIlraith was given an RCMP memorandum which pointed, without specifics, to illegal acts, both those that had happened and those that were prospective. Moreover, notes taken of a Security and Intelligence Committee meeting specifies that Starnes indicated that the RCMP had engaged in illegal acts for the 'last twenty years.' While there is some dispute over whether others recalled this information being given by Starnes, Starnes himself, and the commission counsel in Paper 11, insist that the words were indeed uttered – but mysteriously failed to find their way into the formal record of the committee. That conclusion apparently was enough for the commissioners to sink the paper out of sight, out of mind, and even to deny that it had ever been conceived.

What we have here is evidence not of any political direction to the security service to use illegal methods, but instead evidence that ministers and deputy ministers had been made aware of illegal activity but preferred not to know any details, and did not wish to leave any record that they had such knowledge. In short: plausible deniability. This deniability was made even more plausible by the willingness of the public inquiry the same politicians had appointed to suppress evidence to the contrary. It has become less plausible with time.

10

'I'm Shocked, Shocked to Find That Gambling Is Going on in Here!': The Creation of the Canadian Security Intelligence Service

In the classic 1942 film *Casablanca*, Captain Renault (Claude Raines) of the Vichy police is forced by the Gestapo to order the closure of Rick's nightclub. Incredulous, Rick (Humphrey Bogart) asks: 'How can you close me up? On what grounds?' Renault replies: 'I am shocked, shocked to find that gambling is going on in here!' At this point the croupier hands Renault a roll of bills: 'Your winnings, sir.' 'Oh, thank you very much,' says Renault, pocketing the money: 'Everybody out at once!'

In the early 1980s, following the findings of the McDonald Commission, the federal government embarked upon a major reform of its security service. Like Captain Renault, the politicians were forced to act, and they were 'shocked, shocked' to find that gambling had been going on. Like Captain Renault, they were quite happy to pocket their winnings even as they shut down the nightclub.

The Rocky Road from Mackenzie to McDonald: The Starnes Interlude

The Mackenzie Commission had reported in 1969 to little public notice, and relatively little official policy response. As we indicated in chapter 8, buried in the Mackenzie Report was the recommendation that the security service be taken out of the RCMP and civilianized. This recommendation was supported in a somewhat cursory fashion: about six pages were devoted to an explanation of the advantages of civilian organization. Little was done to prepare public or parliamentary opinion for such a drastic reconstruction; it is not surprising that concerted opposition by the RCMP behind the scenes in Ottawa shot down the proposal, since there was no organized bureaucratic counterweight to the zealous Mountie brass protecting their turf. Nor was public or parliamentary opinion prepared for the fallback position of appointing a civilian as director general of the security service. Even this appointment was a scaled-back response, since the initial idea had apparently been to make John Starnes commissioner of the entire force – an idea that Starnes himself thought inappropriate, or at least premature. Yet, even when Starnes stepped into the lesser position of directing the security service, he was very much on his own, a 'suit' stepping into the lion's den of uniformed paramilitary officers with a highly developed esprit de corps and a deep suspicion of outsiders, whether politicians or civilian bureaucrats, being imposed on their command structure. There was also a 'deep distrust' that had grown up between the RCMP and the Liberal government, a distrust coming from both sides, which Starnes learned about too late to draw the necessary lessons for his own prospects in bringing about civilianization: 'Had I been aware of this deep distrust, I would have been a good deal more cautious and might even have turned down the job. I probably should have attached more significance than I did to the failure (inability) of the government to tackle Mackenzie's recommendations and to have drawn the appropriate lessons.'[1] When one adds to this the traditional notion of 'police independence' from direct political control that the RCMP had always jealously guarded, it is easy to see that Starnes's authority in his new position would have been in doubt from the beginning.

Starnes did come with a mandate of sorts from the prime minister, poorly defined though it was. In a speech to the House of Commons on 26 June 1969, Trudeau had indicated his intention to make the security service 'increasingly separate in structure and civilian in nature.' This would include 'new and more flexible policies in relation to recruiting, training and career planning' to enable it to be 'capable of dealing fairly and effectively with the new and complex problems which we undoubtedly face in the future.' He further indicated his personal interest in ensuring that the service 'will grow and develop as a distinct and identifiable element within the basic structure of the Force.' Starnes as civilian director was the Liberal government's idea of how to implement this vision, but as Starnes quickly realized, his appointment in itself accomplished nothing, and his civilian status was an obstacle to enacting change. As he later, ruefully, suggested:

The government should have been much firmer in dealing with the RCMP's largely emotional and sometimes unrealistic objections to the idea of a security service divorced from the RCMP. It should have paid

far more attention to Mackenzie's detailed proposals and to their effective implementation. I should have been quicker to note the warning flags
and to have insisted on receiving direction when none existed. I was a
compromise candidate and, as it turned out, not a very propitious one – a
stop-gap, not a lasting solution.

The lack of clear direction reminded me of a characteristic of many regimes in the Middle East – the assumption that simply because something
is announced (in this case making the RCMP Security Service 'more civilian and separate in character') it will happen without any further actions
being taken by ministers or interest shown. This attitude became a characteristic of Trudeau's governments, especially in their handling of security
and intelligence.[2]

As Starnes strove to recruit and promote civilians, he came up against
the force's rigid personnel policies, as well as the opposition of Commissioner Len Higgitt, whom Starnes had pledged at the outset to serve
loyally. It was an impossible position. The best that could be done for
reform was to pass the question of personnel policy over to independent
management consultants, a blow to traditional Mountie autonomy to
which Higgitt perhaps reluctantly agreed. By mid-1972, Starnes had become quite discouraged: 'I had come reluctantly to the conclusion that
I had failed to make any real progress in changing the Security Service.'
Consequently, he decided to take early retirement: 'I hoped a fresh mind
and a different approach might succeed where I had failed.'[3]

The 'fresh mind' was that of Michael Dare, another civilian, named
as his replacement in 1973. As a parting gift to his successor, Starnes arranged through Gordon Robertson, the cabinet secretary, for a meeting
with the prime minister – to be attended by himself, Dare, and Commissioner Higgitt – to bring Trudeau up to speed on what had and had
not been accomplished in Starnes's tenure and with the hope of gaining
some fresh direction from the top for Dare to carry with him into the
job. The meeting was held on 16 March 1973 in the Prime Minister's
Office.[4]

Trudeau opened by repeating his stated objective in his 1969 speech
to Parliament that the security service should become increasingly
separate in structure and civilian in nature. Starnes added that, while
much had been done to reach Trudeau's objective, much remained to
be done. He was sure that the commissioner would agree that the security service was 'very nearly autonomous in operational matters' (given
what was unfolding in Quebec at this time, autonomy in operations

might actually have been more a problem than a solution). But on the key question of human-resource management and finances, movement was slower than he would have liked. The service awaited the results of the management study, as well as a study commissioned on computerization of operations, the results of which would have a 'far-reaching effect' upon future capabilities and organization. After completion of these studies, Starnes significantly suggested, it would be possible to identify jobs in the security service 'which could perhaps be more appropriately done by civilians hired from outside.' At this point, the prime minister intervened to ask what proportion of the security service was now civilian. It was about half-civilian, and half-RCMP, but 'by far the largest' civilian component was in relatively junior positions. When asked about the obstacles to recruiting suitable civilians, Starnes was clear: the 'principal' obstacle was the service structure, its 'rigid framework.' It needed to be restructured in ways that would 'offer job satisfaction and adequate career opportunities to persons with suitable academic qualifications.'

Commissioner Higgitt must have been very uncomfortable having to hear this criticism in front of the prime minister. In Starnes's record, Higgitt intervened at this point to insist on the 'high degree of professional excellence' of the 'invaluable' RCMP members of the security service: 'Indeed, the Security Service would not be able to function without this considerable body of expertise.' 'Many' of the Mountie members even had university degrees. Of course, there could be improvements, Higgitt allowed; he would look at the consultants' reports, and he wished to assure the prime minister that 'he would do everything possible to see that the government's wishes were carried out.' This seems to have constituted less than a ringing endorsement of even limited civilianization.

Trudeau responded that 'since 1970' security service reports were satisfactory in quality, although he pointed out that 'prior to that, there had perhaps been certain shortcomings.' He went on to talk about how the work of the service had to be reoriented, in light of new threats supplanting the old ones that had preoccupied the service in the past. Unfortunately, over a page of discussion that follows has been entirely redacted, so we are uncertain what directions were being given with regard to targeting and threat assessments. What we are left with is an indication of what Starnes and his successor Dare, not to speak of the prime minister and the Liberal government, faced in trying to civilianize the security service so long as it remained within the RCMP.

The Spillover Effect from Quebec

As we have indicated in the previous chapter, the main thrust of intrusive security service activities after 1970 was in Quebec, directed at
the separatist threat to national security and national unity. But a blank
cheque issued the security service in one jurisdiction could not fail to
have ramifications outside that jurisdiction. The new threats to security
that had emerged in the 1960s had not been confined to Quebec, even
if they had taken on the greatest urgency in the context of widespread
support for Quebec independence. New Left movements supplanting
the old left Communist Party among young people were as much a
feature of English Canada as of Quebec.[5]

Close attention to these movements in the security service began in
earnest as early as 1967, when the 'Key Sectors' program was initiated
by 'D' Branch. The reason for a new program was that, since the nature
of subversion seemed to be changing, 'it is apparent that "D" Branch
investigative procedures must also undergo considerable change and
adjustments to cope with this situation.' Key Sectors focused on subversion in three areas of Canadian society: government at all levels;
mass media; and schools and universities. The program's aims were
to measure the extent of subversive penetration into the key sectors;
to assess what threat was posed by this penetration; and 'to attempt
to counter or at least contain that threat.' Information collected in the
regions was channelled to headquarters where a new analytical section dedicated to the program made overall assessments.[6] Typically for
the security service, collection tended to outrun analysis and evaluation, and entries in the penetration files had to be drastically winnowed
down in the early 1970s to permit closer analysis of the important ones
remaining.[7] A New Left Desk, later a section, was created in 'D' Branch
to coordinate reporting and analysis.[8]

In seeking to get a handle on these post-Cold War forms of protest,
the security service proved all too ready to take advantage of the wide
latitude afforded intrusive surveillance operations by the politicians'
exhortation to 'counter' and disrupt the separatists, by whatever means
might appear efficacious. Some of the programs employed in Quebec,
such as the illegal mail openings (CATHEDRAL) and unauthorized access to government records on individuals, were always Canada-wide
in scope. Some of the worst examples of unlawful behaviour in Quebec
such as break-ins and theft of data (HAM and BRICOLE) were matched
by operations outside Quebec against left-wing political targets. One
that stands out is the still murky Praxis affair.

A Break-In, a Fire, a Theft, and an Enemies List

In 1970 the Toronto offices housing Praxis Corporation, a left-wing group organizing a national conference of poor people, as well as some other small left-wing organizations, were broken into; Praxis files were stolen and a fire lit. The break-in and fire remain to this day unsolved. Suspicion was rife at the time that this was a police operation aimed at disrupting or preventing the conference from taking place. In 1977 it became publicly known that the stolen files, or at least some of them, had mysteriously come into the possession of the RCMP security service, which indeed retained those of interest for use in the Counter-Subversion Branch, New Left Section. The *Toronto Sun* proclaimed that the RCMP was responsible for the break-in and theft, an action of which the right-wing newspaper thoroughly approved.[9]

The McDonald Commission, acting on a complaint from a lawyer concerned about possible RCMP involvement in a 'break-in, arson, and theft of documents,' investigated the Praxis affair.[10] It found that, approximately two months after the occurrences, some of the documents were handed over to the security service 'by a source of the RCMP.' Peter Worthington, editor of the *Toronto Sun*, admitted that he, too, had been a recipient of some of the documents and had handed them over to the security service. The service 'retained both sets of documents for some seven years.' Commission investigators found no evidence to contradict the findings of criminal investigations by provincial and municipal police forces that 'no member of the RCMP or agent at their request was involved.' They did point out that the retention of the documents by the RCMP might have violated the Criminal Code provision concerning the unlawful possession of property obtained by crime. No criminal investigation of the security service was ever undertaken into that aspect of the Praxis affair.

Whatever the truth about responsibility for the Praxis break-in, there is no doubt that the security service had an interest in investigating Praxis. There is a record of an inquiry to the RCMP from the undersecretary of state for external affairs in the spring of 1969 about the New Left politics of the organization, with which Assistant Commissioner Higgitt was happy to comply, forwarding information on Praxis members from security service files. Higgitt even suggested that External Affairs assign a research fellow to Praxis to gather more details on the organization.[11] Nor is there any doubt that the security service made use of the stolen documents, first as the basis of a detailed report on Praxis by a security service sergeant in June 1972,[12] then incorporating them into its ongoing counter-subversion investigation of the New Left. Adding to suspicions about security service involvement is that the Praxis files were part of a broader investigation of what the service called the 'Extra-Parliamentary Opposition (EPO).'

The story of the EPO threat is a cautionary tale of how security service surveillance could spin out of control when information from its files got into the political sphere. In the late 1960s, 'D' Branch's New Left Section was tracking the emergence of a new tactical and strategic concept on the left associated with the anarchist magazine *Our Generation* in Montreal, which looked to the building of forms of radical political activity outside parliamentary structures. What particularly worried security service analysts was the idea that people advancing the EPO concept might be infiltrating and subverting government. On 11 May 1971 the security service produced a threat assessment entitled 'The Changing Nature of the Threat from the New Left – Extra-Parliamentary Opposition, Penetration of Government.' This document was thirty-two pages in length, much of which, but not all, has been released under the Access to Information Act. After analysing the strategy of the EPO, the document focused on ties between *Our Generation*, Praxis, and other groups, and their links to the federal government, which had given a research grant to Praxis. The security service was especially interested in a group called the Ottawa Committee for Socialist Activities (OCSA), made up of former student activists now working in the federal government – a matter of 'increasing concern to security.' The security problem posed by the EPO/OCSA group in government is 'complex and worrisome,' the report noted. Even though there was as yet 'no direct evidence of manipulation of policy and decision-making functions in the federal government,' the EPO 'members are not weekend radicals, but true revolutionaries dedicated to a long term goal of bringing about a socialist revolution. They are willing to quietly work within the system to subvert it, and due to their anonymity their actions go largely undetected.'

They would not remain anonymous for long. The assistant RCMP commissioner forwarded the report to the solicitor general, Jean-Pierre Goyer, who may have asked for its production in the first place. On the advice of Robin Bourne in SPARG, Goyer then wrote on 15 June 1971 letters marked 'Personal and Secret' to five fellow cabinet ministers warning them about EPO supporters in government employment who required watching 'with more than normal care.' Attached was a list of twenty-one persons extracted from the security service report and identified as working in seven departments, under the ministers contacted. There was no further communication with the security service on this, nor was the matter taken up with the Security Panel, nor were deputy ministers or departmental security officers contacted. What if anything should be done about the list was up the ministers alone to decide. In fact, nothing seems to have been done. But, when the letter found its way into the press in 1977, it came out as the Liberal government's 'Enemies List.'

With the 'Enemies List' now in the public domain, the security service was asked to review the status of the twenty-one names. It turned out that none were of any continuing 'operational interest' to the service, and none since the report had appeared. About half had received security clearances in the normal way, while the remainder either did not require clearances or had left the public service. This was in 1977. A longer-term look at the names reveals that, if the intention had been to establish a blacklist, it was extraordinarily ineffective. Four of the number subsequently rose to the rank of assistant deputy minister and one became the youngest-ever deputy minister in the government of Canada.

The McDonald Commission looked at the EPO episode in detail and made a number of critical comments.[13] First, as to the quality of the security service analysis of the EPO threat, the commissioners were caustic: 'We consider it to be an inadequate analysis, inflammatory in tone, and, at times, faulty in its logic … [demonstrating] an insensitivity to the difference between a threat to Canada's security on the one hand and legitimate dissent on the other.' They also found objectionable the circulation of this paper outside the security service, as well as the fact that the naming of individuals in the paper was on the basis of their political views rather than any actions they had taken. The paper was, they suggested, a 'prime example of the dangers which a security intelligence agency can pose to two cherished values of our society – the right of association and the right to privacy,' not to mention the risk of harming the careers of those named. Worse yet was that the security service had circulated the paper, with the names, to four foreign intelligence agencies without informing the minister or his officials. The security service, McDonald rightly pointed out, 'has no way of controlling the subsequent utilization of the information by the foreign country.'[14]

The EPO matter was a disgraceful affair. No one in government, from the RCMP to the ministers, emerged with any credit. The only redeeming factor is that little damage appears to have been done to the individuals targeted.

The Mounties' Waffle Breakfast: Targeting the NDP

In 1977 there were questions in the Ontario legislature about the RCMP allegedly investigating the New Democratic Party in the earlier part of the decade. This was one of the most sensitive issues to emerge concerning RCMP excesses, for the NDP was a major party in the Canadian Parliament and a party, moreover, that was or had been in office in three provinces. Like the targeting of the PQ in Quebec, this raised serious issues of interference in the legitimate democratic political process. As a professed social-democratic party, the NDP, and its predecessor, the CCF, had always had an ambiguous relationship during the Cold War years with the conservative political policing of the RCMP. In practice a supporter of the Cold War, and often itself a target for both competition and occasionally infiltration by the Communists and other sectarian leftists, the mildly social democratic CCF-NDP nonetheless found itself from time to time considered a suspect party in the black-and-white world of Communism versus capitalism. Had steadfast adherence to NATO and NORAD not been enough to protect the NDP from the RCMP counter-subversion squad?

The truth turned out to be more complicated. The RCMP had mounted an investigation that went inside the NDP, but it seemed they were really not that interested in the NDP as such. Rather, they were after the Waffle movement that was, according to the security service, trying to infiltrate the relatively respectable NDP. They were even after certain factions within the Waffle faction, even smaller numbers of subversives who were trying to infiltrate the group that was trying to infiltrate the NDP. Or so they said.

The Waffle was a left-wing grouping within the NDP dedicated to the achievement of an 'independent, socialist Canada' that began in 1969. The group tried to combine extra-parliamentary activities with electoral politics; it firmly eschewed violence. The Waffle contested the NDP leadership at the national convention of the party in 1971, Waffle candidate Jim Laxer losing to David Lewis with about 40 per cent of the vote on the final ballot. In 1972 the Ontario NDP, indicating that it could no longer tolerate organized factions inside the NDP, formally expelled the Waffle from the provincial party. The Waffle continued as a separate movement for a few years before terminating itself.

On 7 December 1977 the attorney general of Ontario, Roy McMurtry, following consultation with the federal solicitor general and the RCMP, rose in the legislature with a statement responding to reports about

RCMP surveillance of the NDP.[15] There had been no investigation of the NDP by the RCMP, McMurtry reported, no agents had broken into party offices. He did state that, between 1970 and 1973, the RCMP had investigated 'certain members of the Waffle group.' He quoted directly from an RCMP report that pointed to ex-members of the Communist Party and the Trotskyist League for Socialist Action having joined the Waffle. The RCMP had established that these 'subversive elements' had 'penetrated the NDP through the Waffle in order to gain more respectability, credibility and influence.' But once the Waffle had been expelled from the NDP in 1972, these subversives lost interest in the Waffle, and consequently the RCMP lost interest in the Waffle.

There was an additional reason for the RCMP's preoccupation with the Waffle. In the period from 1970 to 1973, the force's interest in the Waffle 'increased' when it was found that a 'Canadian news media person' (unnamed by McMurtry but in fact Mark Starowicz of the CBC), who was 'closely associated with leading people in the Waffle,' was meeting 'clandestinely' with Konstantin Geyvandov, a KGB intelligence officer operating undercover as a *Pravda* correspondent who would later be declared persona non grata by the Canadian government. RCMP investigation 'confirmed' that Starowicz had been paid to provide information, including reports on the Waffle and the NDP. The purpose of these meetings was, the RCMP believed, to assist the KGB in deciding whether the Waffle or any of its members were 'worthy of further attention by the KGB.' The Mounties even considered laying a charge against Starowicz, but concluded that this was not feasible.

In short, the Mounties were claiming two tried (and tired) Cold War justifications for intruding into a legal political party: Communist subversives and Soviet espionage. Neither justification held water. The Waffle did have former Communists and Trotskyists among its members. They openly acknowledged their former affiliations and were welcomed to the degree that they adhered to the principles of the Waffle, which in terms of democratic political process were also the principles of the NDP. Policy views, whether socialist and/or Marxist, that may have been at variance with the NDP mainstream were no business of the state. As for the alleged KGB connection, there was a good reason why no charge of espionage was ever laid against Starowicz: there was no espionage, and no clandestine meetings. Starowicz the journalist was simply helping out a foreign correspondent from the USSR (who may have been a KGB agent, but undercover) figure out who was who in Canada.[16] The use of this alleged connection to justify spying on the NDP was a case of guilt by association, at third or fourth hand – a mighty stretch even by RCMP standards of the early 1970s.

The McDonald Commission had other ideas about why the Waffle/NDP had been targeted.[17] The commissioners noted that, in the late 1960s, interest shifted within the Counter-Subversion Branch away from the old left to the diverse New Left movements then emerging. They quote the officer in charge of the branch in 1972 instructing field units that, against new violent threats (including 'Maoists and Trotskyists'), 'intelligence coverage and counter-measures … will entail expanded human and technical source coverage … and any such other measures deemed necessary by the Security Service to contain, defuse or neutralize the threat posed by such individuals or groups.' A second focus of interest was on 'essentially non-violent elements whose major strategy, whether individually or collectively, is to infiltrate or penetrate existing groups or institutions for the purpose of promoting dissident or subversive influence aimed ultimately at promoting revolutionary activity.' McDonald found 'such a wide definition of subversion dangerous and unacceptable because it does not clearly distinguish radical dissent from genuine threats to Canada's security.' The commission was also 'deeply disturbed' by the attitude revealed in the phrase 'any other such measures deemed necessary by the Security Service,' especially after what the commission had learned about the countering measures and CHECKMATE.[18]

Given this context, the McDonald investigators were not surprised that the security service's interests in the Waffle were actually broader than what had been admitted in the McMurtry statement. They quote a memorandum from the Counter-Subversion Branch to other divisions dated 29 December 1970:

> We are obviously not interested in the normal activity of any legitimate political party as such, however, we do have a responsibility to investigate information of a potentially subversive or espionage nature within such parties. Because of its socialist nature, the NDP has always attracted subversive and radical elements in society. However, it has become increasingly apparent that these elements are now polarizing around the Waffle Group in even greater numbers, particularly in view of the willingness of the Waffle leadership to accept dissident Communists, Trotskyists and 'leftists' generally in an attempt to unite the 'left.'

The memorandum goes on to direct investigation of the 'objectives of the Waffle as a group,' as well as to report on subversive penetration, the influence subversives may exert over other party members, any policy resolutions sponsored by subversives, and recruitment within parties by subversives. Another branch memorandum dated 25 February 1972 admonished Waffle investigators to cease reporting 'largely innocuous matters' about party activity and instead focus on providing 'more penetrating insight and analysis.' The branch was particularly concerned by the 'extreme left posture' adopted by the Waffle, and wanted to hone in on the 'aims, strategies and planned tactics of the Waffle leadership, especially when insights we develop go beyond their open, public announcements. That is, do they have designs which exceed their publicly declared aims and, if so, by what means (strategies) do they hope to attain them.' In other words, having failed to turn up much of interest, investigators were being encouraged to find hidden subversive agendas.

McDonald comments that a non-violent political group's espousal of what the security service considered an extreme left posture should provide 'no rationale whatsoever for a security intelligence agency to use intrusive intelligence-gathering techniques' against it. Even more objectionable to McDonald was the fact that such a rationale was 'used to justify the collection of information about an element of a legitimate political party which is in opposition to the party in power.' The latter concern was underscored when it was learned that, in a 5 March 1971 letter to the solicitor general, Jean-Pierre Goyer, the security service provided the minister with a briefing on the Waffle which included background information on specific individual Waffle members deemed to be 'subversive and radical elements.' McDonald reminded the RCMP that it was undesirable to provide politicians in office with information about individuals in other parties, unless criminal investigations were about to be launched, and that a 'security intelligence agency must exercise extreme care when circulating information about individuals.'[19]

As with the intrusive surveillance in the early 1970s of the Parti Québécois under the guise of hunting subversive separatists, the surveillance of the Waffle NDP failed to make the fundamental distinctions between political dissent and subversion required in a liberal-democratic society. Unlike the PQ, the NDP did not achieve office, however, and thus lacked the tools to investigate the security service's intrusion into its affairs, as the PQ did with the Keable Inquiry. Since the NDP itself expelled the Waffle, it perhaps harboured some of the same doubts about the movement that the security service held. But that did not excuse intrusive surveillance of a legitimate political party, however ill-defined the guidelines provided the security service might be. The episode was just one more black mark against the RCMP security service in a growing dossier in the late 1970s.

In any event, we cannot take RCMP excuses for watching the CCF/ NDP at face value. In 2006 investigative reporter Jim Bronskill, using the Access to Information Act, showed that the RCMP spied on Tommy Douglas for decades. The premier of Saskatchewan from 1944 to 1961, the national NDP leader from 1961 to 1971, the 'father of Medicare' who was voted 'the greatest Canadian of all time' in a 2004 national poll, Douglas was the subject of an apparently voluminous RCMP dossier. The declassified security service file on him shows that the Mounties surreptitiously attended his speeches, analysed his words for evidence of subversion, and even eavesdropped on his private conversations. RCMP interest was triggered by Douglas's association over the years with various left-wing causes and peace movements, and the alarming fact that he occasionally was seen to speak (publicly) with known Communist Party members. Even as he neared retirement in the late 1970s, the Mounties recommended keeping his file open based on the notion 'there is much we do not know about Mr. Douglas.' And these revelations may only be the tip of the iceberg: the government has refused to declassify large amounts of the Douglas surveillance material, citing protection of secret sources among other grounds for exempting material, even when censored documents go back as far as the 1930s. A court challenge to this decision has yet to be resolved.[20] An inescapable question arising from this situation is: Just who is the government seeking to protect? Could it be persons within the CCF/NDP who were reporting to the Mounties on Douglas, their leader? If so, it would simply reconfirm just how far intrusive surveillance penetrated into the associations of civil society – in this case into a leading and legitimate political party and the Parliament of Canada.

Targeting the Trotskyists with Dirty Tricks

Operation CHECKMATE and its predecessors ODDBALL and TENT PEG were at the heart of the 'countering' activity. One of the difficulties in assessing the extent and the nature of the operations carried out under CHECKMATE is that near the end of 1974 a decision was made in the Special Operations Group (SOG) to eliminate the CHECKMATE files. The bulk of the material was destroyed, with summaries kept of completed operations but no record whatever of planned operations not yet implemented. The McDonald Commission found this unacceptable, and clearly an attempt to destroy evidence of wrongdoing. This interpretation was strengthened by the admission of Staff Sergeant Ron Yaworski in SOG, who had been in overall charge of CHECKMATE, and the author of the decision to destroy the files, that the 'principal reason' for file destruction was that many of these operations were 'wrong.' He drew this observation from the example of the FBI'S COINTELPRO program (see below) and especially from the harm done to the FBI by the public exposure of dirty-tricks operations against Americans. Were the 'very sensitive' and 'very explosive' CHECKMATE files to be publicly disclosed, Yaworski worried, the security service could suffer serious embarrassment.[21] The McDonald Commission investigators had difficulty in reconstructing these operations after the elimination of the paper record. In part, they had to rely upon the memory of Yaworski, which was not always reliable: he claimed to have forgotten some operations. But what is known tends to confirm Yaworski's judgment that they were 'wrong.'

One example drawn from material originally withheld from the McDonald Commission public report, but later declassified, is of a dirty-tricks operation against the leader of the League for Socialist Action (LSA), a Canadian Trotskyist organization.[22] This is not the worst of the CHECKMATE cases from the point of view of illegality, but it stands as a good instance of behaviour on the part of the state repugnant to accepted standards of decency.

Even as dissident Communists – so deviant that mainline Communists routinely denounced them as traitors and heretics – the Trotskyists were deemed under Cold War rules legitimate targets for security service surveillance and countering. The hook for intruding into the NDP was that the Waffle faction was allegedly infiltrated by Trotskyists. In the eyes of the security service, that was apparently a blank cheque for spying on one of the main political parties in the country. So it comes as no surprise to learn that CHECKMATE 'Operation No. 13' was a dirty-tricks campaign against a leading Trotskyist, John Riddell.

The operation, approved by Sergeant Yaworski and authorized by Superintendent Murray Chisholm, was developed jointly by headquarters and the Toronto field unit. The purpose was to discredit Riddell, leader of the LSA, by exploiting a division between him and the former leader, Ross Dowson. Anonymous letters purporting to come from an LSA member were drafted in security service offices stating that Riddell was suffering from 'extreme emotional anxiety and instability' and was being treated by a psychiatrist. Some of this information was drawn illegally from confidential Ontario health records (another instance of security service wrongdoing in this era), some was disinformation designed to denigrate Riddell's capacity to lead the organization. The letters were sent to Riddell, to his wife, and to leading members of the LSA who were holding a meeting in Toronto. Similar letters were drafted in French and distributed to LSA members in Quebec. Other letters were sent later to Mrs Riddell when she was in Europe, suggesting that she return immediately to Canada in light of her husband's allegedly deteriorating mental condition. Before the McDonald Commission, Chisholm admitted that the SOG never considered the 'possible ill effect that this type of action could have on the state of physical or mental health of either Mr. Riddell or his wife.' McDonald considered that charges could be brought against the officers under Criminal Code provisions against 'false messages' and 'defamatory libel' and sent on the commission's material on the case to the Ontario attorney general. Even if no offence was committed, McDonald regarded the conduct of Yaworski and Chisholm as 'wrong and unacceptable, particularly the letter written to Mrs Riddell, which was designed to alarm her.' Not only wrong and unacceptable, some might say, but petty and malicious. No wonder Yaworski had the files destroyed to prevent embarrassment to the RCMP if the truth about such operations got out.

The operation may have worked. The LSA did split, with former leader Ross Dowson and a small splinter group exiting. How much of this may be attributed to RCMP meddling and how much to sectarian divisiveness is anybody's guess. But Dowson, who was himself targeted by the security service, decided to take the matter to court once he found out, claiming damages. The case failed in court after court. Finally, in late 1985, an Ontario provincial court dismissed Dowson's claims yet again, adding that 'even if the defendants could be said to have acted wrongfully, they were clearly acting in the performance of their functions or role.' Dowson's lawyer, Harry Kopyto (himself a militant member of Dowson's splinter group whose law office had earlier been infiltrated by an RCMP plant), told the press that 'this decision is a mockery of justice. It stinks to high hell ... The courts and the RCMP are sticking so close together, you'd think they were put together with Krazy Glue.' Kopyto was cited for contempt of court, convicted, and ordered to apologize to the court. If he refused, he would be disbarred. This was later reversed by a higher court, but within a few years Kopyto was disbarred on other grounds.[23] By the time the last ruling on this matter had come down, the security service was no longer part of the RCMP and was operating on an autonomous civilian basis, in part as a result of operations like this. Nonetheless, the courts still found that the ex-SOG dirty tricksters had simply been performing their 'functions or role.'

Whether or not the individual Mounties responsible for executing this particular operation could or should have been sanctioned by the law, there were much bigger issues at stake in this and other such countering and disruption operations. As the McDonald Commission argued, when security service officers deliberately engaged in illegal actions, they were willfully disregarding the fundamental principle of the rule of law. Even where counter-measures designed to 'disrupt the activities of groups or individuals regarded as subversive' were not unlawful but were still 'objectionable and unacceptable,' the commission found it 'entirely inappropriate for the Canadian state, through an agency the operations of which are essentially secret, to take coercive measures against Canadian citizens and put them at a serious disadvantage.' Not only did 'secret attempts to manipulate political events and the news media' and the infliction of damage on Canadian citizens constitute violations of important precepts of Canadian democracy, they also, McDonald warned, seriously harmed the agency itself. 'First there is the corrupting effect which the carrying out of such "dirty tricks" is likely to have on the ethos of the security intelligence organization. Secondly, there is the loss of public respect which the disclosure of such tactics is likely to engender.'[24]

Reading Other People's Mail, Other People's Tax Records

Like other security intelligence agencies, the security service had long used certain methods of operation that existed in a grey area of legality. Surreptitious entry into private premises for various purposes, particularly for planting electronic listening devices (bugs), had always been an accepted part of the job, at least as long as the targets of such actions remained unaware of the intrusions, or the targets were considered so unpopular or illegitimate that little or no concern was raised when such methods came to public notice. The latter condition obtained throughout the early Cold War years, and as late as the Mackenzie Commission in 1969, the view of the commissioners was that the 'special steps' security intelligence agencies need to take to obtain required information (such as wiretaps and other forms of communication intercepts) are 'often the only effective means of countering espionage and subversion.' The sole legal recommendation Mackenzie made was that, if legislation were to be enacted controlling wiretaps, it should exempt intercept operations for security purposes.[25] By the 1970s, however, these kinds of methods were becoming more contentious. The surreptitious entries at the APLQ and the PQ offices in Quebec and the Praxis affair in Toronto raised serious questions. So did the dawning realization that bugging of private premises was far more widespread than previously believed. It was one thing when listening devices were planted to catch Soviet spies or Communist 'subversives,' but quite another when the targets were widened to include a range of associations and groups that had never previously considered themselves among the usual suspects. Some form of regulation and warranting of these methods was on the agenda of the McDonald Commission, as was greater control over the use of human sources, always a more sensitive issue than technical intrusions. In all these instances, there was probably a wide consensus that, while some such methods were no doubt necessary under specific conditions, giving a blank cheque to the RCMP to be used when and how they wished was no longer acceptable under the rule of law.

There were two specific security service methods of obtaining information that particularly raised warning flags: unauthorized mail openings and unauthorized access to privileged data in the possession of other government departments, particularly tax records and unemployment-insurance records. Canadians have always held expectations that the privacy of their personal mail is inviolate. Yet, during the Second World War, the RCMP routinely enlisted postal personnel to open mail under the authority of the Defence of Canada Regulations. These Regulations remained in place until their expiry in 1954. Under the umbrella of Operation CATHEDRAL, the security service continued after 1954 to have mail opened without legal authorization. CATHEDRAL encompassed three levels of scrutiny, the first two of which involved only examination of envelopes, addresses, and so on. CATHEDRAL 'C' involved interception and content examination. Allegedly, 'C' was used only in cases of suspected terrorism or espionage. In 1970 a senior RCMP officer reviewing the operation admitted in an internal memorandum that postal workers cooperating with CATHEDRAL were acting without legal authorization and were thus risking their livelihoods. When Michael Dare took over as director general of the security service in 1973, he was not informed of the existence of CATHEDRAL 'C,' and he helped draft a misleading response for Solicitor General Warren All-mand to a question about mail opening from Allan Lawrence, a Conservative MP (and later solicitor general). The McDonald Commission commented that withholding this information from the director general 'reflected irresponsible conduct on the part of those who reported directly to him.'[26] By extension, the minister was left in the position of signing a misleading letter denying the existence of a program that in fact did exist. When Dare did eventually find out about the program, he failed to inform his minister. The minister had been lied to.

With the 1973 questions, the cat was out of the bag. CATHEDRAL operations were ordered suspended, although a few 'C' operations were authorized over the next year. Finally, when Murray Sexsmith became deputy director general of operations (DDG/Ops) in 1975, he ordered all further 'C' operations halted, citing the example of Watergate in the United States and damage to the security service if mail openings were publicly revealed (some ex-Mounties were starting to talk about the practice). He added that efforts to legalize mail opening had gone nowhere; it was unfair to expose Mounties to possible prosecution. It appears, however, that some field operations went ahead without the authorization of the DDG/Ops.[27]

The program did have some support. Some successful counter-espionage cases (Bower Featherstone and Victor Spencer, for instance) did demonstrate the usefulness of CATHEDRAL in securing evidence not otherwise available. There was also the example of a Japanese Red Army terrorist, Omura, whose planned surreptitious entry into Canada was foiled by an unauthorized CATHEDRAL 'C' operation.[28] But did the ends justify the means?

Less ambiguous than the mixed messages arising from CATHEDRAL were the cases of unauthorized security service access to tax and unemployment records. Security of the personal information of citizens held by government departments and agencies was becoming an important privacy issue in the 1970s. With the rapid growth of electronic storage and retrieval technologies, and the potential for data matching and data mining, this is a privacy-protection issue that has grown exponentially since the 1970s. But even in that decade, the idea that citizens' personal financial information, compulsorily disclosed by law to the tax authorities but supposedly kept strictly confidential, might be accessed by police operating outside the constraints of law and with the secret complicity of the very officials designated to protect confidentiality was bound to cause a stir. Yet that is exactly what was happening between the security service and the Department of National Revenue and the Unemployment Insurance Commission (UIC). The McDonald Commission found that the RCMP had 'as a Force policy' or with the 'tacit approval' of senior officers systematically breached the privacy-protection provisions surrounding the records of these two agencies, that indeed 'this practice of law-breaking became institutionalized within the RCMP.'[29]

In the case of tax records, the Criminal Investigation Branch of the RCMP could lawfully access information only for the purpose of enforcement of the Income Tax Act. For any other purposes, including national security, the Mounties would be party to a criminal offence by aiding and abetting sources within the department to disclose protected information. In the case of the UIC, matters were more complicated, especially after the introduction of the Canada Pension Plan and the Social Insurance Number system in the 1960s, which greatly expanded the scope and sensitivity of information held by the UIC. McDonald found that the Mounties had been using sources within the UIC for three decades to access records illegally, even though they had failed to take advantage of statutory provisions that might have provided them with lawful access.

It is known that some of this information was used in questionable countering operations by the security service. For instance, the attempts by 'G' Ops to coerce FLQers into becoming police sources used information about unemployment records of the targeted individuals as inducements. As the McDonald Commission acknowledged, there were clearly circumstances under which some security service access to such records could be justified as in the national interest (counter-espionage and counter-terrorism cases come to mind). But the ad hoc, illegal manner in which employees of National Revenue and the UIC were drawn into cooperation left them in jeopardy, as well as contributing to a general ethos within the security service that the law could be casually disregarded in getting the job done. The situation cried out for better regulation and control.

The Mounties Go to School

One of the three 'Key Sectors' of Canadian society identified by 'D' Branch in the late 1960s as primary targets for subversive penetration was education. In the late 1960s and 1970s, 'Mounties on campus' became one of the more sensitive issue areas where the protection of national security clashed with other deeply rooted Canadian values, in this case academic freedom, the autonomy of universities from political interference, and the youthful tendency to protest and dissent. These clashes added yet another dimension to the image problems of the security service's counter-subversion efforts and hastened the coming of reform. Luckily, we have an excellent and thoroughly documented account of the Mounties on Canadian campuses in the twentieth century, Steve Hewitt's *Spying 101*,[30] which we rely upon for the following brief discussion.

Universities had always been an area of particular interest to those concerned with threats to the security of the established order. As Hewitt observes, 'fearing for students and being fearful of them were both sentiments that were predicated on the idea of a threat.'[31] 'Fearing *for* students' meant viewing them as impressionable innocents who were putty in the hands of teachers with the power to shape or misshape them for good or ill – this fear of teachers corrupting the young was as old as the charge upon which Socrates was put to death by Athens, and as recent as the security service investigations of subversive professors. But by the late 1960s, with student revolts and occupations at Simon Fraser and Sir George Williams universities, students morphed into potentially serious subversive threats themselves, and hence radical student organizations became targets for security service surveillance and perhaps at times more active counter-measures.

Prior to the 1960s, the Mounties had managed to avoid an important lesson: that publicity about their very presence on university campuses would be a red flag to critics. Campus surveillance predated the war.[32] By the 1950s, Mounties were carrying out on-campus investigations of security-clearance applicants, quietly establishing cooperative relations with trusted sources among the professoriate, and keeping a watchful eye on left-wing professors whose public utterances occasionally ruffled conservative feathers. But this was done almost entirely in secret, to virtually no public notice – which was a good thing for the RCMP security service, since the Mounties of that era generally lacked university education and were hardly at home in the ivory tower milieu. What they failed to grasp was that the idea of cops listening in on lectures, labelling certain academic ideas as subversive, and spying on student politics was anathema to all those who saw universities as places where free thought, free inquiry, and free expression were fundamental values.

In the 1960s two things began to change. First, in the early 1960s, security service officers were encouraged to take paid time-out to gain university degrees. The presence of government 'snoops' in lectures led to speculation that professors were being monitored for their political opinions. This was actually unfair, since the officers in question were simply there to further their education, and thereby to improve the intellectual quality of the service itself. But this public notoriety only partially hid the fact that the service had been gathering data on universities, teachers, and students alike for decades, indeed from before the war. This involved the use of sources on campus reporting what went on in their classes. The potentially chilling effect on academic freedom and free speech of such monitoring by the police was obvious and disturbing to the principles of the university. The knowledge, for instance, that graduates might be applying for public-service positions that required security clearances could certainly cast a chill over free expression of ideas in a setting where a student's words might be noted down and sent for inclusion in the files of the secret police.

Second, the emergence in the early 1960s of an active peace movement on university campuses – the Combined Universities Campaign for Nuclear Disarmament (CUCND) – set off alarm bells in the security service, which had been aggressively investigating the Canadian Peace Congress for years as an alleged Communist-front organization. It set about probing the CUCND with the idea in mind that the movement was, if not Red-led, at least vulnerable to manipulation by the Communists. To this end, it tried to recruit on-campus sources within the CUCND to report on their fellows. Predictably, in the changing political environment of the era, this soon came to public notice, first at Laval University in 1961 and then elsewhere. The security service found itself in the unaccustomed position of having to defend publicly counter-subversion operations suddenly dragged into the harsh light of day. The Diefenbaker Conservative government, which had its own internal divisions over issues of nuclear weapons that would intensify in 1962–3 and lead to defeat in the House of Commons, reacted with the usual public defence of the RCMP, but behind the scenes Justice Minister Davie Fulton ordered a halt to campus investigations while permitting the service's continued use of existing sources. The commissioner called for a review, and pending the results cautioned his men against any actions that could lead to public discussion or complaints to the minister. Continued warnings about the dire threat of Communist takeover of student organizations failed to convince Fulton to back down, although Fulton's successor as minister in charge of the RCMP, Donald Fleming, proved to be a strong supporter of the force. Meanwhile, controversy continued to mount, with the Canadian Association of University Teachers (CAUT) joining the fray as vocal critics of the RCMP's university activities.

With the change in government in 1963, Ottawa pushed the RCMP to compromise with the CAUT, and, as recounted in chapter 8, the CAUT and the National Federation of Canadian University Students (NFCUS) met with the RCMP and Prime Minister Lester Pearson in November 1963 and agreed informally on what became known as the Pearson-Laskin Accord. Each side went away with widely different interpretations of what had been agreed. The CAUT and NFCUS thought they had put an end to 'general surveillance' of university campuses, limited only by continued background checks on job applicants and investigations where there were 'definite indications' of espionage or 'subversive activities' (these terms left undefined). The RCMP, thinking that the status quo had been maintained, continued to operate as usual. Hewitt concludes: 'The notion that the 1963 meeting had accomplished anything of substance was a mirage.'[33] Indeed, he finds that university reporting actually increased in the years after 1963, although the Mounties' advocates in the right-wing media asserted that they were hamstrung by the Liberals from following up subversive leads at universities – a convenient cover for stepped-up surveillance.

Even the principle that ideas in classrooms should be beyond the reach of the service's ears and eyes does not appear to have been honoured. To take just one example, files on surveillance of York University contain reports on the alleged political ideologies of both faculty and students, as demonstrated in particular classrooms.[34] Sometimes this information was reasonably accurate, sometimes less so. But in all instances, the question of the relevance to national security of this kind of spying remains highly questionable. No doubt official Mountie policy specified that Communism and other subversive activity was the target. But how could you find the Reds under the university residence beds without watching everyone and carefully and compiling the information in files that naturally accumulated and fattened over time with all sorts of names of persons and organizations of every variety?

The security service's presence on campuses heated up even further in the late 1960s and early 1970s, and once again it was Quebec that was the catalyst. The emergence of separatist unrest and the violence unleashed by the FLQ and other terrorist groups led the security service to Quebec universities, where FLQ organizers and sympathizers were undoubtedly present. Clearly, university gates could not provide sanctuary for terrorists, so there was justification for enhanced surveillance. Then the student occupation of Simon Fraser in 1968 and the destructive occupation of Sir George Williams in 1969 showed unrest spreading to English Canadian institutions. In a federal cabinet meeting on 23 December 1970, the ministers, still apparently believing the mythology surrounding the 1963 Pearson-Laskin Accord, voted to rescind campus 'immunity' but kept the decision secret, deliberately not informing the CAUT. A few months later, in September 1971, there was another change of course: the cabinet rescinded the mildly effective 1961 decision and reinstated the useless 1963 accord. In a memorandum to his cabinet colleagues, Solicitor General Jean-Pierre Goyer informed them that this was 'satisfactory' to both the RCMP commissioner and the director general of the security service. Goyer did require ministerial approval for installing technical surveillance devices on campuses (not actually used at the time), which roused rebellious grumbling among the security service ranks, but Director General John Starnes mollified them by pointing out that they now had 'complete authority' to 'intensify or maintain, as the situation warrants, our coverage of the university milieu.'[35]

On 24 September 1971, just as the government was in the process of giving the security service the 'complete authority' to which Starnes perhaps over-enthusiastically alluded, the Cabinet Committee on Security and Intelligence gathered to receive an audio-visual presentation from the security service on 'The Threat to Security from Violence Prone Revolutionary Elements in Canada.' Including crudely drawn alarmist slides (one showing a bomb under the Peace Tower), this Mountie presentation warned that the radical virus that had infected the universities in the late 1960s was now moving 'from campus to community,' spreading revolutionary ferment to other institutions of Canadian society via graduating 'Typhoid Mary' radicals.[36]

As Hewitt points out, it is ironic that this focus on student radicalism actually coincided with a decline of radicalism on campus and a growing conservative student backlash against the always small number of activists, a trend noted in continuing security service reports from the universities. It is doubly ironic that, having shifted gears successfully from the outmoded search for old left Communist ties to examining New Left movements, the security service found itself bypassed by yet another societal shift. Yet, even as the campuses became more quiescent, Hewitt indicates that the security service's campus operations ground on through the mid-1970s: 'Budgets and personnel had been allotted, rationales for new emphases developed, and a parallel reality created.'[37] The hunt for student subversives continued, even as the quarry began to resemble an endangered species. But in a parallel reality, threats always remained, and thus the need to counter those threats remained as well.

The Mounties' university experience was emblematic of a deep problem in the security service's focus on subversion. 'Having a security service dedicated to ferreting out subversion,' Hewitt writes, 'will inevitably lead to it discovering subversion.'[38] Or as the old saying goes: to a man with a hammer, everything looks like a nail.

Biting the Hand That Feeds: Bugging the Solicitor General

The Liberal governments of the 1970s had an ambiguous relationship with the Mounties and their security service. On the one hand, Liberal ministers, and indeed Prime Minister Trudeau, had on occasion been critical of the performance of the security service, especially in Quebec. On the other, as the seemingly perpetual governing party, the Liberals were protective of 'their' national police force and naturally defensive when it came to criticism. Liberal ministers had to stand up in Parliament and answer questions about security service activities. Their stance was normally to defend, justify, and, on occasion, rationalize the behaviour of the security service. Trudeau was particularly adept at using the principle of police independence to rationalize a policy of maintaining deliberate ministerial distance from knowledge of security service operations. His best-known expression of this argument occurred before Parliament in 1977:

> I have attempted to make it quite clear that the policy of this government, and I believe the previous governments in this country, has been that they … should be kept in ignorance of the day to day operations of the police force and even of the security force. I repeat that this is not a view that is held by all democracies but it is our view and it is one we stand by. Therefore in this particular case it is not a matter of pleading ignorance as an excuse. It is a matter of stating as a principle that the particular minister of the day should not have a right to know what the police are doing constantly in their investigative practices, what they are looking at, and what they are looking for, and the way in which they are doing it … That is our position. It is not one of pleading ignorance to defend the government. It is one of keeping the government's nose out of the operations of the police at whatever level of government. [39]

Despite this laissez-faire stance, as John Starnes learned when he was named by the Liberals as the first civilian director general, the security service tended to view the Liberals with suspicion. Partly this was a result of the right-wing political attitudes that tended to predominate at all ranks, and the perception in conservative circles of the Trudeau Liberals as dangerously leftish. The most vociferous supporters of the RCMP security service in the media, the *Toronto Sun*, edited by the veteran Cold Warrior Peter Worthington, featured columnists who regularly accused the Liberals of being pro-Communist and soft on Soviet subversion. It does not stretch credibility to imagine that these views were sometimes shared by security service officers. After all, Pierre Trudeau himself had been the subject of a FEATHER BED file, and even after becoming prime minister he had been carefully kept in ignorance of RCMP participation in the secret CAZAB group.[40] His predecessor, Lester Pearson, had been the subject of a long-standing FBI file under the heading 'Espionage R[ussian].'

It thus comes as no surprise that senior security service officers were, to borrow a phrase, 'economical with the truth' with successive Liberal solicitors general. The McDonald Commission was dismayed to hear an assistant commissioner assert that hiding the truth from a minister did not amount to lying: 'I see a great difference between lying to a Solicitor General, if he asks you a question, and not volunteering information.' The same officer expressed surprise that the commission had apparently not figured out the 'obvious,' that the security service 'kept certain operational things from the Solicitor General.' The commissioners pressed for clarity: 'Are you stating today openly and unequivocally that the Force had meant never to let the Solicitor General, whoever he was, know of practices or operations that were not authorized or provided for by law?' The officer replied: 'Yes, sir.'[41]

Some solicitors general, even Liberal ones, were seen more favourably than others. Jean-Pierre Goyer, more than his colleagues, appeared often on the same wavelength as the security service.[42] Others fared less well. None fared as poorly as Warren Allmand, a politician of uncommonly liberal principles on human-rights issues. The degree to which Allmand was distrusted, even held in contempt, by the security service emerged from the shadows and into a cruel light of publicity when it was learned that a security service source had secretly taped a 1974 meeting with the minister. Withholding from a minister of the crown the fact that an individual attending a meeting was a security service source, and that the minister's words were being clandestinely recorded by that source, was in and of itself a serious breach of confidence. Worse yet was the attitude of supercilious disrespect shown by security service officers for their ostensible political master in sworn testimony before the McDonald Commission.

The players in this little drama, besides minister Allmand, were: Roosevelt ('Rosie') Douglas, a former university student from the Caribbean who had taken a leading role in the notorious student occupation and $2-million destruction of the computer centre at Montreal's Sir George Williams University in 1969, and a target of security service surveillance; an American, Warren Hart, a security service source who had been 'borrowed' from the FBI to penetrate the Black Power movement in Canada; Hart's RCMP handlers, Sergeant Plummer and Corporal McMorran; and the latters' superiors, Chief Superintendent Belgalki and Assistant Commissioner Howard Draper. Douglas had served a prison sentence for his part in the destruction of the computer centre, but had been released. Hart was acting as his bodyguard as well as reporting to Plummer and McMorran. When the latter learned, likely through a wiretap of Douglas's telephone, that Douglas had been invited to a meeting with Allmand and that there was a possibility that Allmand would offer Douglas a job writing a report on prison reform, alarm bells went off all over the security service. On learning, too, that Hart would accompany Douglas to the meeting, his handlers equipped him with a body-pack recording device. The 2 December meeting, which lasted about a three-quarters of an hour, was verbally reported on by Hart and was backed by the surreptitious recording Hart had made.[43]

Plummer and McMorran's superior, Belgalki, denied giving approval for recording the minister, and, after he had heard about it, Assistant Commissioner Draper gave orders that the tape should be destroyed. The duo, as it turned out, 'just happened' to have the equipment at hand to transcribe and listen to the tape as soon as it was received; the duplicate that was made was retained, despite Draper's order. Whatever conflicting instructions may have been given regarding the taping, it does not appear that any indication was given by senior management that Hart's presence at the meeting was in any way improper, nor was there ever any intention of informing the minister of Hart's status as a security service source. Nor did Director General Dare ever inform the minister, which led the McDonald Commission to observe that his 'imprudent' failure to do so 'either manifested an attitude of distrust of his Minister or was motivated by a desire to protect his subordinates.

The former is unacceptable; the latter is misplaced loyalty if it results in a lack of candour with the Minister.'[44]

Particularly interesting are the apparent motives for spying on the minister. At an initial meeting between Hart and his handlers on the operation, Hart reported that Plummer had said of Allmand: 'I bet the S.O.B. will offer Douglas a job.' Plummer testified that it was possible he said that. Hart also reported that either Plummer or McMorran asked: 'Should we tape the bastard?' The duo further expressed their opinion of their minister to Hart by referring to him as a 'Red, being a Communist, and being against the RCMP.' Hart understood that he was to tape the minister because Allmand was a 'Communist.' Plummer denied calling Allmand a Communist but admitted referring to his 'socialist tendencies.'[45]

Although the Liberals retained a certain amount of ambivalence towards the security service until its final removal from the RCMP, the Hart-Allmand affair could hardly have endeared the service to its political masters. It was an additional small nudge down the road to reform.

The Times They Are a-Changin

During the 1970s a gathering legitimacy crisis began to envelop the RCMP security service, first in Quebec and then across Canada. But spreading distrust of the 'secret police' spying into the nooks and crannies of Canadian society, and anxiety about the abuse of extraordinary police powers, were not isolated or unique Canadian phenomena in this era. There was a wider context to the times, especially in the United States, always a major influence and point of reference for Canadians. The radicalism of the late 1960s had been more pronounced and more violent in the United States, with the civil-rights struggle boiling over into the assassinations of Martin Luther King and Malcolm X, bloody uprisings in urban black communities, mass protests against the Vietnam War, and violent confrontation at the 1968 Democratic convention in Chicago. The president of the United States, and later his brother seeking the presidency, had both been gunned down by assassins. In the decade that followed, with America suffering a historic military defeat in Southeast Asia, widespread disillusion with the institutions of American government grew apace. In 1971 the *New York Times* published parts of the secret 'Pentagon Papers,' which demonstrated that the White House had systematically lied to the public and Congress about the Vietnam War.[46] In 1972 a break-in at Democratic Party offices in the Watergate building in Washington, D.C., took place; it was later revealed by investigative reporting that the break-in had been run by the Nixon White House. Within two years, President Richard Nixon was forced to resign the presidency to avoid impeachment. 'Watergate' became a symbol of how the imperial national security state could be turned on democracy and the rule of law.[47]

In 1971 COINTELPRO, a vast secret FBI program of disruption, countering, and dirty tricks against dissenting, mostly left-wing, Americans which had its origins in the early 1950s, had its cover blown. In the face of fierce public criticism, the program was soon shut down by the FBI.[48] FBI Director J. Edgar Hoover, who died in 1972, had been an untouchable icon well into the 1960s, but now his reputation as a heroic crime fighter was overturned and replaced with that of a ruthless racist reactionary who had cynically abused his powers to spy, intimidate, and blackmail Americans all the way up to the president of the United States[49] In 1975–6 a Senate committee under Senator Frank Church cast a harsh spotlight on CIA and FBI domestic spying.[50] The committee famously referred to the CIA as a 'rogue elephant.' Congressionally imposed restrictions on both foreign and domestic intelligence activities followed.

All this was in stark contrast to preceding decades. In the late 1940s and early 1950s, congressional interest in security and intelligence was characterized by the likes of the House Committee on Un-American Activities, the Senate Internal Security Subcommittee, and Senator Joseph McCarthy. Legislative oversight meant the triumph of the witch hunters over responsible agencies like the CIA and FBI, which liberals sought to protect from congressional depredations.[51] The key difference between the 1950s and the 1970s was the turn of security intelligence away from the external, alien threat of the Cold War years and towards domestic political interventions. In the late 1950s the FBI began to focus on the black civil-rights movement and in the 1960s on the anti-Vietnam War movement. When the FBI was no longer seen primarily as the shield protecting America from Communism, but as a divisive and partisan force armed with abusive state powers, the picture for many Americans became very different. The reality of political policing in a democracy was now apparent to more Americans than ever before.

Canada has never been immune to social, cultural, and political developments in the United States. The American example resonated strongly north of the border, all the more so as it reinforced developments within Canada. The RCMP security service began shifting in public perception from the non-partisan shield against Communism of the 1950s to a force that had inserted itself into the internal politics of Quebec, and of English Canada as well. Here, too, the reality of political policing was being seen more clearly, shorn of some of the legitimating cloak of the past. Canadian media, perhaps inspired by the investigative reporting of Watergate in the United States, began taking a more critical approach to reporting the RCMP's national-security activities. Once ex-Corporal Samson had blurted out his dark intimations about the RCMP on the witness stand, slowly but surely more investigative reporting began to probe the shadowy activities of the security service. While there were no revelations as shocking as the Watergate story that brought down a president, the cumulative effect of reporting that no longer took the RCMP at its word was a gradual fraying of the once untouchable image of the Mounties. Parliament began hearing uncomfortable questions directed at ministers answering for the RCMP, and then heard ministers backtracking and qualifying their defences of the force. The blistering congressional investigations of the FBI and CIA that took place in the American Congress were not replicated in the more tightly executive-controlled Canadian parliamentary system, but with the Keable inquiry in Quebec and then the McDonald inquiry in Ottawa, revelations of Mountie wrongdoing began pouring forth, amplified by a media now attuned to a new narrative that scripted the Mounties more like the Watergate 'plumbers' than like the heroic red-coated national icons of the past.[52]

In brief, the 1970s in North America witnessed a legitimation crisis for the institutions of the Cold War national security state. The institutions would survive, but not in the same form they had held for the first three post-war decades. Under these circumstances, reform had become as much a conservative as a liberal cause, as some shrewder heads in the security service would understand.

There were two additional contextual factors in Canada hastening the path to reform. First was the broad societal trend towards a greater rights consciousness among Canadians.[53] Prime Minister John Diefenbaker had enacted his long-cherished project of a Bill of Rights in 1960, but this legislation, not entrenched in the constitution, seems only to have whetted the appetite of Canadians for a more American-style entrenched charter. This was answered in the Charter of Rights and Freedoms, entrenched by the Trudeau Liberals in the patriated Canadian constitution in 1982. The Charter as much reflected a greater rights consciousness as it fostered it. This focus on guaranteeing individual rights as a restraint on state power had obvious implications for the debates of the 1970s about the role of the security service and the scope of national-security powers. The shift in public perceptions was subtle, not to speak of slow, but in the end was unmistakable: more Canadians began to see the security service as threatening as opposed to protecting their rights. It would be a considerable exaggeration to suggest that this shift was complete, or that a majority of the population had lost faith in the RCMP. But the terms of the debate had shifted onto terrain that was less comfortable for the RCMP than it had been in the past.

A second contextual factor arose from a peculiarly Canadian set of circumstances, the specific form of federal-provincial and inter-governmental relations in the 1970s. Issues about the RCMP security service had arisen first in Quebec with its sharp conflict between separatism and federalism. The role of the security service as a federal agency operating on provincial territory, and the attendant ambiguity about whether it was protecting national security or national unity, inevitably were caught up in the larger issues of federalism. The 1970s saw not only the emergence of a secessionist party and, after 1976, a secessionist government in office in Quebec, but also severe strains on federal-provincial relations more generally, between the English Canadian provinces and Ottawa as well as between Quebec and Ottawa. For instance, a bitter conflict over taxation of energy resources divided the federal Liberal government and the Conservative provincial government in Alberta, but this was hardly the only deep cause of friction in federalism outside Quebec. There might be little if any sympathy outside Quebec for Quebec's secession. Yet, when English Canadian premiers and English Canadian attorneys general looked at the questions raised in Quebec about the operations of the security service against a provincial governing party, they did not simply see a case of separatists complaining about federal opposition to their plans to break up the country. They also saw issues of federal intrusion into provincial jurisdiction that resonated potentially as much in English Canadian provinces as in Quebec. Battle-hardened by jurisdictional quarrels with Ottawa, many English Canadian premiers found no problem in forming common fronts with PQ Premier René Lévesque against Ottawa when it suited their purposes. Thus, the broader canvas of federal-provincial rivalry and controversy cast the narrow security intelligence policy field into a new, reflected light. When the federal government successfully challenged in the courts the constitutional capacity of the provincial Keable Inquiry to investigate a federal police force (see below), Quebec was joined in its legal defence by six out of the nine English Canadian provinces. Here again, the RCMP found themselves wrong-footed in facing what had been, before the turbulent late 1960s and 1970s, a familiar and friendly governmental landscape in which to operate. The force could no longer rely quite so readily on the kind of semi-automatic bureaucratic and governmental support for the status quo it could still count on as late as 1969, when it smartly headed off the Mackenzie Commission's civilianization recommendation.

The Trudeau Liberals Back into Reform

Marshall McLuhan once said that we drive into the future using only our rear-view mirror. This would certainly apply to the Trudeau Liberal government's handling of the burgeoning RCMP scandals and its convoluted path to reform of the security intelligence system. It is very difficult to discern a coherent strategy in the disjointed process at play in the late 1970s and early 1980s. At the far end of this process came the landmark CSIS Act of 1984, but reading backward from that result it would be difficult to reconstruct a strategic policy-making trajectory spanning the previous seven years.[54] Like Captain Renault in *Casablanca*, the Liberals were only reluctantly forced into action, and like Renault, when they did act, they did so under cover of unconvincing justifications.

The problem for the government was seen from the beginning mainly in terms of damage control. This is, of course, not unusual for governments embattled by bad publicity. But the usual recipes for damage control never seemed to work, and indeed just led to worse problems. Ministers were assured by the RCMP that there was no problem, and they passed on those assurances, only to find themselves contradicted by new revelations that led to even more convoluted assurances. After the PQ government in Quebec launched the Keable Inquiry, previous Liberal denials of charges against the RCMP were being shredded in full public view. The Liberal response was to win a court injunction to prevent the provincial inquiry from investigating a federal agency. But this only deepened distrust and inflamed suspicions of a federal cover-up. The Liberals than launched their own inquiry, the McDonald Commission, to pre-empt the Quebec inquiry. When the McDonald Commission threatened to embarrass not only the RCMP but government ministers with further revelations, the government tried to cripple its own inquiry by invoking what amounted to a Canadian version of

Richard Nixon's Watergate defence of executive privilege to block the commission's investigation of ministerial responsibility. The commission stood up to the government, calling a news conference to declare that, if the government wished to change the commission's methods of inquiry, it would have to change its terms of reference.[55] It was the government that backed down.

Whatever the Liberals' hesitations, it became clear that McDonald was the preferred political route to reform. A well-worn path that governments had followed for generations was to utilize a commission of inquiry as a method to keep discussion of scandal out of Parliament and permit a decent lapse of time to defuse the charged political atmosphere before an independent and non-partisan set of recommendations could be presented. It was also apparent that it suited the two Opposition parties to find a way to depoliticize the national-security issue, though for different reasons: the Conservatives were uncomfortable being seen attacking a conservative institution like the RCMP; the left-of-centre New Democrats feared being branded as soft on subversion. The royal commission was a classic Canadian device for dealing with scandal by removing it from the political forum.[56]

Bureaucratic politics also played an important part in pushing the McDonald Commission forward as the chosen policy instrument, and in the forefront here were four senior RCMP security service officers, led by Superintendent Archie Barr, head of the Counter-Espionage Branch. As indicated in the previous chapter, these officers argued that an impartial inquiry was better for the force than trial by media and criminal charges against individual Mounties. Barr and his fellow officers were even prepared to accept civilianization as the price that might have to be paid to salvage the greater good: the reputation and place of the RCMP as a whole. They also recognized that a separated security service could be reconstituted on a basis that would provide an appropriate mandate for the agency and for its officers, something that it and they had lacked within the RCMP. Just how important this intervention was is indicated by Barr's later reincarnation as a key member of the transition team appointed to implement the McDonald Commission's recommendations, at the centre of which was civilianization.[57]

The Liberals had always been ambivalent about the commission they had created and had unsuccessfully tried to hamstring it once it was in operation. Nonetheless, one way or the other, the Liberals had backed themselves into a situation where McDonald's recommendations would set the stage and frame the debate for serious reform of the security service.

Dr McDonald Prescribes

In its 1981 report, the McDonald Commission recommended a new institutional architecture to achieve a greater degree of accountability and control over the security service. Its most significant recommendation was civilianization with accountability. Three years later, Parliament responded with the CSIS Act creating a civilian security intelligence agency and mandating several new accountability procedures broadly inspired by McDonald, but its provisions occasionally departed – in some cases significantly – from McDonald's recommendations. Major elements of the McDonald recommendations were as follows:

- *Civilianization*: A civilian security intelligence agency, separate from the RCMP, and without law-enforcement powers, should be created.
- *Legislative mandate*: The new agency should operate strictly within a legislative mandate specifying the threats to security it is empowered to investigate. These threats should be defined as espionage, sabotage, foreign interference, political violence and terrorism, and 'revolutionary subversion.' The latter category should be differentiated from the former categories, and, in combating this threat, the agency should be limited to the use of non-intrusive techniques to collect information.
- *Ministerial responsibility*: Overall security policy and priorities should be the responsibility of the cabinet, with the prime minister having special responsibilities in overseeing national security. The solicitor general should be the minister directly responsible for the security service. McDonald insisted that accountability must be ensured by an effective system of communications, within the agency and between the agency and the deputy-solicitor general, 'to ensure that the Minister is informed of all those activities which raise questions of legality or propriety.'
- *External review*: A joint parliamentary committee on security and intelligence should be able to examine the activities of the agency in camera. Ministers and parliamentarians should 'endeavour to provide the public with all information possible about the security of Canada, the threats to it and steps taken to counter those threats.'[58] An Advisory Council on Security and Intelligence should assist the

minister, cabinet, and Parliament in assessing the 'legality, propriety, and effectiveness' of the agency. A Security Appeals Tribunal should consider appeals regarding security-clearance decisions.

- *Judicial Oversight and Control*: Applications for intrusive surveillance should be submitted to a judge of the Federal Court for specific approval.

Along the passage from McDonald to the CSIS Act some changes were added and new byways taken; some recommendations disappeared completely.[59] The tortuous path to legislation illustrates the conflicting political pressures at play around the security service in the early 1980s.

Parliament Considers, Cabinet Dithers

The day that the McDonald *Second Report* was published, Solicitor General Robert Kaplan announced the appointment of a transition team to draft the legislation that would establish the new civilian agency. The transition team would in turn form the nucleus of the new organization. The make-up of this team was obviously crucial; behind the scenes, advising on appointments, was an éminence grise who was to play a critical role in the process: Michael Pitfield, clerk of the Privy Council and cabinet secretary. Pitfield was seen as close to Prime Minister Trudeau, who had named him, at age thirty-seven, the youngest cabinet secretary ever in 1975. Four years later, the incoming minority Conservative government of Joe Clark made a point of not reappointing Pitfield whom it regarded as partisan. Pitfield briefly left the public service to teach at Harvard, but when Trudeau's Liberals were returned to power in the surprise 1980 winter election, he was quickly called back and resumed his duties. He advised the appointment to the transition team of T.D. (Ted) Finn, who had served under him as assistant secretary to the cabinet for security and intelligence.

At first the team was headed by Fred Gibson, who had been the deputy minister of justice and who brought the views of someone at a critical distance from the RCMP and the spy world. Gibson believed that the time was propitious, in the absence of any overarching international security threat in 1981, to provide a 'unique opportunity to carry out the formalized establishment of a Security Service in a rational and thoughtful and politically safe environment.' Within a year, Gibson was pulled from the transition team and made deputy solicitor general. He was replaced as team head by Finn, who would later become the first

director of the civilian agency his team had shaped. Finn's views about
the role of security intelligence proved to be less liberal than those of
Gibson, and these were reflected in what was to prove a disastrous
first draft of the CSIS legislation to emerge from the transition team.
A third member of the team, in retrospect perhaps the key member,
was Chief Superintendent Archie Barr of the security service, who had
earlier played the crucial role in gaining the RCMP commissioner's assent to calling for a federal commission of inquiry in order to head off
worse alternatives for the force. As head of counter-espionage in the
security service, Barr had built up an extensive network of contacts in
the Western intelligence community. As James Littleton points out, Barr
'therefore knew what would be acceptable to the sister security and intelligence agencies. Given the intimate and secret relationships among
these organizations, the ability to bring their influence to bear on the
process of drafting a mandate for CSIS had considerable effect.'[60] Needless to say, this influence was not directed towards greater transparency. Barr's footprint, and by extension the footprint of Canada's senior
partners in the spy world, was all over the first draft of the CSIS Act.

Bill C-157, an act to establish the Canadian Security Intelligence Service, was tabled in the House of Commons on 18 May 1983. It caused
an immediate uproar on all sides. Carefully crafted to reflect the conservative views of the security intelligence establishment in Ottawa
and among Ottawa's allies, designed to protect the RCMP by detaching
the scandal-prone security service while minimizing constraints on the
new organization, C-157 turned out to be a political disaster. The draft-
ers had failed to grasp the deep changes in the Canadian environment
in the decade and a half since the Mackenzie Commission had charted
a similarly conservative passage to safety for the security service.

C-157 roused instant antipathy from civil libertarians, labour leaders, churches, and social movements.[61] While these might have been
dismissed as ill-formed views of the usual suspects, perennial critics of
police and security powers, it was more difficult to ignore the view of
the distinguished scholar Peter Russell, who had served as the director of research for the McDonald Commission. Russell declared that
the government had perversely responded to the McDonald recommendations by actually expanding the powers of the security service
while decreasing political controls over it.[62] Another source of biting
criticism was even more difficult for the federal government to reject
– the unanimous voice of the attorneys general of all provinces of the
federation. Coordinated by the government of Saskatchewan, and led

by Roy McMurtry, the attorney general of the largest province, Ontario, the Attorneys General Conference of May 1983 unanimously declared C-157 to be 'an assault on democracy':

> It jeopardizes Canada's traditional reliance on the rule of law and our open and public system of law enforcement and justice. It calls into question the commitment of the federal government to the principles of the Canadian Charter of Rights and Freedoms. The act is so structured that the law of the land, which every Canadian must obey, could be broken in secret by members of the security service. Their conduct would never be scrutinized by police forces, Crown attorneys, defence counsel, or courts of law.
>
> The ordinary safeguards of our criminal law have been eliminated. The force is given carte blanche to break any law completely free from any independent publicly accountable scrutiny or review … The federal legislation sets up an agency which is not properly accountable and possesses dangerous powers. [63]

McMurtry, who declared that C-157 was a 'legislative monster which places freedom in actual jeopardy,' went so far as to help organize a public protest rally in Toronto at which he himself was a leading speaker.

In assessing the intense opposition of the provinces, it is possible to detect a certain partisan element. In 1983 there were no Liberal provincial governments. Saskatchewan and Ontario were under Conservative Party rule at a time when the Conservatives were poised to return to office nationally. Perhaps more telling was the context of federal-provincial relations. The bruising battle over the patriation of the constitution in 1980–1 (in which eight of ten provinces had opposed the federal initiative) had made the provinces sceptical of any measure giving a federal agency special powers that could intrude on provincial jurisdiction. Never before had national security become an object of federal-provincial conflict, but now that it was, the political dynamic had changed dramatically.

Politics aside, the critics had a number of very pointed, substantive complaints about the deficiencies of C-157. One set of criticisms lay in the definitions of threats to the security of Canada that the new agency was empowered to investigate. Most threats under the draft bill were non-controversial (espionage/sabotage, foreign interference, terrorism), although critics bristled when the coverage of these threats was extended to include 'threats against any state allied or associated with Canada.' But most criticism was directed at the fourth category, subversion, or 'activities directed toward undermining by covert unlawful acts, or directed toward or intended ultimately to lead to the destruction or overthrow of, the constitutionally established system of government in Canada.' Critics were alarmed at the phrase 'intended ultimately to lead to,' suggesting that this could empower the security service to spy on people for their ideas alone, with the state judging the 'intentions' of individuals without the need to find actual acts. McDonald had warned against giving the agency intrusive powers to investigate subversive activities, but C-157 made no distinction about investigative powers between the categories of threat. Most of the scandal associated with the security service in the 1970s had come from the activities of the Counter-Subversion 'D' Branch, in Quebec and elsewhere. C-157 seemed to provide legislative cover for more cowboy-style 'D Ops.'

This concern was deepened by another perceived deficiency in the bill. To investigate threats, the bill directed the new agency to obtain warrants that would enable its officers to 'intercept any communication or obtain any information, document, record or thing,' as well as 'to do any other act or thing that is reasonably necessary.'[64] Warrants would be issued if a judge were to be 'satisfied by evidence on oath that a warrant is required to enable the service to perform its duties and functions under this act.' In effect, in the face of scandal over illegal and improper acts carried out by the security service, the government was proposing simply to legalize these acts, with only minimal judicial constraint. There were also concerns that the powers of the two review bodies proposed by the bill, the independent Security Intelligence Review Committee and the internal Inspector General's Office, might be inadequate, and also that that the McDonald recommendation of a strong parliamentary security intelligence committee had been left out of C-157.

Civilianization had finally come to be seen as the indispensable answer for all, even the Mounties. The Liberals may have initially seen civilianization as a way of getting themselves off the hook and of providing legislative cover for a new security service with enhanced powers to do legally what the RCMP security service had been caught doing illegally. If so, they had to think again. In the face of the storm of criticism, they realized that using their majority to ram through C-157 as it stood would serve only to deepen inter-governmental divisions and public distrust: this was a lose-lose proposition. The cabinet briefly toyed with simply giving up the effort and withdrawing the bill. But Prime Minister Trudeau insisted that this was something he wanted to get done in his remaining time in office, soon drawing to a close as he had already announced his retirement. Rather than bring an amended version of the legislation back before the House, the government instead devised an elegant parliamentary manoeuvre. It sent the unamended bill directly to the Senate.

The Senate Saves the Government

This turned out to be an adroit political move. The appointed upper chamber now housed former cabinet secretary Michael Pitfield, who was made chair of a special committee to consider the bill. Pitfield had extensive experience as the senior public servant dealing with security and intelligence matters, and his close ties to Trudeau gave him the opportunity to draw the sting out of the critics' attacks by offering concessions that moderated the problems in the bill while still being acceptable to the prime minister. He held extensive public hearings[65] and then produced a report[66] that met many of the criticisms, in some cases part way but in others almost completely. The government mainly, though not entirely, accepted thirty-two specific recommendations for change, incorporating them into a new bill which passed into law in June 1984 as the CSIS Act with far more restrained debate than had greeted C-157 (the New Democrats strenuously opposed the CSIS Act, but the Conservatives, poised to take office after the 1984 election, voted in favour). It was the last legislative act in Pierre Trudeau's sixteen years as prime minister.

Among the many changes introduced by the Pitfield committee, none were perhaps more significant than the changes to the definition of threats to security, although these, too, fell short of many critics' suggestions. The definition of subversion (the word itself does not appear in the law) read, following Pitfield:

> 2(d): activities directed toward undermining by covert unlawful acts, or directed toward or intended ultimately to lead to the destruction or overthrow *by violence* of, the constitutionally established system of government in Canada

This definition left subversion as a legitimate target, which for many critics was a fundamental mistake. Others were mollified by the introduction of the qualifying phrase 'by violence,' since it limited the scope of subversive activities subject to investigation. However, it did not contain the crucial qualifier recommended by McDonald limiting the service to non-intrusive surveillance against this threat, as opposed to the other, more serious, threats.

Again, following Pitfield, the act added a highly important qualification: 'but does not include lawful advocacy, protest or dissent, unless carried on in conjunction with any of the activities referred to in paragraphs (a) to (d).' The line between activities described in 2(d) and 'lawful advocacy, protest or dissent' might not always be easy to draw in practice. But, by defining legitimate and illegitimate targets, the law provided CSIS with a legal baseline for judging the appropriateness of its targeting. Following its excesses in Quebec in the 1970s, the newly reconstituted security service after 1984 has been able to maintain a clear policy that it does not target threats to *national unity*, such as the lawful forms of the Quebec sovereignty movement, unless it has reason to believe they are being carried out in conjunction with other defined threats to *national security* such as espionage, terrorism, foreign-influence activities, or the still contentious 'subversion.' This may not be an ironclad guarantee of non-intervention against the peaceful sovereignist movement, but it should act as a deterrent against the kind of thing practised by the security service in the 1970s. Another improvement in the CSIS Act was that the judicial warrant system was considerably strengthened from the inadequate method proposed in C-157.

With regard to *internal controls*, the ministerial and administrative lines of responsibility suggested by McDonald were largely followed. The director of the service was expressly made responsible for its control and management under the 'direction of the Minister.' Following U.S. practice, an additional set of 'eyes and ears on the Service' was established through the Office of the Inspector General (IG) of CSIS. In terms of *external review*, the Security Intelligence Review Committee exhibits some significant differences from the model proposed by McDonald, the most significant divergence being the decision not to follow up on the recommendation regarding a joint parliamentary committee to examine security and intelligence issues in camera. Ironically, even as the Pitfield Senate committee was demonstrating the usefulness of parliamentary institutions by pulling the Trudeau cabinet's irons out of the fire set off by C-157, it was rejecting the parliamentary oversight proposed in McDonald. Instead, as Solicitor General Robert Kaplan said several times during the debates over the CSIS Act in the House of Commons, SIRC was to be a 'surrogate for parliament,' given that its membership was supposed to reflect broadly the party make-up of Parliament. Yet, apart from presenting its *Annual Report* to the House of Commons – after the minister has cleared it – SIRC has remained in an ill-defined and sometimes strained relationship with the legislative arm of government. The lack of an established parliamentary presence has proved to be a long-term problem down to today.

The CSIS Act was passed in tandem with the Security Offences Act. This latter legislation authorizes the attorney general of Canada to conduct proceedings in respect to any criminal offence arising out of conduct constituting a threat to the security of Canada within the meaning of the CSIS Act. The RCMP are designated as the criminal law-enforcement agency responsible for investigating such offences. Despite the creation of CSIS as a civilian security intelligence agency, the RCMP thus never vacated the field of criminal law enforcement with regard to national-security offences. This was necessary, of course, since CSIS was deliberately not given any law-enforcement powers.

The Pitfield committee had laid particular stress on the differences between security intelligence and law enforcement, and on the 'severe consequences on a person's life' that security investigations could have: 'Thus the question of control and accountability becomes important, because there is no impartial adjudication by a third party of the appropriateness of an investigation. Since it is so open-ended and confidential in nature, security intelligence work requires a close and thorough system of control, direction and review, in which political responsibility plays a large part. Such close direction is at odds with traditional Canadian notions of law enforcement.'[67]

Parliament, the Senate Committee, and the McDonald Commission before them had all proceeded on the assumption that accountability, both as control/oversight and as review, was incompatible with the principle of police independence and an arm's-length relationship between the executive and law enforcement. Directly related to this issue of police independence was one of the most significant problems identified by the McDonald Commission: the lack of clear ministerial responsibility for the activities of the RCMP security service. Ministers of the crown had indicated repeatedly that the principle of police independence compelled them to remain in ignorance of security service operations. Separation of the security service from its mother law-enforcement agency was thus seen as the crucial element in permitting both executive control and better external review of its operations, as well as enhancing the principle of ministerial responsibility. Unfortunately, a by-product of this separation was that the RCMP, which remained in place to enforce national-security law, were untouched by any reform to their almost non-existent accountability. Years later, especially after 2001, this would prove to be a major deficiency in the overall framework of national security accountability (see chapters 12 and 13).

Nor was ministerial responsibility as clear as it might be. In one sense, the entire exercise from McDonald to CSIS had been an exercise in evasion of ministerial responsibility for the security service scandals of the 1970s. Blank cheques had in effect been given the service to 'counter' the separatists under vaguely defined and sometimes contradictory guidelines, with the clear implication that, while ministers expected results, they did not expect or wish to know the details of how the results were achieved. When scandal erupted, inquiries were launched not into how the political masters had run the show but rather into how the hired help had performed. The violent separatists had been beaten, and the Liberal Captain Renaults pocketed their winnings even as they blew the whistle on the operation that had produced their winnings. The McDonald commissioners had cooperated with this evasion of ministerial responsibility by following up on ministerial behaviour much less studiously than they did on the behaviour of the security service officers. Nevertheless, the new architecture for national security put in place in 1984 did provide a better, if still imperfect, framework for checking ministerial responsibility in the future.

The Long and Winding Road Comes to an End

It had been a long and winding road from Mackenzie through McDonald to the CSIS Act. At its end, the long anticipated civilianization of the security service was finally accomplished, no longer contentious in principle although still contested in form and detail. A civilian security service was established on a legal mandate that specified what it was empowered to investigate, and what it should not investigate, and it was endowed (or burdened, according to differing viewpoints) with new mechanisms of accountability to the executive, to the courts, and to Parliament and the public. How these new structures have worked out in practice will be the subject of the final three chapters.

11

Old Wine into New Bottles:
CSIS, 1984–2001

Protection of Canada's national security had been entrusted to the RCMP since the force's inception. The civilianization of the security service that came into effect in 1984 with the CSIS Act was widely seen at the time as heralding sharp discontinuity in national-security policy and a clear break with the past. Yet, in important ways, past practices and past ways of thinking persisted long after the changeover. The first few years of CSIS as a fledgling organization finding its feet both within the Ottawa bureaucracy and within the wider international world of security intelligence is a story both of continuity and discontinuity, of persistence and change, of old wine poured into new bottles.[1]

Its new statutory mandate aside, perhaps the single most important fact about the 'new' CSIS at its inception was that the employees who had closed the office doors at the end of the last day of the old RCMP security service were the same people who showed up the next morning to work for CSIS. There had been some time to prepare for the new civilian agency: RCMP intelligence officers had been given the opportunity either to opt to become CSIS officers or to maintain their careers in the RCMP in other capacities. A number chose the latter option, but despite ambitious plans for recruitment in the new agency, inevitably the operational core and the preponderant numbers in the first few years were directly carried over from the Mounties: after all, they had the experience, the contacts, and the inside track on the key senior posts. Younger talent, drawn from university graduates with no intervening police training or police culture, would come in increasing numbers as time went by, but for the era of transition they would largely be junior to what can best be described as an overlaying 'old boy's network.' Indeed, 'boy' is chosen deliberately. By the late 1980s, recruitment would be increasingly sought along lines of gender, ethno-cultural, and linguistic diversity, adding yet another layer of potential organizational friction between old and new employees. In fact, the earliest evidence of such conflict was a flurry of official-language complaints brought by francophone employees reacting to what many apparently perceived as rigidity on the part of a largely anglophone hierarchy carried over into the new agency.

The continuity in personnel from the RCMP to CSIS had some paradoxical effects. There was an undeniable degree of resentment and suspicion among those who remained behind in the Mounties towards those who had opted to turn in their uniforms and join the new civilian agency. After all, the Mounties had suffered public embarrassment at having their security component civilianized, when it was plain that the rationale for change derived from the perception that they had botched their national-security role. Although wise heads in the senior ranks had understood that civilianization of the security service was actually in the long-term interests of the force, appreciation of this strategic public-relations vision was perhaps less evident farther down the ranks. There may even have been some score-settling against Mounties who made the switch to CSIS.[2] Among the new agency's officers, there was the double stress of defining their new roles and responsibilities under unfamiliar rules while at the same time having to stake out their turf in a competitive environment, especially when their competitors were their former colleagues.

CSIS-RCMP tensions were exacerbated by the lack of clear demarcation of responsibilities. On 10 July 1984, on the eve of the inception of CSIS, Solicitor General Robert Kaplan addressed a lengthy memorandum to the first CSIS director and to the RCMP commissioner laying out the division of responsibilities between the two agencies under the new legislation. Despite the organizational separation, there could be no watertight jurisdictional divisions in national security. Kaplan had to admit that

> the creation of a separate, specialized security intelligence agency creates a potential for overlap and duplication between security intelligence (CSIS) and law enforcement (RCMP) functions. Investigative responsibilities overlap and may conflict, thus necessitating careful specification of relationships. In practice, a clear demarcation is not always possible between a 'security intelligence' investigation and a 'security enforcement' investigation undertaken under the *Official Secrets Act* or under Part IV [the *Security Offences Act*].[3]

At this early point it was recognized that one of the more difficult issues was that, since CSIS intelligence 'is unlikely to be useable in enforcement work,' the RCMP would be required to collect evidence for court proceedings yet at the same time 'rely on CSIS to provide intelligence information in respect of a threat to the security of Canada which may constitute a security offence.' The minister therefore recommended a set of principles to guide the exchange of information required for each agency to fulfil its responsibilities. He also recommended that a liaison component be established at RCMP headquarters and in each division dedicated to consultation with CSIS, and encouraged the coordination of joint investigations. For a good many years, these ministerial admonitions remained in the realm of good intentions, fitfully and unevenly acted upon.

Much later, after the 9/11 attacks and the passage of the Anti-Terrorism Act 2001, some media commentators mused about the RCMP being brought 'back' into the national-security field, but in fact the RCMP had never left it. The basis of the separation was the creation of a civilian security intelligence agency without law-enforcement powers. It was little noted at the time that the CSIS Act was passed in tandem with the Security Offences Act,[4] which gave the RCMP responsibility for investigating criminal offences arising out of conduct defined as a threat to the security of Canada under the CSIS Act (as well as for offences against diplomats and foreign government officials). While CSIS is charged with responsibility for providing threat assessments to the government of Canada on espionage, terrorism, sabotage, and so on, criminal law enforcement of such offences remains entirely within the jurisdiction of the Mounties. Moreover, given that the dominant policing philosophy by the 1980s had become 'intelligence-led,' the RCMP soon established its own organizational unit with intelligence capacity to target national-security offences – nowhere as large or significant as the old security service but nonetheless a separate player in the intelligence field.

While CSIS had to grapple with a range of new accountability mechanisms monitoring the fledgling agency's actions with a critical eye, the RCMP national-security unit faced little or no effective oversight, indeed, little or no public notice. Much later, in the first decade of the twenty-first century,[5] the lack of effective external review of RCMP activities would come back to haunt the force, but for the first decade and a half it offered the Mounties what amounted to a free ride, while CSIS operated under relatively greater scrutiny. In fact, strained relations between CSIS and its watchdog review body, the Security Intelligence Review Committee, were a leading, and sometimes embarrassingly public, feature of the early years of the new civilian agency. There were times when it seemed as if CSIS was waging a two-front war, not against the enemies of Canada, but against the RCMP on one side and SIRC on the other. Neither conflict was necessary or desirable; both would be greatly alleviated in the longer run. In the short run, these strains made life difficult for a young agency finding its own legs.

The problems would be compounded by some significant philosophical differences in the way the RCMP and CSIS approach national security, differences rooted in the nature of their responsibilities and the kind of tasks they are assigned. Security intelligence agencies tend to see their job as building networks of sources of information for the purpose of drawing fuller and more precise pictures of threats to security; consequently, they prefer in most circumstances to maintain their intelligence assets in place as long as possible. Criminal law-enforcement agencies, on the other hand, are more likely to strike with arrests and criminal charges at the point where they believe they have sufficient evidence to act. Serious differences also exist between security intelligence and law-enforcement agencies over disclosure of evidence in court, especially the use of secret sources as witnesses in criminal proceedings. Security intelligence agencies fear seeing their hard-won assets revealed in open court and thus rendered useless in future. Law-enforcement agencies will be anxious to seize upon every available resource to secure convictions. These differences extend to the matter of retention of surveillance records (law-enforcement agencies are more interested in retaining anything that might be of potential use in court; security intelligence agencies more in retaining only the intelligence gist of surveillance records). All this would later contribute to the fiasco of the 1985 Air India bombing investigation, which resulted in particular public embarrassment for CSIS, but the problems would persist for many more years.

RCMP-CSIS tensions would also extend abroad to make difficulties for the new agency in international liaison. Former RCMP officers who had donned civilian CSIS hats were to find that the easy, informal access to allied agencies they had previously enjoyed with their Mountie hats was not always as readily available – especially when the RCMP continued their traditional close liaison in criminal investigations with agencies like the FBI. The new guys had to earn their trust. And the Mounties might from time to time remind their international contacts that CSIS officers were under scrutiny from external review bodies that yet had no track record of assurance that they could be trusted to protect intelligence passed in confidence from abroad. Such fears were to prove quite groundless in fact, but in the early years of CSIS they may have added to the difficulties in facilitating the same level of international cooperation as before.

The paradoxes of continuity/discontinuity inherent in the transition from the RCMP to civilian status did not stop with organizational rivalries. One crucial element of continuity that was passed directly from the old to the new agency was the fundamental philosophical orientation, the organizational mission as it were. The RCMP officers who came over to CSIS at its inception brought with them not only their professional experience and tradecraft but also the decades-old Cold War mindset that saw threats to national security arising, not exclusively but primarily, from the Communist states and their allies and sympathizers. Intellectual habits of a lifetime would hardly be shed as easily as the Mountie hats. Nor was there much external pressure for them to do so. When CSIS began its existence, the global context was one of renewed Cold War. With Ronald Reagan in the White House inveighing against what he called the 'Evil Empire,' and Margaret Thatcher (the 'Iron Lady') in Downing Street as co-crusader against Communism, East-West tensions had risen higher than at any time since the Cuban Missile Crisis in 1962. Fears of nuclear war rose precipitously in the first half of the 1980s. Incidents such as the 1982 Soviet downing of a Korean airliner that had crossed into Soviet airspace whipped up public anti-Soviet sentiment in Canada as much as in its neighbour. The new agency was expected to carry on the same fight against the same enemy that the RCMP had targeted since the Bolshevik Revolution.

Nor was this simply a matter of countering East Bloc espionage. The old Counter-Subversion Division (once even called straightforwardly the 'Anti-Communist' Branch) was carried over into the new agency, along with its voluminous files on left-wing Canadians, signalling that Reds-under-the-bed were still on the surveillance agenda despite the more restrictive statutory definition of threats to security in the CSIS Act. The first director of CSIS made public speeches identifying the mission of the new agency essentially in the Cold War terms favoured by its predecessor. The issue here was not that the new agency was blind to other kinds of threats; rather, it was a matter of focus and allocation of resources. For the first decade and a half of CSIS's life, it was the ancient Cold War antagonist that continued to take priority.

Ironically, the very scandals of the 1970s that had made civilianization inevitable had been associated not with Cold War threats but rather with the made-in-Canada problems of violent Quebec separatism. Indeed, it had been the tendency occasioned by Cold War blinkers to focus on alleged connections between Quebec separatists and international Communism that had distracted attention from the homegrown causes of political violence, which in turn led to the overreaction and excesses of the 1970s. Some of the lessons had been learned, to the extent that non-Cold War threats were beginning to be examined in a more clinical, less ideological light. The new agency nonetheless began its young life with the Cold War still looming very large on its horizon. For example, the threat of Soviet espionage remained high on the CSIS agenda. Necessarily, of course: the threat had hardly abated (and indeed continued Russian and Chinese espionage operations in Canada remain even today a problem and a priority for CSIS). But it was also a question of organizational inertia tied up in a disposition of resources that reflected an earlier age when the Communist threat stood virtually unchallenged. Even to the extent that that threat remained, it was itself changing from the old military concerns to economic espionage, a trend that the old spy catchers were perhaps a little slow to pick up. This reflected the changing realities of the Cold War itself during its last decade, as the Communist states wound down their role as global military, diplomatic, and political antagonists of the West to a much shrunken role as failing economies seeking, among other desperate measures, to steal Western technology to shore up their chronic underperformance, and to protect themselves against growing internal dissidence and disenchantment based not only police-state repression but on a manifest failure to deliver the material benefits promised by command economies.

CSIS faced a double-edged challenge to its inherited Cold War mentality during its first half-decade. Not only did the persistence of ancient antagonisms tend to divert attention away from new, non-Cold War threats, but as the 1980s drew to a close, the Cold War itself drew to a stuttering, confused, but ultimately definitive end. With the benefit of hindsight – the knowledge of how history actually unfolded – it would be easy to dismiss the persistent Cold War mentality of the late 1980s as hopelessly anachronistic. We should remember, however, that in the context of the time there were fierce debates over the actual course of international relations. Critics insisted that the old maxims of East-West conflict were tired shibboleths that had to go. Yet there were voices in the West confidently asserting that the leopard never changes its spots; that the Soviet Union remained the antagonist, despite all the talk about perestroika and glasnost under the reforming Soviet leader Mikhail Gorbachev. It now turns out that Ronald Reagan wanted peace and was actually reaching out to Gorbachev, despite all his previous bellicose rhetoric.[6] But the advocates of endless confrontation persisted. Even the dramatic fall of the Berlin Wall and the collapse of all the Communist regimes of Eastern Europe, with no Soviet interventions à la Hungary 1956 or Czechoslovakia 1968, did not immediately convince the diehard Cold Warriors. Only the implosion in the early 1990s of the Soviet Union itself and the collapse of the ideology that that ruled that country since the 1917 Revolution finally put paid to the Cold War. Years of global turmoil and transformation meant that a fledgling security intelligence agency born out of a veteran Cold War force spent its first few years facing a kind of existential *crise de conscience*: Who was the main enemy from which threats to the security of Canada emanated? Or was there no longer a single identifiable enemy to counter?

This existential crisis afflicted all the Western security and intelligence agencies. What to do when the once monolithic enemy vanishes? With the end of the Cold War, the 1990s were curiously formless years, exemplified by the vacuous name often assigned to this decade: the 'post-Cold War era,' or more hopefully but even more meaninglessly, the 'New World Order.' A formless era without a clearly defined adversary did not imply an era of security. Rather, insecurity was being redefined, in new and often alarming ways. In 1993 the director of the CIA, James Woolsey, memorably declared: 'We have slain a large dragon. But we live now in a jungle filled with a bewildering variety of poisonous snakes. And in many ways, the dragon was easier to keep track of.'[7] Among the poisonous snakes were 'rogue states,' failed states, nuclear proliferation, economic/corporate spies, money-laundering trails, international criminal organizations, and terrorist networks. This was a new order paper for CSIS, but one that was much more challenging than the relative simplicities of the old Cold War. After the fall of Communism, the mission changed, but where it was heading was unclear, and remained so through the end of the 1990s until the terrorist attacks of 11 September 2001 set a new national-security agenda.

The 1990s were unsettling for CSIS in another way. The fall of Communism at the beginning of the decade had occasioned calls for a 'peace dividend.' Like the calls to bring the boys back home after victory in the Second World War, the peace dividend from victory in the Cold War foresaw substantial budget savings from demobilization and a return to lower peacetime levels of defence and security spending. This dividend never really materialized. The international situation remained unstable and volatile: Canada made a small military commitment to the Gulf War, and followed with peacekeeping forces that were really peacemaking forces in the Somali, Bosnia, and Kosovo conflicts. With the horrific Air India bombing in 1985 and the continued importation into Canada of violent ethnic conflicts generated in the Middle East and South Asia, there was little political appetite for winding down domestic security vigilance.

What did change, however, with no little impact on CSIS, was the relationship between the security service and the budgetary process. Under the RCMP, the specific allocation of resources to the service was obscure, if not hidden. Buried within the overall funding for the national police force, the specific domestic-security allocation was far from transparent, and the process whereby taxpayer dollars were directed to these, as opposed to other purposes, was opaque – by design. Budgeting by subterfuge was an artifact of the Cold War. The Cold War adversary should not be allowed any insight into how its aggressive intelligence activities were being countered, including any gratuitously released information on how intelligence dollars were spent, or even the total amount allocated to intelligence. Any bits of information, however innocent they might appear by themselves, might be placed by a clever adversary within a 'mosaic' picture that would assist the adversary's capacity to wage damaging attacks on our security; the more bits of information, the more complete the mosaic, and thus the weaker national security. The same logic, of course, also kept taxpayers and the parliamentarians who were supposed to represent them as much, or perhaps more, in the dark about the disposition of their tax dollars.

Cold War decisions had always been made in secret, behind firmly closed doors. Countering the enemy, whether abroad or at home, was an objective that by virtually common consent should stand above the hurly-burly and give-and-take of everyday politics. So it was at least through the 1970s. But with the CSIS Act, the notion that an intelligence agency should be held publicly accountable for its actions, and that there should be at least some degree of transparency in relation to its activities, was introduced for the first time. As long as the Cold War dragged on, much of the old deference towards the automatically closed door remained. However, the collapse of the Communist dragon and the emergence in the 1990s of Woolsey's bewildering array of snakes made the process of secret decisions, secretly arrived at, less defensible. By the mid-1990s, the Office of the Auditor General began a series of annual audits of national-security expenditures, offering an unprecedented degree of scrutiny in this hitherto secret terrain.[8]

Nor could CSIS count on the more-or-less automatic consent of those who held the purse strings to meet the requirements of the service. The Communist threat had always been an effective persuader, especially when backed by the spectre of a Soviet Union armed to the hilt with nuclear weapons and intercontinental missiles to deliver them at a moment's notice. The messy and confusing world of the 1990s, on the other hand, seemed to call out for reflection and debate before the cheques were written.

Another contextual factor with considerable impact on CSIS in this era was the growing influence of neo-liberal economics over policy makers. Deficit elimination, debt reduction, and downsizing of the state became leading watchwords in public discourse, as were the policy instruments of deregulation, privatization, and a 'reinvented' government based more on market criteria. In 1984 the Progressive Conservatives came to office pledged to issue bureaucrats 'pink slips and running shoes.' While they had little success slaying the deficit dragon, the same could not be said for the Liberals after 1993 who did re-establish the nation's finances in a surplus position. The implication for agencies like CSIS was seemingly endless rounds of program reviews and cutbacks, and a new imperative to fight for their budgets before somewhat sceptical eyes. In this chillier climate,[9] CSIS found itself required to behave in an unaccustomed way for a hitherto secret agency: it had to cultivate outside support and play the Ottawa appropriations game. Here the new demands for accountability and transparency dovetailed with organizational needs. The result was a certain aura of glasnost as the closed doors began to open slightly, and very hesitantly, to the curious eyes of academics and journalists – who were now armed with the access-to-information and privacy acts, which came into effect as CSIS was taking over from the RCMP.

Encouraged by the civilian watchdog SIRC, CSIS participated in a series of seminars with outside experts in the 1980s and early 1990s.[10] The Canadian Association for Security and Intelligence Studies (CASIS), which brings together Canadian and international academics and practitioners from the intelligence world, began in the late 1980s and continues to the present, drawing the participation of CSIS as well as other elements of the Ottawa secret world.[11] As well, CSIS directors give public speeches from time to time about what their organization is doing and why, and CSIS occasionally releases studies about threats to Canadian security: modest enough forays into the public arena but in striking contrast to the inscrutable face of the old RCMP security service. Greater engagement with the public has changed perceptions. As early as the hearings conducted by the five-year parliamentary review of the CSIS Act in 1989–90, it was becoming apparent that CSIS was winning support from some groups in civil society – especially among ethnic and religious communities who, fearing the effects of conflicts abroad being imported into Canada, actively seek the protection of the Canadian state from violence and intimidation targeting their communities. The other side of this is suspicion and distrust of CSIS among those communities that find themselves suspect because of possible connections with threats from abroad. In some ways, CSIS has become more like an ordinary player on the bureaucratic landscape, although its privileged access to secrecy continues to set it apart.

These, then, are some of the parameters of continuity/discontinuity in the transition between the RCMP and CSIS over the first decade and a half of the new agency's existence. We now turn to some of the specific issues and crises that marked the development of the civilian agency over this period.

The First and Worst Crisis: The Air India Disaster

The first crisis to strike CSIS was its worst. On 23 June 1985 Air India Flight 182, from Toronto and Montreal to London and Delhi, exploded and plunged into the Atlantic Ocean just off the southwest coast of Ireland, with the death of all 329 passengers and crew, most of them Canadians. The explosion was caused by a bomb in a suitcase loaded onto a Canadian Pacific flight from Vancouver to Toronto that had been transferred to Air India 182, even though the putative passenger who had insisted on placing the suitcase never accompanied it, and indeed did not even have a confirmed reservation on the Air India flight. At the same time, a bomb contained in baggage on a Canadian Pacific flight from Vancouver to Tokyo interlined to an Air India flight to Bangkok exploded at Japan's Narita Airport, killing two baggage handlers. Sikh separatist extremists (with elements active in Canada) targeting the Indian government and Indian institutions like the national airline were quickly identified as being behind these atrocities.

The age of terrorism had come home to Canada with a vengeance. The death toll in this disaster was the worst recorded for any terrorist incident in civil aviation history. In proportion to Canada's population at the time, it was the grim equivalent of the American civilian toll recorded on 11 September 2001 by the Al-Qaeda terrorist attacks, which prompted the United States to declare a global 'War on Terror.' Yet the impact of the Air India bombings on Canadian opinion at the time was strangely mild – not indifferent but almost detached – a peculiar attitude that would later be re-examined critically in light of the visible-minority ethnicity of most of the victims. The government of Canada initially seemed more concerned about limiting its liability and keeping good relations with the Indian government than with assessing the policy failures that had allowed the mass murder of hundreds of Canadians. Years later, in 2005, the only criminal proceedings ever initiated for direct culpability in the bombings, the trials of Ripudaman Singh Malik and Ajaib Singh Bagri, failed owing to the weakness of the evidence assembled by the crown.

Despite official evasions of responsibility, one hard fact could not be denied: Air India represented the worst intelligence failure in Canadian history. CSIS, as a fledgling security intelligence agency less than a year in operation, was squarely at the centre of any inquiry into the causes of the disaster.

An Intelligence Failure Like No Other

The intelligence failure was clear: no specific threat to Air India Flight 182 on that fateful day had been picked up and transmitted to the appropriate authorities as a warning that could have averted the disaster, despite the fact that there had been a general warning that Air India might be targeted by Sikh extremists. A close examination of the intelligence situation surrounding the disaster shows multiple wider failures that permitted the specific failure to occur.[12] The identification of the overall threat posed by Sikh extremism to Indian government targets and the identification of particular individuals who posed such threats did take place. But the intelligence process was lacking in coordination and direction at the top, wanting in effective cooperation at the ground level, and disorganized in communicating threat information to those in a position to act on it: failure was virtually assured. Security intelligence in the broad sense worked, to some degree, but *actionable* intelligence that could have prevented a tragedy from taking place was woefully wanting.

Part of the problem lay in the organizational infancy of CSIS and in the poor relations between the newly autonomous CSIS and its former organizational home, the RCMP. These poor relations – later, under cruel public scrutiny, the cause of public embarrassment to both agencies – were in part the result of the kind of turf wars that plague intelligence agencies with separate mandates everywhere (CIA/FBI tensions have become legendary over the years; Britain's MI5 and MI6 have not always been on the same page). Turf wars were exacerbated by the timing of the Air India disaster within the first year of CSIS's life and the jostling between the two agencies as each sought to stake out for the first time its respective jurisdiction. Much of the difficulty lay in the unresolved issues of how intelligence collected for criminal evidence was to be melded with security intelligence collected for secret threat assessments. Some of the difficulties lay in different analysis and interpretation of the same intelligence by each of the agencies. Neither the RCMP nor CSIS, contending over the trees, could quite see that they had added up to a forest, that 'Birnam Wood to Dunsinane'[13] had come, that international terrorism was about to strike Canadians with ferocity and exact a terrible toll.

Beginning with the structural deficiencies in the organization of intelligence in 1985, it is apparent that the system in place was simply inadequate to deal with a threat of this gravity. The main problem was the lack of a single centralized coordinating body that could assess intelligence from all sources and make authoritative decisions as to how intelligence was to be put into action. This structural gap was particularly problematic in light of CSIS-RCMP tensions and the lack of an international profile for CSIS. Intelligence that originated from the Indian government – obviously a crucial source for information relating to Sikh separatists – was relayed primarily through Canada's Department of External Affairs and through the RCMP, an agency with which the Indians were familiar, but not always directly through CSIS. Yet there is reason to believe that, unlike the RCMP, which took Indian government threat warnings broadly at face value, CSIS took a different tack, tending to be more suspicious of the activities of Indian intelligence in Canada and more sceptical of Indian motives.[14]

CSIS was certainly aware that Sikh terrorism posed a threat within Canada, but the full extent of that threat and the imminence of violence on an unprecedented scale were not appreciated. It should be understood that the rapid escalation of Sikh extremism in India was, as the Air India Commission of Inquiry (chaired by retired Supreme Court justice John Major) later commented, 'the result of events in the Indian sub-continent that took place in the same time frame as the transition from the [RCMP] Security Service to CSIS.' The commission went on to admit that, 'even in a relatively stable institutional environment, keeping up with the rapidly changing landscape of Sikh extremism in Canada would no doubt have proved challenging. The impact of the transition from the RCMP Security Service to CSIS made a difficult situation that much worse.'[15]

Cold War preoccupations with counter-espionage still accounted for the lion's share of resources in the young agency. But of resources devoted to counter-terrorism, more were devoted to the threat of Armenian terrorist actions against Turkish interests in Canada (there had been an Armenian terrorist attack on the Turkish Embassy in Ottawa in March 1985; one diplomat was murdered in Ottawa traffic and another gravely injured in an assassination attempt)[16] than to the emergent Sikh threat. At CSIS headquarters, there was a 'Sikh Desk' in the Counter-Terrorism Branch, which was in retrospect woefully understaffed, never managing even to fill all the positions allocated. Even this complement was reduced further during the critical period leading up to the bombing by employees on leave. In the crucial BC Region, there were only two investigators available for the Sikh extremist file, and these two lacked any specific training with regard to Sikh culture and politics. Most CSIS intelligence on the Sikh community was from foreign, mainly Indian, sources.

Watching the Sikh Extremists ... Intermittently

By 1984, CSIS knew Talwinder Singh Parmar to be the leader of the extremist Babbar Khalsa movement in Canada, and it had also identified Ajaib Singh Bagri as a potential terrorist. Yet the agency failed to build on that intelligence into the critical 1985 period. The major reason for this gap, according to the Air India commission, 'lay in the state of the warrant approvals process that had been put in place by the *CSIS Act* in June 1984.'[17] British Columbia investigators had been unsuccessful in recruiting human sources within the Sikh community, and therefore concluded that they required surveillance and electronic intercepts. But applications for warrants received no priority at headquarters. The reasons for lengthy delays in producing warrants lay in the background to the creation of CSIS.

It was the expectation of those who had created CSIS as a civilian agency that it would develop mechanisms to limit the impact of intrusive surveillance on the civil liberties of Canadians. After all, civilianization was in large part driven by reaction to the excesses of the RCMP security service in Quebec in countering the separatists. The RCMP obtained surveillance warrants simply by asking the solicitor general. CSIS was required to obtain judicial as well as ministerial approval for warrants from the Federal Court. This applied not only to new warrants but also to the conversion of previous ministerial-only warrants. In order to expedite ongoing operations, CSIS prioritized approval of existing warrants first, and left new applications at the back of the queue. It was possible to speed up new applications that were considered urgent, but this urgency was never attached to the Parmar warrant application. As the commission of inquiry comments, this 're-flects the lack of appreciation of the true urgency of the threat of Sikh extremism.'[18] Five months elapsed between the application and its final approval, precious time lost. And poor use was made of physical surveillance and electronic intercepts once approval was obtained.

Surveillance of Parmar was continuous for some time yet was withdrawn on 17 June 1985, at the most crucial moment in the terrorist bombing preparations. The watch on Parmar's residence was also withdrawn on the day of the bombing. Surveillance resources were redirected to a counter-espionage operation – a commentary on the relatively low priority placed on counter-terrorism at the moment when the terrorist threat was about to strike.

The conduct of the surveillance while it was in place was less than exemplary. Sometimes the trail was lost because the surveillants were unable to distinguish between different turbaned Sikh men, reflecting the ethno-cultural limitations of CSIS staff at that time. Then there was the bungling of the so-called 'Duncan blast,' which ironically might have represented a signal success. On 4 June 1985 half a CSIS surveillance team followed Parmar and an unidentified man onto a BC Ferry to Vancouver Island (a second vehicle missed the ferry). The remaining car followed Parmar's car to the Duncan home of Inderjit Singh Reyat, later the only man ever convicted in the Air India case. Near Duncan, Parmar and Reyat walked into the woods, followed by a loud explosive sound coming from their direction. The CSIS watchers mistook as a shotgun blast what was in fact a test of the detonator for the bomb to be used in the Air India attacks. Astonishingly, although on a surveillance operation, the watchers lacked a camera and thus were unable to photograph Parmer's travelling companion, whose identity remains unknown to today. The surveillants were unable to gain authorization to continue the operation the next morning, and so returned to the mainland, with the suspects' further activities left unobserved.

The misidentification of the detonator blast supported a mistaken belief in CSIS's BC Region that the main danger posed by Parmar's group was assassinations. Yet even this intelligence failed to make it into the formal CSIS threat-assessment process. The incident was reported to CSIS headquarters the following day, and to the RCMP Vancouver Division. But, when SIRC later examined the matter, it concluded that 'the significance of the incident does not appear to have been realized at the time and we saw nothing in the CSIS files to indicate if any comprehensive analysis of the incident was immediately undertaken.'[19] Even though the RCMP were informed of possible criminal acts, the Vancouver RCMP division did not report the matter in a way that could be disseminated to all the RCMP units that might have needed it, nor did the report enter the RCMP threat-assessment process. CSIS also shared the information with the Vancouver Police, who also passed it on to the Vancouver RCMP, but again the information failed to reach RCMP headquarters.

Listening in on the Sikh Extremists ... Or Not

If physical surveillance was inadequately carried out, the electronic intercepts were, if anything, handled even less expertly. Electronic surveillance of Parmer was finally approved in March 1985. The planting of intercept devices was not the problem. It was the human resources for transcription, translation, and analysis that were inadequate. Strict security requirements drastically limited the pool of potential translators. There were in fact no Punjabi translators available to CSIS in British Columbia, which had the largest concentration of Sikhs in Canada. Thus, the Parmar intercepts were shipped to Ottawa, where they were dumped onto an already overextended Punjabi translator at CSIS headquarters: not surprisingly, a serious backlog developed. Intercepted calls that linked plots to kill Indian Prime Minister Rajiv Gandhi during his North American visit to potential leads in the Air India plot were left unattended as they were not translated and transcribed until three months after the bombing.

But this was not the full extent of the problem. The distance between those in the field and the translator in Ottawa precluded useful ongoing interaction with the transcription and translation process. The translator was left to her own devices to extract what was useful from the tapes. A Punjabi translator did begin work in the BC Region on 8 June 1985, but there never appeared to be any creative synergy between investigators and the translator. English transcripts, with summaries of what was deemed relevant material, were prepared by another person who worked apart from the translator. The tapes were erased shortly after they were processed, so there never was any opportunity to check the actual tapes for deficiencies in the process. Much potentially useful information was lost. Information that was acquired was all too often ignored. The commission of inquiry concludes: 'What is beyond doubt is that no material from the Parmar intercepts made its way into the CSIS, or any other, threat assessment process in April–May or June of 1985.'[20]

The Parmar intercepts were later the basis for one of the most embarrassing errors in CSIS history: the erasure of many or most of the Parmar surveillance tapes collected between March and July 1985. Thirty-three of eighty-three tapes sent by BC Region to Ottawa for translation before shipments were curtailed in April 1985 were in fact transcribed and translated. The originals of the thirty-three translated tapes were later erased. Those translated in British Columbia were also being erased prior to the June bombing. Following the bombing, the RCMP claim to have made an informal request to CSIS that all tapes be retained for possible evidentiary purposes, but in the absence of any formal request, CSIS continued its policy of erasure, although some tapes were retained. CSIS record keeping was so deficient that it is difficult to gain a precise appreciation of the proportion of tapes erased. By mid-October 1985, all the tapes CSIS recorded from Parmar's phone line since March had been erased, with the exception of fifty-four, fifty of which had been reviewed by an RCMP officer rather than CSIS. In November 1985 BC Region told the RCMP that almost all of its tape holdings prior to 4 November had been erased; the director of CSIS told SIRC that all of the tapes recorded between 23 June and 6 February 1985 had been erased. SIRC did its own painstaking but incomplete reconstruction and concluded that it is 'impossible, in our view, to attest that all of the recorded tapes from the March 27–July 1 period were reviewed for their intelligence content before erasure.'[21]

When the erasures were made public, the reaction was predictably one of astonishment and anger. The obvious questions are whether intelligence that might have warned of the bombing was missed and subsequently lost, and whether criminal evidence that might have assisted in gaining convictions after the event may have been erased. SIRC's conclusion was that 'it is impossible to determine independently if any evidence was lost through erasure. We consider it unlikely that any information in the erased tapes indicating plans to bomb the aircraft would have escaped the attention of the monitors, translators, and investigators.'[22] This is, however, only an assumption. The real embarrassment is that the tapes were erased, and we will never know definitively if key information was lost.

No individual appears to be responsible for the decision to erase, nor is there any evidence of a deliberate cover-up. The erasure embarrassment was the result of confused and inconsistent internal policy that appeared to insist on the erasure of surveillance records once they had been scrutinized for usable intelligence from a CSIS perspective. It is doubly ironic that the context for this policy lay in the reaction against the intrusive excesses of the old RCMP security service as publicized in the McDonald Commission, and in a CSIS mandate and cabinet guidelines that directed the new civilian service to take greater account of civil liberties and privacy concerns in their record-keeping practices. To the extent that CSIS was determined to distance itself from scandal and keep within its mandate, there was a new emphasis on limiting information retention, to avoid the impression of police-state surveillance. Moreover, to distinguish itself from the RCMP, CSIS insisted that it did not collect evidence. This 'mantra,' as the Air India Commission of Inquiry was to call it, justified the erasure of old raw surveillance data, even when criminal activity might have been flagged. As the commission observed, 'CSIS continued to mechanically destroy its raw materials regardless of their content, a practice that came to have serious consequences for the Air India trial.'[23]

Threats General and Specific and the Bigger Puzzle

CSIS was only one of a number of departments and agencies of government with roles in play in determining the security status of Air India flights out of Canada. The RCMP were the federal law-enforcement agency, with criminal intelligence capacity as well as the policing authority at airports. The CSE was the channel for electronic-intelligence intercepts from Canada's allies. External Affairs was the channel for diplomatic intelligence from abroad. Transport Canada had responsibility for regulating overall aviation security as well as for administering airports. Individual air carriers were specifically responsible for the security of their flights, including screening passengers and luggage. The problem was putting all these actors together in a way that channelled threat assessments into effective security responses at airports.

The heart of the tragic intelligence failure of Air India was not a failure to recognize an enhanced threat environment surrounding Air In-

dia flights, but the failure to recognize a *specific* threat to Flight 182, a
failure in which CSIS, along with many others, had some share. The
missing element, as already said, was not intelligence but *actionable* intelligence. In retrospect, it is clear that, as the Air India inquiry concluded, there were 'enough disparate pieces of information that, had
they been assembled in one place, would have not only pointed to the
nature of the threat, but would have provided corroboration for the
seriousness of that threat, thereby highlighting the need to implement
measures aimed specifically at responding to the possibility of sabotage by means of explosive devices concealed in checked baggage.'[24]
With the worsening political situation in India in 1984–5, there were numerous warnings from various quarters that pointed to serious threats
against Air India, and even to the specific form that this threat eventually took in bombs loaded in checked luggage. But such was the chaotic
and disorganized state of overall security planning in 1985 that many
warnings reached only some, not all, actors in the process. Security actually worked against itself, with crucial intelligence deliberately being
withheld from key players who lacked appropriate security clearance:
the 'need to know' principle trumped the 'need to share' principle,
ironically undermining rather than enhancing security. And no single
agency, including CSIS, had the authority and responsibility to put all
the pieces of the puzzle together into one coherent picture.

During the Air India Inquiry's public hearings, startling testimony
was received from the former lieutenant governor of Ontario, James
Bartleman, who at the time had been in charge of security liaison for
External Affairs. Bartleman testified that a memory had been triggered
by media reports about the inquiry hearings. Bartleman now recalled
having read a CSE document, an intercept by an allied agency shared
with Canada, that contained what he took to be a specific threat against
Air India just prior to the doomed Air India 182. He remembered taking
this to the RCMP officer in charge of security coordination to make sure
that the significance of the intelligence not be missed. He recalled that
the reception he received was hostile, with the unnamed officer in effect
telling Bartleman to mind his own business, that the RCMP were quite
capable of making their own threat assessments. Apparently, Bartleman's advice was ignored, with the tragic results we know.

The Bartleman evidence caused consternation, since no evidence of
any document precisely answering to his description could be located.[25]
Although the commission of inquiry eventually did locate some additional CSE intelligence after the conclusion of the hearings, it never did

find precisely what Bartleman recalled seeing. However, as the commission quite sensibly argued in its final report, this was not the point. The main point is that the government's definition of 'specific threat' in 1985, and in retrospect, was and is deficient. Given the number of general threat warnings by June 1985,[26] and given that Air India only flew once a week out of Canada, it might have seemed prudent to escalate the threat level – here was a 'specific' enough threat, to Flight 182 – and taken the special measures required to ensure that when Flight 182 did take off, it was with full assurance of security. Every player in the process, including Air India itself, was in effect complicit in the failure to take the threat warnings seriously enough.

How much blame should be assigned to CSIS in this cascade of failings? Apart from the expected problems of a fledgling agency struggling to find its place in the Ottawa landscape, the turf war in which the young service found itself immersed contributed negatively to its ability to fulfil its mandate. Put bluntly, the RCMP failed to provide CSIS with key pieces of intelligence, both their own and those from other sources available only to the RCMP, thus impeding CSIS's capacity to see the full picture of the emergent threat of Sikh extremism. The Air India commission concluded: 'In terms of the most important information regarding threats to Air India in the year leading up to the bombings, CSIS appears to have been provided with very few of the essential pieces of the mosaic possessed by other government agencies.'[27]

A striking instance of the impairment of CSIS's ability is a 1 June 1985 telex that Air India's chief vigilance and security manager in Bombay sent to the airline's offices worldwide, warning of 'the likelihood of sabotage attempts being undertaken by Sikh extremists by placing time/delay devices etc. in the aircraft or registered baggage.' It specified security precautions to be implemented, including 'explosive sniffers and bio-sensors [dogs]' as well as physical random checks of registered baggage, at least until 30 June 1985. Air India forwarded the telex to the RCMP at Pearson Airport, who sent it on to RCMP headquarters, requesting instructions. Headquarters asked CSIS for an updated threat assessment in relation to Air India. CSIS responded with a threat assessment dated 18 June indicating that, while the threat level from Sikh extremists against Indian targets remained high (repeating the information that one militant had promised something big in two weeks), it was unaware of any 'specific' threats against Air India. Ironically, this assessment bore a 'secret' security designation which precluded it being shared with the Transport Canada officials at Pearson.

But an even greater irony was that the RCMP, which had asked for the assessment, had failed to provide CSIS with the 1 June telex from Air India that would have put the CSIS assessment in a different, and more menacing, light. The Major Commission was angered when it discovered that the RCMP had told Bob Rae, who did the preliminary investigation that led to the calling of the commission, that their request to CSIS for an updated threat assessment was accompanied by the 1 June telex – which was simply untrue. Indeed that telex appears not even to have been sent to the RCMP branch that developed the Mounties' own threat assessments. As the commission observed, the 1 June telex was a key piece of intelligence that was never integrated into the threat-assessment process. The former CSIS investigator in charge of the BC Region's investigation into Sikh extremism stated that, if he had known about this telex, CSIS would have put the Duncan blast into a more meaningful context as a test explosion, rather than a gunshot.

There was also CSE intelligence indicating that Air India was to undertake specific security measures for its flights as a result of threats by Sikh extremists. Airport security was being beefed up in India in June. Yet the RCMP, CSIS, and Transport Canada tended to view Indian demands for better security in Canada as an attempt to get the Canadian government to assume more of Air India's security costs. In the wider context of credible threat warnings about Sikh extremism, if the Indian government's airline-security precautions had been made widely known to the relevant Canadian players, a significant risk of a bomb being planted on Flight 182 might have been recognized. Remarkably, however, the CSE intelligence seemed to have gone nowhere, and certainly not to CSIS. The Major Commission summed up the bleak picture:[28]

> The consequence of these deficient arrangements was that CSIS, the government agency that was given the primary responsibility for threat assessment, did not have sufficient access to facts about the threat of Sikh extremism. Lacking good access to sources of its own within the Sikh community, CSIS was heavily dependent on other agencies, both foreign and domestic, for the information it needed to understand the threat. CSIS had an abundance of threat information from the Indian government about the situation in India and about what was going on in the Sikh community in Canada, but it was unable to corroborate it. Without corroborating information, however, the large volume of information from the Government of India gave the impression that it was 'crying wolf.'

CSIS's lack of access to sufficiently detailed information, perhaps compounded by a lack of necessary technical skill, compromised CSIS's ability to identify the nature of the danger and to determine, with any degree of reliability, the likelihood that it might materialize. The result was the production of threat assessments that provided a qualitative assessment of the danger as 'high' or 'elevated,' with little detail that would allow a recipient of the assessments to make intelligent decisions as to how to deploy, or how to prioritize the deployment of, scarce protective resources, which is, ultimately, the purpose of threat assessment.

In terms of the lamentable turf war between CSIS and the RCMP, and notwithstanding the bitter comments of retired RCMP witnesses at the Air India hearings, the truth is that the two agencies were engaged in parallel threat-assessment processes, and CSIS had as good, or in some cases, better intelligence than the RCMP – despite being kept in the dark by the Mounties about some key pieces of the puzzle. But this is beside the point. Parallel assessment processes – each inadequate, poorly communicating with one another – substituted for a single centralized location for the analysis of all-source intelligence that alone might have provided the basis for actions that could have prevented the atrocity that was Air India.

Turf Wars and Post-Bombing Investigative Futilities

To make matters worse, interagency rivalries continued into the post-bombing era, impeding the capacity of the government of Canada to carry out a criminal investigation that identified and convicted those responsible for the worst mass-murder case in Canadian history. CSIS shares responsibility with the RCMP for this egregious example of governmental dysfunction, but the problem started with the overall government response in 1985: in the first two years after Flight 182 went down, the government's primary concern was less about mounting an effective criminal investigation than about assessing how best to limit the government's liability. In this context of what can best be described as a culture of narrow corporate self-interest, marshalling appropriately coordinated institutional machinery for criminal investigation was not a front-burner concern. Instead, the RCMP and CSIS were left to their own devices in working together. Their own devices were not good enough.

At the core of the investigative tension between the two agencies lies the perennial issue of evidence, or more precisely, the differing interpretations of evidence held by security intelligence and law-enforcement agencies. And along with this issue lay another associated problem: the protection of human source 'assets.' When CSIS turned over security intelligence to the RCMP, it became evidence for criminal prosecution and CSIS sources became potential witnesses. Consequently, CSIS sometimes delayed turning over information, wishing to exploit the source of that information to the maximum before relinquishing control. Moreover, even when sources were produced, it turned out that CSIS record keeping was not designed to facilitate the evidentiary use of that source's information. A telling example is the use or misuse of a statement of one source ('Ms. E') who told CSIS that, the night before Flight 182, Ajaib Singh Bagri had come to her door, asking to borrow her car to go to the airport and telling her that only the luggage would be travelling. CSIS held off passing on this remarkable piece of potential evidence to the RCMP, based on an assumption that the RCMP would scare off the source, resulting in the end of her usefulness. Eventually, the bare minimum of information was given to the RCMP; it was enough to ensure that CSIS met its legal obligations but not enough to alert the RCMP to the gravity of the information. Needless to say, when the full significance did appear later, CSIS behaviour did little to allay RCMP suspicions about lack of cooperation.

Yet subsequent mishandling of 'E' by the RCMP amply confirms CSIS fears about the force's methods. Despite warnings by her CSIS handler that she would be fearful if approached by the RCMP, the Mounties in 1990 went ahead undeterred. She was subjected to an aggressive taped interview at RCMP headquarters, during which she expressed anxiety about her personal safety (considering that several potential witnesses were murdered, attacked, or intimidated by threats of violence, her fears seem entirely justifiable). The RCMP investigators showed reckless disregard for protecting her identity, with the consequence that she ultimately refused further cooperation and feigned memory loss when called to testify at trial.[29] CSIS-RCMP tensions worked at cross-purposes in 'E's' case in another way: lengthy interviews with 'E' by her CSIS handler over a number of years with inadequate record keeping by criminal-investigation standards may have 'contaminated' 'E's' testimony at trial. At least that allegation by defence counsel was hard to refute.

In another case ('Mr A'), a source with possibly significant information about the bombing was approached as a joint RCMP/CSIS opportunity. CSIS was given first go, but was so impressed with the source's potential that it decided to keep him as a CSIS source with assurances of confidentiality, later revealing 'A's' information to the RCMP without indicating the actual source. Yet, when CSIS was finally compelled to hand over 'A' to the RCMP for questioning, a brief, unsympathetic interview by the Mounties left 'A' fearful for his safety and henceforth uncooperative, while the RCMP dismissed his usefulness almost out of hand. Neither agency 'won,' while the investigation lost.

The cases of 'E' and 'A' were not the only examples of the RCMP placing potential sources and witnesses in jeopardy by not protecting them and keeping their identities secret. The Air India inquiry sums up the bleak picture with clarity:

> Sources have rightfully been described as CSIS's lifeblood. CSIS's long-term investigation into Sikh extremism in the late 80's and early 90's depended on its ability to develop long-term relationships with individuals who could provide the Service with insight into what was happening in the Sikh community. Time and again, when CSIS did pass criminal information it received from a source to the RCMP, it ended up being forced to terminate its relationship with that source entirely. This was usually in order to protect the evidentiary value of the source's potential testimony from 'contamination' and from allegations of 'coaching' by CSIS, though at times it was simply the result of the source's refusal to cooperate further with anyone because of the RCMP's heavy-handed approach. The RCMP's concerns about the impact of CSIS involvement on eventual prosecutions were not unfounded, especially in light of CSIS's constant failure to preserve records of its dealings with its sources. On the other hand, the RCMP's bull-headed approach burned bridges for both agencies to the sources. The repeated loss of some of its most promising sources had, not surprisingly, a significant negative impact on morale among the CSIS investigators. CSIS's reluctance to pass information with potential criminal relevance over to the RCMP can accordingly be understood, if not condoned. The combination of the RCMP's aggressive approach and its tendency to quickly discount sources often led to a lose/lose outcome: CSIS lost its source and the RCMP failed to gain any 'evidence,' or even any information, from the source.
>
> Like opposing teams running in pursuit of the ball around a soccer field without goalposts, CSIS and the RCMP continued to actively pursue exclusive access to sources, without much clarity as to exactly what they thought they were trying to accomplish. A simplistic and inflexible view

that CSIS was concerned with 'intelligence' whereas the RCMP dealt with 'evidence' led the agencies to approach their investigations mechanically. Without stopping to think about whether their 'usual' methods made sense, both agencies as often as not ended up sabotaging their own interests as much as each other's.[30]

CSIS officers did succeed better than the RCMP in gaining information from human sources during the post-bombing era, perhaps because their interviewing technique was better, perhaps simply because they were not the police. As the commission wryly comments: 'It then proceeded to render that information essentially useless for the purpose of bringing the perpetrators for the bombing to justice as a result of its stubborn and unreflective insistence on not collecting "evidence."'[31]

Accountability Delayed, Accountability Denied

CSIS, unlike the RCMP, had a public watchdog to impose accountability. The Security Intelligence Review Committee was the appropriate body to review CSIS's role in relation to the Air India bombing, and it did begin to investigate in the late 1980s. Government united across the board to successfully oppose a SIRC review, however, citing possible interference with the ongoing criminal investigation and the trial of Inderjit Singh Reyat. Less creditably, government was closing ranks to cover its own mistakes, and persisting in its initial concern to limit its liability in civil litigation from the victim's families. Against SIRC Chair Ron Atkey's better judgment, SIRC bowed to the pressure and delayed any investigation. After the conviction of Reyat in 1991, the only criminal conviction to this date secured in the case, calls once again mounted for a public inquiry.[32] Once again, government agencies aggressively fought against any external review. An Interdepartmental Working Group prescribed a common front against a possible SIRC review on the basis of potential damage to the ongoing RCMP investigation, unimpressive though that investigation actually was. When SIRC finally did begin a formal review, the RCMP and other players deliberately limited the amount of information they provided to the SIRC review. Looking back on a seven-year delay, Ron Atkey later admitted that Air India did not represent SIRC's 'finest hour.'[33] In any event, SIRC's review mandate was strictly limited to CSIS activity alone, and its review made only tangential comments on the RCMP and other agencies' roles in what was, after all, a generalized governmental failure. For a full accounting, the families of the Air India victims had to wait until a public inquiry was called in 2006. The final report of this inquiry was published on the twenty-fifth anniversary of the bombing – a full quarter of a century later. The government responded to the wide-ranging recommendations of the commission in a manner that disappointed former Commissioner Major, as well as independent observers and the families of the victims. It made vague promises to look into and examine Major's reform proposals – though rejecting outright his central recommendation for a national-security 'czar' to coordinate security intelligence across agencies and departments – but it showed little interest in expanding external accountability mechanisms apart from a previously indicated intention to beef up the RCMP complaints process.[34] Thus, on top of all the other failures in the Air India disaster, one can add a failure of accountability.

Air India was the perfect storm. CSIS would survive the storm, but in part because the multiple, cascading failures, including those of CSIS, were hidden for so long. There were, clearly, few or no encouraging signs for the new agency to be found in the Air India fiasco. At the same time, pessimism was compounded by troubles at the top of CSIS.

A 'Venomously Dangerous Reptile' Loses Its Head

The first director of CSIS was, fittingly, a civilian rather than an old RCMP man. Thomas D'Arcy (Ted) Finn was a career public servant with some experience in the secret world. A protégé of Michael Pitfield, he had served in various capacities in the Privy Council Office, including a stint in the late 1970s and early 1980s as secretary to the Cabinet Committee on Security and Intelligence, overseeing the government response to the McDonald Commission. In 1981 he was named executive director of the transition team that set up CSIS (see chapter 10), later taking over the team and finally being given the job of running the new agency at its inception. Despite Finn's credentials, it was to prove an infelicitous choice. Some of the problems could be attributed directly to Finn's administrative style, but more were rooted in deeper organizational and personnel problems that Finn was unable to resolve.

Ted Finn was the son of a crime reporter for the *Ottawa Citizen*, Joe Finn. A tough-talking, hard-drinking, humorous, larger than life Ottawa valley Irishman, the elder Finn was something of a legend in his own time. His son, by contrast, was quiet, serious, somewhat dour – the perfect civil servant. But there was one gap in his public-service résumé: he had never had responsibility for running a large organization. Finn had a lot on his plate, running a new agency drawn out of the paramilitary RCMP organization that carried the scars and baggage of the security service's past and required, under public and parliamentary scrutiny, fundamental redirection. The task called for both toughness and imagination. Finn didn't have enough of either.

Finn's problems started with his senior management team. Four out of his five deputy directors were ex-RCMP security service men.[35] On the one hand, the lengthy RCMP service records of senior CSIS managers were hardly surprising. Where else would the fledgling agency turn for the necessary experience and expertise? But, despite the civilian director, the heavy RCMP hand at the top set a tone for the agency as a whole, consistently favouring ex-RCMP personnel in recruitment and promotion over the kind of new civilian blood that CSIS obviously required. This was a problem quickly identified by the service's new watchdog, SIRC. Ironically, another major problem also identified by SIRC was the intense rivalry and turf-war mentality that set in between the RCMP and CSIS. Just as CSIS was struggling against the hostility of the Mounties from the outside, it was being criticized for being dominated on the inside by old Mounties and by the old Mountie mentality. Strong leadership was needed to deal with these problems, but not enough was forthcoming.

Part of the administrative shortfall lay in Finn's style, part lay in the senior management structure he set up. Rather than dividing up responsibilities with clear lines of demarcation between his strong-minded deputies, Finn seems to have deliberately planned for overlapping jurisdictions. This system, instead of fostering creative tensions, exacerbated disputes and prolonged decision making. Finn seems to have failed to impose consistently his own decisive hand. The predictable result was delay, confusion, and indirection. Big issues required decisive action; when that did not come, the issues just got bigger. To make matters worse, all his senior management team was headed for the exits sooner rather than later, most through retirement. There was a senior management transition trap opening up.

Finn seems to have shared the Cold War ideological orientation of the old RCMP security service.[36] Certainly, his leadership did not challenge the grip of old Cold War thinking on the service, even as the Soviet empire was rapidly crumbling and, as Air India had demonstrated in shocking fashion, Reds under the bed could no longer claim primary attention.

The general persistence of the RCMP culture had concrete implications for CSIS performance. The Counter-Subversion Branch continued to carry out surveillance and compile files on perfectly legitimate groups and individuals just as the old RCMP security service had done to the displeasure of the McDonald Commission, despite the CSIS Act's exclusion of 'lawful advocacy, protest and dissent' from its mandate. Based on a six-month study of CSIS operations, SIRC pointed out the persistence of an inappropriate anti-left wing bias that could not be justified under the act, and called for the closure of the branch.[37]

In fairness to Finn, there was one important break with the old RCMP culture. Under pressure from Parliament and from SIRC, Finn indicated in 1985 that homosexuality would not be a bar to employment in CSIS. In keeping with the new realities of the Charter of Rights and a broader transformation of social values, Finn's decision effectively cut off a line of ugly continuity in national-security culture from the 1950s, what Gary Kinsman and Patrizia Gentile call the state-sponsored 'War on Queers.' Battles over the 'security' status of gays and lesbians continued through the 1980s, but the battlefield now was the Armed Forces and, to an extent, the RCMP; the security service had largely exorcised this particular demon simply by whisking the spectre away.[38]

SIRC's public finger pointing at the service highlighted another failing of Ted Finn: an inability to adapt to the new age of greater transparency and accountability. CSIS began life with a series of accountability mechanisms imposed upon it that were alien and incomprehensible to the old RCMP officers who were used to almost complete insulation from parliamentary or public scrutiny. Finn, the civilian who had presided over the transition to civilianization brought about by RCMP lawlessness and wrongdoing in the name of national security, should have forced the service to accept and work within the new accountability framework. Instead, he encouraged diehard resistance, particularly to SIRC, which reported many of its findings publicly.

For its part, SIRC under the aggressive leadership of its first chair, former Tory cabinet minister Ron Atkey, was intent upon carving out a substantive, as opposed to merely symbolic, role for itself vis à vis the agency it was reviewing. In hindsight, this was a crucial first stage in establishing SIRC's credibility and effectiveness for the future.[39] Atkey once described his role as that of being a 'pain in the ass' to CSIS.[40] Difficult as this may have been, on both sides, it ultimately paid off as SIRC has established itself not merely as a public watchdog over the security service but, equally important, as a positive force for improving CSIS performance and compliance with law and ministerial direction. Much later, in 2004, a future director of CSIS would tell a public inquiry that, on balance, SIRC has made CSIS a better organization than it would have been in the absence of an external review body, and that CSIS, to its own benefit, has internalized many of the lessons of accountability.[41] But this is wisdom that comes from experience and growing familiarity between the reviewer and the reviewed. It was not present in the first few years.

When Atkey's SIRC produced its critical evaluation of the Counter-Subversion Branch, and parliamentary critics of CSIS stepped up their attacks, Finn's response was to come out slugging. On 14 July 1987 he sent a letter to Atkey that was intemperate in tone and reckless in judgment. The SIRC report, Finn angrily asserted, had 'distorted reality, was full of half-truths, and outright errors and misrepresentations.' Worse, he darkly hinted that SIRC might have compromised national security by undermining confidence in CSIS and 'leaving the Service unable to carry out its very important responsibilities.' 'The characterization of former policemen as insensitive and disrespectful of individual rights has attacked morale and generated a dangerous inner turmoil within the Service.' In rhetoric that must be described as over the top, he wrote that SIRC had fostered an image of CSIS as a 'venomously dangerous reptile.'[42]

Dangerous or not, the 'reptile' was about to lose its head. In precisely the kind of scenario that SIRC had warned against, sloppy corner cutting and disregard for the law on the part of CSIS led to the collapse of an important legal case against Sikh terrorism. Harjit Singh Atwal had been charged with criminal conspiracy in an attack against a visiting Punjabi cabinet minister on Vancouver Island in 1986. CSIS electronic intercepts implicating Atwal were the main basis of the crown's case. But on 11 September 1987, in the Federal Court of Appeal, instead of applying for the usual national-security exemption from the disclosure of CSIS intelligence in open court, CSIS instead offered the court a startling apology, admitting that the application for the warrant authorizing the Atwal intercepts had been riddled with errors, some blatantly obvious, and was based on allegations by a discredited informant previously sacked by another branch of CSIS.[43] Yet various levels of officials had signed off on the application without questioning it, finally including Director Finn and the solicitor general. All this had been known within CSIS as early as 26 August, and the agency was now steeled for the inevitable aftermath. The same afternoon that the warrant fiasco was revealed publicly in court, Finn took responsibility and resigned. By the time he departed, virtually all of his senior management team was also gone. Three years into CSIS's life as a separate agency, it was time for serious renovation.

The bungled warrant application and the Finn resignation simply hastened a process of forced renovation already in motion. The solicitor general, James Kelleher, had received the highly critical SIRC report in June. A month later, Kelleher appointed an Independent Advisory Team, headed by a highly respected former senior public servant, Gordon Osbaldeston, which was charged with investigating the management difficulties at CSIS as well as the problem of its counter-subversion operations and making recommendations for reform. Even before the Osbaldeston team began work, Kelleher had decided that disbanding the Counter-Subversion Branch was inevitable and desirable, as SIRC had publicly recommended. Kelleher, a Conservative with decidedly liberal views, had clashed with CSIS before. The ex-Mounties at the top of the new service treated him with open contempt, rather as they had treated the liberal Solicitor General Warren Allmand in the late RCMP era. Kelleher, who had little or no prospect of re-election in his own constituency, which was normally solidly Liberal, seems to have decided to do the right thing regardless of consequences. The combination of the liberal Tories Kelleher and Atkey and the public servant Osbaldeston overpowered the old Mountie contingent. That the latter were in the process of self-destructing hastened the reform agenda. In retrospect, this was a decisive moment. SIRC had laid down the challenge publicly over counter-subversion. In effect, the external review body had prescribed a major institutional change within CSIS. If the government had ignored the SIRC recommendation, CSIS would have been confirmed in its course of resistance to change. Accepting the recommendation, on the other hand, meant that in effect SIRC was helping to shape the CSIS agenda.

By the time Osbaldeston reported to Kelleher in late October, Finn and many of the senior ex-Mounties were gone. The organization was ripe for new direction, now under a new director, Reid Morden, a career public servant coming out of the PCO and External Affairs, with a strong record in defence, trade, and foreign-policy issues. Osbaldeston provided an extensive agenda for him to work on.[44]

Although Osbaldeston cautioned that SIRC's public criticism had hurt morale in CSIS, his report in all essentials agreed with SIRC, and indeed put some bureaucratic flesh on SIRC's recommendations. SIRC had found serious problems in CSIS management, specifically a failure to progress towards a broader mix of skills, education, and background appropriate to a civilianized service and reflective of Canadian social realities. In brief, CSIS was found to be sticking to a white male anglophone Mountie model. SIRC had pointed to the underrepresentation of francophones and the resulting problems of bilingualism. Osbaldeston rightly added women and ethnic minorities, in regard to whom it found CSIS even more wanting. While this was an agenda for recruitment that would take many years to fulfil, Morden was ready to set the process in motion.

But this was only one set of management deficiencies. When Osbaldeston looked at CSIS as an organization, he found a serious problem at the very top, in leadership. 'We have observed,' he wrote, 'a formal, hierarchical decision-making process that has tended to isolate the Director and that is unsuited either to the redefined security intelligence activities or to the management of people in today's world.' There was no overall direction in integrating policy and programs according to corporate-planning objectives. The compartmentalized management committee structure 'inhibits the accommodation of new or different points of view.' The director, Osbaldeston insisted, 'must chair important internal management committees for his leadership to be manifest.' Morden followed this advice and chaired all important committees. Osbaldeston also identified an endemic communication problem at all levels, which could be traced to 'an inbred proclivity for secrecy as well as to the organizational structure itself.'[45]

Besides enhancing the control of the agency in the hands of the director, Osbaldeston stressed the 'primacy' of the minister in the decision-making process: 'He is the linchpin in both the legal framework and the Government policy framework. It is essential that the Solicitor General continue to exert political control.'[46]

CSIS was seen to be an organization 'uncomfortable in the limelight and not used to close political scrutiny.' Damningly, Osbaldeston found that, 'after three years of transition, CSIS still looks very much like the [RCMP] Security Service. Compartmentalization and secrecy stifle communication; priorities are driven by operational rather than strategic considerations … There has been much resistance to change.' CSIS itself, Osbaldeston insisted, 'must take responsibility for dealing openly with its people in this climate of change. Only in this way can an appropriate set of values be developed and the self-esteem of the Service and its people be established.'[47] There followed detailed prescriptions for organizational restructuring along more modern administrative lines, all of which were more or less followed under Morden. Of particular interest was advice to beef up the analytical and research capacities, with some downplaying of the dominant operational orientation.

Finally, there was a straightforward recommendation to close down the Counter-Subversion Branch. When Osbaldeston examined the concept of counter-subversion in the CSIS culture, he argued that this 'soon leads one to the entire targeting process and thereby illuminates one of the weaknesses in the Service's corporate culture.' The problem was that there were no priorities for targeting being set by analysis, and the skills for distinguishing subversion from dissent were lacking. In polite bureaucratic language, Osbaldeston concluded that the targets of the Counter-Subversion Branch were mostly not worth the resources devoted to them, and certainly not worth the intrusive methods of investigation habitually employed by this branch. Osbaldeston did not emphasize the civil-liberties issues, beyond a general admonition that the rule of law must be respected, but the implications were clear: the McDonald Commission had found that the RCMP Counter-Subversion Branch had been tipping the balance dangerously away from liberty in a misguided attempt to maintain security from 'threats' that were never really threats at all; the new civilian agency was following much the same path. Osbaldeston, SIRC, and the solicitor general all now agreed that it was time to blow the whistle. The branch was to be closed; a few files with relevance to threats as defined in the CSIS Act were to be dispersed to the Counter-Espionage and Counter-Terrorism branches. The fate of the remainder was uncertain, and might have been slated for destruction until scholars intervened and secured their transfer to the national archives for the historical record (some of the records referred to in this book are drawn from these collections).

Although the management changes were of more long-term importance to CSIS as an organization, it was the closure of the Counter-Subversion Branch that had the highest public visibility and the greatest symbolic impact. In many ways it was this, more than the actual inception of CSIS, that closed the door on the RCMP Cold War past. Even under CSIS auspices, the Counter-Subversion Branch never really emerged from under the weight of all those files on all those Canadians considered 'left-wing' by politically unsophisticated Red hunters. Just two years before the closure, 329 people, mostly Canadian, had perished as a result of an all-too preventable terrorist attack motivated by issues that had nothing to do with Communism. And within a couple of years, the Berlin Wall would fall and Communism would collapse. It was definitely time for CSIS to move on, but it required external pressure to make the changes.

Following the closure of the Counter-Subversion Branch, SIRC raised the issue of the continued presence of section 2(d) of the CSIS Act, the so-called 'subversion' clause, defining as a threat to the security of Canada activities directed towards undermining by covert unlawful acts, or directed towards or intended ultimately to lead to the destruction or overthrow by violence of, the country's constitutionally established system of government. SIRC argued that the government should make the act consistent with the reasoning behind the counter-subversion decision by repealing 2(d). 'We realize that there can be a real threat to security posed in any democracy from domestic sources. But we believe that other parts of the mandate offer adequate protection to the security of Canada.'[48]

SIRC was not the only source of criticism of 2(d) – the parliamentary five-year review of the CSIS Act (see below) also recommended repeal, as did many independent critics – but arguments for altering the legislative mandate met an unsympathetic response from government. In 1991 the government issued its definitive answer: the controversy over 'subversion' was not due to 2(d) but 'to the way in which the definition had been implemented during the transition period.' Noting that ministerial direction had subsequently significantly limited the scope and intensity of the service's activities under 2(d), the government went on to state that 'while a particular threat may not be considered especially serious at a given time, this would not, in the Government's view, justify removing it altogether from the mandate of the Service, thereby precluding the Government from ever receiving advice on the issue in the future.'[49] In other words, better safe than sorry. That logic has continued down to the present day: 2(d) remains, unaltered.

In Transition, in Flux, or on Course?

The next test for CSIS was the parliamentary review of the provisions and operations of the CSIS and Security Offences acts after five years that had been mandated in the CSIS Act. The McDonald Commission had recommended a permanent parliamentary committee on national security, but the government had instead chosen to exclude Parliament and go the route of an independent review body, that is, SIRC. The sole provision for a parliamentary role was the five-year review.

A Special Commons Committee was set up in 1989. It was an interesting exercise from a parliamentary point of view. Armed with a small but energetic research staff, the committee was able to function in a remarkably non-partisan fashion.[50] The government, however, opted to treat parliamentarians as lacking the qualifications for access to CSIS people and records that SIRC or Osbaldeston enjoyed. Staff members were excluded from briefings in secure locations, and the MPs were not granted the equivalent of security clearance: to gain required information, the committee was reduced to using the same Access to Information Act as the inquisitive public – with the same limited results. It was denied access to ministerial directives to CSIS; CSIS annual reports to the minister; the Inspector General certificates; or SIRC special reports, especially those concerning how the various branches of the service functioned. There was no policy of general cooperation with the committee from the various agencies and departments examined, and some record of obfuscation and evasion. Yet the government managed a well-coordinated inter-departmental process to develop a response to the committee that was budgeted at close to seven times the dollars available to the committee.[51] Not surprisingly, the committee complained that it lacked confidence that 'it has been able to assess how the *CSIS Act* is operating ... the Committee believes that it has been unable to review adequately the roles of key government participants in the security and intelligence process.'[52]

Given these limitations, the committee was unable to follow up the searching probes of CSIS management and internal organization that SIRC and Osbaldeston had accomplished. Drawing on their work, the committee recognized that CSIS in its first three years had experienced 'difficult moments with respect to the management of human resources' largely due to the inherited RCMP subculture with its 'lack of political acumen and analytical refinement.' In the two years since Reid Morden had taken over, with a mandate for administrative and cultural reform set by Osbaldeston, the committee noted that CSIS had 'undertaken a number of initiatives to correct some of the problems with its human resource management practices.' Armed with a management plan and agenda that set priorities on official-languages promotion, employment equity, improved staff relations, continuous training and skills development, and executive development programs, CSIS was moving in a 'positive' direction. Nonetheless, the committee still found a number of issues and problems that remained to be addressed. Among them, it found that representation of francophones, women, and visible minorities at the senior management and intelligence officer levels, although improving, was still slow to realize appropriate proportions. The committee pointed out that this was not simply a matter of equity. The limitations of CSIS intelligence on Air India and on Sikh extremism had demonstrated that more hiring from minority communities, and a wider range of minority-language skills, would be of positive benefit to CSIS intelligence capacities. Finally, there was the issue of the wider educational backgrounds and skill sets that CSIS should have been emphasizing to accomplish fully the promise of civilianization. Here, too, the committee found a work in progress, but far from completion.

The internal targeting and warrant-application process, the failures of which had led to Ted Finn's resignation, was also in the process of being revamped and reworked. Again, the restraints on the committee's access to internal CSIS information left it unable to assess the new targeting and warrant-application systems confidently, but it did see matters moving in the right direction, towards more controls and more stages in the process that would filter out more mistakes and discourage corner cutting.[53]

The committee was able to assess the strengths and limitations of the CSIS Act, suggest some changes, and make some sensible recommendations about the overall direction and orientation of security intelligence in what was already seen, as the committee reported in 1991, the beginnings of the post-Cold War era. In this latter regard, there was a 'note of caution': 'The Committee believes the Service requires a specific type of intelligence officer and analyst: someone capable of understanding the dramatic changes now taking place in the world and their impact on the security of Canada. In particular, the Service needs recruits who can grasp the social, cultural, political and economic contexts from which the changing threats to the security of Canada emerge.'[54] This was a tall order, although a standard that continues down to the present day. Civilianization was always directed towards encouraging the emergence of more intelligent intelligence. In practice, of course, CSIS has always fallen short of this recruitment ideal, but the best that can be said is that, by the late 1980s and after, there were more persistent efforts to achieve it. Reflecting an appreciation both of the difficulties of transforming and modernizing the old RCMP security service and of the reform efforts being made, the committee, perhaps commenting on Osbaldeston's earlier *In Transition*, called its report *In Flux but Not in Crisis*.

The government seemed relatively unimpressed by the earnest efforts of the parliamentary committee. Bolstered by its vastly superior resources and its privileged access to secrets denied the committee, the government responded in early 1991 with a document somewhat smugly titled *On Course*. This document offered 'a detailed presentation on how the system has been working – the most detailed presentation ever made public by the Government ... The conclusion reached is that the system is sound, has served the nation well and should be preserved. Though some refinements can be contemplated and policy development continues, the framework created by the Acts has proven to be both durable and flexible in times of change.'[55] *On Course* presented a skeletal picture of the bureaucratic system of command and control over security and intelligence then in place. Ironically, this included some information not volunteered to the parliamentary committee. When it came to evidence of organizational shortfall, as in the repeated concerns expressed about poor staff relations and the faltering employment equity and recruitment programs in CSIS, the tone was relentlessly upbeat, expressed in bland bureaucratese:

> The Service has made marked progress in putting in place human resource and labour-management programs that demonstrate management's commitment to creating a quality working environment in step with the challenges of the 1990s ... Within the constraints of a set human resource base ... the Service has now established realistic strategic and numerical objectives to reflect the government's employment equity objectives ... Internal CSIS publications defining managers' responsibilities emphasize the importance of ensuring that employees must be developed, challenged and prepared for the future.[56]

Although most of the special committee's recommendations were rejected, *On Course* did announce one change that was positive for CSIS: it promised to increase substantially the service's budget and to build a new headquarters appropriate for the requirements of an intelligence agency in the late twentieth century. By 1993–4, the CSIS annual budget had doubled from 1985–6, reaching $229 million, some of the increase accounted for by the costs of the new headquarters.[57] This, it should be noted, was during a period of fiscal austerity and general belt tightening in Ottawa.

Changing Course

The government might insist for public-relations reasons that everything was on course for CSIS, but major changes were in process behind the closed doors of the agency's headquarters. While ex-Mounties,

unused to receiving advice from outsiders, might have found it hard
to take the various external shocks that had been administered to the
agency, the criticisms were all advanced in a constructive spirit – how
CSIS could be made to work better. The new leadership under Reid
Morden was committed to implementing the recommended changes.

In late 1989 one important step was taken when Morden sat down
with RCMP Commissioner Norman Inkster in the office of their minister, Solicitor General Pierre Blais, and signed a Memorandum of Understanding (MOU) between the two agencies. The MOU spelled out
in formal detail how the two should coordinate their operations. It de-
lineated in broad terms their respective jurisdictions and responsibilities. It brought together in a single document a number of ministerial
directives issued to both agencies since the inception of CSIS. Importantly, it specified terms for information exchange – when and under
what conditions information should be passed from one agency to the
other – and also provided for procedures to protect the information exchanged. Much of this should have clear from the start, but both agencies had chosen to interpret their respective mandates in differing and
often overlapping ways. On a number of occasions these differences
of interpretation had spilled over into open conflicts that threatened
to undermine their joint raison d'être, the protection of national security. We have already recounted the disastrous record of both agencies
before and after the Air India bombing. There were other incidents of
counter-productive tension and conflict.

In 1985 Armenian Canadian terrorists attacked the Turkish Embassy
in Ottawa. Post-incident investigation uncovered problems of coordination that impeded proper handling of the situation. Early in 1986 a
bomb scare became public involving a threat of a Libyan attack on a
flight out of Ottawa Airport. It turned out to be a hoax, but the investigation had been upended by a turf war between CSIS and the RCMP
over the control of the only witness.

There was also the curious case of Mahmoud Mohammed Issa Mohammed, a member of the Popular Front for the Liberation of Palestine
convicted in a deadly terrorist attack on an El Al jet in Athens in 1968,
who had arrived in Canada in 1987 and was accepted as a landed immigrant even though his name was on a CSIS terrorist watch list. News
about his past hit the media, possibly leaked by Israeli intelligence
which had been tracking him for decades, possibly by CSIS which was
cooperating closely with Israel's Mossad. The government was embarrassed and deportation proceedings were initiated against Mohammed.

Mohammed himself agreed to an RCMP scheme to depart the country voluntarily in 1988 and was put on a jet under RCMP escort to London from whence he would transfer to Tunisia. CSIS was not consulted. But, when Mohammed's presence at Pearson Airport's international departure gate was mysteriously made known (Israeli intelligence was a suspect here), CSIS agents showed up. Though Mohammed departed with his RCMP escort, when his plane landed in London, the arrivals area was crawling with spies from all over the world, not to speak of media cameras and microphones. At this point the plan fell apart as the connecting airline refused to carry Mohammed, fearing for security. Mohammed and his RCMP escort returned to Canada. Mohammed, denied voluntary exit, filed a refugee claim. He still remains in Canada, after more than two decades of quiet, unobtrusive life in southern Ontario and numerous failed efforts to remove him. There are elements of this story that still remain unexplained, but what was clear at the time was that the RCMP-CSIS turf war had seriously bungled a matter of national security.[58]

These and other lesser known incidents of tension had led SIRC to focus critical attention on this wholly unnecessary institutional conflict. The 1989 MOU was supposed to be a kind of peace treaty, and the solicitor general undertook to act as the guarantor of peace, insisting that any differences should be promptly reported to him for ironing out. This was all very well, and undoubtedly represented a step forward. Yet even this MOU failed to resolve one fundamental issue. As SIRC realistically commented, there was one 'unavoidable source of tension between CSIS and the RCMP. Criminal proceedings concerning security offences, a key RCMP role, sometimes carry the risk of public exposure for CSIS operations in areas where secrecy is essential to effectiveness. As a result, CSIS is sometimes unable to tell the RCMP all that it knows.'[59] This problem was not solved in 1989, nor is it yet solved.

On other fronts, CSIS was also moving to respond to the SIRC-Osbaldeston-parliamentary agenda for reform. As director, Morden imposed the kind of internal controls from the top that Osbaldeston had prescribed. A second generation of senior managers succeeded the Finn-era echelon. Morden departed after his term and was succeeded in 1992 by Raymond Protti, another career civil servant with no experience in security intelligence. Protti seems to have made little impression on the organization in a brief tenure before leaving to head the Canadian Bankers Association in 1994. The same could not be said for his successor, Ward Elcock, who was to serve an unprecedented ten years as director, from 1994 to 2004. Elcock came to the job with a background in intelligence in the PCO. He also brought his own decisive style of leadership. Tough, confident, self-assured, Elcock was able to assert effective control over all aspects of the agency and put his own distinctive stamp on all its operations and activities. Under Elcock's firm hand, there were no rogue elements allowed to pursue their own agendas. His was precisely the kind of administrative leadership that Osbaldeston had prescribed. Equally important, he was an extremely effective spokesman for CSIS interests in the Ottawa policy-making process, as adept at inter-departmental bureaucratic infighting as he was at speaking on behalf of the agency before Parliament and the public – indeed, under Elcock there were no other CSIS public voices permitted.

The critics had also focused much attention on the faltering CSIS recruitment agenda, and the glacial pace in the early years of effective, as opposed to merely formal, civilianization. This, too, was about to turn a corner under Morden and his successors. In 1991 CSIS was able to report that more than half of its employees had joined since 1984. New employees each year now made up 8 per cent of the total CSIS complement, bringing with them some of the required skills and educational backgrounds that had been generally lacking among the ex-RCMP veterans. On representational issues, CSIS reported that a workforce that in 1984 had been 85 per cent anglophone was now 66 per cent anglophone and 34 per cent francophone. In terms of gender, women were making up more and more of the overall workforce, from 36 per cent in 1984 to 43 per cent in 1991. More significantly, the intelligence-officer category was 20 per cent by 1991, three times what it was in 1984. Only 8.3 per cent of senior management was female in 1991, but this was an improvement over 1984 when there were no female senior managers. Visible minorities had risen from 0.6 per cent to 2.45 per cent in 1991.[60] These figures present a glass-half-full, glass-half-empty, picture, depending on the observer's point of view. Progress was slow, to be sure, but the trajectory was correct. For another, later snapshot, we can turn to 1997, when it was reported that the number of women in the senior-management category had risen to 11.5 per cent, and in the intelligence-officer category to 27.3 per cent.[61] Recruitment of visible minorities, on the other hand, seemed to show little progress, perhaps reflecting the service's image problems with minority communities.

Personnel issues involved trade-offs between the requirement for new, and more representational, blood and the need for the experience of the ex-RCMP white male anglophone echelon. Gradually, time and attrition would do their work, but it would not happen overnight.

The Most Intrusive Technique – Secret Informers

One issue that everyone, CSIS, SIRC, the parliamentary review, seemed inclined to skate around was the use of human sources or undercover informers as an essential technique of gathering security intelligence on targeted groups. Everyone recognized the crucial importance and value of such sources; everyone recognized the serious legal difficulties and moral ambiguities that surround their use; everyone recognized the delicate issues involved in handling such sources; and everyone seemed at a loss when it came to proposing more effective controls and regulation of their use. Unlike the intervention of technical interception methods (bugs), the use of human sources has never required warrant applications. In the 1980s CSIS twice faced public embarrassment when undercover human sources were 'outed.' It is worth examining these cases in detail.

The Boivin Affair: CSIS Sentenced to Hard Labour?

On a weekend in May 1987, Marc-André Boivin, ostensibly a long-time labour organizer for the Quebec-based Confédération des syndicats nationaux (CSN) but secretly an undercover source within the Quebec labour movement for CSIS and, prior to that, for the RCMP security service, reported to his CSIS handler that he possessed a cache of detonators (some of which had been used in a recent bombing in Chicoutimi), and that bombings against a company in Drummondville and Montreal were planned for the coming Monday evening. CSIS alerted the Sûreté du Québec late Monday. Boivin was arrested, and on 29 June he appeared in court and pleaded guilty to a series of charges, including bombings and conspiracy to carry out bombings. He was sentenced to eighteen months' imprisonment. Even before his court appearance, media reports had disclosed his lengthy career as an informer for both the RCMP and CSIS. Media speculation was rife that CSIS was infiltrating the labour movement and that Boivin may have been an agent provocateur. This was a serious potential embarrassment to CSIS, since its mandate clearly excluded intrusive surveillance of the legitimate trade-union movement, let alone clandestine interference in its operations. It was time to call for accountability.

In this case, both the inspector general and SIRC were called into action, the latter in a special 'section 54' report to the minister in March 1988.[62] Neither had much difficulty in putting to rest fears about the more extreme forms of interference, such as the use of agents provocateurs to disrupt the labour movement. However, a 'thorough' airing of CSIS investigative powers in relation to labour did leave SIRC 'in no doubt that the information made public through the media since Mr. Boivin's arrest has had a chilling effect on normal human relations within the labour movement.' Of course, this was an inevitable result of the disclosure of the identities of undercover sources. But the knowledge that security and police agencies do use undercover informants, knowledge widespread throughout the labour movement for decades, itself had a chilling effect on human relations among those targeted. Indeed, in the absence of public identification, the knowledge that some among one's colleagues *might* be informing could be a festering human-relations problem that was in some senses worse than that occasioned by a public unmasking.

Boivin's double life had begun in 1973 when he was recruited by the RCMP to report on labour organizations, with an emphasis on 'suspected criminal and "subversive" elements' in the labour milieu. Despite repeated brushes with the law resulting from picket-line violence and other union activities, Boivin continued to report to the RCMP. His Mountie handlers were 'extremely concerned' about his becoming involved in criminal activities but failed to take specific measures to prevent recurrences. In the early 1980s, the RCMP security service refocused its attention away from the labour movement, as such, towards the presence in its ranks of 'subversives,' which in the context of the time meant Communists and other left-wing activists. In 1983 a senior Counter-Subversion official at security service headquarters characterized Boivin's value as deriving from a 'privileged position in the labour movement to give us informed assessments of what subversives are up to ... in their perpetual efforts to penetrate and influence labour to their Marxist ideologies.'

As an aside, it is interesting to note that RCMP rethinking of its role in relation to labour went back at least to the period when Boivin was first recruited. In 1974 the security service organized an in-camera conference involving security officers along with representatives from various relevant departments of government for the purpose of trying to sort out just what their role should be in relation to labour. In a post-conference report to senior management, one officer asked a Delphic question: 'How can you chart a course when you know not where you are headed?' 'Some fundamental issues were raised, such as: was our work in this area really necessary or were we searching for a role that was beyond our mandate.' There were lingering concerns expressed about violence and illegal strike activity apart from any Communist connections, although it was 'difficult to determine where our interests should begin.' Some felt subversion was 'our only mandate.' Others, however, felt that the RCMP had a 'valid role to play in the area of violence, confrontation and civil disorder (although the latter is hard to define).' Caution was expressed about using regular RCMP policing as a 'cover for the security service,' since this could jeopardize the entire policing program. The reporting officer concluded that 'we cannot go much further in this field without a new mandate and even with one, we would have to be extremely careful since we are dealing with a powerful and legitimate element of society.'[63]

These very pertinent concerns persisted, and so CSIS – with its new mandate – was faced with real problems in handling sources like Boivin who operated undercover in this 'legitimate element of society.' While SIRC could not find evidence that Boivin had been mandated 'to report either on union activities, as such, or on the activities of individual union members, as such,' 'nevertheless, in reporting on the "non-union" targets against which he was directed, the information provided by Mr. Boivin at times touched upon certain activities of either his union or its members, or otherwise related to labour union activities generally.' The ambiguity of reporting on 'subversive' activities within unions while not reporting on unions was also borne out by the findings of the inspector general, who found that the RCMP security service had, by the late 1970s, consigned union files to the 'passive collation' category. Nonetheless, by the time CSIS took over in 1984, it inherited the pre-CSIS RCMP files on unions and, added to this, 'information incidentally collected under the mandate or from open sources … relating to unions ("passive collation").' This information was 'fully accessible' and continued to grow, even though much of the transferred information 'could not now be collected as investigative information under the CSIS Act.' Despite the lack of evidence that CSIS was deliberately targeting human sources against trade unions, SIRC and the IG warned that the continued retention of this information could be in contravention of the act.

SIRC looked at other cases of CSIS sources in unions and concluded that Boivin was 'the most worrying case we found.' His known involvement in violence set his case apart. And there was an additional embarrassing fact to which SIRC drew attention. A delay of almost two

days before Boivin's warning about the planned bombings in Drummondville and Montreal were reported to the SQ, at the very last moment, 'not only breached CSIS policy but also ordinary standards of
common sense.' No doubt, CSIS was showing the usual reluctance of a
security intelligence agency to disclose its sources to law enforcement,
but in this extreme case of an imminent threat of violent criminal acts,
such hesitation was simply unacceptable. There was, moreover, the pri-
or question of the degree of diligence exercised by Boivin's handlers in
ensuring that their source did not engage in unlawful acts.

On 22 June 1987 the solicitor general, James Kelleher, received the
SIRC *Annual Report 1986/87*, which recommended the closure of the
Counter-Subversion Branch of CSIS. The bad publicity surrounding the
Boivin affair that month only added to the sense of urgency in government that something had to be done. Late the same year, Kelleher announced the closure of the Counter-Subversion Branch. The logic that
led the government to this decision also led SIRC in its investigation
of Boivin to question the use of this kind of union source even more
searchingly:

> Mr. Boivin was targeted, essentially, against communists. During the same
> period, much of the CSIS Counter-Subversion Branch's human resources
> were targeted against communists. This operational activity in the field
> had, as a backdrop, a great many RCMP Security Service files on Canadian
> unions in CSIS Headquarters.
>
> Such an emphasis on communists and unions does not lend itself to
> logical analysis by reference to specific provisions of the *CSIS Act*. The
> RCMP Security Service before 1984, and to a lesser extent CSIS since then
> have had more to do with attitudes of mind than provisions of the law.
> Clearly, the *CSIS Act* had very little effect on this situation until CSIS re-
> ceived direction from the Solicitor General in 1987.

'It is difficult to avoid the conclusion,' SIRC noted sharply, 'that Mr.
Boivin was retained simply because he had worked for many years under the aegis of the RCMP Security Service, and that work was found
for him in order to justify his retention.'

'I was a Nazi for CSIS': The Grant Bristow Affair

In the late summer of 1994, CSIS hit the headlines in a way that an
intelligence agency never likes to see. It was reported that a paid CSIS

source or informant, publicly named as Grant Bristow, had been op-erating within a racist neo-Nazi organization known as the Heritage Front. Allegations flew that Bristow had been acting out of the control of his CSIS handlers, and had incited racist and violent acts; that Bris-tow, with CSIS support and funds, had been instrumental in setting up and financing the front; that he had gathered intelligence on Canadian Jewish groups and passed this on to violent American neo-Nazis; that he had infiltrated and attempted to disrupt a mainstream political par-ty while acting on behalf of another party. As the affair heated up, the accusations grew wilder: that CSIS itself was acting in a reckless and ir-responsible manner, infiltrating and spying on legitimate trade unions and the CBC, and that the Conservative government was using CSIS to advance its own partisan goals.[64]

Bad publicity generated by a media feeding frenzy was bad enough. Worse yet was the public naming of a covert source. Absolute secrecy surrounding the identity of covert sources is the holy of holies for in-telligence agencies. Without ironclad assurances of lifelong anonymity, sources will never be recruited. In some situations, their very lives may be placed at risk if their identity is disclosed.[65] It has never been pub-licly revealed who unmasked Bristow's undercover role, or for what motives. But the result, apart from setting off a media extravaganza and causing a bureaucratic flap in Ottawa, was a great deal of heat if very little light. Most of the swirling accusations against CSIS and Bristow were recklessly exaggerated, and in some cases simply unfounded. But the affair did serve to pinpoint the inevitable ethical ambiguities in-volved in planting undercover sources within violent extremist groups, raised some legitimate questions about the handling of human sources, and inadvertently pointed to some unforeseen problems in the account-ability mechanisms set up in the CSIS Act.

On closer examination, and with the benefit of hindsight, CSIS behav-iour in running Bristow inside the Heritage Front appears to have been eminently defensible. The racist, neo-Nazi right was driven by hatred of identifiable ethnic and religious minorities; used intimidation against its enemies; and potentially threatened the lives and well-being of in-nocent persons. Any impression that CSIS was still mired in a Cold War mentality to the exclusion of attention to right-wing threats is dispelled by the Bristow case. In fact, it seems that Bristow's career as a secret source on the neo-Nazis actually predated the fall of the Berlin Wall. In 1986 Bristow introduced himself to CSIS when, in his capacity as a pri-vate security consultant, he had been contacted by apartheid-era South

African intelligence to assist in providing security for South African officials in Canada from anti-apartheid demonstrators – including spying on Canadian opponents of South Africa's racist regime. Bristow found this objectionable and in effect offered his services to CSIS to report on this instance of covert foreign interference in Canada. The result of this operation was the expulsion of one South African diplomat and the barring of another. In the course of his undercover work, Bristow met several Canadian white supremacists, and in 1988 Operation GOVERNOR was born, whereby Bristow agreed to lead a double life as an apparent racist activist while reporting to CSIS as its primary human source inside the burgeoning extremist right, which represented a definite threat of violence and intimidation against Jewish and other minorities.[66] Bristow was involved in the founding of the Heritage Front, which soon became a leading neo-Nazi organization, and in Bristow, CSIS had its own foot on the ground floor of the extremist movement.

To be sure, there are always ethical conundrums in running sources within groups like this: in order to be fully accepted, agents need to say and, worse, do, things that may be morally and legally ambiguous, even in some cases having to stray right over the line into criminal activity. In Bristow's case, he organized an harassment campaign against Jews and other targets of racist hatred, in order, he later claimed, to deflect the front's energies away from more violent actions. There is also the human cost to undercover sources of being compelled, on a daily basis, to behave in a way that may be repugnant to their own values. These are issues that have particularly bedevilled undercover operations in today's age of terrorism, but they were already apparent when the Bristow affair hit the front pages.[67] Accusations of CSIS complicity in right-wing extremism stemmed from the inherent ambiguities involved in maintaining a valuable human source within a group where members must behave badly to keep the trust of their fellows.

Eventually, the strain of keeping up this double life proved too wearing on Bristow's health and psychological well-being. At the same time, there were elements within the group he had infiltrated that were growing more extreme and more violent to a degree that made his continued role as an activist increasingly problematic. Consequently, he and his handler in Operation GOVERNOR agreed to close it down, and in 1994 Bristow left the Heritage Front while politely rebuffing an offer from his handler to look at more permanent CSIS employment. Within weeks his cover had been inexplicably blown and his faux career as a neo-Nazi extremist was suddenly on parade on television news.

Once the cat was out of the bag, the government quickly grasped that while stuffing it back in was not an option, effectively managing the spin could at least limit the damage. The solicitor general, Herb Gray, was advised by his deputy minister, Jean T. Fournier: 'The use of confidential informants or "human sources" as CSIS refers to them, is recognized as one of the most effective means of collecting security intelligence.' However, it is 'one of, if not *the* most "intrusive" means of investigation available to CSIS.'[68] The problem is that the use of this indispensable investigative technique may undermine the fundamental obligation of governments to protect the constitutionally guaranteed rights and freedoms of citizens. Those who innocently associate with targeted groups (which may conceal their aims from the public) are unwittingly at risk of scrutiny by CSIS. Fournier advised his minister that, where effectiveness has come into conflict with rights, effectiveness has won. This 'one-sidedness' is explained by the state of law with regard to informants and by the recommendations of successive public inquiries, both parliamentary and non-parliamentary, to limit accountability and transparency in regard to secret informants. Only one inquiry – a commission appointed by a Parti Québécois Quebec government in the 1970s and opposed by Ottawa – had recommended that warrants be extended to cover police and security service use of human sources. The courts, too, had granted 'extraordinary latitude' to law-enforcement agencies to protect the identities of secret informants. CSIS is 'essentially unrestricted in its use [of] human sources as an investigative technique, so long as it does not infringe on any other law, and complies with whatever Ministerial directions may apply, and with its own internal policies.'

The minister was advised that the earlier Boivin affair, which had been submitted to SIRC and the IG, might be a useful template to apply in the Bristow case. Inquiries had their shortcomings, not least of which was the need to prevent the public disclosure of some information under the access-to-information and privacy acts. But Fournier concluded: 'Experience with past cases of human source disclosure suggests that the ease with which the resulting SIRC report can be made public (and the climate in which it is released) are critical factors in managing the issues inherent to matters involving human sources.' The government agreed, and SIRC in effect was designated to take a lead role in the handling of the Bristow affair via a section 54 report that would be made as public as possible, consistent with the law.[69]

As SIRC began its investigation, it had at hand some material regarding internal government policy on the handling of human sources. Even before the Boivin case, the Osbaldeston report on CSIS's first few years had pointed to human-source handling as an area requiring close attention. Though Osbaldeston concurred with the McDonald Commission that human sources were an 'essential component of a security intelligence collection program,' the use of this 'very intrusive investigative tool' must be centrally directed and controlled at the Director's level.' Most importantly, Osbaldeston concluded that 'the use of human sources should be the subject of comprehensive ministerial direction.'[70] This advice was followed with a ministerial directive on 30 October 1989.[71] While the directive recognizes the crucial role of human sources in CSIS collection, it also points to the potential damage to 'societal relationships and institutions, given the intrusion into the privacy of individuals and groups which this technique necessarily involves.' The minister laid out six basic principles to guide the service in its handling of human sources:

1) to be used only when and to the extent 'reasonable and necessary' in meeting the service's statutory responsibilities;
2) the need to use to be 'carefully weighed' against possible damage to civil liberties;
3) use must be centrally directed and controlled;
4) sources should not engage in illegal activities, and should conduct themselves as not to 'discredit the Service or the Government of Canada';
5) sources to be managed to protect both the security of the service's operations and the personal safety of sources; and
6) sources should be treated 'ethically and fairly' by the service in terms of both compensation and handling.

The text of the directive is sufficiently censored as to obscure some of the important details, but it seems that CSIS sources were enjoined from acting as agents provocateurs or in any way inciting or encouraging illegal activity.

In 1993 – a year before the Bristow affair became public – the Office of the Inspector General had carried out a review of CSIS human-source files. 'Comparatively few instances of non-compliance' were discovered, 'most of which resulted from varying interpretations of ministerial directions and policy.' In general, the IG found that 'the relevant operational policy framework appears adequate.' Concern was expressed that human sources were not being given instruction about the methods they might use to collect information in the light of court decisions applying section 8 of the Charter of Rights (the right to be secure against unreasonable search or seizure). 'Human sources may not use methods that CSIS could not use without Federal Court authorization.'[72]

SIRC's Heritage Front report was some two hundred pages in length.[73] Among its findings: the Heritage Front had been appropriately targeted, in conformity with CSIS internal guidelines and with the CSIS Act definition of threats to security; Bristow had been a valuable asset in the infiltration of the extreme right-wing movement; and, although not all his actions undercover could be fully justified in retrospect, most of the media charges about his misbehaviour were unfounded. There can be little to quarrel with in these findings, especially if the inevitable ambiguity surrounding undercover participation in extremist groups is recognized. To put matters in blunter language than SIRC permitted itself, undercover operations are always messy; everybody's hands get a little dirty. But the critics' view that CSIS through Bristow had been sponsoring extremism while purporting to investigate it simply does not stand up to scrutiny. Interestingly, Bristow himself has later re-emerged as a public defender of human-rights commissions and laws against hate propaganda, and he received a warm and supportive response from the Canadian Jewish Congress when he addressed the group to explain his infiltration of the anti-Semitic extremist movement.[74]

The SIRC report seemed to have the desired effect of deflating the media critics. Shortly after its appearance, the Bristow affair began to disappear from the front pages, then from the back pages as well. This process was perhaps helped by the fact that SIRC had confronted the media, in the form of the CBC, head on, criticizing some of the public broadcaster's coverage as reckless and irresponsible. One of the CBC stories targeted for particular criticism was that CSIS had been spying on the Canadian Union of Postal Workers (CUPW), which, if true, would have been in violation of the CSIS mandate. We will return to this story in a moment, but at the time the CBC did appear to have been caught off-base. Once burned, the media proved twice shy, and quickly backed off further pursuit of the leads that had previously been hotly followed.

At this point it might seem that the affair had, from the government's point of view, been satisfactorily wound down from CSIS scandal to media embarrassment. However, there were a number of loose ends in the SIRC inquiry, and some of these possibly reflected back on CSIS. In particular, there were some hints of partisan political involvement. SIRC's efforts to snuff out these rumours of partisan bias were not entirely successful. And SIRC itself became entangled in partisan conflict, and in an unfortunate confrontation with Parliament.

To understand how the Bristow affair became tarred with partisan politics, it is necessary to understand the ramifications of the political cataclysm that struck the federal political landscape with the election of 1993. The ruling Progressive Conservatives, following two successive majority governments, were not merely swept out of office but virtually eradicated, being reduced to a derisory two MPs, a blow from which the old party would never recover. Although the Liberals formed a majority government in the new Parliament, the PCs, along with the NDP, lost official party status. The opposition benches were now dominated by two new parties, the sovereignist Bloc Québécois (BQ) and the Western-based Reform Party. The political composition of Parliament should have been irrelevant to the handling of accountability in the Bristow affair, but instead it presented a problem.

When SIRC was set up in 1984 as an independent watchdog over CSIS, it was envisaged that the privy councillors appointed to head the new review body would in some broad sense reflect the political make-up of Parliament, which itself was transformed by the election of that year. The first chair, appointed by the new Progressive Conservative government of Brian Mulroney, was a former Conservative cabinet minister, Ron Atkey. He was joined by another former Conservative minister and one non-partisan appointment, but after consultation with the leader of the Liberal Opposition, a former Liberal minister was added, as was a former NDP provincial cabinet minister after consultation with the leader of the NDP. Although this arrangement was not formalized, it continued to be reflected in later appointments to SIRC by Prime Minister Mulroney. It was accepted that in future SIRC should broadly reflect the parties in Parliament. There was a specific reason for this: in passing the CSIS Act, the Trudeau government had chosen to ignore one of the recommendations of the McDonald Commission, that a parliamentary standing committee on national security be a central component of the new accountability mechanisms for CSIS. The practical political make-up of SIRC was thus an attempt informally to have the body reflect the political composition of Parliament, thus enhancing SIRC's legitimacy in the eyes of the elected members.

An ad hoc Commons subcommittee on national security did begin to operate in the early 1990s as a carry-over from the committee that had carried out the five-year review of the CSIS Act, completed in 1990.[75] By the end of the second Mulroney government, a complementary arrangement seemed workable. SIRC, which enjoyed full access to CSIS, would report annually to the subcommittee, whose members chose not to seek security clearance and thus remained 'outside the loop'; these members instead would rely upon the security-cleared review body, broadly reflective of the political composition of Parliament, to provide MPs with partially censored but trustworthy 'inside the loop' perspectives on CSIS operations.

The 1993 election results blew this accommodation apart. SIRC was a body that now featured three Conservatives, including the chair, a total that exceeded the number of elected Tory MPs. The NDP, also no longer an official party in the Commons, retained one member. But neither of the two new official Opposition parties was represented on SIRC. To make matters more difficult, one of these parties, which from 1993 to 1997 served as the Official Opposition, was the sovereignist Bloc Québécois, which was effectively excluded from participation on SIRC because of its members' publicly professed lack of loyalty to the Canadian state. No present or past BQ supporter has sat on SIRC to this day. The other new party, Reform, was locked in a fierce struggle with the Progressive Conservatives for partisan mastery of the centre-right of the federal political spectrum, a struggle that would continue until 2004 when the two parties finally merged in the new Conservative Party of Canada. It was the Reform-PC conflict that was most disruptive to relations between SIRC and Parliament, and this was exacerbated by the specific partisan fallout from the Bristow affair.

Preston Manning: Target?

Bristow in his undercover guise had been involved in attempts by the Heritage Front to infiltrate the Reform Party in Ontario beginning as early as 1991. Indeed, Bristow, along with other front members, had signed on to provide security for the party leader, Preston Manning, at Reform rallies in the 1993 election campaign.[76] Media leaks about neo-Nazis and racists in Reform ranks proved extremely embarrassing to the party, and may have cost them votes.[77] When news broke about Bristow's status as a CSIS undercover source, Reform suspicions were raised concerning possible CSIS involvement in Tory 'dirty tricks' against their rivals on the right. The party pointed out that the minister in charge of CSIS at the time also happened to be the Tory minister designated to counter the Reform challenge in southern Ontario, Doug Lewis. Was it not possible that CSIS intelligence was being misused for partisan purposes, or at least that partisan benefit may have been derived from privileged access to CSIS intelligence? These suspicions, hotly denied by the Conservatives, were further fuelled when a CSIS briefing document was leaked to the media by a former press aide to Minister Lewis. This aide did not possess appropriate security clearance to see the document he leaked; worse, he had taken other classified CSIS documents with him when he left his position in the defeated government. Reformers wanted to know what kind of access to CSIS documents political staffers might have had under the previous government, and for what purpose.

In its Heritage Front investigation, SIRC made short work of the partisan allegations, to its satisfaction at least, although Reformers remained sceptical. Yet in its report, SIRC actually added to Reform suspicions when it revealed a troubling new piece of evidence: in 1989–90 CSIS had opened an investigation of alleged South African financial contributions to Reform leader Preston Manning in his bid to defeat Joe Clark, foreign minister in the Mulroney government, in Clark's Alberta constituency. Clark had allegedly been targeted for his outspoken criticism of the apartheid regime. SIRC concluded that such an investigation could be justified under the section 2(b) definition of clandestine or deceptive foreign-influenced activities as a threat to Canada. Yet CSIS subsequently admitted that, for three months in 1989–90, it had kept a file under the heading 'Preston MANNING,' raising doubts whether it was foreign influence or the Reform Party that was being targeted. If the latter, this would be in clear violation of the CSIS mandate and would confirm Reform suspicions of partisan use of CSIS. The Tory appointee as SIRC chair, Jacques Courtois, insisted that the file designation was no more than a mistake, with no sinister connotations. Yet the SIRC report would have been more credible if it had noted this 'mistake' when it drew attention to the investigation of Manning. Manning demanded that 'his' file be released to him. This was finally done in the spring of 1995, although it came in heavily censored form in accordance with the access-to-information and privacy acts.[78]

Examination of the Manning file suggests that the basis for opening it was dubious. The sole source was one that CSIS described as of 'unknown reliability' and as 'self serving and very opportunistic particularly if it benefits himself.' The source cited only hearsay that South Africa *might* be contributing to Manning's campaign fund. The argument for foreign influence was, in CSIS's own words, 'to say the least … difficult to support.' Since no evidence was found of any actual foreign money, it is difficult to see why the investigation continued, given the political sensitivity of targeting an opposition political party. Nor was there any evidence in the file that attention had been paid to the 1989 ministerial directive cautioning against precisely this kind of investigation into legitimate political activity.

CSIS, SIRC, and Parliament: The Jealous Triangle

The Reform Party was particularly aggrieved at the way in which the Bristow affair had been handled, but in the new circumstances post-1993 the relationship between SIRC and Parliament had been damaged. The House subcommittee on national security, now with a majority of Liberals, Reformers, and BQ members, called SIRC before it to demand answers and brought in television cameras to cover the proceedings. The atmosphere was strained, and sometimes openly antagonistic. SIRC stuck to the position that its report on the Heritage Front affair was to the solicitor general, not to Parliament, and the subcommittee could be permitted to see only what the minister decided it should see. This was technically correct, since it was a section 54 report, but the perception of the MPs was that they were arbitrarily being denied access to important information to prevent them understanding the affair. Reform and Bloc MPs vented their anger at SIRC, but it was clear that behind the apparently obdurate face of SIRC was the Liberal solicitor general, who was unwilling to allow any flexibility to SIRC to share more of its information with the subcommittee, even in camera. The Liberal government was no more willing than its predecessor to open up CSIS to potentially hostile parliamentary scrutiny.[79] More meetings were held, and SIRC was brought back for another, no less strained, appearance. But in the end, the subcommittee failed to get its act together as the Liberal chair, Derek Lee, indicated a desire to put the issue 'to bed.' No final report ever issued from the subcommittee. The Reform members issued their own bizarre, almost paranoiac, minority report, one that tellingly led with a quote ('The Truth Is Out There') from the occult television series *The X Files*.

In the end, when SIRC confronted Parliament, it was Parliament that blinked. While SIRC was able to quarterback the investigation through to what the Liberal government saw as a reasonably successful conclusion, the bad blood between the new opposition parties and SIRC did not portend an easy future for the legitimation of CSIS activity when scandal, or the appearance of scandal, reached the public eye. Nor was the awkward relationship between Parliament and SIRC a good sign.[80] In a few short years from its inception, SIRC had evolved from an antagonistic relationship with CSIS under SIRC Chair Atkey and CSIS Director Finn into a more professional and respectful relationship on both sides. But just as this was developing, new suspicions and fissures were opening up between SIRC and Parliament, calling into question SIRC's viability as a shield for CSIS against unfair criticism.[81]

National security was being politicized, a process that, if not discouraged, could weaken the insulation of CSIS from partisan pressures. That all this had flared up from an issue of a human source in a political movement was no accident. Political policing Canadian society is a process fraught with danger, as the security service's countering of the separatists in Quebec had already shown. When it is not an issue of foreign powers or groups acting upon Canada from the outside, but domestic political groupings, however extreme, political policing becomes a more divisive matter. It becomes more difficult to draw clear lines of demarcation between the extremists and more moderate political expressions, and more likely that CSIS may stray over the line into spying on legitimate political groups, on 'lawful advocacy, protest and dissent.' Hence the targeting in the 1970s and early 1980s of the Parti Québécois when the violent separatist groups were the appropriate focus – and the slippage between the Heritage Front and the Reform Party.

The Inspector General Calls

Behind closed doors, the government also received another report on CSIS handling of human sources from the Office of the Inspector General, a follow-up on its 1993 report that had predated the public outing of Bristow. The copy released has been so heavily censored that it is difficult to determine even the broad outline of what was concluded. A covering letter from the IG to the solicitor general that seems to have escaped the censor's hand is upbeat. 'Based on our review,' he assured his minister, 'I believe that you can have confidence that CSIS's system for the direction and control of confidential sources is working well.' He did suggest that 'certain refinements to the system will further assist handlers and improve the operation of the system.' He noted in particular that the interpretation of the ministerial directive in operational policy 'could be clarified and amplified in some important areas' and that there were a few areas 'where operational policy or practice should be re-examined.'[82] Both review bodies, SIRC and the IG, seem to be in agreement that, however messy the Bristow affair may have been, it did not indicate serious problems with the way CSIS was handling its secret human sources.

A final note with regard to the Bristow affair: as indicated above, one of the contentious charges raised in the media was that CSIS was spying on the postal workers union, CUPW. Bristow had had a brief stint in a postal station while undercover, and CSIS documents leaked by the former press aide to the solicitor general had hinted at CSIS's worry that word would get out that the service had spied on union activities and passed on the information to Canada Post managers – during a labour dispute. This seemed inherently implausible given the CSIS mandate and the insistence of the service that trade-union activities were not in themselves legitimate targets for surveillance (unless they are carried on in conjunction with the specified threats to security, like terrorism or sabotage). As it happened, CUPW had recently gained the release of documents on the old RCMP security service's activities against the postal unions in the 1970s. The 'worry' by CSIS related more to its concern about the impact of these revelations from the past than to any ongoing operations involving the union in the 1990s.[83] SIRC not only dismissed the union-spying accusations as baseless but characterized them as a 'terrible slur' on CSIS.

Except for continued union complaints,[84] there the matter rested until in 2002 investigative journalist Andrew Mitrovica, who had been very active in pursuing the Bristow story, published a book based largely upon the testimony of a disgruntled former CSIS agent, John Farrell. Farrell had worked as an intelligence officer for Canada Post before enlisting with CSIS and claims that he continued his spying on the post office for the service. SIRC's denial that the postal union was a target is dismissed by Farrell: 'They don't know shit.'[85] However, despite Mitrovica's vehement insistence that SIRC got it wrong, the evidence in his book is too slippery (blurring the lines between Canada Post management and CSIS, and between different CSIS programs, such as a mail-intercept program against extremist groups like the Heritage Front), and too much weight rests upon the credibility of the claims of one aggrieved former employee. In our view, therefore, Mitrovica's charge remains unproven.

'Three-Ring Circus': The Meredith/Pratt Affair

In the mid-1990s a bizarre affair briefly touched CSIS with accusations of betrayal and cover-up. It featured an alleged Russian mole within CSIS, allegations of a second, highly placed mole in a senior position who had covered this up, and a MP sued by a veteran CSIS investigator for defamation.

Information, or misinformation, concerning an alleged Russian mole in CSIS was leaked to a Reform Party MP, Val Meredith, by a former CSIS staffer, Rick Fraser, who was employed in her parliamentary office. Fraser brought into her office in 1996 a man who had worked as a contract employee doing security screening for CSIS in 1991, Pierre Roy. Roy had an apparently shocking tale to tell of moles and cover-ups; Meredith was to be the whistleblower, protected by parliamentary immunity. In media interviews and in press releases, outside parliamentary immunity, Meredith made sensational charges: that Roy, in his brief three-month stint as a contract security screener, had uncovered a 'never-ending trail of questionable activities and associations.' There were unreported contacts with service espionage targets by a CSIS translator, unauthorized travel, questionable financial dealings, a 'dishonest security interview,' and a failed polygraph exam. Attention focused on the head of the Russian translation section of CSIS in its Montreal regional office, who in Meredith's view was worse than suspect. In apparent exasperation, Meredith asked: 'If this guy wasn't a mole, then what was he?'[86] Then the accusations darkened: there might be a Russian 'super-mole' planted near the top of CSIS who was covering up the affair. If there were anything in Meredith's accusations, CSIS might be facing another Gilles Brunet scandal, but in real time. Unfortunately for Meredith, but fortunately for CSIS, the MP's enthusiasm for scoring a publicity coup outran her prudence, perhaps even her common sense.

Her office issued an eleven-page statement outlining the case against the translator, prepared by her staffer Fraser.[87] She indicated that Roy, in his short contract stint, had tried to raise his suspicions with the CSIS hierarchy. Up the chain of command at CSIS headquarters, the service's 'senior trouble shooter' was asked to review the case. His response: 'So what?' The translator was given a polygraph, which he failed, but a second polygraph was cancelled by the 'trouble-shooter,' who suspiciously terminated the investigation while vouching for the integrity of the translator. Meredith's finger was now pointed at the senior 'trouble-shooter,' who was referred to by the pseudonym 'Tom Masters.' But Meredith and Fraser made one very sloppy, and very damaging, error. In the passage containing the reference to the termination of the security investigation, the 'Masters' pseudonym was inadvertently replaced by 'Pratt,' evidently the real name of the senior CSIS official in question. It did not take much sleuthing to discover that 'Pratt' was Frank Pratt, a CSIS (and RCMP security service) veteran who had had an illustrious record in counter-espionage – he had uncovered the Soviet agent Hugh Hambleton – and had ended his long career as director general of operations. Pratt had been described as 'one of the greatest investigators Canada had ever produced.'[88] Now in retirement he found himself described as a super-mole and traitor to the service and his country. Pratt sued for defamation and severe damage to his reputation.

In court,[89] it soon became apparent that the Meredith accusations were more McCarthy than whistleblower. Roy was an aggrieved ex-employee with an axe to grind, whose contract had been terminated when his persistent stories of moles and conspiracies left his employers fed up.[90] An earlier formal complaint to SIRC had elicited an admission from CSIS that 'this particular case at times had the air of a three-ring circus.'[91] It did not get any better once the matter was splashed over the media. But there was no smoking gun, no evidence of a mole, and certainly no evidence that Pratt, an honourable veteran of the service, was some kind of Kim Philby. The espionage case having collapsed, Meredith was forced to back down and apologize to Pratt. She later lost the nomination in her constituency for the newly formed Conservative Party of Canada in 2004 and is no longer an MP. Pratt emerged with his reputation unscathed, as did CSIS.

The Russians Are (Still) Coming!

The Cold War may have waned and then flickered out at the beginning of the 1990s. The Berlin Wall may have fallen; Communism may have collapsed; the Soviet Union may have imploded; the KGB may have given way to the SVR. But the Cold War spies lingered on, like the smirk of the Cheshire Cat after the rest of the beast had vanished. CSIS had warned that the espionage apparatus of the old Soviet Union would outlast its state sponsor. Critics tended to dismiss this as old-style thinking and unwillingness to shift CSIS investments and assets from a disappearing market. But the warnings were not misplaced.

In the United States in the 1990s there were a series of dramatic arrests of American intelligence officers – Aldrich Ames and Harold Nicholson at the CIA; Robert Hanssen and Earl Edwin Pitts at the FBI – for spying for the Soviet Union, and for its Russian successor state after the disappearance of the USSR. Clearly, the old Soviet intelligence apparatus had no intention of curtailing its business-as-usual operations and giving up its hard-won intelligence assets in the United States. Nor has this pattern run its course: in 2010 the media were agog with the news that almost a dozen alleged Russian deep-cover 'illegals' had been arrested as the result of a massive, long-term FBI counter-espionage operation. For CSIS, successor to the RCMP security service that had chased Soviet spies through the 1950s, 1960s, and 1970s like the coyote chasing the roadrunner (see chapter 8), it was still the same old story in Canada. But the coyote had one very big counter-espionage success to brag about in the 1990s. With a distinctive Canadian touch, CSIS dubbed it Operation STANLEY CUP.

On 27 May 1996 CBC television reporter Neil MacDonald broke a sensational story: an unobtrusive young married couple going by the name of Ian and Laurie Lambert, living in a toney apartment in an affluent neighbourhood in Toronto, had been arrested days earlier as Russian spies. The pair had arrived separately from Russia as Yelena Olshevskaya and Dmitriy Olshevsky in the 1980s, assumed false Canadian identities (taking the names of Canadian children who had died in infancy), then got together in Toronto where they were married in 1991, carefully building 'legends' as 'sleeper' agents, all the while following the instructions of Moscow Centre.[92] While it was unclear whether any espionage had actually been committed, CSIS had scored a major coup in snagging the pair. Catching illegals with carefully prepared identities is no easy task: they leave few clues to the deep deception, and until overt acts are undertaken there is little to trigger the attention of spy catchers. While the specific methods whereby the Lamberts were uncovered remain hidden, one possible explanation is that in Quebec, where Yelena/Laurie obtained the name of a long-dead child to begin her Canadian false-identity trail, a routine review of parish demographic records turned up the puzzling match of a social security number for a girl who had died in infancy. A request for further information from the federal government may have twigged CSIS to this intriguing anomaly. Warrants for surveillance of the pair were obtained, and as more discrepancies appeared on closer examination, CSIS realized that it had a real counter-espionage prize in its sights.

Although Moscow was unaware that CSIS was watching, the SVR spymasters were perhaps disappointed that the Lamberts were proving to be less than the ideal spy couple. Their marriage was not merely a convenient façade but a real relationship. When Ian started taking up with another woman, the impact on the arrangement was devastating, both personally and professionally. The CSIS surveillants became aware that the pair were exchanging increasingly heated words, and when Laurie finally ordered her unfaithful husband out of the apartment and out of her life, both CSIS and the SVR must have wondered if the whole operation was about to fall apart. Now living in separate residences with other partners (Laurie soon developed a close relationship with a Toronto physician), the pair nonetheless were recalled together for a visit to the SVR headquarters in Moscow in early 1996. CSIS might have struck at this point, fearing that the pair might never return. Instead, it chose to await developments, but when the pair closed their bank accounts upon their return to Canada, CSIS decided that they were either about to leave definitively or be activated. It was time to act, and both were arrested and brought in for intensive interrogation.

Although details of their interrogations remain murky, for obvious reasons, journalist Andrew Mitrovica suggests that Ian Lambert was ready to do a deal with his captors. This would have offered CSIS the classic counter-intelligence opportunity to turn an agent and use him against the adversary agency. Mitrovica claims that such a deal was shot down by the 'politicians' in Ottawa, who feared diplomatic repercussions with the apparently friendly Russian successors to the Soviets were such a double agent later uncovered.[93] It is impossible to verify this. Shortly after, their arrests were leaked to the media, and any bridges to mutually satisfactory arrangements were irreparably burned. If politicians get the blame for this less useful result, Mitrovica also suggests, somewhat inconsistently, that CSIS itself refused to play along with walk-in offers from other potential Russian defectors from SVR operations, since CSIS suspected they might be set-ups. He does, however, report that in the early 1990s CSIS initially welcomed another walk-in who turned out to be a genuine prize. Anatoli Gayduk, a disgruntled KGB officer under diplomatic cover, offered his services in exchange for political asylum: in return he 'gave up the entire KGB "residency" in Ottawa to CSIS.'[94] It is unclear, however, to what degree CSIS acted on his information, perhaps harbouring lingering doubts about his reliability. As always in the wilderness of mirrors that is counter-intelligence, appearances can be deceiving, and nothing is what it seems.

As for the Lamberts, they were hustled out of Canada under security certificates. Each appealed fruitlessly against their deportation. They divorced before departure, and once back in Russia their saga took a turn to yet more tabloid-journalism form. Ian Lambert's girlfriend – the immediate cause of the marriage break-up – soon joined him in Moscow, where they wed. Then Laurie's doctor boyfriend, who had appealed unsuccessfully on her behalf against her deportation, joined her in Moscow, where they were married at a ceremony attended by Ian and his new wife. Ten years later, Laurie, now known as Elena Miller, with the assistance of her Canadian husband, launched a suit against the government of Canada, seeking permission to return to this country as an immigrant and claiming that she had renounced her past as a spy and no longer represented a threat to Canadian security. The suit failed in the Federal Court, where the chief justice upheld the security certificate and rejected her plea.[95]

In its *1997 Public Report*, CSIS summed up the implications of the Lambert affair blandly but straightforwardly:

> Occasionally, the public is reminded in the press that traditional intelligence activities continue as before. Last year, for example, the case of Dmitriy Olshevsky and Yelena Olshevskaya, the Russian illegals living in Toronto under the developing legends of Ian and Laurie Lambert, hit the headlines for a few days ...
>
> The persistence of traditional intelligence activities in the post-Cold War environment should not surprise Canadians. Several countries have passed legislation to adjust to the new security environment and have assigned new tasks to their intelligence services. Canadians can expect that countries with a perceived security gap, reduced or limited research and development capabilities, or hegemonic ambitions in their own region, will continue to seek political, military, scientific and technical intelligence.

The relatively smooth handling of the Lamberts contrasts with a murky affair early in CSIS history that seems to suggest clumsy bungling of a counter-intelligence opportunity in relation to what was then still Communist East Bloc spy operations.[96] This involved a bizarre story about a former member of Polish intelligence, Ryszard Paskowski, who defected by hijacking an airplane, escaped from prison in West Germany, made his way to Canada, and signed up with CSIS in the mid-1980s to spy on the Polish embassy and the Polish Canadian community. He claims that CSIS allegedly sent him on a mission to Europe to join an international plot to blow up an Air India plane to discredit the Sikh Canadian community, but that he deliberately blew his cover, fell out with CSIS, returned to Canada under a false name, and was then allegedly persecuted by CSIS, which tried to force his deportation by framing him with false criminal charges. It is impossible to check this story out, and parts of it, especially the alleged Air India plot, are inherently implausible. However, there seems little doubt that Paskowski was mishandled, with CSIS showing a lack of professionalism. This was in the mid-1980s; by the time of the Lamberts affair, CSIS appears to have been more competent, but then again the espionage threat from the East had morphed into something different from what it was in 1984 when CSIS began its organizational life.

Round up the Usual (Chinese) Suspects: Project SIDEWINDER

Russia was not the only former Cold War antagonist that continued to hold the attention of CSIS counter-espionage. Unlike Russia, China had never formally renounced Communism (although in the 1980s and 1990s it was building up a form of authoritarian capitalism that would challenge Western economic dominance in the twenty-first century). There were persistent suspicions that the Chinese were spying on Canada in an effort to steal Canadian technology and business secrets. Chinese diplomats and those with whom they had ongoing contacts in Canadian society were always on the radar of the Counter-Espionage Branch. But there were never any cases that came to court, never any Chinese diplomatic officials declared persona non grata, nothing that materialized in the public eye. That does not mean that CSIS had no substantive information about Chinese espionage. It might have meant that decisions were made not to prosecute for counter-intelligence reasons, or that cases never met the evidentiary standards required for successful prosecution. But it is hard to escape the impression that the Chinese were like the usual suspects who are rounded up whenever an unexplained crime occurs but somehow never wind up being charged. This impression becomes stronger when Chinese targeting shifted away from espionage to another threat to security in the CSIS Act, 'foreign influenced activities.' In the wake of this shift came embarrassing revelations about a joint CSIS-RCMP intelligence report on Chinese intelligence activities in Canada that had been scrapped or severely revised by CSIS, leading to an interagency battle and charges

that CSIS was covering up serious threats to Canadian security for political reasons.

In the CSIS Act, threats to the security of Canada include the familiar
threat of espionage:

> s. 2(a) espionage or sabotage that is against Canada or is detrimental to
> the interests of Canada or activities directed toward or in support of such
> espionage or sabotage.

This is followed by a second, more contentious, threat definition:

> s. 2(b) foreign influenced activities within or relating to Canada that are
> detrimental to the interests of Canada and are clandestine or deceptive or
> involve a threat to any person.

When SIRC offered recommendations on amending the CSIS Act in
1989,[97] it spent some time puzzling over the ambiguities of 2(b). What
exactly are 'the interests of Canada'? SIRC noted that the great debate
over the Canada-United States Free Trade Agreement the year before
showed that 'even well-intentioned, patriotic citizens can differ strongly on what is "detrimental to the interests of Canada."' 'Foreign' is not
limited to foreign states and can include corporations, associations,
or groups that are not Canadian but operate in Canada. 'Influenced'
is very ambiguous, raising the general limitation of 'lawful advocacy,
protest and dissent' exempted from CSIS scrutiny. SIRC recommended
that 2(b) be repealed and replaced by 'foreign *directed* activities within
or directly relating to Canada that are surreptitious or deceptive and
that are detrimental to the interests of Canada or involve a serious
threat to any person.' Although the five-year parliamentary review of
the CSIS Act, as well as the Canadian Bar Association, echoed this recommendation,[98] the government was unmoved. Clause 2(b) remains
on the books, unrevised.

'Agent of influence,' as opposed to espionage agent, was always an
ambiguous category, linked to the ideological underpinnings of the
Cold War. The Soviet KGB had sought to cultivate ideologically sympathetic persons in sensitive positions in Western countries to advance
views that were friendly towards Soviet policies and interests. But the
'smoking gun,' as it were, of foreign control or direction was elusive:
What if the person simply held views that happened to coincide with
this or that aspect of Soviet policy? 'Agent of influence' was a charge

that almost always issued from the right wing of the ideological spectrum, directed against those with more left-wing views. The hunt for agents of influence could look very much like a witch hunt, rather than a spy hunt.

In the post-Cold War era, the hunt for agents of influence opens a different can of worms, one that in some ways is even more unsettling for a multicultural country like Canada. If foreign influence is seen as being primarily directed towards members of diaspora communities in Canada from their ethnic homelands, is there not a danger of the official construction of 'suspect communities'? If members of diaspora communities advance views that happen to be favourable to the policies of their country of national origin, are they thereby acting as agents of foreign influence? How to distinguish the expression of honestly held views from those controlled by foreign ventriloquists? If Canadian citizens of a certain ethnicity are to be investigated for their views on public policy, does this not amount to a form of ethnic profiling? None of these questions deny the serious nature of foreign-*directed* activities in Canada that deceptively advance the interests of foreign countries at Canada's expense – these ought to be the legitimate object of CSIS attention. They do, however, indicate some of the pitfalls awaiting the casting of too wide a net. These pitfalls would become painfully obvious for a future director of CSIS in 2010 (see chapter 13), but they were already evident in the late 1990s in the ill-fated RCMP-CSIS joint assessment project dubbed SIDEWINDER.

In 1996 CSIS and the RCMP signed a 'Joint Analytical Plan' for only the second joint intelligence analysis project ever undertaken by the two agencies. The object was to assess the threat to Canada posed by Chinese national interests. The draft submitted to the RCMP-CSIS Joint Review Committee on 24 June 1997 bore the title 'Chinese Intelligence Services and Triad Financial Links to Canada,' thus linking the Chinese state to the Chinese-based criminal networks known as the 'Triads.' The project bore the codename SIDEWINDER. SIDEWINDER referred originally to a venomous rattlesnake found in the American southwestern desert. It was also the name given to a heat-seeking, air-to-air American missile designed to search out and kill enemy aircraft. Why this particular codename was given to the project remains unknown, but the connotation of a lethal threat infiltrating by stealth is unmistakable. The initial draft report exemplifies this imagery: everything that the Chinese do in relation to Canada is given the most sinister interpretation.

The authors[99] of the draft[100] claimed not to present 'theories but indicators of a multifaceted threat to Canada's national security based on concrete facts drawn from [RCMP and CSIS] databanks … classified reports from allied agencies and various open sources.' On this basis they claim to have uncovered 'the tip of the iceberg with only a minute portion of a much more complex situation showing.' Contrary to these assertions, there was a lot of theory that informed their interpretation of the 'concrete facts.' The authors made a number of largely unsupported assumptions: that Hong Kong immigration to Canada, especially through the 'entrepreneur' and 'investor' class, is marked by a significant presence of 'Chinese organized crime elements'; that Chinese business routinely combines legitimate and criminal activities; that both are closely tied to the Chinese state intelligence service; that expanded Chinese ownership of business in Canada is part of a master plan by 'the Chinese government to gain influence on Canadian politics by maximizing their presence over some of the country's economic levers' and stealing Canadian technology. Every takeover by Chinese entrepreneurs, the authors argued, leads to yet more takeovers: 'An effective domino effect ensues that acts like a well-spun web or network at strategic points.' Chinese Triads, tycoons, and state companies have in this way taken over 200 Canadian companies. Through the tycoons and the Triads (apparently pretty much the same people wearing different hats), the Chinese intelligence service is directing the steady expansion of 'direct or indirect influence over the Canadian economy and politics.' China, the SIDEWINDER analysts asserted, 'remains one of the greatest ongoing threats to Canada's national security and Canadian industry.'

This draft never made it to the joint review board. Instead, the director general of the Analysis and Production (RAP) Branch of CSIS stepped in to declare that the findings were 'based on innuendo, and unsupported by facts,' ordering the report shelved. The RCMP were not pleased; after negotiations between the two agencies over a few months, work on the project was resumed, but this time more closely under CSIS's wing. A significantly revised second draft then met with criticism from the RCMP. Even so, the director general of CSIS's RAP Branch was still uncomfortable with the remaining unsupported innuendo. SIDEWINDER was beginning to resemble an unlovely duckling rejected by both parents. In January 1999 a final draft was completed and approved by both agencies, although the RCMP told SIRC that it was 'not fully satisfied' since, unlike the first draft, the final version 'fails to raise key strategic questions and to outline some of the more interesting avenues for research.'[101]

Eventually, the first draft made its way mysteriously onto the Internet in unredacted form, amid journalistic charges that SIDEWINDER had been terminated because CSIS was bowing to political pressure from a Liberal government that was anxious to extend ties with China; that CSIS had ordered all the materials gathered by SIDEWINDER to be destroyed; and that a serious threat to the security of Canada was being ignored.[102] SIRC was called in to investigate, and it concluded that none of the charges of political interference were supported by evidence and that the project had not been scrapped, nor its records destroyed (although it rapped CSIS's knuckles for poor information management and some lost records). It compared the final version favourably with the first draft, which SIRC insisted was 'deeply flawed and unpersuasive in almost all respects,' employing 'leaps of logic and non sequiturs to the point of incoherence ... rich with the language of scare-mongering and conspiracy theory.' We cannot assess the final version, which remains classified, but SIRC's strong criticism of the leaked draft seems fully justified. We would agree that 'at its core, the Sidewinder first draft lacked essential definitional clarity: if one purports to examine the extent of illegal and threat-based activities allegedly taking place alongside entirely legal and benign ones, it is vital to be able to tell the difference between the two.'[103] The SIDEWINDER first draft signally failed that test. Of course, to the supporters of SIDEWINDER, the SIRC investigation was a whitewash and cover-up. Over the years there have been persistent efforts to vindicate SIDEWINDER as a courageous warning to a negligent and insouciant government and a security service that bent its own judgment to political expediency.[104] What can we make of the entire SIDEWINDER imbroglio and the deeper issue of Chinese-influenced activities in Canada? Apart from noting that the issue was far from exhausted in the late 1990s, and indeed continues unabated today, perhaps the most judicious conclusion is that once again the usual suspects were rounded up; once again, no charges could be proven; and once again the usual suspects had to be released.

CSIS at the Millennium

As the year 2000 approached, Canada, like other countries, was in a state of high anxiety over the 'Y2K' threat – the idea that computer systems would crash and the infrastructure of economy and society crumble with the turn of the millennium. At an earlier turn of a millennium, the year 1000 AD, there had been similar waves of anxiety and foreboding, based on the idea that this would be the second coming of Christ, the Final Judgment, and the end of days. Of course, neither apocalyptic event actually happened, and life went on, pretty much as before the turn of the millennium.

CSIS was consulted about the Y2K threat, and the agency had to think about the security eventualities that might follow a catastrophic infrastructure failure. By 1999, it was an organization somewhat better prepared to deal with unexpected contingencies and eventualities than the barely reshaped RCMP security service that had stumbled into new organizational form in 1984. It was getting its own house in better order, with a more professional group of intelligence officers and a better-educated analytical core. It had improved its relations with the rest of the security intelligence bureaucracy, including the RCMP, and was playing with greater confidence and self-assurance on the wider Ottawa stage.

Yet millennial hysteria aside, CSIS stood on the brink of a major challenge to business as usual. A glimpse of this future came in late 1999 when Ahmed Ressam, an Islamic terrorist who had entered Canada under an undetected false identity, boarded a ferry in Victoria, arriving in the United States at Port Angeles where his nervous demeanour sparked the suspicions of a U.S. border guard. Ressam was found to be carrying explosive materials with which he intended to bomb the Los Angeles Airport. The so-called Millennial Bomber was part of a plot organized by a then shadowy Islamic terrorist network, Al-Qaeda. Canada, and CSIS, had failed to detect and prevent this serious threat to the United States, an embarrassment that would last for many years, damaging the reputation of Canada both in official circles and in American public opinion. Then, on 11 September 2001, Al-Qaeda operatives took control of commercial aircraft and turned them into weapons of mass destruction directed at the symbols of American economic and military might, the twin towers of the World Trade Center in New York and the Pentagon in Washington. This was the real millennial challenge, and CSIS would wake up the day after 9/11 to face a radically different world.

PART FIVE

After the Twin Towers

12

After the Deluge: In the Shadow of the Twin Towers, 2001–11

We begin this chapter on 11 September 2001, one of those turning points in history that demarcate one era from another. If the years from 1989 to 2001 represented a somewhat formless 'post-Cold War' era, the terrorist attacks on New York and Washington on that fateful day sharply set off the succeeding years as falling under a new description of global security in which violent non-state actors contest the hegemony of states in the global system. It is not necessary to fall into the trap of those who over-excitedly argued, as the United States still reeled from the impact of the attacks, that the world had somehow changed forever. The Americans declared a global War on Terror, a grandiose but theoretically jejune concept that implicitly replaced the old totalizing logic of the Cold War with a new totalizing logic that saw terrorist networks led by Al-Qaeda as a latter-day version of the Communist International. The global War on Terror, as such, did not survive the Bush administration that coined the phrase. Nor did the Bush administration ever make operational sense of this 'war' as a strategic doctrine. States make war on other states. Declaring war on an abstract noun is a logical absurdity which only obscured thinking about effective counter-measures to the challenges posed by violent non-state actors.

We can now see a great deal more continuity pre- and post-9/11, as well as the sharp discontinuity that was immediately evident. Nonetheless, 9/11 was a crucial divide, especially for a security intelligence agency like CSIS that found organizational opportunities arising from the new realities but also faced organizational adjustments, some fairly wrenching, and the challenge of having to rethink its role fundamentally. In particular, CSIS would have to adjust to the possibilities, and perils, of the integration of its security intelligence functions with the

efforts of other agencies charged with responsibilities in combating terrorism.

After 9/11: Towards Fortress North America?

The immediate impact of 9/11 on CSIS as an organization was bracing. First, it forced a refocusing of threats to security into a narrower
but more intense band: so-called Sunni Muslim extremist elements,
sometimes misleadingly referred to as violent Islamic jihadist movements, or, in short form, Al-Qaeda and similar networks. The focus was
not new to CSIS, which had been looking into this area with increasing interest through the 1990s, but in the wake of 9/11 American pressure became intense to target almost exclusively the specific threat that
brought about the 9/11 devastation. Later in the decade, focus partially
shifted from Al-Qaeda and other global networks to homegrown 'radicalization' of Muslims, especially younger Muslims, in Canada, but the
global emphasis remained.

The Americans were demanding, not unreasonably under the circumstances, that international intelligence and law-enforcement cooperation be brought to bear on the perpetrators of 9/11 in a concerted effort
to 'connect the dots' – to use the fashionable contemporary phrase – of
the global terrorist network. In the Canadian case, American pressures
were particularly insistent because of the widespread although errone-
ous belief in many American quarters that the 9/11 conspirators had
entered the United States through the allegedly 'lax' Canadian border.
The pre-9/11 spectre of Ahmed Ressam, caught slipping into the United States in 1999 on his way to bomb the Los Angeles airport,[1] was one
that Canadian officials found impossible to remove from the consciousness of Americans, who tended to ignore the substantial post-9/11 investments in and upgrading of security by the Canadian government.[2]

Neither CSIS nor the Canadian government was under any illusion
that Canada itself was exempt from the reach of terrorism. Indeed, terrorism in various forms, especially Sikh and Fenian, extended back to
the nineteenth century and had much to do with the origins of the Canadian security service, as this book has recounted. As recently as 1970
with the FLQ crisis and the tragic bombing of Air India by Sikh extremists in 1985, Canada had been forced to confront the potential of violent
nationalist/ethnic/religious movements to carry out assassinations on
Canadian soil and bloody attacks on innocent Canadian civilians. Certainly, if Canada presented softer targets for twenty-first-century ter-

rorists than a United States suddenly galvanized by 9/11 into high alert and draconian security precautions, there was no reason to expect the attention of planners of such attacks not to settle on Canada – especially given the high degree of economic integration of North America and the dependence of the United States on vulnerable Canadian infrastructure for delivering vital energy supplies to the American economy. The Canadian public was shocked and terrified by the spectre of 9/11 and would demand that its government do everything possible to prevent any such calamity befalling Canada. In short, there was a genuine made-in-Canada basis for refocusing the concentration of CSIS on the kind of specific threat that was embodied in 9/11, even at the expense of lessening attention to some degree on other sorts of threats that lacked the kind of compelling headline-grabbing notice of 9/11 and the hegemonic direction of the United States in its global War on Terror.

As powerful as the domestic logic compelling Canada to give the greatest priority to the terrorist threat, the American dimension offered even more bracing reinforcement. In the immediate aftermath of 9/11, a traumatized American state in effect began closing down the 'world's longest undefended border' and lengthy backlogged lines of commercial and visitor traffic on both sides of the suddenly stiffened border persisted long after the first shockwaves had subsided. The spectre of American security concerns – however exaggerated in the case of the Canadian border – in effect trumping the dollars-and-cents logic that had integrated the two economies on a continental scale could be measured in huge economic losses both actual and potential. Such losses were to be counted on both sides of the border but loomed proportionately much larger on the Canadian side given the country's lopsided dependence on exports to the United States. Americans seemed prepared to bear the costs of putting security first, which, in light of persistent American myths about their insecure northern border, sent a chilling message to Canadian business and government.

The immediate response from various quarters – the Official Opposition in Parliament, many provincial premiers, some academics, editorial writers and media commentators, and, above all, corporate Canada – was to throw up the alternative of a North American security perimeter. Never clearly articulated in detail, such an arrangement might mirror the common security boundary around Europe in which individual member states erase internal borders but join together in enforcing a unified entry and exit policy around Europe as a whole. Later versions of this idea were broadened to include a security-for-economics swap, in which intensified economic integration of North America was exchanged for a common security perimeter, thus finally guaranteeing Canadian business unfettered access to the American market.

A security-for-economics swap has been strongly advocated by business lobbies, conservative think tanks, and some politicians in both the Conservative and Liberal parties. But in practice it never commended itself to either the Liberal governments of Jean Chrétien and Paul Martin, nor, it would seem, initially to Stephen Harper's Conservative Party once it achieved office in 2006. The reason for this practical reluctance is simple: Europe maintains a set of supranational governmental institutions to hammer out common immigration and refugee policies among member states, but NAFTA has no provision for shared governance and thus little if any voice for distinctive Canadian concerns in any common security perimeter. Beyond the huge (10:1) disproportion in the size of the two countries, Congress and the executive during the administration of George Bush were notably hostile to any diminution of American sovereignty, and there has been little evidence of change in the 'America First' stance of Congress after the 2009 change in administrations. On the other side of the border, meanwhile, there have been persistent fears that, in any continental-security integration, distinctive Canadian policies would have little chance of survival, and this is a price that governments have been reluctant to pay. The Chrétien government's Smart Borders agreements opted instead to mollify American security concerns on a case-by-case basis. While this pragmatic approach had only limited success in removing impediments and irritants to cross-border flows of goods and people – indeed, the irritants rose in number during the latter years of the Bush administration – it succeeded for a few years in keeping the spectre of a sovereignty-stifling security perimeter deal off the table. By 2011, however, the Harper government was poised to sign a wide-ranging security-perimeter deal with the United States, although until the precise outlines of such an agreement are publicly revealed, and approved by both Parliament and Congress, the implications for Canadian security remain unclear.

A common North American security front against the threat of terrorism would be based on ongoing cooperation of the security and intelligence agencies of the two countries and deeper and more effective intelligence sharing. If Canada is to succeed in convincing the United States that it is a trusted partner in the fight against terrorism, that the northern border does not in its present form constitute a vulnerability to U.S. homeland security, then CSIS has a key role at the cutting edge of counter-terrorism cooperation and intelligence sharing with the Americans. From the Canadian standpoint, access to the intelligence gathered by the much larger and more amply resourced American agencies is crucial, but this in turn rests on the reputation and trustworthiness in American eyes of their Canadian partner agencies, attributes that must be constantly earned and carefully maintained. Catching a glimpse of the kind of thing that might be routinely involved in such close cooperation, a WikiLeaks release of American diplomatic correspondence in 2008 shows CSIS Director Jim Judd boasting to State Department official Eliot Cohen that 'CSIS had responded to recent, non-specific intelligence on possible terror operations by "vigorously harassing" known Hezbollah members in Canada' – bearing in mind that the United States has identified Hezbollah as one of the leading terrorist threats in the world today.[3]

New Resources for National Security

Following 9/11, the Chrétien cabinet put just under $8 billion of new resources into national security and enforcement over five years. Of this, $1.6 billion was allocated to intelligence and policing, and $1 billion to immigration screening and enforcement, both areas in which CSIS plays a leading role.[4] The impact on CSIS as an organization has been notable. The CSIS annual budget increased from $179 million in 1999–2000 to $389 million in 2007–8, a gain of 117 per cent over eight years.[5] The CSIS workforce expanded from 2,061 in 1999–2000 to 2,529 in 2007–8, an increase of 23 per cent.[6] In the process, CSIS has acquired a more modernized workforce, with an average age in 2007–8 of forty-one; half of these employees were women, and 42 per cent of them spoke a language other than English or French (over two-thirds were bilingual, English and French, a matter of some note given the early problems with bilingualism in the 1980s).

New financial resources are, of course, always welcomed by any organization, but more efficient administration and clearer direction from the political level above are equally welcome, and these, too, were forthcoming in the aftermath of the 9/11 crisis. The Chrétien and Martin governments redesigned the architecture of national-security policy making at the cabinet and bureaucratic levels. Most notable was the creation of the new omnibus Department of Public Safety and Emergency Preparedness Canada (later Public Safety Canada), which included under its umbrella CSIS, the RCMP, and most of the intelligence community, with the exception of the CSE, defence intelligence, and the Privy Council Office. Moreover, in 2004 the government published a national-security policy, offering a philosophy and policy framework for the area for the first time.[7]

New Powers to Fight Terrorism – and More

In the wake of 9/11, the Bush administration unveiled a mammoth, omnibus piece of legislation called the USA Patriot Act that considerably extended the powers of the federal government to carry out intrusive surveillance of American society in the name of fighting terrorism. Although pushed through with almost no opposition, or even criticism, by a traumatized Congress, the Patriot Act later proved highly controversial. In Canada, the Liberal government of Jean Chrétien believed the moment right for its own special legislation, which bore the more mundane title of the Anti-Terrorism Act 2001[8] and received royal assent on 18 December 2001 – but not before extensive hearings, wide debate inside and outside Parliament,[9] and forty-seven votes against passage in the House of Commons.

This legislation extended state powers to deal with an emergency, the new threat of terrorism that had extended into North America. Terrorism was defined in a manner that critics consider overbroad but proponents consider necessary for more effective criminal law enforcement against a new kind of threat for which existing law is allegedly inadequate. Among the controversial aspects of this definition is the criminalization of motive: terrorism is defined as activity undertaken for 'political, religious or ideological purpose, objective or cause,' thus breaking with a long tradition in Canada in which the law is indifferent to the motive underlying a crime.[10]

Most controversial were special emergency powers – preventive arrest and investigative hearings – that went beyond traditional powers by authorizing the detention of individuals on suspicion and the compelling of answers in interrogation. So controversial were these new powers that after public hearings they were subjected to 'sunset' clauses that required parliamentary renewal after five years. In 2007 the combined Opposition parties in the minority Parliament allowed the powers to elapse, amid a rancorous debate rather uncharacteristic of Canadian discussion of national-security issues; charges from the government benches that the Opposition parties were 'soft on terrorism' were traded with charges from the Opposition that the government was 'soft on Charter rights.'[11] However, both powers were later reintroduced, and with a Conservative majority after the 2011 election, their return was virtually guaranteed.[12] A curious aspect of this debate is that, along with sunset clauses, an additional requirement is that the government must report to Parliament annually on the instances of invocation of these powers. Surprisingly, in light of the insistence of law-enforcement and security officials on the necessity of the new powers, it turns out that neither has ever been used. The one attempt was retroactive, in connection with the trial of two individuals in the Air India bombing (that ended with acquittals) when the crown sought court approval of the constitutionality of investigative hearings – yet dropped the matter after getting a favourable ruling.

Another controversial part of the Anti-Terrorism Act is its list of terrorist entities, being defined as a group that 'has as one of its purposes or activities facilitating or carrying out any terrorist activity.' The government merely has to establish that it has 'reasonable grounds to believe' that a group fits its definition to permit its listing. Yet listing has the serious consequence of criminalizing the group, and of criminalizing any support for that group by individuals. In other words, a whole new category of criminal activity has been created by the legislation. Charitable organizations that make any resources available, 'directly or indirectly,' to a listed entity will find their charitable status revoked. Listing has inevitably become a controversial, politically charged process. For instance, the Lebanese group Hezbollah, with branches in Canada, was listed under intense pressure from pro-Israeli groups and media, despite the fact that the political wing of Hezbollah is a regular participant in Lebanese government, with cabinet seats, and notwithstanding opposition to listing from some Muslim groups.

These and other changes to the Criminal Code enacted under the Anti-Terrorism Act and specifically directed towards terrorist threats have placed new and potentially intrusive powers in the hands of the authorities. The effect of the new powers on existing agencies is varied. To the extent that the legislation focuses primarily on law enforcement, it is the RCMP that potentially gains the most in terms of expanded powers. CSIS, on the other hand, saw neither expansion of its mandate nor any loosening of the requirements to get approval and warrants for surveillance. More subtly – and this would only emerge later – the emphasis in the legislation on the criminalization of activities in support of or associated with terrorism would not only expand the role of the RCMP as a law-enforcement agency in national-security matters, but would also put pressure on CSIS to provide more of its security intelligence for law-enforcement purposes in court. This is a burden that CSIS has found increasingly difficult to bear, as we shall see. The same legislative thrust also pointed in the direction of greater coop-eration and integration of CSIS activities with those of the RCMP and other law-enforcement agencies in tracking and interdicting terrorist actions. While this was in one sense long overdue and indeed welcome, it would also pose new challenges to the way CSIS does its job.

One specific challenge to CSIS's use of human sources lies in the criminalization of activities supporting terrorism, as well as the listing of terrorist entities. The problem is that CSIS sources operating secretly within terrorist organizations might find themselves on the wrong side of the provisions of the Anti-Terrorism Act. This is an old conundrum for human sources implanted in groups with the potential to carry out criminal acts (which, of course, is the very reason for their targeting in the first place). The new legislation, by virtue of widening the defini-tion of criminal activities, also widened the likelihood of CSIS sources having to break the law to maintain their cover. The burden was on CSIS to ensure that its human-source program was within the law. Ac-countability in this matter is either internal, to CSIS, or external, to the minister of public safety. In reviewing CSIS human-source manage-ment, SIRC found that 'there was no venue by which it [CSIS] could inform the Minister of the implications of the *Anti-Terrorism Act* on hu-man source operations.' SIRC suggested regular ministerial updates. As SIRC commented: 'As Canada's list of terrorist entities grows longer [over forty in 2009], commensurate growth is expected in the number of CSIS human source operations that could benefit listed organizations. It is important that CSIS be held to account for these actions.'[13] This is a complex issue for which there are no easy answers. Accountability in this area will never be public, but it remains important even within the government.

The Anti-Terrorism Act contains more than its name implies, even if most of the political and media attention during its passage was direct-ed at its specific anti-terrorist provisions. It may also be seen as, in ef-fect, an omnibus 'National Security Act.' A virtual wish list of legislative changes compiled by various agencies and offices had been in existence for a number of years but had failed to gain any priority status from successive governments. This wish list was suddenly on the agenda under the capacious umbrella of the new legislation. Among changes not directly or only indirectly connected to terrorism as such were: the replacement of the antiquated Official Secrets Act with a modernized Security of Information Act; the provision of a legal mandate for the activities of the Communications Security Establishment, along with a new offence of 'economic espionage'; amendments to the Proceeds of Crime (Money Laundering) Act; and restrictive changes to the access-to-information, privacy, and personal information protection and electronic documents acts. Again, few of these changes directly affected the CSIS mandate. Even in the crisis atmosphere post-9/11, CSIS appears to have already had, or thought it had, the powers it needed to do its job.[14]

Integrated Intelligence: The New Watchword

Two major global trends in policing and security coincided with the impact of 9/11 to change the practice of security intelligence in Canada. First is the rise of 'intelligence-led policing.'[15] This developed out of the 'community policing' concept popular in the 1980s and 1990s, which stressed crime prevention and closer police relations with the community. The RCMP sees intelligence-led policing as 'the collection and analysis of information to produce an intelligence end product designed to inform police decision-making at both the tactical and strategic levels. It is a model of policing in which intelligence serves as a guide to operations, rather than the reverse … It is predicated on the notion that a principal task of the police is to prevent and detect crime rather than simply to react to it.'[16] While this primarily relates to the RCMP's criminal law-enforcement and crime-prevention mandate, it also bears significance for the force's law-enforcement responsibilities in the area of national security. The detection and prevention of terrorism is dependent upon relations with the communities in which the terrorist networks operate, and the collection of intelligence on the threat is essential to prevent terrorist planning from being put into action. The clear implication is that CSIS, which collects security intelligence on threats to the security of Canada, must have its work coordinated more closely with an increasingly intelligence-led RCMP if counter-terrorist operations are to be successful. The kind of self-defeating organizational rivalry that so unfortunately characterized the Air India fiasco in the 1980s was a luxury that Canada could no longer afford in an age of yet more lethal threats.

Integration of operations is the second major global trend in policing and security. Integration is understood at many levels. First, it involves increasing integration of efforts across borders and between agencies and departments of different nation-states. International cooperation of security and intelligence agencies under American leadership in the Cold War had already led to what some saw as a 'Western intelligence community' – or perhaps more appropriately, several Western intelligence communities – which had a certain life of their own apart from the separate national institutions that constituted them. The events of 9/11 added considerable urgency to the need for international cooperation, since terrorist networks like Al-Qaeda are non-state actors operating in the age of new information technology that renders national boundaries almost irrelevant to the planning and execution of actions with global consequences. While the invasion of Afghanistan and the forcible removal from office of the Taliban in 2001 was predicated on the idea that the regime had offered a base for Al-Qaeda's strike against the United States, subsequent history suggests that traditional territorial bases are not in fact crucial to global terrorist networks, which can operate terrorist 'franchises' from virtual bases in cyberspace while inspiring start-ups among radicalized minority communities in Western countries. National stand-alone agencies jealously guarding their sovereign prerogatives will not be enough for this kind of threat, but neither will the intelligence cooperation of the Cold War past, when the antagonist was another bloc of states, any longer be sufficient. Newer and closer forms of integrated operations, it was widely agreed, would have to be the new norm. Unfortunately, the Americans under the clumsy leadership of the unilaterally disposed Bush administration undermined their own credibility in achieving workable multilateral integration of intelligence. For the RCMP and later for CSIS, closer co-operation with a reckless U.S. administration and with new and uncertain allies with dubious human-rights records would turn out to be a minefield, as we shall see later. But, whatever the unanticipated fallout, the principle of closer integration across borders in the post-9/11 world was unassailable. The problem was: How could integration be made to work effectively while minimizing the collateral damage to human rights and liberal democracy, as well as national sovereignty?

In the Canadian context, integration also meant integration across the institutional stovepipes within the federal government's national-security activities, and integration across federal, provincial, and municipal jurisdictions. The need to work together across these lines had already begun to spur cooperation well before 9/11, but these efforts accelerated after the shock administered the system on 11 September 2001.

These efforts got off to a bad start with the Maher Arar affair and the ill-fated Project A-O Canada, which highlighted some disastrous decisions on intelligence sharing with the Americans and led to strained relations between the RCMP and CSIS (this is discussed in more detail in chapter 13). However, integrated operations were soon put on a more workable basis with the emergence of Integrated National Security Enforcement Teams (INSETs) and Integrated Border Enforcement Teams (IBETs), the latter including U.S. federal and state agencies. INSETs are under RCMP direction and control but include members from other federal agencies such as CSIS, the Canadian Border Services Agency (CBSA), Citizenship and Immigration Canada, and so on, as well as from relevant provincial and municipal police forces. By 2010, INSETs were operational in Montreal, Ottawa, Toronto, and Vancouver.

Another important initiative in cooperation is the establishment of a CSIS/RCMP Joint Management Team to deal with coordination of strategic direction and joint protocols and to minimize conflicts where CSIS and the RCMP are investigating in the same area. Joint Operational Workshops encourage employees of each organization to 'share ideas, learn about each other's mandates, and find ways of working in a more cooperative and effective manner.'[17]

The Arar Commission looked at one example of such interagency cooperation, O-INSET, located in the Toronto area in 2004, and found that it comprised fifty-three regular RCMP members, two civilian RCMP employees, and twenty-two others on secondment from other agencies.[18] O-INSET is the unit that accounts for the greatest success so far in Canadian counter-terrorism: the arrest of the so-called 'Toronto 18,' a group of mainly very young plotters intending to carry out bombings on several targets, including the Toronto Stock Exchange and the CSIS regional headquarters in downtown Toronto. Despite some criticism in the media that the alleged plot was overblown – eventually, of the eighteen originally charged, only eleven were brought to court – it is apparent from evidence in the court documents, and indeed from the contrition of a few defendants who pleaded guilty, that this was an attempt to replicate on Canadian soil the kind of bloody terrorist acts undertaken in Britain by similarly homegrown Islamic extremists that did not have direct ties to Al-Qaeda or other global networks. Even though the young accused often appear in the surveillance evidence as somewhat clueless teenagers playing war games, there is no doubt that their intentions were malign, and that if they had succeeded, many innocent lives might have been lost. The case stands as a partial vindication of the much-criticized Anti-Terrorism Act, under which most of the accused were charged. The apprehension of the plot and the arrest of its protagonists must be seen as a major success for counter-terrorism – although CSIS Director Richard Fadden warned a House of Commons committee in 2010 that his agency continued to hold some two hundred individuals in Canada under surveillance as terrorist suspects.[19] Whether this number represents the bulk of the potential threat, or merely the tip of a dangerous iceberg, remains to be seen.

As significant as the arrests were the investigative methods used by O-INSET. As has been widely discussed since 9/11, the old Cold War methods of intelligence collection, especially the technologically sophisticated communications and imaging intelligence used to great effect against a superpower antagonist like the old Soviet Union, were next to useless against small, highly disciplined, closely knit terrorist cells that offered few targets for spy satellites and communication intercepts. Old-fashioned human-intelligence sources (individual cell members turned by fair means or foul to become agents of the state, or undercover agents planted inside the networks) once again assumed a pre-eminence not seen in decades of technological espionage rivalry between superpowers. But terrorist cells have proved to be hard targets, very difficult to penetrate. The Toronto 18 were an exception. These inept plotters, hardly exemplars of Al-Qaeda-style discipline and counter-intelligence tradecraft, were vulnerable to penetration by human sources. Two undercover agents were in fact essential to the prosecution case. They also proved controversial when details about their activities, and the moral ambiguities inherent in such undercover work, became public knowledge.

One of the agents, Mubin Shaikh, was originally employed by CSIS, which tasked him to infiltrate the group in November 2005 but passed him over to the RCMP the following month. He apparently 'preferred to work as an informer, rather than an agent, because he wished to remain confidential and did not want to testify.'[20] Whatever reticence Shaikh may have initially shown, however, soon vanished when the case led to criminal charges, as he sought out the media spotlight to demonstrate his services to Canada as the undercover agent who helped break the plot.[21] More seriously, questions were raised about Shaikh's possible role in entrapping the apparently impressionable young men, as surveillance transcripts seemed to suggest. However, when defence counsel brought this matter to trial, the court ruled that there was no entrapment or abuse of process. This question does point to a perennial dilemma of undercover informants or agents: to maintain their bona fides, they may from time to time have to play an ambiguous role on the margins of criminality. Bizarrely, a U.S. document 'WikiLeaked' in 2011 revealed that CSIS had passed on Shaikh's name to the American authorities for inclusion on terrorist watch lists (along with incorrect information referring to him as foreign-born). This might represent reckless sloppiness on the part of CSIS, with serious personal consequences for a crucial source. It could indicate that the crown's key witness in gaining convictions in the 'Toronto 18' trials was not what he had been represented to be in court. Defence counsel for the convicted was soon talking about reopening cases on the basis of the crown's failure to offer full disclosure concerning its key informant.[22]

The other informant gained notoriety in the media when it was learned that he was not only paid by the RCMP for his services – as was Shaikh – but may have been paid very large sums far beyond the normal stipend for undercover sources. Shaher Elsohemy, it now appears, was initially paid half a million dollars, but when the full costs of placing him under witness protection are counted in, he may have by now rung up a bill of close to $4 million (this is speculation, not confirmed). Still, he might be 'worth every penny, at least as far as prosecutors and security services are concerned,' since his testimony has been particularly devastating to the defence. Convictions 'might well have been impossible, had police not installed a man on the inside.'[23] This, too, illustrates another ambiguous aspect of undercover operations: if informants cannot be recruited for idealistic reasons alone, they may be blackmailed into cooperation by holding threats over their heads (such as the threat of deportation, if available); or they may be paid handsomely enough that they become willing to betray their erstwhile comrades. There are really no other options. Payment has an advantage that recommends it as a preferred option to spymasters: it establishes a link that places the informant under an obligation to his handlers. Elsohemy proved to be a valuable tool for the prosecution; his employment resulted in a key conviction, and the court ruled that he had in fact acted not as an agent provocateur entrapping the suspect but rather as a valuable source of information for the crown.[24]

By June 2010, the last of the Toronto 18 prosecutions resulted in more convictions, a record of unrelieved success in the courts.[25] These cases were no sooner taken care of than a new case of homegrown terrorist activity broke: a number of men were arrested in an alleged Internet-based conspiracy to carry out bombings, in Canada as well as abroad, as a result of another INSET operation centred in Ottawa employing electronic surveillance, possibly with the assistance of a tip-off by Pakistani intelligence.[26]

The Toronto 18 case represents a success for the model of integrated enforcement. To the extent that CSIS has played an important role within the INSET operations, its actions demonstrate a marked improvement over the turf wars and petty rivalries that too often characterized relations between the RCMP and CSIS in years past, and that the Air India Commission of Inquiry would expose once again with its report on terrorist acts of the 1980s. There is a downside for CSIS, however. Integrated-enforcement operations stress criminal investigation and law enforcement. The security intelligence that CSIS collects is not in the first instance for purposes of law enforcement, and if forced into the courtroom it may endanger the security of CSIS sources, operational methods, or protected information from foreign sources. Thus, although integrated operations are a logical step forward, they are not without cost for an agency like CSIS, which must adjust its traditional sense of its role and purpose to the new realities and new requirements of the age of terrorism. Later in this chapter, we will examine more closely some of the strains imposed on CSIS by this new dispensation.

Another important innovation in the national-security architecture is the Integrated Threat Assessment Centre (ITAC), which rose out of directions laid down in the 2004 National Security Policy. ITAC, which is housed within CSIS for administrative purposes and is staffed mainly although not exclusively by CSIS personnel, supplemented by secondments from other government agencies with national-security responsibilities, is designed to be a community-wide resource. Although the CSIS director is accountable for ITAC's performance, he is advised on strategic directions for ITAC by the national-security adviser to the prime minister and by ITAC's Management Board, made up of the heads of departments and agencies represented on ITAC. This rather complicated arrangement results from the strong integrative thrust that underlies ITAC. Its mandate is to produce 'integrated, comprehensive and timely threat assessments for all levels of government with security responsibilities, first-line responders such as law enforcement and, as appropriate, critical infrastructure stakeholders in the private sector.'[27] ITAC evaluates terrorist threats and distributes assessments to the appropriate places. Importantly, ITAC attempts to address a persistent problem in government by making classified intelligence available in usable form to officials who may lack appropriate security clearance but need actionable intelligence to fulfil their obligations (the inability to distribute pertinent intelligence to those who most needed it but lacked clearance was one of the problems leading to the Air India disaster). ITAC also contributes to international integration of counter-terrorism operations by cooperating with its counterpart foreign integrated-threat-assessment centres in the United States, the United Kingdom, Australia, and New Zealand, among other countries. It makes foreign-intelligence assessments available to Canadian officials (sometimes with Canadian perspective added) and Canadian assessments to its allies. At this point, and from outside government, it is not possible to assess ITAC's performance, but on paper it represents a step forward towards a more effective national-security community.

One of the recommendations of the Commission of Inquiry into the Air India bombing that reported in 2010 was to enhance the role of the national-security adviser to the prime minister to that of a virtual intelligence czar who would coordinate the national-security activities of the entire community, including CSIS and the RCMP.[28] Despite some favourable press reception,[29] the government rejected this recommendation, preferring to rest responsibility for anti-terrorist coordination instead on the shoulders of the minister of public safety.[30] Such a revamped office would provide more centralized direction, although there are other administrative concerns about such reorganization. The American experience in implementing the 9/11 Commission's recommendation for a new office of director of national intelligence (DNI) to supplant the old dual role of the director of central intelligence as both head of the CIA and overall boss of the U.S. intelligence community has not been an entirely happy one, with a succession of DNIs either quitting or being replaced by the president, amid much agency grumbling and turf protection.

CSIS Plays Cop: Mohammed Mansour Jabarah

Shortly after 9/11, a curious story surfaced briefly in the media about a Canadian individual handed across the border into U.S. custody not by the RCMP in the course of its law-enforcement role but by CSIS, the security intelligence service.[31] An admitted Al-Qaeda member, Mohammed Mansour Jabarah had planned to bomb American and Israeli embassies in Southeast Asia, working with Jemaah Islamiah, the notorious Indonesian terrorist network. Apprehended in Oman, Jabarah was handed over to CSIS officials in April 2002 and returned to Canada.

While there could be no doubt about Jabarah's terrorist record, there was a problem: he could not be charged in Canada, since all of his terrorist activities pre-dated the passage of the Anti-Terrorism Act.

It seems that Jabarah then presented himself as someone willing to be cooperative with authorities, and the prospect of gaining intelligence from someone as well connected to Al-Qaeda as he was (he was linked, for example, to Khalid Sheik Mohammed, one of the highest-value Al-Qaeda figures and a principal architect of the 9/11 action) was difficult to resist. So cooperative was Jabarah that he apparently agreed voluntarily (or so it was claimed) to be turned over to the Americans as a golden source of intelligence on the Al-Qaeda network. He even signed an agreement to facilitate his entry into the United States. And so it was that in May 2002 CSIS had him transported to the United States on a Canadian government-owned aircraft, marking the first time that the security service, with no law-enforcement powers, had performed what amounted to an extradition of a Canadian citizen to another country without any appropriate authority. In other words, CSIS had carried out an extraordinary rendition (to use the soon-to-be notorious American term) of a Canadian citizen to the United States.

Whether or not Jabarah was ever sincere in his willingness to cooperate remains unclear. It appears that he was indeed a useful source to the Americans – for a time. Then something happened either to change his mind or to reveal his continued allegiance to Al-Qaeda. His guise of cooperation with authorities long since dropped, Jabbarah in 2008 was sentenced to life imprisonment in a U.S. court.[32]

The curious role of CSIS in this affair drew the attention of the service's watchdog, SIRC, which launched a special review of the case. It began by enlisting the services of retired Supreme Court justice Gérard La Forest, a recognized expert on the Charter of Rights. SIRC was not pleased by what it found:

> SIRC's review raised questions regarding CSIS's contention that Jabarah's decisions were made freely and voluntarily. The Committee concluded that Jabarah was 'arbitrarily detained' by CSIS in violation of section 9 of the Charter and that his right to silence as protected by sections 7 and 11 (c), as well as his right to counsel under section 10, was breached. Furthermore, his right to remain in Canada as protected by section 6 of the Charter (mobility rights) was violated. SIRC believes that section 12 of the CSIS Act does not authorize all aspects of this investigation, and that CSIS strayed from its security intelligence mandate into the area of law enforcement.[33]

Using 'Terrorism' as a Recruitment Tool:
The Case of Suleyman Govan

Another case that pitted SIRC against CSIS went back well before 9/11 and demonstrates the continuity of issues surrounding the CSIS role in immigration security. In 1994 a Kurdish refugee from a Turkey in the midst of a brutal internal conflict with Kurdish separatists was seeking landed immigrant status in Canada. Suleyman Govan was called to a CSIS security interrogation and told that the agency had information that he was a 'member' of the PKK, the Kurdish Workers Party, identified by the government of Canada as a terrorist organization. Govan was given a choice, one offered many times in the past by CSIS to individuals caught in the security mesh: he could be cooperative with CSIS and become an intelligence source on the PKK and its activities in Canada; if, on the other hand, he chose to be uncooperative, the possibility that his application would be refused on security grounds was on the table. Govan denied that he was or had been a member of the PKK and did not take up the offer to act as a source. His application was refused, deportation was threatened, and what was to prove a fourteen-year ordeal for the refugee began. Believing the issue of PKK membership to be the result of a secret accusation by a fellow Kurd with a personal axe to grind, Govan fought to clear his name and stay in Canada. His complaint against CSIS eventually went before SIRC, where it was heard by then SIRC member Bob Rae. In a case that saw the discrediting of the CSIS source against Govan and a document produced in evidence by CSIS that Rae described as an evident 'forgery,' SIRC finally reported in April 2000 – three years after Govan's complaint against CSIS was initiated – that there was no evidence that Govan had ever been a PKK member or a member of any terrorist organization, and that he should be granted his landed papers. For its part, CSIS simply redoubled its efforts to force Govan out of the country, challenging SIRC's jurisdiction and pressuring Immigration Canada to ignore the review body's findings. It took six more years of struggle by Govan and his lawyers and supporters, but finally, on 18 May 2006, the beleaguered refugee received a letter from Immigration Canada indicating he had been granted permanent resident status, even though, as the letter indicated with considerable understatement, 'your application has taken some time.'[34]

Sadly, it seems that CSIS harassment of Govan continued even after this decision. The agency was relentless in its determination to punish a man who had refused its offer. Officially, CSIS denies, as it always has denied, that it uses the threat of security-clearance refusals as a tool to recruit spies within immigrant communities, but this denial is no more than a fictional cover. The threat of clearance refusal has been a primary recruitment tool over the years, and remains so today.

'Inexcusable and a Matter of Profound Concern': Security Certificates

Along with other problems clinging to CSIS from its post-9/11 responsibilities, serious embarrassment arose with regard to three well-publicized security-certificate cases, those of Adil Charkaoui, Mohamed Harkat, and Hassan Almrei. Security certificates pre-date 9/11 and the Anti-Terrorism Act 2001, although they have caused perhaps as much or more controversy than any other aspect of the government's counter-terrorist policies. Under the process, the minister of immigration and the minister of public safety together may sign a certificate declaring a foreign national or a permanent resident inadmissible to Canada on security grounds.[35] Between 1991 and 2006, security certificates were used twenty-seven times.[36] Normally, someone subject to a security certificate would be deported. Much of the controversy results from legal constraints on the government's ability to deport individuals held under security certificates to countries where the risk of torture or cruel and unusual treatment is judged as more significant than the danger the person presents to the security of Canada. This humanitarian consideration has ironically led to a human-rights issue: what amounts to a process of indefinite detention without charge for those individuals who remain in Canada but who are held to be threats to security if left at large.[37] Five men, all judged to be associated with Islamic terrorism, were detained indefinitely under what seemed to critics to be harsh conditions. Sympathetic accounts in the media and reasonable concerns from civil libertarians about indefinite detention without charge combined to raise public awareness, and resulted in campaigns to free the five individuals. Legal and constitutional questions proved sufficiently troubling that in 2007 the Supreme Court of Canada declared significant parts of the security-certificate process unconstitutional, and gave the government a period of time in which the process had to be fixed, according to guidelines set down by the court.[38] A revised process is now in place, and as a result of further judicial intervention, those being held indefinitely under security certificates were released under very stringent – critics would say onerous – conditions.

It is, of course, a fundamental principle of the liberal-democratic rule of law that no one can be imprisoned without due process, habeas corpus, and so on. Indefinite detention on mere suspicion is in violation of fundamental justice, yet that is what the situation of the five security-certificate cases amounted to. Advocates for reform, and the men themselves, made the argument that if there were charges against them, they should have their day in court. But security certificates were not issued on the basis of evidence that would lead to criminal charges; if such evidence existed, criminal charges would have been laid in preference to security certificates.

CSIS, rather than the RCMP, was the main source of intelligence upon which the certificates were issued. Security intelligence collected by CSIS, of course, is different in nature from the kind of evidence gathered by the RCMP for the purposes of criminal proceedings. Much of it cannot be disclosed in open court without jeopardizing national-security confidentiality (sources, methods, foreign caveats). This also means that much of the basis upon which security certificates are issued cannot be disclosed to the individual and his counsel – one of the most controversial aspects of the process inasmuch as people subjected to indefinite detention are never allowed to see the full case against them, or have the opportunity to cross-examine sources of damaging information. One result of the Supreme Court decision in *Charkaoui* was the appointment of special advocates with greater access to protected information (but with limited communication with the detainee or his counsel) who can cross-examine government evidence in camera. The cases against the five individuals were also made public, but based on open sources only.[39] The security-certificate process is heavily dependent upon trust, trust that the largely secret case can be accepted in confidence; trust by the courts that the agency providing the information is professional and observant of high standards; trust, in short, in CSIS, its standards and its methods. According to CSIS in 2005, five conditions must be met before it submits a security intelligence report on an individual suspected of constituting a threat:

- the individual must be assessed as posing a significant threat to the security of Canada;
- CSIS must have sufficient threat-related information and intelligence;
- that information must be reliable and from multiple sources;
- the removal must be of strategic value in light of CSIS's investigative priorities; and

- CSIS must have sufficiently releasable open-source information to support the unclassified summary document.[40]

Confidence and trust in CSIS and in the security-certificate process was thrown into confusion in 2009 when some startling revelations reached Federal Court judges hearing the cases.

Adil Charkaoui

Of the five security-certificate cases, that of Adil Charkaoui has the highest legal profile. It was Charkaoui who took the constitutionality of the process to the Supreme Court of Canada and forced a major set of changes, in two separate decisions.[41] In the second of these decisions, a legal landmark much to the discomfort of CSIS,[42] the highest court ordered CSIS to stop destroying tapes and notes that form part of terrorism investigations. This practice, dating from the inception of CSIS in 1984, largely kept CSIS intelligence out of open court. CSIS argued that it was obliged by its legal mandate to proceed in this fashion, but the Supreme Court disagreed:

> The destruction of operational notes is a breach of CSIS's duty to retain and disclose information, which derives from s. 12 of the Canadian Security Intelligence Service Act and a contextual analysis of the case law on the disclosure and retention of evidence. Section 12 provides that CSIS must acquire information to the extent that it is strictly necessary in order to carry out its mandate, and must then analyse and retain relevant information and intelligence. The CSIS policy on the management of operational notes rests on an erroneous interpretation of that provision. Section 12 does not require that collected information be destroyed, but instead demands that CSIS retain its operational notes when conducting an investigation that targets an individual or group. The retention of notes, which include drafts, diagrams, recordings and photographs, must serve a practical purpose. As a result, the meaning of the word 'intelligence' in s. 12 should not be limited to the summaries prepared by officers. The original operational notes are a better source of information and of evidence.

The Supreme Court would not rule on whether the destroyed evidence prejudiced the case against Charkaoui. Rather, it indicated that the designated Federal Court judge would be in a position to make that determination, as he will have all the evidence before him and will be able to summon and question as witnesses those who took the interview notes. If he concludes that there is a reasonable basis for the security certificate but that the destruction of the notes had a prejudicial effect, he will then consider whether Mr. Charkaoui should be granted a remedy … The only appropriate remedy is to confirm the duty to disclose Mr. Charkaoui's entire file to the designated judge and, after the judge has filtered it, to Mr. Charkaoui and his counsel.

This decision forced the hands of CSIS and dramatically raised the stakes with regard to disclosure of secret intelligence in court.

Moreover, Charkaoui has raised serious doubts about the evidentiary basis for the certificates. A dispute about disclosure to the special advocates assigned to his case of material received in confidence from foreign governments which had not given permission for this disclosure led to court orders to the government to seek such permission. But Federal Court Justice Danièle Tremblay-Lamer was not content to take the government at its word with regard to secrecy. A series of decisions[43] had the effect of challenging the government's capacity to keep most of its information secret. It was not clear precisely what information was being ordered disclosed, but in the face of the court decisions the government simply abandoned much of its case against Charkaoui rather than risk disclosure in open court. A much thinner open case was then provided from which many items in the original open case were withdrawn (including claims that he had attended a Pakistani terrorist-training camp and had been overheard discussing seizing an airliner).[44] At the heart of the original case was the claim by CSIS that Charkaoui was an Al-Qaeda 'sleeper agent' (an agent who could be activated at any time to commit terrorist acts). Yet under cross-examination 'CSIS senior manager Ted Flanigan admitted in court that the spy agency has no evidence of that. Rather, Flanigan said, CSIS believed that Charkaoui "meets the profile" of a sleeper agent – which is to say, he *could* be one. "A (real) sleeper agent would be completely different," Flanigan acknowledged.'[45]

In February 2008 the crown declared that it would no longer rely on hearsay evidence against Charkaoui from Abu Zubayda, the repeatedly tortured and mentally unstable Guantanamo prisoner whose untrustworthy evidence had placed another unfortunate Canadian, Abousfian Abdelrazik, on the UN terrorist list and in bizarre limbo at the Canadian Embassy in Sudan (see chapter 13).[46]

Justice Tremblay-Lamer in early August 2009 questioned whether she should evaluate the certificate against Charkaoui in light of the government's admission of insufficient evidence, or whether the government should simply withdraw the certificate on its own.[47] The following month, after CSIS had pulled almost all its human-source and wiretap evidence, it admitted that the remaining evidence was insufficient to justify the certificate. The judge abruptly stayed further proceedings and declared the security certificate void. Moreover, she refused to agree with the crown's request to send the case on to the Federal Court of Appeal. After years of detention followed by onerous restrictions on release, Adil Charkaoui has finally been declared a free man.[48]

Mohamed Harkat

The case of Mohamed Harkat has been particularly embarrassing for CSIS, which was caught out in misrepresentation before the Federal Court. On 26 May 2009 a Top Secret letter from CSIS was delivered to the Federal Court where Justice Simon Noël had been hearing the security certificate case of Harkat.[49] The letter gave new information dating from 2002 and 2008 concerning the reliability of a human source that had furnished information in relation to the Harkat investigation. The court had been provided with a source matrix 'designed to provide a frank view' of human sources used in compiling the case against Harkat. Both positive and negative information is supposed to be included, 'in order to assist the Court in making a fair assessment of the source's credibility and the reliability of the information they have provided.' CSIS cited the Supreme Court on this subject as insisting that 'the evidence presented must be complete and thorough and no relevant information adverse to the interest of that party may be withheld.'[50] Unfortunately for CSIS, it now had to admit that a polygraph test of a source used against Harkat had been incorrectly reported as indicating the source had been truthful. In fact, the source had in 2002 actually failed a polygraph test on certain questions, leading an independent examiner to conclude that the results were inconclusive – a conclusion not communicated to the court and to the special advocates in the case. CSIS had to admit that the latter 'should have been made aware of the complete results of the polygraph examinations and the failure to do so is a serious matter.'

In response, Justice Noël referred to 'this troubling situation' and noted that a CSIS witness had testified in 2008 that the certificate was reasonable 'even when specifically questioned on the reliability of the source by the Court.' During closed hearings, the court had reminded the government of its 'obligation to act in utmost good faith' and in particular its 'duty to provide all information which would tend to weaken their case against Mr. Harkat.' Justice Noël felt it necessary to emphasize that the 'rule of law is an essential component of any functioning democratic society ... Persons in positions of authority within government whose actions impact on the rights and liberties of Canadians must be held to account for even the slightest disregard for this principle.' In this regard, he drew attention to the question of the compliance of CSIS with previous court orders; 'possible prevarication by CSIS witnesses called to testify concerning the reliability of the information provided by the human source'; and CSIS compliance with 'the obligation of utmost good faith required by the jurisprudence in the context of the ex parte proceedings.'[51]

In a previous decision[52] the court had recognized one exception to the 'absolute bar to the identification of a human source in the public domain': that is, when 'evidence is adduced demonstrating that the identity of the covert human intelligence source must be disclosed to prevent a flagrant breach of procedural justice which would bring the administration of justice into disrepute.' As a result of the new CSIS disclosure, Justice Nöel concluded that the special advocates have a 'need to know the contents of the human source file even if this results in the revelation of the source's identity. The rule of law requires no less.' Hence, he issued an order that 'complete and unredacted copies of the human source file' be filed with the court and that the special advocates 'will be provided with full access to the unredacted file.'

In response to this order, the senior general counsel for CSIS wrote to the chief justice of the Federal Court, admitting that the 'failure to include relevant information' was 'inexcusable and a matter of profound concern to the Service.' He added that 'to the extent "this troubling situation" has given the Court any cause to doubt the integrity of the Service's evidence and question the credibility of its employees, the Service is resolute in its determination to restore judicial confidence in that integrity and credibility.' A senior CSIS manager was assigned to review the entire situation with a mandate to recommend changes in practices or policies as a result. Moreover, CSIS was also embarking upon an 'exhaustive review of all security certificate-related human source matrices and the supporting human source files,' involving at least two experienced officers and with the results to be challenged by a three-person team of two senior managers and a Justice Department counsel. The service will also review human sources used in the warrant-application process, and engage in a 'broader review of its practices concerning the presentation of evidence in legal proceedings generally.' Additionally, CSIS would carry out a critical assessment of current practices and was considering several options, including 'the need for more robust internal checks and balances as well as the possibility of employing a check and balance mechanism external to the Service.'[53]

As if the CSIS mea culpas over Harkat were not embarrassing enough to the government, the Canadian Border Services Agency created a further public-relations fiasco with a heavy-handed search-and-seizure raid on the Harkat residence, where he had been confined on release from detention under highly exacting conditions. This raid occurred on 12 May 2009, nineteen days before Federal Court hearings on the reasonableness of the security certificate were scheduled to begin. Federal Court Justice Noël determined that the search had only two purposes: to exercise the power given the CBSA under the conditions of Harkat's release (in effect, a 'use it to lose it' purpose); and to gather intelligence that might be relevant to a risk assessment of Harkat's compliance with the conditions of his release. Justice Noël was unimpressed with either rationale. 'This Court cannot condone the type of intrusive search undertaken by the CBSA. Mr. Harkat may have a diminished expectation of privacy, but that does not give the state a "*carte blanche*" to unreasonably intrude on what privacy is left to him.' The court ordered the return of all items seized in the raid and the destruction of any copies retained by the CBSA.[54]

On 21 September 2009 an agreement was reached between government lawyers and the court to ease greatly the restrictive conditions imposed on Harket, including surveillance inside and outside his home and the monitoring of his mail and communications; he was now to be permitted at least limited mobility outside his home, although with continued use of an electronic GPS tracking bracelet. In effect, the government – presumably including CSIS – now agreed that Harkat represents a much diminished threat.

On 15 October 2009, after the government had agreed to ease the restrictive conditions imposed upon Harkat,[55] Justice Noël took CSIS to task for failing to respond properly to the issue of the incompletely reported polygraph tests. He found the various CSIS witnesses' explanations to be incomplete and inaccurate. He did not find that there was any deliberate intent on the part of CSIS to mislead the court, but rather that CSIS had failed to offer the appropriate level of institutional support for its witnesses and had left too much discretion to individual officers to make decisions for which they had inadequate preparation. The CSIS officers appearing in the case had assumed that their expertise as intelligence officers entitled them to interpret the information according to their professional standards. Justice Noël sharply criticized this as 'filtering' the evidence before the court and the special advocates: 'When human source information is used to support serious allegations against an individual, the Court and the special advocates must be able to effectively test the credibility and reliability of that information.' The 'failure of CSIS and its witnesses to disclose the polygraph information has seriously damaged confidence in the current system.' The remedy: the human-source files used in the case against Harkat must be produced for the court and for the special advocates (in no circumstances, however, would they be made available to Harket, his counsel, or the public).[56] If CSIS disliked this remedy, and disliked having to testify in the presence of the special advocates, Justice Noël was blunt. The law post-Charkaoui had been changed, and CSIS would simply have to comply: 'This,' he wrote, 'is the new reality.'[57]

Harkat's supporters, perhaps expecting that his case would eventually be resolved along the same lines as that of Charkaoui, were bitterly disappointed when Justice Noël finally ruled on the validity of Harkat's security certificate at the end of 2010. In three separate judgments, Noël went some distance to rehabilitating the security-certificate process despite the errors in which CSIS had participated. Harkat's motion to stay proceedings on the basis of abuse of process was rejected, on the grounds that remedies had already been provided by the crown.[58] Noël ruled that the security-certificate process is constitutional, and that the post-Charkaoui changes safeguard the principles of fundamental justice and do not violate section 7 of the Charter. Moreover, limits imposed on rights are demonstrably justifiable in a free and democratic society and are therefore saved under section 1 of the Charter.[59] Finally, and crushingly for Harkat and his supporters, Noël ruled that Harkat's certificate was reasonable. Harkat was found to have engaged in terrorist activities and to constitute a diminished but still remaining danger to Canadian national security. In his own testimony he was not, Noël concluded, 'truthful, honest or transparent.'[60]

Hassan Almrei

The Harkat case has had a double effect, at once reinforcing the legitimacy of the certificate process while undermining the credibility of elements of the process. Yet more questions about the role of CSIS in the process have surfaced in another case, that of Hassan Almrei.[61]

On 26 June 2009 Federal Court Justice Richard Mosley, who had been hearing the case, wrote to Almrei and his counsel[62] concerning information disclosed to the court and to the special advocates during the closed portion of the proceedings. Following the Harkat revelation, a review of the human-source material in each of the security-certificate cases had been undertaken by CSIS. In Almrei, 'significant errors' had come to light relating to human sources. A CSIS witness who had previously given evidence was cross-examined over three days. It was discovered that

> one human source had not been subjected to a polygraph examination by CSIS as had previously been reported … In addition, the circumstances surrounding a 2007 polygraph examination of a second human source were in question and were being investigated. Consideration was being given at that time to the individual's re-employment as an active source and questions had arisen about the source's reliability. As a result of the further disclosures and the cross-examination of the Service witness, it is now clear that the source was found to have been deceptive in providing answers to each of the specific questions on which his reliability was in doubt.

Mr Justice Mosley was then asked by counsel for Almrei to quash the certificate, a decision opposed by the government. In late 2009 he did just that, indicating that in his opinion much of the case against Almrei, while valid at the time the certificate was first issued, no longer held. Almrei had been changed by his experience, by the generous assistance offered to him by supporters throughout his ordeal, by his wide reading, and by the reinterpretation of his religious faith to exclude terrorist acts. Because of the high visibility attaching to him as a result of the publicity surrounding the case, he no longer represented a realistic threat of re-engaging with active terrorists. Worse from CSIS's point of view was Justice Mosley's finding that 'the Service and the Ministers were in breach of their duty of candour to the Court.'[63] Subsequent to Mosley's decision, Almrei launched a lawsuit against CSIS, the RCMP, the CBSA, and Citizenship and Immigration Canada for negligence and false imprisonment.[64]

Even prior to the decision, one of Almrei's lawyers, Lorne Waldman, reflected on the larger implications of CSIS miscues in the security-certificate process:

> In all of the cases, the government has relied on secret evidence provided by CSIS that is not disclosed to the men. That extraordinary power requires that the agency be vigilant in ensuring that all of the information it provides in secret is absolutely beyond reproach.
>
> The finding that CSIS failed to provide accurate information to the court in secret proceedings is a serious blow to the agency's credibility. While providing inaccurate information to a court of law is always an extremely serious matter, it is especially so in the case of secret hearings where the accused cannot answer to the allegations.[65]

The real problem, Waldman argued, is the federal government's failure for three years to respond to the policy recommendations of Mr Justice O'Connor in the Arar Inquiry (see chapter 13) for a modernized accountability process not only for CSIS but for all those government agencies with national-security responsibilities: 'Their silence sends CSIS and Canadians an ominous message. It is that the problem isn't that CSIS misled the court ... The problem is only that it got caught – and the problem will go away if it is ignored. That's the wrong message: It leaves us with serious doubts about the integrity and competence of federal security agencies. And it leaves us with equally serious doubts about the position of our government on these serious matters.'

The Inspector General Calls

With criticism of CSIS piling up from the courts and from SIRC, in the spring of 2009 a partially redacted report from the Office of the Inspector General was released under Access to Information, drawing some further unfavourable attention. The IG is an independent office created in 1984 under the CSIS Act to serve as the eyes and ears of the minister with regard to the service, a support for ministerial responsibility. Each year the IG is required to provide the minister of public safety with a certificate indicating that the IG is satisfied with the CSIS director's *Annual Report*.[66] This also serves as an opportunity for the IG to indicate whether the service has acted within the law, according to ministerial directives, and has not used its powers unreasonably or unnecessarily. The annual certificates are not public documents and are normally classified Top Secret. However, they are routinely requested under Access to Information, and the declassified versions, with numerous redactions, are made available on the IG's website.

The 2008 certificate proved to be somewhat more contentious than earlier ones. Although the IG, Eva Plunkett, in her fifth year on the job, assured the minister that CSIS 'has not acted beyond the framework of its statutory authority, has not contravened any Ministerial Directives, and has not exceeded its powers unreasonably or unsuccessfully,' she also pointed to a number of 'areas of concern.' Her office 'identified a larger number of instances of non-compliance with CSIS operational policy than noted in my four previous Certificates' and also a higher number of errors in CSIS records. These instances appeared in 'key core activities.' Another concern was 'the length of time taken to develop or amend operational policies to reflect changing requirements and operational activities.' Several aspects of this policy, she found, are 'incompatible and unworkable.' She was particularly concerned that 'without an established policy framework to offer guidance, actions can be taken with the best of intentions that ultimately may have far reaching results and possibly negative consequences.' With regard to the warrant-acquisition and execution process, the IG found the rate of errors 'disconcerting.' She referred as well to issues of factual accuracy before the Federal Court. This, she indicated pointedly to the minister, 'is an area that merits close monitoring by you during the coming year given the intrusive authorities provided by warrants and the implications of these authorities on the civil liberties and privacy interests of individuals.'[67]

It is not possible from the heavily redacted document to grasp fully all the issues that the IG raises. She was at pains to pay tribute to the calibre of CSIS employees, their dedication and commitment, and to note that 'the new generation of employees are very representative of the demographic and geographic diversity of Canada.' But, even if her concerns were being advanced in a constructive spirit, they were still troubling. In a media interview, Plunkett indicated that 'the spy service has not moved quickly enough to create up-to-date guidelines for an era when it is operating around the world against terrorism, not just keeping an eye on spies at home.' 'Any organization has a hard time keeping its policies up to date,' she said, 'but when you have the kind of intrusive powers that the service has, I think it's essential that there's a guidebook for people to follow.'[68]

The Russians (and the Chinese) Are Still Coming ...

Not everything on the CSIS plate in the first decade of the twenty-first century was directly related to 9/11 and its aftermath. The Anti-Terrorism Act 2001 specified for the first time a statutory responsibility to protect the 'political, social and economic security of Canada.'[69] Economic spying is rife in the contemporary world, ranging from commercial espionage carried out by corporations, sometimes against their own national competitors, sometimes against competitors from abroad; to economic espionage carried out by states against the economic interests of other states. States targeted for economic intelligence may just as likely be diplomatic allies as antagonists. Even the closest of allies may not forgo opportunities to steal a march on each other when it comes to economic advantage. Friends and allies are also commercial competitors, of course, and allegations of nefarious activities by old allies on the commercial front have sometimes been whispered but rarely articulated in public. During the negotiations that led up to the Canada-United States Free Trade Agreement in 1988, one of the chief Canadian negotiators recalls a concern that the Americans were surreptitiously listening in on Canadian strategy sessions; the CSE was called in to provide an intercept-free safe location.[70] With these considerations in mind, CSIS obviously faces some delicate issues when confronting threats of economic espionage, especially in getting political approval for counter-espionage operations against friendly powers.

Less sensitive grounds are the economic-espionage efforts mounted by Canada's old Cold War antagonists, Russia and China, both motivated by the desire to steal technology that could assist their own economic competitiveness. Nor have either of these states abandoned political and military espionage as a regular arm of their overseas operations. The Cold War may be ancient history in the era of a global War on Terror, but this does not mean that the two principal antagonists of years past have disappeared from the radar of Canadian intelligence.[71]

It is widely believed that the post-Communist Russian regime has flipped over much of its old KGB (now SVR) apparatus to a contemporary role in trying to play catch-up in commercial competition, where its enterprises are at a considerable disadvantage to more sophisticated and innovative Western corporations. At the same time, renewed concern about Russian intentions abroad under the increasingly autocratic rule of Vladimir Putin, former KGB officer, has further focused attention on possible Russian activities contrary to Canadian national interests. Suspicions are deepened by Russian involvement in another threat to economic security, international organized crime. It is known that so-called Russian *mafiosi* have been operating in Canada for a number of years. Links between these criminals and Russian state intelligence are shadowy at best; however, there is a general suspicion that 'Russian' activities are often threatening, whether they emerge from the state or the frontier-style Russian private sector.

There is one case against a Russian operative that did gain public view, that of 'Paul William Hampel,' a Russian 'illegal' who resided in Montreal for fifteen years under false identity before being nabbed in 2006.[72] Hampel was served with a security certificate and on the basis of secret intelligence from CSIS was deported to Russia. As indicated earlier, security certificates have become a highly controversial and in-effective element of Canadian post-9/11 counter-terrorism. In this case, Hampel was quickly dispatched to his country of origin. Since the CSIS intelligence was presented in camera and never disclosed in public, we are left with speculation as to precisely what activities led to Hampel's expulsion.[73]

The Hampel case does point out a persistent pattern of Russian spy operations that goes back far into the Cold War past: the use of stolen or forged Canadian identities to establish 'legends' for operatives, more often than not to facilitate their eventual entry into the United States, ultimately a more attractive target than Canada. This Canadian secu-rity problem was highlighted once again in 2010 with the news of the arrests of ten alleged secret Russian agents attempting to penetrate the U.S. government. At least four members of the alleged spy ring claimed to be Canadian and apparently used Canadian identity documents, ac-cording to court records.[74] Needless to say, this is an issue of continuing concern for Canada, and always a source of potential embarrassment for the country in its relations with the United States.

In the post-9/11 world, Russian concerns, while still important, are less significant than the perceived threat of Chinese espionage and Chi-nese interference in Canadian affairs. 'Communist' China's emergence as a global capitalist superpower and heavyweight diplomatic and commercial player on the world stage has been accompanied by the widespread perception that an army of Chinese spies have been surrep-titiously (and illegally) advancing Chinese political and economic in-terests at the same time as the growth of competitive Chinese enterprise has been winning the respect and apprehension of the rest of the world. This is more than perception: in the United States a number of serious espionage charges against the Chinese have been brought to court, and several convictions secured, involving both military and economic information. Canadian targets include commercial technology but also Chinese dissidents abroad, who are singled out for intimidation and silencing. The Falun Gong group, persecuted in China and with followers in Canada, falls into the latter category. Both industrial espionage and covert foreign interference in Canada are appropriate categories of threats to security as defined under the CSIS Act.

One case that has surfaced publicly regarding possible Chinese intelligence operations in Canada is the somewhat peculiar matter of Haiyan Zhang, a Chinese-born woman who was fired from a sensitive position in the Privy Council Office in 2003 after her security clearance was removed on the advice of CSIS. Zhang was informed by CSIS that, as a former employee of the state-run Chinese news service, 'you may have engaged in intelligence collection activities on behalf of a foreign state. Secondly, we are concerned that you appear to maintain regular contact with foreign representatives who may be involved in intelligence collection activities.'[75] Instead of simply placing her in a less sensitive position elsewhere, the PCO sought her removal from the public service altogether. On review of the security-clearance decision, SIRC found no fault with CSIS, but a public-service tribunal ruled that she should be allowed to remain in government employment, although in a non-sensitive job. However, she was then sent home without responsibilities, although still maintained on the public payroll.[76]

There is an unresolved ambiguity about the issue of Russian and Chinese espionage in Canada. As noted in the previous chapter, for all the concerns expressed both officially and in the media about a significant threat posed to Canadian security, apart from the Hampel security-certificate case, no espionage cases related to the two old Cold War antagonists have come before the courts. This is in striking contrast to the experience in the United States. The question that naturally arises is why, if estimates of the threat are valid, so few results have been achieved? Does this record indicate a failure of Canadian counter-espionage? Or does it simply indicate that CSIS as a security intelligence agency has been playing a longer-term game, rather than handing cases over early to the RCMP for the law-enforcement process? We are in no position to answer these questions. The contrast between the public warnings and the public evidence of remedial actions does leave CSIS with something of an image problem.

In June 2010 CSIS Director Richard Fadden took the opportunity of a major story on CSIS for the CBC TV national news to refurbish the CSIS image in counter-espionage. Offering the seemingly awe-struck CBC 'unprecedented' camera access to CSIS headquarters and an 'exclusive' interview with the director, CSIS seemed to think that it could shape the narrative. Intent on downplaying the terrorist threat while emphasizing the persistent and growing threat of espionage – by friends and allies as well as by countries more distant from Canada – Fadden made clear that he viewed state-sponsored economic espionage as a very major but under-resourced problem on CSIS's plate. If he had left it at that, his remarks might have elicited little new attention. But he went much further when he cited a different kind of threat: foreign-influenced covert infiltration of the Canadian political process. In an extraordinary public pronouncement, Fadden indicated that CSIS was worried about at least two unnamed provincial cabinet ministers from 'diaspora' communities, along with some public servants and municipal politicians in British Columbia, and MPs in Ottawa, who were in effect acting as agents of influence for unspecified foreign governments. Fadden coyly implied but did not spell out that China might be one of these, a sensitive allusion given an impending state visit of the Chinese president the next day.[77]

It turned out that Fadden had not contacted the governments in question before going public. Provincial and municipal officials, especially in British Columbia, were irate, as were spokespersons of Chinese Canadian associations, who felt that their community was being targeted by a McCarthyite attack.[78] Despite an initial claim, subsequently retracted, that the warning had gone to the Privy Council Office, the Prime Minister's Office was quick to indicate that it had 'no knowledge' of the issue. Faced with a firestorm of criticism from all sides, Fadden backed down the next day, withdrawing his earlier insistence on the importance of the alleged foreign infiltration, and then, bizarrely, stating that there would be no more comments on this 'operational matter' (that he had divulged the day before for a national television audience).[79] The question of the truth behind the allegations was overshadowed by criticism of the manner in which the CSIS director had brought the issue forward, and calls were heard for his resignation or sacking by the prime minister.[80] In the last dying days of the fortieth Parliament in 2011, the Opposition majority on a parliamentary committee called for Fadden's removal, but the government minority rejected the demand as unsupported by evidence. The merits of the case were lost in partisan rancour as another election loomed.[81]

In July, Fadden did address the minister on the subject with a confidential assessment outlining the nature of the threat of foreign interference as understood by CSIS. A partially declassified version of this report indicates concern that long-term strategies by unspecified foreign governments aimed at cultivating individuals from diaspora communities might indeed succeed in exercising influence even where the individuals remained unaware of the real objectives of the foreign agents manipulating them. Electoral support, financial or otherwise, for candidates for public office could, for instance, be an investment in buying longer-term influence over policy making. On a less subtle note, Fadden also pointed out evidence of direct intimidation and coercion against dissidents in ethnic communities: although details were redacted, a well-known example of this is the attacks mounted against the dissident Chinese Falun Gong sect by the Beijing government on Canadian soil.[82]

It is hard to know what to make of this incident. It is certainly possible that elected officials in Canada may be advancing (even unknowingly) the clandestine objectives of foreign powers (not limited to China), which would be a legitimate concern for CSIS, within its mandate. But a public accusation couched in vague and unspecific terms on national television by the director of CSIS that spreads a net of suspicion over a whole group of elected and unelected officials, not to speak of entire ethnic communities, could be interpreted as a kind of officially sanctioned McCarthyism. That it was so quickly retracted seems to imply that the claim may have been overstated. In either case, the political judgment of Director Fadden must be seriously questioned. An unfortunate by-product of his inept intervention is that calm, objective evaluation of the threat of covert foreign-influenced activity has now been rendered more, rather than less, difficult. This fact was underlined when flirtatious e-mails were made public between the parliamentary secretary to the minister of foreign affairs, MP Bob Dechert, and a woman correspondent for China's state-controlled news agency that some have likened to an arm of intelligence. While this may have indicated an inappropriate relationship, any breach of Canadian security was less clear, and the prime minister refused to consider asking for Dechert's resignation, which was not offered.[83]

CSIS and the Anti-Globalization Protests

CSIS has had some public entanglement with contemporary protest movements that has tested its statutory limitation on surveillance of 'lawful advocacy, protest, and dissent.' So-called anti-globalization, or sometimes 'global justice,' movements (actually an umbrella term for a number of groups and tendencies with anti-corporate capitalist orientation protesting the policies and actions of the institutions of global economic governance such as the G-8 and G-20, the North American Free Trade Agreement, the International Monetary Fund, World Bank, and so on) have posed a number of challenges to security at international meetings hosted by Canada.

The right of Canadians to advocate, protest, and dissent lawfully is, of course, fundamental to democratic practice. In dealing with anti-globalization protests, however, some classic dilemmas of political policing have been in evidence. First is the definition of 'lawful' in the context of policing of international events with visiting foreign leaders – often the targets of considerable criticism from protestors – as the guests of Canada expecting the full protection of Canadian law and security while on Canadian soil. The right of Canadians to protest against such events or against visiting officials runs up against Canada's security obligations. Special protection of visiting VIPs and foreign diplomats ('internationally protected persons') is enshrined in Canadian law, with the RCMP given lead responsibility.[84] Protestors can be barred from close access to and potentially threatening contact with visiting foreign officials by an exclusionary area set by the government. As a consequence, protests can be moved so far away as to be rendered out of sight, out of mind. This was accomplished at the Kananaskis, Alberta, G-8 conference in 2002. But more difficult issues of policing and suppression of dissent come to the fore when conferences are held in urban areas with geographically narrower exclusion zones. On three occasions – APEC 1997 in Vancouver, Summit of the Americas 2001 in Quebec City, and G-20 2010 in Toronto – clashes with police have resulted, along with serious questioning of the degree to which lawful protest was being curtailed.

The Vancouver APEC clash, with its notoriously iconic image of 'Sgt. Pepper' of the Mounties spewing apparently peaceful protestors with pepper spray, led to extensive condemnation of excessive police action, two inquiries by the RCMP Public Complaints Commission (the first was aborted), and criticism of the RCMP by its review body.[85] The Chrétien government was dismissive of the criticism. The same Liberal government later presided over a 2001 Quebec City summit that was characterized by widespread clashes between police and demonstrators, and again by widespread protests about the crushing of legitimate dissent. By this point, anti-globalization demonstrations at global meetings involving clashes with police were becoming fixtures of the international scene: meetings in Seattle in 1999 and Genoa in 2001 were particularly violent – one demonstrator in Genoa had been killed by police. What was also evident by the time of the Quebec City clashes was the presence among the largely peaceful demonstrators of highly aggressive, masked, helmeted, black-clad individuals, sometimes with truncheons and projectiles, seeking confrontation and determined to push demonstrations towards violence, with the apparent objective of provoking police overreaction and thus revealing the repressive nature of the capitalist state. The 'Black Bloc' is not an organized party as such but rather an anarchist tendency which favours provocative and menacing tactics. Whatever its dimensions and future, its presence at these international meetings poses major problems, both for the authorities and for the peaceful majority of anti-globalization demonstrators.

These problems were exemplified by the G-20 summit in Toronto in the summer of 2010. Concerned about the inevitable appearance of Black Bloc-like anarchist actions, the federal government in effect shut down much of the downtown of Canada's biggest city for the duration. Whether through police negligence or by design, Black Bloc demonstrators were able to run wild outside the exclusion zone, smashing store windows, setting police cars ablaze, and so on. Operating under a regulation quietly enacted under the authority of an obscure 1939 wartime security law, police struck back the following day with mass arrests, but of largely peaceful protestors. In total, 1,105 people were arrested, the largest mass arrest in Canadian history; some seven hundred were eventually released without charge after enduring sometimes appalling conditions of temporary detention. Many of the remaining charges were later stayed or withdrawn, eventually leaving only 99 cases before the courts.[86] Class action and individual lawsuits have been filed claiming millions in damages from police violence. It was, by almost all accounts, a policing fiasco on an unprecedented scale. Yet demands for a full public inquiry have fallen on deaf ears both in Ottawa and at Queen's Park. The Ontario government asked former Ontario chief justice Roy McMurtry to conduct a narrow and confidential inquiry into the use or misuse of the 1939 wartime law, but his recommendation that the province scrap the law fell far short of critics' broader concerns.[87] A particularly damning report was filed by the Ontario ombudsman focusing on the role of the Toronto Police, pointedly entitled *Caught in the Act*.[88]

If the Black Bloc had deliberately sought to provoke overreaction, it had perhaps exceeded its own expectations. On the side of the anti-globalization majority, there were darker theories finding circulation – that the Black Bloc had been no more than pretext, perhaps even a tool – for a massive police assault on legitimate protest. Video evidence circulated on YouTube of Quebec undercover-police agents provocateurs attempting to inspire violence at the Quebec City summit fed conspiracy theories about the Toronto events. Towards the latter, scepticism is in order: a general rule for theories like this is that, for large and unwieldy organizations like states, cock-up usually trumps conspiracy as explanation. Moreover, policing of the 2010 Winter Olympic Games in British Columbia (where overall direction of security was under former CSIS director Ward Elcock) had been largely successful, if highly expensive, despite some anti-Olympic protestors intent on confrontation. Peaceful demonstrations in Vancouver had taken place at the same time as potential violence had been contained with reasonable restraint. But, even if the notion that the state has plotted to smash the anti-globalization movement lacks credibility, the uncomfortable fact remains that, for the security and policing establishment, the media images of reckless repression have not been flattering; and the claims of the protestors that legitimate and lawful dissent has been to some degree criminalized do have plausibility.

CSIS has not been a major player in this process; the RCMP and provincial and municipal police forces have been at centre stage. But security intelligence on the potential threat posed by the protests is obviously a central resource for policing, and much of this has come from CSIS. The service must tread a fine line in such matters. Forbidden to use intrusive surveillance against 'lawful advocacy, protest and dissent,' CSIS is at the same time directed to assess whether there are those who pose possible threats of violence hiding, as it were, among the lawful protestors. Just as in the 1970s, when the RCMP security service was tasked to flush out the violent separatists and foreign agents among the peaceful democratic sovereignists in the Parti Québécois while respecting the immunity of law-abiding separatists, the task of separating out the bad guys while avoiding apparent interference with the acceptable face of protest has not proven easy. This kind of dual scrutiny can also lend itself to derision when forced into the light of day. Thus, when CSIS security reporting became subject to open proceedings at the RCMP Public Complaints Commission hearings into the APEC affair, CSIS was subjected to ridicule for keeping tabs on the Raging Grannies and other harmless protestors. Of course, CSIS did not believe that the Raging Grannies were a threat to security, but it had been tasked to assess the potential threat posed by the protest movement as a whole, and therefore it had to examine all components of the movement. Intelligence analysis of the real threat posed by the Black Bloc at Quebec City and Toronto could hardly be undertaken without scrutiny of the various schools of inoffensive fish among whom the sharks were swimming.

It is a dilemma for an agency with a legal mandate with which it must comply, and an abiding concern not to alienate unnecessarily members of the civil society it is supposed to protect. The case of the anti-globalization protests harks back to the bad old contentious days of the 1970s. It must have been with a sense of relief, then, that CSIS could turn to countering the threat of terrorism, which commands broad support in the society, although the global War on Terror has revealed its own hidden, dark side, as the next chapter will indicate.

13

No More Mr Nice Spy:
CSIS and the Dark Side of the War on Terror

In 2010 CSIS Director Richard Fadden was photographed in Saudi Arabia meeting with King Abdullah, occasioning a certain amount of surprise that a head of a domestic security service should be visiting a foreign country and be received almost as if he were a political leader or a head of state.[1] Such an event just a decade or two earlier would have been unimaginable, but CSIS's standing in the wider world of security and intelligence beyond Canadian borders was dramatically transformed in the post-9/11 world. Enhanced visibility and prestige was obvious. But there was another element as well to the Fadden-Abdullah meeting. Saudi Arabia has a very poor reputation for human-rights abuse of the people in its prisons. The intelligence sharing between Canada and Saudi Arabia in the global battle against terrorism that the meeting exemplified could be a double-edged sword, raising questions about CSIS complicity in torture.

To understand how CSIS has arrived at this unaccustomed position, it is necessary to retrace some steps. In the wake of 9/11, a gap in the Canadian intelligence architecture that had hitherto been the subject of merely academic debate suddenly appeared as urgent. Canada had refrained from setting up a central human-source foreign-intelligence service at the end of the Second World War, on what had appeared at the time as sound and reasonable policy grounds. Rather than undertake the risks and costs of launching a fledgling mini-CIA or MI6, as the Australians did in the 1950s with their Australian Secret Intelligence Service, Canada had chosen to rely largely on its allies for relevant foreign intelligence. Intelligence sharing is generally done not on the basis of interstate generosity but on the basis of exchange, quid pro quo. In Canada's case, during the Cold War years, the exchange worked for the most part through two vehicles. The first was Canada's sole external intelligence-gathering agency, the signals intelligence agency the Communications Security Establishment, formerly the Communications Branch National Research Council. Plugged into the U.K.-U.S. network of electronic eavesdropping agencies in the English-speaking countries, Canada did have foreign intelligence to provide in exchange.[2] The second vehicle was the security service, first in the RCMP and then as CSIS. Here, Canada could offer security intelligence on Canadians and on clandestine activities mounted on Canadian soil. These two vehicles hardly equipped Canada to be an equal partner with the United Kingdom and the United States, but they did at least put the country on the same playing field. Besides, in the Cold War years, there was a deep degree of common commitment and a wide range of shared assumptions about the nature of the overarching conflict with the Communist world. Occasional issues arose that briefly threatened this cooperation, such as the 1957 suicide of diplomat Herbert Norman (see chapter 8), but these quickly flickered out and the business as usual of close cooperation, on an admittedly unequal basis, continued.

The events of 9/11 came as such a surprise to the political masters in Ottawa that questions were asked about Canada's inability to identify this new and alarmingly undocumented threat, one that was being framed in a particular way by the Bush administration that might or might not be fully suited to Canada's own national interests. The minister first put in charge of the special quasi-wartime cabinet committee on security, John Manley, publicly mused about the lack of a central foreign-intelligence capacity that might have provided some Canadian perspective on this new threat, although he later backtracked on any need for a new agency.[3] The opposition Conservative Party in its 2006 election platform specifically called for the creation of a foreign-intelligence service. No actions were in fact taken by either Liberal or Conservative governments to move in this direction in even a preliminary fashion. A large part of the reason for this inaction is that, in this context of a felt need for better foreign intelligence, CSIS stepped into the breach, offering itself as a relatively low-cost and already established alternative to an uncertain new agency. Ward Elcock, CSIS director prior to and during the first crucial post-9/11 years, undertook an aggressive campaign to pre-empt the bureaucratic space in Ottawa opening up for foreign-intelligence gathering.[4] Elcock's argument was that, since the leading threat to security on the world stage now came from global terrorist networks, the CSIS mandate to investigate threats to the security of Canada gave it legitimate grounds to investigate these threats wherever they appeared. Who better than CSIS to gather intelligence on, say, terrorist networks originating in the Muslim world that would erupt on Canadian soil, threatening Canadian security as well as the global security that Canada was pledged to defend in cooperation with all nations similarly threatened? This did not effectively answer the academic argument that political and economic foreign intelligence from a Canadian perspective, much or most of it unrelated to counter-terrorism, was required to enhance Canadian foreign policy, but in the post-9/11 atmosphere Elcock's strategic move into foreign activity took full advantage of the usual hesitations and confusions of successive minority governments in Ottawa. If possession is nine points of the law, Elcock simply claimed possession of this new space. Since no bureaucratic rival appeared to contest his move, CSIS de facto became Canada's new foreign-intelligence agency. Foreign intelligence not directly related to terrorist threats to Canadian security would continue to be gathered and analysed by a range of departments and agencies, but not systematically by a single centralized bureau.

Throughout the first decade of the new century, a growing number of CSIS officers operated abroad. At the time of writing, CSIS operates three known foreign stations, in London, Paris, and Washington. Locations of other foreign stations are classified, but CSIS has acknowledged publicly its involvement in Afghanistan, Iraq, and Lebanon. In Afghanistan, CSIS offers intelligence support to the Canadian military mission. In a 'WikiLeaked' report of a secret conversation with the U.S. Embassy in Ottawa, CSIS Director Jim Judd indicated that CSIS intelligence was far from being in 'high-five mode' on Afghanistan, based on low marks for the Karzai government's incompetence and corruption. He asserted that CSIS had seen an embarrassing Taliban-engineered Sarpoza prison break coming but had been unable to 'get a handle on the timing.'[5] In Lebanon its involvement in the operation to extract Canadian citizens from that country during the Israeli invasion in 2006 became public knowledge. Traditionally, CSIS officers serving abroad were focused on liaison with their foreign counterparts and in immigration-security screening. It is apparent that the agency's current activities extend beyond these routine tasks, but the precise nature of its enhanced role remains classified. Even the number of CSIS agents abroad remains secret, but what is not a secret is that CSIS has transformed itself into something more than a traditional security intelligence agency with an exclusive domestic focus. One 'WikiLeaked'

American document on Guantánamo detainees asserted that an alleged Al-Qaeda operative with a record as an assassin had been a source recruited by British intelligence and CSIS.[6] In an age of borderless terrorist networks, counter-terrorism has to become borderless as well, and the agency charged with gathering security intelligence on terrorism must operate *sans frontières*.

Reviewing changes in CSIS post-9/11, the Security Intelligence Review Committee noted in its 2009–10 *Annual Report* that 'nothing has changed so markedly as the pushing outwards of Canada's security intelligence activities.'[7] Tellingly, SIRC observed that

> periods of intense change often result in substantial policy gaps – events move more quickly than the ability of policy makers or parliamentarians to make appropriate or necessary statutory or policy reforms. This can lead to incrementalism in which a series of relatively small policy or operational adjustments made over time can culminate in large overall change – all in the absence of cohesive direction from government and without active public engagement … CSIS needs government direction … to ensure that it is operating overseas in a way that reflects government priorities. SIRC accepts that the CSIS Act permits CSIS to collect security intelligence outside of Canadian borders. However, the nature of that activity has been changing – from one strictly of liaison to one that allows for operational activity … SIRC committed in its last annual report to remain vigilant in reviewing this aspect of the Service's activities. SIRC also knows that as CSIS expands its operations internationally, these questions will become more pressing.

SIRC noted a general 'spike' in the demand for CSIS intelligence assessments across government, and especially for foreign intelligence – a 'secondary mandate' for CSIS. This has led to extensive changes in the de facto mandate, greatly expanding CSIS attention to foreign intelligence as against its core responsibilities for domestic security intelligence. To SIRC, this raised the old question of a dedicated foreign-intelligence service for Canada, 'consistent with past thinking on the need to maintain a distinction between foreign and security intelligence, as well as international practice in this regard,' a question the committee put to the minister of public safety directly through a section 54 review of CSIS's foreign-intelligence program. This review pointed to a tension between the two distinct mandates for foreign-intelligence collection in the CSIS Act. Section 12, which authorizes CSIS to collect intelligence on *threats to the security of Canada*, does not restrict collection to Canada. Section 16, on the other hand, defines 'foreign intelligence' as 'information about the capabilities, intentions or activities of a foreign state, foreign national or foreign organization' but restricts CSIS collection within Canada and prohibits collection on Canadian citizens or permanent residents. In most Western democracies, security intelligence and foreign intelligence are carried out by separate agencies, with those focused on the latter operating exclusively in foreign jurisdictions, where they break the laws of those jurisdictions in order to collect information covertly. Parliament has never approved the creation of a dedicated foreign-intelligence agency in Canada, but in SIRC's view 'cumulative changes have affected the once-rigid distinctions between Section 12 and Section 16' to the extent that CSIS 'has increasingly linked Section 12 and Section 16 priorities – what CSIS refers to as blended collection.' SIRC is 'concerned at the potential implications': 'If this were to continue, CSIS could become what Parliament never intended it to be: namely, a Service with equal security intelligence and foreign intelligence mandates. Such a development would not only go against public arguments to the contrary, but would additionally ignore the longstanding practice of respected allies who intentionally separated these divergent intelligence functions to help ensure government control and accountability.'[8]

In the spring of 2010, CSIS Director Richard Fadden testified before a Commons committee on a decade of intensified CSIS involvement abroad.[9] Fadden made a reasonable case for why CSIS has to operate abroad in an age of terrorism, and added to the already public knowledge of its foreign activities a key role in resolving kidnappings of Canadians by extremist forces in dangerous parts of the world. The best-known of these cases is that of retired Canadian senior diplomats Robert Fowler and Louis Guay, held hostage in Africa for months before their release was negotiated.[10] In such cases, Fadden maintained, the local intelligence agencies upon whom Canadian officials rely to secure the release of their nationals may insist that CSIS alone be the point of contact with Canada. Proud as Fadden was of the CSIS role, he also entered a caution that the service 'has little choice but to engage with foreign intelligence agencies, wherever they may be, if it is to protect Canadians.' He granted that 'our arrangements with certain foreign agencies have sometimes been criticized' but insisted that the service must continue to 'cultivate and maintain a large network of intelligence relationships – currently involving over 275 agencies in approximately 150 countries.' The allusion was delicate, and diplomatic, but it points to a difficult set of issues with CSIS involvement abroad: involvement with regimes that have poor human-rights records and few scruples about methods used to extract intelligence. We will return to this thorny set of issues.

One legal challenge faced by CSIS in its foreign operations lay in the problem of acquiring judicial warrants for intrusive surveillance of Canadian targets while operating abroad. In a Federal Court decision of 2007, it was determined that the court lacked jurisdiction under the CSIS Act to authorize intrusive investigation by CSIS of Canadians *outside* Canada.[11] The difficulty was the likelihood, admitted by CSIS, that extension of surveillance to foreign countries would violate foreign laws if prior consent of the foreign country had not been obtained. This posed a serious limitation on CSIS in the event that surveillance already authorized within Canada would have to be dropped while the targets moved outside Canadian national jurisdiction.

In 2008 a test case appeared. The previous year, the Federal Court had issued warrants under sections 12 and 21 of the CSIS Act with respect to two Canadians whose activities were believed on reasonable grounds to constitute threats to the security of Canada, authorizing for one year the use of intrusive investigative techniques at locations within Canada. On 24 January 2009 CSIS filed an application urgently seeking the issuance of an additional warrant authorizing the CSE to conduct surveillance of the targets regarding threat-related activities that it was believed they would engage in while travelling outside Canada. The court was asked to revisit its 2007 decision on the basis of new facts and a different legal argument by the crown. CSIS ordinarily tasks the CSE for intercepts of communications of targets constituting possible threats to the security of Canada for which CSIS has acquired appropriate judicial authorization. Although the CSE itself is prohibited from intercepting communications within Canada, unless specifically related to the CSE's foreign-intelligence-collection mandate, it may do so when acting for CSIS, under section 24(b) of the CSIS Act.[12] Now in question was CSE assistance to CSIS on CSIS warrants applied to Canadians abroad.

On 5 October 2009 Mr Justice Richard Mosley noted that, in light of current technology, terrorists can move rapidly from country to country while maintaining continuous lines of communication with their networks.[13] 'Information,' he argued, 'which may be crucial to prevent or disrupt the threats may be unavailable to the security agencies of the country if they lack the means to follow those lines of communication.' The court ruled that it has jurisdiction to authorize CSIS to intercept communications when individuals lawfully targeted within Canada travel abroad, so long as the surveillance is executed within Canada (the CSE listening posts are located on Canadian soil, while the communications intercepted originate and are received abroad). Needless to say, this decision was welcomed with relief by CSIS, which stated in a press release that the ruling 'provides CSIS with the additional means necessary to exercise its mandate.'

Moving over to the 'Dark Side'?

The extension of CSIS activity abroad is a significant development for the security service, the implications of which are at this stage not entirely apparent. But the first flush of enthusiasm, as witnessed in Elcock's adroit manoeuvring of CSIS onto the world stage, has over subsequent years met a series of setbacks and difficulties that have raised questions about CSIS behaviour and operational standards abroad. There are a number of matters that might have given pause to anyone soberly contemplating this expanded role. First, there is the question of the training and expertise of CSIS officers to move into the complex and ambiguous environments they would encounter in conflict-ridden regions abroad. One instance of this ambiguity is the issue of arming CSIS agents operating in dangerous foreign areas. Under the CSIS Act, it was never contemplated that agents would be armed, that being left to law-enforcement officers. However, since CSIS agents deployed in combat zones like Afghanistan have been fired upon, officers in these situations have been provided with firearms of their own. This raises a host of potential liability and accountability issues, few, or any, of which appear to have been addressed.[14]

More challenging are the ethical issues raised by the Bush administration's unrestricted war on terrorism, apparently largely unexamined in the rush by Canada to cooperate with the Americans. The apparent moral clarity of 11 September 2001 soon gave way to widespread doubts about the methods adopted to counter terrorism, sharply signalled by the unsanctioned American invasion of Iraq in 2003, an action that the government of Canada refused to support, with the backing of a large majority of the Canadian public. Revelations of the warrantless surveillance of American citizens; the abuse of human rights at Abu Ghraib prison in Iraq; the Guantánamo camp for so-called enemy combatants,

in contempt of international law and the Geneva convention on prisoners of war; disclosures of the extraordinary rendition of suspects to be
tortured or murdered in countries with no regard for human rights; reports of a secret gulag of shadow prisons around the world into which
people had disappeared; the admission that the United States itself via
the CIA had employed torture at Guantánamo, a practice stopped by
the Bush administration and denounced by the new president, Barack
Obama: all these matters and more have gravely sullied the name of the
United States and its War on Terror.

   In the immediate aftermath of 9/11, getting visibly onside with the
United States in its global crusade against terrorism and winning a
more substantial place in the anti-terrorist coalition abroad appeared
as positive steps to CSIS. As the collateral human damage caused by
what U.S. Vice-President Dick Cheney once ominously referred to as
America's necessary move over to the 'dark side'[15] began to mount up,
close cooperation with the Americans began to seem double-edged.
Once Canada had taken an independent, critical position on the 2003
Iraq invasion, the optics in the public mind began to shift, and the deep
unpopularity of the Bush administration in Canada, and across the
Western world, took its toll on public acceptance of the rules of engagement in the War on Terror. Trust began to be shadowed by distrust;
consensus by controversy.

Torture in the Name of Fighting Terrorism

Of all the issues raised in the debate over the global War on Terror, none
has had greater resonance than the use of torture in the name of fighting terrorism, whether indirectly, through outsourcing to states with
few scruples about the harshest forms of interrogation, or directly by
the United States. Torture has been so associated in the Western public
mind with barbarous totalitarian police states that its linkage to 'our'
side is deeply shocking to many. Yet in post-9/11 America there has also
arisen a certain populist acceptance of the idea that, in the face of an
enemy as limitlessly murderous as contemporary terrorists, we should
use whatever methods will yield results, eschewing old moral qualms
rendered irrelevant by the magnitude of the new threat. This acceptance
is reflected in the words of former vice-president Cheney, and in popular culture by the figure of 'Jack Bauer,' the fictional TV anti-terrorist
operative (ironically played by Canadian actor Kiefer Sutherland), who
regularly tortured and even performed extra-legal executions to protect

Americans from potentially catastrophic attacks. The Bauer philosophy has been cited enthusiastically as a legal model by U.S. Supreme Court justice Antonin Scalia,[16] and it has been given quasi-respectability by renowned Harvard law professor Alan Dershowitz, who argues for the legalization and judicial regulation of certain torture practices to combat terrorism.[17]

In Canada, the former leader of the Liberal Party, Michael Ignatieff, in his previous role as a Harvard human-rights professor, presented a nuanced rejection of the argument for torture, albeit one not without controversy.[18] Those who object to opening the door to torture rest their case on both ethical and empirical grounds. Torture, it is persuasively argued, is antithetical to the fundamental principles of liberal democracy, the rule of law, and adherence to international commitments to protect human rights. The deliberate infliction of extreme pain and suffering on helpless captives morally corrupts those who employ it, as well as the society that condones such cruelty against human beings. The Supreme Court of Canada has pronounced in a decisive manner on this in *Suresh v. Canada*: 'Torture has as its end the denial of a person's humanity; this end is outside the legitimate domain of a criminal justice system. *Torture is an instrument of terror and not of justice.*'[19]

Beyond the ethical objections, there are powerful empirical reservations. Evidence gained by torture has time and again proved unreliable: subjected to extreme duress, prisoners will confess to whatever they think will make their torturers stop, even when such 'confessions' are entirely untrue. Thus, counter-terrorist intelligence may actually be rendered suspect by dependence on evidence gathered by torture. Moreover, the use of torture has had the perverse effect of deepening hatred of the torturing states among those targeted, and so of widening the ranks of potential terrorists. Practically, even indirect reliance on intelligence tainted by torture, as *The Economist* reminds us, over time 'chokes the defences of democratic societies, because the courts and political systems cannot digest it. The work of Western intelligence is being gummed up with legal protocol.'[20] A report on Guantánamo detainees tried in U.S. civil courts shows that the application of 'enhanced interrogation techniques' has made it much harder to secure criminal convictions of accused terrorists: 'The government has lost more than half the cases where Guantánamo prisoners have challenged their detention because they were forcibly interrogated irrespective of whether torture was applied by foreign agents at the behest of the United States, or directly by US agents.'[21]

CSIS in the Afghan Quagmire

The torture connection was made all the more sensitive for the Canadian government when the issue of the handing over by Canadian Forces in Afghanistan of detainees to Afghan authorities became a major point of contention in the minority Parliament in 2009–10. Despite widespread and credible allegations that suspected Taliban prisoners in Afghan jails are routinely subjected to abuse and torture, Canadian Forces had for some eighteen months from 2006 to 2007 transferred detainees into Afghan control without adequate monitoring. It was only when award-winning investigative journalism by the *Globe and Mail* in 2007 drew attention to the problem that Ottawa began to follow through with closer checks on the process.[22] Then diplomat Richard Colvin testified at a parliamentary hearing that he had vainly tried to alert Foreign Affairs and the Canadian mission throughout 2006 and 2007 of the likelihood of detainee abuse. This potentially represents a very serious issue, since knowingly handing over prisoners to torture may be considered a war crime under the Geneva Conventions Act, as well as in contravention of the War Crimes Act and the Criminal Code section on aiding and abetting torture.[23] In the fall of 2011, the United Nations reported 'compelling evidence that … 46 percent of the detainees interviewed who had been in NDS [Afghan] detention experienced interrogation techniques at the hands of the NDS officials that constituted torture, and that torture is practiced systematically in a number of NDS detention facilities throughout Afghanistan.'[24]

The government refused all calls for a public inquiry into the matter, actively sought to block or impede the hearings being carried out by the arms-length Military Police Complaints Commission, and insisted that documents could be disclosed only in heavily censored form to protect national-security confidentiality and the conduct of Canadian military operations. Government stonewalling raised suspicions among Opposition parties, the press, and the public that some kind of cover-up of serious wrongdoing might be involved. The dispute over disclosure of unredacted documents finally escalated into a full-blown constitutional crisis when the House of Commons in December 2009 moved a motion to demand the release to Parliament of unredacted documents on the subject. The government refused, setting up the potential for censure of the government for contempt of Parliament.[25] Opposition MPs referred the question of whether their privileges had been breached to the speaker of the House of Commons, Peter Milliken, who in a landmark ruling on 27 April 2010, citing parliamentary supremacy, ordered the disclosure of all documents but required the government and Opposition to negotiate a method whereby sensitive documents could be viewed by a select number of MPs without public disclosure.[26] The alternative of continued confrontation and intransigence was so pitted with uncharted dangers for parliamentary democracy[27] that an all-party agreement was finally announced setting out a mechanism whereby four security-cleared MPs, one put forward from each party, could view unredacted documents, backed by a panel of three expert and eminent jurists agreed upon by all parties to advise on which documents could be safely released to the public.[28] As always, however, the devil is in the details: by the time the ground rules had been agreed on, the terms had been changed so drastically on behalf of the government that the NDP refused to take part in an exercise it believed had been emptied of real meaning. Then the 2011 election resulted in a Tory majority; a small percentage of the total number of documents were released to the public and the committee, and the panel of jurists was simply shut down.[29]

Most of the public controversy had been over the question of what the military personnel and senior command in the Canadian Afghan mission knew or did not know about what happened to the detainees handed over to Afghan authorities; and the crucial issue of ministerial knowledge and thus of ministerial responsibility (the latter shared by ministers in successive governments, first Liberal and then Conservative). There was, however, another element in the mix, one with potentially explosive implications: the role of CSIS in interrogating Taliban suspects in Canadian custody for intelligence on Taliban operations. Once it became known that CSIS had been operating on the ground in support of the Afghan mission since 2002,[30] the issue of document disclosure could be viewed in an even more problematic light.

Testifying before the special parliamentary committee on the detainee issue, Michel Coulombe, assistant director of foreign collection at CSIS, asserted that the service's intelligence gathering in Afghanistan 'has led to the disruption and dismantling of insurgent networks planning "imminent" bomb attacks against soldiers and civilians.' There were accusations (including one raised by a former Afghan interpreter for the Canadian mission) that CSIS may have deliberately colluded with the military to hand detainees to Afghanistan's National Directorate of Security (NDS) so that the agency could extract more information from them by more coercive methods than Canadians were willing or able to employ. Coulombe was equivocal in denial. He granted, however, that it was possible CSIS obtained intelligence from the NDS that came from questioning of prisoners transferred from Canadian hands, and that the notorious intelligence agency may have extracted information through the 'abusive interrogation of detainees.'[31]

The problem for CSIS and for the Canadian government is that, if CSIS agents knowingly transferred detainees to the Afghans in the expectation that the latter would be more successful in extracting information through reliance on interrogation methods abusive of human rights, there could be serious legal repercussions, not to speak of a black mark against the Canadian mission.[32] This might help to explain the persistent reluctance of the government to open unredacted documents, whether to the Military Police Complaints Commission or to Parliament. Intelligence shared between allies has always been considered exempt from public disclosure, accompanied as it normally is by caveats as to restricted access. The threat of withdrawal of intelligence exchange by foreign governments or agencies that object to the disclosure of material that carries caveats has always been one that frightens Canadian governments of any political stripe. The dilemma is this: the government of Canada rightly fears the consequences of unauthorized disclosure of intelligence received in confidence, yet if secrecy can be seen as covering up Canadian complicity in torture, the political consequences can be just as damaging.

In July 2011 SIRC submitted a review of CSIS's role in the interviewing of Afghan prisoners. It reported that the CSIS role was in fact quite limited.[33] Although CSIS interviews had taken place, CSIS officers were removed from any direct role in the transfer of detainees to the Afghans and did not have first-hand knowledge of any abuse. SIRC did suggest that CSIS should have 'appreciated the complexities of the environment in which they were operating,' and that the agency could have put in place more quickly guidelines to ensure accountability. SIRC pronounced itself unimpressed with sometimes sketchy CSIS record keeping, and recommended that if CSIS intends to operate more abroad, it ought to improve its record-management practices. In short, there was no smoking gun indicating CSIS complicity in torture. But the Afghan experience was a reminder of just how messy foreign involvement could become.

Touching the Third Rail

Torture has become the deadly third rail of Canadian national security: everyone and every agency that comes in contact with torture, however indirectly or however at arm's length, emerges somehow damaged or under a cloud of suspicion. Torture is something that most Canadians find alien and repellent, beyond the boundaries of Canadian traditions and values. It is not practised in Canada, but it is widely practised outside our borders by countries with less regard for human rights. As Canada in fulfilment of its post-9/11 commitments to global security is drawn more actively into a conflict-ridden world, it finds itself increasingly entangled in relationships with countries whose values and practices sometimes differ sharply from its own. Even more problematic for Canada are situations in which its closest and most trusted ally, the United States, is itself implicated directly and indirectly in torture. Canadians with responsibilities abroad have not welcomed this challenge to core national values but they cannot escape it. Torture is like the proverbial 'tar baby': the more one struggles with it, the more ensnared one becomes.

U.S. President Barack Obama has struggled with the torture problem since assuming office in 2009. The practice of torture under the previous Bush administration has been forthrightly condemned and investigations launched into how the United States had become enmeshed in a process so repugnant to basic decency and respect for human rights. Yet early promises to close down Guantánamo quickly bogged down in public suspicions about terrorists being unleashed on the American homeland and endless political squabbling. Renditions continue to be officially sanctioned American policy, and there are no guarantees that torture is not still being outsourced to regimes with no compunctions about abuse of human rights and international law.

The post-9/11 world of security and intelligence thus faces a series of difficult conundrums. CSIS, an agency well down the chain of the global hierarchy of counter-terrorist organizations, is unable to rely on its relatively low profile abroad to avoid these conundrums. Closer ties between CSIS and the American and allied security and intelligence agencies prosecuting this new kind of 'war' with few reservations about methods may have promised CSIS tangible benefits in enhanced cooperation and intelligence sharing. Yet these thickening ties also sowed a series of dangerous landmines in the agency's path. Beginning with the Maher Arar affair, passing through cases spun out of the Arar affair, and culminating in other cases that drew critical judicial and public attention from 2008 through 2010, CSIS has suffered an escalating series of embarrassments and questions about its competence to act on the wider world stage without becoming complicit in the excesses and human-rights abuses of the American-led global War on Terror. We will now examine each of these cases in turn.

'Extraordinary Rendition' and the Maher Arar Affair

The Maher Arar affair has already entered into Canadian mythology. It is a compelling narrative of the young Canadian computer engineer of Syrian origin who was kidnapped by American authorities[34] while in transit at a New York airport in 2002 en route home to Canada from an innocent trip abroad and then taken by force first to Jordan and finally to Syria, where he was imprisoned in a notorious jail, tortured, and subjected to horrifying conditions. The brave and at first lonely campaign of his wife to find out what fate had befallen her husband and to gain his return[35] slowly gathered force in the face of what began as public and political indifference to the fate of an Arab Muslim terrorist 'suspect.' Following Arar's release and return to Canada, his story of terror and abuse caused a sensation. Demands for a public inquiry rose in volume, and government resistance finally crumbled with the spectacle of a ham-fisted RCMP raid on the home of a reporter who had acted as a conduit for security officials attempting to smear Arar with selective leaks from secret files.[36] With the story apparently spinning out of control, the Paul Martin government appointed Ontario justice Dennis O'Connor to head an inquiry which in 2006 found clear evidence of complicity of Canadian officials with an abusive process; indicated firmly that there was no evidence linking Arar to terrorism; and further recommended a wide-ranging reform of the accountability mechanisms for national security.[37] The Stephen Harper government accepted all of the recommendations of the factual inquiry, issued an official apology to Arar and his family, and paid Arar himself $10.5 million in compensation.

The Arar affair and inquiry had serious consequences for the world of national-security operations in Ottawa.[38] Arar's experience at the hands of the Americans and the Syrians came as the direct result of the abuse of intelligence sharing with the U.S. authorities. O'Connor found that the RCMP in the joint counter-terrorist operation Project A-O CANADA had provided an unauthorized 'data dump' of all the material in the project files to the FBI in the United States – including much material with caveats attached such as 'for Canadian eyes only,' or specification from the originating source that the material was not to go beyond the recipient without authorization. Arar, who had appeared in the files merely as a peripheral 'person of interest' (that is, someone who knew or was known to have associated with someone else who was the target of the investigation), was thus brought to the attention of the U.S. authorities in a highly misleading context of suspicion, made worse by an explicit – and false – characterization supplied by the RCMP to the Americans that Arar and his wife were Muslim 'extremists.' The result was that Arar fell into the clutches of the American extraordinary-rendition program, whereby terrorist 'suspects' were rendered to countries like Syria with infamous human-rights records and no compunctions about the most brutal methods of interrogation (the O'Connor report was the first official documentation by any Western government of this notorious American program which amounts to the outsourcing of torture). O'Connor found that Canadian officials were complicit to a degree in a process that was abusive of Arar's constitutional rights as a Canadian citizen, not to speak of his human rights under international law. He laid down a series of recommendations regarding the appropriate conduct of Canadian officials in the future, including more strict interpretation of what intelligence should and should not be shared even with close allies like the Americans, as well as tighter conditions imposed upon any intelligence cooperation with regimes with doubtful human-rights records.

CSIS as an organization largely escaped critical attention, while the RCMP in its role as the law-enforcement agency responsible for investigating terrorist criminal activity came in for most of the unfavourable publicity. Project A-O CANADA was among the first tentative efforts at a more integrated, cross-agency approach to counter-terrorist operations in the immediate post 9/11 atmosphere of urgency and anxiety. Later, Integrated National Security Enforcement Teams institutionalized this integrated investigative process on a more professional basis[39] (see chapter 12). The O'Connor Inquiry in its second, policy-review, phase recognized that A-O CANADA was not representative of the developing integrated way of investigating terrorism, and it did not base its recommended accountability innovations on this early, hastily drawn-up, and poorly executed project. But the Arar damage was done, and it was the RCMP that bore chief responsibility. Indeed, in the aftermath of O'Connor's findings, the commissioner of the RCMP was forced to resign, to be replaced by the first civilian commissioner in the history of the force. CSIS, it should be noted, was especially displeased by the Mountie 'data dump' at the time it happened, since it included CSIS information with caveats against precisely such redistribution. The public notoriety arising from the commission's published findings attached mainly to the RCMP, as well as to some Canadian diplomats. CSIS, however, had no grounds for self-congratulation.

In fact, CSIS did not escape entirely from O'Connor's criticism: CSIS had travelled to Syria and obtained information on Arar extracted by the Syrians. As O'Connor wrote:

> CSIS did not do an adequate reliability assessment of the information provided by the SMI [Syrian military intelligence], particularly with respect to whether that information could be the product of torture. Moreover, CSIS shared this information with other agencies without giving a warning about the likelihood of torture. As a result, any reliance on this information by CSIS and others was misguided and misplaced. CSIS relied on this information to the prejudice of Mr. Arar on at least two occasions in circumstances that I heard in camera … if CSIS had done an adequate assessment, it would have concluded that the information was likely the result of torture and therefore of questionable reliability … The CSIS visit seems to have provided Syrian officials with a platform to take the position, even if concocted, that CSIS had said it did not want Mr. Arar returned.[40]

Equally damaging information was disclosed when passages in the report that the government had blocked from publication were later released by Federal Court order.[41] One would-be censored passage acknowledged that CSIS had indeed understood the nature of the American extraordinary-rendition program, about which the Canadian government had professed ignorance at the time of Arar's detention and disappearance. In fact, at the time of Arar's seizure by the United States, the CSIS liaison officer in Washington had reported that 'when the CIA or FBI cannot legally hold a terrorist subject, or wish a target questioned in a firm manner, they have them rendered to countries willing to fulfill that role. He said Mr. Arar was a case in point.' More damning yet was the testimony of Jack Hooper, assistant director of operations, who stated flatly in a memorandum on 10 October 2002: 'I think the U.S. would like to get Arar to Jordan where they can have their way with him.'[42]

The Arar affair disclosed a worrying aspect of CSIS operations overseas: engagement with dubious, human-rights-abusing regimes and with an American ally that was prosecuting its War on Terror with reckless disregard for the rights of individuals caught up, innocently or not, in this war. When such individuals were Canadian citizens, CSIS was treading on thin ice. Another, more subtle, result of the Arar affair and the inquiry was to shift public attention and support to a degree away from the remorseless and righteous pursuit of terrorist suspects

– identified as belonging to a suspect Arab/Muslim community – towards some balancing sympathy for members of this suspect community whose human and constitutional rights were being flouted by state excesses. Arar himself was transformed from an individual whose shadowy fate during his imprisonment in Syria elicited little public interest and some media and political suspicion into one whose status of respect earned him the *Globe and Mail*'s 'Canadian of the Year' award for 2006. This signalled a cultural shift with implications for a secret Canadian spy agency enlisted on the front lines of George Bush's War on Terror.

Almalki, Elmaati, and Nureddin: The Syrian Three

One recommendation of the Arar Inquiry had been that the government should inquire further into the actions of Canadian officials with regard to three Canadian citizens – Abdullah Almalki, Ahmad Elmaati, and Muayyed Nureddin – who had also suffered imprisonment and mistreatment in Syrian and, in one case, Egyptian jails but fell outside O'Connor's terms of reference. None were victims of the rendition program but each had unwisely visited the countries that detained them as terrorist suspects. Almalki, it should be noted, had been the main target of A-O CANADA, although he has never been charged with any criminal offence.[43] Almalki has since managed to force the disclosure of RCMP surveillance documents that shockingly reveal just how weak a case A-O CANADA actually had on him. In an RCMP memorandum dated 4 October 2001, an investigator concludes: 'O Div. (Ontario Division) task force are presently finding it difficult to establish anything on him other than the fact *he is an arab running around.*' Yet the same day, in a letter to the Syrian intelligence agency, the RCMP labelled Almalki 'an imminent threat' to Canada's national security and linked him to Al-Qaeda.[44]

In response to O'Connor's recommendation, the government instituted an 'internal inquiry' under retired Supreme Court of Canada Justice Frank Iacobucci with no mandate to make policy recommendations.[45] Although widely criticized for the closed nature of its proceedings, the Iacobucci inquiry concluded that these three Canadians had indeed suffered mistreatment that fell under the United Nations definition of torture. While their treatment could not be directly attributed to Canadian security intelligence and consular officials, the latter had contributed indirectly and thus bore some responsibility for the abuse of the rights of Canadian citizens.[46] In the case of Elmaati, his mistreatment resulted indirectly, in Iacobucci's view, from the actions of Canadian officials, including CSIS, which, by sending questions to Syrian intelligence to be put to Elmaati in detention, and by notifying Egyptian authorities about its concerns regarding Elmaati's possible release, may have contributed to his mistreatment in Egypt. These actions, Iacobucci concluded, were 'deficient in the circumstances.'[47] Over a year after the release of his Report, Justice Iacobucci released a supplement as a result of further negotiation over disclosure of information initially deemed harmful to national security. This additional material indicates that CSIS officers travelled to Egypt to interview Elmaati in 2002, without notifying Foreign Affairs, without consideration of the effect of their visit on his treatment by the Egyptians, and with no concern over the possibility of his mistreatment in either Syrian or Egyptian custody. In Iacobucci's view, this visit 'likely contributed indirectly to Mr. Elmaati's mistreatment in Egypt.' He found CSIS interaction with Egyptian authorities in 2002 deficient in two respects. First, CSIS did not consider the potential consequences of its actions for Elmaati. Second, several witnesses, from both CSIS and the RCMP, told the inquiry that it 'was not the responsibility of intelligence or law enforcement officials to be concerned about the human rights of a Canadian detainee, which were for Foreign Affairs alone to consider' – a position Iacobucci considered unsatisfactory. 'No Canadian officials should consider themselves exempt from the responsibility' to consider the effects of their actions on a detainee and to attempt to minimize these effects, he stated, adding: 'I find the apparent compartmentalization of human rights concerns within agencies of the Canadian government to be troubling.' Iacobucci did note that CSIS and Foreign Affairs had since established a Memorandum of Understanding on national-security consular cases to ensure that consultation and collaboration does take place.[48] A senior CSIS official later acknowledged to the inquiry that 'in hindsight' agents should have asked questions about abuse because it would have been relevant in deciding how reliable Elmaati's statements were.

In the case of Nureddin, a similar conclusion of deficiency in certain respects on the part of CSIS was reached. The service had shared information on its suspicions about Nureddin with several foreign agencies, including American; it also shared his travel itinerary, which indicated a stop in Damascus. All of this likely contributed to his mistreatment.[49]

The case of Almalki was more ambiguous. Although there was no specific finding of deficiency in CSIS actions in that case, nor indirect responsibility for his mistreatment assigned to CSIS, Iacobucci none-theless indicated his agreement with Justice O'Connor that, while inter-action with regimes with poor human-rights records might sometimes be necessary, such interactions must be as controlled as possible 'to safeguard against Canadian complicity in human rights abuses or the perception that Canada condones such abuses. If it is determined that there is a credible risk that Canadian interactions would render Canada complicit in torture or create the perception that Canada condones the use of torture, then a decision should be made that no interaction is to take place.'[50] It should be noted that, since Iacobucci had been ex-cluded by his terms of reference from making policy recommendations, his endorsement of O'Connor in this context may have been an indirect signalling of a policy preference. While CSIS may have been walking a very fine line with regard to Almalki, in Iacobucci's findings it had strayed over that line in the other two cases. And that line was itself questionable from a human-rights standpoint.

Abousfian Abdelrazik: 'Sudan Will Be Your Guantanamo'

The story of Abousfian Abdelrazik, Canadian citizen caught in a Kaf-kaesque limbo in Sudanese prisons and in the Canadian Embassy in Khartoum, is as bizarre as it is troubling.[51] Abdelrazik was a politi-cal dissident who fled his native Sudan in 1990 and was accepted by Canada as a refugee under the UN Convention on Refugees in 1995. As a resident of Montreal, he was an acquaintance of Ahmed Ressam, who was later convicted of planning to bomb the Los Angeles Airport. He also was acquainted with Adil Charkaoui, who was later detained indefinitely by the Canadian government under a security certificate until ordered freed by the courts (see chapter 12). Despite the fact that Abdelrazik volunteered to give evidence for the prosecution in Res-sam's trial, despite the fact that these two acquaintances were the only apparent grounds for any suspicion about him, and despite the fact that both CSIS and the RCMP later indicated that neither agency had any basis for associating him with terrorism, it is evident that Abdelrazik fell under surveillance by Canadian authorities as a possible threat to national security.[52] According to Abdelrazik, CSIS harassed him and his family while he resided in Canada. When in 2003 Abdelrazik made what proved to be a very unwise decision to travel to his native Sudan to visit his ailing mother, he claims that a CSIS officer hinted darkly that 'he would see' when he arrived in Sudan.

After arriving in Sudan, Abdelrazik was subsequently imprisoned and subjected to what he described as torture and what the Federal Court of Canada agrees conforms to the definition of torture under international conventions. While he was incarcerated, he was interrogated by two CSIS officers twice for a total of eight hours. The interrogation was taped, and witnessed throughout by two of his Sudanese captors, according to Abdelrazik.[53] One of the CSIS officers was the same one who had warned him in Canada prior to his trip to Sudan. This officer now reminded him of the earlier warning, adding: 'Now you see.' Even more chilling was the CSIS man's alleged response to Abdelrazik's plea to be brought back home and given a fair trial: 'Sudan will be your Guantanamo.'[54] The Canadian government, in both its diplomatic and political[55] manifestation, seemed equally cool to the plight of its citizen.

Although the Sudanese declared in writing that there was no case against Abdelrazik and released him, the CSIS counter-terrorism chief in Ottawa intervened with Transport Canada to prevent his return to Canada: soon afterward both Air Canada and Lufthansa abruptly cancelled Abdelrazik's ticket home. CSIS documents classified 'Canadian Eyes Only' reveal that it was the Americans who wanted their hands on Abdelrazik. The CIA, CSIS indicated. 'from the very beginning ... have made it known that their preferred option, and one which they will attempt to negotiate with the Sudanese, is to transfer Abdelrazik to the Guantanamo Bay military facility in Cuba.' Delaying or blocking Abdelrazik's return had the intended effect of buying time while the CIA attempted his rendition to the notorious American prison.[56]

Abdelrazik was then detained by the Sudanese a second time. Canadian diplomats were given to believe that, if they did not take Abdelrazik off Sudanese hands by returning him to Canada, he might suffer the fate of many of the Sudanese 'disappeared': this grim latter fate was the alternative 'permanent solution' to his return to Canada.[57] Yet the failure of the Canadians to take up this opportunity kept Abdelrazik in detention for another nine months, before his second release in 2006. On the day of his release, he was designated by the American government as having 'high level ties to and support for the Al-Qaida network,' citing an alleged close relationship with Abu Zubayda, a former high-ranking Al-Qaeda figure by then in U.S. custody. Eleven days later, Abdelrazik was designated by the UN '1267 Committee,' which lists individuals and groups allegedly related to Al-Qaeda and the Taliban,[58] as an Al-Qaeda associate, apparently at the request of the U.S. government.

In late 2006 the Canadian consul in Khartoum met with senior officials from Sudan's National Security and Intelligence Agency (NSI). One partially censored sentence in a dispatch from the Khartoum embassy to Ottawa suggests that Abdelrazik's 2003 arrest may have been on 'recommendation by CSIS.' The same memorandum reported the NSI as insisting that 'initial recommendations for his detention emerged from CSIS.' (The embassy noted parenthetically that 'if this is indeed the case, we had not been told of these communications.')[59] Such an accusation if verified would amount to a Canadian variant of the U.S. extraordinary-rendition program – although Abdelrazik had voluntarily, if very unwisely, travelled to Sudan. CSIS, however, denies that it made any such recommendation in this case, or that it ever seeks the detention of Canadian citizens by foreign states.[60] By 29 April 2008, fearing re-arrest by the Sudanese authorities, Abdelrazik sought refuge in the Canadian Embassy in Khartoum, and was granted safe haven. His real goal was to return to Canada, but it soon became apparent that after granting him haven, the government of Canada was determined to keep him in stateless limbo, living out a sparse and dreary existence in the Embassy compound. The Sudanese wanted rid of him and expected the Canadians to facilitate his return, but the government had no end of excuses as to why this would not be possible. When it was suggested that the destitute Abdelrazik had to provide his own plane ticket, a group of Canadians raised funds (defying the UN list and the Anti-Terrorism Act) and purchased a ticket in his name. It was then claimed that his presence on the UN list prevented his flying home, although the UN official in charge of the committee that had listed him told the media that it was absurd to suggest that he could not fly back to the country of his citizenship.[61] The minister of foreign affairs declared him (without evidence) to be a threat to the security of Canada, and thus inadmissible, even though as a citizen he had the right to return. When Federal Court Justice Russel Zinn (appointed, it should be noted, by Prime Minister Harper) sharply criticized the violation of Abdelrazik's constitutional rights and ordered his immediate return, the government procrastinated for a while longer contemplating an appeal, but finally, gracelessly, it admitted defeat and allowed his return, after spending over $800,000 in a vain attempt to block a Canadian citizen from coming home to his own country.[62]

Abdelrazik's bizarre odyssey took a further turn in the summer of 2009 with his repatriation to Canada. His status under the UN Committee listing and Canadian regulations implementing the UN rules 'prohibit[s] anyone from providing Mr. Abdelrazik with any kind of material aid, including salary, loans of any amount, food or clothing.' 'He can,' one observer wrote, 'barely survive while on this list.'[63] Conditions that the Federal Court referred to as Kafkaesque and 'frightening' for any citizen, and all the more so when based on mere suspicion, continue even in Canada.

In September 2009 Abdelrazik filed claim in Federal Court for $27 million in punitive and aggravated damages against the government of Canada and personally against Foreign Affairs Minister Lawrence Cannon for malfeasance in public office.[64] In the *Statement of Claim*, CSIS figures prominently. The suit alleges that CSIS sought Abdelrazik's detention and mistreatment by the Sudanese in order to extract information from him by methods that are illegal and unconstitutional in Canada; that CSIS shared information with Sudan that 'it knew or reasonably ought to have known would place the Plaintiff at risk'; and that CSIS received interrogation information from the Sudanese authorities that it knew or ought to have known 'had been derived by torture, and that by accepting the information it was condoning or reinforcing the practice of torture.' The suit also alleges that the subjection of Abdelrazik to cruel and unusual punishment by the Sudanese, contrary to the Charter, had been condoned and encouraged by Canada 'at least in part because CSIS agents determined that [Abdelrazik] had not been sufficiently co-operative while on Canadian soil.'[65] A government 'entirely unrepentant' (in the words of Abdelrazik's counsel)[66] tried unsuccessfully to stop the suit on the grounds that Abdelrazik's case was 'mostly frivolous and vexatious.' Prothonotary Federal Court Justice Madam Roza Aronovitch ruled in September 2010 that the case could continue, citing international prohibitions against torture and leaving open the possibility that a private challenge on these grounds could be sustained: 'It is therefore not plain and obvious that the plaintiff cannot succeed, and it is premature to foreclose the debate at this juncture.'[67]

The question remains about the basis, if any, for the suspicions that have entangled Abdelrazik in his endless nightmare. The reliance of the Americans – and by extension the UN Committee acting on American advice – on Abu Zubayda as the apparent sole source linking Abdelrazik to Al-Qaeda is dubious on multiple grounds. Although touted as a very high Al-Qaeda functionary, Zubayda's organizational status pre-detention has been called into serious question, as has his mental state even prior to capture.[68] By 2010, the Obama administration had dropped almost all the original case against Zubayda, in direct repudiation of the extravagant claims made by senior Bush administration officials – including the president – that he was the number two or three man in the Al-Qaeda hierarchy. Instead, he is now being prosecuted as a minor figure, mainly on the evidence of assertions in his personal diary.[69] Whatever his actual importance, his evidence is ineradicably tainted by the fact he was, along with Khalid Sheikh Mohammed, the test case for the use of so-called enhanced-interrogation (that is, torture) methods by the CIA. According to reports based on leaked internal documents, Zubayda was waterboarded at least eighty-three times.[70] Waterboarding is the euphemistic name for simulated drowning used to induce panic attacks that break down a prisoner's resistance, a technique employed by CIA interrogators against Guantánamo inmates that gained such notoriety when revealed that it was stopped by President Bush, who had authorized enhanced interrogation in the first place, and condemned by the incoming Obama administration. The repeated use of this torture technique on Zubayda, a man whose mental state may already have been fragile, calls into severe question the intelligence value of whatever he may have said following these assaults on his sanity.[71] There were officials involved in the process who later questioned whether anything of value was gained from Zubayda by these brutal methods, seeing him as clinically insane after his repeated torture sessions.[72]

Documents disclosed under Access to Information suggest that the U.S. government itself had limited confidence in its evidence against Abdelrazik.[73] On 19 July 2006, the day before the United States officially designated Abdelrazik as a terrorist threat, the U.S. Embassy in Ottawa brought to Foreign Affairs Canada what it termed a 'message from the White House, specifically from senior levels of the Homeland Security Council,' to the effect that the 'US would like Canada's assistance in putting together a criminal case against Abdelrazik so that he could be charged in the US. The US had information on Abdelrazik but at this point, it was not enough to charge him; if Canadian police or security agencies shared what they had, it might prove enough for the US to proceed.'[74] Neither the RCMP nor CSIS in fact possessed adverse information on Abdelrazik that would provide the basis for any criminal proceeding in Canada or in the United States, as both agencies have subsequently attested.[75] Nevertheless, documents were later leaked, very likely by CSIS, to *La Presse* linking Abdelrazik with Adil Charkaoui in an alleged plot to bomb an airliner: information already discredited in Federal Court in the Charkaoui security-certificate proceedings (see chapter 12).[76]

Although the UN Committee eventually posted on its website un-sourced allegations against Abdelrazik (including supposed Afghan and Chechen connections) that he vehemently denies,[77] it would appear that these allegations rest on the Zubayda confessions made under torture. Yet, however tainted the source, once listed by the UN Committee, it is virtually impossible for an individual to get his or her name removed. Indeed, Mr Justice Zinn has stated in his judgment on the Abdelrazik case that the UN Committee regime is 'a situation for a listed person not unlike that of Josef K. in Kafka's *The Trial*, who awakens one morning and, for reasons never revealed to him or the reader, is arrested and prosecuted for an unspecified crime.'[78] Rejected by the U.K. Supreme Court,[79] Canada's '1267' regime is being challenged in the Federal Court by Abdelrazik together with the British Columbia Civil Liberties Association and the International Civil Liberties Monitoring Group.[80] Serious questions have been raised about the legality under international law of the '1267' regime. In response, the United Nations has appointed an ombudsperson – a Canadian jurist[81] – to make recommendations to the Security Council on delisting. Finally, in late 2011, Abdelrazik was formally delisted, wiping out the dark shadow that had hung over him for so long. But even this decision was given no backing from his own government, which chose not to support his delisting, declaring itself 'neutral' and in effect washing its hands of any responsibility.[82]

Inevitably, the issue arose of an inquiry into who in Canada had contributed to Abdelrazik's situation. Since CSIS had figured publicly in the case, the Security Intelligence Review Committee, the independent CSIS watchdog, was the most likely candidate for a review. Since SIRC at first showed little interest in initiating its own study, the ball was in the hands of the minister of public safety, empowered under the CSIS Act to order a section 54 report in which SIRC could be directed to review any matter required by the minister.[83] The then minister, Peter Van Loan, never made such a request, despite the high public visibility of the case and the degree of concern expressed about the role of CSIS. In one of the stranger twists of a very strange tale, this ministerial silence or indifference led the director of CSIS, Jim Judd, to make his own unprecedented section 54 request to SIRC to review CSIS involvement in the Abdelrazik affair.[84] In effect, the head of CSIS was asking the CSIS watchdog to investigate the agency's own behaviour, in the absence of any direction by the minister. One explanation of this most unusual request might be that Judd was sufficiently confident that no wrongdoing had occurred that he wanted a public review for vindication, even without his minister's support. An alternative interpretation, less flattering to CSIS, might be that since Judd would shortly indicate his intention to step down as director before the end of his five-year term,[85] he may have been indicating that an independent review was in fact necessary to address serious issues within the agency.

This speculation was given further purchase when SIRC, perhaps now emboldened by the Federal Court decision and by the government's surrender on the return of Abdelrazik, announced in July 2009 that it would initiate its own comprehensive inquiry into CSIS and the Abdelrazik affair, while specifically rejecting a narrower 'exculpatory' inquiry as requested by the now departed director Judd.[86] Critics were quick to point out that SIRC was limited to studying the role of CSIS and could not provide the kind of wide-ranging inquiry that would also extend to other parts of the government, such as Foreign Affairs, the RCMP, and the Canadian Border Services Agency. The government, by sitting on its hands over implementing the recommendations of the policy-review section of the O'Connor report on Maher Arar affair, had failed to set up the kind of integrated national-security review process that could cross jurisdictional stovepipes to gain the broad picture, leaving yet another special inquiry like O'Connor or Iacobucci as the only alternative to SIRC. It is unlikely that the Conservative government would call such a special inquiry into its own actions. SIRC's report, whenever it is completed, and with all its inherent limitations, will thus almost certainly be the only official review of this murky and troubling affair.

'What Canada Does Not Wish to Know, It Does Not See': CSIS and Torture

Just as the Abdelrazik affair was beginning to unfold publicly, suspicions about CSIS complicity in torture were further fuelled by the testimony of a senior CSIS legal adviser to the House of Commons Committee on Public Safety, Geoffrey O'Brian, who stated that CSIS has 'no absolute ban on using intelligence that may have been obtained from countries with sketchy human rights records on torture.' 'Do we use information that comes from torture? The answer is we only do so if lives are at stake,' O'Brian testified.[87] This 'vague' statement 'deeply troubled' the MPs, the committee later reported.[88] It certainly gained the unhappy attention of the minister of public safety, who quickly issued a rebuke to O'Brian and an affirmation that the government did not condone complicity with torture 'in any circumstances.'[89] CSIS Director Jim Judd was forced to appear before the MPs and repudiate the 'unfortunate' statement by the twenty-five-year veteran of the service: 'Mr. O'Brian may have been confused in his testimony,' Judd said. 'I know of no instance where such use of information has been made by our service ... We do not condone torture. We do not rely on information obtained by torture.'[90]

This was the public face on complicity with torture presented by the CSIS director, one that had gained Judd a degree of respect from human-rights advocates.[91] Yet a WikiLeaks disclosure showed Judd in private conversation with the U.S. Embassy in 2008 in a different light on the subject. At this time, Judd, in the Embassy's words, 'derided' recent judgments in Canada's courts 'that threaten to undermine foreign government intelligence – and information-sharing with Canada. These judgments posit that Canadian authorities cannot use information that "may have been" derived from torture, and that any Canadian public official who conveys such information may be subject to criminal prosecution. This, he commented, put the government in a reverse-onus situation whereby it would have to "prove" the innocence of partner nations in the face of assumed wrongdoing.'[92]

In any event, faced with public repudiation by his boss, O'Brian issued a clarifying mea culpa to the committee that 'CSIS certainly does not condone torture and that it is the policy of CSIS to not knowingly rely upon information that may have been obtained through torture.'[93] But CSIS, even in public documents, had not always been so unequivocal. In its *Annual Report* for 2005–6, SIRC had taken CSIS to task for the way in which it was handling intelligence exchanges with countries with questionable human- rights records. SIRC asked CSIS whether it treated information that might have been obtained 'through human rights violations' differently from information received by other means. In response, CSIS acknowledged that, in most cases, 'it will not know whether a piece of information originated from an abuse of human rights, [but] if suspected, the Service has to balance that against the need to secure information to protect Canadians and Canadian interests'[94] – scarcely a ringing renunciation of relying on information obtained under torture.

The public statements by Van Loan and Judd elicited a scathing critique ('positively bathed in nonsense') from the *Globe and Mail* in an editorial that pointed out that it was no more than the 'plain truth' that CSIS and other Canadian agencies did accept information that may have been tainted by torture. Citing the cases of Arar, Almalki, Elmaati, and Nureddin, the *Globe* sneered that 'what Canada does not wish to know, it does not see.' It went on pointedly: 'A Canadian citizen, Abousfian Abdelrazik, is at this very moment stranded in Canada's embassy in Khartoum. Official Canadian documents show that this country asked Sudan – no bastion of human rights – to arrest and detain him. Canada has most certainly flirted with torturers in gathering intelligence against its own citizens detained abroad.' The *Globe* concluded that 'the simple truth about torture is treated as a scandal, and the actual torture scandals as if they never happened.'[95] Nor has CSIS abandoned the position staked out momentarily by O'Brian before his articulation of it provoked such embarrassment. This is evidenced by internal briefing notes prepared for Director Richard Fadden and released in 2010 to the Canadian Press, which reported that 'CSIS will share information received from an international partner with the police and other authorities "even in the rare and extreme circumstance that we have some doubt as to the manner in which the foreign agency acquired it." The notes say [that,] although such information would never be admissible in court to prosecute someone posing an imminent threat, "the government must nevertheless make use of the information to attempt to disrupt that threat before it materializes."'[96] Despite the notes' acknowledgment of the inadmissibility of torture-derived evidence in the courts, and despite the common-sense appeal of the argument presented there (should CSIS turn a blind eye to a possible terrorist attack because information may have been obtained by abusive methods?), they do not clarify where CSIS finally stands with regard to sharing intelligence with states that may use torture; on the contrary, they actually muddy the waters. Even if torture-tainted information cannot be used in Canadian courts, there are many ways in which such information can be used by CSIS, with dire consequences, as the cases enumerated above demonstrate, for the rights and well-being of Canadians.

O'Brian's apparent gaffe provided one disclosure of value: the minister of public safety provided the parliamentary committee with a ministerial directive to CSIS on 'Information Sharing with Foreign Agencies.' This directive acknowledges that, in combating terrorism, CSIS may enter into formal information-sharing arrangements with foreign agencies 'including those that are generally recognized as having poor human rights records.' The government, however, is 'steadfast in its abhorrence of an opposition to the use of torture' for any purpose, including the collection of intelligence. To avoid any complicity in the use of torture, CSIS must 'not knowingly rely upon information

that is derived from the use of torture,' have in place reasonable measures to identify such sources of information, and 'take all reasonable
measures to reduce the risk that any action on the part of the Service
might promote or condone, or be seen to promote or condone the use of
torture, including, where appropriate, the seeking of assurances when
sharing information with foreign agencies.'[97] The Opposition majority
on the committee declared itself unsatisfied by what the MPs took to
be a lack of clarity and specificity in the directive, and complained that
it applied only to CSIS and not to other agencies involved in national
security; they called for a new directive that would clearly state that the
'exchange of information with countries is prohibited when there is a
credible risk that it could lead, or contribute, to the use of torture.' The
Conservative minority, however, dissented from this conclusion, insisting that the Opposition's condition was already fulfilled.[98]

CSIS has responded to the ministerial directive. A declassified, but
somewhat redacted, internal CSIS memorandum lays out appropriate mechanisms for CSIS to comply with the broad brushstrokes of the
ministerial directive, but it clearly does leave open the possibility of
continued intelligence exchange with countries with questionable human-rights records, under certain circumstances.[99] The director of CSIS
and the deputy minister of foreign affairs signed a protocol between the
two agencies in 2007 'Concerning Cooperation in Respect of Consular
Cases Involving Canadians Detained Abroad as Part of a National Security or Terrorism Related Case.' A caveat regarding human rights is
now attached to information supplied by CSIS to foreign-intelligence
agencies.[100]

That CSIS controls over acceptance of evidence derived from torture may be inadequate is suggested by a Federal Court decision in
another of the security-certificate cases, this time of Mohammed Mahjoub. In June 2010 Federal Court Justice Edmond Blanchard ruled that,
'notwithstanding the policies and practices implemented' by CSIS, the
agency's approach to evidence obtained from countries with poor human-rights records did not meet the admissibility criteria for Canadian
courts, and that, accordingly, much of the secret case against Mahjoub
was unacceptable.[101]

Mustafa Krer: A Canadian in Colonel Gadhafi's Cells

In late 2011, after the fall of Tripoli to rebel forces in the Libyan revolution, the organization Human Rights Watch recovered a cache of
documents in a Libyan security building revealing details of close

cooperation between the United States, the United Kingdom, and other governments with the Libyan intelligence agency. Among these were records of a Libyan-Canadian citizen imprisoned for eight years by the notorious Gadhafi regime; these records revealed that CSIS agents interrogated him while he was in Libyan custody for suspected terrorist ties. Mustafa Krer was detained in Libya from 2002 to 2010. He told Human Rights Watch that Canadian interrogators visited him about three times between 2003 and 2005, even questioning him jointly with a team of Libyans in the room. One of the recovered documents, apparently CIA, requests that the Libyans ask Krer a set of eighty-nine questions. Krer confirmed that he was asked those questions by the Libyans and the CIA, and he was also asked some of those questions by CSIS.

Canada's apparent decision to interrogate a suspect in the custody of Gadhafi's forces is deeply troubling,' said a senior counsel at Human Rights Watch. 'CSIS did not torture Krer, but they must have known that the Libyans probably did.' He added: 'There is no justification for CSIS agents joining in the interrogation of a prisoner by agents of a government well-known for torturing prisoners.'[102] It is also heavily ironic given Canada's enthusiastic diplomatic and military support for the NATO intervention that helped topple the Libyan dictatorship, and the frequent denunciations issued by the prime minister and the minister of foreign affairs against the nefarious and oppressive nature of the Gadhafi regime.

Omar Khadr: Canada's Abandoned Child Soldier

Of all the ugly Canadian spin-offs of the American War on Terror, none has elicited such sharp and pointed criticism of CSIS as the case of Omar Khadr, the Canadian boy of fifteen who was found wounded and near death after a fierce firefight between Taliban fighters and American soldiers in Afghanistan in July 2002. The wounded boy was captured, charged with allegedly throwing a grenade that had killed an American Special Forces sergeant, and ended up as the sole Canadian, and ultimately the sole Westerner, in the camp for so-called enemy combatants at the U.S. base in Guantánamo, Cuba.[103] Although the British and Australian governments had intervened successfully with the Bush administration to secure the release of their nationals from the increasingly notorious Guantánamo facility, no request for Khadr's return to Canada ever emerged from either the Liberal governments of Jean Chrétien or Paul Martin or the Conservative government of Stephen Harper, even though the latter has faced an widening array of demands for Khadr's return, ranging from a united Opposition in Parliament through various groups in civil society and finally the courts. And, in the case of Omar Khadr, concern about Canadian complicity in torture and mistreatment of prisoners has focused on CSIS – including the judicial authorization of public airing of videotapes of CSIS interrogating Khadr in a Guantánamo cell. This concern has led to criticism of CSIS behaviour by its own review body, SIRC.

The Khadr case was always complicated, with a potential political downside for any government that requested his release and return to Canada. Omar Khadr is a member of a family that became notorious for its open support of Al-Qaeda terrorism. Omar's late father, Ahmed Said Khadr, was a kind of terrorist patriarch who moved his entire family, both physically and in spirit, from Canada to Pakistan and finally to the battlefields of Afghanistan in support of the Taliban regime, under the cover of a charitable organization with support from sections of the Canadian Muslim and Arab communities. Khadr Sr had inspired a CSIS dossier on his activities, and the agency considered him a terrorist, pure and simple. However, when the ailing Khadr was detained in Pakistan in 1995 on terrorism charges, he went on a hunger strike, and his 'cause' mobilized a support campaign in Canada. On a 'Team Canada' trade mission to Pakistan, Prime Minister Jean Chrétien was persuaded to meet with the wife and children of Khadr – including the then eight-year-old Omar – and pledged to raise the question of Khadr's treatment with Pakistani Prime Minister Benazir Bhutto when the two leaders conferred. Khadr was subsequently released from custody with charges dropped.

In the circumstances of the time, an expression of prime ministerial concern for a Canadian citizen detained under questionable conditions by a regime with a reputation for harsh and arbitrary actions was not altogether untoward. However, the later notoriety of the Khadr family's associations with Al-Qaeda and the Taliban cast this intervention in a very different and embarrassing light as an 'appalling political error.' The Khadr patriarch was killed in action on behalf of the Taliban in Afghanistan. Omar's youngest brother, Abdul Kareem, was permanently paralysed in the same attack that killed the father; he was allowed to return to Canada where he receives medical treatment. An older brother, Abdullah, was subject to an extradition request by the United States later quashed in Canadian courts (see below). The strangest case is that of Abdurahman Khadr, who was at one point imprisoned along with

Omar at Guantánamo but was released and, after a peculiar odyssey through a number of countries, returned to Canada with a story of alleged cooperation with American intelligence.[104]

Against this background, Ottawa officials would soon refer to the 'Khadr effect' to 'explain why politicians were reluctant to intervene in cases that could become embarrassing.'[105] This effect became even more powerful when Khadr Sr's widow and daughter, only their eyes visible through their black *niqabs,* gave an infamous post-9/11 interview on CBC television proclaiming their identity as an 'Al-Qaeda family'; their contempt for Canadian life; and their view that the 9/11 victims 'deserved' their fate. The Khadr effect goes a long way to explain the later reluctance, if not outright resistance, of successive Liberal and Conservative governments to intervene on Omar's behalf with American authorities.

After his capture, Omar was initially held in the Bagram collection camp in Afghanistan. Physical abuse and intimidation of detainees was routine at Bagram, and Khadr has claimed that he was subjected to treatment there that answers to the international legal definition of torture, even as his wounds were being treated. He had just turned sixteen years of age when he was relocated to Guantánamo in late 2002. Documentation of torture at Guantánamo emerged over the next few years, but even at the outset the decision of the United States to ignore the Geneva Conventions on prisoners of war by inventing a category of 'enemy combatants,' to be held in a military facility offshore outside the jurisdiction of U.S. courts and beyond the protection of the U.S. constitution (or so the Bush administration claimed, although this was later denied under judicial review), drew worldwide concern. The charge against Omar Khadr – the murder of an American officer – has been challenged by his defence lawyers, who have photographic evidence they claim prove that he could not have carried out the alleged act since he was already disabled by bullets in his back and lying under a pile of rubble when the death occurred.[106] In any event, a murder charge is dubious in the context of a war brought about by the American invasion of Afghanistan. Only with the sleight-of-hand construction of the enemy-combatant category could someone like Khadr be charged with murder in a battlefield situation in which both sides were trying to kill the other.[107]

To make matters even more dubious, as an adolescent, Khadr qualified as a 'child soldier,' a category recognized under international conventions and Canadian law as requiring special treatment. Drawn into the conflict by his father and family, the then fifteen-year-old Omar was hardly responsible for his own situation in the way that an adult volunteer might be. Yet not only was Omar put into the Guantánamo system without habeas corpus and, initially, without legal counsel, but he was placed among adult detainees at both Bagram and Guantánamo even though some other young detainees were kept separately. Moreover, there is ample evidence that he was mistreated by his captors, perhaps in the belief that his youth might make him more vulnerable to intimidation and harsh interrogation. His captors apparently believed that his attendance with his father at various Al-Qaeda-linked locations made him a potentially valuable source of information, and had no intention of passing up the opportunity to squeeze the teenager for whatever they might drain from him. One of the methods used on him – since admitted by the Americans – was what they called the 'frequent flyer' program, systematic and sustained sleep deprivation as a means of disorienting a subject and weakening their resistance. Sleep deprivation has been a feature of interrogation by torture since the Spanish Inquisition and has been recognized as a component of torture under international conventions.[108]

Neither the Chrétien nor Martin governments publicly advocated on behalf of Omar Khadr, despite their reservations about his treatment and the entire Guantánamo system. Bureaucratic inquiries and cautions were communicated to the Americans behind the scenes, to no effect.[109] For the Liberals, after the embarrassment of Chrétien's public intervention on behalf of Khadr Sr, it was a matter of once burned, twice shy. For the incoming Conservative government of Stephen Harper, on the other hand, Omar Khadr seems to have offered a political opportunity. Playing consistently to political supporters who revile the Khadr family as a terrorist clan which should enjoy no constitutional rights, the Conservatives refused to follow their British and Australian allies who successfully sought the return of their nationals from Guantánamo, however unpopular these men may have been at home.

The hardening of the official Canadian position after the change in government should be set against a shift in opinion in other quarters. The Liberals in opposition moved to support a united front of all three Opposition parties – a majority in a minority Parliament – calling on Canada to request Omar's return. Civil-liberties associations and the Canadian Bar Association added their voices of concern, as did leading newspapers. Public opinion may not have moved too far from the immediate post-9/11 anti-Khadr family feelings,[110] but elite, informed opinion had moved strongly in favour of Canadian intervention on Khadr's behalf. This did not signal any growing Canadian sympathy for terrorists, or for the Taliban, which by November 2011 had killed 158 Canadian soldiers in Afghanistan's unending conflict. But it did signal a growing revulsion against American counter-terrorist excesses, and a sense of responsibility on behalf of a Canadian youth abused and denied basic human rights, whatever the opinions and actions of his family. The Harper Conservatives alone seemed unmoved by humanitarian or legal concerns. Yet they soon found themselves ranged not only against elite opinion but also against the Canadian courts, a most formidable adversary. And CSIS found itself uncomfortably in the crossfire.

Once formal murder charges were laid against him, Khadr was granted limited legal representation. His Canadian counsel then sought disclosure in Canada of all documents relevant to the charges in the possession of the Canadian crown, including the records of interviews conducted with him at Guantánamo by CSIS agents in 2003, the products of which interviews were subsequently shared with the U.S. authorities. In 2005 a Federal Court judge issued an injunction barring Canadian agencies, including CSIS, from interviewing Khadr further, since the earlier interviews had violated Khadr's Charter rights.[111] The Federal Court of Appeal ordered that unredacted copies of all relevant documents be produced before the Federal Court for review. The crown appealed against this to the Supreme Court, which in 2008 rendered a crucial decision rejecting the appeal.[112] Khadr, the Supreme Court held unanimously, was entitled under the Charter of Rights to disclosure of the records of the CSIS interviews and of any information given the United States as a consequence of the interviews. Normally, the Charter would not apply to the actions of Canadian officials acting abroad but in compliance with local law. However, when Canadian officials participate in processes that 'violate Canada's binding international human rights obligations,' the Charter does apply. The court found that the processes in place at Guantánamo at the time CSIS interviewed Khadr and 'passed on the fruits of the interviews to US officials' have been found by the US Supreme Court 'with the benefit of a full factual record to violate U.S. domestic law and international obligations to which Canada subscribes.' By permitting these actions of Canadian officials, Canada had participated in a process that 'violated its international human rights obligations.' Thus, with Khadr's 'present and future liberty at stake, Canada is bound by the principles of fundamental justice and is under a duty of disclosure pursuant to s. 7 of the *Charter*.' The Supreme Court ordered a designated judge[113] of the Federal Court to review all the relevant documents for disclosure.

In June 2008 Federal Court Justice Richard Mosley reviewed the documents and ordered disclosure consistent with the national interest.[114] Among the items disclosed were documents relating to the CSIS interviews.[115] In these records, Canadians were clearly made aware of allegations by Khadr that he had been tortured at Bagram and continued to fear further torture at the hands of his Guantánamo captors. The 'smoking gun' that implicated Canadian officials in complicity with legally unacceptable treatment was an acknowledgment by the director of the Foreign Intelligence Division, Department of Foreign Affairs, that when an official from that division was allowed to meet with Khadr in early 2004, the prisoner had been systematically subjected to sleep deprivation prior to and during the visit: 'In an effort to make him more amenable and willing to talk, [redacted] has placed Umar on the "frequent flyer program" for the three weeks before Mr. Gould's visit. Umar has not been permitted more than three hours in any one location. At three hour intervals he is moved to another cell block, thus denying him uninterrupted sleep and a continued change of neighbours. He will soon be placed in isolation for up to three weeks and then he will be interviewed again.'[116]

The most sensational of the court-ordered disclosures were videotapes of the CSIS interview sessions, which were soon aired internationally as the first public video records of Guantánamo interrogations. As CSIS Director Jim Judd predicted to the American Embassy, DVD release 'would likely show three (Canadian) adults interrogating a kid who breaks down in tears.' He observed that the images would no doubt trigger 'knee-jerk anti-Americanism' and 'paroxysms of moral outrage, a Canadian specialty,' as well as lead to a new round of heightened pressure on the government to press for Khadr's return to Canada. He also predicted that the Harper government would nonetheless continue to resist this pressure. Judd was right on both scores.[117]

The videotaping had been done by the Americans, and is often of poor quality, the audio at times indecipherable. Nonetheless, beyond the novelty of a first public exposure of life inside Guantánamo, the airing of the videos did have an impact on public perception of the case. The image of a lost and confused teenager ensnared in the by now notorious Guantánamo process being bullied and prodded by Canadians, who were apparently hand-in-glove with his American captors, was less than impressive. The unnamed CSIS agent questioning Khadr does not come off well: sneering, taunting, and dismissive of all Khadr's complaints about his treatment, the agent seems more like a small-town cop berating a juvenile offender than an intelligence agent skillfully playing a subject to elicit hidden truths.

Canadian officials knew that Khadr's subjection to sleep deprivation was part of his interrogation process – a key point for the Canadian courts. When Khadr's Canadian lawyers brought suit against the government of Canada to force it to seek his repatriation to Canada, the Federal Court upheld his argument that his section 7 Charter rights had indeed been infringed, and that the appropriate remedy was to seek his return. His Charter rights had been violated by refusal to recognize his special status as a minor, by his lack of legal counsel until 2004, and by the decision of Canadian officials to interrogate him in 2004 while fully aware that sleep deprivation had been imposed upon him prior to and during their interviews.[118] When the Harper government insisted upon appealing this ruling, its appeal was rejected by the Federal Court of Appeal in a two-to-one decision. The majority judgment stated that 'the purpose of the sleep deprivation mistreatment was to induce Mr. Khadr to talk, and Canadian officials knew that when they interviewed Mr. Khadr to obtain information for intelligence purposes. *There can be no doubt that their conduct amounted to knowing participation in Mr. Khadr's mistreatment.*'[119] The Conservative government appealed this decision to the Supreme Court, pointing to the dissenting Appeal Court judgment that, despite the need for a remedy for the violation of Khadr's rights, the courts had no business directing the government in matters of foreign policy.

In early 2010 the Supreme Court issued an opinion that upheld the finding of the lower courts that Khadr's rights had indeed been violated but refrained from calling for the specific remedy of ordering the government to request his repatriation. While the court did find that a remedy was required, it chose not to order the specific remedy of a repatriation request. Warning that the 'executive is not exempt from constitutional scrutiny,' the unanimous court nonetheless argued that the 'appropriate remedy in this case is to declare that K[hadr]'s *Charter* rights were violated, leaving it to the government to decide how best to respond to in light of current information, its responsibility over foreign affairs, and the *Charter.*'[120] Predictably, the government took this as a vindication of its position, although it did propose a remedy that fell short of repatriation: it sent a diplomatic note to Washington asking that any information gained from Canadian interviews not be used in any legal proceedings against Khadr.[121] In the summer of 2010, the U.S. government opened a military trial for Khadr in Guantánamo. In pre-trial proceedings it simply brushed off the Canadian government request and indicated it would use any information gathered from Khadr by Canadian officials, including CSIS, against him.[122] Critics argued that this U.S. government's rejection of the pro forma Canadian request, along with its refusal to consider the child-soldier issue, rendered compliance with the Supreme Court order questionable.[123]

On 5 July 2010 Mr Justice Zinn of the Federal Court (the same judge who had rendered the Abdelrazik verdict that forced Abdelrazik's return to Canada) ruled that 'Omar Khadr was entitled to procedural fairness by the executive when making its decision as to the appropriate remedy to take. I further find that the executive failed to provide Mr. Khadr with the level of fairness that was required when making its decision.' Justice Zinn then gave the government seven days to provide 'other potential remedies that may cure or ameliorate the breach of his Charter rights, and as to whether those being considered by Canada, in his view, are potential remedies that may cure or ameliorate the breach.'[124] However, further legal proceedings in Canada were overtaken by events in Guantánamo.

As if to spell out the widespread impression that the military tribunal is little more than a kangaroo court, Canadian reporters, including Michelle Shephard of the *Toronto Star* who had published a book on the Khadr case, were banned from covering the so-called trial. And the military judge simply waived aside objections to admitting so-called confessions compelled by beatings and threats of rape brought against a severely wounded and terrified fifteen-year-old by American interrogators.[125] The entire proceeding resembled nothing so much as the 'trial' in *Alice in Wonderland*: '"Let the jury consider their verdict," the King said. "No, no!" said the Queen. "Sentence first – verdict afterwards."'[126] The *New York Times* referred to the proceedings as 'warped justice.'[127] The squalid denouement was finally played out in late 2010 when Khadr was compelled to plead guilty (to a 'crime' that would be recognized by no other court in the world) in order to permit an obviously embarrassed Obama administration to finally unload its unwanted poster boy for American injustice onto a grumbling and recalcitrant Harper government. Although the military court jury pronounced a punitive forty-year sentence, a plea bargain arrangement forced by U.S. Secretary of State Hillary Clinton on Foreign Affairs Minister Lawrence

Cannon instead would see Khadr serve one final year in Guantánamo and then be returned to Canada for an additional seven years. Once in Canada, he would, however, have recourse to an appeal to the National Parole Board, which could take account of his eight years of confinement prior to conviction, not to speak of recourse to Canadian courts that have already indicated severe violations of his rights. In any event, once on Canadian soil, the Americans will have effectively washed their hands of him.[128] True to form to the bitter end, the Harper government tried to claim that it had not negotiated Khadr's return, a claim met with incredulity and derision in the media.[129] A year earlier the same government had admitted spending $1.3 million of taxpayer dollars in its futile attempt to deny recourse for the wrongful prosecution – not to speak of persecution – of its own citizen: the bill will no doubt be much higher in a final accounting.[130]

The full negative impact of Khadr on CSIS became apparent in the summer of 2009 when the CSIS watchdog review body, SIRC, issued a critique of the agency's behaviour in the case.[131] Apart from media reports and court decisions, SIRC represents the only inquiry into the Khadr affair at arm's length from the executive, and one that has been at least partially opened to the public. Although sections of the report (originally designated Top Secret) are redacted, what remains is as critical of CSIS as any review previously done by SIRC throughout its twenty-five-year history. Of course, given SIRC's relatively narrow jurisdictional remit, it is CSIS that is the sole target of the inquiry. The actions of Canadian diplomats and other officials fall outside the committee's mandate. This may have the effect of unduly taxing CSIS for what was a joint, coordinated failure of the government of Canada, up to and including ministers of the crown, to take Khadr's rights seriously.[132] That said, SIRC's criticism of CSIS is pointed and relevant precisely to an agency in the process of expanding its foreign operations and its cooperation with a range of states, some with doubtful records on respect for human rights.

SIRC indicated that CSIS had, from the first news of Khadr's arrest in Afghanistan, acted as a 'valuable conduit of information by gathering and relaying intelligence from foreign partners to domestic agencies' and providing informed advice to the government on the Khadr case. SIRC granted that CSIS had a legitimate intelligence purpose in interviewing Khadr. It also found that the sharing of intelligence gathered from these interviews with domestic partners was 'lawful and appropriate.'[133] With the exception of exchanges with the Americans, under conditions set by the U.S. authorities, SIRC found no indications that CSIS had shared any information emanating from the interviews with any other foreign agency.

SIRC did find a great deal to criticize in other, crucial, aspects of the CSIS-Khadr interaction. For one thing, the conditions set by the Americans compelled CSIS to ignore its own operational policy for conducting interviews, which insisted on the confidential nature of the process. The audio and video recording by the Americans clearly violated the confidentiality condition. Of much greater concern was SIRC's finding that CSIS had clearly ignored what CSIS Director Jim Judd referred to as the 'challenge' for CSIS in 'dealing with countries with poor human rights records.'[134] SIRC pointed out that, at the time of the interviews, there was already 'widespread media reporting on allegations of mistreatment and abuse of detainees in US custody in Afghanistan and Guantanamo Bay.'[135] As an intelligence agency, CSIS had ignored open-source intelligence relevant to its activities. CSIS protestations that it had acted in good faith and had no adverse information concerning the American treatment of Khadr did not impress SIRC, which declared that the agency 'failed to give full consideration to Khadr's possible mistreatment by US authorities before deciding to interact with them on this matter.'[136] It appeared that CSIS had given no thought to the legality of its interviews, and had not sought legal advice from CSIS Legal Services before interviewing Khadr.[137]

A crucial point about any interviews with Khadr, SIRC pointed out, was his age. After detailing Canada's legal obligations with regard to the special treatment of children and child soldiers, SIRC expressed its 'concern that Khadr's age did not appear to factor into CSIS's decision to interview him, nor influence its interview methodology,' adding that this concern was 'compounded by the fact that Khadr had been kept incommunicado since his arrival at Guantanamo Bay,' thus violating CSIS's own operational policy with regard to the right to counsel for interviewees. CSIS told SIRC that 'policy would not prevent an interview from taking place if there were compelling operational reasons to go ahead.'[138] SIRC granted that the unusual conditions in place made it impossible for CSIS to comply with its own policy, but insisted nonetheless that there were 'certain underpinnings in policy which CSIS should make every effort to uphold and consider part of its decision-making process: one such principle is that an individual should have the opportunity to receive legal counsel prior to undertaking discussions in which information provided could lead to him or her being placed under investigation or, at some point in the future, even prosecuted. This principle is especially important in the case of youth, who lack the maturity, judgement and understanding to appreciate the consequences of their actions.'[139]

In considering the significant issues (Khadr's age, detention conditions, and legal status), SIRC was 'disconcerted' to discover that there had been no 'meaningful discussion of these issues within CSIS' prior to going to Guantánamo, indeed no concrete evidence that that these 'important issues' had ever been raised or considered.[140] CSIS had considered Khadr as an interview subject solely from the point of view of his intelligence value (and claimed that its mission to Guantánamo had been 'highly successful, as evidenced by the quality intelligence' gained from the interviews).[141] While CSIS is primarily an intelligence-gathering agency, SIRC was not prepared to accept that intelligence acquisition alone should govern CSIS decisions. Post-9/11 and post-Arar directives, guidelines, and protocols have been applied to CSIS activities with regard to relations with countries with poor human-rights records and on information obtained by torture. There is, SIRC pointed out, a 'contradiction' between the government's public position on not condoning torture and its 'own direction to the Service on this issue.' Unfortunately, redactions in the SIRC report make it unclear what exactly this direction is, and why it is in contradiction to the stated policy – a rather significant gap in the argument.[142] Importantly, SIRC specified that 'until the Service receives clear direction form the government as to how to interact and share information with countries that have poor human rights records, this very difficult issue will continue to plague CSIS decision-makers.' What is more, it will place the organization in an uncertain and vulnerable position when legal proceedings arise, as seen in the Khadr matter.[143]

Closely related to this concern is the challenge CSIS faces with the growing 'judicialization' of intelligence which is 'forcing intelligence agencies into courtrooms.' The investigation of terrorist threats since 9/11 has blurred the line between intelligence and law-enforcement agencies and thus between intelligence and evidence admissible in criminal proceedings. Intelligence gathered by CSIS is now 'undeniably being relied upon more often in criminal proceedings' even though its collection follows different rules than the collection of evidence in criminal law enforcement. The Khadr affair as it has proceeded through the courts has demonstrated the difficulties CSIS faces in collecting intelligence that may end up in a context for which it was never intended. 'Intelligence that is found to have been gathered in circumstances that violated domestic laws or international conventions will not only be rendered useless in the courtroom, but more importantly, will bring discredit to the Service.'[144]

While not unsympathetic to the difficulties faced by CSIS, SIRC's final (heavily redacted) conclusions on the Khadr affair were very pointed with regard to how far the agency has fallen behind in adapting to the new realities:

> Changes in policies and procedures are but one component of a broader transition. The time may have come for CSIS to undertake a fundamental re-assessment of how it conducts business and to undergo a cultural shift to keep pace with the political, judicial and legal developments of recent years. Indeed there is mounting pressure and expectation that CSIS will consider extra-intelligence matters in fulfilling its mandate and carrying out its activities. As a result, *it is incumbent upon CSIS to implement measures to embed the values stemming from recent political, judicial and legal developments in its day-to-day work in order to maintain its own credibility, and to meet growing and evolving expectations of how an intelligence agency should operate and perform in a contemporary democratic society.*[145]

SIRC also made it clear that, in light of the agency's steadily expanding role in foreign-intelligence gathering, 'it is also important for the Service to demonstrate that it has the professionalism, experience and know-how required to make the difficult decisions that arise when conducting operations abroad.'

Just as it had addressed CSIS deficiencies, SIRC specified that 'it would be helpful if CSIS received guidance and advice from the Minister on how to accomplish this task,' making a useful point about the importance of ministerial responsibility and direction. SIRC, chaired by Gary Filmon, a former Conservative premier, was pointing a finger not just at CSIS but at a Conservative government that has tried consistently to evade all responsibility for Omar Khadr. The onus was being placed on the public safety minister to oversee the 'cultural shift' in CSIS that SIRC believes necessary and that had been highlighted by CSIS involvement in the Khadr affair.[146]

The Spies' Dilemma

This is perhaps an appropriate point to offer some reflections on the very real difficulties faced by an agency like CSIS tasked with countering the threat of global terrorism. We have enumerated some of the shortcomings spotlighted by the Arar, Abdelrazik, Khadr, and other cases, as well as the security-certificate issues and the admonitions offered by the courts, SIRC, the IG, and critics inside and outside Parliament. All these are important and useful. They may not add up to a comprehensive indictment of incompetence or malfeasance, but they certainly indicate outstanding issues that require remedial action. Similar difficulties have cropped up in recent years for CSIS's equivalents in the United States and the United Kingdom. Indeed, the CIA has suffered far more scathing criticism for its direct role in torture. In the United Kingdom, fierce controversies over alleged British complicity in harsh interrogation techniques beset the Labour governments that under Tony Blair and Gordon Brown had presided over close British cooperation with the Americans in the War on Terror and the invasions of Iraq and Afghanistan. In 2010 the incoming Conservative-Liberal coalition government announced an unprecedented inquiry into evidence and allegations of British complicity in the torture and abuse of terror suspects. The inquiry was to be comprised of a judge, a journalist, and a civil servant, who were said to be appointed to 'remove the "stain" on Britain's reputation.'[147] There seem to be endemic problems in countering terrorism.

Margaret Thatcher once remarked apropos of Western intervention in the Balkan conflicts that 'there are just wars, but there is no just way to wage war.' There is virtually a unanimous consensus in Western countries, including Canada, that combating the threat of terrorism is an important and appropriate goal of public policy. *How* to combat terrorism is a question that yields no consensus, and much dispute. The current generation of terrorists has seemingly eschewed all scruples about causing harm to innocents; indeed, they have assumed the objective of maximizing death and suffering among the innocent. This threat is thus felt more directly and acutely by the population than the threat of Soviet Communism ever was during the Cold War. The latter was always more a contest between states and state elites, while the former is deliberately directed against civilians. In this circumstance, there is some presumption that citizens will be inclined to give the benefit of the doubt to the police and security agencies that protect them when it comes to granting enhanced powers and tipping the delicate balance between security and liberty more to the security side. Where the threat has materialized in actual attacks with heavy tolls in death and injuries, not to speak of economic costs, as in the United States and the United Kingdom, the temptation of the state to assume more intrusive powers and abridge traditional individual liberties has been felt most strongly.

In Canada, where no toll has been exacted as yet by post-9/11 terror, this temptation has been reduced and the readjustment of the security/ freedom balance has been less noticeable. This could, of course, change in the instant of a terrorist attack on Canadian soil. Even if it does not, there is another side to the post-9/11 equation which is as much in evidence in Canada as in the United States and the United Kingdom. This has to do with the expectations the public holds of its police and security agencies, and the obligation felt by the agencies to perform up to these expectations. If traditional liberties are to be limited in the name of assuring greater security, then the public expects that the state will live up to its side of the bargain and keep them safe. The problem for the agencies is that little attention is paid by the public to success, which appears simply as business as usual. A great deal of attention is paid to visible failures. Politicians understand that they will win little credit for maintaining security but can expect voter wrath if things go badly wrong. When the latter occurs, the politicians' instinct is to shift attention away from their own responsibility and focus instead on the accountability of their appointed officials. The classic example of this phenomenon is the aftermath of the RCMP scandals of the 1970s, as discussed earlier in this book.[148]

In short, CSIS is expected to get results, and not mess up. Pressures come not only from its Canadian political masters but directly and indirectly from its U.S. allies. The spectre of Ahmed Ressam and his explosives entering the United States after having eluded threadbare Canadian security continues to haunt Canadian counter-terrorism. In order to get results, the boundaries of permissible methodology tend to become elastic, especially when the Americans are pushing the enve- lope of the acceptable in their own pursuit of the terrorists.

The cost of failure is all too clear. Air India, a quarter of a century in the past but the subject of a well-publicized public inquiry as late as 2009, continues to offer CSIS a lesson in the price of failure: the air- ing of dirty laundry, and consequent public humiliation for the agency; recriminations and finger pointing from different agencies of govern- ment; and a burden of guilt that 331 lives that could have been saved were lost. There is unfairness, to be sure, in the criticism. 'Connecting the dots' is always easier in retrospect when we know what events ac- tually took place, and when, than in the messy, uncertain present when it is not so clear which are the relevant dots, let alone the lines connecting them, and there are never enough resources available to follow all possible leads. Yet, in the aftermath of failure, political masters and the public are likely to be unforgiving.

Integrated anti-terrorist operations, obviously the best way to respond to the threat of globalized, borderless terrorist networks, present their own difficulties to a security intelligence agency like CSIS. There is a presumption in integrated operations that law enforcement is the primary focus, that anti-terrorism is above all a matter for criminal investigation and the intervention of the police and courts to prevent terrorist plots from reaching their unacceptable fruition. There may be pressure from governments to show success in the fight against terrorism, which usually means media announcements of apprehended conspiracies, arrests, criminal charges, and public trials, as in the case of the Toronto 18. This is the order of business with which the RCMP as a law-enforcement agency are familiar and comfortable. The RCMP gather information always with an eye to what can at an appropriate point be presented in court as evidence of criminal activity.

For CSIS, however, matters are not so straightforward. Charged with preparing threat assessments for the government, CSIS collects intelligence that it often would not wish to see subjected to the public scrutiny of the legal process. As usual with official secrecy, there are both good and bad reasons for this attitude towards disclosure of security intelligence in court. Reluctance to face hostile cross-examination of the intelligence product might be placed in the latter category of poor reasons, if the object is to avoid possible embarrassment. But this reluctance has more reasonable grounds as well. Failure to protect information provided by foreign agencies under clear caveats against disclosure could result in damaging loss of confidence in CSIS among its partners, and the loss of access to valuable if not crucial intelligence. The unmasking of human sources or assets in order to secure criminal convictions could potentially destroy penetration operations designed for longer-term intelligence benefits than might be gained in the short term by quick convictions of small cogs of a larger network. The same could be said for disclosure of operational methods employed by the agency that could give valuable clues to the targets as to how to better evade surveillance and penetration. The spectre of the *Stinchcombe*[149] decision of the Supreme Court, which obliges the crown to disclose all relevant and non-privileged evidence, whether favourable or unfavourable, to the accused in criminal proceedings, has haunted CSIS. Some attempt was made in the Anti-Terrorism Act 2001 to limit the impact of *Stinchcombe* on disclosure of intelligence, but serious issues remain.[150] CSIS has found its intelligence increasingly drawn into the courtroom, whether in the context of efforts by government to seek criminal convictions or of civil-liberties concerns about fundamental justice for individuals. An example of the latter is the security-certificate cases, where the fate of an accused depends on evidence never disclosed to them in full. These cases, where the accused is denied the right to a real defence, may well involve life-or-death decisions, in the case of deportation; short of deportation, they may involve indefinite detention or indefinite restraint on liberty. They strike at the very heart of fundamental justice and due process.

The CSIS dilemma is that it must disclose its intelligence to the extent that it endangers the security of its sources, or it holds fast to non-disclosure on grounds of national-security confidentiality and sees its case crumble in the courts and in the docket of public opinion. That CSIS has had to admit to errors in the preparation of its in-camera evidence in some cases has undermined its credibility in general. Further court demands for wider disclosure may simply cause CSIS to withdraw its security reports in some cases, as has already happened, even if CSIS believes that this might endanger national security.

The dilemma is made more acute by the difficulties attendant upon the wider and deeper interaction with other intelligence services abroad. The issues surrounding dealings with states with dubious human-rights records (that is, those notorious for torture and abuse) have been difficult enough when these are states with which CSIS and the RCMP have at best distant and qualified relations. When it is the United States and its agencies – the closest allies and partners of CSIS – that are called into question for human-rights abuse, the dilemma becomes a conundrum.

This situation is obviously not appreciated by CSIS. In his first public remarks after taking over as CSIS director, Richard Fadden (like his predecessor Jim Judd, a career public servant) appears to have taken the view that the best defence is a good offence. Rightly pointing to the relative lack of informed debate on national security in Canada, Fadden criticized the tendency of the 'elites' to 'avert their eyes' when national-security issues were concerned. Worse, he detected a 'serious blind spot as a country': 'Many of our opinion leaders have come to see the fight against terrorism not as defending democracy and our values, but as attacking them. Almost any attempt to fight terrorism by the government is portrayed as an overreaction or an assault on liberty.'

After describing the gravity of the terrorist threat, Fadden hit out at critics in the legal profession, the media, and 'elites' in general for, in effect, romanticizing the terrorists (or more precisely, but questionably, those 'accused' of terrorism) while demonizing CSIS. A 'loose partnership' of 'single issue NGOs, advocacy journalists and lawyers has succeeded, to a certain extent, in forging a positive public image for anyone accused of terrorist links' even though 'terrorism is still the most important threat we face.' He attacked unnamed members of the Canadian 'elites' for being aloof to the threat of terrorism entirely:

> Why then, I ask, are those accused of terrorist offences often portrayed in media as quasi-folk heroes, despite the harsh statements of numerous judges? … Why are they always photographed with their children, given tender-hearted profiles, and more or less taken at their word when they accuse CSIS or other government agencies of abusing them? It sometimes seems that to be accused of having terrorist connections in Canada has become a status symbol, a badge of courage in the struggle against the real enemy, which would appear to be, at least sometimes, the government.[151]

Fadden also pointed out the specific challenges posed by what he described as the 'turbulent legal environment in which CSIS finds itself.' When CSIS was created in 1984, there were three core assumptions underlying how the new agency would be expected to operate:

> that we would be separate from police work and would not collect evidence; that to protect civil liberties, we would only retain what we strictly needed in order to do our jobs; and that we would appear in court rarely and in a very, very focused manner.

Each of these core assumptions, Fadden explained, has been questioned or modified by legal rulings. The legal ground has 'shifted under our feet,' with 'profound implications on how we work at every level.' Criminal cases under the Anti-Terrorism Act, three commissions of inquiry, civil litigation, security-certificate cases, and SIRC and IG reviews covering some of the same ground – all have all contributed, in Fadden's view, to a redirection of CSIS energies towards 'fighting legal battles.' When CSIS began operations, it employed a single legal counsel. Twenty-five years later, no less than eighty employees were now dedicated to legal issues. For the three commissions of inquiry alone,

130,000 CSIS documents had to be reviewed and 108 current or former employees were interviewed or testified in public.

There are unanticipated consequences of these pressures. The original assumption that information collected by CSIS would not be retained beyond what was strictly necessary was motivated by concern for protecting the privacy and civil liberties of citizens. The Supreme Court *Charkaoui* decision has turned this 'founding principle on its head.' All operational materials must now be retained in cases that could involve future litigation – and, as Fadden rightly pointed out, 'because it is difficult to predict what an investigation will lead to, we have made the decision to retain virtually all the material we collect.' 'Retaining everything is now seen as the best defence of our civil liberties.' This led Fadden to the sardonic prediction that in future 'someone will accuse us of acting like the Stasi because of the information we are now compelled to keep.' The irony of this observation was lost on the media that reported his speech; instead, it was viewed as institutional self-pity.[152] But he was only describing a very real dilemma: 'Our employees have spent too much of their time thinking about where we stand rather than what the bad guys are up to.'

Fadden was giving public voice to a complex of concerns that had animated CSIS management for some time prior to his assumption of leadership. In 2008 former director Judd confided secretly to U.S. diplomat Eliot Cohen that an '"Alice in Wonderland" world view was held by Canadians and their courts, whose judges have tied CSIS "in knots," making it ever more difficult to detect and prevent terror attacks in Canada and abroad. The situation ... left government security agencies on the defensive and losing public support for their effort to protect Canada and its allies.' He even went so far as to admit that 'CSIS was increasingly distracted from its mission by legal challenges that could endanger foreign-intelligence sharing with Canadian agencies.' Judd complained that judges had inappropriately treated intelligence agencies like law-enforcement bodies. CSIS, he ruefully confided, was 'sinking deeper and deeper into judicial processes,' making its Legal Affairs Division the fastest growing in his organization. Legal challenges, he added, were becoming a 'distraction' that could have a major 'chill effect' on intelligence officials.[153]

Fadden's remarks were a plea for a 'smart, balanced debate' on how national security should best be protected. Unfortunately, his attacks on the 'elites' caught most of the media attention, which served only to distract attention from the real issues. Nor did he perhaps expect that the following day at the Canadian Association for Security and Intelligence Studies meeting where his speech was delivered, his counterpart at the RCMP, Commissioner William Elliott, would join the debate by posing a direct challenge to CSIS.

According to the first civilian commissioner of the Mounties, security intelligence (that is, CSIS) may have received too large a chunk of the expanded resources devoted to national security post-9/11. Elliott posed a question: 'Has the focus on enhanced intelligence overshadowed the role of law enforcement in protecting Canada's national security?' In his view, 'the time has come for law enforcement to be even more active in the realm of national security.' This shift in emphasis relates to the specific nature of the terrorist threat, which poses imminent danger to the safety and security of Canadian citizens, but also to the fact that the very methods used to combat terrorism may endanger the rights and freedoms of Canadians:

> People often speak of a balance between national security and human rights. That implies we have to choose between the two. I believe we can have both and that this will be more achievable by a greater reliance on law enforcement … It must be recognized that in the presence of a credible and imminent threat, our first job is to protect Canadians. That sometimes means disrupting threats to national security before sufficient evidence can be gathered to justify criminal charges. However, *counter-terrorism measures based exclusively on intelligence that falls short of the evidentiary threshold are fraught with danger and difficulty*. I believe that law enforcement and criminal prosecution will be the new paradigm of national security in democratic nations the world over.[154]

Elliott's point is double-edged. The most effective response to terrorism is to put the terrorists behind bars, but intelligence that cannot be used in court will not achieve that end. At the same time, the legal process offers some protection of rights and freedoms of citizens that the state's use of secret intelligence does not. 'Most democratic nations have realized that infringing on the very rights and freedoms we seek to protect from terrorism is ultimately untenable, it is also not very effective in countering terrorist threats.' The commissioner quoted a 2006 British parliamentary committee report on human rights that stressed criminal prosecution of terrorists as an obligation of government and the preferred recourse to threats of terrorism. The report acknowledges that one of the problems of the criminal-justice approach is the fact that security intelligence may not always meet the evidentiary standard required for it to be admissible in court: 'If protection of the public through criminal prosecution is genuinely to be the first objective of counter-terrorism policy, then turning information into evidence should be uppermost in the minds of all those involved in acquiring intelligence at the earliest possible stage in that process. Intelligence should always be gathered with one eye on the problem of how to turn it into admissible evidence before a judge in a criminal court.' Elliott closed his remarks with the admonition that 'the next chapter in Canada's unfolding history of national security must be written by law enforcement … The time has come to step up law-enforcement in closing the loop on national security.'

To the extent that Elliott's speech might be read as a plea for redistributing scarce resources away from CSIS towards the RCMP, this might suggest yet another round of RCMP-CSIS sparring over turf, which no one would welcome. While Elliott was at pains to point out the much more effective degree of cooperation between the two agencies than in the past and the increasing number of integrated operations, the return of a more competitive approach at the strategic level of structuring public policy in national security was nonetheless unmistakable. At the same time, the credibility of Elliott in inter-bureaucratic power struggles was compromised by an unprecedented public revolt of senior RCMP brass against their civilian commissioner's management style, and a ministerial appointment of a special investigation into RCMP management – by former CSIS director Reid Morden.[155] Finally, Elliott announced he would step down and urged that his replacement come from within the Mountie ranks.[156]

Despite the civilian commisisoner's fate, there may be more to his words than is apparent on the surface. The old argument about the appropriate balance between security intelligence and criminal intelligence that ran through the McDonald Commission Report and was the subject of academic debate was largely framed within the parameters of the Cold War when espionage and the activities of foreign states constituted the most pressing security threats. Cold War espionage and counter-espionage was largely a game between state elites, a game that had little direct or pressing impact upon ordinary people. There was considerable force and logic in emphasizing the key role of security intelligence in circumstances in which developing a wider intelligence appreciation of the extent of adversary networks could take priority over a quick but limited law-enforcement hit that might cost important counter-intelligence assets. Cold War wisdom held that the best counter-intelligence effort was the one that the public never heard about, the one where, for example, a detected foreign agent was 'doubled' and turned into a counter-intelligence weapon against the adversary. Law enforcement might be the last, rather than the first, recourse. Even when trials did take place, there could be circumstances under which the state would withhold important evidence for fear of risking its intelligence assets, even at the cost of lessening the odds of conviction.[157] There is good reason to believe that this balance in favour of intelligence over law enforcement has to be readjusted when terrorism has become a predominant security threat, a point already becoming apparent in the 1970s and 1980s[158] but rendered starkly visible after 9/11.

There is a persuasive argument that terrorism is first and foremost a criminal-law-enforcement matter. Unlike state-to-state Cold War threats to security, terrorists target civilian populations for the infliction of maximum death and destruction. Canadians expect their state to prevent terrorist acts against them, and this is best done by identifying and arresting terrorists, breaking up their conspiracies, and bringing them to justice (as with the Toronto 18). In the immediate aftermath of 9/11, arguments were made that Al-Qaeda, as a global terrorist network directed from a command centre, parallels to a degree the tightly controlled top-down KGB espionage networks of the Cold War era. In this optic, intelligence had a key role in building counter-terrorist knowledge of the architecture of the networks and to this end may have to protect its assets from being revealed in court proceedings. This may be valid reasoning in the abstract, but given the imminence of the threat of terrorism to public safety, the interdiction of terrorist acts through criminal law enforcement should perhaps take priority over the protection of intelligence where the two claims are in conflict. This argument takes on greater force in relation to the post-9/11 evolution of the terrorist threat, which has shifted from the centralized, hierarchical Al-Qaeda model to more self-starting and self-directed threats from radicalized homegrown extremist groups. CSIS has in fact been arguing for some time that the terrorist threat now comes primarily from homegrown sources, a point reiterated in 2010 by CSIS Director Richard Fadden.[159] Whatever might be said about patiently gathering intelligence on global terrorist networks with only secondary focus on criminal law enforcement, the same cannot be said for homegrown groups like the Toronto 18 whose plans are directed towards immediate violent acts against the local civilian population. Intelligence is certainly required to identify such groups, but priority must be placed on intelligence that can be converted quickly into evidence that can be used in criminal proceedings.

Another argument weighing in the balance against CSIS's insistence on cleanly separating security intelligence from criminal evidence is that time and again, as in the security-certificate cases and in the cases of intelligence sharing on persons held abroad, CSIS intelligence has been brought to bear on individuals in circumstances that directly threaten their fundamental constitutional and human rights. CSIS cannot realistically expect to have it both ways, to submit their intelligence in building cases against suspected terrorists or terrorist supporters yet at the same time enjoy impunity from the kind of scrutiny and cross-examination that is required when fundamental rights are at stake.

The RCMP have been tasked with prevention of terrorism as its highest national-security priority. There is reason to believe that resources for the force's national-security functions have been largely channelled into the terrorism file. This leaves its responsibilities for fighting espionage and nuclear proliferation thinly funded.[160] CSIS continues to collect intelligence on espionage (especially economic espionage attributed to the Chinese and Russian governments) and is concerned with the threat posed by nuclear proliferation. When there are reasonable or probable grounds to believe that criminal acts have taken place or are about to take place with regard to espionage or proliferation, it would be the responsibility of CSIS to pass on its intelligence to the RCMP for law-enforcement purposes, but in these areas it would seem that CSIS is in effect the lead agency for the federal government. On terrorism, however, the RCMP are the appropriate lead agency, and the difficulties experienced by CSIS in terms of the use of its intelligence in open court proceedings is perhaps an indication that CSIS should play a more subordinate role to the RCMP in countering terrorism. Burned badly by the Arar affair and the O'Connor Commission, the RCMP have subsequently responded with major changes both to the way in which they handle terrorist cases and to the way in which they handle relations with states that abuse human rights.[161] Since most of the recent criticism of CSIS has rested on its role in counter-terrorism, a less visible public presence in this area might serve the interests of both the service itself and the fight against terrorism. Alan Borovoy, the doyen of the Canadian civil-rights movement, has argued that perhaps separation of the two agencies was a mistake that should now be rectified:

'Why not put the intelligence gathering performed by CSIS and the related law enforcement performed by the RCMP into the same agency?
Jurisdictional disputes, turf wars and organizational jealousies would
be less likely to develop and could be more readily overcome if both
of these functions were responsive to a central command and shared
culture.'[162] Not too many, perhaps, would support such a move, but
Borovoy's provocation did contribute to renewed debate.

The current situation places CSIS in a public-relations 'lose-lose' position. Given the conflicting pressures on the agency, it is no wonder
that its reputation has been damaged. Less clear is how the damage can
be repaired.

Accountability: The Vanishing Dimension

Over the years since its inception, CSIS has learned to live relatively
amicably with its independent review body, SIRC. After a very bad
patch in relations when CSIS was under its first director, Ted Finn, and
SIRC was under its first, activist chair, Ron Atkey, relations have progressed to the point where former CSIS director Ward Elcock, when
asked by the Arar Commission counsel if he felt that CSIS was a 'stronger organization' because of SIRC's presence in reviewing its operations, replied, 'Yes, I do.'[163]

Accountability, however, has not kept up with the changes that have
followed 9/11. The Arar Commission made extensive recommendations for overhauling accountability over the entire national-security
and intelligence community in Ottawa, especially the RCMP.[164] The
commission especially stressed that the new reality of integrated operations had not been matched by any equivalent integration of external review, and proposed various mechanisms to achieve this. The
government procrastinated for years in responding to these proposals,
citing the awaited report of the Air India Inquiry. However, when Justice John Major issued his report on the Air India affair with several
pointed recommendations for policy changes with regard to accountability, the government announced that it was taking into consideration
only the specific proposals for revamping and strengthening the RCMP
complaints process; it had no interest in pursuing more integrated or
coordinated accountability for national security as a whole, apart from
a vague promise to address 'internal' (that is, non-public, non-trans-
parent) accountability.[165] To make matters worse, in the fall of 2011 the
chair of SIRC, the review body that would feature prominently in any

revamped accountability system, was forced to resign as a result of conflict-of-interest questions about his relationship with questionable foreign connections, leaving SIRC with a cloud surrounding its credibility.[166] Effective accountability represents a major unfulfilled agenda for national-security policy.[167]

The courts have stepped into this vacuum. As our account of the Khadr, Abdelrazik, and security-certificate cases has shown, the Federal Court and the Supreme Court have not shrunk from setting legal precedents in how national-security cases can and should be handled, especially in terms of the rights of those on the receiving end of state action. At one level, this judicial activism in an area where judges traditionally tended to defer to the executive is to be welcomed. The application of the Charter of Rights to those targeted as suspected terrorists forces the state to consider more carefully how its actions may impinge upon human rights and fundamental justice. In a liberal- democratic society that professes devotion to the rule of law, that is all to the good. However, judicial intervention is inevitably one-sided: it focuses primarily on the *propriety* of the activities of agencies like CSIS, not on the crucial policy question of *efficacy*. Canadians may wish to be protected from the excesses of national-security agencies, but they are more concerned that they be protected from the threats posed by those forces that the national-security agencies are trying to counter. The question of how well the agencies are performing in counter-terrorism and against other threats to security, and the large policy questions of what kind of national-security protection the country wants and needs, go well beyond the scope of judicial review. They do fall legitimately within the jurisdiction of appropriate accountability mechanisms set up to examine both propriety and efficacy. With regard to the latter, Parliament is the most appropriate forum for debate over policy directions. Yet Parliament has been allotted only a sporadic and marginal role in national-security accountability. Over the Afghan detainee issue, Parliament has won an important, precedent-setting victory in gaining unrestricted access to documents, but its continuing role in assessing the government's national-security performance remains a leading item on the unfinished agenda.

The issues plaguing CSIS that represent fallout from the global War on terror need addressing in a more comprehensive manner than is possible under the existing patchwork of uneven, and often non-existent, outside scrutiny. Ironically, CSIS actually has the best external review process in SIRC, but this in itself has invidious implications for CSIS, since other departments and agencies that may also be implicated in the same problems that dog CSIS escape the kind of public scrutiny that CSIS receives. Comprehensive accountability reform, if properly conceived and executed, can improve not only the human-rights records but also the performance of the agencies scrutinized.

Conclusion:
Policing Canadian Democracy

Political policing has been a persistent feature of Canadian political life from the origins of national government in the mid-nineteenth century through to the twenty-first century. At all times and under all circumstances, governments have felt the need to police the frontiers of political activity and political expression, drawing enforceable lines separating the legitimate from the illegitimate, maintaining and reinforcing deference to authority. Policing in democracies like Canada, while officially about criminal law enforcement, is also about the surveillance and control of particular groups and communities, in the name of public safety and national security. In this latter guise, policing is not only political but always to some degree carried out in secret. While there are invariably technical and practical justifications advanced for maintaining secrecy in political policing, there is another, less neutral, reason: coercive intervention by the liberal-democratic state into the political life of its citizens should always be a matter for concern. The fundamental liberal-democratic values of freedom, equality, and the rule of law are all challenged by political policing. A dominant strain of thinking among officeholders over the years has been: better to let the sleeping dogs of political opposition lie, rather than awake them to an uncertain reaction.

In a totalitarian or authoritarian state, the secret police are unashamedly the props of the ruling party or dictator. But in a democracy, policing is supposed to be in defence of public liberties, even as political policing enforces a dominant ideology and protects the dominant classes and communities. The secrecy surrounding political policing serves not only to facilitate its operations but to mask its multiple roles and tactics, some less presentable on their face than others. Political

policing has been justified as the necessary means to protect the democratically elected regime from the enemies of democracy who aim to
impose minority rule through force, and as such has usually found
widespread public support. But beyond protecting the country from
espionage, sabotage, terrorism, political violence, and covert foreign
interference – threats generally recognized as reasonable targets for policing – state security has also targeted groups and individuals said
to be 'seditious' or 'subversive,' terms whose vagueness and lack of
definition have been inversely matched by corresponding fervour and
passion on the part of those hunting subversives, whoever or whatever
they might be.

Those targeted as subversives assert that it is they who are seeking to achieve the democratic ideals of equality and freedom against a
state and society that unfairly denies them full access to these goods,
and then subjects them to political policing when they protest injustice. Thus, along with Communists and Fascists who might plausibly
be seen as attempting to impose totalitarian rule, or terrorists visiting
violence and destruction upon innocent civilians, political policing
has over the years also targeted a long list of those labelled extremist
threats that includes, among others, workers striking for higher wages
and better working conditions, refugees fleeing political conflict and
persecution abroad, gay men and lesbian women, religious sects like
the Doukhobors and Jehovah's Witnesses, democratic socialists, Quebec separatists, First Nations activists, anti-globalization protestors,
and so on.

The secrecy surrounding political policing not only serves to cover
potential embarrassment over political biases but also masks methods
and techniques that are not in keeping with liberal-democratic norms
and even to a degree mimic the methods of authoritarian regimes. Political surveillance involves the routine gathering of a vast amount of
information, much of which is apparently harmless but may acquire
more sinister connotations when matched and juxtaposed in police
dossiers to other seemingly innocuous information or when shared
with other agencies possessing little restraint and less oversight. Beginning with the infiltration of political gatherings, political policing inevitably expands into the penetration of the private world of individuals
targeted – listening in on their conversations, reading their mail, tracking their purchases, monitoring their personal relationships. The enlistment of human sources to spy on co-workers, associates, and friends
carries the penetration of intimacy even deeper. At times the state has

sought actively, but covertly, to counter and disrupt the activities of associations of civil society labelled subversive or politically dangerous.

That this extension of the state's eyes, ears, and fists into civil society is carried out largely in secret is an invitation to abuse, which – as this analysis has shown – has not always been avoided. Yet the secret state has not had a free run in Canada. A liberal democracy has counterweights in the form of an elected Parliament, an independent judiciary, due process, a relatively free press, and public opinion. Under certain circumstances, such as in wartime or in emergencies triggered by apprehended threats, these counterweights have often tended to bend together in deference to the silent exercise of the powers of the political police. Yet they are also resilient, returning at other times to more assertive insistence upon checking and regulating political policing, and even shining light on the process. Sometimes the sleeping dogs are aroused.

What we have written to this point about political policing could be applied not only to Canada but to other liberal democracies like the United States or Britain. Our survey of the evolution of political policing in Canada presents as well many features that are specific to the Canadian historical experience.

Canadian Political Policing in a Global Framework

One striking observation, in light of Canadian evolution from colony of the British empire to self-governing nation to junior partner in the American empire, is that political policing in Canada has always been framed within a wider, imperial architecture of global policing. The surveillance of Fenian threats to Canada in the nineteenth century was carried out largely on American soil in conjunction with British imperial forces. Surveillance of South Asian activists similarly was carried on in cooperation with American authorities by Canadians working under the direction of the India and colonial offices in London, with links to the police in India. Amid the gathering clouds of Great Power rivalries that were to erupt in the First World War, British intelligence detected German efforts to mobilize Irish and Indian extremists to instigate colonial revolts against the empire. Political policing in Canada was part of broader imperial strategy, and Ottawa – dutifully – was preoccupied with 'subversive' groups and individuals whose real enemy was the mother country rather than Canada.

The imperial framework was further reflected in the means adopted by Canada to play its part: Canada's embryonic secret service, both in the 1860s and early 1900s, relied heavily on Britain's extensive diplomatic presence in the United States to target its enemies. The role of the British diplomatic corps was supplemented by many imperial civil servants, most notably the various governors general who served as Canada's head of state and were instrumental in getting the Canadian spy service up and running. Regular communication channels between the Canadian and U.K. governments on matters of security and intelligence were established, material flowing first via the governor general and, as time went on, by a more direct route between the RCMP and the appropriate British agency.

The creation of the RCMP, with its exclusive responsibility for surveillance and intelligence-gathering operations, produced the first made-in-Canada national political police force. But the RCMP were far from autonomous. While the importance of the 'Old Country' declined after the First World War, it did not disappear. Throughout the Great Depression, the ideological mission of the RCMP was the defence of 'British values' and 'British traditions' against Communist subversion, an appeal easily understood by most English-speaking Canadians. The significance of British values as a touchstone for political debate in Canada did not diminish until well after the Second World War.

The RCMP were also moving into another external relationship that would prove more long lasting. By the mid- to late 1920s, regular intelligence exchanges between Canada and the United States were developing, including lists of deported radicals and suspected Communists, fingerprint records, and photographs. The relationship between the RCMP and FBI was formalized in 1937. The Second World War greatly accelerated cooperation and the succeeding era of the Cold War firmly established the close integration of Canadian security intelligence operations within the Western alliance under American leadership. On crucial issues, among them the Gouzenko spy affair and the Herbert Norman suicide, the links between the RCMP and their American counterparts proved as strong as or stronger than the ties between the police and their Canadian political masters. A thick web of interrelations survived the end of the Cold War and the civilianization of the security service, and continued into the post-9/11 era of the global War on Terror. By this time, the American ties of both CSIS and the RCMP had become highly controversial, as the ugly impact of the 'dark side' of the War on Terror on individual Canadians, like Maher Arar, became widely known.

The political policing of Canadian society has never been detached from the wider framework of Canada's international alliances, which have deeply coloured Canadian practices. But these international ties have also been at the root of persistent tensions, as Canadian national feelings have resisted subordination to outside influences.

Security Intelligence versus Law Enforcement

The internal organization of the Canadian government's security intelligence function also shows some continuities, as well as evolution. One constant source of tension in organization has been between intelligence collection and law enforcement. From the prosecution of the Fenians in the nineteenth century to the security-certificate cases in the twenty-first century, the question of how much intelligence collected should be divulged in criminal prosecutions before sources are compromised has been posed time and time again. Until the creation of CSIS in 1984, both functions, intelligence collection and criminal investigation, were contained uneasily within the same organizational structure. Since 1984 the tension between the two has been embodied in two separate institutional structures, CSIS and the RCMP. The problem has never been resolved, as the Air India disaster suggests.

Throughout the period, security intelligence has benefited from special legislation, often passed during wartime or in perceived emergencies, that bestow extraordinary powers for the policing of politics. The typical pattern is the emergence of a threat – the Fenians and South Asians in the nineteenth century, enemy aliens and Bolshevik and anarchist revolutionaries during and after the Great War, Communism from the Great Depression through the Cold War era, violent Quebec separatists in the 1960s and 1970s, Islamic terrorists after 9/11 – often followed by the passage of emergency legislation through panicked legislatures. Characteristics of this legislation are the bestowal of extended and expanded police powers; tremendous harassment of suspect populations; and then, somewhat surprisingly, leniency in sentencing offenders, and often non-application of the new powers. There is a historical catalogue of special powers enacted and then either little or lightly used, or even allowed to lapse into dead letters on the statute books. There appears to be an element of symbolic politics here: the Canadian state, drawing on its tradition of deference to authority, often seems satisfied with the symbolic exercise of power, while at the same time, drawing on another Canadian tradition, liberal cooptation, often pulls back from heavy-handed repression that serves only to generate violent reactions. Besides, the political police have usually had enough power to fulfil their assigned tasks without special legislation.

One reason why authorities under pressure have reached for unnecessary special legislation is that forewarned is not always forearmed. Intelligence failures arise either from the shortcomings of the collection agency or from the inability or unwillingness of governments to take appropriate action on receipt of intelligence, or from some combination of both. Beginning with the Fenian raids on Canada, poor communication between government, its secret service, and military or civilian officials on the ground, coupled with conflicting intelligence reports, have often generated a mix of confusion and complacency in official circles, sometimes followed by overreaction and reaching for new powers when failure became apparent.

In two high-profile cases (the arrest of the 'Communist 8' in 1931 and the deportation proceedings against eleven others in 1932), the intelligence process worked seamlessly. This was soon marred by subsequent intelligence failures based on limited coverage, difficulties of maintaining sources in place, and weak analysis, coupled with resistance and counter-intelligence practised by the targets of surveillance – especially evident in the RCMP's mishandling of the On-to-Ottawa Trek, which ended with violence in Regina. In the post-war era, there have been two major intelligence failures of serious proportions, each entailing grave consequences: the October Crisis in 1970 and the Air India disaster in 1985. In each case, the apportionment of blame between the security service and its political masters is an ongoing debate, but one in which politicians have shown greater agility in evading responsibility. In the case of the October Crisis, overreaction during and after the crisis involved excesses in the political policing of Quebec that in turn led to damaging consequences for the security service and for Canadian federalism. In the case of Air India, it was rather the curious lack of reaction that eventually led, a quarter of a century later, to an official inquiry with far-reaching recommendations for the structuring and accountability of security intelligence.

A poor fit between security intelligence and the rest of government has been a lasting difficulty, exacerbated in the late nineteenth and early twentieth centuries by a blurring of jurisdiction. Sir John A. Macdonald's intelligence agent and lands agent, Gilbert McMicken, played a dual role vis-à-vis the security threat posed by the Métis in the West, his policy advice undermining arrangements made by other civil authorities. Other civil servants also gathered intelligence outside McMicken's direction; similar dynamics defined William Charles Hopkinson's tenure as the Canadian government's über-agent on the Pacific coast in the early 1900s. The jurisdictional issue was partially resolved with the creation of the RCMP and subsequent moves to centralize the security and intelligence functions previously undertaken on an informal basis by other government departments. But this by no means settled the structural issue. With the growth in size and complexity of government during the twentieth century, systematic intelligence collection has inevitably spread to a wide range of departments and agencies. Still unresolved by the early twenty-first century are the matters of how the government's overall intelligence collection can be effectively coordinated, and how intelligence is communicated to government decision makers.

Organizing and Funding the Political Police

The question of how the security service should best be organized goes back to the initial creation of the RCMP. The government at the time was searching for a way to undertake political policing on a wider and more sustained basis that would be affordable, politically viable, and effective. In the Union government of Prime Minister Borden, there were opposing views, coming from an influential Conservative, C.H. Cahan, and a Liberal minister, Newton Rowell. Cahan liked the American model of the FBI then emerging within the U.S. Department of Justice, particularly the advantages of combining criminal law enforcement with the political policing of revolutionary unrest and subversion, which he wished the new force to pursue with a vengeance. Rowell disliked a policy of excessive repression that could only alienate 'progressive' but moderate elements in the community who 'insist on freedom of thought and freedom of speech on social and economic questions.' Rowell's view prevailed, and Cahan, who lacked the entrepreneurial talent of J. Edgar Hoover, failed to create a Canadian FBI clone.

The RCMP security service that did emerge was just as focused on hunting Reds as Hoover's FBI, but it did so in a political culture that was less permissive of enterprising and self-aggrandizing bureaucrats like Hoover politicizing security, building political alliances, and cultivating extravagant personal media images (not to speak of using secret files to intimidate and blackmail potential opponents). The RCMP brass always preferred to keep anti-Communism under the sober aegis of the crown, and out of the volatile political realm, even during the McCarthy era of the early 1950s. Although the RCMP had always benefited from its iconic public image, as celebrated in film, in print, and in self-promotional 'shows' like the Musical Ride, its brass proved sometimes surprisingly inept in practising effective media spin when public-relations difficulties beset the force. Certainly, the Mounties proved less than effective in building political and public support when the security service became tainted with scandal in the 1970s.

The internal organization of the security service has evolved with time. In the early days, regional districts collected intelligence while a central staff collated and deployed the information obtained. Under wartime pressures in the 1940s – for instance, the requirement for lists of politically suspect German and Italian Canadians to be rounded up for internment – this structure became more streamlined, a process that continued through the post-war era with the need for massive security-clearance programs in the public service and among immigration and citizenship applicants. In carrying out these duties, the RCMP increasingly utilized science, such as the use of fingerprinting technology, which went back to the pre-war era.

All these activities, along with the requirements for Cold War counter-espionage operations, demanded more sophisticated organization, better information management (including, by the 1960s, computerization) over the burgeoning files, and more sophisticated, better-educated intelligence officers. The latter requirement heated up the growing post-war calls for the civilianization of the security service, which appeared unsuccessfully in the 1969 Mackenzie Commission and successfully in the 1981 McDonald Commission. As with many intelligence agencies, the security service's capacity for collection tended to outrun its capacity for analysis and evaluation, a disparity that has persisted down to today. Even as CSIS analytical capacities have improved over the RCMP era, so too has the ever expanding technological capacity for amassing largely unprocessed information.

Given irresistibly growing demands on the security intelligence bureaucracy, and given the high importance attached by successive governments over the years to the tasks assigned the security service, it comes as something of a surprise to learn that that the service was until recent decades habitually underfunded and understaffed, always struggling with perennial backlogs of security clearances and mountains of accumulated information waiting to be processed for its voluminous files. As early as the 1920s, RCMP senior management was complaining about the penurious attitude of the political masters, and the same complaints echoed, less convincingly, through the Cold War years. In the 1960s and 1970s, funding and staffing seriously stepped up under the threat of Quebec separation, only to fall partial victim to general government downsizing and belt tightening in the 1980s and 1990s. Of course, police, like the military, are always demanding more resources, but the sporadic effectiveness of RCMP lobbying for funding remains a bit of a puzzle. Perhaps the reluctance of the force to engage in political alliance building outside the bureaucracy left them vulnerable to the cost cutters. It was only after the terrorist attacks on 9/11 that CSIS's budget was significantly and consistently augmented.

The funding issue points to another continuity: extreme secrecy surrounding the funding of political policing. This began with Macdonald's secret service funds, spent at his personal discretion. Alexander Mackenzie's Liberal government investigated Macdonald's misuse of the secret service fund but never questioned the fund's legitimacy, purpose, or secrecy. The oversight later established by Parliament fell far short of equivalent standards found in England at the same time. With the establishment of the RCMP, funding of the security service was buried in the general appropriations for the force, and at no time in the succeeding decades did Parliament or the public get to see any breakdown of how Mountie money was spent on security intelligence: this information was considered privileged, since any details could assist Canada's enemies. Only in the 1990s was the Office of the Auditor General authorized to begin examining value for money in Ottawa's security intelligence expenditures, but much remains locked away from parliamentary and public scrutiny even today.

Inside the bureaucracy, rudimentary inter-departmental structures for liaison and exchange were begun in the 1920s but were effective only intermittently. During the Second World War, closer coordination of intelligence efforts, both domestic and foreign, was instituted as part of a total war effort, and this momentum carried over into the Cold War era with the Security Panel of senior bureaucrats overseeing security and intelligence operations. Within the small, hermetically sealed world of the 'secureaucrats,' the Mounties could be relatively effective in getting their point of view across, and occasionally in exercising a veto over civilian policy decisions. They were quite successful in promoting their point of view on key security issues during the war, and the scotching of the Mackenzie Commission recommendation for civilianization was a good example of effective bureaucratic politics. When a decade and a half later, civilianization was imposed, it came with the endorsement of senior RCMP officials who actually assisted the separation of the security service as an act limiting damage to the force as a whole. The same officials participated in shaping the new civilian agency at least partially to their liking.

The Indispensability of Human Sources

Turning to methods of operation, one lesson drawn from history is that the most important source of intelligence available to the security service has always been human sources placed within the groups or organizations targeted. In the nineteenth and early to mid-twentieth centuries, human sources were not only invaluable but indeed virtually the only sources. In the late twentieth century, advances in surveillance technologies have permitted much wider use of technical sources – 'wiretaps,' 'bugs,' communication intercepts of various kinds from low-tech mail openings to high-tech e-mail and Internet surveillance, satellite imagery, and so on. Yet, even with the application of what Sir Winston Churchill enthusiastically dubbed the 'Wizard War,' human sources remain indispensable to political policing. High-tech surveillance techniques usually require dependence upon other agencies like the Communication Security Establishment, with elaborate protocols attached; and difficulties arise from the imposition of extensive judicial and other forms of regulation and external review and control of the use of technical sources. Human sources come with the smallest burden of accountability. They are high risk, yet high gain, propositions.

For all their advantages, however, human sources have presented major problems for the spymasters handling them. Human sources have human flaws and human weaknesses. Human sources live double lives and systematically betray those with whom they associate closely. This may lead even their controllers to suspect their motives. When the colourful, and very effective, undercover agent Henri le Caron was first hired, Sir John A. Macdonald, as noted earlier, warned his handler: 'A man who will engage to do what he offers to do, that is, betray those with whom he acts, is not to be trusted.' Yet by the latter part of the nineteenth century, with Irish threats still at the forefront, the use of undercover agents had become routine and uncontroversial among Canada's political leaders. Intelligence gathering on South Asian groups in the early twentieth century relied to a greater extent on informants, many paid, within that specific immigrant community. This was necessary given the ethnicity of the police operatives readily available on the Pacific coast at that time: most were white. The difficulty of securing sources within ethno-cultural communities has been a persistent problem for political policing, persisting down to the notorious failure to gain access to the Sikh extremist groups behind the Air India bombing.

Another recurrent problem with human sources is the extreme reluctance to use their evidence in criminal proceedings, for fear of revealing their identities and thus destroying their usefulness for ongoing intelligence gathering. In the wake of the Winnipeg General Strike in 1919, a debate raged between the RCMP and the chief prosecutor in the cases brought against the strike leaders over the use of undercover agent 'Harry Blask' (a.k.a., Zanetti, Zaneth) as a star witness: in the end, law enforcement won the argument, and the Mounties lost their top labour spy. The most famous case of an undercover source publicly unveiled was in 1931 when undercover Communist 'Jack Esselwein,' wearing Mountie red serge as Sergeant John Leopold, stepped into the Toronto courtroom hearing the 'Communist 8' case. Despite this publicity coup, the depletion of effective and reliable sources within the Communist and other left-wing groups was demonstrated within a few years by the debacle of the On-to-Ottawa Trek.

Human sources retained their critical value through the Cold War years, when the Communist Party was effectively infiltrated and extensive networks of informers were built among trade unions, ethnic and immigrant communities, and other civil associations as part of a massive counter-subversion campaign. When the FLQ and other violent separatist groups made their appearance in the 1960s, the security service recruited informants in the initially unfamiliar milieu of Quebec nationalist ferment. So skilled did the service become that it enlisted as a paid RCMP source the second-highest ranking member of the Parti Québécois government, Claude Morin.

However important, even indispensable, such sources might be, the problems associated with recruiting and running them persist. Recruitment of sources may draw on ideological belief or 'public spiritedness,' on monetary incentives, or, more dubiously, on intimidation or what amounts to virtual blackmail by the state. In this latter regard, security screening, especially of immigration and citizenship applicants, has been a tool for recruitment of human sources in groups to which the security service wishes to gain access. Ethical questions abound in such cases. Another issue: the more dangerous and threatening the groups targeted by human sources are, the more challenging becomes the handling and control of those sources. A source within a terrorist group, for instance, may have to engage in criminal or at the very least questionable acts to maintain their credibility, thus casting suspicions on the agency that controls them. CSIS was caught in this trap over the Grant Bristow/Heritage Front affair in the 1990s. Human sources planted in non-violent groups raise different, but equally troubling, issues of Big Brother *Stasi*-like surveillance of civil society. When such sources are revealed, as in the Morin affair, the result is embarrassment for the state, not to speak of potential political backlash.

Many of the same issues with human sources also arise with regard to counter-espionage and counter-intelligence, with agents, double agents, disloyalty, and betrayal. Canada came late to this game, stumbling badly in the Second World War with the *Watchdog* fiasco. The Gouzenko affair placed Canada squarely at the centre of the Cold War spy game but the RCMP experienced continuing difficulties coping with the complexities of the 'wilderness of mirrors,' as the frantic Mountie coyote pursued the maddeningly elusive KGB roadrunner around the back streets and backrooms of Ottawa. The mad mole hunt of the 1970s that consumed so many across the Western intelligence community struck in Canada as well, where an innocent outsider, Jim Bennett, was fingered as a KGB mole, while 'one of us,' Gilles Brunet, got away with betraying his service and his country for KGB gold. Of course, successes in the murky world of counter-espionage may remain in the shadows, while mistakes tend to break out on the front pages. But, whatever the final score by the close of the Cold War, counter-espionage was only one aspect, and the least controversial, of the security service's job description. Far more controversial, with far greater impact on Canadian society and Canadian democracy was its political policing of *subversion*, in all the protean forms that elusive concept could take in the minds of those charged with hunting it.

Policing Ethnicity

One of the most consistent themes throughout the period covered by this book is the mission of the political police to identify, intrusively observe, and even actively counter 'subversive' organizations formed among minority communities. The concept of 'suspect communities' in a country like Canada is inherently controversial and certainly potentially divisive. The evolution of Canada from a 'British' society in which state institutions unabashedly reflected white anglo supremacy to the multiethnic and multicultural pluralism of today is an oft-told story. But the place within this story of the political policing of ethnic and cultural diversity is less familiar.

Sometimes, the targeting of particular communities as suspect has arisen simply from racial or religious prejudice. The treatment of Asian immigrants in the nineteenth century and later, from denial of the franchise to the internment of the entire Japanese Canadian population in the Second World War, is illustrative of how difference could lead to the state construction of suspect communities. However, for the security intelligence resources of the state to be deployed against particular ethnic or immigrant organizations, a more specific threat was required that had some degree of plausibility. The Fenians did threaten Canada with military attack, however derisory, and with assassination of public officials; it is highly likely that the Fenians killed D'Arcy McGee. Some early South Asian groups were violent, murdering the government agent Hopkinson and threatening further violence not only in Canada but in their Indian homeland, then part of the empire. In both cases, entire communities, Irish Catholic and South Asian, were constructed as suspect and subjected to surveillance and intelligence gathering operations; and in both, the civil servant in charge of policing the suspect community combined above-board government duties with surreptitious secret service work. The state presented many faces simultaneously. In the case of the surveillance of South Asians in the early 1900s, the civil servant in question, Hopkinson, paid for the visibility that came with his multiple roles with his life. Later, such operations would be more circumspect.

Another pattern set in the early period was the discriminatory and divisive nature of the policing of ethnicity. Spying on the Irish Catholic community was not only a reinforcement of the British hegemony evident in the anglo domination of the political and economic spheres of late-nineteenth- and early-twentieth-century Canada, it was also an intervention that favoured one community over another: in this case, the Protestant Irish Loyalists represented by the Orange Order, which was not the subject of systematic state surveillance. In effect, the state bestowed legitimacy on the Protestant Irish community while delegitimizing the Roman Catholic Irish as suspect. Ironically, the two most prominent political assassinations in Canadian history were drawn out of intra-community conflict: McGee the loyalist Irishman, as just noted, was likely murdered by the Fenians; over a century later, Pierre Laporte, the federalist Québécois and provincial minister of labour, was killed by the FLQ.

Discriminatory ethnic bias broke down during the Great War when generalized suspicion was cast over entire 'enemy alien' communities, that is, communities drawn from nations with which Canada was at war, with wholesale detentions following. The RCMP showed more selectivity in their interventions among immigrant communities in the 1920s and 1930s, in part because of a political dimension being added to the ethnic. The case of South Asian activists associating with emergent left-wing and radical movements in the early twentieth century points the way to an important theme. When suspect ethnicity is allied to suspect politics, the political police redouble their attention. This became evident in the 1930s when the RCMP honed in on ethnic organizations associated with the Communist Party: left-wing political and cultural centres such as the Finnish Organization of Canada and the Ukrainian Labour Farmer Temple Association as well as various Jewish organizations. The discriminatory element now turned on politics rather than religion. During the Second World War, left-wing Finns, Ukrainians, and Jews faced more of the sharp edge of the Defence of Canada Regulations than their less radical brethren. In the post-war era, it was the same story as the security service closely watched the pro-Communist Ukrainians and Finns while treating more conservative ethnic organizations as Cold War allies.

On the other side, charged with rounding up pro-Fascist Italian and German Canadians at the beginning of the war, the RCMP proved relatively proficient at singling out enemy sympathizers, as distinct from members of the Italian and German communities (unlike in the previous war). Yet their interest waned precipitously with the end of hostilities, as Nazi war criminals and collaborators fleeing from justice entered the country, hiding successfully among anti-Communist ethnic groups.

A final twist in ethnic policing is noteworthy in the contemporary era. Regional conflicts in various parts of the world, particularly the Middle East and South Asia, have been imported into Canada along with refugees and immigrants from these regions. Homeland lines of division have been reproduced in the diaspora communities. Antagonists abroad continue to be antagonists in Canada: Sikh 'Khalistan' separatists versus India, Tamil versus Sinhalese Sri Lankans, Jewish supporters of Israel versus Palestinians. CSIS has been accused of bias in its interventions. For example, in the wake of the end of the Sri Lankan civil war, Tamils seeking refugee status in Canada have been suspected of association with the Tamil Tigers, a banned group, while accusations of CSIS being too close to the Sinhalese-dominated Sri Lankan government have also been voiced. Similarly, in the post-9/11 era, Palestinians and other Arabs and Muslims have been treated as suspect communities, which complain of unwanted CSIS attention, while Jewish groups have appeared as supporters of CSIS, lobbying successfully to ban Islamic groups like Hezbollah and Hamas as terrorist. The point here is not to disentangle and adjudicate these arguments, but simply to note that policing ethnic politics in an era of explosive and bitter regional ethnic conflicts is bound to cast the political policemen in an uncomfortable light: what is seen favourably by one group is seen as ethnic bias by another.

The Remarkable Persistence of the Red Menace

Issues of ethnic, cultural, and religious bias aside, the overriding bias exhibited by political policing over the entire period of study, until very recent years, has been an ideological bias against the left. This is not surprising in light of the police mission to maintain order, which is most often interpreted as maintaining existing social structures and institutions. What is more surprising is that, when threats to the existing order have come from the opposite direction of the political spectrum, they have seemingly had little long-term effect on the conservative profile of the security service.

In the 1920s the Ku Klux Klan made inroads into rural Canada, presenting a threat to order and to liberal-democratic values. Yet the RCMP, obsessed with revolutionary agitators, collected no intelligence on the Klan and had no interest in it. In the 1930s, extreme right-wing and pro-Nazi movements competed with Communist and other left-wing groups in political protest, but the police concentration on the threat from the left was virtually exclusive. Indeed, the RCMP had to be nudged by senior bureaucrats to start tracking the Italian pro-Fascists in the late 1930s. And, even while they rounded up Fascist sympathizers in the war, the RCMP was publicly asserting that Communists were the most dangerous enemies, notwithstanding the military struggle then being waged against Fascism. On the RCMP's advice, Communists remained interned while the USSR was a wartime ally. At war's end, the RCMP returned enthusiastically to the task of focusing exclusively on the Communist threat under the new post-Gouzenko Cold War rules. Under these rules, Communism was the fifth column for the Soviet Union, which posed an all-fronts threat to the Western world.

What is particularly striking about the security service's focus on anti-Communism is that it was always less about the Soviet military threat or Soviet espionage and more about Communism as subversion. Perhaps the metaphor invoked by C.H. Cahan in 1918 just after the Russian Revolution – the Bolshevik menace as a many-headed poisonous Hydra symbolizing anarchic disorder brought on by the 'wretched of the earth' – was an enduring text for the narrative of political policing. Cahan, and the Mounties who followed, were auditioning to play the part of the mythic hero Hercules, who finally slew the Hydra. In 1919 they put down the Winnipeg General Strike, but other Hydra heads of unrest arose in its place. In 1931 they hauled the Communist leaders before the courts and sent them to prison or deported them, but the party grew more heads. In 1945 the Gouzenko detainees brought to the RCMP barracks were hauled before Inspector (later Commissioner) Clifford Harvison, who declared: 'We've tangled with you Reds before, but this time, by God, we've got you!' Three decades later, the Mounties were still struggling with revolutionary subversion, this time in the form of 'New Left' movements, Quebec separatists, even homosexuals. The Hydra persisted but Hercules never appeared.

From the time of the Bolshevik Revolution, there was one source of potential Communist support that demanded policing: labour militancy. The spectre of the Winnipeg General Strike, where labour unrest appeared to escalate into a potential threat to the capitalist system, haunted the defenders of order for decades. Indeed, it was the combined wallop of the national labour revolt and the Great War that led to the creation of the RCMP's security service in the first place. As the 1920s gave way to the 1930s and 1940s, labour unions and strike activity were constant preoccupations of the security service. Although the service always insisted that trade-union activity was a legitimate activity, it also held fast to the belief that Communist-inspired or Communist-led labour activity was subversive and had to be stopped, or at least contained and quarantined – even if suspected Red leaders were democratically elected by a union's rank-and-file members. In this new Cold War context, older distinctions between good unions (conservative) and bad unions (radical) – which had dominated debates about labour relations for decades – hardened and sharpened, as the considerable resources of the security service were now put at the disposal of those who tangled with the *bad* unions: recalcitrant governments, hostile employers, and Cold Warriors within the labour movement itself. To be sure, the 'good' unions were not always good in any sense other than their acceptable politics: the worst case was the American SIU takeover in the late 1940s of the Canadian waterfront from the Communist CSU under the direction of the notorious labour racketeer and thug Hal Banks. But as the Mounties might say, in war you take – or make – what allies you can.

The demarcation between good and bad unions was paralleled by distinctions the political police had to draw between different varieties of left-wing political parties. There were early difficulties over 'Socialist' and 'Social Democratic' parties, and after the founding of the CCF in 1932 they had to contend with a respectable social-democratic party with representation in Parliament and after 1944 the government of Saskatchewan, a party, moreover, that was in direct competition with the Communists for left-wing votes and for trade-union support. Usually the Mounties were able to distinguish CCF socialists from Marxist Communists. On the other hand, there was always some blurring of the lines on the left wing of the CCF and its successor after 1961, the NDP, a grey area where the CCF/NDP could also be subject to surveillance, and indeed a general watchful eye on the party and its leaders. Hence the targeting of the NDP in the 1970s, ostensibly on the pretext of targeting the left-wing Waffle faction of the party. And in 2010 a battle in the courts is being waged to force disclosure of jealously guarded security service files on CCF leader Tommy Douglas – a man voted in a national poll the 'Greatest Canadian' but clearly a suspect figure to a generation of security service watchers.

There was a problem with the Mountie obsession with Communist subversion, a very big problem. However much Communists might be painted as foreign, alien, un-Canadian, they were part of Canada as much as the Mounties were. And it was impossible to draw lines around the Reds as fit subjects for political policing while exempting all others. The very nature of subversion, to the extent that we can nail down any clear definition, is that it is directed at undermining *from within* the institutions and values of the society. To the Mounties, the Communist problem was primarily one of subversive infiltration and penetration of the institutions of civil society. The Communist Party did view infiltration as a tactic, but the 'infiltrators' were just as likely to see themselves as good trade unionists, working for their members, as well as indirectly for the interests of the party, which would benefit from gains for the members. Yet, seeing the infiltrators simply as subversive, the security service found it necessary to bring these 'infiltrated' institutions under the same surveillance directed at the 'infiltrators.' If the worry is Communist infiltration of respectable trade unions, or citizen-advocacy groups, or student councils, or peace groups, or any of the other myriad associations the Communists might target, then the security service had to have sources of information on these groups, or, to speak plainly, had to spy on them. Hence the network of informers honeycombed in organizations across the country, reporting to the security service on the everyday activities of civil society, from the executive of the Canadian Labour Congress to the Ladies Auxiliary, Mine, Mill and Smelter Workers, Sudbury Local. Hence the public shock when the McDonald Commission reported at the end of the 1970s that the RCMP security service held files on 800,000 individuals and groups.

Public distaste for this kind of infiltration of civil society began to rise in the 1960s and crested in the 1970s when a number of developments came together. The security service, under cabinet direction, went to war against Quebec separatism and failed to make the necessary distinctions between threats to national security and threats to national unity. For the first time, political policing had become a seriously divisive factor in domestic politics. Intrusive surveillance of political life in English Canada also spilled into the media, and into public consciousness, at a time when concern for guarantees of individual rights was on the rise, culminating in the Charter of Rights and Freedoms. Distrust of the Cold War national security state had risen sharply in the United States and in Canada. The old Mountie war against subversion had to be cut back, qualified, and moderated in the face of these new realities. CSIS was created, with limits placed on its reach into Canadian society and mechanisms of accountability imposed upon it. The Counter-Subversion Branch of CSIS was ordered closed, its files dispersed to the national archives. And then, at the end of the 1980s, the Soviet Communist enemy collapsed and disappeared, and the Cold War came to an end.

History does not run in straight lines. While the developments of the 1970s and 1980s pointed to an end to state surveillance of subversion, and refocusing on more politically neutral and less controversial targets, the terrorist attacks of 11 September 2001 inaugurated a new era of a global War on Terror under hegemonic American leadership that parallels in eerie ways the Cold War. Once again emergency powers have been added to the state security arsenal, suspect communities constructed, and surveillance stepped up. Accountability mechanisms appropriate at the time of their inception now appear patchwork, threadbare, and outdated.

In some ways the world of the twenty-first century would appear strange to the political police of the twentieth century. The spectre of Red revolution no longer haunts the world, and left-wing subversion has diminished to the vanishing point. Cahan's Communist Hydra was never slain but fled the field and is now out of sight, out of mind. But new, unfamiliar Hydras have appeared, spouting not Marxist-Leninist ideology but verses from the Koran and weapons-making instructions from Internet jihadist manuals. Political policing has had to discard its old field manuals, but new ones are on the way. *Plus ça change, plus c'est la même chose?*

Violence and Subversion: Joined at the Hip?

There is one thread that runs from the origins of political policing in the nineteenth century to the twenty-first century, a consistent source of both continuity and tension. State security intelligence is called into action by the perception of threats to national security and public safety. In a pluralist democratic society like Canada, political policing has never been acceptable on its own terms or as a good in itself, but rather as a kind of necessary evil required to protect liberal democracy from its enemies. The text of political policing – the defence of public safety, security, and the national interest – is widely proclaimed and widely applauded. The subtext – drawing boundaries that exclude some groups, whether ideological, ethnic, religious, or national, from full legitimacy as members of the Canadian community – is less often displayed publicly and is less widely approved.

Those who criticize political policing often question the text as a way of drawing attention to the subtext. Official reports of threats to national security have been portrayed as greatly exaggerated, or deliberately concocted, or even imaginary: the imagery of 'witch hunts' taken literally suggests either deliberate invention or social panic. However suspect the subtext, it would be a grave mistake to dismiss the text as deliberately duplicitous, or merely misguided. In looking over the broad historical sweep in Canada, it is striking that the perceived threats to security that have triggered expanded political policing have, at some level, always had substance. *Violence* to force political change is a threat that no liberal democracy can tolerate, and there have been many such threats to the Peaceable Kingdom, some more menacing than others but all triggering a response.

Violence was inherent to both the radical Irish and South Asian movements of the late nineteenth and early twentieth centuries. The violent political imagery of Fenian and South Asian militants, sometimes reflected in their actions, derived from an anti-imperialism that identified the Canadian state as an enemy and relied on force to achieve their goals. The spectre of revolutionary unrest threatening the existing economic and political system was made real in the 1917 Bolshevik Revolution in Russia, with its apparent echoes in Canada with the Winnipeg General Strike and the formation of a Canadian Communist Party. Exaggerated as the Red Menace appears in retrospect, the Leninist model of the violent seizure of power by revolutionary militants was not one that could be tolerantly assimilated by any liberal democracy. Given the faithful pro-Moscow line followed by the Canadian Communists from their inception, suspicions that the party harboured Bolshevik dreams of violent revolution had some plausibility, despite the actual absence of any revolutionary actions by Communist militants over decades of activity. In the Cold War years, the threat of domestic revolution had vanished, but now Canadian Communists were tied to the very real external threat of a hostile nuclear-armed superpower. Similarly, during the Second World War, the threat of fifth-column activity based on ideology or ethnicity in support of Canada's battlefield enemies could hardly be ignored. When the idea of Quebec sovereignty burst upon Canada in the 1960s, it appeared in a dual guise, with one pursuing a lawful and legitimate route via the existing political process and another that believed it could force independence through bombing and killing. The era of international terrorism, in which non-state actors attempt to advance political/ideological agendas exogenous and alien to Canada through violence against civilians, was ushered in with the terrible Canadian toll of Air India, and continues in a post 9/11 world in which Canada and Canadians could well be targets for the death and destruction already inflicted in New York, Washington, London, Madrid, Mumbai, and elsewhere.

The text of security and public safety has a convincing solidity, an authenticity that has persuaded generations of Canadians readily and often unquestioningly to accept the political policing of the borders of the public realm. This reality is ignored at critics' peril. Text is never, as some might have it, mere pretext, a cloak to cover the state's cynical manipulation of public anxieties, permitting the expansion of intrusive powers over civil society. Whatever the verdicts of revisionist history on the origins and causes of the Cold War, it is clear that if the 'Soviet threat' had been entirely conjured up out of nothing, it could not have maintained its hold on the public for so many decades. Similarly, 9/11 conspiracy theorists, who downplay or even deny the reality of Al-Qaeda-type threats, fail to appreciate the entirely understandable anxiety of ordinary people in the face of violence directed at them that appears inexplicably irrational, whatever grievances of the Muslim world against the West are cited in the apocalyptic rhetoric of the Islamist extremists against the 'infidels.'

Matters cannot, however, be left there. Text has indeed been transformed into pretext, again and again. Precisely when the text is authentic, and thus convincing, the danger of its abuse is greatest. A common pattern throughout Canadian history is the appearance of a real threat to security and public safety, followed by a state response that identifies and isolates the source of the threat (security intelligence), acts to eliminate or contain the threat (national-security law enforcement), and then goes on to construct suspect communities – ideological, ethnic, religious – from which the threats are said to emanate, and to marginalize, stigmatize, exclude, and delegitimize these communities (political policing).

There seems to be a peculiar alchemy whereby *terrorism*, *espionage*, and *covert foreign interference* – legitimate threat categories – are too often transmuted by political policing into the dubious, ill-defined, and thus remarkably elastic category of *subversion*. Combating the former threats should be an activity that commands a broad consensus; combating 'subversion' is always an invidious political intervention in civil society. The search for Soviet spies during the Cold War was unexceptional. When the search turned to 'agents of influence,' the stakes grew more ideological. As the security service began spying on Communist, leftist, and even sexual 'subversives,' the search became a witch hunt. Even with the closure of the Counter-Subversion Branch of CSIS in the 1980s, the alchemical process continues in the post 9/11 world, as recent CSIS controversies over alleged Chinese agents of influence, as well as the anxieties of Muslim and Arab communities over public and official suspicions of disloyalty, can testify.

The question of subversion points to another contested dimension of political policing, the closure of public debate over the legitimate grievances and concerns that may have helped spark the kind of violent protests that lead to the targeting of suspect communities. When Irish republicans and South Asian radicals entered into violent or potentially violent confrontation with the Canadian state in the late nineteenth and early twentieth centuries, the extremism of their actions grew out of legitimate grievances against racist oppression by British imperialism of Irish Catholics and colonized Indians. Yet the effect of the political policing of their violent tactics was to strengthen oppression and deepen further the very sense of injustice that had caused them to turn to violence. The Irish Protestant opponents of republicanism represented in the aggressive Orange Order were legitimized by linkage to British imperial hegemony, even as the Irish Catholic community was being defined as suspect and disloyal on the basis of the actions of the Fenians. British rule in India was reaffirmed along with the racial exclusion of Asians from equality in Canada as the state acted to counter the Asian radicals. When the RCMP targeted Communists in trade unions, they also targeted legitimate working-class demands for better wages and working conditions, while at the same time intervening in effect on behalf of business: however obfuscated in official rhetoric, the bias in favour of capital over labour was unmistakable. The inability to distinguish reliably between legitimate Quebec sovereignists threatening national unity and violent separatists threatening national security bedevilled Canadian federalism from the 1960s to the 1980s.

The existence of legitimate aspirations and justifiable grievances on the part of communities from which violent movements emerge does not, of course, excuse violence, or offer exemption from the laws of the land, even when these laws may be oppressive, as with the old section 98 of the Criminal Code or the now repealed War Measures Act. Pointing out that political violence may result from oppression and injustice is rational social science, not a philosophical justification for violence. Nor do all violent movements arise from legitimate causes. But where it does exist, the link between violence and injustice should not be missed because of the light it casts on the bias of political policing. CSIS in the twenty-first century, operating on a statutory mandate with imposed restraints on its reach and methods, and with layers of accountability surrounding its operations, has shed some, although not all, of the ideological baggage of the old RCMP security service. But there may be inherent limitations on how far this liberalization can proceed in practice.

A political slogan with some currency in recent years has been: 'Tough on crime, tough on the causes of crime.' Agencies like CSIS and the RCMP can deal only with the first part of that formulation; it must be left to other parts of government and society to deal with the latter. Security and policing services are not social-service agencies and are not equipped to deal with economic, social, and cultural grievances. But when they are called upon to intervene in the political life of the society, and especially when their intervention extends beyond genuine threats to security to encompass the alleged subversion of the established order, they appear all too frequently as agents of political repression, defenders of wealth and power against dissent and resistance. In short, they appear as the praetorian guard of conservatism. Moreover, they are guards with access to extraordinary powers who operate in privileged secrecy. It is no surprise that they tend to feature in conspiracy theories and popular culture as secret, sometimes almost occult, powers behind the throne.

An Invisible Government?

Images of the 'invisible government' or the 'secret state' – particularly prominent in depictions in popular culture and sensationalist journalism on the intelligence services of the Cold War superpowers (the KGB, the CIA, the FBI, the NSA) – have stoked fears of sinister, shadowy, ruthless, all-powerful organizations with global reach, stunning technological armory, and absolutely no scruples. Oddly enough, this image competes with another, contradictory image of intelligence services, one that rises to the surface each time a major intelligence failure is witnessed. In this alternative universe, the intelligence services are the bumbling incompetents who never saw the Japanese attack on Pearl Harbor until the bombs struck; who failed to catch even a glimpse of the Al-Qaeda terrorists who commandeered the planes that brought down the Twin Towers; who were too busy chasing phantom Reds under beds to notice the FLQ terrorists who precipitated the October Crisis; who sleepwalked through the planting of the bombs on the Air India flights that killed 331 innocent people, and were too busy stumbling over each other to bring the perpetrators to justice.

The Canadian secret service has not shared as much as its American counterparts in the extravagant image of fearful secret powers, although for many decades the celebrated Mountie mystique of 'always getting their man' clung to the RCMP security service – only to suffer the embarrassment in the 1960s and after of a newer, competing image among sections of the public of the Mounties as incompetents frantically searching for non-existent Reds under beds, while missing real life spies – an image cemented by the Trudeau government's disdainful characterization of the RCMP's alleged failure to counter Quebec terrorists. To some at least, the Hollywood image of the Mounties shifted from the indomitable Sergeant Preston of the Yukon to the Royal Canadian Air Farce's comical Sergeant Renfrew. Yet continuing to co-exist with this unflattering image was another, more menacing view drawn from the scandals of the 1970s, that of *Stasi*-like secret police compiling sinister dossiers on innocent citizens while targeting legitimate political activities for disruption and dirty tricks.

CSIS has never enjoyed the cultural cover of Mountie symbolism and has thus been especially vulnerable to facile popular imagery of laughable incompetence. In 2011, for example, CBC TV unveiled a new sitcom, *InSecurity*, featuring a thinly disguised CSIS made up of 'bumbling spies who protect the country one mistake at a time,' according to the co-producer.[1] Yet the contradictory image of a menacingly efficient secret power has never been entirely absent from the mind of critics.

These competing images are mutually exclusive. They cannot both be right, but perhaps both are, in important ways, wrong. Our history of the secret service from the nineteenth to the twenty-first century suggests that neither polarized image meets the evidentiary test. Incompetence has been in evidence occasionally, as one would expect in any bureaucratic organization over time. However, one must always beware the propensity of politicians to deflect responsibility for failures onto their appointed officials, which results in an appearance of bureaucratic incompetence not always earned. Yet the opposite image, that of an all-powerful shadowy agency secretly shaping events and manipulating elected officials like marionettes, is clearly over the top. There is a paradox in the political policing of democracies. It is the competence of the security service in performing the tasks assigned by their elected political masters that sparks the fears of critics that the 'secret state' threatens liberal democracy. Yet shortcomings in carrying out these assigned tasks are sure to be greeted by ridicule or, in serious cases of intelligence failure, severe condemnation.

Political policing in a liberal democracy is inherently controversial. Separating the uncontroversial elements of the protection of national security and public safety from the contentious elements of political policing is as complex as finding the famous delicate balance between freedom and security that successive Canadian governments have striven to achieve. Perhaps the most optimistic observation we can make in the early twenty-first century is that the process is now more in the open than it ever was in the past.

Notes

Introduction: Political Policing in Canada

1 Commission of Inquiry into the Actions of Canadian Officials in Relation to Maher Arar, *Report of the Events Relating to Maher Arar: Analysis and Recommendations* (hereafter *Arar Report: Analysis and Recommendations*) (Ottawa: Public Works and Government Services 2006), 9.

2 The Amnesty International report is archived at http://circ.jmellon.com/docs/view.asp?id=390.

3 *Arar Report: Analysis and Recommendations*, 13–14.

4 'I think the U.S. would like to get Arar to Jordon where they can have their way with him,' the agency's deputy head remarked on 10 October 2002, two days after Arar had been secretly flown to the Middle East by the CIA. See 'Arar Tortured after RCMP Handed Files over to CIA,' *Globe and Mail*, 10 August 2007, 1.

5 A useful timeline can be found at www.theglobeandmail.com/news/politics/tracking-afghan-detainee-transfers/article1393402/.

6 'CSIS Secretly Interrogated Afghan Prisoners,' *Toronto Star*, 8 March 2010.

7 A video of Milliken's ruling can be found at www.cbc.ca/politics/story/2010/04/27/afghan-detainee-documents-speaker-milliken-privilege-ruling.html#ixzz0rnJImF5W.

8 'CSIS Admits to Spying Abroad,' *National Post*, 20 October 2003, 1.

9 A former CSE employee has written a controversial memoir about the activities of the agency: Mike Frost, as told to Michel Gratton, *Spyworld: Inside the Canadian and American Intelligence Establishments* (Toronto: Doubleday 1994). An excellent introduction can be found in Bill Robinson, 'Intelligence, Eavesdropping and Privacy: Who Watches the Listeners?' in Craig McKie, ed., *The System: Crime and Punishment in Canadian Society: A Reader* (Toronto: Thompson Educational Publishers 1996).

10 Two books that try to cover the general topic of espionage and Canada confirm the absence of any serious foreign-intelligence dimension are J.L. Granatstein and David Stafford, *Spy Wars: Espionage and Canada from Gouzenko to Glasnost* (Toronto: Key Porter Books 1990); and Graeme S. Mount, *Canada's Enemies: Spies and Spying in the Peaceable Kingdom* (Toronto: Dundurn Press 1993).

11 On this point see John Herd Thompson and Stephen J. Randall, *Canada and the United States: Ambivalent Allies*, 3rd ed. (Montreal and Kingston, Ont.: McGill-Queen's University Press 2002).

12 Richard Hofstadter, *The Paranoid Style in American Politics and Other Essays* (New York: Knopf 1966).

13 Robert K. Murray, *Red Scare: A Study in National Hysteria, 1919–1920* (Minneapolis: University of Minnesota Press 1955).

14 David Oshinsky, *A Conspiracy So Immense: The World of Joe McCarthy* (New York: Free Press 1983).

15 Commission of Inquiry concerning Certain Activities of the RCMP (McDonald Commission), *Second Report, Volume 1, Freedom and Security under the Law* (Ottawa: Minister of Supply and Services 1981), 518. According to the 1971 census, the total population of Canada was 21,568,000: 800,000 files represent information on more than one out of every twenty-seven Canadians.

16 See Gary Kinsman and Patrizia Gentile, *The Canadian War on Queers: National Security as Sexual Regulation* (Vancouver: UBC Press 2010).

17 For a comparative study of this phenomenon in a contemporary setting, see Peter Gill, *Policing Politics: Security Intelligence and the Liberal Democratic State* (London: Frank Cass and Company 1994).

18 David Mamet, 'Some Thoughts on Writing in Restaurants,' *Writing in Restaurants* (New York: Viking Press 1986).

19 Franca Iacovetta, *Gatekeepers: Reshaping Immigrant Lives in Cold War Canada* (Toronto: Between the Lines 2006).

20 On this point, see N. Ward, *Public Purse: A Study in Canadian Democracy* (Toronto: University of Toronto Press 1962).

21 Reg Whitaker, 'Canada: The RCMP Scandals,' in Andrei S. Markovits and Mark Silverstein, eds., *The Politics of Scandal: Power and Process in Liberal Democracies* (New York: Holmes and Meier 1988), 38–61.

22 See Peter Wright, *Spycatcher: The Candid Autobiography of a Senior Intelligence Officer* (New York: Viking 1987); David Leigh, *The Wilson Plot* (London: Heinemann 1988); and Stephen Dorrill and Robin Ramsay, eds., *Smear! Wilson and the Secret State* (London: Harper Collins 1991).

23 For the most comprehensive examination of this issue, see Laurence Lust-

garten and Ian Leigh, *In from the Cold: National Security and Parliamentary Democracy* (Oxford: Clarendon Press 1994).

24 'CSIS Admits to Spying Abroad,' *National Post*, 20 October 2003, 1.

25 John Sawatsky, *Men in the Shadows: The RCMP Security Service* (Toronto: Doubleday 1980), and *For Services Rendered: Leslie James Bennett and the RCMP Security Service* (Toronto: Doubleday 1982).

26 James Littleton, *Target Nation: Canada and the Western Intelligence Network* (Toronto: Lester and Orpen Dennys 1986).

27 Richard Cleroux, *Official Secrets: The Story behind the Canadian Security Intelligence Service* (Scarborough, Ont.: McGraw-Hill Ryerson 1990).

28 Larry Hannant, *The Infernal Machine: Investigating the Loyalty of Canada's Citizens* (Toronto: University of Toronto Press 1995); Steve Hewitt, *Riding to the Rescue: The Transformation of the RCMP in Alberta and Saskatchewan, 1914–1939* (Toronto: University of Toronto Press 2008), and *Spying 101: The RCMP's Secret Activities at Canadian Universities, 1917–1997* (Toronto: University of Toronto Press 2002); and Kinsman and Gentile, *The Canadian War on Queers*.

29 Carl Betke and Stan Horrall, 'Canada's Security Service: An Historical Outline, 1864–1966' (Ottawa: RCMP Historical Section 1978), CSIS Access Request #117-90-107. For background and assessment of this very useful source, see Larry Hannant, 'Access to the Inside: An Assessment of "Canada's Security Service: A History,"' in Wesley K. Wark, ed., *Espionage: Past, Present, Future?* (Ilford, U.K.: Frank Cass and Company 1994), 149–59.

30 The *Report of the Royal Commission on Security* (Ottawa: Minister of Supply and Services 1969), the Mackenzie Commission, is a rather thin and uninformative document, but that can certainly not be said of the weighty (and meaty) McDonald Commission, especially its *Second Report: Freedom and Security under the Law*, and its *Third Report: Certain RCMP Activities and the Question of Governmental Knowledge* (Ottawa: Minister of Supply and Services 1981). The O'Connor inquiry into the Maher Arar affair (see n.1, above) has much valuable information in its second part, 'A New Review Mechanism for the RCMP's National Security Activities,' on the post-9/11 national-security bureaucratic landscape. The Major inquiry into the 1985 Air India bombing (Commission of Inquiry into the Investigation of the Bombing of Air India Flight 182, *Final Report, Air India Flight 182: A Canadian Tragedy*, 5 vols. [Ottawa: Public Works and Government Services 2010]) is an invaluable source of information on that tragic event). One of the authors (Whitaker) had the benefit of acting as an adviser to both the O'Connor and Major inquiries. Finally, there is somewhat more limited

interest to be found in Honourable Frank Iacobucci, commissioner, *Internal Inquiry into the Actions of Canadian Officials in Relation to Abdullah Almalki, Ahmad Abou-Elmaati and Muayyed Nureddin* (Ottawa: Public Works and Government Services Canada 2008).

31 House of Commons Special Committee on the review of the CSIS Act, *Report: In Flux but Not in Crisis* (Ottawa: Supply and Services 1990).

32 The authors of this book have already published books and articles relating to various aspects of this history. See Gregory S. Kealey, 'The Surveillance State: The Origins of Domestic Intelligence and Counter-Subversion in Canada, 1914–1920,' *Intelligence and National Security*, 7, no. 3 (1992): 179–210; Gregory S. Kealey, 'State Repression of Labour and the Left in Canada, 1914–1920,' *Canadian Historical Review*, 73, no. 3 (1992): 281–314; Gregory S. Kealey, 'The Early Years of State Surveillance of Labour and the Left in Canada: The Institutional Framework of the RCMP Security and Intelligence Apparatus, 1918–26,' in Wark, *Espionage*, 129–48; Andrew Parnaby and Gregory S. Kealey, 'The Origins of Political Policing in Canada: Class, Law, and the Burden of Empire,' *Osgoode Hall Law Journal*, 41, no. 3 (2003): 211–40; Andrew Parnaby and Gregory S. Kealey with Kirk Niergarth, '"High-Handed, Impolite, and Empire-Breaking Actions": Radicalism, Anti-Imperialism, and Political Policing in Canada, 1860–1914,' in Barry Wright and Susan Binnie, eds., *Canadian State Trials, Volume III, Political Trials and Security Measures, 1840–1914* (Toronto: University of Toronto Press, 2009), 483–515; Reg Whitaker: *Double Standard: The Secret History of Canadian Immigration* (Toronto: Lester and Orpen Denys 1987); Reg Whitaker and Gary Marcuse, *Cold War Canada: The Making of a National Insecurity State, 1945–1957* (Toronto: University of Toronto Press 1995); Reg Whitaker and Steve Hewitt, *Canada and the Cold War* (Toronto: Lorimer 2003), and 'Official Repression of Communism during World War II,' *Labour/Le Travail*, 17 (1986): 135–68; and Reg Whitaker and Steve Hewitt, 'Apprehended Insurrection? RCMP Intelligence and the October Crisis,' *Queen's Quarterly*, 100, no. 2 (1993): 383–406.

33 This project and the present book are examples of the scholarly resources now available to researchers willing to pursue hitherto secret documentation via the Access to Information Act. Using this statute is not always easy, and the results are not always what we would like, but repeated complaints to the information commissioner and even court action have succeeded in releasing more information than was sometimes forthcoming in the first instance. CSIS and the RCMP have not perhaps been enthusiastic participants in this exercise of counter-surveillance by three scholarly researchers, but we can report that they have generally behaved quite

correctly and appropriately in responding according to the letter of the act, even if they have tended to be quite literal in interpreting our specific requests.

1 The Empire Strikes Back

1 This chapter borrows heavily from Andrew Parnaby and Gregory S. Kealey with Kirk Niergarth, '"High-Handed, Impolite, and Empire-Breaking Actions": Radicalism, Anti-Imperialism, and Political Policing in Canada, 1860–1914,' in Barry Wright and Susan Binnie, eds., *Canadian State Trials, Volume III, Political Trials and Security Measures, 1840–1914* (Toronto: University of Toronto Press and Osgoode Society 2009), 483–514.

2 Greg Marquis, 'The "Irish Model" and Nineteenth-Century Canadian Policing,' *Journal of Imperial and Commonwealth History*, 25, no. 2 (1997): 193–218, provides an excellent discussion of policing in British North America, including the colonies of Vancouver Island and Newfoundland. See also: Elinor Senior, *British Regulars in Montreal: An Imperial Garrison, 1832–1854* (Montreal: McGill-Queen's University Press 1981); Allan Greer, 'The Birth of the Police in Canada,' in Allan Greer and Ian Radforth, eds., *Colonial Leviathan: State Formation in Mid-Nineteenth-Century Canada* (Toronto: University of Toronto Press 1992), 17–49; Brian Young, 'Positive Law, Positive State: Class Realignment and the Transformation of Lower Canada, 1815–1866,' in Greer and Radforth, eds., *Colonial Leviathan*, 50–63; Allan Greer, *The Patriots and the People* (Toronto: University of Toronto Press 1993); and Hereward Senior, *Constabulary: The Rise of Police Institutions in Britain, the Commonwealth, and the United States* (Toronto: Dundurn Press 1997). The objectives of the rural police are contained in *Rule for the Government of the Rural Police: Circular Memorandum for the Information and Guidance of the Inspecting Stipendiary Magistrate ... in the Montreal District* (Montreal: n.p., 1839), 2.

3 Britain's antipathy to political policing during the Victorian era, and the very different practices undertaken in the colonies, is taken up by Bernard Porter in his groundbreaking *The Origins of the Vigilant State: The London Metropolitan Police Special Branch before the First World War* (London: Weidenfeld and Nicolson 1987), 188–94.

4 The literature on the Fenians is massive. One of the best places to start is John Newsinger's slim volume *Fenianism in Mid-Victorian Britain* (London: Pluto Press 1994). Also useful are: Neidhardt, *Fenianism in North America*; Keith Amos, *The Fenians in Australia, 1865–1880* (Kensington: New South Wales University Press 1988); Brian Jenkins, *Fenians and Anglo-American*

Relations during Reconstruction (Ithaca, N.Y., and London: Cornell University Press 1969); and Christy Campbell, *Fenian Fire: The British Government Plot to Assassinate Queen Victoria* (London: Harper Collins 2003). Interestingly, Fenian leader James Stephens was also a member of the International Working Man's Association, the so-called First International which included Karl Marx. See Hereward Senior, *The Fenians in Canada* (Toronto: Macmillan 1978), 40–1.

5 Quoted in Jenkins, *Fenians and Anglo-American Relations*, 23.

6 Library and Archives Canada (LAC), John A. Macdonald Papers (JAMP), MG 26, Letterbooks, vol. XI, John A Macdonald to Col. Ermatinger, 8 February 1868. On the wider American political context at this time, and its link to Fenianism, see Jenkins, *Fenians and Anglo-American Relations*; David Montgomery, *Beyond Equality: Labor and Radical Republicans, 1862–1872* (New York: Vintage Books 1967); and Eric Foner, 'Class, Ethnicity, and Radicalism in the Gilded Age: The Land League and Irish-America,' *Marxist Perspectives*, 1, no. 2 (1978): 6–55.

7 In the Canadian context, the Fenian question has been framed in many ways: as an important moment in Canadian military history; as a significant dimension of Irish immigrants' experience in the New World; and as key variable in the debates associated with the act of Confederation in 1867. See: C.P. Stacey, 'A Fenian Interlude: The Story of Michael Murphy,' *Canadian Historical Review*, 15 (1934): 133–54, and 'Fenianism and the Rise of National Feeling in Canada at the Time of Confederation,' *Canadian Historical Review*, 3 (September 1931): 238–61. See also Peter M. Toner, 'The Military Organization of the "Canadian" Fenians, 1866–1870,' *Irish Sword*, 10, no. 38 (1971): 26–37; Peter M. Toner and D.C. Lyne, 'Fenianism in Canada,' *Studia Hibernica*, 12 (1972): 27–76; Peter M. Toner, 'The Rise of Irish Nationalism in Canada, 1858–1884,' PhD thesis, National University of Ireland, 1974; Senior, *The Fenians in Canada*; Hereward Senior, 'Murphy, Michael,' *Dictionary of Canadian Biography (DCB)*, vol. 9 (all *DCB* entries cited here are also available at http://www.biographi.ca); George Sheppard, '"God Save the Green": Fenianism and Fellowship in Victorian Ontario,' *Histoire Sociale–Social History*, 20, no. 39 (1987): 129–44; Jeff Keshen, 'Cloak and Dagger: Canada West's Secret Police, 1864–67,' *Ontario History*, 79 (1987): 353–77; Peter M. Toner, 'The Home Rule League: Fortune, Fenians, and Failure,' *Canadian Journal of Irish Studies*, 15, no. 1 (1989): 7–19; Oliver Rafferty, 'Fenianism in North America in the 1860s: The Problems for Church and State,' *History*, 84, no. 274 (1999): 257–77; and Brian Clarke, *Piety and Nationalism: Lay Voluntary Organizations and the Creation of an Irish-Catholic Community in Toronto, 1850–1895* (Montreal and Kingston,

Ont.: McGill-Queen's University Press 1993). The quotations from the *Irish Canadian* are taken from Clarke, *Piety and Nationalism*, 175.

8 See Senior, 'Murphy, Michael.'

9 Quoted in Campbell, *Fenian Fire*, 62.

10 Quoted in W.S. Neidhardt, *Fenianism in North America* (University Park: Pennsylvania State University Press 1975), 35.

11 Hereward Senior, *The Last Invasion of Canada: The Fenian Raids, 1866–1870* (Toronto: Dundurn 1991), 45–57.

12 LAC, JAMP, MG 26, McMicken Correspondence, Gilbert McMicken, 'Special Order,' 31 December 1864.

13 McMicken was involved in the construction of the Queenston Suspension bridge and the extension of Canada's first telegraph line from Toronto to Lewiston, New York. In 1835 he married Anne Theresa Duff, granddaughter of Alexander Grant, who, in Carl Betke's words, 'dominated the early fur trade, the shipping industry, and the Provincial Marine in the Detroit region.' See Carl Betke, 'McMicken, Gilbert,' *DCB*, vol. 12.

14 Quoted in ibid. McMicken developed an especially close relationship with Alan Pinkerton, head of Pinkerton's Detective Agency, and personally intervened, as a magistrate, to facilitate extraditions when Pinkerton detectives had pursued fugitives into Canada. See Dale and Lee Gibson, 'Railroading the Train Robbers: Extradition in the Shadow of Annexation,' in Dale Gibson and Wesley Pue, eds., *Glimpses of Canadian Legal History* (Winnipeg: Legal Research Institute, University of Manitoba, 1991), 71–93.

15 The number of spies is derived, in large part, from LAC, JAMP, MG 26, McMicken Correspondence, vol. 236, McMicken to Macdonald, 5 December 1865, and vol. 238, McMicken to Macdonald, 20 July 1866. See also the various letters between British, Canadian, and American officials in *Correspondence Relating to the Fenian Invasion and the Rebellion of the Southern States* (Ottawa: Hunter Rose 1869), in particular: Simon Cameron, U.S. secretary of war, to the Right Honourable Sir Edmund Head, 24 October 1861; Lord Lyon to Lord Monck, 8 August 1864; Lord Monck to E. Cardwell, MP, 23 September 1864; British Legation, Washington, to Seward, U.S. secretary of state, 26 December 1864.

16 LAC, JAMP, MG 26, Letterbooks, vol. 511, Macdonald to McMicken, 22 September 1865. On the counterattack undertaken by British officials in 1865 and 1866, see Newsinger, *Fenianism in Mid-Victorian Britain*, 40–7. Stephens eventually escaped from jail with the assistance of two Fenian jailers, a development that, according to Newsinger, 'highlighted the extent of the IRB's penetration of the police, the prison service, and government department generally' (44).

17 The backgrounds and numbers of spies have been pieced together from the voluminous spy reports contained in LAC, JAMP, MG 26, McMicken Correspondence, vols. 234–40, and Wayne Crockett, 'The Uses and Abuses of the Secret Service Fund: The Political Dimension of Police Work in Canada, 1864–1877,' MA thesis, Queen's University, 1982, 31–4. Also useful on this question is Jeff Keshen, 'Cloak and Dagger: Canada West's Secret Police, 1864–1867,' *Ontario History*, 79, no. 4 (1987): 353–81.

18 LAC, JAMP, MG 26, McMicken Correspondence, vol. 237, McMicken to Macdonald, 9 April 1866.

19 W.L. Morton, 'Lord Monck and Nationality in Ireland and Canada,' *Studia Hibernica*, 13 (1973): 77–100.

20 Archibald's time in Newfoundland corresponded with the colony's transition to responsible government; see Leslie Harris's entry for Archibald in the *DCB*, vol. 11. This paragraph is based on: Edith J. Archibald, *The Life and Letters of Sir Edward Mortimer Archibald* (Toronto: G.N. Morang 1924); William D'Arcy, *The Fenian Movement in the United States* (New York: Catholic University of America Press 1947); Crockett, 'The Uses and Abuses of the Secret Service Fund,' 66–70; Leon O'Broin, *Fenian Fever: An Anglo-American Dilemma* (London 1971), 41–51; Harold A. Davis, 'The Fenian Raid on New Brunswick,' *Canadian Historical Review*, 36, no. 4 (1955): 316–34.

21 Quoted in Crockett, 'The Uses and Abuses of the Secret Service Fund,' 40.

22 Keshen, 'Cloak and Dagger,' 365.

23 Ibid., 366.

24 The links between Archibald and the lieutenant governor of New Brunswick are discussed in Davis, 'The Fenian Raid on New Brunswick,' 316–34; and Carl Betke and Stan Horrall, 'Canada's Security Service: An Historical Outline, 1864–1966' (Ottawa: RCMP Historical Section 1978), CSIS Access Request #117-90-107, 67–70.

25 Peter M. Toner, 'The "Green Ghost": Canada's Fenians and the Raids,' *Eire-Ireland*, 16, no. 4 (1981): 37–41; Davis, 'The Fenian Raid on New Brunswick'; Newsinger, *Fenianism in Mid-Victorian Britain*, 46.

26 Toner, 'The "Green Ghost,"' 37–41.

27 The connection between the Fenian invasion and Confederation is a staple of the Canadian literature. See C.P. Stacey, 'Fenianism and the Rise of the National Feeling in Canada at the Time of Confederation' and 'A Fenian Interlude'; Davis, 'The Fenian Raid on New Brunswick,' 332–4; Senior, *The Fenians in Canada*. The quotation is from Davis, 'The Fenian Raid on New Brunswick,' 333.

28 The poem appears in John A. Cooper, 'The Fenian Raid of 1866,' *Canadian Magazine*, 10, no. 1 (1897): 47.

29 Quoted in Jenkins, *Fenians and Anglo-American Relations*, 140.

30 According to Keshen: 'At the most crucial moment of his career as Stipendiary Magistrate for Canada West, McMicken failed miserably. His presence and that of the frontier force changed nothing. The Fenian raid proceeded as planned, and the government was unprepared.' See 'Cloak and Dagger,' 368.

31 Members of the Parti Patriote, middle-class reformers who led the Rebellions of 1837–8 in Lower Canada, often compared themselves to those Irish professionals who backed Daniel O'Connell. On the Fenians and Lower Canada, see: John W. Dafoe, 'The Fenian Invasion of Quebec, 1866. With Several Valuable Historical Illustrations,' *Canadian Magazine*, 10 (1898), 339–47; Hereward Senior, 'Quebec and the Fenians,' *Canadian Historical Review*, 40, no. 1 (1967): 26–44; Greer, *The Patriots and the People*, 134–5 and 147; Robert C. Daley, 'The Irish of Lower Canada and the Rise of French Canadian Nationalism,' paper presented at the annual meeting of the Canadian Historical Association, June 1984, in the possession of Gregory S. Kealey; David A. Wilson, 'The Fenians in Montreal: Invasion, Intrigue, and Assassination,' *Eire-Ireland*, fall–winter 2003, 109–33.

32 Each of these battles is examined in Senior, *The Last Invasion of Canada*, 59–129; the fatality and wounded numbers appear on p. 100; the quotation on p. 101.

33 Ibid., 131–86. The arrests are the subject of R. Blake Brown, '"Stars and Shamrocks Will Be Sown": The Fenian State Trials, 1866–7,' in Wright and Binnie, eds., *Canadian State Trials, Volume III*, 38.

34 Ibid., 38–41.

35 Betke and Horrall, 'Canada's Security Service,' 77–9; Keshen, 'Cloak and Dagger,' 353–77; Philip Stenning, 'Guns and the Law,' *The Beaver*, December 2000–January 2001, 6–7.

36 LAC, JAMP, MG 26, McMicken Correspondence, vol. 328 [?], McMicken to Macdonald, August 1866.

37 Brown, '"Stars and Shamrocks Will Be Sown,"' 38–45.

38 W.S. Neidhardt, 'The Fenian Trials in the Province of Canada, 1866–7: A Case Study of Law and Politics in Action,' *Ontario History*, 66, no. 1 (1974): 34n.73.

39 Quoted in Brown, '"Stars and Shamrocks Will be Sown,"' 70.

40 This observation regarding Clarke is based on his correspondence with McMicken. See Clarke's reports in LAC, JAMP, MG 26, McMicken Correspondence, vol. 238 (July 1866), vol. 238 (August, September, October,

November, and December 1866), vol. 239 (January, February, and March 1867). The final quotation appears in Clarke to McMicken, 23 March 1867. The emphasis is in the original.

41 Toner, 'The "Green Ghost,"' 41; Betke and Horrall, 'Canada's Security Service,' 77–9; Keshen, 'Cloak and Dagger,' 353–77; Crockett, 'The Use and Abuses of the Secret Service Fund,' 70–1.

42 David A. Wilson, 'The D'Arcy McGee Affair and the Suspension of Habeas Corpus,' in Wright and Binnie, eds., Canadian *State Trials, Volume III,* 85–92.

43 Bill Kirwin, 'The Radical Youth of a Conservative: D'Arcy McGee in Young Ireland,' *Canadian Journal of Irish Studies,* 10, no. 1 (1984): 51–62; Wilson, 'The Fenians in Montreal.' The most in-depth treatment is Wilson, *Thomas D'Arcy McGee, Volume 1: Passion, Reason, and Politics, 1825–1857* (Montreal and Kingston, Ont.: McGill-Queen's University Press 2008).

44 Wilson, 'The Fenians in Montreal,' 92–5.

45 Toner, 'The "Green Ghost,"' 40–4; LAC, JAMP, MG 26, Letterbooks, vol. 11, Macdonald to Anderson Hebert, 13 April 1868.

46 'In calmer times, he might well have been acquitted,' Senior concluded in his 'Quebec and the Fenians' (39). Senior also provides an intriguing thumbnail sketch of James Patrick Whelan and an analysis of the trial. See as well Wilson, 'The Fenians in Montreal.'

47 Charles Curran suggests that Beach adopted this name in jest: 'Le Caron is argot for "slice of fat bacon." Beach was lean and wiry. It has been suggested that he took the name by way of a joke.' See his 'The Spy behind the Speaker's Chair,' *History Today,* 18 (1968): 745–54.

48 Henri le Caron, *Twenty-Five Years in the Secret Service* (London: Heinemann 1892), 29–55.

49 LAC, JAMP, MG 26, McMicken Correspondence, vol. 240, McMicken to Macdonald, 8 June 1868.

50 Quoted in D'Arcy, *The Fenian Movement,* 297.

51 Le Caron, *Twenty-Five Years in the Secret Service,* 57, 60.

52 Peter Edwards, *Delusion: The True Story of Victorian Superspy Henri Le Caron* (Toronto: Key Porter 2008), 87.

53 LAC, JAMP, MG 26, McMicken Correspondence, reel 244A, Coursol to Macdonald, 1 April 1870.

54 Quoted in Edwards, *Delusion,* 94.

55 J.M. Bumsted, *Louis Riel v. Canada: The Making of a Rebel* (Winnipeg: Great Plains Publications 2001), 172–8.

56 In the aftermath of the raid, three Métis were arrested for assisting the raiders. Two, Isadore Villeneuve and Andre Jerome, were not convicted,

but the third, Louison Letendre, was found guilty and sentenced to hang (his sentence was later commuted to twenty years' imprisonment and in January 1873 he was exiled to the United States). Ruth Swan and Edward Jerome explore the context of these arrests and the harsh treatment of those arrested in 'Unequal Justice: The Métis in O'Donoghue's Raid of 1871,' *Manitoba History*, 39 (2000): 24–38.

57 Gilbert McMicken, 'The Abortive Fenian Raid on Manitoba: Account by One Who Knew Its Secret History,' *Historical and Scientific Society of Manitoba*, transaction no. 32 (1887–8) (Winnipeg: Winnipeg Free Press [?] 1888). See also Swan and Jerome, 'Unequal Justice'; D.N. Sprague, *Canada and the Métis, 1869–1885* (Waterloo: Wilfrid Laurier University Press 1988), 75–107; A.H. de Trémaudan, 'Louis Riel and the Fenian Raid of 1871,' *Canadian Historical Review*, 4 (June 1923): 132–44; J.P. Pritchett, 'The Origin of the So-Called Fenian Raid on Manitoba in 1871,' *Canadian Historical Review*, 10 (March 1929): 23–42.

58 McMicken to Macdonald, 12 November 1871 and 22 December 1871, as cited in Sprague, *Canada and the Métis*, 98.

59 See Sprague, *Canada and the Métis*, 96–8.

60 Quoted in Betke and Horrall, 'Canada's Security Service,' 133.

2 You Drive Us Hindus out of Canada and We Will Drive Every White Man out of India!

1 Portions of this chapter are taken directly from Andrew Parnaby and Gregory S. Kealey with Kirk Niergarth, '"High-Handed, Impolite, and Empire-Breaking Actions": Radicalism, Anti-Imperialism, and Political Policing in Canada, 1860–1914,' in Barry Wright and Susan Binnie, eds., *Canadian State Trials, Volume III, Political Trials and Security Measures, 1840–1914* (Toronto: University of Toronto Press and Osgoode Society 2009), 483–514. The opening section on the British in India from 1857 to 1914 is drawn from Judith M. Brown, *Modern India: The Origins of an Asian Democracy* (New York: Oxford University Press 1994), 1–193. The 'desperadoes' quotation appears in Richard J. Popplewell, *Intelligence and Imperial Defence: British Intelligence and the Defence of the Indian Empire, 1904–1924* (London: Frank Cass 1995), 32.

2 British Library (BL), Asia, Pacific, and Africa Collection (APAC), Indian Office Records (IOR), L/PJ/12/1, '[Confidential] Note on the anti-British Movement among Natives of India in America,' 1908.

3 On the development of the Indian radical tradition abroad, see Arun Coomer Bose, *Indian Revolutionaries Abroad, 1905–1922: In the Background*

of International Developments (Patna, India: Bharati Bhawan 1971); Robert
G. Lee, 'The Hidden World of Asian Immigrant Radicalism,' in Paul Buhle
and Dan Georgakas, eds., *The Immigrant Left in the United States* (Albany,
N.Y.: SUNY Press 1996), 256–88; Maia Ramnath, 'Two Revolutions: The
Ghadar Movement and India's Radical Disapora, 1913–1918,' *Radical History Review*, 92 (spring 2005): 7–30. James Campbell Ker's *Political Trouble in India, 1907–1917* (Delhi: Oriental Publishers 1917 [1973]) is an indispensable source. Ker was a senior officer in the Home Department of the Indian
government; he also worked as personal assistant to the director (DCI)
of the Criminal Investigation Department (CID). This book is a collection
of the confidential documents he amassed during his tenure at the CID.
As such, it details the activities of radicals operating outside India. Ker's
analysis was continued in a 'sequel' by H.W. Hale, *Political Trouble in India, 1917–1937* (Allahabad, India: Chugh Publications [1974]).

4 On the emigration of South Asians to British Columbia, see Hugh Johnston, *The Voyage of the Komagata Maru: The Sikh Challenge to Canada's Colour Bar* (Oxford: Oxford University Press 1979); R. Sampat-Mehta, *International Barriers* (Ottawa: Canada Research Bureau 1973), 125–91; Norman Buchignani and Doreen M. Indra with Ram Srivastiva, *Continuous Journey: A Social History of South Asians in Canada* (Toronto: McClelland and Stewart 1985), 4–70; Gucharn S. Basran and B. Singh Bolaria, *The Sikhs in Canada: Migration, Race, Class, and Gender* (Oxford: Oxford University Press 2003), 95–103; Hira Singh, 'The Political Economy of Immigrant Farm Labour: A Study of East Indian Farm Workers in British Columbia,' in Milton Israel, ed., *The South Asian Diaspora in Canada: Six Essays* (Toronto: Multicultural History Society of Ontario 1987), 87; Achana B. Verma, 'Status and Migration Among the Punjabis of Paldi, BC and Paldi, Punjab,' PhD thesis, Simon Fraser University, 1994; Ninette Kelley and Michael Trebilcock, *The Making of the Mosaic: A History of Canadian Immigration Policy* (Toronto: University of Toronto Press 1998), 142–56.

On anti-Asian agitation in British Columbia, see especially Patricia Roy, *A White Man's Province: British Columbia Politicians and Japanese Immigrants, 1858–1914* (Vancouver: University of British Columbia Press 1989); W. Peter Ward, *White Canada Forever: Popular Attitudes and Public Policy towards Orientals in British Columbia*, 2nd ed. (Montreal and Kingston, Ont.: McGill-Queen's University Press 1990); Mark Leier, *Red Flags and Red Tape: The Making of a Labour Bureaucracy* (Toronto: University of Toronto Press 1995), 125–42. It is important to note that not all white British Columbians endorsed the politics of Asian exclusion; the radical labour movement and Protestant missionaries were important voices of tolerance. On the former, see Mark Leier, *Where the Fraser River Flows: The Industrial Workers of the World in British Columbia* (Vancouver: New Star Books 1990); on the latter, see Ruth Compton Brouwer, 'A Disgrace to "Christian Canada": Protestant Foreign Missionary Concerns about the Treatment of South Asian in Canada, 1907–1940,' in Franca Iacovetta, Paula Draper, and Robert Ventresca, eds., *A Nation of Immigrants: Women, Workers, and Communities in Canadian History, 1840s–1960s* (Toronto: University of Toronto Press 1998), 361–83.

5 In October 1907 Prime Minister Wilfrid Laurier told Deputy Minister of Labour Mackenzie King that imperial authorities would act on Canada's behalf to stop immigration from India. According to King's account, Laurier 'thought the Chinese were met now by the tax, the Japs wd. be limited by understanding, and the Hindoos would be stopped by an ordinance in India preventing their immigration and which wd. be arranged thro British office.' Laurier had clearly been disappointed in this hope by January 1908, as his government's adoption of specific orders-in-council to prohibit South Asian immigration attests. See the entry for 7 October 1908, LAC, Diaries of Prime Minister William Lyon Mackenzie King [hereafter King Diaries], MG 26-J13, http//www.king.collectionscanada.ca/EN/Default. asp.

6 According to the *Report of the Committee Appointed to Investigate Revolutionary Conspiracies in India* (London: His Majesty's Stationery Office 1918), 'an agitation of unparalleled bitterness was started in both provinces and especially in the eastern [after partition]. It was proclaimed through newspapers, pamphlets and orators that Bengal was a motherland once rich and famous and now dismembered; she had been torn in two despite the protests of her children.' See p. 17 of the report; it can be found in BL, APAC, IOR, Mss. Eur, F161/152. For an even-handed assessment of Curzon and the partition question, see David Gilmour, *Curzon: Imperial Statesman* (New York: Farrar, Strauss, and Giroux 2003), 271–3, 322–4, 345, 378, 405–7.

7 BL, APAC, IOR, L/PJ/6/1137, file 320/1909, governor general of Canada to Colonial Office, 11 December 1908. Governor General Lord Grey quotes a letter from Prime Minister Laurier dated 8 December 1908.

8 BL, APAC, IOR, L/PJ/6/888, file 3168/1908, 'Confidential Memorandum Accompanying Report of W.L. Mackenzie King … On the Subject of Immigration to Canada from the Orient,' 1908.

9 Ibid.

10 Ibid.

11 Quotations are from King's published report, 'Immigration to Canada from the Orient,' Sessional Paper no. 36a, *Sessional Papers*, 7–8 Edward VII, 1908.

12 Aside from the 'continuous journey' requirement, which will be discussed below, King pointed out that a close reading of the Indian Emigration Act (1883) allowed for the emigration of contract labourers only to a country 'certified' by the governor general in council to have had 'made such laws and other provisions as the Governor General in Council thinks sufficient for the protection of emigrants to that country during their residence therein.' Since no such certification would be made for Canada, King suggested that Canada could 'prohibit the landing in Canada of immigrants who come in violation of the laws of their own country' and thereby eliminate any prospect of contract labourers arriving from India. King was also pleased that the government of India had issued public warnings about the 'risks involved in emigration to Canada.' Finally, King noted that the regulation requiring immigrants to possess $25 could also pose a justification for barring some South Asian immigrants, but 'should this amount prove inadequate it could be increased.' On 3 June 1908, a month after King submitted his report, an order-in-council required South Asian immigrants to be in possession of $200 on arrival. See King's report 'Immigration to Canada from the Orient'; Johnston, *The Voyage of the Komagata Maru*, 138; and Sampat-Mehta, *International Barriers*, 131–42.

13 On the arrangement made with the CPR, King recorded in his diary that the minister of labour, Rodolphe Lemieux, told him that 'Canada had doubled her subsidy to the CPR. England not paying as much, a tacit understanding was that immigration from India was not to be encouraged by the Co.' See the entry for 27 April 1908, King Diaries. The immigration figures cited here are contained in Kelley and Trebilcock, *The Making of the Mosaic*, 142–56.

14 The British Columbia judgment, in the case of *Re Narain Singh et al.*, principally determined that the provincial British Columbia Immigration Act (1908) was inoperative because ultra vires. Judge J. Morrison, however, noted that while the governor in council had power to 'prohibit the landing in Canada of any specified class of immigrants,' those South Asians who had arrived in British Columbia aboard the *Monteagle* had not been so specified and had a right to land in Canada according to sections 35 and 53 of the Immigration Act. See *Reference Re Narain Singh* (1908) 13 British Columbia Reports 477 (Supreme Court); Johnston, *The Voyage of the Komagata Maru*, 138; and Sampat-Mehta, *International Barriers*, 138, 140–2.

15 The biographical information on Hopkinson is drawn from the following sources: Hugh Johnston, 'The Surveillance of Indian Nationalists in North America, 1908–1918,' *BC Studies*, 78 (summer 1988): 5 and n.4; Johnston, *The Voyage of the Komagata Maru*, 1, 7, 137n.1, 138n.13; Buchignani, Indra,

and Srivastiva, *Continuous Journey*, 25, 30n.42; Popplewell, *Intelligence and Imperial Defence*, 150–1, 163n.25. The *Vancouver Province*, 22 October 1914, states that Hopkinson was 'police chief at Lahore.'

Details of Hopkinson's father's career in the army vary widely. Popplewell states that he 'had been one of the military escort of Sir Louis Cavagnari massacred at Kabal in 1879,' leaving Hopkinson and his mother 'stranded at Lahore in the Punjab.' Buchignani, Indra, and Srivastiva suggest that 'Hopkinson's father was a non-commissioned officer in the British Indian army, who was reputed to have been killed by Afghan raiders when Hopkinson was young.' As a result, they suggest, Hopkinson was 'raised in India by his Brahmin mother' and was 'fiercely anti-"seditionist."' Johnston, whose work is perhaps the most comprehensive, states in *Voyage* that Hopkinson's father was 'a sergeant instructor of volunteers at Allahabad.'

Information about the composition of the Calcutta police force is contained in Giriraj Shah, *History and Organisation of Indian Police* (New Delhi: Anmol Publications 1999), 116.

16 The information on Taraknath Das is taken from: BL, APAC, IOR, L/PJ/6/1137, file 320/1909, '(Confidential) Memorandum on Matters Affecting the East Indian Community in British Columbia, by Colonel E.J.E Swayne; Information as to Hindu Agitators in Vancouver'; L/PJ/12/1, '[Secret] Circular No. 12 of 1912, Indian Agitation in America,' by J.C. Ker, personal assistant to the director, Department of Criminal Intelligence. See also: N.N. Bhattacharya, 'Indian Revolutionaries Abroad,' *Journal of Indian History*, 50 (1972): 415; Arun Coomer Bose, 'Indian Nationalist Agitation in the US and Canada until the Arrival of Har Dayal,' *Journal of Indian History*, 43 (1965): 227. According to Das, *Free Hindusthan* 'advocates the liberal principles of man and puts forth undeniable facts and fights about the exploiting principles of the British government in Hindustan.' This quotation appears in Brij Lal, 'East Indians in British Columbia, 1904–1914: An Historical Study in Growth and Integration,' MA thesis, University of British Columbia, 1976, 60–1. On Das, see Bose, *Indian Revolutionaries Abroad*, 48–52; Ker, *Political Trouble in India*, contains translations of various articles that appeared in *Free Hindusthan* (see 108–11).

17 There is some disagreement among scholars as to whether or not Hopkinson was sent to British Columbia by Indian authorities. Popplewell argues strenuously that 'the initiative in the surveillance of Indian agitators on the Pacific Coast at this time came entirely from the Canadian side and not from India, let alone from the British government in London.' In *Voyage*, Johnston states flatly that 'he had turned up in Vancouver in 1908 ... an In-

spector of the Calcutta Metropolitan police ... officially on leave, but pursuing investigations for the Criminal Intelligence Department in India.' These statements are not necessarily contradictory: it is possible that he was sent by the CID in India, but the proposal to place the South Asian community under constant surveillance came first from the Canadian government. On the emergence of the CID in India, see Brown, *Modern India*, 137–9; Popplewell, *Intelligence and Imperial Defence*, 8–164, especially 147–64.

18 BL, APAC, IOR, L/PJ/6/1137, file 320/1909, J.B. Harkin to superintendent of immigration, 29 July 1908.

19 The rise and fall of the British Honduras scheme is chronicled in J.B. Harkin's own *The East Indians in British Columbia: A Report regarding the Proposal to Provide Work in British Honduras for the Indigent Unemployed among Them* (Ottawa: Department of the Interior 1908). See also: BL, APAC, IOR, L/PJ/6/1137, file 320/1909, Harkin to superintendent of immigration, Ottawa, 29 July 1908; Harkin to Ministry of Interior, 16 October 1908 and 6 November 1908; Wilfred Collet, officer administering the government, British Honduras, to secretary of state of Canada, 19 and 26 November 1908; Collet to Colonial Office, 2 and 3 December 1908; and 'Certified Copy of a Report of the Committee of the Privy Council, Approved by His Excellency the Governor General on 10 December 1908.'

The final quotation in this paragraph is from BL, APAC, IOR, L/PJ/6/1137, file 320/1909, governor general of Canada to Colonial Office, 21 December 1908. Along with his confidential letter, Lord Grey included a detailed memorandum prepared by W.W. Cory, the deputy minister of immigration, about the relocation plan. The memo (hereafter Cory memorandum) includes excerpts from the telegrams and letters exchanged between Hopkinson, Harkin, and ministry officials after the delegation returned from Belize; see Hopkinson to Harkin, 20 and 23 November 1908; Harkin to Cory, 23 November 1908. Johnston takes up the issue of Hopkinson's alleged corruption in 'The Surveillance of Indian Nationalists,' 6n.11. 'Hopkinson was loyal to British India and Anglo Canada and behaved accordingly,' he concludes. 'One does not need evidence of personal corruption to explain the part he played.'

20 This brief biography of Teja Singh is based on: BL, APAC, IOR, L/PJ/6/1137, file 320/1909, '(Confidential) Memorandum on Matters Affecting the East Indian Community in British Columbia, by Colonel E.J. E Swayne'; Buchignani, Indra, and Srivastiva, *Continuous Journey*, 26–7; Johnston, *Voyage*, 12; Bose, *Indian Revolutionaries Abroad*, 52–5. Harkin certainly did not think much of Teja Singh, referring to him as the 'absolute dictator of the community.' See his *East Indians in British Columbia*, 4.

21 BL, APAC, IOR, L/PJ/6/1137, file 320/1909, Hopkinson to Harkin,
   20 November 1908; Cory to Harkin, 4 December 1908; *Vancouver Province*,
   23 November 1908; Cory memorandum.

22 BL, APAC, IOR, L/PJ/6/1137, file 320/1909, Governor General Lord Grey
   to Prime Minister Wilfrid Laurier, 3 December 1908. See also Carman Miller's entry for Lord Grey in the *Dictionary of Canadian Biography* (*DCB*), vol.
   15 (all *DCB* entries cited here are also available at http://www.biographi
   .ca/).

23 BL, APAC, IOR, L/PJ/6/1137, file 320/1909, Lord Grey to Colonial Office,
   9, 10, 11, and 21 December 1908; secretary of state for the colonies to
   Lord Grey, 23 December 1908; and Colonial Office to India Office, 30 December 1908. See also Johnston, 'The Surveillance of Indian Nationalists,'
   9.

24 BL, APAC, IOR, L/PJ/6/1137, file 320/1909, Laurier to Lord Grey,
   8 December 1908.

25 BL, APAC, IOR, L/PJ/6/1137, file 320/1909, '(Confidential) Memorandum
   on Matters Affecting the East Indian Community in British Columbia, by
   Colonel E.J. E Swayne.'

26 Ibid. On the links between the IWW, SPC, and East Indian community in
   British Columbia, see: Peter Campbell, 'East Meets Left: South Asian Mili-
   tants and the Socialist Party of Canada in British Columbia, 1904–1914,'
   International Journal of Canadian Studies, 20 (fall 1999): 35–65.

27 BL, APAC, IOR, L/PJ/6/1137, file 320/1909, '(Confidential) Memorandum
   on Matters Affecting the East Indian Community in British Columbia, by
   Colonel E.J. E Swayne.'

28 Quoted in Popplewell, *Intelligence and Imperial Defence*, 129.

29 This brief section on the general nature of Hopkinson's duties is based
   on the following: BL, APAC, IOR, L/PJ/6/930, file 1309/1909, Hopkinson
   to Cory, 10 September 1908, 19 December 1908, 4 and 18 January 1909,
   15 April 1909, 18 May 1909, 14 January 1910; L/PJ/6/1064, file 568/1911,
   Hopkinson to Cory, 10, 23, and 29 March 1911, 7 June 1911, 4 August 1911,
   7 and 8 December 1911.

30 The reference to Kumar being a 'Punjabi Buddhist' is taken from Johnston,
   'The Surveillance of Indian Nationalists,' 9.

31 BL, APAC, IOR, L/PJ/12/1, J.C. Ker, '[Secret] Circular No. 12 of 1912,
   Indian Agitation in America.'

32 BL, APAC, IOR, L/PJ/6, file 4917/1911, secretary to the government of
   India to Sir Richmond Ritchie, His Majesty's undersecretary of state for
   India, 25 November 1911. The final quotation in this paragraph is taken
   from a report entitled 'History Sheet of G.D. Kumar' attached to the secre-

tary's letter. Copies of *Swadesh Sevak* – the newspaper – can be found in BL, APAC,IOR,L/PJ/6/1064, file 568/1911.

33 On the use of informants see: BI, APAC, IOR, L/PJ/6/1137, file 275/1912, Hopkinson to Cory, 11 July 1911; Hopkinson to Cory, 5 October 1912.

34 BL, APAC, IOR, L/PJ/6/1064, file 568/1911, Hopkinson to Cory, 8 May 1911. Additional information about *Bande Mataram* can be found in: Johnston, *Voyage*, 10; Ker, *Political Trouble in India*, 102–6.

35 On the changing nature of Canadian immigration policy at this time, see Kelley and Trebilcock, *The Making of the Mosaic*, 111–63; Barbara Roberts, *Whence They Came: Deportation from Canada, 1900–1935* (Ottawa: University of Ottawa Press 1988), 1–70. The 1910 revisions to the Immigration Act sought to further insulate boards of inquiry created under the auspices of the immigration branch from judicial scrutiny; section 23 of the revised act stated that 'no court or judge could interfere with a decision of a Board of Inquiry.' See Johnston, *Voyage*, 18.

36 BL, APAC, IOR, L/PJ/6/1064, file 568/1911, Hopkinson to Cory, 28 June 1912.

37 This brief biography of Rahim is taken from BL, APAC, IOR, L/PJ/12/1, J.C. Ker, '[Secret] Circular No. 12 of 1912, Indian Agitation in America,' See also Buchignani, Indra, and Srivastiva, *Continuous Journey*, 36–47; Johnston, *Voyage*, 9–12; and Campbell, 'East Meets Left.' Johnston is dismissive of Rahim's left-wing politics, writing that he 'assimilat[ed], in a half-digested way, the language of class warfare.' For a more sympathetic reading, see Campbell's 'East Meets Left' and *Canadian Marxists and the Search for the Third Way* (Montreal and Kingston, Ont.: McGill-Queen's University Press 1999), 10–11, 18, 74, 247n.2, and 248n.25.

38 BL, APAC, IOR, L/PJ/6/1064, file 568/1911, J.H. MacGill, immigration agent, to Cory, 28 October 1910.

39 BL, APAC, IOR, L/PJ/12/1, J.C. Ker, '[Secret] Circular No. 12 of 1912, Indian Agitation in America.'

40 BL, APAC, IOR, L/PJ/6/1064, file 568/1911, J.H. MacGill, immigration agent, to Cory, 28 October 1910; Hopkinson to Cory, 3 November 1910 and 17 February 1911.

41 Quoted in Lal, 'East Indians in British Columbia,' 65–6. G.D. Kumar was the organization's secretary-treasurer.

42 Rahim's letter appeared in the *Vancouver News Advertiser* on 14 May 1912 under the headlines 'Should Canada Exclude Hindus?'

43 BL, APAC, IOR, L/PJ/6/1064, file 568/1911, Hopkinson to Cory, 26 March 1912.

44 BL, APAC, IOR, L/PJ/6/1064, file 568/1911, 1 April 1912. Rahim's involve-

ment in the SPC is detailed in Campbell, 'East Meet Left,' 46–50. More on the IWW can be found in Mark Leier, 'Solidarity on Occasion: The Vancouver Free Speech Fights of 1909 and 1912,' *Labour/Le Travail*, 23 (1989): 39–66, and *Where the Fraser River Flows; Rebel Life: The Life and Times of Robert Gosden, Revolutionary, Mystic, and Labour Spy* (Vancouver: New Star Books 1999).

45 BL, APAC, IOR, L/PJ/6/1137, file 275/1912, James Bryce to immigration secretary [?], 19 September 1911. Bryce's career is chronicled in *John T. Seaman, A Citizen of the World: The Life of James Bryce* (London: Tauris Academic Studies 2006).

46 BL, APAC, IOR, L/PJ/6/1137, file 275/1912, Hopkinson to Cory, 5 October 1911.

47 BL, APAC, IOR, L/PJ/6/1137, file 275/1912, Hopkinson to Cory, 23 October 1911.

48 The quotation about Das is from BL, APAC, IOR, L/PJ/6/1137, file 275/1912, Hopkinson to Cory, 5 October 1911. The details about Lala Har Dayal are found in BL, APAC, IOR, L/PJ/12/1, J.C. Ker, '[Secret] Circular No. 12 of 1912, Indian Agitation in America.'

49 Ramnath, 'Two Revolutions,' 22. Har Dayal was leader of the campus Bakunin Club. See BL, APAC, IOR, L/PJ/12/1, '[Secret] Criminal Intelligence Office, Draft Circular, 1914, Indian Agitation in America.'

50 Popplewell, *Intelligence and Imperial Defence*, 150–61.

51 BL, APAC, IOR, L/PJ/12/1, T.W. Holderness, undersecretary of state for India, to undersecretary of state, Colonial Office, 22 July 1913; M.C. Seton to undersecretary of state, 28 August 1913; M.C. Seton to 'Dear Wheeler,' 4 September 1913; secretary to the government of India, Home Department, to undersecretary of state for India, 21 May 1914.

52 BL, APAC, IOR, L/PJ/12/1, 'Note on the Personal Views of J.A.W. [J.A. Wallinger],' 22 May 1912.

53 Quoted in Popplewell, *Intelligence and Imperial Defence*, 158.

54 Ibid., 150–61.

55 Quoted in Buchignani, Indra, and Srivastiva, *Continuous Journey*, 53.

56 Ramnath, 'Two Revolutions,' 13. According to '[Secret] Criminal Intelligence Office, Draft Circular, 1914, Indian Agitation in America,' copies of *Ghadar* were moving into India from many points around the Pacific Rim: 'Many copies which have been intercepted show signs of having passed through many hands.' The circular can be found in BL, APAC, IOR, L/PJ/12/1.

57 BL, APAC, IOR, L/PJ/12/1, '[Secret] Criminal Intelligence Office, Draft Circular, 1914, Indian Agitation in America.'

58 Quoted in Johnston, 'The Surveillance of Indian Nationalists,' 15–16.

59 BL, APAC, IOR, L/PJ/12/1, '[Secret] Criminal Intelligence Office, Draft Circular, 1914, Indian Agitation in America.' Har Dayal's experiences in Germany during the war changed his perspective on Indian nationalism radically: 'During that one year I learned that the triumph of Germany would be a great calamity for Asia and the whole world,' he wrote in 1920. 'England is free and great, and we can share in this freedom and greatness as worthy citizens of the greatest state that the world has yet seen.' This quotation is from: Lala Har Dayal, *Forty-Four Months in Germany and Turkey: February 1915 to October 1918* (London: P.S. King and Son 1920), 73, 103.

60 Johnston, *Voyage*, 37–8.

61 By all accounts, he carried out his duties well and was largely responsible for keeping a tight leash on the more belligerent and pugnacious elements within government ranks.

62 See Johnston, *Voyage*, 125–36.

63 BI, APAC, IOR, L/PJ/6/1341, file 5372/1914, Reid to Scott, 22 October 1914.

64 BI, APAC, IOR, L/PJ/6/1341, file 5372/1914, clipping from the Vancouver *Province*, 22 October 1914.

65 BI, APAC, IOR, L/PJ/6/1341, file 5372/1914, Malcolm Reid to W.W. Cory, 27 October 1914.

66 BI, APAC, IOR, L/PJ/6/1341, file 5372/1914, clipping from the Vancouver *News Advertiser*, 14 January 1915.

67 BI, APAC, IOR, L/PJ/6/1341, file 5372/1914, photographs 439 and 431.

68 BL, APAC, IOR, L/PJ/12/775, Lewis V. Harcourt to the governor general of the Dominion of Canada, 4 November 1914; W.W. Cory to M.C. Seton, 2 December 1914.

69 Johnston, 'The Surveillance of Indian Nationalists,' 22–7.

70 Quoted in Popplewell, *Intelligence and Imperial Defence*, 161.

71 Ramnath, 'Two Revolutions,' 7.

72 On this point see Matthew Plowman, 'Irish Republicans and the Indo-German Conspiracy of World War I,' *New Hibernia Review*, 7, no. 3 (2003): 81–105.

73 MI6 was preceded by the Secret Service Bureau, which was created in 1909. A joint project of the Admiralty and the War Office, the Secret Service Bureau was particularly concerned with imperial Germany. See Keith Jeffrey, *MI6: The History of the Secret Intelligence Service, 1909–1949* (New York: Penguin 2010).

74 Karl Hoover, 'The Hindu Conspiracy in California, 1913–1918,' *German*

Studies Review, 8, no. 2 (1985): 245–61; Karla K. Gower, 'The Hindu-German Conspiracy: An Examination of the Coverage of Indian Nationalists in Newspapers from 1915–1918,' paper presented at the Association for Education in Journalism and Mass Communication conference, 1997, accessed at AEJMC archives, http://www.list.msu.edu/cgi-bin/wa.

75 Johnston, 'The Surveillance of Indian Nationalists,' 21–7.

76 Har Dayal, *Forty-Four Months*, 98, 101.

77 BL, APAC, IOR, L/PJ/6/1137, file 4803/1911, *Free Hindusthan*, March–April 1910.

78 BL, APAC, IOR, Mss. Eur, F161/152, *Report of the Committee Appointed to Investigate Revolutionary Conspiracies in India*, 17.

79 BL, APAC, IOR, L/PJ/6/1137, file 4803/1911, *Free Hindusthan*, March–April 1910.

3 A War on Two Fronts

1 Zaneth's career is documented in James Dubro and Robin Rowland, *Undercover: Cases of the RCMP's Most Secret Operative* (Markham, Ont: Octopus Publishing 1991), especially chapter 2. See also Library and Archives Canada (LAC), CSIS Records, RG 146, RCMP Personnel file 5743, Access to Information and Privacy Request 88HR-2533.

2 On the labour revolt, see G.S. Kealey, '1919: The Canadian Labour Revolt,' *Labour/Le Travail*, 13 (1984): 11–44; Allan Seager, 'Nineteen Nineteen: Year of Revolt,' *Journal of the West*, 23, no. 4 (1984): 40–7; and the collection of essays in Craig Heron, ed., *The Workers' Revolt in Canada, 1917–1925* (Toronto: University of Toronto Press 1998).

3 David Edward Smith, 'Emergency Government in Canada,' *Canadian Historical Review*, 50 (1969); 429–48; Roger Craig Brown, '"Whither Are We Being Shoved?" Political Leadership in Canada during World War I,' in J.L. Granatstein and R.D. Cuff, eds., *War and Society in North America* (Toronto: T. Nelson 1971), 104–19. For an excellent discussion of the implications of this act, see F. Murray Greenwood, 'The Drafting and Passage of the War Measures Act in 1914: Object Lessons in the Need for Vigilance' (Unpublished paper, University of British Columbia, 1987). Details of these and other orders-in-council can be found in Frances Swyripa and John Herd Thompson, eds., *Loyalties in Conflict: Ukrainians in Canadian during the Great War* (Edmonton: Canadian Institute of Ukrainian Studies 1985), 171–81.

4 Arthur Lower, *Colony to Nation* (Toronto: Longmans 1969), 473.

5 For details see Robert H. Coats, 'The Alien Enemy in Canada: Internment Operations,' in *Canada and the Great War: An Authoritative Account of the*

Military History of Canada from the Earliest Days to the Close of the War of Nations (Toronto: N.P. 1919), 144–61; Desmond Morton, 'Sir William Otter and Internment Operations in Canada during the First World War,' *Canadian Historical Review*, 55 (1974): 32–58; Desmond Morton, *The Canadian General: Sir William Otter* (Toronto: Hakkert 1974), 315–68; Jean Laflamme, *Les Camps de Detension du Quebec* (Montreal: N.P. 1973); Joseph A. Boudreau, 'Western Canada's Enemy Aliens of World War I,' *Alberta History*, 12, no. 1 (1964): 1–9, and 'The Enemy Alien Problem in Canada,' PhD thesis, University of California at Los Angeles, 1965. While most of these internees were released in 1916, at the same time as the Canadian economy recovered and a general labour shortage developed, the entire experience understandably embittered Canadian Ukrainians. For first-hand experiences, see Helen Potrobenko, *No Streets of Gold: A Social History of the Ukrainians in Alberta* (Vancouver: New Star Books 1977), 131–6; Watson Kirkconnell, 'Kapuskasing – An Historical Sketch,' *Queen's Quarterly*, 28 (1921): 264–78. See also Bill Waiser, *Park Prisoners: The Untold Story of Western Canada's National Parks* (Saskatoon: Fifth House Publishing 1995), especially chapter 1.

6 Ernest J. Chambers, *The Duke of Cornwall's Own Rifles: A Regimental History of the 43rd Regiment, Active Militia in Canada* (Ottawa: E.L. Ruddy 1903), 37, 44–5.

7 Ibid., 20, 29, 35, 51.

8 Ibid., 44; 'And He Who Loves God Loves His Brother Also,' *Ottawa Citizen*, 6 June 1953, 2.

9 Don MacGillivray, *Captain Alex MacLean: Jack London's Sea Wolf* (Vancouver: University of British Columbia Press 2008), 117–27. Sherwood was particularly interested in the infamous Cape Breton sealing captain Alex MacLean, whose exploits in the fishery were well known among seafarers up and down the coast.

10 The pertinent orders-in-council are: PC 2070 (6 August 1914); PC 2821 (6 November 1914); PC 1330 (10 June 1915); Consolidated Orders Respecting Censorship (17 January 1917); and PC 1241 (22 May 1918). See also LAC, RG 18, vol. 2380; Ernest J. Chambers, *Revised List of Publications the Possession of Which in Canada Is Prohibited* (Ottawa: Department of the Secretary of State 1918). The most thorough discussion of this issue can be found in Jeffrey A. Keshen, *Propaganda and Censorship during Canada's Great War* (Edmonton: University of Alberta Press 1996), especially chapters 3 to 5. See also Allan L. Steinhart, *Civil Censorship in Canada during World War I* (Toronto: Unitrade Press 1986); Herbert Karl Kalbfleisch, *The History of the Pioneer German Language Press of Ontario, 1835–1918* (Toronto: University of Toronto Press 1968), 105–6; Werner A. Bausenhart, 'The Ontario Ger-

man Language Press and Its Suppression by Order-in-Council in 1918,' *Canadian Ethnic Studies*, 4, nos. 1/2 (1972): 35–48; W. Entz, 'The Suppression of the German Language Press in September 1918,' *Canadian Ethnic Studies*, 8, no. 2 (1976): 56–70; and Arja Pilli, *The Finnish-Language Press in Canada, 1901–1939* (Turku: Institute for Migration 1982), 85–95. The general discussion in John Herd Thompson, *The Harvests of War: The Prairie West, 1914–1918* (Toronto: McClelland and Stewart 1978), 33–5, fails to take this issue seriously.

11 Of the 36,267 members of the first contingent of the Canadian Expeditionary Force, fully 42 per cent were English-born and another 22 per cent were Scottish-, Irish-, and Welsh-born. English Canadians composed 26 per cent and French Canadians about 3 per cent. See J.L. Granatstein and J.M. Hitsman, *Broken Promises: A History of Conscription in Canada* (Toronto: Oxford University Press 1977), 23. See also Thompson, *Harvests*, 12–44.

12 Borden to Walters, et al., 27 December 1916, as quoted in Granatstein and Hitsman, *Broken Promises*, 45.

13 Granatstein and Hitsman, *Broken Promises*, 51ff., and Elizabeth Armstrong, *The Crisis of Quebec, 1914–1918* (New York: Columbia University Press 1937), chapter 7.

14 Quoted in Bryan D. Palmer, *Working-Class Experience: Rethinking the History of Canadian Labour, 1800–1991* (Toronto: McClelland and Stewart 1992), 199.

15 The 1917 campaign is ably narrated by Granatstein and Hitsman, *Broken Promises*, 70–83, and Michael Bliss, *Right Honourable Men: The Descent of Canadian Politics from Macdonald to Chrétien* (Toronto: Harper Collins 2004), 63–91.

16 Trades and Labor Congress, *Proceedings*, 141–2.

17 Trades and Labor Congress, *Proceedings*; Toronto *Globe*, 20–21 September 1917.

18 Further options, of course, existed outside the law and many took these steps as well, if they were actually ordered to report. In Montreal, for example, of the first 500 conscripts, 35 per cent of the English Canadians and 56 per cent of the French Canadians failed to report. By the end of the war, almost 25,000 Canadians had succeeded in remaining 'unapprehended defaulters' under the MSA. Statistics are from Granatstein and Hitsman, *Broken Promises*, 64–96.

19 LAC, RG 24, C-5660, HQC 2358, 'Disturbances in Quebec over the Enforcement of the Military Service Act, 1918.' For a description of the dead men, see LAC, RG 24, C-5660, HQC, report by Douglas Kerr of the Dominion Police, 12 April 1918. In this report, Kerr refers to 'tough young element' and notes that 'no person of consequence' was involved in the disturbances.'

Accounts of the riots can be found in Jean Provencher, *Quebec sous la loi des Mesures de Guerre 1918* (Trois Rivières: Boréal-Express 1971); Mason Wade, *The French Canadians*, vol. 2 (Toronto: Macmillan 1968), 764–9; Armstrong, *Crisis*, 228–37.

20 On the Vancouver General Strike, see Allen Seager and David Roth, 'British Columbia and the Mining West: A Ghost of a Chance,' in Heron, ed., *Workers' Revolt*, 231–67; Paul Phillips, *No Power Greater: A Century of Labour in British Columbia* (Vancouver: Boag Foundation 1967), 67, 71–3; Working Lives Collective, *Working Lives: Vancouver, 1886–1986* (Vancouver: New Star Books 1985), 169. The life and death of Ginger Goodwin is treated in Susan Mayse, *Ginger: The Life and Death of Albert Goodwin* (Madiera Park, B.C.: Harbour Publishing 1990); for a critique of Mayse, see Mark Leier's 'Plots, Shots, and Liberal Thoughts: Conspiracy Theory and the Death of Ginger Goodwin,' *Labour/Le Travail*, 39 (spring 1997): 215–24. Also important is Roger Stonebanks, *Fighting for Dignity: The Ginger Goodwin Story* (St John's: Canadian Committee on Labour History 2004).

21 Quoted in Seager and Roth, 'British Columbia and the Mining West,' 255; Kealey, '1919: The Canadian Labour Revolt,' 15.

22 Gregory S. Kealey and Douglas Cruikshank, 'Canadian Strike Statistics, 1891–1950,' *Labour/Le Travail*, 20 (1987): 85–145, sets out the general contours of the strike wave. The final quotation is from LAC, Department of National Defence, RG 24, vol. 3985, N-S-C 1055-2-21, Secret, 'Memorandum on Revolutionary Tendencies in Western Canada,' prepared by assistant comptroller, RNWMP.

23 Gregory S. Kealey, 'State Repression of Labour and the Left in Canada, 1914–20: The Impact of the First World War,' *Canadian Historical Review*, 73, no. 3 (1992): 308.

24 Palmer, *Working-Class Experience*, 155–213.

25 Most mainstream historical writing about the internment of Ukrainians during the Great War has diverged dramatically from the discussion of Japanese internment during the Second World War, which has been universally deplored. Writing in *A Nation Transformed*, Brown and Cook argue that the Borden government actually aimed to 'safeguard the rights of aliens' against nativist hostility.' In a final rationalization, they conclude that 'the government's actions held in check the unrestrained enthusiasm of native Canadians to persecute their fellow citizens.' Not surprisingly, scholarship undertaken by Ukrainian Canadian historians have not shared this sympathetic view of the Borden government. See Ramsay Cook and Robert Craig Brown, *Canada 1896–1921: A Nation Transformed* (Toronto: McClelland and Stewart 1974), 224–7 at 226; Potrobenko, *No Streets of Gold*,

103–30; Myrna Kostash, *All of Baba's Children* (Edmonton: Hurtig Publishing 1977), 45–55; Melnycky, 'Internment of Ukrainians,' in Frances Swyripa and John Herd Thompson, eds., *Loyalties in Conflict: Ukrainians in Canada during the Great War* (Edmonton: Canadian Institute of Ukrainian Studies 1983), 1–24.

26 For the text of this order-in-council, see Swyripa and Thompson, eds., *Loyalties in Conflict*, 190–2. According to the ban, 'publication' included 'any book, newspaper, magazine, periodical, pamphlet, tract, circular, leaflet, handbill, poster or other printed material'; 'enemy language' meant 'German, Austrian, Hungarian, Bulgarian, Turkish, Roumanian, Russian, Ukrainian, Finnish, Estonian, Syrian, Croatian, Ruthenian, and Livonian.' Several radical and left-wing newspapers that were published in English but, in Chambers's opinion, espoused subversive ideas also came under intense scrutiny; these included: *Canadian Forward* (Social Democratic Party), *Western Clarion* (Socialist Party of Canada), and *Marxian Socialist* (Socialist Party of North America).

27 Kealey, 'State Repression of Labour and the Left,' 293–8.

28 For the text of PC 2384, see Swyripa and Thompson, eds., *Loyalties in Conflict*, 193–6. Under this order-in-council, illegality, in effect, became retroactive, for the order presumed 'in the absence of proof to the contrary' that the accused was a subversive if, since the outbreak of the war, he or she had 'repeatedly' attended meetings of a banned group, spoken publicly about its ideals, or distributed its literature. Additional clauses made it illegal to attend any meeting, except religious services, 'at which the proceedings or any part thereof are conducted in the language of any country with which Canada is at war or ... the languages of Russia, Ukraine, or Finland.' All such offences were punishable by fines up to $5,000 and prison sentences of not more than five years.

29 LAC, Borden Papers, MG 26, vol. 104, file Oc519, Cawdron to minister of justice, 5 March 1918.

30 LAC, Borden Papers, MG 26, vol. 104, file Oc519, Cawdron to minister of justice, 21 March 1918; Temiskaming mine managers to Frank Cochrane, 22 March 1918; R. Allen, special agent, Hollinger Consolidated Gold Mines, Timmins, Ont., to Percy Sherwood, 8 April 1918; Davis, Military Intelligence, to Mewburn, 17 April 1918; Sherwood to Acland, Department of Labour, 9 May 1918. The final quote in this paragraph is from Cawdron to minister of justice, 23 May 1918.

31 Archives of Ontario (AO), Ontario Provincial Police Papers, RG 23, E30, file 1.6, Major Joseph E. Rogers, superintendent, OPP, to F.H. Whitton, general manager, Stelco, 24 February 1919.

32　LAC, RCMP Records, RG 18, vol. 2380, W.H. Routledge to officer commanding, Regina, 16 August 1919, CIB 104, 'Bolsheveki Propaganda – List
of Parties Prosecuted in connection with.'

33　On the Mounted Police's history of policing the 'other,' see the following
essays in William N. Baker, ed., *Mounted Police and Prairie Society, 1873–
1919* (Regina: Canadian Plains Research Center 1988); R.C. McLeod, 'The
NWMP and Minority Groups,' 119–36; William M. Baker, 'The Miners and
the Mounties: The Royal North-West Mounted Police and the 1906 Lethbridge Strike,' 137–72; and Steve Hewitt, 'Malczewski's List: A Case Study
of Royal North-West Mounted Police-Immigrant Relations,' 297–306.

34　LAC, RCMP Records, RG 18, vol. 83–84/321, file G-26-22, comptroller
to commissioner, 25 July 1914; 'Memorandum, re: Secret Agents' by G.T.
Hann, 14 February 1949. See also vol. 490, file 433-15; vol. 524, file 38-17;
and Department of Justice Records, RG 13, vol. 216, file 1962/1917, deputy
minister of justice to chief commissioner, Dominion Police, 21 November
1917.

35　LAC, Borden Papers, MG 26 H, vol. 216, file RLB 1281, Perry to Borden,
11 October 1916.

36　The '80' figure is taken from Stan Horall, 'The Royal North-West Mounted
Police and Labour Unrest in Western Canada, 1919,' in William M. Baker,
ed., *Mounted Police and Prairie Society* (Regina: Canadian Plains Research
Center 1998), 309. For an in-depth examination of this era, see Steve
Hewitt, *Riding to the Rescue: The Transformation of the RCMP in Alberta and
Saskatchewan, 1914–1939* (Toronto: University of Toronto Press 2006).

37　LAC, Borden Papers, MG 26 H, vol. 218, file RLB 1374, Perry to Borden, 11
June 1917; Gwatkin [?], Memo, 19 June 1917; Perry to Borden, 23 June 1917;
Borden to Perry, 3 July 1917; Borden to Kemp, 21 January 1918; Kempt
to Borden, 26 February 1918. See also RCMP Records, RG 18, vol. 1930,
Comptroller A.A. McLean, memorandum on an increase of the force from
1,000 to 2,000 men, 10 December 1918. On the Siberian draft, see vol. 1929.

38　Vernon A.M. Kemp, *Scarlet and Stetson: The RNWMP on the Prairies* (Toronto: Ryerson Press 1964), 7–8.

39　This brief biography of Cahan is derived from the following sources: LAC,
Borden Papers, MG 26, vol. 104, file OC19, Cahan to minister of justice,
20 July 1918; Christopher Armstrong and H.V. Nelles, *Southern Exposure:
Canadian Promoters in Latin America and the Caribbean, 1896–1930* (Toronto:
University of Toronto Press, 1988), 43–4, 97–110; A.J.P. Taylor, *Beaverbrook*
(London: Hamish Hamilton 1972), 32–6; Jules Witcover, *Sabotage at Black
Tom: Imperial Germany's Secret War in America, 1914–1917* (Chapel Hill,
N.C.: Algonquin Books 1989), 194–5; *The Canadian Who's Who 1938–39*,

vol. 3 (Toronto, 1939), 103; W.S. Wallace, *Macmillan Dictionary of Canadian Biography* (Toronto: Macmillan 1963). During the R.B. Bennett administration, he served as secretary of state. Defeated in the 1940 federal election, the staunch Conservative retired from public life; he died four years later in Montreal at the age of eighty-three.

40 LAC, Borden Papers, MG 26, vol. 104, file OC519, Cahan to Borden, 11 May 1918; Borden to Cahan, 19 May 1918. On German spies in Canada, see Grant W. Grams, 'Karl Respa and German Espionage in Canada during World War One,' *Journal of Military and Strategic Studies*, 8, no. 1 (2005): 1–17.

41 This brief discussion of the APL is based on David M. Kennedy, *Over Here: The First World War and American Society* (New York: Oxford University Press 1982), 45–92; all of the quotations are taken from this source. On this subject, see also: David Montgomery, *Fall of the House of Labor: The Workplace, the State, and American Labor Activism, 1865–1925* (New York: Cambridge University Press 1987), 376; Tom Copeland, *The Centralia Tragedy of 1919: Elmer Smith and the Wobblies* (Seattle and London: University of Washington Press 1993), 27; Julian F. Jaffe, *Crusade against Radicalism: New York during the Red Scare, 1914–1924* (New York: Kennikat Press 1972), 1, 49; Robert Justin Goldstein, *Political Repression in Modern America, 1870 to the Present* (Boston: G.K. Hall and Company 1978), 110–12, 116, 140, 149, 264; Joan M. Jensen, *The Price of Vigilance* (Chicago: Rand McNally, 1968); Robert H. Wiebe, *The Search for Order, 1877–1920* (New York: Hill and Wang 1967), 298–9; Emerson Hough, *The Web: The Authorized History of the American Protective League* (Chicago: Reilly and Lee 1919).

42 LAC, Borden Papers, MG 26, vol. 104, file OC519, Cahan to minister of justice, 20 July 1918; Cahan to Borden, 27 August 1918; Borden to Cahan, 29 August 1918. See also LAC, RCMP Papers, RG 13, vol. 229, file 2471/1918, Sherwood to Cahan, 22 July 1918; Cahan to Doherty, 24 July 1918.

43 This entire paragraph is drawn from LAC, Borden Papers, MG 26, vol. 104, file OC519, Cahan to minister of justice, 14 September 1918.

44 LAC, RCMP Records, RG 18, vol. 83–84/321, file G-270-2, PC 2213, 7 October 1918. See also Greg Marquis, 'Police Unionism in Early Twentieth-Century Toronto,' *Ontario History*, 81 (1989): 109–28.

45 LAC, Department of Justice Records, RG 13, vol. 86-87/361, file 166/1919, Cahan to Doherty, 1 October 1918, and minister of justice to governor general in council, 2 October 1918.

46 LAC, Department of Justice Records, RG 13, vol. 229, file 2472/1918, Cahan to Doherty, 7 November 1918.

47 LAC, Department of Justice Records, RG 13, vol. 229, file 2472-18, Cahan to minister of justice, 7 November 1918.

48 LAC, RG 24, vol. 2543, file HQC 2051, Part 1, 'Socialistic Propaganda in Canada: Its Purposes, Results, and Remedies – Address Delivered by C.H. Cahan, K.C., before St. James Literary Society, Montreal, on December 12th, 1918.' The emphasis in the text is ours.

49 This short section is deeply in debt to the recent work by Peter Linebaugh and Marcus Rediker, *The Many-Headed Hydra: Sailors, Slaves, Commoners, and the Hidden History of the Revolutionary Atlantic* (Boston: Beacon Press 2000); see their introduction, 1–8.

50 Margaret Prang, *N.W. Rowell* (Toronto: University of Toronto Press 1975), 266–8; Horall, 'The Royal North-West Mounted Police and Labour Unrest in Western Canada,' 309–12.

51 LAC, Borden Papers, MG 26, vol. 104, file Oc519, Rowell to Doherty, 18 October 1918; Cahan to Borden, 21 October 1918; Cahan to Borden, 22 October 1918; Cahan to Doherty, 22 October 1918; Rowell to Borden, 29 October 1918.

52 LAC, Borden Papers, MG 26, vol. 104, file Oc519, Rowell to Borden, 29 October 1918.

53 LAC, Borden Papers, MG 26, vol. 245, file RLB 2848, Borden to Crerar, 4 November 1918, and Crerar, memorandum, 1 November 1918. Crerar's position throughout these debates showed his increasing discomfort at the repression of civil liberties. See Queen's University Archives, Crerar Papers, F.J. Dixon to Crerar, 12 October 1918; Crerar to Dixon, 25 October 1918; Dixon to Crerar, 9 November 1918; Crerar to Dixon, 15 November 1918; Dixon to Crerar, 3 December 1918.

54 LAC, Department of Justice Records, RG 13, vol. 86–87, file 166/1919, Cahan to Doherty, 29 October 1918; Cahan to White, 15 November 1918; Doherty to Newcombe, 15 November 1918; Doherty to Cahan, 15 November 1918; Cahan to Meighen, 18 November 1918; deputy minister of justice to undersecretary of state for external affairs, 2 January 1919; 'PC 104,' 16 January 1919.

55 On the career of the young Hoover, see Richard Gid Powers, *Secrecy and Power: The Life of J. Edgar Hoover* (New York: Free Press 1987), especially chapters 3 to 6; and Athnan G. Theoharis and John Stuart Cox, *The Boss: J. Edgar Hoover and the Great American Inquisition* (Philadelphia: Temple University Press 1988), especially chapters 2 to 4.

56 LAC, RCMP Records, RG 18, vol. 1927, file 150, A.A. McLean to Perry, 28 October 1918; Perry to A.A. McLean, 30 October 1918.

57 LAC, Borden Papers, MG 26, vol. 246, file RLB 2854, Meighen to Borden and Doherty, 3 December 1918; Borden to Meighen, 11 December 1918.

58 LAC, Borden Papers, MG 26, vol. 246, file RLB 2854, Meighen to Borden and Doherty, 3 December 1918; Borden to Meighen, 11 December 1918.

59 LAC, Borden Papers, MG 26, vol. 1930, 'PC 3076,' 12 December 1918, and memorandum of A.A. McLean, 10 December 1918; RCMP Records, RG 18, vol. 83–84/321, file G–2–6, McLean to Sherwood, 16 December 1918; Cawdron to McLean, 3 January 1919; Spalding, OC [Officer Commanding] Calgary, to Perry, 11 January 1919; Cawdron to Reid, 11 January 1919; Cawdron to McLean, 13 January 1919; Perry to McLean, 14 January 1919.

60 LAC, RCMP Records, RG 18, vol. 83–84/321, file G-2-6, Rowell to McLean, 11 January 1919.

61 LAC, RCMP Records, RG 18, vol. 83–84/321, file 2-6-1951, Perry to comptroller, 14 January 1919; comptroller to commissioner, 22 January 1919; McLean to Rowell, 14 January 1919; Perry to McLean, 14 January 1919; McLean to Perry, 22 January 1919; McLean to Cahan, 24 February 1919.

62 LAC, RCMP Records, RG 18, vol. 1003, Cahan to Newcombe, 9 January 1919; Stevens to Calder, 18 March 1919; Perry to McLean, 10 April 1919; McLean to Rowell, 15 April 1919. Also, vol. 2169, file 16/3, Perry to Lieutenant-Colonel Primrose, 20 February 1919.

63 LAC, RCMP Records, RG 18, vol. 599, file 1328, Circular Memo No. 807 and 807A, 6 January 1919.

64 LAC, RCMP Records, RG 18, vol. 2380, memorandum CIB No. 10, Routledge to OCs, 28 February 1919; Circular Memorandum CIB No. 10A, Routledge to OCs, 14 March 1919.

65 A list of the personal-history files created between 1919 and 1924 can be found in Gregory S. Kealey and Reg Whitaker, eds., *RCMP Security Bulletins: The Early Years, 1919–29* (St John's: Canadian Committee on Labour History 1992).

66 LAC, RCMP Records, RG 18, vol. 1931, OC Edmonton to Perry, 31 January 1919. For a complete list of RNWMP secret agents identified to date, see the appendix in Gregory S. Kealey, 'The Royal Canadian Mounted Police, the Canadian Security and Intelligence Service, the Public Archives of Canada, and Access to Information: A Curious Tale,' *Labour/Le Travail*, 2, no. 1 (1988): 199–226.

67 On the use of returned men as strike-breakers, see Andrew Parnaby, *Citizen Docker: Making a New Deal on the Vancouver Waterfront, 1919–1939* (Toronto: University of Toronto Press 2008).

68 LAC, RCMP Records, RG 18, vol. 1931, Horrigan to Perry, 13 March 1919.

69 This portrait of Gosden is taken from the meticulous research conducted by Mark Leier. See his 'Portrait of a Labour Spy: The Case of Robert Raglan

Gosden, 1882–1961,' *Labour/Le Travail*, 42 (fall 1998): 55–84, and *Rebel Life* (Vancouver: New Star Books 2000).

70 Leier, 'Portrait of a Labour Spy,' 55–66.

71 Ibid., 68–9.

72 Ibid., 73–5.

73 LAC, Borden Papers, vol. 104, file Oc519(A) 1, McLean to White, 12 April 1919, with enclosures: Perry to McLean, 2 April 1919; 'Notes for Commissioner's Perusal of SA No. 10 Report on the Calgary Convention'; and 'Report of SA No. 10,' 19 March 1919. Gosden's identity as Secret Agent No. 10 is confirmed in British Columbia Archives (BCA), Records of the Attorney General, GR 1323, B2300, file L-125, 'RCMP Assistant Commissioner J.W. Spalding to Officer Commanding "E" Division,' and 'S.T. Wood, Superintendent, BC District, RCMP, to Commissioner, BC Provincial Police.'

74 LAC, Borden Papers, vol. 104, file Oc519(A) 1, McLean to White, 12 April 1919, with enclosures: Perry to McLean, 2 April 1919; 'Notes for Commissioner's Perusal of SA No. 10 Report on the Calgary Convention'; and 'Report of SA No. 10,' 19 March 1919.

75 LAC, Borden Papers, vol. 104, file Oc519(A) 1, McLean to White, 12 April 1919, with enclosures: Perry to McLean, 2 April 1919; 'Notes for Commissioner's Perusal of SA No. 10 Report on the Calgary Convention'; and 'Report of SA No. 10,' 19 March 1919.

76 LAC, CSIS Records, RG 146, RCMP Personnel file 5743. See also Dubro and Rowland, *Undercover*, chapter 2.

77 Palmer, *Working-Class Experience*, 200–5.

78 Tom Mitchell, '"Repressive Measures": A.J. Andrews, the Committee of 1000, and the Campaign against Radicalism after the Winnipeg General Strike,' *left history*, 3, no. 2/4, no. 1 (1995–6): 133–67, and '"The Manufacturing of Souls of Good Quality": Winnipeg's 1919 Conference on Canadian Citizenship, English-Canadian Nationalism, and the New Order after the Great War,' *Journal of Canadian Studies*, 31, no. 4 (1996–7): 5–28.

79 'Judge Metcalfe's Charge to the Jury,' in Winnipeg Defence Committee, ed., *Saving the World from Democracy* (Winnipeg 1919), 230–69. The quotation is on page 231–2.

80 Ibid., 254.

81 LAC, CSIS Records, RG 146, RCMP Personnel file 5743; Dubro and Rowland, *Undercover*, chapter 2.

82 On these changes, see Kealey, 'State Repression of Labour and the Left'; and Barbara Roberts, '"Shovelling out the Mutinous": Political Deportation from Canada before 1936,' *Labour/Le travail*, 18 (1986): 77–110.

4 The RCMP, the Communist Party, and the Consolidation of Canada's Cold War

1 On the post-war 'return to normalcy,' see: Bryan D. Palmer, *Working-Class Experience: Rethinking the History of Canadian Labour, 1800–1991* (Toronto: McClelland and Stewart 1992), 214–19; Carolyn Strange and Tina Loo, *Making Good: Law and Moral Regulation in Canada, 1867–1939* (Toronto: University of Toronto Press 1997), 103–23; Cynthia R. Comacchio, *The Infinite Bonds of Family: Domesticity in Canada, 1850–1940* (Toronto: University of Toronto Press 1999), 65–89.

2 Palmer, *Working-Class Experience*, 226–9; John Manley, 'Does the International Labour Movement Need Salvaging? Communism, Labourism, and the Canadian Trade Unions, 1921–1928,' *Labour/Le Travail*, 41 (spring 1998): 147–80. See also Library and Archives Canada (LAC), MG 28, IV 4, vol. 48, file 48-5, 'Rules for Underground Party Work.'

3 Carl Betke and Stan Horrall, 'Canada's Security Service: An Historical Outline, 1864–1966' (Ottawa: RCMP Historical Section 1978), CSIS Access Request #117-90-107, p. 413.

4 LAC, RG 13 A2, vol. 328, file 832-1929 (Consolidated), Cortlandt Starnes to deputy minister of justice, 15 November 1922; Starnes to Sir Lomer Gouin, 'minister controlling the R.C.M. Police,' 17 July 1922; Starnes to deputy minister of justice, 28 March 1923.

5 Betke and Horrall, 'Canada's Security Service,' 231, 350; entry for Perry in Henry Morgan, *Canadian Men and Women of the Time* (Toronto: William Briggs 1912). See also: Gregory S. Kealey, 'Spymasters, Spies, and Their Subjects: The RCMP and Canadian State Repression, 1914–39,' in Gary Kinsman, Dieter Buse, and Mercedes Steedman, eds., *Whose National Security?* (Toronto: Between the Lines 2000), 18–33.

6 LAC, RG 18, vol. 3440; entry for Starnes in *Canadian Who's Who*, 1938–61.

7 *The Legionary*, March 1938; *Ottawa Journal*, 2 June 1935; *Ottawa Citizen*, 27 January 1927; Normam Hillmer and William McAndrew, 'The Cunning of Restraint: General J.H. MacBrien and the Problems of Peacetime Soldiering,' *Canadian Defence Quarterly*, 20, no. 1 (1990): 45–52; Betke and Horrall, 'Canada's Security Service,' 436–7; MacBrien entry in *Canadian Who's Who*, 1938–61.

8 Betke and Horrall, 'Canada's Security Service,' 384–7; Morgan, *Canadian Men and Women*; see also Jeffrey A. Keshen, 'All the News That Was Fit to Print: Ernest J. Chambers and Information Control in Canada, 1914–1919,' *Canadian Historical Review*, 73, no. 3 (1992): 315.

9 Betke and Horall, 'Canada's Security Service,' 390–1.

10 Charle Rivett-Carnac, *Pursuit in the Wilderness* (London: Jarrolds 1967), chapters 1 and 8.

11 This observation is indebted to: Mark Moss, *Manliness and Militarism: Educating Young Boys in Ontario for War* (Toronto: University of Toronto Press 2001), 1–35; Mike O'Brien, 'Manhood and the Militia Myth: Masculinity, Class, and Militarism in Ontario, 1902–1914,' *Labour/Le Travail*, 42 (fall 1998): 115–41; Steve Hewitt, 'The Masculine Mountie: The Royal Canadian Mounted Police as a Male Institution, 1914–1939,' *Journal of the Canadian Historical Association*, 7 (1996): 153–74; Catherine Hall, *White, Male, and Middle-Class: Explorations in Feminism and History* (New York: Polity 1992); Keith Walden, *Visions of Order: The Canadian Mounties in Symbol and Myth* (Toronto: Butterworth 1982), 27–69; Desmond Morton, 'The Cadet Movement in the Moment of Canadian Militarism,' *Journal of Canadian Studies*, 13 (1978): 56–67; James Eayrs, *In Defence of Canada: From the Great War to the Great Depression* (Toronto: University of Toronto Press 1967), 62–148.

12 LAC, RG 18, vol. 3722, file G 449-3 (part 1), '[Speech to] Chicago Convention'; Hewitt, 'The Masculine Mountie,' 160–1.

13 LAC, RG 18, vol. 3722, file G 449-3 (part 1), '[Speech to] Chicago Convention.'

14 The quotation is from LAC, RG 18, vol. 3722, file G 449-3 (part 1), '[Speech to] Chicago Convention.' As late as 1941, training contained a cavalry/military-style component and a practical police component. See Hewitt, 'Masculine Mountie,' 165; Walden, *Visions*, 27–69; and C.W. Harvison, *The Horsemen* (Toronto: McClelland and Stewart 1967). The McDonald Commission noted that the RCMP, 'through its recruiting, training, and management practices, engulfs its members in an ethos akin to that found in a monastery or religious order.' See Commission of Inquiry concerning Certain Activities of the Royal Canadian Mounted Police, *Second Report, Volume 1, Freedom and Security under the Law* (Ottawa: Minister of Supply and Services, 1981) para. 18, 102.

15 This paragraph is informed by Michael Dawson, *The Mounties: From Dime Novel to Disney* (Toronto: Between the Lines 1998), 1–49; Walden, *Visions*, 27–69; Robert Thacker, 'Canada's Mounted: The Evolution of a Legend,' *Journal of Popular Culture*, 14, no. 2 (1980): 298–312; Pierre Berton, *Hollywood's Canada: The Americanization of Our National Image* (Toronto: McClelland and Stewart 1975).

16 The 'dapper' quote is from Thacker, 'Canada's Mounted,' 307. On the connection to the British crown, see Doug Owram, *Promise of Eden: The Canadian Expansionist Movement and the Idea of the West, 1856–1900* (Toronto 1992), 140.

17 Dawson, *From Dime Novel*, 39.
18 Canada, *Report of the Royal Canadian Mounted Police for the Year Ended September 30, 1929* (Ottawa: King's Printer 1927), 5. Other complaints can be found in LAC, RG 18, vol. 3180, File G-1235-1-24.
19 Gregory S. Kealey, 'The Early Years of State Surveillance of Labour and the Left in Canada: The Institutional Framework of the Royal Canadian Mounted Police Security and Intelligence Apparatus, 1918–26,' *Intelligence and National Security*, 8, no. 3 (1993): 132–3.
20 This observation about the condition of the force in the early 1920s is based on the following: Larry Hannant, *The Infernal Machine: Investigating the Loyalty of Canada's Citizens* (Toronto: University of Toronto Press 1995), 63–9; Stephen J. Harris, *Canadian Brass: The Making of a Professional Army, 1860–1939* (Toronto: University of Toronto Press 1988), 141–91; Lorne and Caroline Brown, *An Unauthorized History of the RCMP* (Toronto: Lorimer 1973); Nora and William Kelly, *The Royal Canadian Mounted Police: A Century of History, 1873–1973* (Edmonton: Hurtig Publishers 1973); Eayrs, *In Defence of Canada*, 224–69; Vernon A.M. Kemp, *Without Fear, Favour, or Affection: Thirty-Five Years with the RCMP* (Toronto: Longmans 1958); T. Morris Longstretch, *The Silent Force: Scenes from the Life of the Mounted Police in Canada* (New York: Century Company 1927), 313–23. On the 'external' and 'internal' dimensions of this consolidation process, see Gregory S. Kealey, 'The Surveillance State: The Origins of Domestic Intelligence and Counter-Subversion in Canada, 1914–21,' *Intelligence and National Security*, 7, no. 3 (1992): 179–210, and 'The Early Years of State Surveillance,' 129–48.
21 Public Record Office (PRO), CO 42/1011/192554, especially 250–7, 455–61; CO 42/1014, secretary of state for the colonies to governor general, 26 July 1919; CO 708/7A, Register, 1919–20, especially entries for 21 May and 23 June 1919; CO 335/29, 30, and 31. These registers document clearly the regularity of information supplied by the RCMP to British intelligence; see November 1920, three reports; December 1920, four reports; January 1921, five reports; March 1921, five reports; April 1921, four reports; May 1921, six reports; June 1921, four reports; July 1921, three reports; August 1921, five reports; September 1921, five reports; October 1921, five reports; November 1921, six reports; December 1921, eight reports. LAC, RG 18, vol. 3182, file G355-1-2, Basil Thomson, Scotland House, to A.B. Perry, 31 March 1921; vol. 3182, file G-553, director of naval intelligence, Admiralty, to director of naval service, Canada, 8 March 1922, 'Comintern Circular to the Bureau of the Western European Secretariat for Propaganda, 8 December 1921.' Examples of routing through the governor general can be found throughout LAC, RG 7.

22 PRO, CO 42/1044, 192408; excerpts from this file appear in *Labour/Le Travail*, 30 (fall 1992): 169–205; LAC, MG 26, J4, vol. 63, file 419, Duke of Devonshire to Lord Byng, 5 March 1923; Office of the Under-Secretary of State for External Affairs, Canada, to F.A. McGregor, private secretary to the prime minister, 28 March 1923; Office of the Under-Secretary of State for External Affairs, 'Memorandum for the Prime Minister,' 20 March 1923.

23 LAC, RG 18, vol. 1003, Maclean to Rowell, 11 September 1919, and Rowell to Maclean, 12 September 1919.

24 'The R.C.M. Police receives information of a confidential nature ... to some extent from the United States,' C.F. Hamilton reported in the early 1920s. 'This deals largely with social unrest.' The quotation comes from LAC, RG 18, vol. 3181, file G-355-3-1925, 'Memorandum on Sources of Information [for the sub-committee on Intelligence],' likely prepared by C.F. Hamilton. On photographs and fingerprints, see Hannant, *The Infernal Machine*, 38–9, 50.

25 Betke and Horall, 'Canada's Security Service,' 405–7.

26 Kealey, 'The Early Years of State Surveillance,' 138–40.

27 Ibid.

28 Ibid.

29 LAC, RG 18, vol. 3181, file G-355-1-22, Proceedings of the Defence Committee, Tenth Meeting, 15 December 1921.

30 LAC, RG 18, vol. 3181, file G-355-3-1925, 'Memorandum for Submission to the 1st Meeting of the Intelligence Sub-Committee of the Defence Committee,' prepared by H.H. Mathews, assistant director of military intelligence, 12 January 1922. For a general history of military intelligence, see Major S.R. Elliot, *Scarlet to Green: A History of Intelligence in the Canadian Army, 1903–1963* (Toronto: Canadian Intelligence and Security Association 1981), especially 56–62; Wesley Wark, 'The Evolution of Military Intelligence in Canada,' *Armed Forces and Society*, 16 (1989): 77–98.

31 LAC, RG 18, vol. 3181, file G-355-3-1925, 'Memorandum on Sources of Information [for the Subcommittee on Intelligence],' likely prepared by C.F. Hamilton.

32 LAC, RG 18, vol. 3181, file G-355-1-22, Proceedings of the Defence Committee, Eleventh Meeting, 5 February 1922.

33 Donald Avery, *Reluctant Host: Canada's Response to Immigrant Workers, 1896–1994* (Toronto: McClelland and Stewart 1995), 82–90.

34 Barbara Roberts, '"Shovelling out the Mutinous": Political Deportation from Canada before 1936,' *Labour/Le travail*, 18 (1986): 80n.8. Commissioner Perry was disappointed by the amendments; he wanted them to go further. See ibid., 84–5n.15.

35 Stephen Hewitt, 'Old Myths Die Hard: The Transformation of the Mount-
    ed Police in Alberta and Saskatchewan, 1914–1939,' PhD, University of
    Saskatchewan, 1997, 130. According to Hannant, 'the vetting of potential
    citizens became one of the RCMP's undertakings. RCMP records show that
    in 1926 applicants for naturalization were being fingerprinted and the re-
    sults compared to the RCMP's criminal records.' See Hannant, *The Infernal
    Machine*, 69.
36 LAC, RG 18, vol. 2382, file C.I.B. 405–455, 1921–1924, Cortlandt Starnes to
    the officer commanding, RCMP Southern Saskatchewan District, 9 August
    1922.
37 Betke and Horrall, 'Canada's Security Service,' 377–9.
38 LAC, MG 27, II 19, vol. 9, file 'RCMP Report, Sept. 1920,' D.M. Ormand to
    the commissioner, 28 August 1920.
39 LAC, MG 27, II 19, vol. 9, File 'RCMP Report, Sept. 1920,' D.M. Ormand to
    the commissioner, 28 August 1920. This file also contains various clippings
    from the Ottawa *Citizen*: 'Dominion Police Claim Agreement Not Carried
    Out'; 'Royal Mounties and New Members Seem to Have Certain Troubles.'
    The RCMP's *Rules and Regulations* (Ottawa: King's Printer 1928) forbade
    rank-and-file Mounties from 'making any anonymous complaint to the
    government or the Commissioner ... [and] communicating without the
    Commissioner's authority, either directly or indirectly, to the public press
    any matter or thing touching the force.' Unionization in the force was
    banned in 1918 under a wartime order-in-council. See Hewitt, 'Old Myths,'
    51nn.64, 69.
40 Hannant, *The Infernal Machine*, 45–61.
41 LAC, RG 18, vol. 3722, file G-449-3 (part 1), '[Speech to] Chicago Conven-
    tion.'
42 LAC, RG 18, vol. 3181, file G-1346-4-24, 'Quarters for C.I.B. Staff, Vancou-
    ver, BC'; vol. 2382, file CIB 1-42, Circular Memorandum No. 40B, assistant
    commissioner to officer commanding all divisions, 1 June 1921; vol. 2381,
    file CIB 351-404, Circular Memorandum 391, A.B. Perry to officer com-
    manding Southern Saskatchewan District, 'Re: Detective Badges.'
43 LAC, RG 18, vol. 2382, file CIB 1-42, Circular Memorandum No. 40C, com-
    missioner to officers commanding, 'Mail submitted to Headquarters,' 22
    February 1922.
44 Michael Butt, 'Superintendent Duffus, Herbert Darling, and the early
    CIB: The Generation of RCMP Secret Service *Intelligence Reports* and the
    Processing of Information at the District Level, 1920–23,' unpublished
    paper presented at the 'Canada's Legal History: Past, Present, and Future'
    conference, Faculty of Law, University of Manitoba, 1997, 6–12.

45 For Ontario, see Hewitt, 'Old Myths,' 2–4. The year it was created, 'O' Division's complement stood at twenty-four. The creation of new divisions in Alberta and Saskatchewan is detailed in Hewitt, 'Old Myths.'

46 Kealey, 'The Early Years of State Surveillance in Canada.'

47 Harvison, *The Horsemen*, 14–60.

48 LAC, CSIS records, RG 146, Personal File – John Leopold, file 0333, 'Leopold – Medical Record, Medical Examination, 8 August 1921.'

49 Kealey, 'Spymasters, Spies, and Their Subjects.'

50 Ibid.

51 Kealey, 'The Surveillance State,' 205, appendix 1.

52 Gregory S. Kealey and Reg Whitaker, eds., *RCMP Security Bulletins: The Early Years, 1919–29* (St John's: Canadian Committee on Labour History 1992), 15–17, 452–651. An extended discussion of these registries can be found in Gregory S. Kealey, 'Filing and Defiling: The Organization of the State Security Archives in the Interwar Years,' in Franca Iacovetta and Wendy Mitchinson, eds., *On the Case: Explorations in Social History* (Toronto: University of Toronto Press 1998), 88–108.

53 Kealey and Whitaker, eds, *RCMP Security Bulletins: The Early Years*, 15–17, 452–651.

54 Martin Robin, *Shades of Right: Nativist and Fascist Politics in Canada, 1920–1940* (Toronto: University of Toronto Press 1992); Stanley Barrett, 'The Far Right in Canada,' in C.E.S. Franks, ed., *Dissent and the State* (Toronto: University of Toronto Press 1989), 224–46.

55 Kealey and Whitaker, eds., *RCMP Security Bulletins: The Early Years*, 296, 305–6, 335, 342, 578, 622, 624–8, 630–2, 635–48.

56 Hewitt, 'Old Myths,' 202. The quotation is from Robin, *Shades of Right*, 63.

57 See the announcement for a Klan meeting in Radville, Saskatchewan, in 1929 which is reproduced in Robin, *Shades of Right*, Preface. This paragraph draws on the general insights of: Ninette Kelley and Michael Trebilcock, *The Making of the Mosaic: A History of Canadian Immigration Policy* (Toronto: University of Toronto Press 1998), 209–15; Avery, *Reluctant Host*, 82–107 ('slag and scum' quotation); Gerald Friesen, *The Canadian Prairies: A History* (Toronto: University of Toronto Press 1987), 403–6; Steve Hewitt, 'Malczewski's List: A Case Study of Royal North-West Mounted Police-Immigrant Relations,' in William N. Baker, ed., *The Mounted Police and Prairie Society, 1873–1919* (Regina: Canadian Plains Research Center 1998), 297–306 ('large alien population' quotation).

58 The low figure is taken from Manley, 'Does the International Labour Movement Need Salvaging?' 161; the high estimate is from Palmer, *Working-Class Experience*, 227.

59 Quoted in Palmer, *Working-Class Experience*, 228–9.
60 Manley, 'Does the International Labour Movement Need Salvaging?'
   147–80.
61 On this point see Donald Avery, 'Divided Loyalties: The Ukrainian Left
   and the Canadian State,' in Lubomyr Luciuk and Stella Hryniuk, eds.,
   Canada's Ukrainians: Negotiating an Identity (Toronto: University of Toronto
   Press 1991), 271–87; J. Peter Campbell, 'The Cult of Spontaneity: Finnish-
   Canadian Bushworkers and the Industrial Workers of the World in Northern Ontario, 1919–1934,' *Labour/Le Travail*, 41 (spring 1998): 117–46.
62 Manley, 'Does the International Labour Movement Need Salvaging?'
   166–77; Palmer, *Working-Class Experience*, 221–9; Andrew Neufeld and Andrew Parnaby, *The IWA in Canada: The Life and Times of an Industrial Union*
   (Vancouver: New Star Books 2000), 28–40; David Frank, *J.B. McLachlan: A
   Biography* (Toronto: Lorimer 1999). The final quotation is from Neufeld and
   Parnaby, *The IWA in Canada*, 29–30.
63 Kealey and Whitaker, eds., *RCMP Security Bulletins: The Early Years,
   1919–1929*, 18–19.
64 For the full text of this registry, see ibid., 652–68. The role of secret agents,
   post office and customs officials, and organizations such as the Great War
   Veterans Association is detailed in LAC, RG 13 A2, vol. 328, file 832-1929
   (Consolidated), Number 1847; Number 294; Number 624; Number 1250.
65 LAC, RG 13 A2, vol. 328, file 832-1929 (Consolidated), Number 1189,
   Cortlandt Starnes, assistant commissioner, to deputy minister of justice, 1
   June 1921. It appears that Knowles first came to the attention of the force
   in 1920; see the 'Intelligence Bulletin' for 14 October 1920 in Kealey and
   Whitaker, eds., *RCMP Security Bulletins: The Early Years*, 232.
66 LAC, RG 13 A2, vol. 328, file 832-1929 (Consolidated), Number 252, Mary
   L. Bollert, National Secretary, IODE, to minister of immigration and
   colonization, 27 June 1921. 'In this period of economic stress, unrest, and
   reconstruction, good will between all classes of the community is essential and only sane measures and methods can be helpful,' a resolution
   passed at the IODE's annual convention in 1921 began. 'And whereas it
   is most undesirable that seditious or treasonable utterances ... should go
   unpunished, particularly when addressed to the foreign born who are less
   fortified by knowledge and the British spirit to resist such appeals ...' Subsequent clauses took aim at Canada's lax immigration laws, the failure of
   recent arrivals to assimilate, and the value of the Dominion government's
   crackdown on 'treasonable anti-British sentiments' during the Great War,
   all of it a prelude to a final demand that 'we request in particular that
   those responsible for the writing and publication of ... *Ukrainian Voice* be

forthwith deported.' On the IODE see also: Nancy Sheehan, 'Philosophy, Pedagogy, and Practice: The IODE and the Schools in Canada, 1900–1945,' *Historical Studies in Education*, 2, no. 2 (1990): 307–21; Lorraine Coops, '"Strength in Union": Patterns of Continuity and Change within the Sir Robert Borden Chapter (IODE), 1915–1965,' *Atlantis*, 20, no. 1 (1995): 77–86; Julie Guard, 'Women Worth Watching: Radical Housewives in Cold War Canada,' in Kinsman, Buse, and Steedman, eds., *Whose National Security?* 73–92.

67 LAC, RG 13 A2, vol. 328, file 832-1929 (Consolidated), Number 252, A.B. Perry to deputy minister of justice, 15 July 1921; Frank W. Wilson to chief of Dominion Police, 2 March 1921; deputy minister of justice to A.B. Perry, 22 March 1921.

68 Roberts, 'Shovelling out the Mutinous,' 86.

69 LAC, MG 28, IV 4, vol. 48, file 48-70, 'The King vs. Arvo Vaara,' *Canadian Railroad Employees' Monthly*, March 1929, 6.

70 Kealey and Whitaker, eds., *The RCMP Security Bulletins: The Early Years*, 36, 409, 480, 659, 661.

71 LAC, MG 28, IV 4, vol. 48, file 48-70, 'The King vs. Arvo Vaara,' 6.

72 LAC, RG 13 A2, vol. 328, file 832-1929 (Consolidated), Number unknown, 'Memorandum for the Minister of Justice,' prepared by W. Stuart Edwards, deputy Minister of Justice, 28 July 1922.

73 LAC, RG 13 A2, vol. 328, file 832-1929 (Consolidated), no. unknown, 'Memorandum for the Minister of Justice,' prepared by W. Stuart Edwards, deputy minister of justice, 28 July 1922.

74 LAC, MG 28 IV 4, vol. 48, file 48-5, 'Rules for Underground Party Work.'

75 LAC, RG 13, vol. 291, file 1429, deputy minister of immigration and colonization to E.L. Newcombe, deputy minister of justice, 7 August 1924.

76 LAC, RG 146, ATIP 117-94-003, Percy Reid, division commander, to R.S. Knight, commanding officer, BC District, RCMP, 31 May 1924.

77 LAC, RG 146, ATIP 117-94-003, A.L. Joliffe, commissioner of immigration, to commissioner, RCMP, September 1924; 'Report, re: Samuel Scarlett,' 9 September 1924; Joliffe to the commissioner, RCMP, 11 September 1924; 'Report, re: IWW Activities,' 14 September 1924; 21 September 1924; copy of resolution adopted 21 September 1924; Canada Steamship Lines to Colonel Courtlandt Starnes, 13 April 1925; 17 April 1925; 25 April 1925; 8 May 1925. Scarlett would later join the Communist Party and play a significant role in the deadly Estevan miners strike in 1931.

78 Andrée Lévesque, *Red Travellers: Jeanne Corbin and Her Comrades* (Montreal and Kingston, Ont.: McGill-Queen's University Press 2006), 10–26.

79 Kealey and Whitaker, eds., *RCMP Security Bulletins: The Early Years*, 309,

437; Joan Sangster, *Dreams of Equality: Women on the Canadian Left, 1920–1950* (Toronto: McClelland and Stewart 1989), 68; Hewitt, 'Old Myths,' 191–2.

80 On this point see Steve Hewitt, *Spying 101: The RCMP's Secret Activities at Canadian Universities, 1917–1997* (Toronto: University of Toronto Press 2002); Marcel Martel, '"They Smell Bad, Have Diseases, and Are Lazy": RCMP Officers' Reporting on Hippies in the Late 1960s,' *Canadian Historical Review* 90, no. 2 (2009): 215–45.

81 Butt, 'Superintendent Duffus, Herbert Darling, and the Early CIB,' 11.

82 'This report shows the dissension within the ranks of the Communists here, and there can be no doubt but that until one or other of the factions gain complete supremacy, the incessant bickering will hamper their work,' Duffus observed in 1922, demonstrating a clear grasp of this characteristic of party life. Quoted in Butt, 'Superintendent Duffus, Herbert Darling, and the Early CIB,' 14–15. See also Butt's 'Surveillance of Canadian Communists: A Case Study of Toronto RCMP Intelligence Networks, 1920–39,' PhD thesis, Memorial University of Newfoundland, 2003, for further analysis of repression in 'O' Division.

83 Hewitt, 'Old Myths'; Betke and Horall, 'Canada's Security Service,' 445–8; the activities of British Columbia's 'E' Division are chronicled in LAC, RG 146, Subject Files, 117-91-68.

84 By 1929, the city's Police Commission had banned any 'communist or bolshevist public meeting' that was conducted in a language other than English. This section on Draper is based on: A.E. Smith, *All My Life: An Autobiography* (Toronto: Progress Books 1949), 98–113; Michiel Horn, '"Free Speech within the Law": The Letter of the Sixty-Eight Toronto Professors, 1931,' *Ontario History*, 72, no. 1 (1980): 27–48; LAC, MG 28 IV 4, vol. 8, file 8-10, Canadian Labor Defence League to the Royal Commission Appointed to Investigate the Actions of the Police in Toronto, January 1936. Vancouver's 'Red Squad' is discussed in Greg Marquis, 'Vancouver Vice: The Police and the Negotiation of Morality, 1904–1935,' in Hamar Foster and John McLaren, eds., *Essays in the History of Canadian Law: British Columbia and the Yukon* (Toronto: University of Toronto Press and Osgoode Society 1995).

85 Paula Maurutto, 'Private Policing and Surveillance of Catholics: Anti-Communism in the Roman Catholic Archdiocese of Toronto, 1920–60,' in *Whose National Security?* 37–54.

86 For Vancouver, see Marquis, 'Vancouver Vice,' and Andrew Parnaby, 'On the Hook: Welfare Capitalism on the Vancouver Waterfront, 1919–1939,' PhD thesis, Memorial University, 2001, 356–66.

87 William Rodney, *Soldiers of the International: A History of the Communist Party of Canada, 1919–1929* (Toronto: University of Toronto Press 1968), 44–7.

88 Kealey, 'Spymasters, Spies, and their Subjects,' 22.

89 Archives of Ontario, RG 4–32, file 1927/2267, 'In the Police Court for the City of Toronto, R. v. Oscar Ryan, Trevor Maguire, Michael Buhay, John W. Esselwein, Amos T. Hill.'

90 LAC, CSIS records, RG 146, Personal File – John Leopold, file 0333, vol. 2, Leopold to 'DCI,' 16 July 1940.

91 Tom McEwen, *The Forge Glows Red: From Blacksmith to Revolutionary* (Toronto: Progress Books 1974), 120.

92 Andrew Parnaby and Gregory S. Kealey, 'How the "Reds" Got Their Man: The Communist Party Unmasks an RCMP Spy,' *Labour/Le Travail*, 40 (fall 1997): 260.

93 Laurel Sefton MacDowell, *Renegade Lawyer: The Life of J.L. Cohen* (Toronto: University of Toronto Press and Osgoode Society 2001), 32–3.

94 Parnaby and Kealey, 'How the "Reds" Got Their Man,' 253–9.

95 LAC, CSIS records, RG 146, Personal File – John Leopold, file 0333, vol. 1, Leopold to 'The Commissioner,' 15 November 1931.

96 The party sent Esselwein a formal letter of dismissal on 17 May. 'This is to inform you that the C.E.C [Central Executive Committee] at a recent meeting decided to expel you from the Party. You are aware that there have been suspicions against you for some time, but we were not in possession of any evidence,' it read. 'We now have incontrovertible evidence that you are and have been for some considerable time in the employ of a certain department of the Government. We are notifying your group secretary and the general membership and also through the columns of the Worker the labor movement at large.' The letter is reproduced in Betke and Horall, 'Canada's Security Service,' 439–40.

97 LAC, CSIS records, RG 146, Personal File – John Leopold, file 0333, Supplement 'A,' Leopold to A.B. Allard, 24 May 1928.

98 LAC, CSIS records, RG 146, Personal File – John Leopold, file 0333, Supplement 'A,' Leopold to A.B. Allard, 24 May 1928.

99 *The Worker*, 26 May 1928.

100 These statistics are taken from: Michiel Horn, Canadian Historical Association booklet, *The Great Depression of the 1930s in Canada* (Ottawa: Canadian Historical Association 1984), 3; Palmer, *Working-Class Experience*, 241; Margaret Conrad and Alvin Finkel, *History of the Canadian People*, vol. 2, 3rd ed. (Toronto: Pearson 2000), 232 (Table 11.1) and 236 (Table 11.2).

101 Quoted in James Struthers, *No Fault of Their Own: Unemployment and the*

Canadian Welfare State, 1914–1941 (Toronto: University of Toronto Press 1983), 74.

102 The strike statistic appears in E.R. Forbes and D.A. Muise, eds., *The Atlantic Provinces in Confederation* (Toronto: University of Toronto Press 1997), 245; the description of McLachlan is quoted from Frank, *J.B. McLachlan*, 161. Wallace's role in the Halifax Unemployed Council is described in LAC, CSIS Records, RG 146, vol. 1937, 'Conditions Unemployment, Halifax, NS.'

103 Hannant, *The Infernal Machine*, 63.

5 'Redder Than Ever': Political Policing during the Great Depression

1 Merrily Weisbord, *The Strangest Dream: Canadian Communists, the Spy Trials, and the Cold War* (Toronto: Lester Orpen Dennys 1983), 34–40; A.E. Smith, *All My Life: An Autobiography* (Toronto: Progress Books 1949), 130–9; Library and Archives Canada (LAC), RG 146, vol. 907, 'Case History – Tim Buck,' *Record of Proceedings: The King v. Buck, et al. (Communist Party of Canada)*, 3–9. The nine men who were arrested were: Tim Buck, Tom Ewen, John Boychuk, A.T. Hill, Malcolm Bruce, Sam Cohen (Sam Carr), Mathew Popovich, Mike Golinsky (Mike Gilmore), and Thomas Cacic.

2 On Campbell, see: British Columbia Archives (BCA), Records of the Attorney General, L-1-125-1931, 'Record – Allan Campbell,' Chief Constable's Office, 26 January 1931; Eric W. Hichens, special constable, to Chief Constable W.J. Bingham, 'Ref: Allen Campbell alias Mcewen,' 22 January 1931; Jas. L. Malcolm, Canadian government emigration agent, to director of European emigration, 17 January 1930; A.E. Skinner, division commander, to W.J. Bingham, chief of police, 21 December 1929; 'In the Supreme Court of British Columbia, Oyer and Terminus and General Gaol Delivery,' 1931. Campbell is mentioned in John Manley, '"Starve, Be Damned!": Communists and Canada's Urban Unemployed, 1929–39,' *Canadian Historical Review*, 79, no. 3 (1998): 466–91 at 468.

3 On this point, see Dennis G. Molinaro, '"A Species of Treason?": Deportation and Nation-Building in the Case of Tomo Cacic, 1931–1934,' *Canadian Historical Review*, 91, no. 1 (2010): 71.

4 Manley, '"Starve, Be Damned!"'; Andrew Parnaby, 'On the Hook: Welfare Capitalism on the Vancouver Waterfront, 1919–1939,' PhD thesis, Memorial University, 2001, 285–7; Barbara Roberts, *Whence They Came: Deportation from Canada, 1900–1935* (Ottawa: University of Ottawa Press 1988),

126–7; Michael Butt, 'RCMP "O" Division Surveillance of the Communist Party of Canada's Attempts to Mobilize Toronto Unemployed, 1929–1931,' paper presented at the annual meeting of the Canadian Historical Association, 1996; David Bright, '"The Lid Is Tight Now": Relations between the State, the Unemployed, and the Communist Party in Calgary, 1930–1935,' paper presented at the annual meeting of the Canadian Historical Association, 1996; Peter MacKinnon, 'Conspiracy and Sedition as Canadian Political Crimes,' *McGill Law Journal*, 23, no. 4 (1977): 622–43; Michiel Horn, '"Free Speech within the Law": The Letter of the Sixty-Eight Toronto Professors, 1931,' *Ontario History*, 72, no. 1 (1980): 27–48; F.R. Scott, 'Communists, Senators, and All That,' *Canadian Forum* (January 1932): 127–9; F.R. Scott, 'The Trial of the Toronto Communists,' *Queen's Quarterly*, 39, no. 3 (1932): 512–27.

5 LAC, RG 146, vol. 3322, 'C.P. of C – Radicals for Deportation,' J.W. Phillips, officer commanding Quebec District, to commissioner, 19 November 1931; 'Five Communists' Appeal Dismissed,' *Montreal Gazette*, 29 February 1932.

6 Ian McKay, ed., *For a Working-Class Culture in Canada: A Selection of Colin McKay's Writings on Sociology and Political Economy, 1897–1939* (St John's: Canadian Committee on Labour History 1996), 332.

7 Quoted in Lorne Brown, *When Freedom Was Lost* (Montreal: Black Rose Books 1987), 33.

8 Molinaro, '"A Species of Treason?"'

9 LAC, RG 146, vol. 907, 'Case History – Tim Buck,' *Record of Proceedings*, 12.

10 Ibid., 13–16; Scott, 'The Trial of the Toronto Communists,' 517. 'It is needless and endless repetition to introduce evidence now to show that their principle is to destroy the present parliamentary system,' the judge stated at one point. 'The issue is, how they propose to do it, whether by lawful or unlawful means; that is the whole inquiry.' Quoted in ibid., 520. For a different interpretation of Leopold's 'heroic' testimony, see A.E. Smith's humorous description in *All My Life*, 137.

11 This very question has been the subject of considerable scholarly debate; see, for example, John Manley, 'Canadian Communism, Revolutionary Unionism, and the "Third Period": The Workers' Unity League, 1929–35,' *Journal of the Canadian Historical Association*, 5 (1987): 167–94; Bruce Nelson, 'Unions and the Popular Front: The West Coast Waterfront in the 1930s,' *International Labor and Working-Class History*, 30 (fall 1986): 59–78.

12 Quoted in Scott, 'The Trial of the Toronto Communists,' 524.

13 LAC, RG 146, vol. 907, 'Case History – Tim Buck,' *Record of Proceedings*, 16.

14 Ibid., 24.

15 LAC, RG 146, vol. 907, 'Case History – Tim Buck,' *The King vs. Buck and Others: The Judgement of the Court of Appeal of Ontario concerning the Communist Party in Canada.*

16 Ibid., 2.

17 LAC, RG 146, 'Communist Party of Canada – Vancouver,' untitled song sheet, 11 September 1933. More conservative Canadians were not altogether comfortable with the Mounties' attack on British liberties either; see J. Butterfield, 'The Common Round,' *Vancouver Daily Province*, 28 April 1932.

18 LAC, RG 146, vol. 907, 'Case History – Tim Buck,' *Record of Proceedings*, 12.

19 LAC, RG 146, 'Communist Party of Canada – Vancouver,' S.T. Wood, superintendent commanding B.C. District, to commissioner, 13 January 1931. The letter includes a report from Detective/Constable J.A. Bourdeau describing a 'newspaper cut-out ... all punctured with pin and needle holes.'

20 Smith, *All My Life*, 146. See also LAC, MG 28 IV 4, vol. 8, file 8-10, A.E. Smith to the Royal Commission Appointed to Investigate the Actions of the Police in Toronto, January 1936.

21 The use of the Immigration Act for the purposes of political deportation sparked considerable debate among legal scholars at the time; see F.R. Scott, 'Immigration Act – False Arrest – Illegal Treatment of Arrested Person [headnote],' *Canadian Bar Review*, 1 (1936): 62–7; Maxwell Cohen, 'The Immigration Act and Limitations upon Judicial Power: Bail,' *Canadian Bar Review*, 14 (1936): 405–11; Moffatt Hancock, 'Discharge of Deportees on Habeas Corpus,' *Canadian Bar Review*, 14 (1936): 116–36. For an overview of this topic, see Shin Imai, 'Deportation in the Depression,' *Queen's Law Journal*, 7 (1981): 66–94.

22 LAC, RG 146, vol. 3322, 'C.P. of C – Radicals for Deportation,' J.H. MacBrien to officers commanding, Vancouver, Edmonton, Lethbridge, Regina, Winnipeg, 16 October 1931; MacBrien to officer commanding 'O' Division, 16 October 1931; MacBrien to A.L. Jolliffe, commissioner, Department of Immigration and Colonization, 10 November 1931; memorandum from commissioner, 1 December 1931.

23 LAC, RG 146, vol. 3322, 'C.P. of C – Radicals for Deportation,' A.L. Jolliffe to MacBrien, 3 December 1931.

24 LAC, RG 146, vol. 3322, 'C.P. of C – Radicals for Deportation,' C.F. Hamilton to V.J. LaChance, 14 November 1931.

25 The 'synchronize' quotation is from LAC, RG 146, vol. 3322, 'C.P. of C – Radicals for Deportation,' commissioner of immigration and colonization to commissioner, RCMP, 3 December 1931.

26 LAC, RG 146, vol. 3322, 'C.P. of C – Radicals for Deportation,' memoran-

dum prepared by MacBrien, 'Deportation of Members of the Communist Party,' 1 December 1931.

27 For preparations in the various districts, see LAC, RG 146, vol. 3322, 'C.P. of C – Radicals for Deportation,' R. Field, commanding Manitoba District, to Commissioner MacBrien, 22 December 1931; S.T. Wood to MacBrien, 28 December 1931; officer commanding Alberta to MacBrien, 30 December 1931. The final quotation is from J.H. MacBrien to commissioner of immigration, 26 February 1932.

28 LAC, RG 146, vol. 3322, 'CP – Radicals for Deportation,' MacBrien to officers commanding, Vancouver, Winnipeg, Edmonton, Toronto, and Montreal, 19 April 1932; G.L. Jennings to officer commanding, 27 April 1932; *Vancouver Province*, 26 April 1932.

29 LAC, RG 146, 'Communist Party of Canada – Vancouver,' S.T. Wood to Commissioner MacBrien, 5 May 1932.

30 This paragraph is based on the following: LAC, RG 146, vol. 3322, 'CPC – Radicals for Deportation,' R. Field, assistant commissioner, commanding Manitoba District, to Commissioner MacBrien, 3 May 1932; 'File No. 175P/2783,' Dan Chomicki or Dan Chomicky; R. Field to Commissioner MacBrien, 22 October 1931, 'Communist Party of Canada re: Deportations'; *Winnipeg Free Press*, 7 May 1932; *Toronto Star*, 7 May 1932.

31 LAC, RG 146, vol. 3322, 'CPC – Radicals for Deportation,' G.L. Jennings to officer commanding 'H' Division, 30 April 1932.

32 *Toronto Star*, 5 May 1932; *Mail and Empire*, 6 May 1932.

33 Quoted in Imai, 'Deportation in the Depression,' 80–1.

34 *Vancouver Sun*, 18 May 1932.

35 Imai, 'Deportation in the Depression,' 82.

36 Quoted in Lorne Brown and Caroline Brown, *Unauthorized History of the RCMP* (Toronto: Lorimer 1973), 63.

37 LAC, RG 146, vol. 3322, 'CPC – Radicals for Deportation,' J. Leopold to officer commanding 'H' Division, 17 May 1932; Leopold to officer commanding 'H' Division, 19 May 1932; 'Memorandum to the Director, CIB, Ottawa,' 30 May 1932; C.D. LaNauze, officer commanding 'H' Division, to Commissioner MacBrien, 1 June 1932; 'Decision of the Honourable Mr. Justice Carroll in the Supreme Court (Halifax 27-5-32).' The detail about Leopold and Holmes is from *Toronto Star*, 7 May 1932.

38 LAC, RG 146, vol. 3322, 'CPC – Radicals for Deportation, Summary of Supreme Court Decision "re: Immigration Act,"' prepared by V.J. LaChance, chief, Bureau of Records, 15 October 1932; Imai, 'Deportation in the Depression,' 84; Ninette Kelley and Michael Trebilcock, *The Making of the Mosaic: A History of Canadian Immigration Policy* (Toronto: University

of Toronto Press 1998), 243–4. One of the deportees, Hans Kist, an activist among the unemployed in Vancouver, appears to have died in a Nazi death camp several years later. See Roberts, *Whence They Came*, 140–6. Despite the deportations, local law-enforcement agencies were still frustrated by the federal government's 'lack of enthusiasm' for political deportations. Writing to the attorney general of British Columbia, the chief of the British Columbia Provincial Police argued that 'our own Immigration officials seem to look upon themselves as semi-judicial ... This attitude is all wrong, and more successful work would undoubtedly be accomplished if the Immigration officials themselves took a more aggressive attitude in picking up and questioning all persons suspected of agitating tendencies.' See BCA, GR 1323, file 1-125-1933, J.H. McMullin, commissioner, BCPP, to attorney general, 23 December 1932. The attorney general passed these sentiments along to H.H. Stevens, member of Parliament for Vancouver and minister of trade and commerce in the Bennett government.

39 LAC, RG 146, vol. 3322, 'CPC Radicals for Deportation,' G.L. Jennings, commanding 'O' Division, to commissioner, 5 December 1931. According to Jennings: 'I am afraid it is going to be a long and difficult matter to get this information, as we have no one here who can talk their language or otherwise converse with these parties in such a way as to not create suspicion as to the object of the conversation.'

40 On MacBrien and 'O' Division, see Butt, 'RCMP "O" Division Surveillance,' 1–28; Gregory S. Kealey, 'Introduction,' in Gregory S. Kealey and Reg Whitaker, eds., *RCMP Security Bulletins: The Depression Years, Part 1* (St John's: Canadian Committee on Labour History 1993), 12. On efforts taken by the party to fend off infiltration, see, for example, LAC, RG 146, vol. 3322, 'CPC Radicals for Deportation,' officer commanding Southern Alberta District, to commissioner, 18 December 1931; S.T. Wood, superintendent commanding B.C. District, to commissioner, 28 December 1931.

41 Larry Hannant, *The Infernal Machine: Investigating the Loyalty of Canada's Citizens* (Toronto: University of Toronto Press 1995), 64, 71, and 76.

42 Carl Betke and Stan Horrall, 'Canada's Security Service: An Historical Outline, 1864–1966' (Ottawa: RCMP Historical Section 1978), CSIS Access Request #117-90-107, p. 394.

43 Kealey and Whitaker, eds., *RCMP Security Bulletins: The Depression Years, Part 1*, 14–15.

44 Quoted in David Bright, 'Street-Fighting Men (and Women): Clashes between the State and the Unemployed in Calgary, 1930–35,' unpublished paper, 15.

45 This paragraph is based on Kealey, 'Introduction,' in Kealey and Whitaker,

eds., *RCMP Security Bulletins: The Depression Years, Part 1*, 15; J. Petryshyn, 'Class Conflict and Civil Liberties: The Origins and Activities of the Canadian Labour Defense League, 1925–1940,' *Labour/Le Travail*, 10 (autumn 1982): 39–63; Tom Mitchell, 'From Social Gospel to the "Plain Bread of Leninism": A.E. Smith's Journey to the Left in the Epoch of Reaction after World War I,' *Labour/Le Travail*, 33 (1993): 125–51; John Manley, '"Audacity, Audacity, Still More Audacity": Tim Buck, the Party, and the People, 1932–1939,' *Labour/Le Travail*, 49 (spring 2002): 9–42; Bright, 'Street-Fighting Men (and Women),' 15.

46 Archives of Ontario (AO), Records of the Attorney General, RG 22, Series D-1-1, file 3188 (1931), 'Resolutions of the Enlarged Plenum of Communist Party of Canada, February 1931,' 13.

47 John Manley, '"Starve, Be Damned!"'

48 LAC, RG 146, vol. 1937, 'Conditions Unemployment, Halifax, NS,' leaflet, 'Camp Workers. Attention,' 1935.

49 LAC, MG 28 IV 4, vol. 52, file 74, Drayton to Tom Ewan, 30 June 1930.

50 John Manley, 'Canadian Communists, Revolutionary Unionism, and the "Third Period"': John Manley, 'Introduction,' in Gregory S. Kealey and Reg Whitaker, eds., *RCMP Security Bulletins: The Depression Years, Part II, 1935* (St John's: Canadian Committee on Labour History 1995), 9–20. See also Gordon Hak, 'Red Wages: Communists and the 1934 Vancouver Island Loggers Strike,' *Pacific Northwest Quarterly*, 80 (July 1989): 82–90.

51 Weisbord, *The Strangest Dream*, 79–96; Bonita Bray, 'The Weapon of Culture: Working-Class Resistance and Progressive Theatre in Vancouver, 1930–38,' MA thesis, University of Victoria, 1990; James Doyle, 'Red Letters: Notes toward a Literary History of Canadian Communism,' *Essays on Canadian Writing*, 55 (spring 1995): 22–39; Dorothy Livesay, *Right Hand Left Hand* (Erin, Ont.: Press Porcepic 1977), 69.

52 John Manley, 'Introduction: From United Front to Popular Front: The CPC in 1936,' in Gregory S. Kealey and Reg Whitaker, eds., *RCMP Security Bulletins: The Depression Years, Part III, 1936* (St John's: Canadian Committee on Labour History 1996), 1; Butt, 'RCMP "O" Division Surveillance'; the final quotation is from Paul Axelrod, 'Spying on the Young in Depression and War: Students, Youth Groups, and the RCMP, 1935–1942,' *Labour/Le Travail*, 35 (spring 1995): 43–63.

53 Steve Hewitt, *Spying 101: The RCMP's Secret Activities at Canadian Universities, 1917–1997* (Toronto: University of Toronto Press 2002), 49.

54 Reporting to the Communist International in 1932, the central executive committee of the party boasted that a 'very wide movement' of 'leftist attitude' was taking hold in British Columbia.' See LAC, Comintern Fonds,

file 176, 'Comrade Morgan to the Anglo-American Secretariat, Report on the Canadian Question – 7/3/32'; Manley, '"Starve, Be Damned!"' 4; Parnaby, 'On the Hook,' 252–309; Jeanne Myers, 'Class and Community in the Fraser Mills Strike, 1931,' in Rennie Warburton and David Coburn, eds., *Workers, Capital, and the State in British Columbia: Selected Papers* (Vancouver: UBC Press 1988), 141–60; Gordon Hak, '"Line Up or Roll Up": The Lumber Workers Industrial Union in the Prince George District,' *BC Studies*, 86 (summer 1990): 57–74; Andrew Neufeld and Andrew Parnaby, *The IWA in Canada: The Life and Times of an Industrial Union* (Vancouver 2000), 38–47.

55 The general assessment of the party is drawn from LAC, RG 146, 'CPC – Vancouver,' report, 'Re: Communist Party of Canada,' 1 January 1931; 10 January 1930 ('creaky'); 31 March 1930; 23 September 1930; 12 May 1930; 7 July 1930; Newson to commissioner of RCMP, 10 February 1930. Mead's assessment is recounted in BCA, GR 1323, file L-125-1, J. Shirran, acting officer commanding 'E' Division, to assistant superintendent, British Columbia Provincial Police, 15 November 1930. In this letter, Shirran also notes that 'the RCMP keep in touch with all the principals in connection with this party, who are reasonably known to Insp. Mead, and each meeting of consequence is covered by an agent of the Dominion government.' Newson's remark appears in BCA, GR 1323, file L-125-1-1931, Newson to commissioner, British Columbia Provincial Police, 28 January 1931. See also Mead's 'Communism in Canada,' *RCMP Quarterly*, 3, no. 1 (1935): 45.

56 LAC, RG 146, 'CPC – Vancouver,' Newson to Commissioner MacBrien, 26 May 1931; 3 August 1932; 7 August 1931; report, 'Re: Communist Party of Canada,' by J.G. Yendell, 8 September 1931; S.T. Wood to commissioner, 10 October 1931; MacBrien to officer commanding, Vancouver, 23 October 1931; MacBrien to officer commanding, Vancouver, 15 [?] April 1932; BCA, GR 1323, file L-125-1, H.M. Newson to R.H. Pooley, attorney general, 7 August 1931; S.T. Wood, to attorney general, 13 November 1931.

57 Betke and Horrall, 'Canada's Security Service,' 395–6.

58 LAC, RG 146, 'CPC – Vancouver,' Report, 'Re: Communist Party of Canada,' 4 September 1930; 27 February 1932; Wood to MacBrien, 3 November 1931; 19 November 1931; 22 January 1932; 30 April 1932; Michael Lonardo, 'Under a Watchful Eye: A Case Study of Police Surveillance during the 1930s,' *Labour/Le Travail*, 35 (spring 1995): 11–41.

59 Parnaby, 'On the Hook,' 334–8; Raymond Frogner, '"Within the Sound of the Drum": Currents of Anti-Militarism in the BC Working Class in the 1930s,' MA thesis, University of Victoria, 1991, chapter 2.

60 Lonardo, 'Under a Watchful Eye,' 11–19. On the communication between the RCMP and the Canadian Legion, see also LAC, RG 146, 'CPC – Vancouver,' Canadian Legion of the British Empire Service League to commissioner, RCMP, 8 September 1933. Veterans registered their dissent in the 1930s in a variety of ways; compare Lara Campbell's, '"We Who Have Wallowed in the Mud of Flanders": First World War Veterans, Unemployment, and the Development of Social Welfare in Canada, 1929–1939,' *Journal of the Canadian Historical Association*, 11 (2000): 125–49, with Michael Kevin Dooley's, '"Our Mickey": The Story of Private James O'Rourke, VC.MM (CEF), 1879–1957,' *Labour/Le Travail*, 47 (spring 2001): 171–84.

61 As one WESL leaflet stated: 'Ex-servicemen! Your comrades who served with you and are now working on the Waterfront ... are being held back from exercising the democratic right they fought for, for the right to have a voice in the administration of the conditions under which they must work.' See Parnaby, 'On the Hook,' 333–6.

62 On the sharing of intelligence, see: BCA, GR 429, box 21, file 2, W.C.D. Crombie, labour manager, Shipping Federation of British Columbia, to G.M. Sloan, attorney general, British Columbia, 20 September 1934; box 21, file 4, J.W. Phillips, assistant commissioner, commanding 'E' Division, to G.G. McGeer, mayor of Vancouver, 11 June 1935.

63 LAC, RG 146, 'CPC – Vancouver,' Report, 'Re: Communist Party of Canada,' 3 August 1933.

64 Parnaby, 'On the Hook,' 252–383.

65 LAC, RG 146, 'CPC – Vancouver,' H.M. Newson to commissioner, RCMP, 7 August 1931.

66 Quoted in Lonardo, 'Under a Watchful Eye,' 20.

67 Quoted in Brown, *When Freedom Was Lost*, 105.

68 Quoted in Ronald Liversedge, *Recollections of the On-to Ottawa Trek* (Toronto: McClelland and Stewart 1973), xvi.

69 Lonardo, 'Under a Watchful Eye,' 20–2.

70 Ibid., 23. The evidence on this final point is contradictory. According to Betke and Horrall, 'Canada's Security Service,' 448, Constable Graham accompanied the trekkers when they left Vancouver. Trek participant Ronald Liversedge makes a similar claim, writing in his *Recollections* that 'on the train with us was an RCMP constable, an undercover man, a member of the Relief Camp Workers' Union. This man had been with us since the relief camp days, was a member of my division (three) and went through the strike with us, and was never exposed. It came as a big surprise when this man stood in his uniform in the court in Regina, after the Dominion Day police riot, giving evidence against the arrested camp workers' (86). At the

Regina Riot inquiry, however, Graham stated that he did not accompany the strikers the entire way; moreover, S.T. Wood testified that the Mounties were 'handicapped' by lack of intelligence after the strikers left Vancouver. On this final point, see Lonardo, 'Under a Watchful Eye,' 23.

71 This paragraph is based on Lonardo, 'Under a Watchful Eye,' 24–5.

72 MacBrien to Wood, 11 June 1935, quoted in Liversedge, *Recollections*, 78; S.R. Hewitt, '"We Are Sitting at the Edge of a Volcano": Winnipeg during the On-to-Ottawa Trek,' *Prairie Forum*, 19, no. 1 (spring 1994): 51–64.

73 Steve Hewitt, *Riding to the Rescue: The Transformation of the RCMP in Alberta and Saskatchewan, 1914–1939* (Toronto: University of Toronto Press 2008), 125.

74 Ibid., 125–30.

75 Liversedge, *Recollections*, 210.

76 Ibid., 210–16.

77 Ibid., 216.

78 Ibid., 115.

79 Lonardo, 'Under a Watchful Eye'; Hewitt, *Riding to the Rescue*, 126–7.

80 In May 1938 about 1,200 protestors, some of them veterans of the On-to-Ottawa Trek, occupied the Vancouver Art Gallery, the Georgia Hotel, and the main post office. The demonstration ended in late June after city, provincial, and federal police attacked the men with tear-gas and batons, a move that prompted about 20,000 people to attend a rally in support of the unemployed. See Patricia Wejr and Howie Smith, eds., *Fighting for Labour: Four Decades of Work in British Columbia, 1910–1950* (Victoria: Provincial Archives of British Columbia 1978), 41–60.

81 Kealey and Whitaker, eds., *RCMP Security Bulletins: The Depression Years, Part III, 1936*, 15; Gregory S. Kealey and Reg Whitaker, eds., *RCMP Security Bulletins: The Depression Years, Part IV, 1937* (St John's: Canadian Committee on Labour History 1997), 1, 10–19. A good case study can be found in Parnaby, '"What's Law Got to Do With It?": The IWA and the Politics of State Power in British Columbia, 1935–1939,' *Labour/Le Travail*, 44 (1999): 9–44.

82 Victor Howard, *The Mackenzie-Papineau Battalion: The Canadian Contingent in the Spanish Civil War* (Ottawa: Carleton University Press 1986); Mark Zuehlke, *The Gallant Cause: Canadians in the Spanish Civil War, 1936–1939* (Vancouver: Whitecap Books 1996); D.P. Stephens, *A Memoir of the Spanish Civil War* (St John's: Canadian Committee on Labour History 2000); Lawrin Armstrong and Mark Leier, 'Canadians in the Spanish Civil War, 1936–1938,' *Beaver*, October–November 1997, 19–26; Myron Momryk, 'Hungarian Volunteers from Canada in the Spanish Civil War, 1936–1939,' *Hun-*

garian Studies Review, 24, nos. 1–2 (1997): 3–13; Martin Lobigs, 'Canadian Response to the MacKenzie-Papineau Battalion, 1936 to 1939,' MA thesis, University of New Brunswick, 1992; Kirk Niergarth, 'Waking up from the "Thirties Dream": A Critical Analysis of Left Wing Canada's Response to the Spanish Civil War,' Honours BA thesis, Queen's University, 2000.

83 In *Renegades: Canadians and the Spanish Civil War* (Vancouver: University of British Columbia Press 2008), 48, Michael Petrou states that 80 per cent of the Canadian volunteers were recent immigrants.

84 This paragraph draws on the following: LAC, MG 27 III, B10, vol. 22, file 70, 'P.C. 1915,' 6 August 1937; O.D. Skelton to Ernest Lapointe, 20 February 1937; Howard, *The Mackenzie-Papineau Battalion*, 11–13; T.E. Frohn-Nielson, 'Canada's Foreign Enlistment Act: Mackenzie King's Expedient Response to the Spanish Civil War,' MA thesis, University of British Columbia, 1982. The final quote appears in Niergarth, 'Waking,' 59; see also LAC, RG 146, ATIP 87-A-6, O.D. Skelton to Commissioner MacBrien, 27 January 1937; MacBrien to Lapointe, 1 September 1937.

85 LAC, RG 146, ATIP 87-A-6, G.L. Jennings, deputy commissioner, to Ernest Lapointe, 20 January 1937; Jennings to undersecretary of state for external affairs, 22 January 1937; 1 February 1937.

86 Quoted in Lonardo, 'Under a Watchful Eye,' 36–7. By early February 1937, Commissioner MacBrien was bragging that 'our latest information is ... that very few, if any, of those applying from Winnipeg have received their passports due to the fact that the Department of External Affairs has been requesting further information from the applicants regarding their qualifications in so far as issuance is concerned.' See LAC, RG 146, ATIP 87-A-6, MacBrien to Lapointe, 2 February 1937.

87 Petrou, *Renegades*, 170.

88 LAC, RG 146, ATIP 87-A-6, MacBrien to Lapointe, 1 September 1937; Lapointe to MacBrien, 15 September 1937; MacBrien to Lapointe, 26 November 1937; W. Stuart Edwards, deputy minister, to MacBrien, 16 December 1937; Blais and Campbell, Barristers and Solicitors, to W. Stuart Edwards, 20 January 1938; Wood to Lapointe, 11 February 1938; Wood to Lapointe, 23 March 1938; Wood to Lapointe, 29 March 1938; Petrou, *Renegades*, 172–3.

89 This paragraph is derived from: LAC, RG 146, ATIP 87-A-6, S.T. Wood to director, Immigration Branch, 2 November 1938; Wood to O.D. Skelton, 1 December 1938; Wood to Skelton, 20 April 1938; Wood to passport officer, 28 January 1938; MacBrien to Lapointe, 25 August 1937; Lapointe to MacBrien, 13 September 1937.

90 In Vancouver, where labour and the left were especially active, anti-Com-

munist propaganda from employers was pervasive. See examples in City of Vancouver Archives (CVA), Shipping Federation of British Columbia Papers, Add. Mss 279, box 67, file 11, typescript of pamphlet 'The Workers Unity League: Agents of Revolution'; University of British Columbia – Special Collections, John Stanton Papers, box 10, file 1, 'Communism in British Columbia'; LAC, Department of Labour, RG 27, Strike and Lockout Files, vol. 369, Strike 87A, copies of various newspaper ads created by the Citizens League.

91 See C.M. Coates, ed., *Imperial Canada, 1867–1917* (Edinburgh: University of Edinburgh Press 1995).

92 The quotation appears is from Liversedge, *Recollections*, 263. Our thinking about this issue was influenced by numerous articles in Christopher Dummit and Michael Dawson, eds., *Contesting Clio's Craft: New Directions and Debates in Canadian History* (London: Institute for the Study of the Americas 2009).

93 On this point, see Jose E. Igartua, *The Other Quiet Revolution: National Identities in English Canada, 1945–71* (Vancouver: University of British Columbia Press 2006).

6 Keep the Home Fires Burning, 1939–45

1 LAC, Ernest Lapointe Papers, vol. 50, f.50, S.T. Wood to Ernest Lapointe, 25 August 1939.

2 CSIS Files, Inspector C.E. Rivett-Carnac to the commissioner, 'Re: Annual Report – Intelligence and Liaison Section,' 22 April 1939; Carl Betke and S.W. Horrall, 'Canada's Security Service: An Historical Outline, 1864–1966' (Ottawa: RCMP Historical Section 1978), CSIS Access Request #117-90-107, 481–2. The *Annual Reports* of the section, part of an internal process that eventually resulted in a public document, have been obtained for the war years under the Access to Information Act (CSIS Access # 117-91-11), with surprisingly few deletions.

3 This contest is the subject of Daniel Robinson, 'Planning for the "Most Serious Contingency": Alien Internment, Arbitrary Detention, and the Canadian State, 1938–39,' *Journal of Canadian Studies*, 28, no. 2 (1993): 5–20, on which our account is based.

4 Wood to Lapointe, 16 May 1939, quoted in Robinson, 'Planning,' 12.

5 Betke and Horrall, 'Canada's Security Service,' 480.

6 Ibid., 480–1.

7 Ibid., 479–80.

8 Ibid., 491–2.

9 Ibid., 512–17.

10 Ibid., 517–19.

11 Larry Hannant, *The Infernal Machine: Investigating the Loyalty of Canada's Citizens* (Toronto: University of Toronto Press 1995), 103.

12 David Stafford, 'The American-British-Canadian Triangle: British Security Co-ordination 1940–1945.' Paper presented to the International Studies Association Conference, London, March 1989, 33.

13 Hannant, *Infernal Machine*, 101.

14 For instance, an issue of the RCMP *Intelligence Bulletin* in 1945 contains a cautionary item about how a Nova Scotia company had tried unsuccessfully (because it had failed to follow proper channels) to use the Mounties against strikers. Gregory S. Kealey and Reg Whitaker, eds., *RCMP Security Bulletins: The War Series, Part II, 1942–45* (St John's: Canadian Committee on Labour History 1993), 407–8.

15 John Bryden, *Best-Kept Secret: Canadian Secret Intelligence in the Second World War* (Toronto: Lester Publishing 1993).

16 C. Masterman, *The Double Cross System* (New Haven, Conn.: Yale University Press 1973), xii. This classic book was initially a secret report by one of the practitioners completed just at the end of the war, and was finally made public some thirty years later. See also F.H. Hinsley and C.A.G. Simkins, *British Intelligence in the Second War*, vol. 4, *Security and Counter-Intelligence* (London: HMSO 1990); and Michael Howard, *Strategic Deception in the Second World War* (London: Pimlico 1992).

17 C.W. Harvison, *The Horsemen* (Toronto: McClelland and Stewart 1967), 119–20.

18 J.L. Granatstein and David Stafford, *Spy Wars: Espionage and Canada from Gouzenko to Glasnost* (Toronto: Key Porter Books 1990), 26–8.

19 Dean Beeby, *Cargo of Lies: the True Story of a Nazi Double Agent in Canada* (Toronto: University of Toronto Press 1996).

20 Ibid., 189.

21 Hinsley and Simkins, *Security*, 228. The RCMP's own correspondence regarding Moonbeam seems to have convinced the RCMP historians that he actually existed: Betke and Horrall, 'Canada's Security Service,' 568n.28.

22 The fullest account of the Kobbé affair is in Graeme S. Mount, *Canada's Enemies: Spies and Spying in the Peaceable Kingdom* (Toronto: Dundurn Press 1993), 91–105.

23 LAC, W.L.M. King Papers, Correspondence, vol. 272, p. 187002, N.A. Robertson to Mackenzie King, 3 November 1943.

24 Ibid., p. 187010, T.A. Stone, 22 January 1944.

25 Bruno Ramirez, 'Ethnicity on Trial: The Italians of Montreal and the

Second World War,' in Norman Hillmer, B. Kordan, and L. Luciuk, eds., *On Guard for Thee: War, Ethnicity, and the Canadian State, 1939–1945* (Ottawa: Canadian Committee for the History of the Second World War 1988), 71–84.

26 Robert H. Keyserlingk, '"Agents within the Gates": The Search for Nazi Subversives in Canada during World War II,' *Canadian Historical Review*, 66, no. 2 (1985): 212–39; and 'Breaking the Nazi Plot: Canadian Government Attitudes toward German Canadians, 1939–1945,' in Hillmer et al., eds., *On Guard for Thee*, 53–7.

27 William Kaplan, *State and Salvation: The Jehovah's Witnesses and Their Fight for Civil Rights* (Toronto: University of Toronto Press 1989); William and Kathleen M. Repke, *Dangerous Patriots: Canada's Unknown Prisoners of War* (Vancouver: New Star Books 1982); Reg Whitaker, 'Official Repression of Communism during World War II,' *Labour/Le Travail*, 17 (spring 1986): 135–66.

28 Betke and Horrall, 'Canada's Security Service,' 484.

29 PC 2363, 4 June 1940; Kaplan, *State and Salvation*, 49–50.

30 Caution and moderation with regard to the 'enemy alien' minorities is quite evident in the annual wartime reports of the security service. During the height of the fifth-column scare in 1940, RCMP headquarters was flooded with denunciations by Canadians of German-origin neighbours, including a list of 'traitors' submitted by the Chamber of commerce. The Mounties handled these complaints with what can best be described as weary forbearance: those checked out invariably proved unfounded. See the papers of the House of Commons Committee for the Defence of Canada Regulations, Office of the Clerk of the House of Commons, Ottawa.

31 Kealey and Whitaker, eds., *RCMP Security Bulletins: The War Series, Part II*, 1 March 1943, 64–6; and Introduction, 22.

32 On the ULFTA, see Whitaker, 'Official Repression of Communism.' The ULFTA's complaint that their property and halls had in some cases been sold by the custodian of alien enemy property to their 'bitter political enemies,' the Ukrainian National Organization (a complaint echoed by a number of respectable civil libertarians in mainstream Canadian society), was dismissed by the RCMP in its internal *Intelligence Bulletin* in the following extraordinary fashion: 'The psychological effect upon the ... membership through loss of their halls to its [*sic*] opposition helps to keep alive the enthusiasm in their organization and produces a state of exuberance [!] so necessary to back their demands to the Government.' Kealey and Whitaker, eds., *RCMP Security Bulletins: The War Series, Part II*, 1 March 1943, 56.

33 Kaplan, *State and Salvation*, 69, 77–80, 93–5, 103; Intelligence Section, *Annual Report*, 1941, 30 July.

34 Intelligence Section, *Annual Report*, 1942, 14 April.

35 J.L. Granatstein, *A Man of Influence: Norman A. Robertson and Canadian Statecraft, 1929–68* (Ottawa: Deneau 1981), 81–90. A. Grenke, 'From Dreams of the Worker State to Fighting Hitler: The German-Canadian Left from the Depression to the End of World War II,' *Labour/Le Travail*, 35 (spring 1995), points out that Robertson's advice overrode the RCMP's intention to intern left-wing German Canadians on the basis of information that they were anti-Nazi and pro-war, despite the Hitler-Stalin pact (94).

36 RCMP, Ottawa headquarters, 'The Organization and Activities of the Italian Fascist Party in Canada,' 20 November 1937.

37 CSIS, Access Request 87-A-130, V.A.M. Kemp, superintendent O Division, to the commissioner, 15 May 1940.

38 Michelle McBride, 'From Internment to Indifference: An Examination of RCMP response to Fascism and Nazism in Canada from 1934 to 1941,' MA thesis, Memorial University, 1997, 170. Some informants, she reports, were secret agents, others vindictive neighbours, while others were simply trying to be good Canadian citizens.

39 Quoted in ibid., 169.

40 In 2010 an Italian Canadian pressure group managed to gain the assent of the House of Commons to a private member's bill calling for a formal apology for the internment of Italian Canadians during the Second World War and requiring a 'commemoration and education fund' worth $2.5 million: Canadian Press, 'MPs vote for Apology to Italian-Canadians, but Tories Opposed,' 28 April 2010. For the contrary view that the Italian Canadian internments were targeted specifically at pro-Fascists, see Franca Iacovetta, Roberto Perin, and Angelo Principe, eds., *Enemies Within: Italian and Other Internees in Canada and Abroad* (Toronto: University of Toronto Press 2000); and in the same volume, Reg Whitaker and Gregory S. Kealey, 'A War on Ethnicity? The RCMP and Internment,' 128–47, and Franca Iacovetta and Robert Ventresca, 'Redress, Collective Memory, and the Politics of History,' 379–412.

41 Keyserlingk, '"Agents within the Gates."'

42 At most, 847 pro-Germans were interned (out of a potential population base of more than a half-million), with most released by late 1944 or early 1945 – in striking contrast to the 9,000 some persons of German and Austro-Hungarian origin interned during the First World War. The total numbers of Italian internees peaked at 632, with most released by the end of 1943. Adding in Communists and Canadian Nazis, the total number

of internees appears to have reached just over 1,200 in 1940. This total excludes the 'relocated' Japanese population of British Columbia, and also the refugees from Hitler's Germany, many of them Jewish, sent from Britain to Canada and kept in confinement for much of the war.

43 S.T. Wood wrote that 'many may be surprised to hear that it is not the Nazi nor the Fascist but the radical who constitutes our most troublesome problem. Whereas the enemy alien is usually recognizable and easily rendered innocuous by clear-cut laws applicable to his case, your "Red" has the protection of citizenship, his foreign master is not officially an enemy and, unless he blunders into the open and provides proof of his guilt, he is much more difficult to suppress ... Most of his work is carried on under cover of other organizations and associations pretending to be, or in reality, loyal to the Constitution.' Wood cites, as examples of such witting or unwitting fronts: labour unions, groups of the unemployed, the 'criminal and weakminded classes,' youth clubs, civil liberties associations, dupes in the press who criticized government policies, and even 'a few parliamentarians, who are apparently sincere but obviously un-informed or indifferent to facts' and who are 'greatly encouraging the subversive elements' by attacking the Defence of Canada Regulations. Wood, 'Tools for Treachery,' *Canadian Spokesman: The Magazine on National Affairs*, 1, no. 2 (1941): 1–6.

44 Early in 1943 Sergeant Leopold told a U.S. Embassy official that there were '18,000 active Communists in Canada.' Adding in sympathizers, the 'total number interested in Communism' reached, in Leopold's no doubt alarmist view, 'more than 350,000.' The 18,000 hard core definitely 'feel a primary loyalty to the USSR and international Communism and not Canada' and would be 'easily mobilized by Stalin in the event of hostilities.' Gratuitously, Leopold reported that 'at least half of the leadership among the Communists is Jewish.' US National Archives, State Department files, Decimal Series, 842.00B/1-1845, CS/HS, Ray Atherton to secretary of state, 18 January 1943.

45 Hannant, *The Infernal Machine*.

46 Betke and Horrall, 'Canada's Security Service,' 509; Intelligence Section, *Annual Report*, 1944–5; Reg Whitaker, *Double Standard: The Secret History of Canadian Immigration* (Toronto: Lester and Orpen Dennys 1987), 25.

47 Hannant, *Infernal Machine*, 209.

48 On Panopticism, see the classic work by Michel Foucault, *Discipline and Punish: The Birth of the Prison* (New York: Vintage Books 1979). See also Reg Whitaker, *The End of Privacy: How Total Surveillance Is Becoming a Reality* (New York: New Press 1999), 32–46.

49 William Stevenson, *A Man Called Intrepid: The Secret War* (New York: Har-

court Brace Jovanovitch 1976), and *Intrepid's Last Case* (New York: Villard Books 1984), is the worst offender, the former book having inspired an entirely fictional film starring David Niven as Sir William. On Stephenson's own self-promotion, see Timothy Naftali, 'Intrepid's Last Deception: Documenting the Career of Sir William Stephenson,' *Intelligence and National Security*, 8 (July 1993): 72–92; and Wesley K. Wark, ed., *Espionage: Past, Present, Future?* (Ilford, U.K.: Frank Cass 1994), 72–99. Solid scholarly background can be found in David Stafford's *Camp X* (Toronto: Lester and Orpen Dennys 1986). A partial and careful vindication of Stephenson's real (as opposed to imaginary) importance is retired CIA historian Thomas F. Troy's *Wild Bill and Intrepid: Donovan, Stephenson, and the Origin of CIA* (New Haven, Conn.: Yale University Press 1996).

50 Troy, *Wild Bill*, 38, 64.

51 Ibid., 68–9.

52 Thomas F. Troy, *Donovan and the CIA: A History of the Establishment of the Central Intelligence Agency* (Frederick, Md.: University Publications of America 1981), 111–19; the bitter relationship between Donovan and Hoover is detailed in Athan G. Theoharis and John Stuart Cox, *The Boss: J. Edgar Hoover and the Great American Inquisition* (Philadelphia: Temple University Press 1988), 188–91.

53 Hinsley and Simkins, *Security*, 187. This official history, published in 1990, primly avoids naming Mills, although his identity had already been disclosed in Nigel West, *A Matter of Trust: MI5, 1945–72* (London: Weidenfeld and Nicholson 1982), 26. He is also referred to by name in Granatstein and Stafford, *Spy Wars*, and in Beeby, *Cargo of Lies*.

54 Betke and Horrall, 'Canada's Security Service,' 529–31.

55 Stafford, 'The American-British-Canadian Triangle,' 33. Stafford points out that Stephenson had wanted a branch office of the BSC established in Ottawa to coordinate Canadian security, but that this, not surprisingly, was vetoed by Ottawa.

56 Betke and Horrall, 'Canada's Security Service,' 521–2.

57 Hannant, *Infernal Machine*, 198–9.

58 Ibid., 195.

59 Granatstein, *A Man of Influence*, 88–9.

60 CSIS, R.L. Cadiz to [addressee blacked out but clearly FBI], 20 October 1942; Norman Robertson to S.T. Wood, 21 October 1942; Cadiz to Robertson, 24 October 1942.

61 LAC, William Lyon Mackenzie King Papers, Memoranda and Notes series [MG 26 J4, hereinafter WLMK: M&N], vol. 328, f.3490, W.J. Turnbull, memorandum for the prime minister, 6 July 1942. In fairness to the RCMP,

if not to Leopold, it should be noted that Turnbull was contrasting obsessive 'Red-hunting' with an apparent lack of counter-espionage against the Nazis. Shortly after this memorandum, the first Nazi spy (*Watchdog*) fell into Mountie hands.

62 H.S. Ferns, *Reading from Right to Left: One Man's Political History* (Toronto: University of Toronto Press 1983), 182.

63 These difficulties are recounted at length in ibid. Some of the problem seems to have stemmed from an alleged mention in one of the documents that Gouzenko stole from the Soviet Embassy: this turns out to be an absurd case of mistaken identity based on a mistaken transliteration of Russian into English. See Reg Whitaker and Gary Marcuse, *Cold War Canada: The Making of a National Insecurity State, 1945–1957* (Toronto: University of Toronto Press 1994), 107–9.

64 LAC, Mackenzie King Papers, J4 Series, vol. 372, file 3913, 'J.A.G.,' memorandum to King, 16 November 1940; Pickersgill, 'Note on a War-Time Intelligence Service,' 27 November 1939, and 'Analysis of the Intelligence Bulletin Issued at R.C.M.P. Headquarters, October 30, 1939' (C257902–C257910).

65 October 1939 – War Series no. 2. The declassified version can be found in Gregory S. Kealey and Reg Whitaker, eds., *RCMP Security Bulletins: The War Series*, Part I, *1939–1941* (St John's: Committee on Canadian Labour History 1989), 30–9.

66 The House Committee on Un-American Activities, which, under the chairmanship of Congressman Martin Dies of Texas, investigated Communism in the United States in the late 1930s with scant attention to fact but a sharp eye for headlines.

67 This would not be the last time that civilian direction or control over RCMP activities in security and intelligence would be suggested. It would take two royal commissions, one reporting in 1968 and the second in 1981, for the RCMP security service to be 'civilianized' under the Canadian Security Intelligence Service Act of 1984. Pickersgill was thus ahead of his time by about forty-five years.

68 The *Bulletins* were continued mainly for the benefit of field officers, to keep them abreast of the wider national and international picture of intelligence and to counteract the tendency to become 'localized in viewpoint.' Officers were instructed to file their copies in binders: 'The format is one lending itself to easy compilation as a ready and comprehensive reference fyle.' Kealey and Whitaker, eds., *RCMP Security Bulletins: The War Series*, Part II, May 1945 (269–70); 1 November 1945 (411).

69 In the spring of 1941 the commander of prisons for England and Wales

testified before the secret hearings of the House of Commons Committee on the Defence of Canada Regulations that 'there was not much trouble in Britain with Communists as the British sense of humour was somewhat inclined to view them as a joke rather than a menace': 20 May 1941, Papers of the Committee, Office of the Clerk of the Committees of the House of Commons.

70 Whitaker, 'Official Repression of Communism,' 163–4.

71 LAC, WLMK: M&N, Pearson to Norman Robertson, 12 October 1941.

72 The most extreme variant of this revisionism is James Barros's Gothic speculation that 'Lester Pearson was Moscow's ultimate mole': Barros, *No Sense of Evil: Espionage, The Case of Herbert Norman* (Toronto: Deneau 1986), 169.

73 Whitaker and Kealey, eds., *RCMP Security Bulletins: The War Series, Part I,* 371–424.

74 Whitaker and Kealey, eds., *RCMP Security Bulletins: The War Series, Part II,* 15 December 1943, 25–43.

75 Ibid., 1 August 1944, 128–33.

76 Whitaker, 'Official Repression of Communism,' 149–52.

7 The Ice Age: Mounties on the Cold War Front Line, 1945–69

1 Reg Whitaker and Gary Marcuse, *Cold War Canada: The Making of a National Insecurity State, 1945–1957* (Toronto: University of Toronto Press 1994).

2 Quoted in P.N. Furbank, 'A Simple Facilitator,' *New York Review of Books,* 43, no. 12 (11 July 1996): 51.

3 Amy Knight, *How the Cold War Began: The Gouzenko Affair and the Hunt for Spies* (Toronto: McClelland and Stewart 2005); Whitaker and Marcuse, *Cold War Canada,* 27–110; John Sawatsky, *Gouzenko: The Untold Story* (Toronto: Macmillan 1984); Robert Bothwell and J. L. Granatstein, eds., *The Gouzenko Transcripts: The Evidence Presented to the Kellock-Taschereau Royal Commission of 1946; the Report of the Royal Commission to Investigate the Facts Relating to and the Circumstances Surrounding the Communication by Public Officials and Others in Positions of Trust of Secret and Confidential Information to Agents of a Foreign Power* (Ottawa: King's Printer 1946). In 1984 Access to Information requests brought about the declassification of a substantial amount of original documentation relating to the affair: see Reg Whitaker, 'Lifting Gouzenko's Cloak,' *Globe and Mail,* 6 November 1984.

4 This judgment must be qualified: some of the people Gouzenko fingered would not have fallen under screening. External Affairs was exempt from RCMP clearances; one convicted person was an employee of the U.K. High Commission. Moreover, actual dismissal or demotion of security risks was

the responsibility not of the RCMP but of the department or agency. Yet there is no available evidence that any of the Gouzenko principals had actually been identified as risks by RCMP screeners in the first instance, even though a number of them did have Communist associations.

5 On Smith's role both in the royal commission and in External Affairs, see Whitaker and Marcuse, *Cold War Canada*, 82–3, 118–26.

6 An Access to Information request to CSIS for surveillance files on the CAScW yielded eighty-eight pages covering the years 1944 to 1949. A month before the Gouzenko affair broke, headquarters rebuked an investigating officer in the Winnipeg division Intelligence Section for failing to grasp the 'proletarian tinge' that adhered to the association: H. Gagnon to O/C 'D' Division, 8 April 1946. The royal commission followed the headquarters interpretation closely. In fact, the CAScW was the offshoot of the British Association of Scientific Workers, which, although undoubtedly 'progressive' in its politics, was not directly linked to the Communists. Ironically, the Canadian government's chief scientific source on the significance of the secrets, including material relating to the atomic bomb, passed to the Soviets, was Dr John Cockcroft, who had been and would continue to be a leading member of the British association. On the CAScW affair, see Whitaker and Marcuse, *Cold War Canada*, 84–103.

7 Library and Archives Canada (LAC), Frank and Libby Park Papers, vol. 9, f.153, Emergency Civil Liberties Committee, 'Report of a Fact-Finding Committee,' n.d., 6. In his own later memoirs, Gordon Lunan recalls a slightly different version in which Harvison said: 'Well, we've tangled with you reds before and you scream your heads off but there's no way you're going to wriggle out of this one.' Lunan, *The Making of a Spy: A Political Odyssey* (Montreal: Robert Davies 1995), 21.

8 LAC, Department of External Affairs (DEA), vol. 2620, file 'Temporary N-1,' Arnold Smith, Interview with Gousenko,' memo II.

9 Igor Gouzenko, *This Was My Choice: Gouzenko's Story* (Toronto: J.M. Dent and Sons 1948).

10 Sawatsky, *Gouzenko: The Untold Story.*

11 Cabinet directive, 'Security Investigation of Government Employees,' 5 March 1948. For an overview of security screening in the public service in the late 1940s and early 1950s, see Whitaker and Marcuse, *Cold War Canada*, 161–87.

12 Indeed, public notice, or notoriety, came as quickly as 1949 from journalist Blair Fraser: 'Backstage at Ottawa,' *Maclean's Magazine*, 1 September 1949. The Mounties had wind of his story and had already tried, with some success, to soften its focus.

13 By 1961, a review of clearance procedures concluded that 'over the years very little, if any, information of value has been obtained from neighbours'; such interviews were deemed 'questionable' (CSIS, Directorate of Security and Intelligence, *Annual Report, 1960/61*). Despite this scepticism, many decades and a new security agency later, Ottawa neighbours were still in the twenty-first century being interviewed by security service officers concerning screening subjects' personal habits, marital relations, and, sometimes, political views.

14 'To Bar Reds from Positions in Public Service,' *Ottawa Journal*, 24 March 1947.

15 House of Commons, *Debates*, 22 June 1948, 5630.

16 CD-332/52, 16 October 1952.

17 Confidential interviews (some of those affected are still unwilling to invite publicity).

18 It is perhaps relevant that the same practice was often followed by the Mounties with regard to ex-convicts trying to get 'straight' work after serving their time, thus perversely encouraging recidivism.

19 Whitaker and Marcuse, *Cold War Canada*, 181–2.

20 DEA, f.50207-A-40, Security Panel minutes, 7 May 1951.

21 Brian Mulroney: 'PM Denounces 1960s Purge of Homosexual Civil Servants,' *Globe and Mail*, 28 April 1992.

22 The definitive account of the anti-homosexual campaign, particularly noteworthy for telling the story through the victims' eyes, is Gary Kinsman and Patrizia Gentile, *The Canadian War on Queers: National Security as Sexual Regulation* (Vancouver: UBC Press 2009). See also Reg Whitaker, 'Cold War Alchemy: How America, Britain, and Canada Transformed Espionage into Subversion,' *Intelligence and National Security*, 15, no. 2 (2000): 177–210.

23 The fruit machine was first described in John Sawatsky, *Men in the Shadows: The RCMP Security Service* (Toronto: Doubleday 1980), 124–37.

24 CSIS, Directorate of Security and Intelligence, *Annual Report, 1960/61*, 20 October 1960. Names are censored in this text, but the reference is obviously to diplomat John Watkins (see below). The official security service historians also mention the Watkins case in this context, and, while indicating that Watkins reported the incident to his superiors, they add that this 'only emphasised the reality of the security risk that had been run': Carl Betke and S.W. Horrall, 'Canada's Security Service: An Historical Outline, 1864–1966' (Ottawa: RCMP Historical Section 1978), CSIS Access Request #117-90-107, p. 598.

25 See Daniel Robinson and David Kimmel, 'The Queer Career of Homosexual Security Vetting in Cold-War Canada,' *Canadian Historical Review*,

75, no. 3 (1994): 319–45, and the CSIS documents on which the article is based, Access Requests #91-088 and #92-008. See also Gary Kinsman, '"Character Weakness" and "Fruit Machines": Towards an Analysis of the Anti-Homosexual Security Campaign in the Canadian Civil Service,' *Labour/Le Travail*, 35 (spring 1995): 133–62. One figure mentioned internally in the early 1960s for civil servants identified as risks was about 500. It is not clear from the context if all these were removed or hounded out, but it is likely that most were.

26 See Dean Beeby and William Kaplan, eds., *Moscow Despatches: Inside Cold War Russia* (Toronto: James Lorimer 1987), especially the Introduction, xiii–xxxii; John Sawatsky, *For Services Rendered: Leslie James Bennett and the RCMP Security Service* (Toronto: Doubleday 1982), 174–83; J.L. Granatstein and David Stafford, *Spy Wars: Espionage and Canada from Gouzenko to Glasnost* (Toronto: Key Porter 1990), 103–14.

27 One of the most notable of these victims was the late John Holmes, whose promising career (which included postings to Moscow) was cut short. Holmes went on to head the Canadian Institute of International Affairs and became one of the most distinguished academic historians of Canadian foreign policy.

28 Betke and Horrall, 'Canada's Security Service,' 598–602.

29 As late as the 1990s, evidence of continuing prejudice against certain 'lifestyles' (read homosexuality) embedded in the military's screening process drew a rebuke from the chair of the Security Intelligence Review Committee, and the notorious 'don't ask, don't tell' policy in the U.S. military remained in place until 2011 when it finally was shelved by the Obama administration under judicial pressure. In the intelligence field, anti-homosexual prejudice appears to have sharply waned. In the 1990s British intelligence hired its first same-sex couple to serve abroad as a team and the CIA was holding annual Gay Pride days for its gay and lesbian officers.

30 See Whitaker and Marcuse, *Cold War Canada*, chapters 10 and 11, 227–60, for a revisionist version supported by newly released documentation. Since that book appeared, yet more records of security service surveillance of the NFB have been declassified. New material is cited here.

31 Daniel J. Robinson, 'Falling into Line: The National Film Board, Foreign Policy, and the Cold War,' *National History: A Canadian Journal of Enquiry and Opinion*, 1, no. 2 (1997): 158–72.

32 See, for instance, J.W. Pickersgill, *My Years with Louis St. Laurent* (Toronto: University of Toronto Press 1975), 146–9.

33 Access to Information Request #93-A-00082, Constable K.G. Stroud to Inspector Sweeny, 14 August 1959.

34 Quoted in Robert A. Divine, *American Immigration Policy, 1924–1952* (New York: Da Capo Press 1972), 177–8.

35 This and subsequent paragraphs, unless otherwise noted, are drawn from Reg Whitaker, *Double Standard: The Secret History of Canadian Immigration* (Toronto: Lester and Orpen Dennys 1987).

36 Betke and Horrall, 'Canada's Security Service,' 607.

37 Ibid., 620, 624.

38 [Deschênes] Commission of Inquiry on War Criminals, *Report* (Ottawa, 1987).

39 CSIS, *Annual Report 1947/48*, Corporal A. Alsvold, 17 March 1948.

40 Christopher Simpson, *Blowback: The First Full Account of America's Recruitment of Nazis and Its Disastrous Effect on the Cold War, Our Domestic and Foreign Policy* (New York: Collier Books-Macmillan 1989); Neal Ascherson, Magnus Linklater, and Isabel Hilton, *The Nazi Legacy: Klaus Barbie and the International Fascist Connection* (New York: Holt, Rinehart, and Winston 1985); Tom Bower, *The Paperclip Conspiracy* (London: M. Joseph 1987); Clarence G. Lasby, *Project Paperclip: German Scientists and the Cold War* (New York: Atheneum 1971).

41 The existence of the Defectors Committee was first revealed in Whitaker, *Double Standard*, 115–19. More detailed information, although heavily censored under the Access to Information Act, was provided by Alti Rodal in an unpublished study for the Deschênes Commission on war criminals, 'Nazi War Criminals in Canada: The Historical and Policy Setting from the 1940s to the Present.'

42 CSIS, Directorate of Security and Intelligence, *Annual Report*, 1959/60.

43 CSIS, Directorate of Security and Intelligence, *Annual Report*, 1960/61, appendix A.

44 Betke and Horrall, 'Canada's Security Service,' 629–30.

45 The Communications Branch, National Research Council, later renamed as the Communications Security Establishment, intercepts and decrypts electronic communications abroad, but it is not and never has been a central intelligence agency, as such.

46 [McDonald] Commission of Inquiry concerning Certain Activities of the Royal Canadian Mounted Police, *Second Report*, *Freedom and Security under the Law*, 3 vols. (Ottawa: Minister of Supply and Services 1981).

47 See Whitaker, *Double Standard*, 148–77.

48 These intra-bureaucratic battles over immigration policy are detailed in ibid.

49 For Canada's place in this community, see James Littleton, *Target Nation: Canada and the Western Intelligence Network* (Toronto: Lester and Orpen Dennys 1986).

50 As early as 1953–4, Special Branch officers spent 144 person days in attendance at international conferences: sixty-six at a Commonwealth Security Conference in London, fourteen days at a secret meeting in Paris (probably NATO), and sixty-four in Latin American countries. Another forty person days were devoted to miscellaneous liaison commitments, and sixty in public appearances. CSIS, *Annual Report 1953/54*, 'International Conferences and Meetings Attended by Officers of the Special Branch in 1953–54.'

51 See, for instance, Athan Theoharis and John Stuart Cox, *The Boss: J. Edgar Hoover and the Great American Inquisition* (Philadelphia: Temple University Press 1988); Richard Gid Powers, *Secrecy and Power: The Life of J. Edgar Hoover* (New York: Free Press 1987).

52 This account is based on Whitaker and Marcuse, *Cold War Canada*, 50–4.

53 The author of the definitive account of the Gouzenko affair, Amy Knight, declares flatly that 'Wood had lied to the Prime Minister': *How the Cold War Began: The Gouzenko Affair and the Hunt for Soviet Spies* (Toronto: McClelland and Stewart 2005), 95.

54 Roger Bowen, *Innocence Is Not Enough: The Life and Death of Herbert Norman* (Vancouver: Douglas and McIntyre 1986); James Barros, *No Sense of Evil: The Espionage Case of Herbert Norman* (Toronto: Deneau 1986). The controversy is covered as well in some detail in Whitaker and Marcuse, *Cold War Canada*, 402–26. On Norman's work, see Roger Bowen, ed., *E.H. Norman: His Life and Scholarship* (Toronto: University of Toronto Press 1984).

55 Peyton V. Lyon, 'The Loyalties of E. Herbert Norman,' 18 March 1990, reprinted in *Labour/Le Travail*, 28 (1991): 219–59.

56 One was a reference Gouzenko had seen in the Soviet espionage traffic suggesting that 'one Norman' *might be* approached, but no evidence that he was, or that he cooperated. The other was the presence of Norman's name in the address book of Israel Halperin, one of the Gouzenko detainees. Not only was Halperin never convicted of any charges arising out of the affair, but it now appears that he had never knowingly passed any information of any kind to the Soviets (on this point see Whitaker and Marcuse, *Cold War Canada*, 103–6, 113–14). Halperin's innocence has recently been confirmed by his only link to the spy operation, Gordon Lunan, who describes him as an 'unwitting victim' (*The Making of a Spy*, 145). Yet Halperin's *notebook* was pronounced guilty by the security forces of Canada, the United States, and Britain, and any name that appeared in it became suspect. The presence of Norman's name was altogether innocuous in any event: the two men had known each other in the past and were both civil servants in wartime Ottawa.

57 See RCMP memorandum, 'The Norman Case: Some Factors and Considerations,' undated but from internal evidence probably 1957. This is among

a number of Norman-related documents released from RCMP files in the 1980s.

58 Bowen, *Innocence*, 214.

59 William A. Rusher, *Special Counsel* (New Rochelle, N.Y.: Arlington House Publishers 1968). Some public notice of the Pearson connection did appear in *Time*, 'The Pearson Case,' 29 April 1957.

60 Pearson file is FBI 65-60356, Freedom of Information Request #262,554.

61 Sawatsky, *Men in the Shadows*, 14.

62 Sawatsky, *For Services Rendered*, 254.

63 Lyon, 'Loyalties,' 23.

64 This was reported by Lyon, and confirmed by Guernsey in an interview with one of the authors (Whitaker) the same year. Guernsey did not, however, go so far as to affirm any positive belief in Norman's innocence, merely that there was an insufficient case against him: this would be an appropriate stance for a police officer involved in a criminal investigation. In the context of a security investigation, it does suggest a very weak case for the prosecution, given that the case merely had to demonstrate credible *doubts* about reliability, not proof of espionage or treason.

8 The Coyote, the Roadrunner, and the Reds under the Bed: Communist Espionage and Subversion

1 John Sawatsky, *For Services Rendered: Leslie James Bennett and the RCMP Security Service* (Toronto: Doubleday 1982), 188.

2 The 1948 cabinet directive establishing the guidelines for post-war screening had stated frankly that 'no system of security investigation which can be devised can provide a sure guarantee against unreliable elements.' In reference to the Gouzenko inquiry, it admitted that 'it is open to question whether the activities of any persons named by the recent Royal Commission would have been discovered by any conceivable system of "screening."' Cabinet directive, 'Security Investigation of Government Employees,' 5 March 1948.

3 Margaret Gowing, *Independence and Deterrence: Britain and Atomic Energy 1945–1952*, vol. 2 (London: Macmillan 1974), 151.

4 Chapman Pincher claims that FBI evidence was suppressed by Kim Philby at the British Embassy in Washington, but cites only 'confidential information' as his source: Pincher, *Too Secret Too Long* (London: Sidgwick and Jackson 1984), 151–2.

5 Robert Bothwell, *Nucleus: The History of Atomic Energy of Canada Ltd.* (Toronto: University of Toronto Press 1988), 30, 78. The most complete account

of Pontecorvo's odyssey is in Montgomery Hyde, *The Atom Bomb Spies* (London: H. Hamilton 1980), 125–42.

6 Reg Whitaker, 'Spies Who Might Have Been: Canada and the Myth of Cold War Counterintelligence,' *Intelligence and National Security*, 12, no. 4 (1997): 25–43.

7 CSIS, Special Branch, *Annual Report 1951/52*, W.L. Higgitt, 31 March 1952.

8 See Tom Mangold, *Cold Warrior: James Jesus Angleton, the CIA's Master Spy Hunter* (London: Simon and Schuster 1991), and Peter Wright's own surrealistic memoir, *Spy Catcher: The Candid Autobiography of a Senior Intelligence Officer* (Toronto: Stoddart 1987).

9 Sawatsky, *For Services Rendered*, 253–5.

10 CSIS, file 120-2-14, RCMP Commissioner R.H. Simmonds to Solicitor General Allan Lawrence, 28 December 1979; CSIS Director T.D. Finn, 'letter file' to Solicitor General Elmer MacKay, n.d.

11 CSIS, file 120-2-14, 'FEATHER BED – TOP SECRET,' 19 November 1979. One former security service officer who claims to have had direct knowledge of FEATHER BED suggests that there was indeed a file on Trudeau but that there was 'nothing in it' (confidential source). There seems little reason to suspect that the RCMP were systematically mounting anything like a J. Edgar Hoover-style operation to gather dirt on the elected head of government. Nevertheless, the propriety of secret police files on the loyalty of political leaders must remain questionable.

12 CSIS, Special Branch, *Annual Report 1952/53*. Emphasis in original.

13 Sawatsky, *For Services Rendered*, 33–85.

14 'The Spy Canada Brought in from the Cold,' CBC, *The National*, 5 June 1997, transcript.

15 Reg Whitaker and Steve Hewitt, *Canada and the Cold War* (Toronto: James Lorimer and Company 2003), 100–2.

16 CSIS, *Annual Report 1949–50*. Sergeant W.L. Higgitt, 'Annual Report, Counter-Espionage Section – Headquarters Special Branch, April 1st, 1949–March 31st, 1950,' 31 March 1950.

17 Carl Betke and Stan Horrall, 'Canada's Security Service: An Historical Outline, 1864–1966' (Ottawa: RCMP Historical Section 1978), CSIS Access Request #117-90-107, p. 703.

18 Sawatsky, *Men in the Shadows: The RCMP Security Service* (Toronto: Doubleday 1980), 29–40.

19 CSIS, Directorate of Security and Intelligence, *Annual Report 1956/57*.

20 Commission of Inquiry concerning Certain Activities of the RCMP (hereafter McDonald Commission), *Second Report, Freedom and Security under the Law, Volume 1* (Ottawa: Minister of Supply and Services 1969), 201–19.

21 We owe this information to Security Panel documents in the Privy Council Office records consulted prior to the coming into effect of the Access to Information Act. Any such records would now be subject to excision of names under the privacy provisions.

22 CSIS, Directorate of Security and Intelligence, *Annual Report, 1960/61*.

23 *Commission of Inquiry into Complaints made by George Victor Spencer. The Hon Mr Justice Dalton Wells, Commissioner*, July 1966. On Spencer generally, see Sawatsky, *For Services Rendered*, 114–38.

24 Mangold, *Cold Warrior*, 255–6.

25 CAZAB was so secret that neither cabinet ministers nor deputy ministers were permitted to know of the RCMP's membership, no one beyond the RCMP commissioner and Prime Minister Lester Pearson, who had agreed to join. That circle grew even smaller when Pearson was succeeded by Pierre Trudeau, who was never initiated. According to John Starnes: 'To have indoctrinated Trudeau would have involved reopening the whole question of Canada's membership – something that the commissioner was reluctant to do.' John Starnes, *Closely Guarded: A Life in Canadian Security and Intelligence* (Toronto: University of Toronto Press 1998), 140.

26 Ibid., 151.

27 Ibid., 150–1. See also Starnes's earlier 'Setting the Record Straight: The Case of Leslie James Bennett,' *Ottawa Citizen*, 2 June 1993.

28 Ian Adams, *S: Portrait of a Spy: RCMP Intelligence, the Inside Story: A Novel* (Agincourt, Ont.: Gage 1977).

29 This quotation and the foregoing biographical background on Brunet is drawn from Sawatsky, *Men in the Shadows*, 215–16.

30 Peter Marwitz, 'Gilles Brunet: A KGB Mole in the RCMP.' Paper presented to the Canadian Association of Security and Intelligence Studies, Ottawa, 31 May 1998.

31 Mangold, *Cold Warrior*, 272–3n.39.

32 CBC, *Fifth Estate*, 30 March 1993; David Wise, 'The Ruin of a Counterspy,' *Washington Post*, reprinted in the *Guardian Weekly*, 22 August 1993.

33 The implications of the Bennett-Brunet affair are examined critically in Reg Whitaker, 'Spies Who Might Have Been,' 25–43.

34 Sources on Hambleton are J.L. Granatstein and David Stafford, *Spy Wars: Espionage and Canada from Gouzenko to Glasnost* (Toronto: Key Porter 1990), 151–86; Leo Heaps, *Hugh Hambleton: Spy* (Toronto: Methuen 1983).

35 McDonald Commission, *Second Report, Freedom and Security under the Law, Volume 1*, 518.

36 See Elizabeth Grace and Colin Leys, 'The Concept of Subversion and Its Implications,' in C.E.S. Franks, ed., *Dissent and the State* (Toronto: Oxford University Press 1989), 62–85.

37 CSIS Files, RCMP *Intelligence Bulletin*, April–May 1947, June.

38 Interview with the late Mark McClung, Ottawa, 1984.

39 Interview with Bill Walsh, Toronto, 1990; Reg Whitaker and Gary Marcuse, *Cold War Canada: The Making of a National Insecurity State, 1945–1957* (Toronto: University of Toronto Press 1994), 359–60. Cy Gonick, *A Very Red Life: The Story of Bill Walsh* (St John's: Canadian Committee on Labour History 2001), contains a detailed picture of Walsh's activities in various unions and his difficulties in gaining any clear perspective on Communist objectives in the union movement.

40 The 'Diefenbunker' was an underground fortress to which top officials would repair for safety in the event of a nuclear war; this bizarre tribute to Cold War paranoia was never used, and eventually closed and sealed, but it reopened later as a tourist attraction.

41 Betke and Horrall, 'Canada's Security Service,' 673–5. Information on the PROFUNC program is also found in the *Annual Reports* for the late 1950s and early 1960s.

42 In 1951 the minister of justice revealed to his cabinet colleagues a good reason for not outlawing the Communist Party, as some voices were demanding at the time: the RCMP were already keeping close tabs on the party's inner operations through agents planted within. 'The communists,' he confided, 'were well aware of the fact that federal agents were active within [their] ranks … During recent years there had been two purges aimed at ridding the Party of such agents. The purges had, however, been unsuccessful in achieving the desired results.' PCO 16, vol. 24, Cabinet Conclusions, 3 May 1951. See also Whitaker and Marcuse, *Cold War Canada*, 200–1.

43 In 1954 the U.S. Consulate in Quebec City sought to ascertain Walsh's status by asking the Quebec police and the RCMP, but 'they indicated they knew nothing whatever about the truth or falsity of Mr Walsh's assertion.' The consul doubted that Walsh was ever a 'full time employee' but believed he may have passed on information. U.S. National Archives, State Department Decimal Files, 742.001/3-353 Tel 9 and 742.001/2-154. For his part, Walsh went so far as to provide what he purported was his 'special agent number,' 208-A, and said his mission was to infiltrate the Canadian Peace Congress, the Canada-Soviet Friendship Association, the League for Democratic Rights, and the Woodworkers Union (742.001/2-1755). In the Herbert Norman file in the Senate Internal Security Subcommittee, there is a letter from Walsh (25 March 1957) claiming that he had worked for the 'RCMP special branch' as an 'undercover agent under Supt. John Leopold and Insp. Lemieux.'

44 Betke and Horrall, 'Canada's Security Service.'

45 Recent Freedom of Information requests in the United States have re-

vealed that by 1960 the FBI, according to its own files, maintained 433 'live informants' within the U.S. Communist Party, or 7.8 per cent of the party's active membership: https://www.sites.google.com/site/ernie124102/cpusa.

46 Whitaker and Marcuse, *Cold War Canada*, 310–63; Irving Abella, *Nationalism, Communism and Canadian Labour* (Toronto: University of Toronto Press 1973).

47 See the eight volumes of the *RCMP Security Bulletins*, Gregory S. Kealey and Reg Whitaker, eds. (St John's: Canadian Committee on Labour History 1989–97).

48 This issue has been exhaustively researched by Steve Hewitt in his superb *Spying 101: The RCMP's Secret Activities at Canadian Universities, 1917–1997* (Toronto: University of Toronto Press 2002).

49 See Len Sher, *The Un-Canadians: True Stories of the Blacklist Era* (Toronto: Lester Publishing 1992), 39–77.

50 CSIS, Special Branch, *Annual Report 1952/53*.

51 Whitaker and Hewitt, *Canada's Cold War*, 94–6.

52 Information based on personal conversations with the late Percy Saltzman.

53 See R.C. Macleod, 'How They "Got Their Man,"' *Literary Review of Canada*, 5, no. 8 (1996): 19–21.

54 CSIS, C.E. Rivett-Carnac to the director of criminal investigation, 'Re: Reorganization – Special Branch, Headquarters and Divisions,' 6 January 1947.

55 Keith Walden, *Visions of Order: The Canadian Mounties in Symbol and Myth* (Toronto: Butterworth 1982), 117–36.

56 Betke and Horrall, 'Canada's Security Service,' 678. We have been unable to obtain a copy of this Leopold memorandum, both CSIS and the RCMP claiming the other must hold it.

57 CSIS, C.E. Rivett-Carnac to the director of criminal investigation, 'Re: Reorganization – Special Branch, Headquarters and Divisions,' 6 January 1947.

58 At this time, Special Branch HQ was comprised of two officers, twenty-one NCOs and members, and five translators. Outside HQ, the branch commanded the services of forty-seven more NCOs and members (many clerical and stenographic), more translators, and an undisclosed number of secret agents.

59 Betke and Horrall, 'Canada's Security Service,' 681–2.

60 Ibid., 686.

61 CSIS, Mark McClung, 'Memorandum on Organization of the Internal Security Service,' 15 March 1955.

62 CSIS, Harvison to Nicholson, 26 July 1955; Nicholson to Harvison, 27 July 1955.

63 Interview with Mark McClung, Ottawa, 1984.

64 Sawatsky, *Men in the Shadows*, 108–9; James Littleton, *Target Nation: Canada and the Western Intelligence Network* (Toronto: Lester and Orpen Dennys 1986), 136; Richard Cleroux, *Official Secrets: The Story behind the Canadian Security Intelligence Service* (Toronto: McGraw-Hill Ryerson 1990), 36–7.

65 McDonald Commission, *Second Report, Freedom and Security under the Law, Volume 2*, 669–71.

66 CSIS, Harvison to commissioner, 'Survey of Special Branch,' 16 July 1956; Betke and Horrall, 'Canada's Security Service,' 689–90.

67 Betke and Horrall, 'Canada's Security Service,' 700, 697.

68 While there is no statistical evidence available on the career paths of the graduates, our observation is based on anecdotal evidence based on personal conversations with a number of these graduates.

69 CSIS, Directorate of Security and Intelligence, *Annual Report 1960/61*.

70 Betke and Horrall, 'Canada's Security Service,' 664.

71 CSIS, Directorate of Security and Intelligence, *Annual Report 1955/56*.

72 McDonald Commission, *Freedom and Security under the Law, Volume 1*, 63.

73 John English, *The Life of Lester Pearson, Volume 2: The Worldly Years, 1949–1972* (Toronto: Alfred Knopf 1992), 351, cites an 'inadvertent' and 'incredible' 'wiring error.' Perhaps, but the chain of contingencies leading to the particular result does make simple error itself seem somewhat 'incredible.'

74 CSIS, minutes of meeting, 30 December. Betke and Horrall, 'Canada's Security Service,' 779–81.

75 J.L. Granatstein, *Canada 1957–1967: The Years of Uncertainty and Innovation* (Toronto: McClelland and Stewart 1986), 290.

76 The Commission of Inquiry into Matters Relating to one Gerda Munsinger, *Report* (Ottawa, 1966).

77 When interviewed in 1966 by one of the authors (Whitaker), Coldwell unhesitatingly responded to a question about the proudest achievement of his political career as a pioneering social democrat: 'Helping bring Canada into NATO.'

78 Sawatsky, *Men in the Shadows*, 194.

79 *Report of the Royal Commission on Security* (abridged) (hereafter Mackenzie Commission, *Report*) (Ottawa, 1969). Further material has been released under Access to Information, but nothing in the declassified portions of the unpublished version adds any new perspectives that one could not find in the public version.

80 Ibid., 5, para. 8.

81 Ibid., 20, para. 56.
82 Ibid., 18, para. 24.
83 Security Panel minutes, 9 June 1969.
84 Ibid., 7 February 1969.
85 In his memoirs, Starnes recounts that the first inquiries he received from the cabinet were in regard to an appointment as RCMP commissioner, although this was later reduced to security service director – a downgrade that Starnes himself believed appropriate. It would not be until 2007 that the first civilian commissioner was appointed after another round of RCMP scandals. Starnes plays down the degree of hostility the Mounties may have shown the first civilian to head the service and attributes much of the difficulties he did experience to the lack of clear direction from the government as to what it actually expected him to do: Starnes, *Closely Guarded*, 138.

9 National Unity, National Security: The Quebec Conundrum, 1960–84

1 *Report of the Royal Commission on Security (Abridged)* (Ottawa: Minister of Supply and Services 1969), 8, para. 21–3.
2 Marc Laurendeau, *Les Québécois violents: la violence politique 1962–1972*, rev. ed. (Montreal: Boréal 1990), offers a survey of a decade of violence; Louis Fournier, *FLQ: The Anatomy of an Underground Movement* (Toronto: NC Press 1984), is the best history of the FLQ; R. Comeau, D. Cooper, and P. Vallières, *FLQ: un projet révolutionnaire: lettres et écrits felquistes (1963–1982)* (Outremont: VLB 1990), assembles the texts and manifestos of the FLQ.
3 Fournier, *FLQ*, 36.
4 One minister, Gérard Pelletier, published a book within a year of the crisis (*La crise d'Octobre* [Montreal 1971]) in which he wrote about the 'inefficacité policière' (157–9). A biographer of the then prime minister, Pierre Trudeau, quotes unidentified ministers as describing an RCMP cabinet briefing as 'pathetic,' 'a farce,' 'unbelievable' (Richard Gwyn, *The Northern Magus: Pierre Trudeau and Canadians* [Toronto: McClelland and Stewart 1980], 122). Trudeau himself is quoted as recalling 'with genuine indignation' that the RCMP were 'so damned ignorant about Quebec' (J.L. Granatstein and David Stafford, *Spy Wars: Espionage and Canada from Gouzenko to Glasnost* [Toronto: Key Porter Books 1990], 208).
5 Commission of Inquiry concerning Certain Activities of the Royal Canadian Mounted Police (hereafter McDonald Commission), *Second Report*,

Freedom and Security under the Law, and *Third Report, Certain RCMP Activities and the Question of Governmental Knowledge* (Ottawa 1981).

6 Foremost among these critics has been John Starnes, who was the director of the security service during the late 1960s and early 1970s: Starnes, 'Trudeau's Critical Judgment of RCMP Unfair and Unjustified,' *Ottawa Citizen*, 28 December 1993; Starnes, *Closely Guarded: A Life in Canadian Security and Intelligence* (Toronto: University of Toronto Press 1998), 158–87. Although some have dismissed Starnes's arguments as special pleading, it is the conclusion of this chapter that there is some considerable justice in his complaints.

7 Reg Whitaker, 'Canada – The RCMP Scandals,' in Andrei S. Marcovits and Mark Silverstein, eds., *The Politics of Scandal: Power and Process in Liberal Democracies* (New York: Holmes and Meier 1988), 48–9.

8 One of the authors (Whitaker) made a series of access requests to CSIS and/or the National Archives regarding security service files on Quebec separatism, the FLQ, and the Parti Québécois for the 1960s and 1970s. Much of the material in this chapter initially appeared in Reg Whitaker, 'Apprehended Insurrection? RCMP Intelligence and the October Crisis,' *Queen's Quarterly*, 100, no. 2 (1993): 383–406, an article that was based on these documents. A large portion of this article is reprinted in Guy Bouthillier and Edouard Cloutier, eds., *Trudeau's Darkest Hour: War Measures in Time of Peace, October 1970* (Montreal: Baraka Books 2010), 80–94.

9 The unilingualism of the Mounties is striking. Not until the 1970s were security service reports on Quebec actually written in French, even in cases where their authors were francophones. In 1963 a constable in Ottawa receiving documents on the FLQ from Montreal noted that most of them were in French and requested 'translated version of any parts which headquarters feel may be of interest to us at this point' (Access Request #1025-9-9130, 24 July 1963). Even as late as the 1970s, surveillance of the Parti Québécois was filed under the quaint heading 'Quebec Party (Parti Quebecois)' with the French name sometimes misspelled. The problems outlasted the RCMP security service; the early years of CSIS as a separate civilian agency were wracked by internal complaints about official-language failings on the part of a still unilingually anglophone senior management (see chapter 11).

10 Project #65, Central Research Branch, 'RCMP Coverage of Quebec Separatist Movement,' n.d.

11 Brief #35. Fournier, *FLQ*, identifies this as having been written by Corporal Maurice Brussières, one of the few francophones employed by the security service at this time. It was, however, written entirely in English.

12 Brief #51, September 1964.
13 Brief #39, 'The Development of Separatism in Quebec,' 18 September 1964.
14 Fournier, *FLQ*, gives evidence of early infiltration by the Montreal Police.
15 Brief #103, 1 December 1965; Cobb-o.i/c/ D Branch, 30 December 1965.
16 Privy Council Office, Minutes of the 76th meeting of the Security Panel, 23 September 1964.
17 CD-35, which provided the security service's terms of reference for security screening in the public service, had come into effect in 1963 and did not mention separatism. CD-63 was not superseded until the 1970s.
18 This practice, condemned by the McDonald Commission (*Second Report, Volume 1*, 545) has always been officially denied by the security service, but anyone familiar with the workings of the security-screening process knows that it has often been employed.
19 Brief #129, 'Quebec Separatism,' 5 August 1966, and #139 (Project #145, Central Research Bureau), 31 October 1966, which is an updated version of the earlier brief, are much more detailed and specific in their familiarity with trends and activities among the various separatist groupings than was the case in earlier reporting.
20 Fournier, *FLQ*, 106: This was Bernard Sicotte, run by Donald Cobb for eighteen months. Sicotte provided dynamite first rendered harmless by the RCMP.
21 Fournier, *FLQ*, 143–4.
22 Access Request #92-A-00043.
23 Fournier, *FLQ*, 145–6. The alleged source was Claude Larivière of the Company of Young Canadians, which also employed Bachand until he was dismissed. Larivière has apparently denied that he was a source.
24 Brief #69, 31 December 1969.
25 Brief #51-1.
26 Dale C. Thomson, *De Gaulle et le Québec* (Saint-Laurent, Que.: Editions du Trécarré 1990). J.F. Bosher, *The Gaullist Attack on Canada, 1967–1997* (Montreal and Kingston, Ont.: McGill-Queen's University Press 2000), takes an expansive interpretation of a sustained surreptitious effort of French 'imperialism' to undermine the Canadian federal state while assisting the emergence of a separate successor state in Quebec. Bosher claims that successive federal governments from Pearson on failed to grasp either the magnitude of the Gaullist threat or the degree to which the PQ were clients of the French.
27 Fournier, *FLQ*, claims that Rossillon had been instrumental in helping an FLQ activist flee to Algeria (41–2). On French involvement generally, see Bosher, *Gaullist Attack*, 128–44; Granatstein and Stafford, *Spy Wars*, 200–10.

28 Interview with James Warren, then director of operations, CSIS, February 1987.

29 Brief #306, April 1971, 'Action Taken by the Force, K.D. Green c/m i/c "K" Branch – Miss J. Keir 21.4.71.'

30 Starnes to Goyer, 14 January 1972, 'K' Branch Project #348 [or #326]. We have two different declassified copies of this same document, with differing exemptions.

31 'Threats against Prominent Individuals by Organizations or Persons of "I" Directorate Interest – Canada,' 14 April 1970.

32 On July 23 1970 Starnes transmitted a paper on 'The Threat to Law and Order and National Unity from Subversive Organizations' to McIlraith that attempted to provide an in-depth analysis of the relation of rapid social change to the deterioration of law and order that would set the background, as it were, of the FLQ's defiance of the state.

33 'Report of the Strategic Operations Centre, December 10, 1970,' reprinted in Gouvernement du Québec, Ministère de la Justice, Jean-François Duchaîne, *Rapport sur les événements d'Octobre 1970*, vol. 2 (Quebec 1980) (hereafter Duchaîne, *Rapport*).

34 Emphasis added. See the excellent discussion on 'Intelligence and Its Customers,' in Walter Laqueur, *A World of Secrets: The Uses and Limits of Intelligence* (New York: Basic Books 1985), 71–109.

35 Duchaîne, *Rapport*, vol. 1, 28, 255.

36 Pierre Elliott Trudeau, *Memoirs* (Toronto: McClelland and Stewart 1993), 146–7.

37 Duchaîne, *Rapport*, vol. 1, 240–1.

38 Ibid., 238.

39 This was alluded to by McDonald Commission, *Third Report: Certain RCMP Activities and the Question of Governmental Knowledge* (Ottawa: Minister of Supply and Services 1981), 203–6.

40 Fournier, *FLQ*, 238.

41 Gwyn, *Northern Magus*, 118.

42 George Radwanski, *Trudeau* (Toronto: Macmillan 1978).

43 Library and Archives Canada, McDonald Commission, in-camera testimony, C-39, 11 January 1979; C-10, 16 May 1978. According to Ferraris, one of the two names that Pelletier questioned was 'Gérard Pelletier.' After assurances that this was another, less respectable, Gérard Pelletier, a journalist, the minister waived his objection. Ironically, the next night police (either Montreal Police or SQ) raided minister Pelletier's Outremont home with a warrant under the War Measures Act for 'Gérard Pelletier, *journaliste*.' It took some persuading to convince them that they had the wrong Pelletier.

We have the benefit of an eyewitness to this bizarre event, a woman who was at the time resident in the Pelletier household.

44 Edward Mann and John Alan Lee, *The RCMP vs. the People* (Don Mills, Ont.: General Publishing 1979), 183. Trudeau recalled that 'we were completely stunned' by the kidnappings, 'caught off guard' and 'badly equipped to deal with it.' He insisted that, when 'left to their own devices,' the police continued to hunt for Communists instead of FLQers; that the 'police were out of their depth, and were on the verge of physical and mental exhaustion.' Consequently, the imposition of emergency powers was necessary 'to prevent the situation from degenerating into chaos.' As for the War Measures Act being a 'sledgehammer,' Trudeau plaintively, but not entirely accurately, claims that the sledgehammer 'was the only tool at our disposal.' Trudeau, *Memoirs*, 134, 137, 143.

45 Pierre Vallières, *The Assassination of Pierre Laporte* (Toronto: James Lorimer 1979).

46 McDonald Commission, testimony, C-10, 16 May 1978.

47 McDonald Commission, testimony, C-39, 11 January 1979.

48 Don Jamieson, *A World unto Itself: The Political Memoirs of Don Jamieson*, vol. 2 (St John's: Breakwater 1991), 81–6; emphasis added. Jamieson also suggests that the particular leadership style of Trudeau imprinted itself on the crisis: once he made up his mind, 'he was inordinately reluctant to change ... having moved – as with the War Measures Act – he was tenacious even to the point of unreasonable stubbornness' (191). Technically, the request for the invocation of war powers had to come from the Quebec government, but accounts that take this request at face value miss the real dynamic of decision making which rested practically in the hands of the prime minister.

49 D Branch, 'Developments Quebec,' 21 October 1970.

50 Jamieson, *A World unto Itself*, 87–90. Emphasis added.

51 The government may have succeeded in crushing terrorist activity in Quebec through this massive show of force. For an admiring portrait of Trudeau's generalship by a military officer involved in the October action, see Dan G. Loomis, *Not Much Glory: Quelling the FLQ* (Toronto: Deneau 1984). Another account by a well-informed insider in the Quebec cabinet at the time is William Tetley, *The October Crisis, 1970: An Insider's View* (Montreal and Kingston, Ont.: McGill-Queen's University Press, new rev. ed., 2010). See also the (self-) revisionist argument of J.L. Granatstein, 'Changing Positions on the October Crisis,' *Cité Libre*, autumn 1999, 71–4, and A. Cohen and J.L. Granatstein, eds., *Trudeau's Shadow: The Life and Legacy of Pierre Elliott Trudeau* (Toronto: Random House 1998). Granatstein protested

the War Measures Act in 1970 but now accepts that its use was justified by the defeat of the FLQ. A rather more nuanced view can be found in Reg Whitaker, 'Keeping up with the Neighbours? Canadian Responses to 9/11 in Historical and Comparative Context,' *Osgoode Hall Law Journal*, 41, nos. 2/3 (2003): 241–65.

52 David E. Murphy, *What Stalin Knew: The Enigma of Barbarossa* (New Haven, Conn.: Yale University Press 2005); Gabriel Gorodetsky, *Grand Delusion: Stalin and the German Invasion of Russia* (New Haven, Conn.: Yale University Press 1999).

53 Duchaîne, *Rapport*, vol. 1, 256.

54 McDonald Commission, *Second Report, Volume 1*, 450.

55 Ibid., 451.

56 Ibid., 452.

57 R. Gordon Robertson, memorandum for the prime minister, 16 December 1969; D.F. Wall, memorandum for the prime minister, 17 December 1969. These and other documents relating to the 19 December committee meeting are reproduced in Starnes, *Closely Guarded*, 207–13. The authors would like to thank John Starnes for drawing their attention to a number of relevant documents that he has had declassified under the Access to Information Act.

58 Memorandum for the Cabinet Committee on Security and Intelligence, 'Current Threats to National Unity: Quebec Separatism,' 17 December 1969.

59 S.14: 'The head of a government institution may refuse to disclose any record requested under this Act that contains information the disclosure of which could reasonably be expected to be injurious to the conduct by the Government of Canada of federal-provincial affairs, including, without restricting the generality of the foregoing, any such information: (a) on federal-provincial consultations or deliberations; or (b) on strategy or tactics adopted or to be adopted by the Government of Canada relating to the conduct of federal-provincial affairs.'

60 D.W. Wall, 'Record of a Meeting of the Cabinet Committee on Security and Intelligence, Dec. 19, 1969,' 5 January 1970. The then head was Assistant Commissioner J.E.M. Barrette, and the future heads were John Starnes and Michael Dare.

61 Trudeau, *Memoirs*, 131–3. Emphasis added.

62 McDonald Commission, *Second Report, Volume 1*, 81–4.

63 Ibid., 90–3.

64 Ibid., 75.

65 Ibid., 77.

66 Ibid., 452–3. Emphasis added.

67 Ibid., 453–4.

68 Elizabeth Grace and Colin Leys, 'The Concept of Subversion and Its Implications,' in C.E.S. Franks, ed., *Dissent and the State* (Toronto: Oxford University Press 1989), argue that it is not to prevent criminal activities that the concept of subversion has been used: 'It is invoked, rather, in order to *create* a "grey area" of activities that *are* lawful, but that will be denied protection from state surveillance or harassment by being *declared* illegitimate, on the ground that they *potentially* have unlawful consequences' (63).

69 McDonald Commission, *Second Report*, *Volume 1*, 7. The Montreal Police were also part of a joint federal-provincial-municipal operation.

70 McDonald Commission, *Third Report: Certain RCMP Activities and the Question of Governmental Knowledge* (Ottawa 1981), 382–91.

71 House of Commons, *Debates*, 17 June 1977, 6793.

72 McDonald Commission, *Second Report*, *Volume 1*, 9–10.

73 House of Commons, *Debates*, 6 July 1977, 7365.

74 Among the sources drawn on are: McDonald Commission, *Second Report* and *Third Report*; Gouvernement du Québec, Ministère de la Justice, *Rapport de la Commission d'enquête sur les opérations policières en territoire québécois* (hereafter Keable Inquiry) (Quebec: Gouvernement du Québec 1981); Duchaîne, *Rapport*; John Sawatsky, *Men in the Shadows: The RCMP Security Service* (Toronto: Doubleday 1980); Robert Dion, *La police secrète au Québec* (Montreal: Editions Québec-Amérique 1978); Jeff Sallot, *Nobody Said No* (Toronto: Lorimer 1979); Marc Laurendeau, *Les Québécois violents: la violence politique 1962–1972* (Montreal: Les Editions du Boréal 1990); Fournier, *FLQ*; Carole de Vault (with William Johnson), *The Informer: Confessions of an Ex-Terrorist* (Toronto: Fleet Books 1982); Richard Cleroux, *Pleins feux sur les Services Secrets Canadiens: Révelations sur l'espionnage au pays* (Montreal: Les Editions de l'Homme 1993); Norman Lester, *Enquêtes sur les Services Secrets* (Montreal: Les Editions de l'Homme 1998).

75 McDonald Commission, *Second Report*, *Volume 1*, 454.

76 PQ membership lists had already been stolen and copied in Operation HAM, two years earlier.

77 McDonald Commission, *Second Report*, *Volume 1*, 455–6.

78 Ibid., 457–9.

79 Ibid., 460.

80 Ibid., 465.

81 Starnes, *Closely Guarded*, 168.

82 Operation HAM has retained high sensitivity for decades. The *Third Report* of the McDonald Commission, on the question of government knowledge

of illegal acts, had a section (part 6, chapter 10) devoted to HAM, which was entirely redacted from the published version since criminal charges were still pending. Yet an Access to Information Request (#886011) for unpublished portions of the *Report* years later resulted in the release of a single page for chapter 10: One word ('Introduction') is followed by a note indicating that the 'remaining portion of this chapter is entirely exempt pursuant to sections 16(1) [criminal investigations, etc.] and 19(1) [personal information] of the *Access to Information Act.*'

83 'Minuet' refers to a social dance of eighteenth-century French origin for two people, described as a slow graceful dance in 3⁄4 time characterized by forward balancing, bowing, and toe pointing (*Merriam-Webster Dictionary*). This seems to describe rather well the lengthy and convoluted relationship between Morin and his successive RCMP handlers. According to Richard Cleroux, one retired Mountie has a more cynical interpretation for why this codename was used: 'Why not? We taught him to dance': Cleroux, 'Mountie Mischief and *l'affaire Morin*,' *Globe and Mail*, 11 July 1992.

84 The best account of the Morin affair can be found in Richard Cleroux, *Pleins Feux*, 213–82. Cleroux extensively interviewed Morin's RCMP handlers and places Morin as a source within a comprehensible context, something missing in most of the other accounts.

85 Bédard made a statement following the public revelation of Morin's role that he had been informed of the relationship by Morin in 1977 and had asked him to continue his meetings two or three more times, in order to gain information on RCMP dirty tricks operations in Quebec (a matter about which the PQ government was understandably interested), but then curtail the relationship – a plan that Morin approved, and indeed followed: Patricia Poirier and Rhéal Seguin, 'Ex-Minister Used Morin Contacts,' *Globe and Mail*, 13 May 1992. There is reason to believe, however, that Premier René Lévesque was not made aware of the Morin-RCMP relationship until 1981, and that he took the news badly. Lévesque's chief of staff has stated that Morin's departure from the PQ cabinet was caused by Lévesque's distress at the potential for blackmail (Sandro Contenta, 'Aide Says Lévesque Feared Blackmail over Morin Affair,' *Toronto Star*, 15 May 1992), but this has not been independently confirmed and is hotly denied by Morin. Bédard made it quite clear in 1992 that he never doubted Morin's loyalty to Quebec, even if he harboured doubts about the propriety of Morin's acceptance of cash.

86 Lester, *Enquêtes sur les Services Secrets*, 139–232. Lester writes from a vociferous sovereignist position: see his three-volume polemic, *Le Livre Noir du Canada Anglais* (Montreal: Les Intouchables 2003–4).

87 Claude Morin, 'Pourquoi j'ai accepté de collaborer avec le GRC,' *La Presse*, 11 May 1992.

88 Claude Morin, *L'affaire Morin: Légendes, sottises et calomnies* (Montreal: Les Editions du Boréal 2006). It is hard to know what to make of this extraordinarily self-serving and self-absorbed book. Morin indignantly refutes numerous errors and exaggerations published by his critics, which is fair enough, but his own justifications sometime stretch credulity. To take just one example, to explain why he took cash, Morin declares that he was simply charging the RCMP an honorarium like any academic might charge for professional consultation or producing a paper for an academic conference.

89 Sandro Contenta, 'Probe Aimed at Spies, Not the PQ: Ex-Mountie,' *Toronto Star*, 15 April 1992. The same logic led the Counter-Espionage Branch to wiretap the office of a minister in the Bourassa Liberal government, François Cloutier, because of contacts with alleged French agents.

90 Cleroux, *Pleins feux* and 'Mountie Mischief.'

91 *Quebec versus Ottawa: The Struggle for Self-Government, 1960–72* (Toronto: University of Toronto Press 1976).

92 Michael McLoughlin, *Last Stop, Paris: The Assassination of Mario Bachand and the Death of the FLQ* (Toronto: Viking 1998).

93 This strain is best exemplified by Normand Lester, who concludes his *Enquêtes sur les Service Secrets* with an epilogue in which he speculates that only a few of the RCMP transgressions of the 1970s have been exposed, that the federal Liberals have deliberately buried these 'squelettes dans les placards' (skeletons in the closet) to cover up their responsibility for the political espionage of the decade: 'Au Canada la loi de l'omertà semble plus respectée à la GRC et au SCRS que dans le mafia!' (In Canada the rule of *omertà* is more respected at the RCMP and CSIS than in the Mafia). To Lester, and other sovereignists, 'le "grand jeu" reste toujours le meme. Il s'agit d'introduire des espions dans les rangs de l'adversaire pour connaître ses intentions et ses moyens véritables, puis de le destabiliser et le désorganiser par les manoeuvres clandestines.' (The Great Game is always the same. It's a matter of planting spies in the ranks of the enemy to learn its intentions and its true strength; then to destabilize and disorganize the enemy by clandestine manoeuvres.) Lester, *Enquêtes sur les Services Secrets*, 349–51.

94 Reg Whitaker, 'Designing a Balance between Freedom and Security,' in Joseph F. Fletcher, ed., *Ideas in Action: Essays on Politics and Law in Honour of Peter Russell* (Toronto: University of Toronto Press 1999), 128-9.

95 Redacted transcript of secret hearings of McDonald Commission, undated,

pages 17038–44. Our thanks to John Starnes for providing a copy of the response to his Access to Information request.

96 Starnes, *Closely Guarded*, 170–6.

10 'I'm Shocked, Shocked to Find That Gambling Is Going on in Here!': The Creation of the Canadian Security Intelligence Service

1 John Starnes, *Closely Guarded: A Life in Canadian Security and Intelligence* (Toronto: University of Toronto Press 1998), 134–5.

2 Ibid., 135, 138–9.

3 Ibid., 145.

4 John Starnes, 'Memorandum for File,' 20 March 1973 (Top Secret, redacted).

5 A case study centred on British Columbia that details the transition from old to new left and the impact of this transition on politics is Benjamin Isitt, *Militant Minority: British Columbia Workers and the Rise of a New Left, 1948–1972* (Toronto: University of Toronto Press 2010).

6 Steve Hewitt, *Spying 101: The RCMP's Secret Activities at Canadian Universities, 1917–1997* (Toronto: University of Toronto Press 2002), 138–9.

7 Ibid., 177.

8 Commission of Inquiry concerning Certain Activities of the RCMP (hereafter McDonald Commission), *Second Report*, *Volume 1*, *Freedom and Security under the Law* (Ottawa: Minister of Supply and Services 1981), 507.

9 *Toronto Sun*, 'RCMP Inquiry?' 29 May 1977.

10 McDonald Commission, *Third Report: Certain RCMP Activities and the Question of Government Knowledge* (Ottawa: Minister of Supply and Services 1981), 322–3.

11 Hewitt, *Spying 101*, 192–3.

12 Ibid., 193.

13 McDonald Commission, *Second Report*, *Volume 1*, 506–11.

14 Ibid., 508–11.

15 Ontario, Legislative Assembly of Ontario, *Debates*, 9 December 1977. Much of this is also reproduced in McDonald Commission, *Second Report*, *Volume 1*, 478–80.

16 Starowicz suffered no harm to his career when his identity in this pseudo-affair was leaked to the media. He went on to take charge of the national TV news program *The Journal*, became the executive director of documentaries for the CBC, and produced the award-winning TV series *Canada: A People's History*.

17 An Access for Information request for files on the Waffle after the closure

of the Counter-Subversion Branch in the 1980s and the dispersal of its files to the National Archives elicited a few pages with such extensive redactions as to make them worthless for historical research. Consequently, we have had to lean on the McDonald Commission investigation.

18 McDonald Commission, *Second Report*, *Volume 1*, 480–1.

19 McDonald Commission, *Third Report*, 482–3.

20 Jim Bronskill, 'Mounties Spied on Tommy Douglas,' *Globe and Mail*, 17 December 2006; Joan Bryden, 'Spy File on Tommy Douglas Is Old, But Not Old Enough for Release: CSIS,' *Canadian Press*, 10 March 2010. A Federal Court decision ordering a review of all documents withheld or censored has been appealed by the federal government: Amy Chung, 'Federal government appeals decision on secret Tommy Douglas dossier,' *Postmedia News*, 29 September 2011.

21 McDonald Commission, *Third Report*, 361–8.

22 Access Request #886011; McDonald Commission, *Third Report*, part vi, chapter 12, paras. 37–40, 'Operation No. 13.' Some of this material was submitted to the Royal Commission of Inquiry (Krever) into the Confidentiality of Health Records in Ontario, *Report* (1980), 40–5. See also *Ross Dowson v. the RCMP*, http://www.rossdowson.com/rcmpvsross.html.

23 Kirk Makin, 'Ex-RCMP Officers Only Doing Their Job, Ontario Judge Decides,' *Globe and Mail*, 18 December 1985.

24 McDonald Commission, *Second Report*, *Volume 1*, 274–5.

25 *Report of the Royal Commission on Security (Abridged)* (Ottawa 1969), 101–2.

26 McDonald Commission, *Third Report*, 235–41.

27 McDonald Commission, *Second Report*, *Volume 1*, 201–9.

28 Ibid., 575.

29 Ibid., 221.

30 See n.5.

31 Hewitt, *Spying 101*, 6.

32 Ibid., 41–65; Paul Axelrod, 'Spying on the Young in Depression and War: Students, Youth Groups and the RCMP 1935–1942,' *Labour/Le Travail* 35 (spring 1995): 43–64.

33 Hewitt, *Spying 101*, 101.

34 CSIS, vol. 2756, 'York University – Toronto, Ont.' York was chosen for attention because one of the authors (Whitaker) was for many years a member of the York faculty and thus knowledgeable about the names and organizations cited in the surveillance reports.

35 Hewitt, *Spying 101*, 116–17.

36 Ibid., 173.

37 Ibid., 178.

38 Ibid., 85.

39 Quoted in J.L.J. Edwards, *Ministerial Responsibility for National Security*, Study Prepared for the McDonald Commission (Ottawa: Minister of Supply and Services 1980), 94.

40 See chapter 8, n.25.

41 McDonald Commission, *Third Report*, 8.

42 Goyer was not pleased to learn that the director general of the security service had a direct pipeline, when needed, to the prime minister, bypassing Goyer as minister answerable in Parliament for the RCMP. This direct pipeline does not seem to have been used very often, however, and Goyer remained on relatively good terms with the service – not the case with Warren Allmand and Francis Fox.

43 The facts surrounding the meeting with the minister are drawn mainly from the McDonald Commission, *Third Report*, 243–57.

44 Ibid., 257.

45 Ibid., 244–5. Allmand subsequently held other cabinet posts and after leaving federal politics in 1997 has pursued a career as an advocate of human rights and democratic causes. Douglas, the alleged Black Power radical, ironically resurfaced years later as a member of the Progressive Conservative Party. Hart, so far as is known, returned to the United States. We have no information on what became of Plummer and McMorran.

46 Daniel Ellsberg, *Secrets: A Memoir of Vietnam and the Pentagon Papers* (New York: Viking 2002).

47 Theodore H. White, *Breach of Faith: The Fall of Richard Nixon* (New York: Atheneum 1975); Carl Bernstein and Bob Woodward, *All the President's Men* (New York: Simon and Schuster 1974).

48 Ward Churchill and Jim Vander Wall, *The COINTELPRO Papers: Documents from the FBI's Secret Wars against Domestic Dissent* (Boston: South End Press 1990).

49 Athan Theoharis, *The Boss: J. Edgar Hoover and the Great American Inquisition* (Philadelphia: Temple University Press 1988). William W. Keller, *The Liberals and J. Edgar Hoover: Rise and Fall of a Domestic Intelligence State* (Princeton, N.J.: Princeton University Press 1989), argues that American liberals in the 1950s wanted to take anti-Communist investigations out of the hands of the congressional witch hunters and depoliticize anti-Communism by placing it under the 'administrative' control of the FBI, without congressional checks. In other words, American liberals wanted to have a situation just as in Canada where the RCMP took care of anti-Communism while the politicians were largely kept at bay. By the 1970s, the politics

around the FBI had been reversed, and the situation in Canada was no longer recognizable by earlier standards.

50 Loch K. Johnson, *A Season of Inquiry: Congress and Intelligence* (Chicago: Dorsey Press 1988).

51 We now know that the witch-hunting congressmen, including McCarthy, were being secretly fed from Hoover's FBI files, but that revelation came only much later, when it simply added to the FBI's newly unfavourable image.

52 The prevalence of this new media narrative should not be overemphasized. Parts of the media, such as the *Toronto Sun*, remained staunch supporters of the RCMP and tended to be dismissive of the revelations of wrongdoing. Other newspapers tended to downplay the RCMP coverage, apparently deeming it not newsworthy enough. However, a study by a graduate student of one of the authors (Whitaker) of editorial content on the issue in nine newspapers and national magazines from 1977 to 1981 shows a growing chorus of criticism of RCMP behaviour, an equal apportionment of blame attached to the Trudeau government for its defence of the force, and a consensus view that something had to be done to rectify the situation even if there was no agreement on whether a civilian agency was the appropriate answer. Thanks to Mark Olyan.

53 Dominique Clément, *Canada's Rights Revolution: Social Movements and Social Change, 1937–1982* (Vancouver: UBC Press 2008).

54 See Reg Whitaker, 'The Politics of Security Intelligence Policy-Making in Canada: 1970–1984,' *Intelligence and National Security*, 6, no. 4 (1991): 649–68, for an overview of the various factors at play.

55 McDonald, *Second Report, Volume 2*, appendix 'F,' 'Reasons for Decision of the Commission, October 13, 1978,' 1175–91.

56 Reg Whitaker, 'Canada: The RCMP Scandals,' in Andrei S. Marcovits and Mark Silverstein, eds., *The Politics of Scandal: Power and Process in Liberal Democracies* (New York: Holmes and Meier 1988), 38–61.

57 McDonald Commission, *Second Report, Volume 1*, 9–10; James Littleton, *Target Nation: Canada and the Western Intelligence Network* (Toronto: Lester and Orpen Dennys 1986), 149–50.

58 McDonald Commission, *Second Report, Volume 2*, 843.

59 For a survey of the evolution of McDonald recommendations into law, see Stuart Farson, 'Restructuring Control in Canada: The McDonald Commission of Inquiry and Its Legacy,' in Glen Hastedt, ed., *Controlling Intelligence* (London: Frank Cass 1991), 157–88.

60 Littleton, *Target Nation*, 150.

61 On the reaction to C-157, see ibid., 152–8; Whitaker, 'Politics of Security Intelligence Policy-Making,' 661–3.

62 Russell not only directed the commission's research but had largely set the agenda for the commission's recommendations with a paper laying out the parameters of the reform debate at the outset of the inquiry: Reg Whitaker, 'Designing a Balance between Freedom and Security,' in Joseph F. Fletcher, ed., *Ideas in Action: Essays on Politics and Law in Honour of Peter Russell* (Toronto: University of Toronto Press 1999), 127–9.

63 Quoted in Canada, House of Commons, Minutes of Proceedings and Evidence of the Special Committee on the Review of the *CSIS Act* and the *Security Offences Act*, 1989/90, no. 17, 5.

64 Canada, House of Commons, 23rd Parliament, 1st Session, Bill C-157, s.22(1).

65 The committee held nineteen days of public hearings and received twenty-five formal briefs.

66 Canada, Senate, Report of the Special Committee of the Senate on the Canadian Security Intelligence Service, *Delicate Balance: A Security Intelligence Service in a Democratic Society* (Ottawa, 1983).

67 Ibid., 6.

11 Old Wine into New Bottles: CSIS, 1984–2001

1 'Neither do men put new wine into old bottles: else the bottles break, and the wine runneth out, and the bottles perish: but they put new wine into new bottles, and both are preserved' (Matthew 9:17).

2 Reviewing CSIS-RCMP cooperation in the investigation of the Air India bombing, SIRC reported that in the BC Region 'CSIS personnel who continued to exercise their membership rights in the RCMP NCO's Mess were subjected to some verbal abuse from the RCMP members there' (Security Intelligence Review Committee, *CSIS Activities in regard to the Destruction of Air India Flight 182 on June 23, 1985*, 16 November 1992, Top Secret File No 2800-5, expurgated by SIRC).

3 Robert Kaplan, Memorandum, 'Bill C-9 and the Conduct of RCMP Security Responsibilities,' 10 July 1984, with covering letter to T.D. Finn, CSIS director, 29 July 1984, annex B to SIRC, *CSIS Activities*.

4 Canada, Revised Statutes (R.S.), 1985, c.S-7.

5 The Maher Arar affair and the O'Connor Inquiry would later put a harsh spotlight on the inadequate accountability of the RCMP's national-security activities (see chapter 12).

6 A point made by John Lewis Gaddis in *The Cold War: A New History* (New York: Penguin 2005), 230–6.

7 R. James Woolsey, testimony before the Senate Select Committee on Intelligence, 2 February 1993.

8 Reg Whitaker and Stuart Farson, 'Accountability in and for National Security,' Institute for Research in Public Policy, *Choices*, 15, no. 9 (2009): 29–30.

9 Reg Whitaker, 'Security Intelligence in a Cold Climate,' in Gene Swimmer, ed., *How Ottawa Spends 1996–97: Life under the Knife* (Ottawa: Carleton University Press 1996), 409–42.

10 Two academic publications resulted from such meetings: C.E.S. Franks, ed., *Dissent and the State* (Toronto: Oxford University Press 1989); and Peter Hanks and John D. McCamus, eds., *National Security: Surveillance and Accountability in a Democratic Society* (Cowansville, Que.: Les Editions Yvon Blais 1989).

11 A publication that came out of a 1989 CASIS conference is A. Stuart Farson, David Stafford, and Wesley K. Wark, eds., *Security and Intelligence in a Changing World: New Perspectives for the 1990s* (London: Frank Cass 1991).

12 Discussion of the Air India intelligence failure is based partially upon the report to the Air India Commission of Inquiry (*Air India Flight 182: Aviation Security Issues*) by the CATSA Act Review Advisory Panel, which one of the authors (Whitaker) chaired. References to this document are limited to the redacted portions of that report as tabled by the commission. Most of the information in this section is drawn from the report of the Air India Inquiry: Commission of Inquiry into the Investigation of the Bombing of Air India Flight 182, *Final Report, Air India Flight 182: A Canadian Tragedy*, 5 vols. (Ottawa: Public Works and Government Services, 2010) (hereafter AICR). Another important source is the (belated) SIRC review of the CSIS role in the Air India affair: SIRC, *CSIS Activities*. Journalistic sources on Air India include Ian Mulgrew, *Unholy Terror: The Sikhs and International Terrorism* (Toronto: Key Porter 1988); Kim Bolan, *Loss of Faith: How the Air India Bombers Got Away with Murder* (Toronto: McClelland and Stewart 2005); and Salim Jiwa and Donald J. Hauka, *Margin of Terror: A Reporter's Twenty-Year Odyssey Covering the Tragedies of the Air India Bombing* (Toronto: Key Porter 2006).

13 The reference is to the prophecy of the three witches in Shakespeare's *Macbeth* that Macbeth will 'never vanquish'd be until Great Birnam Wood to high Dunsinane Hill shall come against him.' Macduff leads an army against Macbeth by deception: his soldiers are disguised as the trees in Birnam Wood while they advance imperceptibly on Macbeth's castle. The witches' threat assessment was technically accurate but misleading as actionable intelligence, fatally so for Macbeth.

14 Tensions between the RCMP and CSIS had surfaced during the visit of Indian Prime Minister Rajiv Gandhi to North America in the spring of 1985,

with the two agencies differing in their interpretation of threat assessments from the Indian government concerning Gandhi's safety. A book by two journalists alleging Indian intelligence manipulation of the Air India attack appears to have been based on two CSIS sources: Zuhair Kashmiri and Bryan McAndrew, *Soft Target: The Real Story behind the Air India Disaster*, 2nd ed. (Toronto: James Lorimer 2005). Along with the Indian government, the RCMP publicly denied any Indian involvement. In 1992 the RCMP informed the chair of SIRC that 'the RCMP does not have any evidence to support this theory': SIRC, *CSIS Activities*, 117–18. This thesis of Indian involvement remains contentious and unproven, but it may well have played a role in straining relations between the two agencies charged with protecting Canadian security.

15 The events that led to the rapid rise of violent Sikh extremism are summarized by the commission as 'the occupation and fortification of the Golden Temple in Amritsar, Sikhism's central shrine, by armed Sikh separatists, the subsequent bloody storming of the Golden Temple by the Indian army, and the resulting massacres and intercommunal violence in the State of Punjab, all of which culminated in the assassination of Indian Prime Minister Indira Gandhi by her own Sikh bodyguards. This chain of events led to a rise in anti-Indian sentiment within the Sikh diaspora, including the Sikh community in Canada.' AICR, 1: 3, 84–5.

16 Incidents of Armenian terrorism directed at Turkish diplomats in Canada can be found in J.L. Granatstein and David Stafford, *Spy Wars: Espionage and Canada from Gouzenko to Glasnost* (Toronto: Key Porter 1990), 252–5.

17 AICR, 1: 3, 86.

18 Ibid., 1: 3, 87.

19 SIRC, *CSIS Activities*, 22.

20 AICR, 1: 3.2, 90.

21 SIRC, *CSIS Activities*, 78.

22 Ibid., 90.

23 AICR, 1: 3.9.2, 119.

24 AICR, 1:3.3, 97.

25 Since one of the authors (Whitaker) reported to the Commission on the Air India on the security situation in 1985 (see n.10), and had unrestricted access to government records in preparation of that report, he can affirm that no document as described by Bartleman seems to have been retained, nor any references to such a document. Of course, it remains possible that such a document might have been destroyed at the time, or lost, although the latter would seem unlikely. The point here is that government witnesses may not have been part of a concerted attempt to undermine Bartleman's

credibility, as the commission seemed to believe, but were simply responding honestly to testimony they found puzzling.

26 These included a record made by the Vancouver Police of a meeting of
Sikh extremists two weeks before the bombing in which one militant, in
response to a complaint by another extremist about the lack of attacks
against Indian targets, promised that 'something would be done in two
weeks.' CSIS and the RCMP were both made aware of this threat.

27 AICR, 1: 3.3, 98.

28 AICR, 1: 3.3, 98.

29 It was E's refusal to testify that led the crown to contemplate the retroactive application of the controversial 'investigative hearing' clause in the
Anti-Terrorism Act 2001 (see chapter 12) to compel her to produce her
information. Curiously, after gaining a court ruling upholding the constitutionality of the power, it was never actually invoked.

30 AICR, 1: 3.9.1, 118–19.

31 AICR, 1: 3.9.2, 120.

32 In *R. v. Reyat*, 2011 BCSC 14, 7 January 2011 (Docket: 23744), Mr Justice
McEwan of the British Columbia Supreme Court sentenced Reyat to nine
years for perjury, multiple examples of which occurred when he was
called as an uncooperative witness at the failed prosecutions of Ripudaman Singh Malik and Ajaib Singh Bagri in 2005.

33 AICR 1:3.12.1, 141. Stuart Farson, 'Accounting for Disaster: The Quest for
"Closure" after Aerial Mass Murder – the Downing of Air India Flight 182
in Comparative Perspective,' in Karim-Ally S. Kassam, ed., *Understanding Terror: Perspectives for Canadians* (Calgary: University of Calgary Press
2010), 67–100.

34 Public Safety Canada, 'Action Plan: The Government of Canada Response
to the Commission of Inquiry into the Investigation of the Bombing of Air
India Flight 182,' December 2010, http://www.publicsafety.gc.ca/prg/ns/
ai182/res-rep-eng.aspx; Tonda MacCharles, 'Air India Inquiry Head Baf-
fled by Ottawa's Response,' *Toronto Star*, 7 December 2010. A critical view
of the government's response to Major can be found in Reg Whitaker, 'Air
India: Still a Policy Debacle after All These Years?' Parts 1 and 2, *PRISM:
The National Security Practices Monitor*, 12 and 31 December 2010, http://
prism-magazine.com/2010/12/air-india-still-a-policy-debacle-after-all-
these-years/. http://prism-magazine.com/2010/12/air-india-still-a-
policy-debacle-after-all-these-years-part-2-of-2/#comment-3590.

35 Journalist Richard Cleroux points out that all four had been involved in
the by-now notorious FEATHER BED file (see chapter 8); the idea that
there may have been a kind of FEATHER BED cabal at the top of the new

service may be exaggerated, but it does point to the continuing Cold War ideological orientation of those directing CSIS. See Richard Cleroux, *Official Secrets: The Story behind the Canadian Security Intelligence Service* (Toronto: McGraw-Hill Ryerson 1990), 90–1.

36 Addressing a 1987 academic conference on national security and the law, Finn made a brief bow to the threat of terrorism (less than two years after Air India), which he acknowledged made it easier for CSIS to arouse public interest, but went on to stress the dominant threat of Soviet espionage and especially 'Communist subversion,' with the Soviets increasingly using 'clandestine and misleading tactics' to convince decision makers to adopt policies favouring the USSR. Ted Finn, 'Domestic Security and the Canadian Security Intelligence Service,' in Hanks and McCamus, eds., *National Security*, 261–9. In private, off-the-record conversation, Finn was, if anything, even more fervent in his hawkish views.

37 SIRC, *Annual Report, 1986–87*, 33–40.

38 The authors of the definitive account of the anti-homosexual bias in Canadian national security seem reluctant to grant that CSIS policy was different from that of its predecessor. They instead recount harrowing tales of continued repression and discrimination in the armed forces, but vaguely lump CSIS into the same bag, as when they write that 'in the 1980s, *major campaigns* against queers continued in the military and the RCMP and CSIS' (Gary Kinsman and Patrizia Gentile, *The Canadian War on Queers: National Security as Sexual Regulation* [Vancouver: UBC Press 2010], 248 [emphasis added]). They provide no evidence of any major, or indeed, minor campaigns of this sort for CSIS, although they certainly do for the military.

39 Peter Gill, 'Symbolic or Real? The Impact of the Canadian Security Intelligence Review Committee, 1984–1988,' *Intelligence and National Security*, 4, no. 3 (1989): 550–75; Reg Whitaker, 'The Politics of Security Intelligence Policy-Making in Canada: II, 1984–91,' *Intelligence and National Security*, 7, no. 2 (1992): 53–76; Reg Whitaker, 'Designing a Balance between Freedom and Security,' in Joseph Fletcher, ed., *Ideas in Action: Essays on Politics and Law in Honour of Peter Russell* (Toronto: University of Toronto Press 1999), 139–41.

40 Quoted in David Vienneau, 'Retiring Watchdog Atkey Doesn't Regret Being "Pain" to Spies,' *Toronto Star*, 1 December 1989.

41 Ward Elcock testimony to the Commission of Inquiry into the Actions of Canadian Officials in Relation to Maher Arar, 21 June 2004, 187.

42 Cleroux, *Official Secrets*, 184.

43 One of Atwal's lawyers, the late David Gibbons, said that the problems

started even earlier when CSIS had breached solicitor-client privilege: David W. Gibbons, 'Criminal Justice, National Security and the Rights of the Accused,' in Hanks and McCamus, eds., *National Security*, 88–91.

44 *People and Process in Transition*, [Osbaldeston] Report to the Solicitor General by the Independent Advisory Team on the Canadian Security Intelligence Service (28 October 1987).

45 Ibid., 13.

46 Ibid., 28.

47 Ibid., 14.

48 SIRC, *Amending the CIS Act: Proposals for the Special Committee of the House of Commons 1989*, 1.

49 Government's Response to the Report of the House of Commons Special Committee on the Review of the Canadian Security Intelligence Service Act and the Security Offences Act, *On Course: National Security for the 1990s* (February 1991), 40.

50 This non-partisan atmosphere was perhaps assisted by the fact of majority government, by contrast to the more rancorous partisan atmosphere in parliamentary committees since the advent of continuous minority parliaments since 2004; but even in the context of a stable Parliament, the degree to which members set aside partisan considerations was unusual.

51 Whitaker, 'Politics of Security Intelligence Policy-Making,' 67.

52 Canada, House of Commons, *In Flux but Not in Crisis*, Report of the Special Committee on the CSIS Act and the Security Offences Act (September 1990), 192.

53 CSIS now has an elaborate multistage internal control process for warrant-application approval. This has led one observer to the view that the main impact of the judicial control of surveillance applications may lie in the internalization of the control process within CSIS: Ian Leigh, 'Secret Proceedings in Canada,' *Osgoode Hall Law Journal*, 34, no. 1 (1996): 173.

54 *In Flux*, 59.

55 *On Course*, 6.

56 Ibid., 31, 33.

57 SIRC, *Annual Report, 1992–93*, 58.

58 Granatstein and Stafford, *Spy Wars*, 245–51. One of the authors (Whitaker) was acting as an adviser to Mohammed's legal counsel and as an expert witness for Mohammed in his various immigration and refugee proceedings. He was personal witness to some of the events described, but such is the obscurity of the affair that he is unable to shed much more light on who was finally responsible for derailing Mohammed's voluntary departure. There is no evidence that Mohammed has been associated in any way with terrorist activity in his two and half decades in Canada.

59 SIRC, *Annual Report, 1989–1990*, 16.

60 CSIS, *Public Report, 1991*, 24–6.

61 SIRC, *Annual Report, 1997–1998: An Operational Audit of CSIS Activities*, 56.

62 SIRC, 'Section 54 Report to the Solicitor General of Canada on CSIS's Use of Its Investigative Powers with respect to the Labour Movement,' 25 March 1988. This SIRC report also drew upon the IG report.

63 CSIS file 1A 195-8-4-1, D Ops, 'Operational Conference – Labour Relations,' 5–7 February 1974; memo to Inspector Walsh, 8 April 1975. A decade later, CSIS called a similar conference, but this time the declassified document is so blacked out as to make it almost impossible to infer anything about any conclusions that may have been drawn: CSIS file 1A 195-8-4-4, 'Work Oriented Operational Conference, Counter Subversion – Labour Unit, Ottawa, Sept. 1985.'

64 The scope of the accusations was summed up in an article by investigative Canadian journalist Richard Cleroux in an American magazine specializing in exposés of national-security scandals: 'Canadian Intelligence Service Abets Neo-Nazis,' *Covert Action*, winter 1994–5, 14–20. In 'Front Man: How CSIS's Neo-Nazi Spy Spiralled out of Control (*This Magazine*, November 1994, 26–9), Cleroux went so far as to imply that the 'floundering' CSIS had kept the front alive for years simply 'to justify CSIS's $206-million annual budget.'

65 Bristow, fearing retaliation from his former comrades, was relocated with his family to another province under a false identity, which in turn was revealed in the media after his brother-in-law shopped the information to the highest journalistic bidder: 'Newspaper Finds Former CSIS Informer in Hiding,' *Canadian Press*, 20 April 1995. It was almost a decade before he finally came out of hiding: Andrew Mitrovica, 'Front Man: Grant Bristow Kept Silent for Almost Ten Years about His Controversial Work as a CSIS Spy in Canada's Neo-Nazi Movement. Now, Finally, He's Ready to Tell His Side of the Story,' *The Walrus*, September 2004.

66 Mitrovica, 'Front Man.'

67 On informers in general and the issues they raise, see Steve Hewitt, *Snitch! A History of the Modern Intelligence Informer* (New York: Continuum 2010).

68 Memoranda, Jean T. Fournier, deputy minister to Hon. Herb Gray, solicitor general, 26 and 29 August 1994, disclosed in part under Access to Information Request #1336-SEC-95012.

69 Section 54 of the CSIS Act indicates that SIRC 'may, on request by the Minister, or at any other time, furnish the Minister with a special report concerning any matter that relates to the performance of its duties and functions.'

70 *People and Process in Transition*, 25.

71 Hon. Pierre Blais, solicitor general, to J.R. Morden, CSIS director, 30 Octo-ber 1989 (SECRET, redacted version released under Access to Information).

72 Inspector General, 'Human Sources' (April 1993) (TOP SECRET, released in redacted form under Access to Information).

73 SIRC, *The Heritage Front Affair*, report to the solicitor general, 9 December 1994.

74 Grant Bristow, 'Witness to the War against Hatred: A Former Undercover Mole for CSIS Describes the Neo-Nazi World He Infiltrated,' *National Post*, 30 July 2008; Mitrovica, 'Front Man.'

75 *In Flux.*

76 The 1993 IG report on human sources, cited above, expressly pointed to concerns about CSIS-source involvement in political parties during an election campaign. Although it is unclear whether the reference is to Bristow, it is likely that this is so. The IG wrote: 'In our opinion, the mere fact that a CSIS source is actively involved in a candidate's election cam-paign, in a political party organization or in party activities might "gener-ate public controversy," if it became public knowledge.' That prediction was certainly borne out the following year. The IG added that 'CSIS should ensure that operational directives are interpreted uniformly, re-gardless of the political party concerned and the type of work done by the source, especially during election campaigns.' For its part, CSIS assured the IG that operational directives dealing with sources who are involved in the activities of political parties would be ready before the next election, although none were in place in 1993.

77 After the Heritage Front infiltration story reached the media, the Reform Party launched its own internal investigation in 1992. See the insider's account in Tom Flanagan, *Waiting for the Wave: The Reform Party and Preston Manning* (Toronto: Stoddard 1995), 92–3.

78 Thanks to Preston Manning for providing a copy of the released portions of the file.

79 The Liberals were acting just like previous Liberal governments on na-tional security. There may also have been a specific political reason why the Liberals chose not to offer any opening for the Reform Party's claims concerning the Mulroney government's politicization of intelligence to un-dermine Reform. The latter was after 1993 a far bigger and more dynamic threat to the Liberals than the fast-fading Conservative Party; there was little advantage to the Liberals in assisting Reform attacks on the lesser threat.

80 When the auditor general carried out the first, landmark, audit of the Canadian intelligence community in 1996, the report was quite specific

in its concern that 'SIRC's continuing effectiveness hinges critically on having Parliament's confidence.' In reference to the Bristow affair, it noted: 'Unfortunately, relations between SIRC and members of the Subcommittee on National Security have become increasingly strained in recent years ... We are concerned by the possibility that continuing strained relations with the Subcommittee could lead to an erosion of Parliament's (and the public's) confidence in SIRC to the point where its effectiveness would be compromised.' Report of the Auditor General of Canada to the House of Commons, chapter 27, *The Canadian Intelligence Community – Control and Accountability* (November 1996), 17–18.

81 A critical examination of the handling of the Bristow affair is Reg Whitaker, 'The "Bristow Affair": A Crisis of Accountability in Canadian Security Intelligence,' *Intelligence and National Security*, 11, no. 2 (1996): 279–305. But see the response from the executive director of SIRC in the same issue: Maurice Archdeacon, 'The Heritage Front Affair,' ibid., 306–12.

82 Inspector general, 'CSIS Handling of Confidential Sources' (April 1995) (TOP SECRET, released in redacted form under Access to Information); H. David Peel, inspector general, to the Hon. Herb Gray, solicitor general, 7 April 1995.

83 CSIS suggested that the reference was in fact to documents on RCMP spying in the 1970s: Jeff Sallot, 'CBC Accused of Making a Mistake in Saying Agency Spied on CUPW,' *Globe and Mail*, 10 September 1994. The heavily redacted documents from the 1970s that were released to CUPW do provide clear evidence of Canada Post management looking for evidence of 'subversive activities' within the postal unions negotiating teams, and receiving the cooperation of the security service in alerting the 'Minister as to the type of persons the Department will be dealing with during negotiations' (M.J. Spooner, inspector officer i/c A Branch, memorandum to file, 'Re: Subversive Activities within the Council of Postal Unions,' 11 June 1974. Our thanks to CUPW for providing copies of files declassified at its Access Request in 1995).

84 Evert Hoogers, 'In Whose Public Interest? The Canadian Union of Postal Workers and National Security,' in Gary Kinsmen, Dieter K. Buse, and Mercedes Steedman, eds., *Whose National Security? Canadian State Surveillance and the Creation of Enemies* (Toronto: Between the Lines 2000), 246–55. Hoogers grants that CSIS surveillance of CUPW is not 'as extensive' as that practised by the RCMP, and admits that the facts are 'difficult to verify,' but nonetheless insists that the union continues to be targeted by CSIS. Yet the evidence he does produce is less than convincing, blurring the line between CSIS and 'law-enforcement' agencies.

85 Andrew Mitrovica, *Covert Entry: Spies, Lies and Crimes inside Canada's Secret Service* (Toronto: Random House 2002), 140–9.

86 Val Meredith, MP, press release, 28 March 1996.

87 'A Review of the Security Screening Investigation of "John Shevnikov" [Pseudonym].' The fullest version of the suspicions against the translator can be found in Normand Lester's rather credulous account: *Enquêtes sur les services secrets* (Montreal: Les Editions de l'Homme 1998), 257–88.

88 Cleroux, *Official Secrets*, 212.

89 Frank Pratt and the Honourable Val Meredith, Ontario Court (General Division) 99756/96. One of the authors (Whitaker) was an expert witness for the plaintiff Pratt in this action.

90 At one point, Roy had taken his accusations about the translator directly to the FBI in Washington without the sanction of his superiors – a clear breach of protocol, not to speak of a violation of the conditions of his security clearance.

91 T.J. Bradley, Director General Secretariat, CSIS, to Maurice Archdeacon, executive director, SIRC, 22 August 1994; *Pratt v. Meredith*, Affidavit of Documents.

92 The most complete account of the Lamberts' story is in Mitrovica, *Covert Entry*, 173–247.

93 Ibid., 233.

94 Ibid., 242.

95 IMM-2499-05 2006, FC 912, *Elena Miller and Peter Miller (Applicants) v. The Solicitor General of Canada and Minister of Public Safety and Emergency Preparedness (Respondent)*, Federal Court, Chief Justice Allan Lutfy, Toronto, 26 April, 24 July 2006.

96 David Kilgour, *Betrayal: The Spy Canada Abandoned* (Scarborough, Ont.: Prentice Hall 1994); Cleroux, *Official Secrets*, 147–64.

97 SIRC, *Amending the CSIS Act*, 2–4.

98 *In Flux*, 19–21.

99 There were originally four members, two from the RCMP Criminal Analysis Branch and two from the CSIS Analysis and Production Branch, assigned to the project. The draft appears to have been the joint production of Josée Thérien from the RCMP and Michel Juneau-Katsuya from CSIS. The latter, who was replaced on the project after the hostile reception accorded the draft by CSIS brass, later left the service and as a private security consultant has become a familiar face on Canadian media as a commentator on CSIS and security issues. He is also co-author of a book (Michel Juneau-Katsuya and Fabrice de Pierrebourg, *Nest of Spies: The Startling Truth about Foreign Agents at Work within Canada's Borders* [Toronto:

Harper-Collins 2009]) that identifies Chinese espionage as the 'greatest threat' to Canada.

100 We are in possession of an unredacted version of the draft ('Sidewinder SECRET RCMP-CSIS Joint Review Committee Draft Submission,' 24 June 1997) that was made available on the Internet in 2000. The provenance of this leak is mysterious, but it seems likely to have come from the RCMP, aggrieved at the hostile reception accorded the draft by CSIS. The rejected draft subsequently took on a life of its own on various right-wing blogs and websites, and was revived once again after CSIS Director Richard Fadden made controversial remarks on CBC TV in 2010 pointing to alleged, but unnamed, Chinese agents of influence in provincial cabinets and municipal councils, remarks linked to the old SIDEWINDER controversy: Andrew Mitrovica, 'Spies Blow in Political Wind,' *Toronto Star*, 7 July 2010.

101 *SIRC Report, 1999–2000: An Operational Audit of the Canadian Security Intelligence Service* (2000), 5–6.

102 See, for instance, Andrew Mitrovica and Jeff Sallot, 'China Set up Crime Web in Canada, Suppressed Federal Study Says,' *Globe and Mail*, 29 April 2000.

103 *SIRC Report, 1999–2000*, 6–7.

104 One of the pro-SIDEWINDER crusaders is former Canadian diplomat Brian McAdam, who claims to have unearthed vast corruption and criminal penetration in the Hong Kong immigration office and fed the SIDEWINDER investigators with information: Donna Jacobs, 'One Man's China Crusade: "I Was Mocked, Demeaned and Threatened in a Hostile Environment While Dealing with Some of the World's Most Ruthless Ciminals,"' *Ottawa Citizen*, 25 August 2008.

12 After the Deluge: In the Shadow of the Twin Towers, 2001–10

1 See Reg Whitaker, 'Securing the "Ontario-Vermont Border": Myths and Realities in post-9/11 Canadian-American Security Relations,' *International Journal*, 60, no. 1 (2004–5): 53–70. The myth of the Canadian-9/11 connection has proved remarkably durable, even resurfacing in the words of the new homeland security secretary in the incoming Democratic administration of President Barack Obama in 2009, words for which she eventually offered a grudging apology. Andrew Mitrovica, 'Former U.S. Spy Linked 9/11 Terrorists to Canada,' *Toronto Star*, 24 April 2009; Mitch Potter and Allan Woods, 'US Security Czar Stops Blaming Canada: Napolitano Says She "Misunderstood" Question about Canadian Connection to Sept. 11 Bombers,' *Toronto Star*, 22 April 2009.

2 Stuart Farson and Reg Whitaker, 'Canada,' in Stuart Farson et al., eds., *PSI Handbook of Global Security and Intelligence: National Approaches*, vol. 1, *The Americas and Asia* (Westport, Conn.: Praeger Security International 2008), 21–51; Reg Whitaker, 'More or Less Than Meets the Eye? The New National Security Agenda,' in G. Bruce Doern, ed., *How Ottawa Spends 2003–2004: Regime Change and Policy Shift* (Don Mills, Ont.: Oxford University Press 2003), 44–58; and Reg Whitaker, 'Made in Canada? The New Public Safety Paradigm,' in G. Bruce Doern, ed., *How Ottawa Spends, 2005–2006: Managing the Minority* (Montreal and Kingston, Ont.: McGill-Queen's University Press 2005), 77–98.

3 WikiLeaks, U.S. Department of State, 08OTTAWA918 2008-07-09 18:06, SECRET//NOFORN Embassy Ottawa SUBJECT: COUNSELOR, CSIS DIRECTOR DISCUSS CT THREATS, PAKISTAN, AFGHANISTAN, IRAN REF: A. OTTAWA 360; Colin Freeze, 'Canadian Spy Secrets Exposed in WikiLeaks Dump,' *Globe and Mail*, 29 November 2010.

4 Farson and Whitaker, 'Canada,' 28.

5 CSIS, *Public Report, 2007–2008*, 30.

6 Ibid., 28.

7 *Securing an Open Society: Canada's National Security Policy*; Reg Whitaker, 'Made in Canada?' 77–98.

8 49–50 Elizabeth II, c.41.

9 Papers critical of the legislation at an academic conference were rushed with unusual speed into print to coincide with parliamentary hearings on second reading: Ronald J. Daniels, Patrick Macklem, and Kent Roach, eds., *The Security of Freedom: Essays on Canada's Anti-Terrorism Bill* (Toronto: University of Toronto Press 2001). See also Kent Roach, *September 11: Consequences for Canada* (Montreal and Kingston, Ont.: McGill-Queen's University Press 2003), 21–114; Craig Forcese, *National Security Law: Canadian Practice in International Perspective* (Toronto: Irwin Law 2008), 261–300.

10 Forcese, *National Security Law*, 268–70. This tradition was not unbroken. It might be argued that the notorious section 98 of the Criminal Code that outlawed teaching, advocating, advising, or defending the use of force to accomplish 'governmental, industrial or economic change' skated close to criminalizing motive. No motive was, however, actually specified, even though Communists were the main target. When section 98 was repealed in 1935, it was replaced by a section that specified a presumption of a 'seditious intention'; M.L. Friedland, *National Security: The Legal Dimensions*, study prepared for the McDonald Commission (Ottawa, 1979), 22–3. Although this muddies the water to a degree, the Anti-Terrorism Act was very specific in singling out motives.

11 Kent Roach, 'Better Late Than Never? The Canadian Parliamentary Review of the *Anti-Terrorism Act*,' Institute for Research in Public Policy, *IRPP Policy Choices*, 13, no. 5 (2007): 9–11.

12 Even before the Conservatives achieved a majority, Liberal defections permitted the return of the two clauses to reach second reading in the House before Parliament was dissolved for the election. C-17, Third Session, Fortieth Parliament, 59 Elizabeth II, 2010, C-17, An Act to Amend the Criminal Code (Investigative Hearing and Recognizance with Conditions); Reg Whitaker, 'Will Preventive Arrests and Investigative Hearings Arise from the Dead?' *PRISM: The Security Practices Monitor*, 5 May 2010, http://www.prism-magazine.com/2010/05/will-preventative-arrests-and-investigative-hearings-arise-from-the-dead/; Craig Forcese, 'Catch and Release: A Role for Preventive Detention without Charge in Canadian Anti-Terrorism Law,' Institute for Research in Public Policy, Study no. 7, July 2010, http://www.irpp.org/pubs/IRPPstudy/IRPP_Study_no7.pdf.

13 Security Intelligence Review Committee, *Annual Report 2008–2009: Accountability in a New Era of Security Intelligence* (Ottawa: Public Works and Government Services Canada 2009), 16. The question of potentially illegal actions undertaken by human sources or agents was raised during the Heritage Front affair over the possibly illegal activities of CSIS source Grant Bristow while posing as a neo-Nazi activist (as discussed in the previous chapter). But, if the Heritage Front had been a listed entity under the Anti-Terrorism Act, any activity in support of the front, even activity otherwise legal, could have been construed as illegal under the act.

14 In 2011 reports indicated that CSIS had warned the government that federal departments were under assault from cyber hackers just weeks before an attack crippled key computers in two government departments: Jim Bronskill, 'CSIS Warned Government of Cyber Attacks Just Weeks before Crippling Hack,' Canadian Press, 30 October 2011. This highlighted the apparent overlap of CSIS responsibilities for cyber crime with those of the CSE, an issue that was addressed in SIRC's *Annual Report* of 2010–11, which concluded that there had been no overstepping of jurisdictional boundaries: SIRC, *Checks and Balances: Viewing Security Intelligence through the Lens of Accountability: Annual Report, 2010–2011* (30 September 2011), 17–19. This extension of CSIS responsibilities did not require any changes in its legislative mandate.

15 Peter Gill, *Rounding up the Usual Suspects: Developments in Contemporary Law Enforcement Intelligence* (Aldershot, U.K.: Ashgate Publishing 2000).

16 Commission of Inquiry into the Actions of Canadian Officials in Relation to Maher Arar (hereafter Arar Commission), *A New Review Mechanism for*

the RCMP's National Security Activities (Ottawa: Public Works and Government Services Canada 2006), 43.

17 Public Safety Canada, 'Action Plan: The Government of Canada Response to the Commission of Inquiry into the Investigation of the Bombing of Air India Flight 182,' 7 December 2010, http://www.publicsafety.gc.ca/prg/ns/ai182/res-rep-eng.aspx.

18 Arar Commission, *New Review Mechanism*, 102.

19 Remarks by Director Richard B. Fadden to the House of Commons Standing Committee on Public Safety and National Security, 11 May 2010, http://www.csis.gc.ca/cmmn/rmrks_hc_stndng_cmmtt_11052010-eng.asp.

20 Isabel Teotonio, 'No Entrapment, Court Rules in Terror Case,' *Toronto Star*, 24 March 2009.

21 'A second informant, Mubin Shaikh, decided to go public. Now you can't shut him up. He's been interviewed by the *Star*, the *National Post*, the *Los Angeles Times*, the CBC and most recently the BBC': Thomas Walkom, 'Terror Trial Proceedings Troubling: Bizarre Allegations about Toronto 18, Unorthodox Decisions Are Raising Questions about Crown's Case,' *Toronto Star*, 25 September 2007.

22 Neil Macdonald, 'Key CSIS RCMP Operative Denounced to US. WikiLeaks: Crown's Star Witness in Toronto 18 Trial Named to US as Conspirator,' CBC News, 19 May 2011, http://www.cbc.ca/news/canada/story/2011/05/18/mubin-shaikh-wikileaks.html; Thomas Walkom, 'CSIS Adds Its Own Mole to Terror List,' *Toronto Star*, 19 May 2011; Wesley Wark, 'No One Wants Another Arar Case,' *Ottawa Citizen*, 21 May 2011.

23 Colin Freeze, 'Toronto 18: How a Police Agent Cracked a Terror Cell,' *Globe and Mail*, 3 September 2009.

24 Thomas Walkom, 'Victory for Crown and Moles,' *Toronto Star*, 17 February 2010.

25 Isabel Teotonio and Bob Mitchell, 'Two Men Guilty in Final Toronto 18 Terror Trial,' *Toronto Star*, 23 June 2010.

26 Chris Cobb and Ian Macleod, 'Wiretap Used to Snag Terror Suspect: Pakistani Intelligence Claims to Have Tipped off Canada,' *Ottawa Citizen*, 1 September 2010. The Pakistani connection has triggered concerns about possible tainting of evidence because of Pakistani interrogation methods deemed abusive by Canadian standards (see chapter 13): Craig Forcese, 'Ottawa Terrorism Arrests: The Derivative Evidence Issue,' *National Security Law Blog*, 1 September 2010, http://www.cforcese.typepad.com/ns/2010/09/ottawa-terrorism-arrests-the-derivative-evidence-issue.html. So 'homegrown' is this second alleged ring that the first man arrested

turned out to have been a one-time contestant on the *Canadian Idol* reality TV show: Michelle Shephard, 'Terrorism's Theatre of the Absurd,' *Toronto Star*, 27 August 2010; Stewart Bell, 'Radicalization in Canada Top Intelligence Priority,' *National Post*, 25 August 2010.

27 Integrated Threat Assessment Centre (ITAC), http://www.itac-ciem.gc.ca (18 February 2010); Arar Commission, *New Review Mechanism*, 141–3.

28 Commission of Inquiry into the Investigation of the Bombing of Air India Flight 182, *Final Report, Air India Flight 182: A Canadian Tragedy*, 5 vols., vol. 3, *The Relationship between Intelligence and Evidence and the Challenges of Terrorism Prosecutions* (Ottawa: Public Works and Government Services 2010), chapter 2, 49–64.

29 'Let's face it: no one is in charge of Canadian security: The job of ensuring Canada's security should belong to Prime Minister Harper, who should give urgent consideration to establishing a national security czar.' *Globe and Mail*, 25 June 2010.

30 Public Safety Canada, 'Action Plan: The Government of Canada Response to the Commission of Inquiry into the Investigation of the Bombing of Air India Flight 182.'

31 Christine Boyd and Allan Woods, 'CSIS Hands over Canadian al-Qaeda Suspect,' *Globe and Mail*, 29 July 2000.

32 Josh White and Keith B. Richburg, 'Terror Informant for FBI Allegedly Targeted Agents, Once-Trusted Jabarah Sentenced to Prison,' *Washington Post*, 19 January 2008.

33 SIRC, 'Mohammed Mansour Jabarah, Section 54 Report, 2006–2007,' Summary.

34 Details on the Govan case are drawn from the fine book by Mary Jo Leddy, *Our Friendly Local Terrorist* (Toronto: Between the Lines 2010), especially 97–116 and 139–41. Leddy was a tireless supporter of Govan; her personal account of the affair is supplemented in an appendix by lawyer Sharry Aiken's more academic 'Manufacturing "Terrorists": Refugees, National Security, and Canadian Law,' 143–74.

35 Immigration and Refugee Protection Act, Statutes of Canada (S.C.) 2001, c.27, s.77.

36 Arar Commission, *New Review Mechanism*, 138.

37 The links between security certificates and indefinite detention are explored in Forcese, *National Security Law*, 569–75.

38 2007 SCC 9.

39 Public-version dossiers on all five were made available for a time on the Federal Court of Canada website, although this is no longer the case.

40 CSIS Backgrounder no. 14, Certificates under the *Immigration and Refugee*

Protection Act (IRPA), revised February 2005. This backgrounder was accessed on the CSIS website in 2008 (http://www.csis-scrs.gc.ca/nwsrm/bckgrndrs/index-eng.asp), but by the summer of 2009, following CSIS difficulties with the Federal Court over its security-certificate intelligence reports, the backgrounder disappeared from the website without explanation.

41 2007 SCC 9.

42 2008 SCC 38.

43 2009 FC 546.

44 Even though the claim that Charkaoui had been heard plotting the bombing of an airliner had been ruled as inadmissible in court, the alleged document on which this allegation was based was leaked, likely by CSIS, to *La Presse* following the quashing of Charkaoui's security certificate. This could only be interpreted as an attempt to smear Charkaoui's reputation after CSIS had failed to sustain the security certificate against him, yet the government showed no interest in pursuing the source of the leak, which was in apparent breach of the Security of Information Act: Reg Whitaker, 'When Governments Take a Leak, It Can Smell Very Bad: The Charkaoui, Abdelrazik Leaks,' *Prism: The Security Practices Monitor*, 12 August 2011, http://prism-magazine.com/2011/08/when-governments-take-a-leak-it-can-smell-very-bad/.

45 Thomas Walkom, 'Six Years in Legal Labyrinth,' *Toronto Star*, 26 August 2009. CSIS's admission that Charkaoui only fits the profile of a sleeper agent, that he *'could be one,'* offers an eerie parallel to the Cold War era with its Communist spies who *might have been* because they fitted a preconceived profile of what a spy might look like – unfortunates like Herbert Norman or Leslie James Bennett (see chapter 8).

46 Colin Freeze, 'R. v. Charkaoui: A David and Goliath Story,' *Globe and Mail*, 24 September 2009.

47 La Cour fédérale, Dossier DES-4-08, Directive écrit de la Cour, Tremblay-Lamer, J., 5 August 2009; Jim Bronskill, 'Federal Terror Case against Charkaoui in Jeopardy,' Canadian Press, 20 August 2009.

48 La Cour fédérale, Dossier: DES 4-08, Tremblay-Lamer, J; Les Perreaux and Colin Freeze, 'Judge Lifts Charkaoui Restrictions,' *Globe and Mail*, 24 September 2009.

49 André Seguin, counsel, CSIS Legal Services, to Nancy Allen, registrar, Designated Proceedings, Federal Court, 26 May 2009. A redacted version of this letter was disclosed in a communication from Mr Justice Simon Noël, Federal Court of Canada, Docket DES-5-08, 5 June 2009.

50 The citation is from *Ruby v. Canada (Solicitor General)*, [2002] S.C.J. No. 73,

at para. 27. The citation is actually slightly misquoted in the CSIS letter by the omission of two words, but it has been presented correctly here.

51 2009 FC 553.

52 2009 FC 204.

53 Michael W. Duffy to the Hon. Allan Lutfy, 4 June 2009 (Federal Court of Canada, Docket DES-5-08, 5 June 2009).

54 The raid involved sixteen law-enforcement officers and three canine units (an 'explosives dog,' a 'weapons dog,' and a 'currency dog'). A number of documents were seized, particularly everything found with Arabic writing, computers, disks, CDs, and videotapes – including material protected by solicitor-client privilege. The supervising officer was a mid-level official who had been told by her superiors that the limits of the search were at her discretion; despite its intrusive nature, the legality of the search had never been discussed. Judge Noël found that, since the CBSA had failed to demonstrate that the search and seizure was authorized, it was unreasonable. In effect (although these are not the court's words), the CBSA had performed an unwarranted search and seizure as a fishing expedition. Judge Noël expressed great concern about the 'intrusive and overbroad nature' of the search, its 'excessive' execution, and the lack of consideration accorded the dignity of the Harkats. FC 659, 2009, Reasons for Order and Order, 23 June 2009.

55 Federal Court of Canada, Docket DES-5-08; Colin Freeze, 'Judge Eases Restrictions on Suspect,' *Globe and Mail*, 21 September 2009.

56 In a later decision, Justice Noël rejected requests by Harkat's counsel for access to a wide range of CSIS information relied upon by the crown, although he noted that this information was available to the special advocates: Federal Court of Canada, Docket DES-5-08, 2009, Reasons for Order, 11 December 2009.

57 Federal Court, Docket DES-5-08, 15 October 2009.

58 FC 1243, DES-5-08, 9 December 2010.

59 FC 1242, DES-5-08, 9 December 2010.

60 FC 1241, DES-5-08, 9 December 2010.

61 2009 FC 314, 24 March 2009.

62 Federal Court of Canada, DES-3-08, Communication to Mr Almrei and his counsel Issued by the Hon. Mr Justice Mosley, 26 June 2009, Entered in Minutes of Hearing Book, vol. 23.

63 Federal Court of Canada, DES-3-08, Reasons for Judgment, 14 December 2009.

64 Jim Bronskill, 'Syrian Canadian Sues for False Imprisonment,' *Canadian Press*, 5 May 2010.

65 Lorne Waldman, 'Troubling Lack of Candour by CSIS: Spy Agency Has Abused Power by Providing Tainted Testimony in Secret Hearings,' *Toronto Star*, 14 July 2009.

66 CSIS Act, s.33(2).

67 Certificate of the Inspector General CSIS – 2008, Submitted to the Minister of Public Safety pursuant to Subsection 33 (2) of the *Canadian Security Intelligence Service Act*, redacted version.

68 Jim Bronskill, 'CSIS Makes Disconcerting Errors, Agency's Inspector-General Finds,' Canadian Press, 27 April 2009.

69 S.C. 2001, c.41, Preamble. The Security of Information Act that supersedes the old Official Secrets Act now includes specific offences related to economic espionage, viz., s.19(1). Every person commits an offence who, at the direction of, for the benefit of, or, in association with a foreign economic entity, fraudulently and without colour of right and to the detriment of Canada's economic interests, international relations, or national defence or national security, (*a*) communicates a trade secret to another person, group, or organization; or (*b*) obtains, retains, alters, or destroys a trade secret. 'Trade secret' is defined in s.19(4) as 'any information, including a formula, pattern, compilation, program, method, technique, process, negotiation position or strategy or any information contained or embodied in a product, device or mechanism that (*a*) is or may be used in a trade or business; (*b*) is not generally known in that trade or business; (*c*) has economic value from not being generally known; and (*d*) is the subject of efforts that are reasonable under the circumstances to maintain its secrecy.'

70 Confidential interview.

71 For a popular exposé of alleged Russian and Chinese espionage and interference in Canada, see Fabrice de Pierrebourg and Michel Juneau-Katsuya, *Nest of Spies: The Startling Truth about Foreign Agents at Work within Canada's Borders* (Toronto: Harper Collins 2009). Unfortunately, despite the fact that Juneau-Katsuya is a former CSIS officer, this books offers little documentation but much in the way of sensational but often unsupported claims.

72 Stewart Bell and Adrian Humphreys, 'Suspected Spy Arrested: False Identity a Russian Technique,' *National Post*, 16 November 2006; Stewart Bell, 'Cold War Spying Never Really Ended: "More Sophisticated,"' *National Post*, 16 November 2006; Doug Struck, 'In Canada, a Sequel to an Old Cloak-and-Dagger Story: Suspect Could Be "Part of the First Post-Soviet Generation" of Spies for Russia,' *Washington Post*, 24 November 2006.

73 The court record is less than informative, with CSIS merely asserting that the Russian SVR is a spy agency, that Hampel is an SVR agent, and that, therefore, he is a threat to Canadian security. CSIS provides no public hint of anything that Hampel might actually have done. *Federal Court in the*

Matter of the Person Alleging to be Paul William Hampel, Statement Summarizing Information Pursuant to Section 78(H) of the IRPA, 20 November 2006, court file no.: DES-3-06.

74 Paul Koring, 'Arrested Russian Spies Accused of Stealing Canadian Identities,' *Globe and Mail*, 29 June 2010.

75 Paul Waldie, 'A Job Given, Then Taken Away: CSIS Feared Zhang Had Ties to Spies,' *Globe and Mail*, 23 December 2005.

76 Colin Freeze, 'Alleged Spying Risk Earns Full Pay – for No Work,' *Globe and Mail*, 7 May 2007.

77 CBC, *The National*, 21–22 June 2010, http://www.cbc.ca/thenational/indepthanalysis/story/2010/06/21/national-insidecsis.html; Dirk Meissner, 'Canadian Politicians Accused of Being under Control of Foreign Governments,' *Toronto Star*, 23 June 2010; Sarah Boesveld, 'Government Infiltrated by Spies, CSIS Boss Says: Intelligence Agency Considers at Least Two Provincial Cabinet Ministers as "Secret Supporters,"' *Globe and Mail*, 23 June 2010.

78 Jonathan Fowlie and Jeff Lee, 'Gordon Campbell Slams CSIS Director over Foreign-Infiltration allegations,' *Vancouver Sun*, 23 June 2010.

79 Statement by Director of the Canadian Security Intelligence Service (CSIS) on Foreign Interference: http://www.csis-scrs.gc.ca/cmmn/dr_mssg_frgn_ntrfrnc-eng.asp. NDP MP Donald Davies later claimed that Fadden had admitted in a letter to a parliamentary committee that he had cleared his comments with the minister of public safety. However, a reading of the letter in question does not indicate any such consultation prior to the airing of the CBC interview: Richard B. Fadden to Roger Préfontaine, clerk of the Standing Committee on National Security and Public Safety, 31 August 2010: http://www.chineseinvancouver.ca/wp-content/uploads/Canadian-Security-Intelligence-Service-2010-09-07-B.pdf.

80 Wesley Wark, 'CSIS Director Blew Himself up,' *Ottawa Citizen*, 25 June 2010; Reg Whitaker, 'Bad Summer for Top Ottawa Secureaucrats,' *Prism: The Security Practices Monitor*, 26 August 2010, http://prism-magazine.com/2010/08/bad-summer-for-top-ottawa-secureaucrats/.

81 Canada, House of Commons, 40th Parliament, 3rd Session, Report of the Standing Committee on Public Safety and National Security, *Report on Canadian Security Intelligence Service Director Richard Fadden's Remarks regarding Alleged Foreign Influence of Canadian Politicians*, March 2011.

82 Jim Bronskill, 'Canada a Target for Foreign Interference, Spy Chief Warns,' *Globe and Mail*, 6 January 2011.

83 Steven Chase, 'Tory MP Apologizes for "Flirtatious" E-Mails to Chinese Reporter,' *Globe and Mail*, 9 September 2011.

84 Security Offences Act (Revised Statutes [R.S.], 1985, c.S-7); An Act to

Amend the Foreign Missions and International Organizations Act (49–50 Elizabeth II 2001–02, c.12).

85 Commission for Public Complaints against the RCMP, Chair's Final Report Following a Public Hearing, 25 March 2002, http://www.cpc-cpp .gc.ca/prr/rep/phr/apec/fr-rf-eng.aspx; W. Wesley Pue, ed., *Pepper in Our Eyes: the APRC Affair* (Vancouver: UBC Press 2000).

86 Rob Ferguson, 'G20 "Secret Law" to Undergo Independent Review,' *Toronto Star*, 22 September 2010.

87 Rob Ferguson, 'Ontario Refuses to Apologize for Secret G20 Law,' *Toronto Star*, 28 April 2011.

88 Ombudsman of Ontario, Report, *Investigation into the Ministry of Community Safety and Correctional Services' Conduct in Relation to Ontario Regulation 233/10 under the Public Works Protection Act: "Caught in the Act,"* André Marin, ombudsman of Ontario, December 2010, http://www.ombudsman .on.ca/media/157555/g20final1-en.pdf. See also: National Union of Public and General Employees and Canadian Civil Liberties Association, *G20 Summit: Accountability in Policing and Governance Public Hearings*, 10–12 November 2010 (Ottawa 2011), http://ccla.org/wordpress/wp-content/ uploads/2011/02/Breach-of-the-Peace-Final-Report.pdf.

13 No More Mr Nice Spy: CSIS and the Dark Side of the War on Terror

1 Colin Freeze, 'CSIS Chief Meets with Saudi King to Discuss Terrorism,' *Globe and Mail*, 20 September 2010.

2 Jeffrey T. Richelson and Desmond Ball, *The Ties That Bind: Intelligence Cooperation between the UKUSA Countries* (London: Allen and Unwin 1985). On the CSE, see Philip Rosen, *The Communications Security Establishment: Canada's Most Secret Intelligence Agency* (Ottawa: Library of Parliament Research Branch 1993). As well, there is a 'tell-all' exposé of limited value by a former CSE employee, Mike Frost, and Michel Gratton, *Spyworld: Inside the Canadian and American Intelligence Establishments* (Toronto: Doubleday Canada 1994).

3 Reg Whitaker, 'More or Less Than Meets the Eye? The New National Security Agenda,' in G. Bruce Doern, ed., *How Ottawa Spends 2003–2004: Regime Change and Policy Shift* (Don Mills, Ont.: Oxford University Press 2003), 51; David Ljunggren, 'No Need for Overseas Spy Service, Manley Says,' *National Post*, 11 April 2002.

4 The debate on foreign-intelligence gathering began with the widespread view that the CSIS mandate limited the service to domestic security-intelligence gathering *in* Canada. In testimony to the House of Commons com-

mittee on national security, CSIS Director Elcock corrected that impression by stating flatly that 'under the *CSIS Act*, threats to the security of Canada can cover either, what some people would describe as foreign intelligence and other people would call security intelligence. It includes both. It includes any kind of intelligence related to threats to the security of Canada wherever it's collected': Canada, House of Commons, Sub-Committee on National Security of the Standing Committee of Justice and Human Rights, Evidence no. 4, Monday, 27 May 2002. Elcock later informed the Canadian Association for Security and Intelligence Studies that 'foreign sources of threat-related information have become predominant ... Events have increasingly required us ... to operate abroad ... Working covertly abroad has become an integral part of the service's operations.' Bruce Campion-Smith, 'Global Spy Role Grows: CSIS Head,' *Toronto Star*, 27 October 2003. In early 2004 it was reported that a panel of senior public servants was mulling over the various options, including a new agency: 'Panel Ponders CIA-Style Spy Service for Canada,' Canadian Press, 25 March 2004. By the end of the year, the Liberal public safety minister, Anne McClellan, was telling the media that CSIS was the 'logical vehicle' for gathering foreign intelligence: Kathleen Harris, 'Minister Calls for More Spies, Foreign Intelligence Crucial: Grit,' *Toronto Sun*, 19 December 2004. The Conservatives dithered for a year and a half before announcing that CSIS would have its foreign mandate expanded to fill the void: 'Not Another Spy Agency,' *Globe and Mail*, 6 June 2007.

5 WikiLeaks, U.S. Department of State, 08OTTAWA918 2008-07-09 18:06, SECRET//NOFORN Embassy Ottawa SUBJECT: COUNSELOR, CSIS DIRECTOR DISCUSS CT THREATS, PAKISTAN, AFGHANISTAN, IRAN REF: A. OTTAWA, 360; Colin Freeze, 'Canadian Spy Secrets Exposed in WikiLeaks Dump,' *Globe and Mail*, 29 November 2010. Three years later, another breakout from the same prison freed almost five hundred Taliban prisoners. This was particularly embarrassing to Canada, since Canadian advisers had been working closely with the Afghan authorities to prevent just such a recurrence: Anna Mehler Paperny, 'Prison Break Throws Canada's Afghan Legacy into Doubt,' *Globe and Mail*, 26 April 2011; Matthew Fisher, 'Hundreds of Prisoners Escape from Kandahar Prison,' *Postmedia News*, 25 April 2011.

6 SECRET//NOFORN//20330708. JTF-GTMO-CDR, 8 July 2008, Memorandum for Commander, United States Southern Command, Subject: Detainee Assessment Brief Guantanamo detainee ISN PK9AG-001452DP(S): http://www.guardian.co.uk/world/guantanamo-files/PK9AG-001452DP?INTCMP=SRCH. Media attention was directed to the American assessment that the detainee in question had misled his British and CSIS

handlers, and perhaps was a double agent for Al-Qaeda (Declan Walsh et al., 'Guantánamo Bay Files: Al-Qaida Assassin "Worked for MI6,"' *Guardian*, 25 April 2011). However, great caution should be exercised in assessing the validity of testimony extracted by the kind of abusive methods employed at Guantánamo. See Annie Machon, 'Guantánamo Bay Files: Was Bin Hamlili Really an MI6 Source?' *Guardian*, 26 April 2011.

7 SIRC, *Annual Report 2009/10: Taking the Measure of Security Intelligence, Time for Reflection* (Ottawa 2010), 5.

8 Ibid., 14–15. National-security law expert Craig Forcese has also drawn attention to the implications: Craig Forcese, 'A Foreign Intelligence Service in Increments?' *National Security Law Blog*, 4 January 2011, http://cforcese .typepad.com/ns/2011/01/a-foreign-intelligence-service-in-increments .html.

9 Remarks by Director Richard B. Fadden to the House of Commons Standing Committee on Public Safety and National Security, 11 May 2010, http://www.csis.gc.ca/cmmn/rmrks_hc_stndng_cmmtt_11052010-eng .asp.

10 The harrowing kidnap is recounted in Robert Fowler, *A Season in Hell* (Toronto: Harper Collins Publishers 2011).

11 Reported in expurgated form in *Re CSIS Act*, 2008 FC 301. The ambiguities and conundrums opened up by this decision have been commented upon by Craig Forcese, 'Spies without Borders: International Law and Intelligence Collection,' *Journal of National Security Law and Policy*, 5 (2011): 179–210.

12 Section 24(b) of the CSIS Act provides that a warrant issued under section 21 may authorize any other person to assist a person acting in accordance with the warrant. The CSE's mandate (National Defence Act, Revised Statutes [R.S.C.] 1985, c.N-5, amended by the *Anti-Terrorism Act*, Statutes of Canada [S.C.] 2001, c.41) authorizes it to acquire foreign intelligence for the government of Canada and to provide technical and operational assistance to federal law-enforcement and security agencies in the performance of their lawful duties, within Canada as well as outside.

13 2009 FC 1058. Federal Court, Docket: CSIS-3-08, 'In the Matter of an Application by [redacted] for a Warrant pursuant to Sections 12 and 21 of the CSIS Act,' R.S.C. 1985, c.C-23; and 'In the Matter of [redacted], October 5, 2009, Amended and Redacted Public Reasons for Order.' It should be noted that redactions in the published order render the precise circumstances of the warrants difficult to decipher, but the legal implications of the decision are clear.

14 Colin Freeze, 'Undercover CSIS Agents Carry Guns in Foreign Flash-

points,' *Globe and Mail*, 25 May 2010. A retired senior diplomat expressed concern about the level of training accorded armed agents abroad: 'Amateurs with guns are dangerous to everyone.' The former chair of SIRC, Ron Atkey, was 'flabbergasted' by the report and indicated that this was something that should be investigated by SIRC, even though it is unclear whether SIRC's mandate extends to CSIS operations outside Canada.

15 On 6 September 2001 Cheney was interviewed by Tim Russert on NBC's *Meet the Press*, in the course of which he said the following: 'We also have to work, though, sort of the dark side, if you will. We've got to spend time in the shadows in the intelligence world. A lot of what needs to be done here will have to be done quietly, without any discussion, using sources and methods that are available to our intelligence agencies, if we're going to be successful. That's the world these folks operate in, and so *it's going to be vital for us to use any means at our disposal, basically, to achieve our objective.*' The emphasized phrase indicates what Cheney, and the Bush administration, meant by working the 'dark side.'

16 Colin Freeze, 'Judge Scalia Cites Jack Bauer as Example in Discussion over Torture,' *Globe and Mail*, 20 June 2007.

17 Alan Dershowitz, *Why Terrorism Works: Understanding the Threat, Responding to the Challenge* (New Haven, Conn.: Yale University Press 2002), 131–64.

18 Michael Ignatieff, *The Lesser Evil: Political Ethics in an Age of Terrorism* (Toronto: Penguin Canada 2004), 133–44. Ignatieff has unfairly been charged with condoning torture, which he ultimately rejects, but his argument is perhaps ambiguous enough about the possibility of exceptions in extreme cases as to invite misunderstanding.

19 *Suresh v. Canada (Minister of Citizenship and Immigration)* 2001 SCC1, [2002] 1 S.C.R. 3 at para. 51. Emphasis added.

20 'Spies under the Thumbscrews,' *The Economist*, 1 August 2009, 12. See also 'The Dark Pursuit of Truth' in the same issue, 20–2.

21 'Legacy of Torture, *New York Times*, 26 August 2010, citing joint research by ProPublica and the *National Law Journal*.

22 Good background on the detainee issue from the Martin to the Harper governments is found in Janice Gross Stein and Eugene Lang, *The Unexpected War: Canada in Kandahar* (Toronto: Viking Canada 2007), 246–58.

23 Military Police Complaints Commission, Afghan Detainee Transfer Investigation, Exhibit MPCC 2008-042: Craig Forcese, *Research Report: Assessment of Complainants' Legal Claims*, March 2010. Posted at Craig Forcese, *National Security Law Blog*, http://www.scribd.com/doc/31192302/MPCC-Research-Report.

24 United Nations Assistance Mission in Afghanistan, 'Mistreatment of
    Conflict-Related Detainees in Afghan Facilities,' 10 October 2011, http://
    unama.unmissions.org/Default.aspx?tabid=1783&ctl=Details&mid=1882
    &ItemID=15279; Alissa J. Rubin, 'UN Finds Systematic Torture in Afghan-
    istan,' *New York Times*, 10 October 2011.

25 Reg Whitaker, 'Prime Minister vs. Parliament,' *Toronto Star*, 18 December
    2009.

26 'Ruling on the Questions of Privilege Raised on March 18, 2010, by the
    Member for Scarborough-Rouge River (Mr Lee), the Member for St John's
    East (Mr Harris) and the Member for Saint-Jean (Mr Bachand) concerning
    the Order of the House of December 10, 2009, respecting the Production of
    Afghan Detainee Documents,' 27 April 2010.

27 Reg Whitaker, 'After the Speaker's Ruling: Where Do We Go from Here?'
    Toronto Star, 29 April 2010.

28 Sessional Paper 8530-403-10, tabled in the House of Commons by the min-
    ister of justice, 14 May 2010. Subsequent interparty negotiations watered
    down the original deal to the extent that NDP walked out of the arrange-
    ment, although the Liberals and the BQ remained on board: Reg Whitaker,
    'Has the Detainee Document Deal Gone Sideways?' *PRISM: The Security
    Practices Monitor*, 21 June 2010, http://prism-magazine.com/2010/06/
    has-the-detainee-document-deal-gone-sideways/.

29 Colin Freeze and Daniel Leblanc, 'Vetting of Afghan Detainee Files Left
    Unfinished, Panel Says,' *Globe and Mail*, 23 June 2011.

30 Testifying before the special committee on the Afghan detainees, CSIS Di-
    rector Richard Fadden spelled out how CSIS became an Afghan player: the
    Canadian Forces 'were not organized' to interview suspects, leaving the
    job to CSIS agents. 'We were frequently brought in to ask them questions,
    usually trying to ascertain their identity, to try and find out what they had
    been up to.' Bruce Campion-Smith, 'Spy Agency CSIS Warns of Homeg-
    rown Terror in Canada,' *Toronto Star*, 12 May 2010.

31 Steven Chase, 'Information from Afghan Intelligence Possibly Tainted by
    Torture, CSIS Official Says,' *Globe and Mail*, 6 May 2010.

32 At the same time as the Canadian controversy was raging, the British gov-
    ernment was facing questioning along very similar lines of its handling of
    detainees in its mission in Helmand province (next to Kandahar where the
    Canadians operate): Doug Saunders, 'British Officers Recorded Claims of
    Detainee Torture, Memos Reveal,' *Globe and Mail*, 21 April 2010.

33 SIRC, *CSIS's Role in Interviewing Afghan Detainees*, Study No. 2010-01 (File
    2800-153 (TO R502), 4 July 2011.

34 It would now appear from testimony before a U.S. congressional commit-

tee and in court proceedings that the decision to render Arar was taken not by the frontline officials at the airport but on instructions sent from senior Justice Department and/or FBI officials in Washington: Sinclair Stewart and Colin Freeze, 'Conspiracy against Arar Reached to Highest Levels, US Court Told,' *Globe and Mail*, 10 December 2008; Paul Koring, Omar El Akkad, and Colin Freeze, 'Porous Border Spurred Arar Rendition: Declassified Report Reveals Motivation for Sending Canadian to Syria – Where He Was Tortured – as U.S. Reopens Probe into His Treatment,' *Globe and Mail*, 6 June 2008.

35 Monia Mazigh, *Hope and Despair: My Struggle to Free My Husband, Maher Arar* (Toronto: McClelland and Stewart 2008).

36 The story in question (Juliet O'Neill, 'Canada's Dossier on Maher Arar: The Existence of a Group of Ottawa Men with Alleged Ties to Al-Qaeda Is at the Root of Why the Government Opposes an Inquiry into the Case,' *Ottawa Citizen*, 8 November 2003) drew extensively on material that was to be found only in the Top Secret files of Project A-O CANADA which had been deliberately leaked by a person or persons within the project. No one has ever been identified and prosecuted for this contravention of the Security of Information Act. Ms. O'Neill did successfully challenge in court the act's application to the recipient of the leak, as opposed to those at the origin of the leak: *O'Neill v. Canada (Attorney General)* [2006] 82 O.R. (3rd) (Ont. Sup. Ct of Jus.). Her view of her role in defence of freedom of the press can be found in O'Neill, 'Rogue Elephants and Press Freedom,' 7th Annual Kesterton Lecture, School of Journalism and Communications, Carleton University, Ottawa, 6 February 2006. A critical view with implications for journalistic ethics in reporting national security is Andrew Mitrovica, 'Hear No Evil, Write No Lies,' *The Walrus*, December/January 2006–7; and Reg Whitaker, 'The Horse's Mouth,' *The Walrus*, March 2007.

37 Commission of Inquiry into the Actions of Canadian Officials in Relation to Maher Arar (hereafter Arar Commission), *Report of the Events Relating to Maher Arar*, 3 vols. (Ottawa: Ministry of Public Works and Government Services 2006); Arar Commission, *A New Review Mechanism for the RCMP's National Security Activities* (Ottawa: Public Works and Government Services 2006). One of the authors, Whitaker, served as a member of the Advisory Panel to Justice O'Connor on the policy-review mandate of the inquiry.

38 Reg Whitaker, 'Arar: The Affair, the Inquiry, the Aftermath,' Institute for Research in Public Policy, *Policy Matters*, 9, no. 1 (2008).

39 Arar Commission, *A New Review Mechanism*, part iv, 3.5, 102–7.

40 Arar Commission, *Report of the Events*, vol. 3, part v, 4.2, 197.

41 Federal Court of Canada, 2007 FC 766, 24 July 2007, *Attorney General of Canada v. Commission of Inquiry into the Actions of Canadian Officials in Relation to Maher Arar*.

42 The additional passages disclosed by court order were in Arar Commission, *Report of the Events*, vol. 1, *Factual Background*, 245.

43 Kerry Pither, *Dark Days: The Story of Four Canadians Tortured in the Name of Fighting Terror* (Toronto: Penguin Books 2008).

44 Andrew Duffy, 'RCMP Documents Indicate Terror Case against Ottawa Man Unfounded and "Racist,"' *Ottawa Citizen*, 25 October 2011. Emphasis added.

45 The Honourable Frank Iacobucci, Commissioner, *Internal Inquiry into the Actions of Canadian Officials in Relation to Abdullah Almalki, Ahmad Abou-Elmaati and Muayyed Nureddin* (Ottawa: Public Works and Government Services Canada 2008).

46 Ibid., 34–9.

47 Ibid., 109–92.

48 Ibid., *Supplement to Public Report*, 23 February 2010.

49 Iacobucci, *Internal Inquiry*, 437–55.

50 Ibid., 397–435. Iacobucci's citation of O'Connor is found at 417.

51 That Abdelrazik's story reached the light of day is almost entirely the result of dogged investigative reporting by the *Globe and Mail*, and in particular reporter Paul Koring. No other media outlets showed any interest until the matter reached the attention of Parliament. The facts of Abdelrazik's predicament are summarized succinctly by Federal Court justice Russel W. Zinn, 2009 FC 580, 4–17, paras. 8–41.

52 Justice Zinn, despite in-camera hearings, states unequivocally: 'There is no evidence in the record before this Court which on which one can reasonably conclude that Mr. Abdelrazik has any connection to terrorism or terrorists, other than his association with these two individuals (i.e., Ressam and Charkaoui).'

53 Federal Court of Canada, T-5080-09, *Abousfian Abdelrazik and Attorney General of Canada and Lawrence Cannon, Statement of Claim*, 21 September 2009.

54 Ibid., 38–42. Abdelrazik gave a press conference upon his return to Canada in 2009. The quotes attributed to the unnamed CSIS officer are according to Abdelrazik and are unconfirmed: 'CSIS to Abdelrazik: "Sudan Is Your Guantanamo"' (*Globe and Mail*, 23 July 2009); Joanna Smith, 'Strange Case of Tortured Canadian,' *Toronto Star*, 24 July 2009.

55 Abdelrazik, *Statement of Claim*, 113–15. Speaking before an unofficial meeting of the House Commons Committee on Foreign Affairs during the prolonged prorogation of Parliament imposed by the prime minister from

December 2009 to March 2010, Abdelrazik told the committee that, when
the Conservative parliamentary secretary for foreign affairs visited him
during his exile at the Canadian embassy, he quizzed him about Osama
bin Laden, Al-Qaeda, and his opinions on Israel. He claimed Deepak
Obhrai told him that, if he didn't answer the questions, 'there's no help.'
Tonda MacCharles, 'Abdelrazik Wants His Name off UN Blacklist,' *Toronto
Star*, 3 February 2010.

56 Paul Koring, 'CSIS Notes Reveal How Canadian Was Kept in Exile,' *Globe
and Mail*, 22 September 2011.

57 Memorandum from Khartoum Embassy to Foreign Affairs, Ottawa, 21
March 2006, Subject: Sudan Consular Case, Abousfian Abdelrazik; Paul
Koring, 'Canada Was Indifferent to Sudan's Threat to Kill Abdelrazik, Files
Show,' *Globe and Mail*, 21 July 2009.

58 The Security Council Committee established this committee pursuant to
Resolution 1267 (1999) on 15 October 1999, subsequently modified numerous times. It is also known as the Al-Qaeda and Taliban Sanctions Committee.

59 Memorandum from Khartoum embassy to Ottawa, 16 December 2006,
Subject: KHGR0532 – Sudan, Meeting with NSI concerning Consular Case.

60 According to then CSIS Director Jim Judd: 'The Service has stated for
the public record that it does not, and has not, arranged for the arrest of
Canadian citizens overseas and that, in this matter, CSIS employees have
conducted themselves in accordance with the CSIS Act, Canadian law, and
policy.' Judd to Gary Filmon, chairman of the Security Intelligence Review
Committee, 5 March 2009.

61 Paul Koring, 'Ottawa's Case for Barring Return of Canadian Citizen
Doesn't Wash, UN Says: Travel Ban Exemption Allows for His Entry,' *Globe
and Mail*, 7 May 2009.

62 In answer to a written question in the House of Commons, the justice minister stated that the 'total costs of the legal case on the part of the government are approximately $808,177.15': Paul Koring, 'Ottawa Spent $800,000
on Abdelrazik Case,' *Globe and Mail*, 16 September 2009.

63 Gerald Caplan, 'Abdelrazik's Next Challenge,' *Globe and Mail*, 31 July 2009.

64 Abdelrazik, *Statement of Claim*; Paul Koring, 'Abdelrazik Sues Ottawa for
$27-Million,' *Globe and Mail*, 24 September 2009.

65 Abdelrazik, *Statement of Claim*, 139–46, 156.a.

66 Paul Koring, 'Ottawa Rejects Abdelrazik Claim That CSIS Knew He Faced
Torture,' *Globe and Mail*, 20 February 2010.

67 'Abdelrazik Gets OK to Sue Canada,' CBC News, 1 September 2010; 'Complicity in Torture Actionable?' Carmen K. Cheung, British Columbia Civil

Liberties Association, *National Security Blog*, 1 September 2010, http://nationalsecurity.bccla.org/2010/09/01/complicity-in-torture-actionable/.

68 Ron Suskind quotes an FBI official describing Zubayda as rendered certifiably insane, someone moreover who had been used by Al-Qaeda as a kind of 'greeter' rather than a functionary, perhaps a kind of glorified travel agent: *The One Percent Doctrine: Deep Inside America's Pursuit of its Enemies since 9/11* (New York: Simon and Schuster 2006), 99–101.

69 United States District Court for the District of Columbia, Civil Action No. 08-cv-1360 (RWR), *Zayn Al Abidin Muhammad Husayn, Petitioner, vs. Robert Gates, Respondent, Respondent's Memorandum of Points and Authorities in Opposition to Petitioner's Motion for Discovery and Petitioner's Motion for Sanctions*.

70 Scott Shane, 'Waterboarding Used 266 Times on 2 Suspects,' *New York Times*, 20 April 2009.

71 Jane Mayer, *The Dark Side: The Inside Story of How the War on Terror Turned into a War on American Ideals* (New York: Doubleday 2008), 171–9, casts grave doubt on the value of Zubayda's confessions after his repeated waterboarding and the marked deterioration of his mental state.

72 David Johnston, 'At a Secret Interrogation, Dispute Flared over Tactics,' *New York Times*, 10 September 2006; Peter Finn and Joby Warrick, 'Detainee's Harsh Treatment Foiled No Plots: Waterboarding, Rough Interrogation of Abu Zubaida Produced False Leads, Officials Say,' *Washington Post*, 29 March 2009.

73 Ironically, in light of the very visible American hand in Abdelrazik's targeting as a 'terrorist,' the U.S. State Department, in its annual global report on human rights for 2010, cited the Canadian government's long refusal to allow Abdelrazik's return to Canada as one of the rare instances of human-rights abuse in Canada: U.S. Department of State, Bureau of Democracy, Human Rights, and Labor, *2009 Country Reports on Human Rights Practices: Canada*, 11 March 2010, http://www.state.gov/g/drl/rls/hrrpt/2009/wha/136104.htm.

74 Memorandum, John Di Gangi to James R. Wright, 19 July 2006, Subject: Abdelrazik US Embassy Demarche.

75 A CSIS letter to Foreign Affairs dated 6 November 2007 states that 'the Service has no current substantial information regarding Mr. Abdelrazik.' For its part, the RCMP informed Foreign Affairs in a letter dated 15 November 2007 that it 'conducted a review of its files and was unable to locate any current or substantive information that indicates that Mr. Abdelrazik is involved in criminal activity.' Cited in Abdelrazik and the Minister of Foreign Affairs, Federal Court, 12, para. 27.

76 Reg Whitaker, 'When Governments Take a Leak, It Can Smell Very Bad: The Charkaoui, Abdelrazik Leaks,' *Prism: the Security Practices Monitor*, 12 August 2011, http://prism-magazine.com/2011/08/when-governments-take-a-leak-it-can-smell-very-bad/.

77 Paul Koring, 'UN Details Allegations on Abdelrazik's Terrorism Links,' *Globe and Mail*, 23 June 2009. For the 1267 Committee's listing of 'details' (including clearly spurious and unsupported information), see http://www.un.org/sc/committees/1267/NSQI22006E.shtml.

78 Abdelrazik and the Minister of Foreign Affairs, 24, para. 53.

79 In *Her Majesty's Treasury v. A, K, M, Q and G* [2010] UKSC, the Supreme Court struck down the Terrorism Order (implementing the UN's terrorism regime) and the Al-Qaeda and Taliban Order (implementing the UN's 1267 sanctions regime). The court held that the order did not provide for effective judicial remedy to challenge an individual's listing by the 1267 Committee.

80 'Rights Groups Challenge United Nations Blacklist in Court,' British Columbia Civil Liberties Association / International Civil Liberties Monitoring Group, press release, 7 June 2010.

81 Paul Koring, 'Canadian Judge Hopes to Shed Light on Terrorism Blacklist,' *Globe and Mail*, 18 January 2011.

82 Paul Koring, 'Canadian Abousfian Abdelrazik Taken off United Nations Terror List,' *Globe and Mail*, 30 November 2011.

83 Section 54 of the CSIS Act specifies that SIRC 'may, on request by the Minister or at any other time, furnish the Minister with a special report concerning any matter that relates to the performance of its duties and functions.'

84 'Top Spy Seeks Probe of Abdelrazik file,' *Canadian Press*, 20 March 2009. In his letter to the SIRC chair, Judd made clear that he sought the clearance of CSIS's name by a report that would clarify the facts: Judd to Gary Filmon, chairman of the Security Intelligence Review Committee, 5 March 2009.

85 Tonda MacCharles and Bruce Campion-Smith, 'Head of CSIS Stepping Down: In Surprise Move, Jim Judd Is Leaving before End of His Term as Chief of Spy Agency,' *Toronto Star*, 15 April 2009.

86 Paul Koring, 'Spy Watchdog to Probe CSIS Conduct in Abdelrazik Case,' *Globe and Mail*, 29 July 2009.

87 Standing Committee on Public Safety and National Security, *Evidence*, 31 March 2009; Tonda MacCharles, 'CSIS Defies Orders on Torture: Spy Agency Says It Uses Intelligence Extracted That Way "if Lives Are at Stake," despite Federal Ban,' *Toronto Star*, 1 April 2009; Daniel Leblanc, 'CSIS Won't Rule out Tips Derived from Torture,' *Globe and Mail*, 31 March 2009.

88 House of Commons, Standing Committee on Public Safety and National Security, *Report: Review of the Findings and Recommendations Arising from the Iacobucci and O'Connor Inquiries*, June 2009, Part 3: D.

89 Tonda MacCharles, 'CSIS Does Not Condone Torture, Tories Insist: Public Safety Minister Moves Fast to Clarify Testimony by Senior Spy Agency Official,' *Toronto Star*, 2 April 2009.

90 Tonda MacCharles, 'Spy Agency Clarifies Torture Policy,' *Toronto Star*, 3 April 2009; Colin Freeze and Bill Curry, 'Spy Chief Dismisses Witness's Remarks on Torture: CSIS Legal Expert Was "Confused" When He Suggested Canadian Spies Can Rely on Intelligence Obtained through Coercive Interrogation,' *Globe and Mail*, 3 April 2009.

91 Allan Woods, 'The Two Faces of Jim Judd,' *Toronto Star*, 1 December 2010.

92 WikiLeaks, U.S. Department of State, 08OTTAWA918 2008-07-09 18:06, SECRET//NOFORN Embassy Ottawa SUBJECT: COUNSELOR, CSIS DIRECTOR DISCUSS CT THREATS, PAKISTAN, AFGHANISTAN, IRAN REF: A. OTTAWA, 360.

93 O'Brian letter submitted to committee, 1 April 2009.

94 SIRC, *Annual Report, 2005–2006: An Operational Review of the Canadian Security Intelligence Service* (Ottawa 2006), 14.

95 'CSIS Disowns the Plain Truth,' *Globe and Mail*, 3 April 2009.

96 Jim Bronskill, 'CSIS Would Use Torture-Tainted Info, Briefing Notes Say,' Canadian Press, 12 September 2010.

97 The undated directive is reproduced in the committee report, *Review of the Findings*, appendix D.

98 Ibid., Part 3: D, and 'Dissenting Opinion from the Conservative Party of Canada.'

99 Charles Bisson, deputy director, Operations, memorandum to HQ and regional directors general, 'Directive on Information Sharing with Agencies with Poor Human Rights Records,' 19 November 2008 (Secret). Thanks to Craig Forcese for declassifying this document.

100 The caveat reads: 'Our Service is aware that your organization might be in possession of threat related information on Canadian citizen [*name of individual*]. As we believe [*name of individual*] will be present in your country, our Service recognizes the sovereign right of your government to undertake reasonable measures under the law to ensure your public safety. Should you deem some form of legal action against [*name of individual*] is warranted, our service trusts that [*name of individual*] will be fairly treated within the accepted norms of international conventions, that he is accorded due process under law and afforded access to Canadian diplomatic personnel if requested. Furthermore, should you be in posses-

sion of any information that originated from our service regarding [*name of individual*], we ask that this information not be used to support [*name of individual*]'s detention or prosecution without prior formal consultation with our service.'

101 Federal Court of Canada, DES-7-08, 'In the Security Certificate Matter of Mohammed Zeki Mahjoub, Ottawa,' 9 June 2010 (released in redacted form, 23 July 2010).

102 Libya's Abuse of Detainees Well-Documented at Time, *Human Rights Watch*, 28 September 2011, http://www.hrw.org/news/2011/09/28/canada-intelligence-service-accused-libya-interrogations; Colin Freeze, 'CSIS Questioned Canadian in Libya, Rights Group Says,' *Globe and Mail*, 28 September 2011; Jeremy Relph, 'A Lifelong Crusade to Bring Down Gadhafi,' *Toronto Star*, 24 September 2011.

103 Michelle Shephard, *Guantanamo's Child: The Untold Story of Omar Khadr* (Mississauga, Ont.: John Wiley and Sons 2008), is the best overall source on Khadr.

104 See Abdurahman Khadr, 'I Am the Usual Suspect,' *Globe and Mail*, 15 March 2004. This article is reproduced in Shephard, *Guantanamo's Child*, 147–50.

105 Ibid., 58. Shephard acknowledges the ambiguities of the issue at the time of Chrétien's intervention. For a much less sympathetic interpretation, see Stewart Bell, *Cold Terror: How Ottawa Nurtures and Exports Terrorism around the World* (Mississauga, Ont.: John Wiley and Sons 2004), 156–86.

106 Michelle Shephard, 'Omar Khadr "Innocent" in Death of U.S. Soldier,' *Toronto Star*, 28 October 2009.

107 Using similar logic, the American definition of enemy combatant could have been used by the British at the time of the American Revolution to describe the irregular American forces mustered to rebel against British rule in the colonies, and to bring charges of murder against those who had killed British troops in battle. Needless to say, this irony was lost upon Bush officials intent on removing any impediment by way of international law to the unilateral prosecution of their War on Terror.

108 Sleep deprivation has been held to constitute torture if it is prolonged, and certainly if used in conjunction with stress positions, also practised at Guantánamo. Sleep deprivation causes general physical deterioration and produces hallucinations, which contribute to mental deterioration. Its use by American police forces to procure confessions in criminal cases was barred by the U.S. Supreme Court in *Ashcraft v. Tennessee*, 1944. CSIS has posted a defence of its conduct with regard to Khadr on its website that

rests heavily on the fact that the application of sleep deprivation was associated with the 2004 Foreign Affairs interviews, in which CSIS did not participate. Canadian Security Intelligence Service, '2003 Interviews with Omar Khadr – Media Coverage, Ottawa, July 21st, 2008,' http://www.csis.gc.ca/nwsrm/nwsrlss/prss20080721-eng.asp. While this is technically correct, it hardly relieves CSIS of responsibility for complicity in the wider context of Khadr's rights violations, as both the courts and SIRC have found.

109 Diplomatic notes began in 2002 seeking consular access to Khadr; all were rejected. Four notes asking for assurances regarding his medical treatment, his status as a minor, and the possibility of the death penalty were sent through 2003, with no formal responses. Seven further diplomatic communications were sent in 2004 and 2005 prior to the defeat of the Martin government, raising a series of issues about safeguards against mistreatment, due process, and diplomatic access, again to little or no effect. The last such diplomatic note, requesting independent medical assessment and access to counsel of choice, was dated 17 April 2006, just a few months after the Harper government came to office. After that, the Conservative government has maintained official silence in relation to the Americans on the matter of the only Canadian in Guantánamo, while turning aside all calls from within Canada for his return. Diplomatic notes are summarized in Federal Court of Appeal, *The Prime Minister of Canada et al. and Omar Ahmed Khadr*, 14 August 2009 (2009 FCA 246).

110 Tonda MacCharles, 'Canadians Still Split on Omar Khadr, Poll Shows,' *Toronto Star*, 2 September 2009. According to an Angus Reid poll taken after the Supreme Court partially upheld the Conservative government's appeal against the Federal Court order to seek Khadr's return, 40 per cent agreed that Khadr's repatriation should be sought, but another 40 per cent preferred to leave him to American military justice. Although only 39 per cent agreed that he could receive a fair trial at Guantánamo, while 47 per cent disagreed, only 33 per cent felt any 'sympathy' for his plight and a clear majority, 54 per cent, expressed no sympathy. In fact, sympathy for Khadr had actually declined slightly since the Federal Court of Appeal decision six months earlier: *Angus Reid Public Opinion*, 3 February 2010.

111 2005 FC.

112 2008 SCC 28.

113 'Designated Federal Court judges' refer to a small group specially designated to hear national-security cases.

114 2008 FC 807.

115 Among the documents released in slightly redacted form were U.S.

Air Force Office of Special Investigations, 'Subject Interview of: (UNK) KHADR, OMAR AHMED,' 17 and 24 February 2003; and memorandum, 'Re: Interviews of Omar Khadr,' 14 April 2003. Both indicate the information gained by American authorities from the CSIS interviews. There were also two memoranda from R. Scott Heatherington, director, Foreign Intelligence Division, Department of Foreign Affairs and International Trade, 'Umar KHADR: Conditions of His Detention etc.,' 20 February 2003, and 'Umar Khadr: A Meeting With,' 20 April 2004, which indicate the knowledge of Canadian authorities about Khadr's treatment by his American captors.

116 Heatherington memorandum, 20 April 2004. The same official went on to suggest that, in his opinion, Khadr's American interrogator was 'not impressive' and 'seemed to be trying to intimidate Umar or force Umar to talk rather than trying to cajole him into cooperation.' Heatherington further maintained that 'certainly Umar did not appear to have been affected by three weeks on the "frequent flyer program,"' which he attributed to the 'natural resilience of a well-fed and healthy seventeen-year old' (even though he also reported that Khadr had been recently 'hospitalized' without medical explanation from the Americans). In his earlier memorandum of 20 February 2003, Heatherington reported that, when interviewed, Khadr exhibited 'great mood swings' and had expressed his fears of a 'resumption of the torture he had undergone while in American custody in Afghanistan,' allegations that Heatherington asserted 'did not ring true' despite evidence of scars and other signs of physical damage which he had shown to his Canadian interviewers.

117 WikiLeaks, U.S. Department of State, 08OTTAWA918 2008-07-09 18:06, SECRET//NOFORN Embassy Ottawa SUBJECT: COUNSELOR, CSIS DIRECTOR DISCUSS CT THREATS, PAKISTAN, AFGHANISTAN, IRAN REF: A. OTTAWA, 360.

118 2009 FC 405.

119 2009 FCA 246, at para. 49. Emphasis added.

120 2010 SCC3, Docket: 33289, 29 January 2010.

121 Sarah Boesveld, 'Ottawa Asks U.S. to Omit Evidence in Khadr Case,' *Globe and Mail*, 17 February 2010; Bruce Campion-Smith, 'U.S. Asked to Ignore Khadr Reports,' *Toronto Star*, 17 February 2010.

122 Michelle Shephard, 'Canada Will Not Push Washington on Khadr case,' *Toronto Star*, 12 May 2010. The *Globe and Mail* denounced what it called an 'abusive process' at Guantánamo and attacked the disgraceful negligence of the Canadian government in failing to stand up appropriately for Khadr's rights: 'If Based on Coerced Evidence the Khadr Trial Cannot Be

Just: The U.S. Prosecutors Are Still Trying to Use Statements Obtained by Extreme Intelligence-Gathering Methods,' *Globe and Mail* editorial, 7 May 2010.

123 Audrey Macklin, Diana Juricevic, and Cheryl Milne, 'A Chance to Do the Right Thing: The Government Must Act When the Land's Highest Court Declares It Is Breaking the Law in the Omar Khadr Case,' *Globe and Mail*, 2 February 2010.

124 2010 FC 715, Docket: T-230-10, 5 July 2010, the Honourable Mr Justice Zinn, Reasons for Judgment and Judgment.

125 Giuseppe Valiante, 'No Evidence Khadr's Confessions Were Obtained through Torture: Judge,' *Postmedia News*, 20 August 2010.

126 Lewis Carroll, *Alice's Adventures in Wonderland*, chapter 12.

127 'Warped Justice,' *New York Times*, 9 November 2010.

128 U.S. Department of State, memorandum for Michael L. Bruhn, executive secretary, Department of Defense, Subject: Mr. Omar Khadr, 24 October 2010; with attached U.S. and Canadian diplomatic notes dated 23 October 2010; *United States of America v. Omar Ahmed Khadr, Offer for Pre-trial Agreement*, 13 October 2010.

129 John Ibbitson, 'Canada Agrees to Take Khadr Back,' *Globe and Mail*, 1 November 2010.

130 Anna Mehler Paperny, 'Cost to Keep Khadr out of Canada: $1.3-Million So Far,' *Globe and Mail*, 29 October 2009.

131 Security Intelligence Review Committee, SIRC Study 2008-05, 'CSIS's Role in the Matter of Omar Khadr,' 8 July 2009, 'Top Secret,' disclosed by SIRC in redacted format. Disclosure was accompanied by a news release, 'SIRC Completes Its Review of CSIS's Role in the Matter of Omar Khadr,' 15 July 2009, with comments by SIRC Chair Gary Filmon. In its *Annual Report* for 2008–9 (*Accountability in a New Era of Security Intelligence*, 30 September 2009, 9–15), SIRC summarized its findings regarding Khadr.

132 SIRC makes clear that the CSIS visit to Guantánamo was 'fully supported' by the government and was part of a 'whole of government' effort: 'CSIS Role,' 9. However, SIRC's mandate does not permit it to examine and assess the actions of other departments, such as Foreign Affairs, despite their key role in the Khadr matter.

133 SIRC, 'CSIS's Role,' 29.

134 Ibid., 14.

135 Ibid., 16.

136 Ibid., 17.

137 Ibid., 10.

138 Ibid., 21–2.
139 Ibid., SIRC, 22. SIRC added a concern that CSIS had identified the 'radi-
     calization' of Muslim youth in Canada as a major security problem and
     recommended that CSIS develop a 'policy framework that guides its
     interactions with youth' that was in keeping with Canadian and interna-
     tional legal principles as they relate to youth.
140 Ibid., 25.
141 Ibid., 13. It should be noted that this citation from CSIS is followed in the
     public version of the SIRC *Report* by a redacted section. It is thus unclear
     whether SIRC accepted this CSIS self-assessment at face value.
142 Ibid., 25.
143 Ibid., 26.
144 Ibid., 27.
145 Ibid., 28. Emphasis in original.
146 Another contemporaneous court case involved yet another Khadr, this
     time Omar's elder brother, Abdullah, who had been captured by Pakista-
     ni forces in 2004 and interrogated by the Pakistanis as well as the Ameri-
     cans and the RCMP and CSIS. In December 2005 he was released, despite
     American demands for his extraordinary rendition. In August 2010, just
     as his brother was awaiting the opening of his so-called military trial, the
     Ontario court ruled that Abdullah Khadr is not extraditable to the United
     States since his self-incriminating statements were manifestly unreliable,
     given the conditions of his imprisonment and interrogation. The govern-
     ment appealed the ruling. *United States of America v. Khadr*, 2010 ONSC
     4338, Court file no.: EX0037/05, 4 August 2010, *Superior Court of Justice be-
     tween: the Attorney General of Canada on behalf of the United States of America,
     Requesting State, and Abdullah Khadr, Person Sought*; Kate Allen, 'Abdullah
     Khadr Freed by Toronto Court: Extradition Hearing Is Stayed in Toronto,
     Just Days before Brother Omar Is Slated to Stand Trial in Guantanamo
     Bay,' *Globe and Mail* and Canadian Press, 4 August 2010; Colin Perkel,
     'Government to Appeal Ruling That Stayed Abdullah Khadr's Extradi-
     tion,' Canadian Press, 31 August 2010.
147 Patrick Wintour, Nicholas Watt, and Ian Cobain, 'Torture Claims Inves-
     tigation Ordered by William Hague,' *Guardian*, 20 May 2010; Richard
     Norton-Taylor and Ian Cobain, 'Government to Compensate Torture
     Victims as Official Inquiry Launched,' *Guardian*, 6 July 2010; Haroon Sid-
     dique, 'Torture Inquiry: Who Is on the Panel?' *Guardian*, 6 July 2010. In
     2009 the Labour foreign minister and home secretary published an article
     in which they more or less said that the U.K. government never condones
     torture – except when they have to (David Miliband, foreign secretary,

and Alan Johnson, home secretary, 'We Firmly Oppose Torture – but It Is Impossible to Eradicate All Risk,' *Telegraph,* 8 August 2009).

148 See chapters 9 and 10.

149 *R v. Stinchcombe*, [1991] 3 S.C.R.

150 For a full discussion of national security in open courts, see Craig Forcese, *National Security Law: Canadian Practice in International Perspective* (Toronto: Irwin Law 2008), 400–21.

151 CSIS, Remarks by Richard B. Fadden, director, Canadian Security Intelligence Service, to the Canadian Association for Security and Intelligence Studies (CASIS) Annual International Conference, 29 October 2009, http://www.csis-scrs.gc.ca/nwsrm/spchs/spch29102009-eng.asp.

152 Colin Freeze. 'Canadians Blind to Terror Threat: Top Spy,' *Globe and Mail*, 29 October 2009.

153 WikiLeaks, U.S. Department of State, 08OTTAWA918 2008-07-09 18:06, SECRET//NOFORN Embassy Ottawa SUBJECT: COUNSELOR, CSIS DIRECTOR DISCUSS CT THREATS, PAKISTAN, AFGHANISTAN, IRAN REF: A. OTTAWA, 360.

154 RCMP, Commissioner William Elliott, 'Closing the Loop on National Security through Law Enforcement, October 30, 2009,' http://www.rcmp-grc.gc.ca/news-nouvelles/speeches-stat-discours-decl/20091109-secur-eng.htm. Emphasis added. Colin Freeze, 'Top Mountie Wants More Money to Fight Terrorism,' *Globe and Mail*, 31 October 2009.

155 Sarah Boesveld, 'Senior RCMP Officers File Complaints over Commissioner's Conduct,' *Globe and Mail*, 27 July 2010; 'Former Top Spy Assigned to Look into RCMP Troubles,' Canadian Press, 30 July 2010; Daniel Leblanc, 'RCMP Brass Shuffle Expected as Elliott Stays on as Boss,' *Globe and Mail*, 4 September 2010. It is only fair to point out that the 2010 attacks on Elliott as RCMP commissioner have been matched by calls for the resignation or firing of CSIS Director Richard Fadden over his ill-judged public accusations concerning Chinese 'foreign-influenced' activities of unnamed public officials and the resultant storms of controversy (see chapter 12): Reg Whitaker, 'Bad Summer for Top Ottawa Secureaucrats,' *Prism: The Security Practices Monitor*, 26 August 2010, http://prism-magazine.com/2010/08/bad-summer-for-top-ottawa-secureaucrats/.

156 Daniel Leblanc, 'Outgoing RCMP Chief Urges Return to Tradition in Choosing Successor,' *Globe and Mail*, 8 Februay 2011.

157 Perhaps the most notorious example of the state withholding crucial evidence in support of an espionage prosecution was in the United States in the trial, conviction, and execution of Julius and Ethel Rosenberg for atomic espionage. Crucial evidence rested on the Venona decrypts,

knowledge of which the American authorities were anxious to keep
from the Soviets. In the absence of the Venona evidence, the government
resorted to a variety of unethical tactics that surrounded the process with
doubts about its legitimacy and left a generation of sceptics convinced
that the Rosenbergs were innocent victims of Cold War hysteria, even
though the Venona evidence demonstrated the culpability of Julius if not
of his wife. See, inter alia, John Earl Haynes and Harvey Klehr, *Venona:
Decoding Soviet Espionage in America* (New Haven, Conn.: Yale University
Press 2000).

158 A. Stuart Farson, 'Security Intelligence vs. Criminal Intelligence: Lines of
Demarcation, Areas of Obfuscation, and the Need to Re-Evaluate Organizational Roles in Responding to Terrorism,' *Policing and Society*, 2 (1991):
65–87; 'Criminal Intelligence vs. Security Intelligence: A Re-Evaluation
of the Police Role in Response to Terrorism,' in David A. Charters, ed.,
Democratic Responses to International Terrorism (Dobbs Ferry, N.Y.: Transnational Books 1991), 191–228.

159 Bruce Campion-Smith, ' Spy Agency CSIS Warns of Homegrown Terror in
Canada,' *Toronto Star*, 12 May 2010.

160 The RCMP performance report submitted to the public security minister
and released in October 2009 lists the reduction of the threat of 'terrorist criminal activity in Canada and abroad' as one of the RCMP's five
operational priorities, and places several initiatives under that rubric; no
mention is made of counter-espionage or counter-proliferation activities:
RCMP, *RCMP Departmental Performance Report 2008–2009*.

161 RCMP, National Security Criminal Investigations, *RCMP Actions in Response to Recommendations Stemming from the Report of the Events Relating to
Maher Arar (O'Connor Inquiry)*. A new unit, the National Security Criminal
Investigations Branch, is up and running and dedicated to counter-terrorist investigations. For a favourable view of the new unit and its future,
see Wesley Wark, 'Back in the Saddle? At the Heart of RCMP Reforms Is a
New National Security Unit,' *Globe and Mail*, 6 February 2009.

162 A. Alan Borovoy, 'Two Heads Not Better Than One on National Security
File,' *Toronto Star*, 2 July 2010.

163 Arar Commission, Public Hearings, 21 June 2004, 137, bcp/commissions/
maher_arar/07-09-13/www.stenotran.com/commission/maherarar/
2004-06-21%20volume%201.pdf.

164 Arar Commission, *A New Review Mechanism*.

165 Public Safety Canada, 'Action Plan: The Government of Canada Response
to the Commission of Inquiry into the Investigation of the Bombing of Air
India Flight 182,' December 2010, http://www.publicsafety.gc.ca/prg/

ns/ai182/res-rep-eng.aspx. A critical view of the government's response to Major can be found in Reg Whitaker, 'Air India: Still a Policy Debacle after All These Years?' Parts 1 and 2, *PRISM: The National Security Practices Monitor*, 12 and 31 December 2010, http://prism-magazine .com/2010/12/air-india-still-a-policy-debacle-after-all-these-years/; http://prism-magazine.com/2010/12/air-india-still-a-policy-debacle-after-all-these-years-part-2-of-2/#comment-3590.

166 Kathryn Blaze Carlson and Brian Hutchinson, 'Canada's Top Spy Watchdog Resigns following National Post Revelations,' *National Post*, 10 November 2011. The *National Post* had reported that Dr Arthur Porter, a financial contributor to the Conservative Party, had lent $200,000 to a notorious international lobbyist who had acted as an agent of Robert Mugabe in an attempt to entrap the Zimbabwean opposition leader in an alleged coup attempt, and as well was acting as the diplomatic representative in Canada of Sierra Leone – activities clearly incompatible with his duties as SIRC chair: Brian Hutchinson, 'Canada's Spy Watchdog's Questionable $200,000 Deal,' *National Post*, 8 November 2011; and Brian Hutchinson, 'Spy Review Board Chief Offered Me Job: Senator,' *National Post*, 8 November 2011. Ironically, in its 2010–11 *Annual Report*, SIRC had made a plea for a much expanded role for itself in widened national-security accountability reform: SIRC, *Checks and Balances: Viewing Security Intelligence through the Lens of Accountability: Annual Report 2010–2011* (30 September 2011), 5–6. In his resignation letter to the prime minister, Porter wrote that 'I am cognizant that the SIRC is in the middle of a significant transition and I worry that the media portrayal has the potential to tarnish the SIRC's credibility.'

167 Reg Whitaker and Stuart Farson, 'Accountability in and for National Security,' Institute for Research in Public Policy, *Policy Choices*, 15, no. 9 (2009), http://www.irpp.org/choices/archive/vol15no9.pdf; Reg Whitaker, 'Enough with the Inquiries: Canada Needs One Permanent Accountability Process for Security and Intelligence Issues,' *Ottawa Citizen*, 31 August 2009.

Conclusion: Policing Canadian Democracy

1 Cassandra Szklarski, 'CBC-TV Sends up Spies in "InSecurity,"' Canadian Press, 3 January 2011; Wesley Wark, 'Get Smarter,' *Ottawa Citizen*, 15 January 2011.

A Note on Sources

As the extensive endnotes to this book suggest, our account of political policing in Canada is the product of decades of intensive and sometimes laborious research. The quantity of published and widely available sources – specialized journalistic and scholarly articles, collections of essays and monographs, and government reports – is quite large; so, too, is the quantity of unpublished and still restricted documents, which are held in Library and Archives Canada (LAC), largely in Record Group (RG) 146, the records of the Canadian Security Intelligence Service. (We've got the bankers' boxes to prove it!) For the uninitiated, finding a way into this material can be somewhat intimidating. The lengthy Bibliography for this book at the University of Toronto Press website (www.utppublishing.com/pdf/Bibliography_Secret_Service.pdf) will be of some assistance in this respect; perhaps the following observations about some of the resources will help too.

This present book notwithstanding, comprehensive and accessible histories of political policing in Canada are few and far between. RCMP historians Carl Betke and Stan Horrall's 'Canada's Security Service: An Historical Outline, 1864–1966' is a good place to start. As 'insiders,' Betke and Horrall had unrestricted access to government documents, some of which are still inaccessible to the public or exist in heavily redacted form. That work also has the added (unintended?) bonus of shedding light on the Mounties' own perception of their controversial past. The problem with this source – and it is a big one – is that it is unpublished and available only through Access to Information at LAC.

In its place, researchers who wish to pursue further topics and issues raised by our book might find it useful to begin with *The Infernal Machine* by Larry Hannant and supplement it with more specialized studies by Steve Hewitt (*Spying 101*) and Gary Kinsman and Patrizia Gentile (*The Canadian War on Queers*), among others. Books published by investigative journalists, like John Sawatsky and James Littleton, examine parts of this history and thus provide accessible entry points. More refined still are the numerous scholarly articles published in academic journals such as *Intelligence and National Security*, the *Canadian Historical Review*, and *Labour/Le Travail*. All of these journals are available and searchable online. Numerous earlier studies conducted by Whitaker, Kealey, and Parnaby can be found there.

Researchers interested in contemporary national-security issues – from the 1960s to the early 2000s – will find the online audio and visual archive created by the Canadian Broadcasting Corporation especially valuable (http://archives.cbc.ca/). Searchable by keyword, the online archive possesses extensive material related to the Second World War, the Gouzenko affair, Quebec separatism, and the Air India bombing. Online resources such as Craig Forcese's 'National Security Law' blog (http://cforcese.typepad.com/ns/), the British Columbia Civil Liberties Association's National Security Blog (http://nationalsecurity.bccla.org/about/), and *PRISM: The Security Practices Monitor* (http://prism-magazine.com/) are equally helpful places to begin studying more contemporary issues.

Also invaluable are the records of the numerous government inquiries and commissions that have studied security questions and institutions in Canada, beginning in 1946. We have drawn heavily on their final reports and supporting documentation, most of which are available online and easily located at libraries, usually in their 'government documents' section. A summary of major parliamentary reports on security and intelligence can be found on the website of the Privy Council Office (http://www.pco-bcp.gc.ca/index.asp?lang=eng&page=information&sub=publications&doc=cpns-cpsn/10-eng.htm). The websites belonging to the Security Intelligence Review Committee (http://www.sirc-csars.gc.ca/) and the Canadian Security Intelligence Service (http://www.csis.gc.ca) are also rich sources of contemporary government-generated information.

While it was relatively easy for us to gain access to the books, articles, and reports (the 'secondary sources') listed above, the same cannot be said for the government documents (the 'primary sources') upon which our most important and original insights rest. There are many reasons for this difference, the most important of which is related to the subject under consideration in this book: security and intelligence.

Of immense importance to this book were the records of the Canadian Security Intelligence Service, which are located at LAC as RG 146. The records of the early Canadian secret service, which form the basis of RG 146, were transferred by the RCMP to LAC in stages over the 1960s and early 1970s; some documents were never transferred (no one knows how many) and others were subsequently seized by the Mounties from the archives, picked over again, then returned for public use. Beginning in 1982, these records – among others belonging to sensitive federal institutions – were brought under the auspices of the Access to Information Act and the Privacy Act, where they remain to this day.

Any researcher who wishes to study the history of the Canadian security service, then, must be prepared to use both pieces of legislation. It can be costly, time-consuming, and occasionally frustrating, especially when the documents are judged either too sensitive to release or arrive heavily redacted ('information … injurious to the national security of Canada'). Protection of personal privacy, while an eminently defensible principle in the abstract, has also proven to be a very serious barrier to research into national-security issues, as the unresolved legal dispute over the release of documents on the decades-long surveillance of the political icon Tommy Douglas testifies.

LAC provides a basic guide to using both acts on its website (http://www .collectionscanada.gc.ca/the-public/005-6010-e.html). Cautionary tales about access are expressed in: Gregory S. Kealey, 'The Royal Canadian Mounted Police, the Canadian Security and Intelligence Service, the Public Archives of Canada, and Access to Information: A Curious Tale,' *Labour/Le Travail*, 21 (spring 1988): 199–226; Larry Hannant, 'Using the Privacy Act as a Research Tool,' *Labour/Le Travail*, 24 (fall 1989): 181–5; and (more recently) Patrizia Gentile, 'Resisted Access? National Security, the Access to Information Act, and Queer(ing) Archives,' *Archivaria*, 68 (fall 2009): 141–58. Researchers interested in the state surveillance and repression of the Canadian labour movement might find the eight-volume series *RCMP Security Bulletins* (St John's: Canadian Committee on Labour History 1989–97) to be a valuable short cut through (or a substitute for) an Access to Information application. Edited by Kealey and Whitaker, the volumes contain reports supplied by the RCMP to the federal cabinet as part of the security briefing process between 1920 and 1949. Each volume contains a thorough scholarly introduction and detailed index of 'subversive' organizations and people. A fully searchable on-line version of the *Security Bulletins* is available at: http://journals.hil.unb.ca/index.php/RCMP.

An additional issue surrounding the sourcing of public records released under the access and privacy acts is that the declassified material is extracted from its original filing position within the originating agency's own records system. In effect, released records become, de facto, newly minted record series determined by the parameters of the request and the response, rather than by how the records were actually organized by the originating agency. This has obvious drawbacks from the standpoint of historical method. It also means that in this book there are references to 'CSIS' or 'RCMP' documents that are the result of Access to Information requests and are identified under ATIP request numbers. Unfortunately, these may not be available for public scrutiny, unless they have been independently published, as in the case of the *RCMP Security Bulletins* referred to above.

The difficulties in gaining access to primary documentation increase as the time frame comes closer to the present. Although cabinet records are in principle disclosable twenty years after their production, and there are no time limits imposed on the declassification of records of government agencies, 'national security' exemption claims become stronger the more recent the records, especially, of course, those that may still be deemed operational. Moreover, in an era in which security intelligence operations have become more global in scope, and ever more linked within international networks of exchange of information, exemptions based on sources originating from foreign governments and international agencies are more frequently invoked. One result of these factors is that the documentary record for CSIS, following its creation in 1984, and especially after 11 September 2001, tends to be somewhat sketchier than that which we were able to establish for the old RCMP security service.

Offsetting these barriers to contemporary research are three important kinds of sources for declassified documentation: public inquiries; oversight reports; and judicial review of security-related cases. Public inquiries into the Maher Arar affair and the Air India tragedy, in particular, revealed a wealth of relevant material – sometimes only after prolonged disputation with government censors that had to be adjudicated by the Federal Court. Independent oversight, although clearly inadequate in terms of scope and powers, has also revealed important information. Finally, the courts have begun playing a much more active role in reviewing, and occasionally rebuking, national-security agencies for their role in relation to the constitutional and human rights of Canadian citizens. In the process, further light has been focused on the workings of the secret state.

There is an unusual twist to this story of declassified records in the writing of this book. One of the authors, Whitaker, was involved in the Arar and Air India inquiries, as well as in an official review of Canadian aviation security in 2005–6. This required security clearance to examine a range of secret documentation on national-security matters. The Security of Information Act holds everyone who has been granted clearance to strict non-disclosure of classified information, in perpetuity. No classified information has been disclosed in this book, with references only to records released under the access and privacy acts, or referred to in published sources.

Near the end of the preparation of this book, the WikiLeaks phenomenon burst on the international scene, with a vast trove of mainly American classified documents being released in defiance of American and other national-secrecy laws. Canada has not figured heavily in these unauthorized releases, but some

American diplomatic correspondence referencing Canadian events and discussions with Canadian officials has proved useful in this study, and these documents are referenced to the WikiLeaks site, although the future of that site may prove problematic in the face of concerted governmental hostility.

While ease of access recommends WikiLeaks and other online resources, that access does come with a significant downside, which researchers might want to keep in mind: the web addresses (or URLs) cited here are active and accurate as of June 2011, but there is no guarantee that they will be so in the future. The locations of websites/pages can and do change often, for reasons beyond our control.

Illustrations Credits

1. McGee Funeral: McCord Museum, M967.138.5.
2. Le Caron: National Portrait Gallery (London), NPG 2238.
3. Sherwood: McCord Museum, M20111.76.
4. Hopkinson: Vancouver Public Library, VPL 6228.
5. Cahan: LAC, E.H. Coleman Collection, C-11600.
6. Zaneth: LAC, RCMP fonds, PA-209544.
7. Underground Party: LAC, MG 28 IV 4, vol. 48, file 48-5.
8. Cash Relief: LAC, RG 146, vol. 1937, 'Halifax.'
9. May Day Rally, B.C.: Vancouver Public Library, VPL 8786.
10. Arthur Evans: Glenbow Museum, NA-3634-1.
11. Italian Interns: Beaton Institute, Cape Breton University, 97-515-28363.
12. Gouzenko Ad: *Globe and Mail*, 15 May 1948.
13. Pearson and Norman: UBC Rare Books and Special Collections, BC-2124-108.
14. Mounties on Parade: Archives of Ontario, 10022183.
15. Hal Banks: National Film Board, Stock Shot Library.
16. 'Drive the War Makers …': McMaster University Library, William Ready Archives and Research Collections, 00000711.
17. Vallières and Gagnon: McMaster University Library, William Ready Archives and Research Collections, Front de libération du Québec collection.
18. Trudeau at Funeral: LAC, Frank Prazak fonds, PA-206661.
19. McDonald Commission: Glenbow Museum, M-8000-593.
20. Counter-Terrorism: 'Commission of Inquiry … Air India,' vol. 2, pt. 1, 136.
21. Air India: CP Photo/Chuck Stoody.
22. World Trade Center: U.S. Navy Photo / Photographer's Mate 2nd Class Jim Watson. Use of released U.S. Navy imagery does not constitute product or organizational endorsement of any kind by the U.S. Navy.
23. Maher Arar: CP Photo/Tom Hanson.
24. Canadian Soldier: CP Photo, John Cotter.

Index